NONPROFIT
MANAGEMENT

This book is dedicated with love to
Maria, my wife
Shane, my son
Lindsey, my daughter

NONPROFIT MANAGEMENT

PRINCIPLES AND PRACTICE

MICHAEL J. WORTH
The George Washington University

Los Angeles • London • New Delhi • Singapore • Washington DC

For information:

SAGE Publications, Inc.
2455 Teller Road
Thousand Oaks, California 91320
E-mail: order@sagepub.com

SAGE Publications Ltd.
1 Oliver's Yard
55 City Road
London EC1Y 1SP
United Kingdom

SAGE Publications India Pvt. Ltd.
B 1/I 1 Mohan Cooperative Industrial Area
Mathura Road, New Delhi 110 044
India

SAGE Publications Asia-Pacific Pte. Ltd.
33 Pekin Street #02-01
Far East Square
Singapore 048763

Printed in the United States of America

Library of Congress Cataloging-in-Publication Data
Worth, Michael J.
Nonprofit management: Principles and practice / Michael J. Worth.
    p. cm.
Includes bibliographical references and index.
ISBN 978-1-4129-3778-8 (cloth)
   1. Nonprofit organizations—Management. I. Title.
HD62.6.W675 2009
658′.048—dc22   2008017869

This book is printed on acid-free paper.

09   10   11   12   10 9 8 7 6 5 4 3 2

Acquisitions Editor:	Al Bruckner
Associate Editor:	Deya Saoud
Editorial Assistant:	MaryAnn Vail
Production Editor:	Laureen A. Shea
Copy Editor:	QuADS Prepress (P) Ltd.
Typesetter:	C&M Digitals (P) Ltd.
Proofreader:	Eleni-Maria Georgiou
Indexer:	Diggs Publication Services
Cover Designer:	Gail Buschman
Marketing Manager:	Jennifer Reed Banando

Brief Contents

Detailed Contents

2 Understanding the Nonprofit Sector and Nonprofit Organizations   31

PART II   Governing and Leading Nonprofit Organizations

3 Nonprofit Governing Boards   61

4 Executive Leadership — 90

PART III   Managing the Nonprofit Organization

5 Accountability and Performance Measurement   **115**

6 Building Capacity and Managing Change   **146**

7 Strategic Planning and Strategic Management 166

8 Managing Paid Staff and Service Volunteers 189

PART IV   Obtaining and Managing Resources

11 Nonprofit Enterprise   266

12 Financial Management   289

PART V   Special Topics

13 Collaborations and Mergers   317

Acknowledgments

Writing a book is a collective enterprise, even when the book has one author. Any author builds on the work of others, and this text reflects the wisdom of the many scholars and practitioners who are cited throughout it.

I am grateful to my editors at Sage, Al Bruckner and Deya Saoud, who encouraged me to undertake this work and who continued to offer support even at times when it seemed questionable if it would ever be completed. I am grateful as well to the reviewers, whose sometimes frank comments added immeasurably to the final product. They are as follows: Phyllis R. Anderson, Governors State University; Anthony J. Filipovitch, Minnesota State University, Mankato; Gary Kirk, James Madison University; Eric C. Martin, Eastern Connecticut State University; Sarah Maxwell, University of Arizona; Stuart C. Mendel, Cleveland State University; Carl Milofsky, Bucknell University; Dorothy Norris-Tirrell, The University of Memphis; Charlene J. Phipps, University of Oregon; and Robert Rex Walters, University of California, Santa Cruz.

I also thank my professional colleague Lilya Wagner, whose comments and suggestions on some chapters were helpful.

I have learned immensely from my students at The George Washington University, from my faculty colleagues, and from the many nonprofit executives who have participated in various of my classes over the years. I thank them for the education they have provided me and hope that they will find this book to be a useful contribution to the field.

Finally, I express my deepest gratitude to my family and friends for their patience and forbearance over the months of my effort with this project.

Michael J. Worth
Professor of Nonprofit Management
The George Washington University
Washington, DC, December, 2007

Introduction

This is a book about the management of nonprofit organizations. The topic begs two fundamental questions: Why do nonprofit organizations need to be managed? And, is management of a nonprofit organization really different from management of a business or government agency? In other words, is there really a need for a book like this, or is management a generic activity that could be learned as well from a textbook in business or public management?

Some may hold a perception of nonprofit organizations as primarily collections of well-intentioned people who struggle with minimal resources to meet human needs, without much attention to the bottom line, and with some disdain for management as an unwelcome distraction from the all-important work of delivering vital programs and services. However, there has been a management revolution in the nonprofit sector in recent decades, and this stereotype, if ever true, does not describe all nonprofit organizations today.

The nonprofit management revolution has been driven by several forces. One overarching force has been the introduction of competition, resulting from changes in funding patterns, the growth of the sector, and increasing demands for accountability. The years since the "Reagan revolution" of the 1980s have seen reductions in federal government funding for many social programs, the devolution of funding to state governments, and increased outsourcing of the delivery of social and human services by government agencies to nonprofit organizations. Nonprofits have been forced to compete for contracts, against each other and, in some cases, against for-profit firms. In addition, many government benefits are now being provided through voucher-type payments made directly to individuals, who are thus transformed into customers, free to purchase the services they need in the marketplace. Such customers are free to select the organizations that will provide services based on perceptions of quality and other considerations; this forces nonprofits to compete for their business. Like the competition for contracts, the competition for empowered customers has forced nonprofits to either become better managed or place their survival at risk.

But government has not been the only force driving change. Other funders, including United Ways, major foundations, and even individual donors, have shown an increased concern with the results achieved by nonprofits through the programs they offer. This has been especially true of many newly wealthy entrepreneurs who amassed their fortunes during the economic boom of the 1990s and the advancing stock market of the mid-2000s. Many view their philanthropic giving as a type of investment from which they expect to see a measurable return in the form of effective programs and services. The requirement that nonprofits meet these expectations for measurable results also has increased the need for management.

There has been a shift in thinking about nonprofit organizations that focuses much more on the organization itself than merely on the programs and services it delivers—a concern with organizations' capacity and sustainability, ideas we will discuss later in this book. The

1990s brought searing critiques of traditional philanthropy and the management of nonprofits. Among them was a *Harvard Business Review* article by Christine Letts, William Ryan, and Allen Grossman (1999b), titled "Virtuous Capital: What Foundations Can Learn From Venture Capitalists." The article essentially made an indictment of traditional foundations' grantmaking practices, arguing that the short-term program grants made by most foundations were not meeting the need for investment in the long-term capacity of nonprofit organizations themselves. Letts et al. advocated an approach to philanthropy that would parallel the approach of venture capitalists to investing in companies, including a more sustained commitment to support along with the requirement that organizations meet performance standards. Bill Shore's book, *The Cathedral Within*, published the same year as Letts's article, echoed some of the criticisms of traditional philanthropy and argued that the emphasis on programs rather than building organizations was in fact preventing many successful programs from "going to scale," that is, growing to a point that they could have significant impact, because the organizations did not have the capacity to expand (Shore, 1999). Letts, Shore, and others contributed to a change in thinking about nonprofits, shifting from the programs they offer to the strength and sustainability of the organizations themselves. It was, in the words of Jim Collins and Jerry Porras (1994), a shift of emphasis from "telling time" to "building clocks." This new emphasis on nonprofit organizational development also has been a force in increasing the demand for professional nonprofit management.

Another reality is that the dramatic growth of the nonprofit sector and its assets has simply raised the stakes. Fueled in part by a wave of philanthropy based on the economic gains of the past two decades and in part by the continued devolution of government programs, nonprofits now employ more people and control more resources than ever before. The nonprofit sector has become a consequential part of the American economy that cannot be ignored. Therefore, it has captured the increasing attention of legislators, the media, and others who demand that nonprofits be accountable for the assets entrusted to them and for the results that they achieve with those assets. This reflects an increased concern with accountability throughout American society, affecting businesses as well as nonprofits. Demands for accountability and the need for systems and procedures to comply with greater scrutiny and regulation also have contributed to the need for trained managers.

In sum, if it was ever true that the typical nonprofit organization fit the image of a well-intentioned but unmanaged endeavor, nonprofit organizations today, other than perhaps the smallest, must be managed. To be otherwise is not only to risk failure in meeting society's needs and expectations but also to place the organization's survival at risk. But the question remains, whether managing a nonprofit organization is different from managing a government agency or a business corporation. Is management generic, or is management in the nonprofit sector a distinguishable endeavor?

Throughout most of the history of management as a recognized discipline, most theorists advocated a generic approach, arguing that common management principles would apply equally to all organizations, whether businesses, government agencies, or nonprofits. And there remain some who are skeptical that management in the nonprofit sector is unique or that it requires particularly distinctive skills.

At an operational level, surely management in the nonprofit sector requires many of the same skills that are also important in government or business. There may not be a particularly nonprofit way of processing payroll or implementing a new information system; and, indeed, many of the techniques of business management have been adopted by nonprofit organizations as well. But this book is predicated on the view that nonprofit management is different from management in the business or governmental sector, in a variety of ways, including the following four.

First, as Herman and Heimovics (2005) explain, nonprofit management uniquely requires the ability to integrate mission, the acquisition of resources, and strategy.

> The choice of a mission for an organization depends on the potential for the acquisition of sufficient resources to carry out that mission. Conversely, the acquisition of certain kinds of resources can influence the mission an organization chooses to undertake. Any mission, no matter how great the cause, is likely to fail if the organization lacks necessary and sufficient resources to pursue it. Moreover, decisions about strategies for acquiring resources must be consistent with the mission and ethical values of the organization. Actions in one realm affect the other realms. The leadership challenge is to see that decisions and actions in one realm are not only consistent with those in other realms but also mutually reinforcing. (Herman & Heimovics, 2005, p. 153)

Managers of government agencies generally have a single source of revenue—for example, the U.S. Congress or a state legislature, and carry out programs mandated by the law. Managers in business receive revenue from the sale of products or services and have the freedom to decide what goods or services they will provide and to which customers. More sales translate into increased revenues, and activities that are not profitable can be discontinued. The same relationships do not always hold true for a nonprofit. Most nonprofits obtain resources from multiple sources and, like businesses, have considerable freedom to determine the activities in which they will engage. However, one important difference is that increased activity may strain resources rather than enhance them. That is because not all of a nonprofit's customers may pay the full cost of producing the good or service, and indeed, some may not pay at all. Judy Vredenburgh, a former executive of Big Brothers Big Sisters and the March of Dimes, describes the dilemma: "'Every time we in nonprofits satisfy customers, we drain resources, and every time for-profits satisfy a customer, they get resources. That sounds very simple, but it has huge implications'" (Silverman & Taliento, 2006, p. 41).

Thus, as Herman and Heimovics (2005) suggest, management of a nonprofit organization requires constant trade-offs among the mission, the acquisition of resources, and strategy. That distinguishes nonprofit management from the management function in the business or public sectors. Management in those sectors, while also complex, at least begins with some fixed points of clear goals and positive relationships between activities and revenues. Managing a nonprofit is more like swimming in the air, with everything variable and in constant motion.

Second, the complex relationships among a nonprofit organization's stakeholders require management that is especially skilled in negotiation and compromise, with a high tolerance for ambiguity. In corporations and in government agencies, the flow of authority from the top down is generally clear. But, as Anheier (2005) describes,

> nonprofit organizations consist of multiple components and complex, internal federations or coalitions among stakeholders . . . [therefore], the structure of nonprofit organizations may require a multi-faceted, flexible approach to management and not the use of singular, ready-made models carried over from the business world or from public management. (p. 245)

Jim Collins (2005) recounts a meeting between Frances Hesselbein, the then chief executive officer (CEO) of the Girl Scouts of America, and a *New York Times* columnist, in which she addressed this unique characteristic of nonprofit management:

[The columnist] asked what it felt like to be on top of such a large organization. With patience, like a teacher pausing to impart an important lesson, Hesselbein proceeded to rearrange the lunch table, creating a set of concentric circles radiating outward—plates, cups, saucers—connected by knives, forks, spoons. Hesselbein pointed to a glass in the middle of the table. "I'm here," she said. Hesselbein may have had the title of Chief Executive Officer, but her message was clear: *I'm not on top of anything.* (p. 9)

Nonprofit management is unique because nonprofit organizations are different from businesses and governmental units—often reliant on the support of donors and the work of volunteers, pursuing missions derived from values and principles, about which there may be disagreement, and engendering a sense of ownership and a desire for influence among multiple constituencies both inside and outside the walls of the organization itself. In this environment, a nonprofit CEO must provide leadership as well as management, a distinction we will explore further in Chapter 4. Robert Higgins, who worked as both a nonprofit executive and a venture capitalist and thus was able to observe the differences between the sectors firsthand, explains,

"In most for-profit organizations . . . people arrive with common goals. The board of directors may have different viewpoints, but shareholder value as a fundamental goal is something shared by the board, by the CEO, and by senior management. You start off differently in the not-for-profit world, with each board member arriving with a different set of goals and often different agendas. To manage that as a CEO is much more complex." (Silverman & Taliento, 2006, p. 38)

Third, managers of nonprofit organizations must measure their success by a double bottom line. A nonprofit exists to pursue a social mission, and success must be measured in terms of its ability to achieve that mission. That's one bottom line. But, in today's competitive environment, nonprofit managers also must pay close attention to the financial bottom line if their organizations are to survive and succeed. Ask a room of people "What's the purpose of Microsoft," and some may quickly reply "to produce software" or perhaps some will joke "to control the world!" But both responses miss the point because Microsoft, like all businesses, has one clear purpose: to increase the value of the business and thus the wealth of its owners. Producing software and controlling the world are but means to that end. To be sure, many corporations today are also guided by principles of social responsibility and ethics, but social progress is not their *purpose*. Indeed, social concerns are properly viewed as constraints on the pursuit of the purpose for which every business exists: to maximize profit in order to increase the value of the owners' equity. Managers may have their own personal, social goals, but if they make them a central element of the company's purpose, they will not fulfill their principal responsibility to the owners of the firm.

In contrast, a nonprofit *exists* to serve a social purpose. But, as we have discussed, in today's competitive environment, financial results also require the executive's attention—he or she must manage the double bottom line of financial and social return. And the latter may be ambiguous in its definition, even a subject of disagreement and dissension among the organization's many stakeholders and/or difficult to measure.

Fourth, and finally, many of the problems that nonprofit managers address are exceptionally difficult and intractable. Andreasen and Kotler (2003) offer a strong example:

> While the "difficulty" of one's management challenges may be a matter of opinion, very few corporate chieftains would think it easier to increase market share two percent than to reduce the number of AIDS cases in an African country with volunteer workers, an antagonistic government, countervailing religious and cultural norms, rampant customer illiteracy, and crumbling public infrastructure. (p. 5)

To say that managing a nonprofit is inherently more complex than managing a business of comparable size is not to demean the skills of business managers nor to disparage their clear focus on profit. The creativity and problem-solving skills of business leaders have built great organizations and propelled economic progress. And it is the wealth created by the business sector that sustains nonprofits and makes social advancement possible. But the need to manage the double bottom line, to relate to disparate and competing constituencies, and often to work against the weight of deep-seated historical and cultural barriers adds complexity to the nonprofit CEO's challenge, a challenge that is too often underestimated by some who observe the nonprofit sector from a business perspective. William Novelli, a former businessman who built the public relations firm Porter Novelli and is now the CEO of the nonprofit AARP, explains the challenge:

> "It's harder to succeed in the nonprofit world. . . . It may be hard to compete in the field of consumer packaged goods or electronics or high finance . . . but it's harder to achieve goals in the nonprofit world because these goals tend to be behavioral. If you set out to do something about breast cancer in the country, or about Social Security solvency, it's a hell of a lot harder to pull that off. [And] it's also harder to measure." (Silverman & Taliento, 2006, p. 37)

This book is based on the premise that nonprofit management is a unique endeavor, distinguishable from management in business or government. It is necessary, however, to acknowledge that some see a convergence of management across the sectors in recent years, as both public managers and nonprofit managers are expected to be more businesslike and business managers are expected to demonstrate more responsibility toward the social and human impact of their actions. As Lester Salamon (2002) observes, If nonprofits are becoming more "business-like," the business methods they are adopting have themselves undergone fundamental change in recent years, and many of the changes have involved incorporating management approaches long associated with nonprofit work—such as the emphasis on organizational mission, service to clients, and the need to imbue staff with a sense of purpose beyond the maximization of profit. In a sense, these longtime nonprofit management principles have now been fused with business management techniques to produce a blended body of management concepts that is penetrating business and nonprofit management alike (p. 6).

The rise of nonprofit management as a field of study

Students taking their first course in nonprofit management might reasonably assume that such courses always have existed. But they are a relatively recent addition to the curriculum at most colleges and universities, and scholarly research in the field, while growing, still does not approach the volume of courses devoted to the study of public or business management.

Indeed, recognition of *management* as an identifiable function—in any organizational setting—is relatively recent in the scope of history. While management-like functions have been performed throughout civilized history, the beginning of management as a field of study dates approximately to the late 19th century and the development of an industrial economy. Stephen Block (2001) credits an 1886 paper by the engineer Henry R. Towne as the first call for the development of management as an independent field of study with its own literature (p. 106). The nation's first school of management, the Wharton School at the University of Pennsylvania, was established shortly thereafter, in 1898. The first two decades of the 20th century saw the growth of professional management societies, books, and university programs. The first doctoral dissertation in management was written in 1915. Interest in management was increased by the experience of American manufacturing during WWII, and the decades since have brought explosive growth in business management education and research, including the development of theories we will explore at relevant points in this book (p. 107). But the early study of management was focused on business organizations, with attention to public management developing later. Interest in nonprofit management has emerged primarily within the past three decades.

As mentioned above, until about the 1960s, most management theorists advanced a "generic approach," arguing that their theories applied equally in all types of organizations, whether businesses, government agencies, or nonprofits. As Hal Rainey (2003), a public administration scholar, emphasizes, "With some clear exceptions . . . the theorists repeatedly implied or aggressively asserted that distinctions such as public and private, market and non-market, and governmental and nongovernmental offered little value for developing theory or understanding practice" (p. 48). However, by the 1960s, some authors began to challenge this approach and to call for more research focused specifically on the management of public agencies. This coincided with a period of growth in the federal government and the development of master of public administration (MPA) degree programs in universities, which for the first time emphasized management skills in government and differentiated the study of public management from the discipline of political science. The National Association of Schools of Public Affairs and Administration (NASPAA) was founded in 1970 and began to accredit such programs.

Attention was drawn to the nonprofit sector by an important national study conducted by the Commission on Private Philanthropy and Public Needs during the period 1973 to 1975. That commission, often called the "Filer Commission" in honor of its chair, issued a report titled *Giving in America* (Commission on Private Philanthropy and Public Needs, 1975), which was the most detailed study of philanthropy in the United States up to that time. The first academic center devoted to the study of nonprofits, the Yale Program on Non-Profit Organizations (PONPO), was founded shortly thereafter, in 1978, and social scientists began to turn their attention to understanding the role of nonprofit organizations in economic and political life. The generic approach was beginning to yield to the view that nonprofit organizations might have unique characteristics that distinguish them from organizations in the other two sectors.

As previously discussed, the 1980s marked a turning point in public policy, with government outsourcing more of the delivery and management of social and human services to nonprofits. That development further increased the need for professional management in nonprofit organizations and captured the interest of some students previously aiming for careers in government. Public administration faculty members saw that a growing number of their students were interested in working in nonprofit organizations and responded by developing programs to teach nonprofit-specific skills (Joslyn, 2004). The number of programs grew throughout the 1980s. The 1980s also saw the establishment of new research centers and programs, including Case Western Reserve University's Mandel Center for Nonprofit Organizations and the Center on Philanthropy at Indiana University.

But the significant attention of management scholars and writers has turned to the nonprofit sector only since the 1990s. Writing in 1990, the management guru Peter Drucker observed a "management boom" going on in nonprofit organizations, but he also noted the lack of recognition of nonprofit management as worthy of attention. "For most Americans," he wrote, "the word 'management' still means business management" (p. xiv). But as the nonprofit sector continued to grow throughout the 1990s and into the 2000s, a burgeoning literature sought to adapt the theories and skills of business management to the planning, managing, and financing of nonprofits. Courses in the strategic management of nonprofits began to proliferate in business schools, and new books applied the techniques used by companies and governments to the nonprofit sector (Oster, 1995; Steiss, 2003). The *Harvard Business Review* came to include occasional articles on the management of nonprofit organizations, with some of the classics collected into a book in 1999 (Harvard Business Review, 1999). The late 1990s brought an economic boom and a boom in the literature of venture philanthropy, social enterprise, entrepreneurial nonprofits, and business techniques applied to nonprofit organizations (Dees, 1998; Dees, Emerson, & Economy, 2001; Kearns, 2000, Letts, Ryan, & Grossman, 1999a; Oster, Massarsky, & Beinhacker, 2004).

Concomitant with the increase in research, educational programs related to nonprofit management grew rapidly in the 1990s. A study by Mirabella and Wish (2000) found that there were only 17 graduate programs in nonprofit management in existence in 1990. But a follow-up study in 2002 found more than a 10-fold increase, with 255 colleges and universities offering courses in nonprofit management. That number included 114 institutions offering a graduate degree with at least a concentration in nonprofit management (Mirabella, 2004). Recent years have seen a virtual explosion in the availability of training for nonprofit managers and professional expertise directed toward the improvement of management practices in nonprofit organizations, including programs offered by educational institutions, regional associations of nonprofits, nonprofit infrastructure organizations, and for-profit consulting firms.

Formalization of the nonprofit management curriculum in universities has progressed, but it is still a work in progress. In 2001, the NASPAA issued "Guidelines for Graduate Professional Education in Nonprofit Organizations, Management and Leadership." The Nonprofit Academic Centers Council, a membership association of academic centers and programs that focus on nonprofit organizations, issued its first "Curricular Guidelines for Graduate Study in Philanthropy, the Nonprofit Sector, and Nonprofit Leadership" in 2004.

Nonprofit management remains an adolescent field. There continues to be a "best-place debate" about whether nonprofit management should be taught in schools of business or management, in schools of public administration and public policy, or in other academic units (Mirabella & Wish, 2000). In her 2004 study, Mirabella found that 49% of graduate programs were offered as concentrations within MPA degrees, 8% were concentrations within MBA programs, and 15% were offered in schools of social work. Other programs led to the MS or MA degree, and just a handful of institutions offered a Master of Nonprofit Management degree.

PHILOSOPHY OF THIS BOOK

A Comprehensive Overview

Students reading this book are likely to have varied backgrounds. Some may be undergraduates who do not yet have substantial work experience and perhaps wish to explore nonprofit management as a possible career direction. Others may be graduate students with an interest in nonprofit careers but who have not previously studied management. Others may have studied management as undergraduates but may have limited knowledge of the unique values, characteristics, and circumstances of the nonprofit sector or how the management principles they know can be applied in the nonprofit environment. Yet others may be individuals with considerable experience working in nonprofit organizations who are pursuing further study to increase and broaden their understanding and professional skills.

Some students reading this book may be beginning a program leading to a master's degree in nonprofit management. Others may be pursuing a master's degree in business, public administration, or public policy, with a concentration in nonprofit management. Yet others may be taking only one course in nonprofit management as an elective in their undergraduate or graduate degree program, seeking only a broad and general orientation to the field.

Given this diversity of backgrounds and goals often found among students taking their first course in nonprofit management, a textbook intended for such a course must include both theoretical concepts and practical applications; it must cover some basics as well as intellectually stimulating issues; it must be both rigorous and accessible to students of varied academic backgrounds; it must provide both a foundation of knowledge that may serve as a springboard to more advanced study and a comprehensive overview for those students whose one experience with the field will consist of a single course.

This book strives to address all these diverse needs and interests, with the author's humble recognition that it may not succeed in meeting all of them for all students. It attempts to provide a comprehensive exposure to topics relevant to the field of nonprofit management, but it obviously must be selective in its discussion of those topics. This intended balance between comprehensiveness in topics and selectivity in their treatment may frustrate some readers. Some may find their appetites whetted but unsatisfied by the quick tour provided in some parts of the book. Others may find that some chapters include ideas they have seen before in other courses.

Students are encouraged to tailor their use of the book to their own interests and backgrounds. Readers who, for example, already have studied some of the organizational and management theories we will discuss are encouraged to read relevant sections as a refresher but to pay closer attention to material that is new to them. Those to whom the theories are new, and who find their discussion in this book to be too brief, are encouraged to explore the additional resources suggested throughout the book. In sum, it is hoped that this book may provide a kind of comprehensive menu, from which students may select the topics or approaches on which they wish to "click" for more information. Both novices and more experienced individuals may find it a foundation on which they can build, seeking appropriate avenues for further information and learning. And, in all likelihood, professors also will elaborate on some topics and skip lightly over others, as they sense the tempo of their individual classes.

A Balanced and Integrated Approach

One goal of this book is to provide a balanced and integrated approach to the field. The literature of nonprofit management reveals a variety of opinions and perspectives. Authors often disagree on specific points—for example, on the appropriate roles and relationships of the organization's board and CEO, on the appropriate balance between being businesslike and remaining focused on the nonprofit mission, or on the standards by which a nonprofit organization's effectiveness or performance should be measured, among others.

There are at least two broad approaches or perspectives reflected in the contemporary nonprofit management literature. Generalization can, of course, sometimes lead to oversimplification; differences in perspective or approach are often nuanced. But students will likely observe that authors writing about nonprofit organizations and nonprofit management today reflect one of two perspectives that are distinguishable, at least in tone and emphasis.

Some see nonprofit organizations primarily as social institutions. The services they provide are important, but nonprofits also are essential for creating civil society, pursuing social change, and sustaining the free expression of values and opinions in a democratic society—indeed, for preserving our most important values as a society. Process and involvement are valued nearly as much as the end result. From this perspective, nonprofit managers often are portrayed as stewards of their organizations or servants of society. With regard to the education of nonprofit managers, those who hold this perspective usually emphasize the need to develop an appreciation of nonprofit values, an understanding of nonprofits' role in society, and a capacity for ethical decision making. In discussing charity and philanthropy, they tend to focus on their cultural and historical roots of giving and view giving as an expression of moral and religious values. They do not necessarily deny the usefulness of business methods in managing nonprofit organizations, but some do express skepticism about the possibility of measuring organizations' effectiveness against sometimes lofty missions. Some express concern that the application of business methods and business thinking holds the risk of undermining traditional nonprofit values and diminishing nonprofit organizations' unique contributions to society. They are often uncomfortable about nonprofits becoming too engaged in commercial activities or forming close relationships with business and concerned that nonprofit culture will be eroded and organizations will lose sight of their social purposes in the pursuit of financial success.

From another perspective, nonprofit organizations are social enterprises, essentially businesses that have a social purpose. Those who hold that view do not dismiss the importance of nonprofits' social missions, nor do they necessarily deny the unique qualities and contributions of the nonprofit sector. Most give at least lip service to the idea that a business approach may not be appropriate for every nonprofit organization. But they tend to emphasize the commonalities between nonprofit organizations and business firms and encourage the use of business principles and techniques in managing nonprofits. They admire nonprofit leaders who are social entrepreneurs and discuss the education of nonprofit managers in terms of developing entrepreneurial and business skills. Their discussions often focus on building the capacity of nonprofits and the application of business methods, such as strategic planning, strategic management, and marketing. They often use the vocabulary of business, discussing a nonprofit organization's "competitive advantage" and "sustainability." Some criticize traditional charity and philanthropy and prefer that nonprofits rely more on earned income—that is, on revenue derived from their own businesslike activities rather than on gifts. They emphasize results, and some even discuss the idea of developing nonprofit capital markets that would allocate funds rationally to nonprofit organizations that show high performance, much as stock markets allocate investment dollars to the companies that produce the highest financial returns.

Again, the above characterizations of these two perspectives are likely oversimplified, and some writers take a moderate stance between the two poles described. But it is usually not difficult to identify a particular book or article as leaning toward one perspective or the other. This text draws on literature from both approaches and strives to present a balanced and integrated understanding. Where disagreements may exist, it attempts to fairly summarize both sides of the argument.

That approach leads to the frequent use of the expression "on the one hand, but on the other hand." Some might prefer to know the "right answer" and learn what is indeed the best way to manage a nonprofit organization. The philosophy reflected in this book is that there is often no right answer and that the best way is often pragmatic and eclectic. It includes viewing a problem from multiple perspectives and drawing from various approaches selectively as situations may dictate. Students will find abundant other materials written by authors who come from one particular viewpoint or another that they may find to be especially attractive or persuasive.

Focus on Management

This book draws upon three bodies of literature: (1) the work of social scientists who study nonprofit organizations as social and economic institutions; (2) organizational theory, theories of organizational behavior, and management theory from the business and public sectors that have particular relevance for nonprofit organizations; and, (3) a rich practitioner literature that offers important understandings.

Nonprofit management, both as a profession and as an academic field of study, is still relatively young. That is reflected in its literature. There is an increasing body of academic research, including the work of economists, sociologists, historians, and other social scientists who have developed taxonomies to identify and track the major components of the nonprofit sector; theories to explain the existence and behavior of the sector; theories describing its relationship to government and the business sector; examinations of its role and impact in the U.S. economy; and analyses of related public policy issues. The management of nonprofits also has been the focus of more applied studies drawn from the fields of public administration and business management.

However, much of the nonprofit management literature is still written by or for practitioners and has a prescriptive, how-to-do-it approach. Consultants, including professionals working in for-profit consulting firms, also have made important contributions to the literature of nonprofit management.

This book is a textbook, not a manual for nonprofit executives. But neither is its purpose to offer an entirely theoretical examination of the nonprofit sector. It is intended to provide students who are considering or pursuing careers in nonprofit management with a broad foundation blending theoretical and practical topics relevant to the work they do or will do. This approach introduces the risk that some pragmatic individuals may find it too academic and that some academics may find it insufficiently grounded, but it is appropriate to provide a comprehensive and useful overview of a field that is still emerging.

Emphasis on Complex Management Challenges

For most people, the term *nonprofit organization* conjures up the image of a small organization, perhaps run by a tiny band of volunteers more focused on delivering services to people in need than on building or managing an organization. Indeed, most nonprofit organizations are small organizations, with perhaps no or limited professional staff. This book incorporates some examples drawn from such organizations. Mention the word *business* and people will likely think first of a large corporation, such as Wal-Mart or Coca Cola, although, in reality, most businesses are small, too. But it is large business enterprises that are the focus of most business texts and MBA case studies. That's because, as in the non-profit sector, the need for management varies with size. The corner dry cleaner needs few management skills beyond perhaps basic accounting and maybe a rudimentary understanding of how to manage a few employees. The young technology entrepreneur starting a new business in his father's garage is not focused on management but on development and delivery of a product, much as the directors of small nonprofits are often more concerned with delivering programs than with building or managing the organization. As a company grows, requiring outside investment and employing more people, its need for professional management increases. Founder entrepreneurs are often replaced by MBAs, who have formal management training. So too, as a nonprofit organization becomes larger, it faces more complex and interesting management challenges, especially if it comes to operate in more than one location across the United States or internationally. For that reason, this book is principally about organizations that have at least some full-time paid staff, and it includes examples and cases drawn from some of the nation's largest and best-known nonprofits.

Focus on U.S. Charitable Nonprofits

As we will discuss in Chapter 1, the nonprofit sector encompasses an amazing array of organizations with different characteristics, structures, and purposes. This book focuses primarily on that category known as charitable nonprofits and, in particular, those that provide services, such as education and research, health care, arts and cultural programs, and social and legal services. Such organizations account for 92.3% of revenues, 95.5% of paid staff, and 97.6% of all salaries and wages in the nonprofit sector (Weitzman, Jalandoni, Lampkin, & Pollak, 2002). The following chapters will sometimes mention member-serving organizations—for example, trade and professional associations—but primarily as points of contrast with charitable nonprofits. Religious congregations make up a significant component of the overall nonprofit sector, but religion is the subsector that is the least professionalized—that is, it employs relatively few professional managers. Thus, we will not devote significant discussion to the management of churches, synagogues, and mosques. We will discuss foundations, but primarily as sources of support for service-providing nonprofits; we will not discuss the management of foundations per se. This book does not exclude, but also does not emphasize, those nonprofits that are primarily advocacy organizations, also known as social welfare organizations. While they are nonprofits, they are also different from charitable nonprofits in important ways, as we will discuss further in Chapter 1. Of course, some principles of governance, leadership, and management discussed in this book apply to all nonprofits and will be of relevance to students intending to work in any component of the nonprofit world.

While this book includes a chapter on nonprofits in the international environment, it primarily addresses the management of nonprofit organizations in the United States. The American nonprofit sector is the largest in the world; it operates under unique cultural, economic, and legal circumstances. It is where most American students of nonprofit management will pursue their careers. However, as governments around the world seek to reduce their expenditures and devolve many functions to nonprofit organizations, many also are looking to relevant aspects of the American model in developing their own nonprofit sectors. Thus, even for students primarily interested in working on the international stage, an understanding of nonprofit management in the United States is both relevant and useful.

PROCEEDING WITH REALISM AND PRIDE

Finally, readers should understand, this book is based on the view that while there is a need to improve the management of nonprofit organizations, it is a misperception to believe, as some do, that they are generically less well managed than businesses.

This misperception is based in part on our society's bias for defining success primarily in financial terms. The results of good business management are evident in bottom-line earnings, while the results of nonprofit management are reflected in progress toward a social mission, which may be less visible or easy to measure.

In addition, the misperception is often reinforced when apples are compared with oranges, which may occur, for example, if someone's image of a nonprofit is as a small organization and that person's image of a business is that of a larger corporation. It may be accurate to observe that some small nonprofits are not well managed. But, it is important to note, the same is true of many small businesses, most of which fail in the first five years of their existence. It might be difficult to demonstrate that a family-run B&B is really better managed than the local homeless shelter, which would be more appropriate than comparing the shelter with Marriott.

When nonprofit organizations and companies are compared fairly, we find poor and excellent management in both. The American Red Cross, one of the nation's largest nonprofits, confronts many problems that have been well publicized. But, it is fair to ask, is it less well managed than General Motors, which at the time of this writing, is making massive cuts and struggling to survive? Or, we might ask, are Habitat for Humanity and Doctors Without Borders less innovative organizations than Microsoft or Google? In a sequel to his best-selling book on business management, which focuses on the social (or nonprofit) sector, Jim Collins (2005) argues that the important difference is not between business management and nonprofit management but between mediocrity and greatness:

> Most businesses—like most of anything else in life—fall somewhere between
> mediocre and good. Few are great. . . . Mediocre companies rarely display the
> relentless culture of discipline . . . that we find in truly great companies. [But]
> a culture of discipline is not a principle of business; it is a principle of greatness.
> (p. 1)

The author's purpose in making this point in this Introduction is to dispel any misperceptions that students may hold that nonprofit management is somehow second rate. Or, as implied by critical articles seen in the popular media, that incompetence and corruption are rampant in nonprofit organizations. Nonprofit managers are in general highly capable and dedicated individuals, worthy of the respect and regard of their counterparts in the other sectors of business and government. They work in organizations that are different from businesses or government; they have different purposes and goals; and they often work with fewer resources available to them. But they are not categorically less able or successful. Students beginning their study of nonprofit management should do so with a pride and confidence equal to that of their classmates who may be preparing for careers in business, government, or other distinguished professions.

At the same time, students should hold no illusions about the challenges of a nonprofit management career. Although salaries are improving, nonprofit managers are unlikely to achieve the wealth of their counterparts in business or the job security of their colleagues who hold civil service positions in the government. The pressures are significant. As Julie Rogers, President of the Agnes and Eugene Meyer Foundation, observes, nonprofit executives face a never-ending stream of advice from their boards, funders, clients, volunteers, and others: "Focus on finding dependable sources of income. Produce measurable results. Evaluate whether you are making a difference. Be strategic, not opportunistic. Build diverse boards. Spend more time on advocacy. Collaborate with other organizations" (Rogers, 2006). And, too often, they are advised to do all this with smaller budgets, smaller staffs, less training, and less recognition than is provided to managers in business or government. Indeed, some recent studies suggest that the complexity of the nonprofit manager's job and the multiple pressures he or she must handle too often lead to frustration and burn out (Rogers, 2006).

But nonprofit managers also enjoy unique rewards, including the satisfaction of knowing that they are working to advance those aspects of human life that many consider to be the most important—the arts, education, the preservation of culture, and the development of young people. They experience the excitement of tackling some of society's most daunting problems and protecting society's most vulnerable members, making a difference in their lives and in the future of society. And they know the camaraderie and fellowship that comes from working alongside others who share their values, priorities, and commitments. For many who have dedicated their careers to advancing nonprofit organizations, the value of such intangible rewards is beyond measure.

OVERVIEW OF THE BOOK

The first two chapters of this book provide an orientation to the nonprofit sector and a theoretical foundation for the more applied topics we will consider later. Chapter 1 offers a look at the structure, boundaries, and characteristics of the nonprofit sector and establishes some basic definitions. Chapter 2 expands our understanding of the nonprofit sector by reviewing theories that explain its existence and its role in relation to government and business. That chapter also examines selected theories that describe the nature of nonprofit organizations and explain their behavior.

The next two chapters consider the roles and responsibilities of governing boards and nonprofit CEOs and the ways in which these two vital actors interact in leading organizations. The nonprofit governing board has functional, moral, and legal responsibilities. Nonprofit chief executives, whether titled "executive director," "president," "CEO," or something else, lead their organizations in a complex and dynamic environment that will be described. The partnership between the CEO and the board is critical to a well-operating and effective organization. That critical relationship will be explored in Chapters 3 and 4.

The next five chapters focus on applied aspects of nonprofit management. Chapter 5 reviews the increasing demands for nonprofit accountability and various approaches to measuring the performance of nonprofit organizations. One response to increased concerns about performance has been a growing emphasis on building the capacity of nonprofit organizations, or, simply put, on enhancing their ability to achieve their missions. There is an extensive and growing literature on the subject of capacity building, which will be considered in Chapter 6. Chapter 7 discusses an important aspect of capacity building, the development of organizational strategy, and the tools of strategic planning and strategic management now employed by many nonprofits. Chapter 8 discusses both the theory and the practice of human resource management in nonprofit organizations. One of the significant differences between many nonprofits and business or government is the substantial employment of volunteers to provide the organization's core services. Management of an unpaid workforce requires an understanding of human motivation and skill in managing effective relationships between an organization's volunteers and its paid professional staff. Chapter 9 considers the management of programs for communication and marketing, essential for organizations that are highly interactive with and dependent on the world around them.

Another section of the book, encompassing three chapters, is concerned with the acquisition and management of resources. Chapter 10 reviews the principles of raising philanthropic funds from individual, corporate, and foundation donors. Chapter 11 explores the subject of nonprofits' earned income—that is, efforts to generate revenue through activities other than traditional philanthropy. That chapter explores the myriad and growing commercial partnerships between nonprofit organizations and corporations, including cause-related marketing, sponsorships, licensing agreements, joint ventures and others. It also considers nonprofit entrepreneurial ventures, the creation of revenue-generating businesses that provide a stream of revenue to support mission programs.

The securing of revenue and the management of financial resources are interrelated activities. Like many of the topics covered in this book, financial management is large, complex, and important. Chapter 12 provides a few basic concepts and directs students to additional sources from which they can obtain the more detailed understanding they may seek.

The final section of the book includes three chapters that will bring our discussion up-to-date with a brief look at some contemporary developments, trends, and issues. Chapter 13 examines recent trends toward collaboration and mergers among nonprofit organizations. Chapter 14 looks at the role of nonprofits as advocates for social change and some of the considerations for managers of such activities. Chapter 15 looks beyond the United States to discuss the work of nonprofit organizations on the world stage. The Conclusion to the book offers some of the author's final reflections and observations.

Students may observe that the book does not include a chapter on nonprofit law. Nonprofits are subject to a large and growing body of law at the local, state, and federal levels, and additional regulation of the sector is under discussion as this volume is written. However, the author decided to discuss aspects of nonprofit law in the various chapters where they are most relevant rather than in a separate chapter. The book provides references to other resources for students who may want to know more. The book also does not include a separate chapter on ethics; rather, ethical issues are addressed at relevant points throughout the text.

Again, all the following chapters draw on the theoretical and academic literature as well as the writing of experienced practitioners and consultants. Where the topic lends itself to examples, key points are illustrated with actual cases, some drawn from the daily headlines. Students are encouraged to include the cases in their reading of each chapter, to consider the Questions for Discussion at the end of each chapter, and to think about the relevance of what they are reading to any nonprofit organizations with which they may have personal experience.

PART I

Understanding Nonprofit Organizations

CHAPTER 1

Overview of the
Nonprofit Sector

America's nonprofit sector is large, complex, and diverse, including organizations very different from one another in purpose, size, and other characteristics. As Simon wrote in 1987, "The sprawling and unruly collection of animals that populate the nonprofit world—from churches to civil rights groups to garden clubs to the National Council on Philanthropy— makes this field hard to grasp and study all at once" (p. 69). And, as we will soon discover, the nonprofit sector is even more sprawling and unruly today than it was in 1987.

In this chapter, we will look at the nonprofit sector as a whole and establish basic concepts and definitions that will help bring some order to our understanding of its structure, boundaries, and characteristics. Let's start by taking a brief imaginary tour around one American city, starting from the author's office on the campus of The George Washington University, located near the center of Washington, D.C. As the nation's capital, Washington, D.C., is home to a significant number of nonprofits, but the variety of organizations that we will see on our tour is typical of what we might find in any American city. A walk through this one city helps give us a sense of the complexity to be found in today's nonprofit sector across the country.

Leaving the author's office at the University, we might walk past the George Washington University Hospital, then turn down the street and pass Western Presbyterian Church, just a few blocks from the edge of the campus. If it were morning, we likely would see men and women waiting to enter the basement of the church to visit Miriam's Kitchen, an organization that serves breakfast and provides other services to homeless people.

Another turn, and we would walk in front of the national headquarters of the American Red Cross and past the headquarters of the National Park Service. Proceeding farther into town, we would see the headquarters of the National Geographic Society and that of the American Federation of Labor and Congress of Industrial Organizations (AFL-CIO). Eventually, we might walk past the Smithsonian Institution, located in several buildings along the National Mall, which extends from the Washington Monument to the Capitol building. If we continued our walk up Capitol Hill, we would pass the Library of Congress and the national headquarters of the Republican and Democratic parties. If the weather were warm, we might stop for some ice cream at Ben and Jerry's on Capitol Hill, before turning back for the return walk to the campus. We could take a slight detour and come back by way of 14th Street, which is home to several nightclubs. Among them we would see HR-57, which offers live jazz performances. Arriving back at The George Washington University, we might think about the various sights we have seen in our day and try to identify which are nonprofits and which are not. But that would not be as easy a task as it may initially seem.

We have indeed encountered a number of nonprofits on our tour, but some seem more nonprofit-like than others. When the word *nonprofit* is used, many people may think first of an organization like Miriam's Kitchen. While it is located in Western Presbyterian Church, it is a separate organization from the church. It is small and supported almost entirely by gifts. Its workforce is predominantly volunteers, and it provides its services to people who pay nothing for them. Most people also would probably recognize the American Red Cross as a nonprofit organization, which it is, although it is chartered by the U.S. Congress and has a mandate from government to provide services to the U.S. military and to the general population in times of disaster. Some might not think of Western Presbyterian Church or other religious congregations as nonprofits in the same way as the Red Cross or Miriam's Kitchen, but religious congregations are indeed a part of the nonprofit sector. Some may be surprised to learn that both the Republican Party and the Democratic Party, and labor unions are also nonprofit organizations.

Some nonprofits don't look or feel like nonprofits. HR-57 is a nonprofit music cultural center in Washington, D.C., which takes its name from a resolution passed by the U.S. House of Representatives in 1987, designating jazz as "a rare and valuable national American treasure." But it doesn't seem that different from any other jazz club on 14th Street. On the other hand, some organizations may seem like nonprofits, but the reality is more complex. For example, The George Washington University Hospital, which we would have passed early on in our walk, doesn't seem any different from other hospitals that are nonprofit. But it is in fact a for-profit hospital owned jointly by The George Washington University (a nonprofit) and Universal Health Services (a for-profit hospital management corporation). Although it is right down the street from Miriam's Kitchen and provides services to some of Miriam's clients, as an organization it is really more like Microsoft than Miriam's.

Several organizations display combinations of nonprofit missions and business operations. Our imaginary tour of Washington, D.C., touched two of these—the Smithsonian Institution and National Geographic. The National Geographic Society is a nonprofit organization dedicated to geographic exploration and education. But National Geographic Ventures is its wholly-owned-for-profit subsidiary that produces television programs, computer software, and other products. The National Geographic Channel is a joint venture with for-profit Fox Entertainment (http://channel.nationalgeographic.com/channel/intl, accessed September 22, 2005). On cable TV, National Geographic competes with Discovery Communications, operator of the Discovery Channel and a for-profit business corporation. Although it looks and feels like any other ice cream shop, the Ben & Jerry's on Capitol Hill is indeed a business franchise owned by the Latin American Youth Center, a nonprofit organization based in Washington, D.C., that uses the shop as the foundation of a job-training program as well as a source of additional revenue to support its mission programs.

The Smithsonian Institution is particularly complex, operating in part like a government agency, in part like a nonprofit organization, and in part like an entrepreneurial business. The Smithsonian receives a significant portion of its support from federal appropriations, but it was founded through a charitable bequest from John Smithson, after whom it was named, and it actively solicits philanthropic gifts for its museum exhibits, educational programs, research, and other nonprofit activities. A division called Smithsonian Business Ventures was created in 1999 and manages the business activities of the Smithsonian Institution, including theaters, museum restaurants, and museum stores. Such business ventures now provide $50 million to $60 million in unrestricted annual revenue to support the Smithsonian's educational and research programs (Trescott, 2005, p. A01).

If the line between nonprofit organizations and for-profit businesses is sometimes difficult to distinguish, the line between the nonprofit sector and government itself is also increasingly blurry. Almost one third of the revenue of the nonprofit sector comes from government contracts and grants (Weitzman et al., 2002, p. xxxii), and some organizations exist primarily as government contractors implementing government-funded programs. But some government agencies also have begun to tap the private sector for support to supplement the funds they receive from tax revenues—including two we would have passed on our journey around Washington, D.C., the National Park Service and the Library of Congress. Both are agencies of the federal government that are increasing their efforts to raise private funds to supplement government appropriations.

Further confusing the landscape, there are for-profit companies that look, feel, and sometimes sound nonprofit-like in the way they describe their missions, programs, and goals. Some compete directly with nonprofits engaged in similar activities. Consider, for example, the following description of services offered by one organization:

> We not only help our government and private-sector clients with their employment and training needs, we offer and deliver key services that address fundamental barriers to employment. These include: child care, transportation, counseling, and eligibility determination for federal programs that include Supplemental Security Income (SSI). (MAXIMUS Web site, www.maximus.com, accessed September 24, 2005)

That sounds like the description of a nonprofit organization's programs, but it is indeed drawn from the Web site of MAXIMUS, a large for-profit corporation that manages government programs and employs 5,500 people in 280 different office locations.

Clearly the lines between the for-profit, nonprofit, and public sectors of our society are sometimes difficult to perceive without close examination. And the popular image of a nonprofit organization as a small band of volunteers intending to do good, working with minimal resources, serving people in need, and sharply distinct from business and government is far from the reality of many nonprofit organizations today. To understand how we came to where we are and make sense of the "sprawling and unruly collection of animals" that is today's nonprofit sector, we will need some understanding of the history that brought us to this point—and perhaps some road maps to lead us through the "zoo" (Simon, 1987).

AMERICA'S NONPROFIT SECTOR: A HISTORICAL OVERVIEW

The roots of America's nonprofit sector lie in the ancient traditions of *charity, philanthropy,* and *voluntarism*. Steven Ott (2001, p. 90) identifies the Greco-Roman emphasis on community, citizenry, and social responsibility and the Judeo-Christian ethic of helping others as "two diverse ideological streams" that influenced these traditions in Western societies. But, indeed, virtually all cultures and religions include some emphasis on the importance of service to others, which includes giving or voluntary action.

The legal foundations of America's nonprofit sector are drawn from English law, particularly the Statute of Charitable Uses and the Poor Law, both passed in 1601. These laws clarified the relationship between the British government and the Church of England, defined the legitimate activities to be supported by charity, and established a means to make the trustees of charitable institutions accountable (Hammack, 1998, p. 5). The philosophy reflected in these statutes influenced the development of U.S. law regarding nonprofits and is still reflected in American legal traditions.

Despite their ancient roots, it is in the United States that the traditions of charity, philanthropy, and voluntarism have reached their most elaborated expression. As early as 1835, the Frenchman Alexis de Tocqueville observed the unique propensity of Americans to form "voluntary associations" to address social and political objectives, which he reported in his famous book *Democracy in America*. Indeed, in a young nation born in revolution against the authority of the British government, voluntary organizations and institutions provided many of the services, from schools to volunteer fire departments. A certain mistrust of government has been a pervasive and continuing aspect of American culture and has provided philosophical support for private, voluntary initiatives throughout the nation's history. As we saw in our tour of Washington, D.C., there appears to be some blurring of the nonprofit sector and government in today's environment. But it is important to recognize that the blur was even greater in the earliest days of the nation, when government supported churches and churches sponsored many of the young institutions that served communities.

The beginnings of our modern nonprofit sector lie in the early years of the 20th century. Amidst the rise of great wealth resulting from the industrial revolution, charity and philanthropy became organized activities undertaken on a large scale. This was the time of great philanthropists such as John D. Rockefeller and Andrew Carnegie, who endowed universities, libraries, colleges, and other institutions across the nation. Carnegie's essay, "The Gospel of Wealth," published in 1900, remains a classic statement of the philosophy underpinning the American tradition of philanthropy. Carnegie expresses the responsibility of wealthy individuals to give back to the society that has enabled their accumulation of wealth, saying that "the man who dies rich dies disgraced." Carnegie's philosophy remains deeply a part of American culture, as evidenced by many contemporary entrepreneurs and investors, such as Bill Gates and Warren Buffet, who have created charitable foundations with similar expressions of obligation.

Carnegie also helped establish a distinction between the concepts of charity and philanthropy. Although the words are often used interchangeably and *philanthropy* is sometimes used as the broader, encompassing term, they describe two different types of giving. *Charity* is appropriately defined as giving intended to meet current individual human needs or to alleviate current human suffering—for example, to feed the homeless or aid the victims of a natural disaster. It is emotionally driven and often impulsive, as evidenced by the outpouring of gifts made through the mail, phone, and the Internet within days of the terrorist attacks of September 11, 2001, and Hurricanes Katrina and Rita in September 2005.

Philanthropy, on the other hand, is a more rational form of long-term investment in the infrastructure of society, seen, for example, in gifts made to construct new hospitals, endow universities, or create new charitable foundations intended to exist in perpetuity. If the goals of philanthropists were ultimately achieved, it is arguable that the need for charity would be eliminated, since there would exist institutions prepared to meet any human needs that might arise. However, in the imperfect world of the present, both types of giving are important and complementary in their impacts.

Some writers differentiate voluntarism (also called "volunteerism") from charity and philanthropy, arguing that "charity and philanthropy may require little, if any, direct involvement with the beneficiaries [of the services provided]," whereas "volunteerism . . . is a very active process that requires active involvement with either the beneficiaries directly or an organization or group that serves a specific population" (Block, 2001, p. 101). Robert Payton (1988), on the other hand, makes *philanthropy* the umbrella term, defining it as "voluntary action for the public good," including both the giving of time and the giving of money.

Despite its ancient roots and long history in the United States, the concept of a definable nonprofit sector, comparable with the for-profit and governmental sectors, is of relatively recent origin, dating to the work of the Commission on Private Philanthropy and Public Needs (the Filer Commission) in 1973 to 1975. The Commission's report, titled "Giving in America," was the first to characterize nonprofits as constituting a recognizable sector of society. The Filer Commission report came at a time when the nonprofit sector was expanding, reflecting in part changes in government policy. The 1960s and early 1970s were a period of increasing government spending on social programs, starting with the Great Society programs of President Lyndon Johnson. In many cases, government funds were channeled to nonprofit organizations, which provided the actual services. "Indeed," Lester Salamon (2002) observes, "much of the modern nonprofit sector as we know it took shape during this period as a direct outcome of expanded government support" (p. 12). Beginning in the 1980s, under President Ronald Reagan, federal spending for social programs was sharply reduced, only to recover somewhat in the 1990s under President Bill Clinton. Since the 1980s, there has been a change not only in the level of government support but also in its form, with important implications for the management of nonprofit organizations. The shift has been away from direct grants to nonprofit organizations and toward providing aid to individuals in the form of voucher-type subsidies. This occurred, for example, in health care, where Medicare and Medicaid reshaped the industry. And, it occurred in higher education, where government funds going directly to colleges and universities diminished, while aid directed to individual students and their families increased. This created a new generation of student consumers and transformed higher-education institutions into competitive, marketing organizations. This shift also was illustrated in the welfare reform legislation of 1996, which brought competition to many areas of human services. This empowerment of individuals as consumers through direct subsidies to them has forced nonprofits to compete for customer dollars not only with other nonprofits but also with for-profit companies that have entered fields previously the exclusive preserve of the nonprofit sector. For example, MAXIMUS is now among the nation's largest managers of welfare-to-work programs.

These changes in government funding also account in part for the growing commercialization of the nonprofit sector itself, the increased need for professional nonprofit management, and the demands that nonprofits demonstrate greater accountability and results. Nonprofit organizations comprise a vital and growing sector of our economy and society, but questions about their effectiveness and accountability are topics of national discussion and debate. Some are even reassessing the meaning of concepts such as "community benefit" and "charitable purpose," and the justification of tax exemption for at least some portions of the sector (see Salamon, 2002, pp. 28–29).

SEARCHING FOR A COMMON VOCABULARY

The nonprofit sector is so diverse and its structure is so complex that it is confusing to some people and there are various ways in which people understand it. Diverse understandings are reflected in the fact that there are multiple terms by which the sector is identified.

As Thomas Wolf (1999) points out, describing an elephant as a "non-horse" would seem to most people an unsatisfactory definition (p. 19). But the term *nonprofit organization* really refers to *one* thing nonprofit organizations do *not* do, rather than capturing much about what they are or the diverse programs and services they offer to society. One thing nonprofit organizations do *not* do is distribute profits to individual owners in the form of dividends or use those profits to enhance the wealth of owners through the increasing value of the enterprise.

It is important to dispel the common misunderstanding that nonprofits cannot earn profits. Defined as simply an excess of revenues over expenses, nonprofits can and do earn profits. But theses profits must be retained within the organization and be used to further its programs rather than enrich individuals personally. This non-profit-distribution requirement, also called the nondistribution constraint, is *one* defining characteristic of nonprofit organizations. But it is clearly not *the* defining characteristic; indeed, by this narrow standard, the Department of Defense and the State of New York might also be called "nonprofits," since they also have no stockholders or owners to whom any profit is distributed.

While the term *nonprofit organization* or just *nonprofit* is the most commonly used term in the United States, organizations that work internationally are generally known as *nongovernmental organizations*, although there is no identifiable nongovernmental sector with the same meaning as the term *nonprofit sector* in the United States. The term *nongovernmental* reflects in part the reality that many such organizations are performing government-like functions in the countries they serve and that most receive a substantial portion of their revenue from government sources. Many are like arms of government operating just outside the public sphere. Like *nonprofit*, the term *nongovernmental* defines organizations by what they are not—they are not government agencies. But this term seems equally inadequate. It could apply as well to profit-making companies such as Intel and General Electric, which are also clearly nongovernmental in their ownership and legal control.

ALTERNATIVES TO "NONPROFIT"

While *nonprofit* is the term most commonly used to describe the sector, there is no shortage of proposed alternatives. Each alternative has its own virtues and shortcomings as well. The term *independent sector* has some prominence since it is also the name of the principal organization representing the interests of nonprofits in Washington, D.C.—Independent Sector (www.independentsector.org). But it raises the question of "independent from what?" Nonprofits are financially dependent on resources derived from both government and private donors and are subject to an increasing array of state and federal law, so independence would not seem to capture their essence.

Some prefer the term *third sector*, placing nonprofits in the universe alongside the commercial economy and government. The term is accurate in terms of size—both the business sector and government employ more people, generate larger revenues, and account for a larger share of economic output. But it also seems to imply a rank order of importance, which would not agree with the values of many people, who may consider religion, education, the arts, medical research, and other purposes served by the nonprofit sector to be among the most important of human endeavors. Furthermore, some scholars suggest that American society encompasses not three but four sectors: business, government, the nonprofit sector, and families and communities. In this broader array, it becomes more difficult to rank the sectors, except by size, in which case families and communities would come first and the nonprofit sector would be fourth rather than third.

The term *charitable sector* is sometimes used, but it is contrary to the reality that charitable gifts, while important, are not the largest source of nonprofit revenues. Nor is the term synonymous with *nonprofit sector*, since there are organizations that qualify as nonprofit under the U.S. tax code but that neither seek nor receive any form of charitable support. This is true, for example, of membership organizations that are funded entirely through dues and those nonprofits whose revenues may consist entirely of grants and contracts received from government. Nor does the term seem appropriate to encompass major institutions, such as Harvard University, that are nonprofit but hardly consistent with most people's understanding of a charity.

Some use the term *voluntary sector*. Voluntarism is one of the foundations of the sector, and many organizations do indeed rely on volunteers, both as members of their governing boards and for at least part of their workforce. But the term does not reflect the reality that in many nonprofits, paid staff members far outnumber volunteers. It also may perpetuate an inaccurate image of nonprofits as universally small and amateurish in their operations, when, indeed, many nonprofits are substantial enterprises and professional management of nonprofits has been a growing trend.

The phrase *tax-exempt sector*, commonly used by accountants, attorneys, and other tax specialists, is similar to *nonprofit*. It identifies organizations entirely in terms of their status under U.S. tax law. Nonprofits are exempt from paying federal income tax and generally from state and local income taxes as well. But, again, *tax-exempt* speaks to the legal status of such organizations and says nothing about what they actually do. As we will discuss shortly, the sector encompasses a variety of organizations with few apparent similarities aside from their tax-exempt status.

Another term that has been proposed is *civil society sector* (Salamon, 1999, p. 9). There are many different definitions of *civil society*, and while "the nonprofit sector provides the organizational infrastructure of civil society," the concept itself is more abstract, including "the sum of institutions, organizations, and individuals located between the family, the state, and the market, in which people associate voluntarily to advance common interests" (Anheier, 2005, p. 9). And as Salamon (1999) acknowledges, the term *civil society sector* is like *voluntary sector* in that it "emphasizes the citizen base" of these organizations, while most are not membership associations and many engage large paid staffs (p. 9).

In recent decades, nonprofits have come to be increasingly managed like businesses, and as we will discuss later, some undertake entrepreneurial ventures either directly, through for-profit subsidiaries, or with for-profit partners. Some have adopted the term *social enterprise* to characterize nonprofits that have a social objective but blend traditional nonprofit methods and commercial principles in their generation of revenue (Dees et al., 2001, p. 9). Although the term *social enterprise* is generally associated with those who especially advocate organizations' operating like a business and undertaking efforts to increase revenues from commercial activities, it could be argued that the term captures the positive essence of *all* private organizations having a social purpose, perhaps better than *nonprofit*. Like companies, nonprofits bring together people, resources, and purposeful effort in pursuit of a mission, and they increasingly operate with plans, goals, and established criteria of success—they are indeed enterprises, but their missions relate to social purposes rather than to the enrichment of private individuals. Were *social enterprise* to become a general designation for all such organizations, the sector that contains them perhaps then would be called the *social sector* to differentiate it from business and government. Or, as Jon Van Til (2000) suggests, perhaps something like the French term *economie sociale*, or *social economy*, would be appropriate (p. 12). Indeed, *social sector* has become popular among some business authors in referring to the nonprofit sector (Collins, 2005). However, this broader meaning of the term has not yet gained universal acceptance, and we generally will use the more common designations of *nonprofit organization* and *nonprofit sector* in the remainder of this book.

SIZE OF THE U.S. NONPROFIT SECTOR

It is difficult to say precisely how many nonprofit organizations exist in the United States. One important type, religious organizations, are not required to register with the Internal Revenue Service (IRS), making it difficult to count their number. Until 2008, organizations with annual revenues less than $25,000 also were not required to register with the IRS and thus were almost impossible to catalog or count. Indeed, many of the latter are not incorporated, and some are little more than informal groups of people who have come together to address some common interest or need.[1]

In the mid-1990s, the nonprofit scholar Lester Salamon (1999) estimated that there were 1,600,000 nonprofit organizations in the United States, including 400,000 that were "member-serving" and 1,200,000 that were "public-serving" (p. 22), terms that we will explain further below. In 1998, it was estimated that nonprofits employed almost 11 million paid staff members, constituting more than 7% of the U.S. workforce. Taken together as an "industry," nonprofits employed three times as many people as agriculture, twice the number in wholesale trade, and nearly 50% more than are engaged in construction and finance, insurance, and real estate (Salamon, 2002, p. 7).

The number of nonprofits in the United States increased dramatically throughout the 1990s and into the 2000s. The total number of organizations grew by 62.4% between 1987 and 1997 (Weitzman et al., 2002, p. 12) and by 5.6% in 2003 alone (Gose, 2005). The years between 1999 and 2003 saw the creation of 35,000 new religious organizations, 30,000 new educational organizations, 28,000 human services groups, and 5,000 new organizations concerned with the welfare of animals (Gose, 2005). Thus, while the number of organizations cannot be precisely measured, it is clear that America's nonprofit sector is large and growing, becoming an ever more important component of the U.S. economy and an increasing area of career opportunity.

The growth of the nonprofit sector is attributable to a variety of forces, including the trend that began in the 1980s toward the devolution of federal programs to state and local governments and outsourcing of the provision of many services to nonprofits by governments at all levels. Also contributing to the growth of nonprofits was the booming economy of the 1990s, which gave rise to an 81% increase in the number of foundations created by wealthy individuals and a doubling of foundation assets, making more money available to fund nonprofit programs (Gose, 2005). And, some argue, the growth of nonprofits has been fueled by a reawakening of the spirit of public service among the current generation of Americans. The requirement of community service for graduation from high school has exposed a generation of young people to the idea of volunteering. Events such as September 11, 2001, the 2004 tsunami in South Asia, and Hurricane Katrina in 2005 have called the nation's attention to human needs and the role of nonprofit organizations in helping alleviate human suffering.

In his influential, although controversial, 1995 article, "Bowling Alone: America's Declining Social Capital," Robert Putnam discussed a decline in civic engagement among Americans, using the metaphor of his title to suggest that Americans were becoming more isolated and more involved in individual pursuits than in collective interests and activities. But a decade later, Putnam and his colleague Thomas Sander reported that young Americans who witnessed the events of September 11, 2001, in their adolescent years appeared more involved in public affairs and community life than their older siblings. As Sander and Putnam (2005) note, "We'll have to wait some years to see if this budding civic engagement blossoms, but it could prove to be the largest civic shift in the past half-century" (p. A23).

DIFFERENTIATING THE NONPROFIT SECTOR

As we saw from our imaginary walking tour of Washington, D.C., nonprofits are a widely diverse group of organizations and institutions. Fortunately, there are ways of bringing order out of the apparent chaos by placing nonprofits into categories. Let's review some of them and see if we can gain a clearer picture of this complex arena.

IRS Classifications

Perhaps the most practical way to divide the nonprofit sector is by the categories (or "classifications") applied by the IRS in recognizing tax exemption.[2] Nonprofits qualify for tax exemption under various sections of the Internal Revenue Code (IRC), depending on the nature of their principal activities.[3] For example, political parties are qualified under Section 527 of the code and farmer's cooperatives under Section 521. But most tax-exempt nonprofits are qualified for tax exemption under one section of the IRC—Section 501 (c). Under Section 501 (c), there are a number of subsections into which a nonprofit may fit, again, based on the nature of its principal activities. About 70% of all nonprofits, including those emphasized in this book, fall under just two subsections of the code: Section 501 (c) (3) and Section 501 (c) (4) (Weitzman et al., 2002). Organizations that qualify under Section 501 (c) (3) are generally called "charitable nonprofits." And organizations that qualify for tax exemption under Section 501 (c) (4) are called "social welfare organizations." There are important differences.

Charitable Nonprofits

It is important at this point to distinguish two concepts: the tax *exemption* of organizations themselves and the tax *deductibility* of gifts made to them. *All* organizations qualified under Section 501 (c) of the IRS code are *tax-exempt*; that is, they are not required to pay federal taxes on their income. (Organizations exempt from federal income tax are usually also granted exemption from state and local income taxes.) However, *only* those classified under Section 501 (c) (3)—the charitable nonprofits—are both tax-exempt themselves and *also* eligible to receive gifts that are tax deductible for the donors. So, for example, the Republican and Democratic parties are tax-exempt organizations—they do not pay federal taxes on their own income. But they do not qualify under Section 501 (c) (3). They are not charitable organizations. If a donor makes a contribution to the Democratic or Republican party, he or she cannot deduct that gift from his or her individual income when calculating his or her own income tax due. But, if that individual makes a gift to a charitable, 501 (c) (3) organization, such as a church, college, or hospital, the gift is tax deductible, within certain limits.

The tax deductibility of gifts made to charitable nonprofits obviously provides a significant advantage to them in their fundraising efforts. Consider an individual donor who is in a 25% federal tax bracket and who makes a deductible gift of $100 to a charitable nonprofit organization. He or she can deduct that $100 from his or her income before calculating the income tax due. The donor's taxable income is reduced by $100, so the donor's tax bill is reduced by 25% of that amount, or $25. This is considered a tax saving, since, but for the gift, the donor would have paid that amount in additional federal income tax. The out-of-pocket cost of the $100 gift is thus reduced, from $100 to $75 ($100 minus the $25 tax saving). Some view the saving as a form of tax subsidy, or tax expenditure, in the form of foregone federal revenue.

The tax deduction for gifts to charitable organizations is intended to encourage charitable giving and sustain the services provided by charitable organizations. Society has determined that the purposes they serve are to the public benefit and that if the nonprofits did not exist, those services might need to be provided by government. Being eligible to receive deductible gifts makes it easier for charitable nonprofits to raise funds, since the donors are, at least theoretically, able to give more because of the tax saving realized from the deduction.

To be recognized as tax-exempt under Section 501 (c) (3), an organization must demonstrate three things; in other words, it must meet three tests. First, it must be *organized and operated* for one or more of eight purposes: charitable, religious, educational, scientific, literary, testing for public safety, fostering national or international amateur sports competitions, and prevention of cruelty to children and animals. (Curiously, the IRC does not specifically mention health care, although, as we will soon discuss, that is one of the largest components of the nonprofit sector.) The term *charitable* may seem somewhat imprecise, but IRS defines it to include certain specific activities:

> relief of the poor, the distressed, or the underprivileged; advancement of religion; advancement of education or science; erection or maintenance of public buildings, monuments, or works; lessening the burdens of government; lessening of neighborhood tensions; elimination of prejudice and discrimination; defense of human and civil rights secured by law; and combating community deterioration and juvenile delinquency. (www.irs.gov/charities/charitable/article/0,,id = 96099,00.html, accessed August 3, 2006)

In addition to demonstrating that its primary purposes include one or more of those discussed above, a 501 (c) (3) nonprofit must meet two additional requirements. It must meet the nondistribution test, ensuring that its assets are not being used to benefit individual owners and that its managers are not being personally enriched through excessive compensation. And it must limit its political activities. A nonprofit qualified under Section 501 (c) (3) cannot support candidates for public office, and it must limit its expenditures on lobbying—that is, efforts to influence legislation.

Social Welfare Organizations

Social welfare organizations are tax-exempt because they work, in the IRS's words, "to further the common good and general welfare of the people of a community (such as bringing about civic betterment and social improvements.)" But how is this different from the work of charitable nonprofits? One big difference between 501 (c) (3) and 501 (c) (4) organizations is that the latter do not face the same limitations on political activity that are imposed on the former. They can spend money on lobbying without limitation (www.irs.gov/charities/nonprofits/article/0,,id = 96178,00.html, accessed August 3, 2006).

Because of that difference, 501 (c) (4) organizations are tax-exempt, but gifts made to them are *not* tax deductible. They often raise funds by encouraging individuals to become members or to make gifts, but the individuals do not earn a tax deduction for those payments.

Because of the different advantages enjoyed and disadvantages experienced by 501 (c) (3) and 501 (c) (4) organizations, in terms of the tax treatment of gifts and the limitations on lobbying, some organizations have two arms—actually two separately incorporated but related organizations. One is qualified under Section 501 (c) (3) and is thus eligible to receive tax-deductible gifts. It pursues education, research, and other activities consistent with that classification. The other organization is qualified under Section 501 (c) (4) and is free to engage in lobbying without restriction. It cannot receive deductible gifts, but it can raise funds through member dues and others types of revenue. Box 1.1 provides an example in the form of mission statements for the Sierra Club, a nationally known environmental organization, and the related Sierra Club Foundation. The Sierra Club itself is a 501 (c) (4) social welfare organization that works to preserve the environment, including lobbying for environmental-protection legislation. The Sierra Club Foundation is a 501 (c) (3) organization that supports certain activities of the Sierra Club. As its description carefully explains, the Foundation limits its support to those activities that are consistent with the "charitable, scientific, literary, and educational purposes" allowed for 501 (c) (3) organizations. Note the subtle differences in the mission statements of the two organizations. The Sierra Club's mission includes "enlisting" humanity, which suggests the possibility of building political coalitions and encouraging individuals to political action, while the Foundation "empowers" the citizenry, something that might be accomplished merely by providing them with information—that is, through education—without any call to political action. These may seem like subtle differences, but facing the possibility of audit by the IRS and wishing to protect the tax status of both entities, most organizations are precise in monitoring their activities for consistency with tax law. Chapter 14 discusses lobbying in more detail, including relevant legal issues.

National Taxonomy of Exempt Entities

The IRS classifications of nonprofit organizations are obviously of practical importance because of the benefits and restrictions they convey. But they are also broad and lump together many organizations that in fact have significant distinctions among them. A more elaborated set of classifications is the National Taxonomy of Exempt Entities (NTEE). Maintained by the National Center for Charitable Statistics (NCCS), a program of the Center on Nonprofits and Philanthropy at the Urban Institute, the NTEE divides the universe of nonprofit organizations into 26 major groups under 10 broad categories. These categories are based on organizations' purposes, activities, and programs and are similar to the industry classification codes used to group for-profit companies.

Box 1.2 lists the 10 broad categories in the NTEE. The complete taxonomy, which runs to two pages, along with explanations of the categories, is available on the Web site of NCCS (http://nccsdataweb.urban.org/FAQ/index.php?category = 73).

Salamon's Anatomy

Both the IRS classifications and the NTEE group organizations according to the principal activities in which they are engaged. Some have sought ways of categorizing nonprofits along other lines. Various scholars have attempted to develop maps to bring greater clarity to our understanding of the structure of the nonprofit sector (Gamwell, 1984; Smith, 1991;

BOX 1.1   Comparison of Charitable and Social Welfare Organizations

Mission of the Sierra Club, a 501 (c) (4) Organization

To explore, enjoy, and protect the wild places of the earth; to practice and promote the responsible use of the earth's ecosystems and resources; to educate and enlist humanity to protect and restore the quality of the natural and human environment; and to use all lawful means to carry out those objectives.

Source: The Sierra Club Web site (www.sierraclub.org/101/3.asp, accessed September 14, 2005).

Mission of The Sierra Club Foundation, a 501 (c) (3) Organization

The mission of The Sierra Club Foundation is to advance the preservation and protection of the natural environment by empowering the citizenry, especially democratically based grassroots organizations, with charitable resources to further the cause of environmental protection. The Sierra Club is the vehicle through which The Sierra Club Foundation generally fulfills its charitable mission.

Description of The Sierra Club Foundation

Working as a funding resource for the environmental community, The Foundation offers its services in receiving, administering, and disbursing funds for tax-exempt charitable, scientific, literary, and educational purposes both to the Sierra Club and to other environmental organizations and projects. Subject to federal tax codes that clearly define the activities with which we can assist, The Foundation is precluded from supporting electoral activities and can expend only a small part of its resources on influencing legislation. While The Foundation is autonomous and is governed by its own Board of Trustees, it works closely with the Sierra Club in pursuing its program and goals.

Source: The Sierra Club Foundation Web site (www.sierraclub.org/foundation/inside/background.asp, accessed September 14, 2005).

BOX 1.2   National Taxonomy of Exempt Entities (NTEE) Major Groups

Arts, Culture, and Humanities	International, Foreign Affairs
Education	Public/Societal Benefit
Environment and Animals	Religion Related
Health	Mutual/Membership Benefit
Human Services	Unknown/Unclassified

Source: NCCS Web site (http://nccsdataweb.urban.org/FAQ/index.php?category=73, accessed August 3, 2006).

Sumariwalla, 1983; Van Til, 1988, 2000). Among them is Lester Salamon's *America's Nonprofit Sector* (1999), which divides the universe of U.S. nonprofits into two broad categories, *member serving* and *public serving*, and then defines various subcategories on each side of that divide (p. 22).

As the term implies, member-serving organizations exist primarily to secure benefits for the people who belong to them or who support them through dues, membership fees, or other contributions. They include, for example, social and fraternal organizations, business and professional associations, and labor unions. In general, their sources of support and the beneficiaries of their programs are one and the same, although society may benefit indirectly— for example, through the improvement of skills among members of a profession that serves the public's needs. These organizations are tax-exempt but not eligible to receive tax-deductible gifts.[4] They are not charitable organizations. Salamon's (1999) definition of public-serving organizations includes churches, the charitable and social welfare organizations we have discussed, as well as foundations and other "funding intermediaries."

Salamon's Anatomy (Salamon, 1999) provides another and a useful way to think about the nonprofit sector, classifying nonprofit organizations not by the nature of their activities, like IRS or the NTEE, but rather by who receives the principal benefit of those activities. But while it adds clarity in certain respects, it also raises questions. For example, Salamon puts churches in the public-serving category. They surely are tax-exempt and eligible to receive tax-deductible contributions—they are 501 (c) (3) organizations, but it seems possible that their activities might more directly serve their own members rather than the general public.[5] He classifies political parties as member-serving organizations. It is true that they are *not* 501 (c) (3) organizations under the tax code. But it isn't clear exactly what benefits their members derive from their affiliation (Anheier, 2005, p. 64). Despite its weaknesses, Salamon's Anatomy (Salamon, 1999) has contributed to the vocabulary of the nonprofit field, and it is not unusual for some to refer to organizations as " member serving" or " public serving."

The Independent Sector

Figure 1.1 provides a way to visualize the nonprofit sector and brings together the various types of organizations that have been mentioned so far. It is based on a diagram illustrating how the organization Independent Sector defines its membership. As mentioned previously, Independent Sector is the principal organization that represents the interests of nonprofits in Washington, D.C. Its membership generally coincides with Salamon's (1999) public-serving organizations.

Figure 1.1 first divides society into the three sectors: government, nonprofits, and for-profit business. The nonprofit sector then is divided into four categories: (1) religious congregations, which are automatically tax-exempt under Section 501 (c) (3) and are not required to register with the IRS (Box A); (2) organizations that do register with the IRS under Section 501 (c) (Box B); (3) organizations that register with the IRS under sections of the tax code *other than* Section 501 (c)—for example, political parties that register under Section 527 (Box C); and (4) small, often informal organizations with minimal revenues (Box D).

Take a look at Box B, the 501 (c)s. They are further broken down into three categories: (1) the 501 (c) (3) charitable nonprofits (Box E), (2) the 501 (c) (4) social welfare organizations (Box F), and (3) other tax-exempt organizations that qualify under Section 501 (c) (Box G).

FIGURE 1.1   The Independent Sector

Source: Adapted from Weitzman et al. (2002, p. 216). Used with permission of John Wiley & Sons, Inc.

The latter includes, for example, some business associations that are under Section 501 (c) (6). Indeed, most of Salamon's (1999) member-serving organizations would be within Box G. You will notice that the 501 (c) (3) organizations are further divided into two categories—*public charities* (Box H) and *private foundations* (Box I). Let's put that point aside for the moment and come back to it shortly.

MAJOR SUBSECTORS

The independent sector as a concept (and Independent Sector as an organization) encompasses Boxes A, F, H, and I in Figure 1.1. It is dominated by five subsectors—*health services, education and research, social and legal services, religious organizations,* and organizations in the fields of *art and culture*—that account for 92% of nonprofit revenues, 96% of paid staff working in the nonprofit sector, and 98% of all salaries and wages paid to nonprofit employees (Weitzman et al., 2002, pp. 46–47). The subsectors differ significantly in their sources of revenue, the degree of commercialization they reflect, and the extent to which their management has been professionalized—that is, the extent to which they are run by paid staff rather than volunteers.

Health Services

The health services subsector is the largest component of the overall nonprofit sector if measured by total revenue, the number of employees, and its share of total wages and salaries. It includes hospitals, home health agencies, outpatient clinics, hospice programs, nursing homes, health maintenance organizations, dialysis centers, community health centers, residential treatment programs for emotionally disturbed youth, and a variety of specialized institutions. The health services subsector is unique in that a small portion of its revenue comes from contributions (just 4% in 1997) and a large portion (42%) comes in the form of government payments. The latter reflects the impact of Medicare and Medicaid programs, which reimburse for services provided to individuals whom they have insured. Another 47% of health services revenue comes from private payments, including those made by private insurance companies and patients themselves, and 7% comes from other sources (Weitzman et al., 2002, p. xxxiv).

As its revenue pattern suggests, health services is the most commercialized of the nonprofit subsectors; that is, its organizations are businesslike in deriving most of their revenue from fees charged for services provided. Health services was one of the first subsectors to become professionalized in its management—that is, to develop large paid staffs rather than depend on volunteers. It is also a field in which nonprofits compete with for-profit firms to a significant extent. In some industries—for example, nursing homes—for-profits have captured the major portion of the market. Health services also has seen the conversion of some nonprofits into for-profit entities, including insurance plans, hospitals, and nursing homes.

Education and Research

Education and research is perhaps the subsector best known to students. It includes colleges and universities, preschool, elementary and secondary schools, correspondence schools, libraries, and various free-standing research institutions (or "think tanks"), such as the

Brookings Institution. It will not surprise students to learn that educational institutions receive a significant portion of their revenues from fees for service, including tuition, which accounted for 56% of this subsector's income in 1997. Government payments provided another 19%; private contributions made up 13%; and 11% comes from other sources, including investment returns on endowment funds (Weitzman et al., 2002, p. xxxv). Higher education is a field in which professional management has increased in recent decades. While the senior executives of colleges and universities are still predominantly drawn from the academic ranks, on most campuses there has been a proliferation of midlevel management in areas such as fundraising, student services, and financial administration. Middle management has grown as colleges and universities have faced increased competitive pressures, greater governmental regulation, and the need to expand revenues through intensified fundraising programs.

While for-profit education firms—for example, the University of Phoenix—have grown in recent decades, most schools, colleges, and universities remain either nonprofit or government controlled.

Social and Legal Services

The social and legal services subsector, encompassing individual and family services, free legal aid, day care, residential care, job training, youth programs, and other such services, includes many of the organizations that many people would think about first when the term *nonprofit* is used. They are often small and community based. Social and legal services grew at a faster rate than any of the other charitable subsectors from the 1970s to the 1990s, reflecting in part the trends we mentioned before—the outsourcing of government programs to the nonprofit sector and government's departure from some areas of activity altogether. Although many people might consider organizations in these fields as among the most "charitable," indeed they are among the most reliant on government funds. Government payments constituted 52% of their revenue in 1997, with private contributions accounting for 20%, private payments making up 19%, and 9% coming from other sources (Weitzman et al., 2002, p. xxxvi). This dependence on government funds makes the social and legal services subsector the most vulnerable when public policy shifts and government social spending declines. For this reason, among others, many of the efforts to diversify revenues by developing alternative sources, including business enterprises, have been in this subsector, and also much of the discussion regarding the need for improved management and accountability in the nonprofit sector as a whole. In recent decades, professional nonprofit management has grown more rapidly in this subsector than in any other, increasing its share of total nonprofit employment from 13% in 1977 to 17.5% in 1998 (Weitzman et al., 2002, p. xxxv).

Religion

As we have noted before, religion is a unique component of the nonprofit sector. It is protected by the U.S. Constitution and the guarantee of religious freedom it provides. The principle of separation of church and state prevents government funds from going directly to religious congregations or to organizations that would use them for religious activities. However, congregations are to be distinguished from faith-based organizations that provide social services, which can receive government funds to support their secular programs. Federal legislation passed in 1996, 1998, and 2000 included *charitable choice* provisions to allow faith-based organizations to receive grants under federally funded programs, and proposals to further increase the ability of faith-based nonprofits to obtain such funding generated controversy during the first term of President George W. Bush.

This book does not specifically discuss the management of religious congregations—that is, churches, synagogues, and mosques. Religious organizations are the least professionalized of the subsectors. Although there has been some growth in the number of church managers, the management of most congregations is still done by the clergy and volunteers. In 1998, religious organizations accounted for just 11.6% of paid employment in the charitable non-profit sector (Weitzman et al., 2002, p. xxxvi). As a subsector, religion is also unique in that most of its revenue, 95% in 1997, comes from private gifts (Weitzman et al., 2002, p. xxxvi). Indeed, it is the largest single recipient of gifts, accounting for 35.5% of all giving in the United States in 2004 (Center on Philanthropy at Indiana University, 2005, p. 20).

Arts and Culture

The arts and culture subsector includes museums, orchestras, botanical gardens, zoos, performing arts groups, art galleries, nonprofit radio and television stations, literary societies, and other such organizations. Although it is the smallest, its revenue growth during the 1990s was the highest of the charitable subsectors (10.4% from 1992 to 1997). Arts and culture organizations receive substantial support through philanthropy, which accounts for 44% of their revenues. Private payments, including ticket sales and admission charges, provide another 28%, 10% comes from government, and about 19% comes from other sources (Weitzman et al., 2002, p. xxxvii).

The subsectors of health services, education and research, social and legal services, religion, and arts and culture account for the largest portion of the charitable nonprofit sector and are likely to be the most familiar to most individuals. They include many of the largest organizations and institutions, and many have a noticeable physical presence—for example, a campus, a hospital, a church, or a performing arts center. But there is another type of non-profit organization that, while perhaps less visible, plays an important role in the nonprofit sector—what Salamon (1999) calls the "funding intermediaries," including foundations and federated funders.

Funding Intermediaries

Funding intermediaries are organizations that exist for the sole purpose of directing money to other nonprofits (Salamon, 1999). They generally do not themselves operate programs that provide services directly to individuals. Rather, their role is, in a sense, to be like the bankers of the nonprofit sector, channeling private giving to other, service-providing nonprofits.

Federated Funders

Federated funders include organizations such as the United Way and the American Heart Association. They raise money from the public and then redistribute it to other organizations that serve their local communities, pursue the fight against certain diseases, or undertake other activities consistent with the purposes and priorities of the funder.

Foundations

Foundations are funding intermediaries, too. They are 501 (c) (3) organizations that, like the federated funders, generally do not operate their own programs but rather make gifts or grants to other nonprofits that do. Foundations are created by individuals, companies, and other donors, who give money to the foundation, generally earning a tax deduction. The way in which foundations then manage and disburse that money varies, but many retain the original gifts, invest them, and use only the income earned on those investments to make grants to operating nonprofits.

Public Charities and Private Foundations

At this point, it is necessary to complicate things still further by introducing two new terms. As we saw in Figure 1.1, there are two different types of nonprofit organizations that are exempt under Section 501 (c) (3)—public charities [Box H] and private foundations [Box I]. There are technical definitions of these terms established in tax law, but it is sufficient to understand that public charities, as the term suggests, are organizations that receive support from the public, meaning that they have a *relatively large number of donors.* They include most of the public-serving nonprofits, both those that provide direct services (e.g., hospitals) and the federated funders (e.g., the United Way). Public charities generally spend a significant portion of the gifts they receive each year.

Private foundations, on the other hand, usually have only one or perhaps a few donors—usually one person, one company, or the members of a family. For example, the Bill and Melinda Gates Foundation was funded through gifts from Bill and Melinda Gates, and the Ford Foundation was created through gifts from Henry Ford. It is a common misunderstanding to think that the Gates Foundation was created by Microsoft Corporation. Indeed, the funds used to establish the foundation were those belonging to Bill and Melinda Gates personally. Likewise, the Ford Foundation was created by Henry Ford with his personal fortune, not by the Ford Motor Company.

Private foundations receive different tax treatment from public charities. One significant difference is that tax deductions allowed to individual donors for gifts to private foundations are more limited than for gifts to public charities. In addition, the investment earnings of private foundations are subject to a tax, and they face a requirement for minimum spending of their investment returns that does not apply to public charities. Indeed, what level of spending should be required of private foundations, and what should be included in the definition of that spending, has been a source of debate and legislation in recent years.

Supporting Organizations

Let's add yet another complication! There are organizations that use the word *foundation* in their name but are really public charities rather than private foundations. One type, community foundations, receive gifts from members of a particular community and make gifts to support a variety of service-providing nonprofits in that community. Another type of foundation that is a public charity is called, under the tax law, a *supporting organization*. These foundations are the fundraising arms of their host or parent organizations. They are public charities because they solicit and receive gifts from a large number of donors. But, unlike the United Way or community foundations, which make grants to multiple organizations, this type of foundation directs its support to just one organization. Such foundations are commonly associated with public universities. For example, the University of Maryland Foundation raises funds for the state university it serves. Some federal government entities also have affiliated foundations that seek private gifts to supplement the funds that the agency receives through public appropriations. An example of this is the National Park Foundation, a fundraising entity that supports the National Park Service. And, as in the case of the Sierra Club and The Sierra Club Foundation, there are foundations associated with nonprofit organizations that do not themselves qualify to receive tax-deductible contributions.

To complicate things yet further, there are private foundations that do not make any, or many, grants to other nonprofits and that may not even have the term *foundation* in their names. For example, Colonial Williamsburg, in Virginia, and Longwood Gardens, in Pennsylvania, are legally private foundations, but all their funds are used to support their own programs and operations. They are thus called *operating foundations* and, with some exceptions, are not sources of financial support for other nonprofits.

We will consider foundations again in Chapter 10 as part of our discussion on fundraising. Students who are interested in how foundations are managed will find many excellent resources, including books and the Web sites of the Council on Foundations (www.cof.org), the Forum of Regional Associations of Grantmakers (www.givingforum.org), and Grantmakers for Effective Organizations (www.geofunders.org), among others.

THE SPECTRUM OF ORGANIZATIONS

So far, we have looked at ways of differentiating nonprofit organizations according to their purposes and activities (the IRS classifications and the NTEE), according to who benefits from their activities (Salamon's [1999] member-serving and public-serving categories), and according to their sources of support (public charities and private foundations). Yet another way to differentiate nonprofits is according to the degree in which they are commercialized— that is, the extent to which they operate like businesses.

In their 2001 book, *Enterprising Nonprofits: A Toolkit for Social Entrepreneurs*, Dees et al. depict a spectrum of nonprofit organizations (which they call "social enterprises"; see Table 1.1). Each endpoint of the spectrum represents an extreme—that is, a pure example of two alternate conditions. The spectrum encompasses every possible point in between. In Dees et.al.'s spectrum, the two extremes are organizations that are "purely philanthropic" and those that are "purely commercial," defined by their "general motives, methods, and goals" and their

TABLE 1.1	The Social Enterprise Spectrum		

	Continuum of Options		
	Purely Philanthropic	*Hybrid*	*Purely Commercial*
General motives, methods, and goals	Appeal to goodwill	Appeal to mixed motives	Appeal to self-interest
	Mission driven	Balance of mission and market	Market driven
	Goal is social value creation	Goal is social and economic value creation	Goal is economic value creation
Key stakeholders			
Beneficiaries	Pay nothing	Subsidized rates and/or a mix of full payers and those who pay nothing	Pay full market rates
Sources of capital	Make gifts and grants	Below-market capital and/or a mix of below-market capital, market-rate capital, and gifts	Charge market rates
Workforce	Volunteers	Below-market wages and/or a mix of volunteers and paid staff	Market-rate compensation
Suppliers	Make in-kind gifts	Special discounts and/or a mix of full price, discounts, and in-kind gifts	Charge market prices

Source: Adapted from Dees et al. (2001, p. 15). Used with permission of John Wiley & Sons, Inc.

relationships with their key stakeholders. In other words, we might think of those at the left endpoint of the spectrum as the most nonprofit-like and those at the right endpoint as the most businesslike. In between, at various points along the spectrum between the two extremes, are most nonprofit organizations today.

Let's walk through Dees et al.'s (2001) spectrum thinking about three organizations, including two we saw on our hypothetical tour of Washington, D.C., and a third that is familiar to all of us—Miriam's Kitchen, The George Washington University, and Microsoft Corporation. Even Miriam's, which is close to what most people would think of as a purely philanthropic nonprofit and thus somewhere close to the left end of the spectrum, is not entirely pure according to Dees et al.'s criteria because it does employ paid staff. But it is close enough to serve as an example for our discussion. Microsoft, most would agree, is close to a pure example of a commercial organization, at the right end of the spectrum. The George Washington University is somewhere in between—in Dees et al.'s terminology, it is a hybrid that is somewhat nonprofit-like and somewhat like a business. This is true of most private colleges and universities and, in some ways, increasingly true of public universities as well.

What characterizes organizations that are purely philanthropic? As Dees et al.'s chart indicates, such organizations *appeal to goodwill* rather than *self-interest*. People engage with Miriam's Kitchen because they hold compassion and concern for homeless individuals. But few would buy Windows because Microsoft needs the money! What about universities? They appeal to *mixed motives*. People do feel altruistic about universities; that's why many alumni continue to make gifts long after they have graduated. But, for most students, attendance at a university is also a practical investment. Although some may value learning for its own sake, most are likely motivated to study at least in part by self-interest—that is, an interest in their own financial futures.

Philanthropic organizations are *mission driven*. If they are purely philanthropic, then, at least theoretically, they pursue the mission without any regard for the financial bottom line. Although this image may comport with the stereotype that some may hold of nonprofits as organizations run by dedicated volunteers unconcerned with money, an example of that purest form would be somewhat difficult to find in today's nonprofit world, for many of the reasons we already have discussed. On the other hand, Microsoft is unlikely to produce software that nobody wants to buy, regardless of what social value it might serve—it is, like all businesses, *market driven*. What about a university? Again, most are mixed, *balancing commitment to a mission with responsiveness to the market*. A university may continue to offer academic programs or to support research efforts that are not profitable, indeed, that require a subsidy, because they are important to its educational mission. But most universities also respond to the market, developing new programs and expanding others that are attracting increased student interest.

Philanthropic organizations are concerned with creating *social value*—in the simplest terms, with improving the lives of individuals and their communities; they are not about making money for its own sake. On the other hand, as we have discussed before, the principal goal of a business is to create *economic value*—in other words, to generate profits and increase its owners' wealth. Again, the hybrids that Dees et al. (2001) define pay almost equal attention to both components of the double bottom line, focusing on the creation of *both social and economic value*, or in the words of Bill Shore (2001), they are "doing good by doing well."

Let's look at our three sample organizations' relationships with some of their key stakeholders–their beneficiaries (clients), those who provide them with capital funds, their workforce, and their suppliers. At purely philanthropic organizations, clients *pay nothing* for the services they receive, like the hundreds of homeless men and women who are served by Miriam's Kitchen. On the other end of the spectrum, people generally pay for their Microsoft software at whatever *market price* prevails. And hybrids? Let's consider a typical undergraduate classroom in a private university. Some students will be attending on full scholarships—they pay nothing in the way of tuition. Others, from more affluent families, may be paying the full tuition price listed in the university bulletin, while still others will be paying some portion of the listed tuition with scholarships to cover the rest. This is typical of hybrid nonprofits, including universities and hospitals, which often serve a *mix of full payers and subsidized clients.*

If Miriam's needs capital to expand or meet special organizational needs, it will obtain it through fundraising for *gifts* or *grants.* Microsoft will issue new stock or borrow money, paying the full *market rate* of interest. Hybrids often mix these methods; for example, a university may have a campaign to raise capital dollars through gifts but may also borrow funds for the construction of new buildings. Nonprofits sometimes can borrow at *less than the market rate of interest,* although some will also borrow at the going market rate.

The purely philanthropic workforce is composed entirely of *volunteers.* As we have discussed, this is the case for some small nonprofits, although many (including Miriam's Kitchen) have paid staff members in addition to a substantial volunteer workforce—they are not, in Dees et al.'s (2001) terminology, "pure." But it is likely that no one volunteers at Microsoft. The company pays *market wages* and, indeed, competes in the marketplace for talent. Universities, as any professor will testify, are somewhere in between; professors do not work for free, but neither do they earn the salaries their talents might command in a purely commercial enterprise.

How do nonprofits obtain needed supplies? A purely philanthropic nonprofit would have all its supplies *contributed*; that is, it would receive them through *gifts-in-kind.* Miriam's does receive such gifts, although it also purchases some of the food it needs for its breakfast program. However, it is doubtful that Microsoft ever receives such gifts, and it likely pays the *market price* for its pencils as well as its PCs (although it may negotiate some discounts based on volume rather than the generosity of its suppliers). As a hybrid, a university may receive some gifts in kind, pay market price for some products, and receive educational *discounts* on others.

Again, it is important to emphasize that the concept of a spectrum includes various points along the line rather than two or three discrete categories, so organizations may be hybrids to a lesser or greater extent. Indeed, the reality in today's nonprofit sector is that relatively few organizations offer an example of the purely philanthropic as Dees et al.'s (2001) chart defines it. Most are hybrids to some degree. Even Miriam's Kitchen. Most private universities are hybrids, commercialized to a considerable degree, and even state universities have moved in that direction, receiving a diminishing portion of their revenues from state funds and an increasing portion from tuition charges and gifts (Selingo, 2003).

Are there examples of purely commercial organizations? Microsoft may come pretty close, but some argue that, indeed, for-profit businesses are becoming more nonprofit-like. While many nonprofits demonstrate increasing degrees of commercialization—that is, they are moving from left to right across Dees et al.'s (2001) spectrum, many corporations are becoming more attuned to their social responsibilities, tempering their pursuit of profit at least somewhat with a concern for social value. In terms of Dees et al.'s spectrum, they may be moving to the left (no political pun intended!). Because of these movements in both directions across the spectrum, some see a blurring of the nonprofit and for-profit sectors. Some celebrate it, while for others it arouses deep concern.

COMMERCIALIZATION CONTROVERSY

Commercialization of nonprofits is a source of controversy. Some observers view the increasing use of business methods in nonprofits and their efforts to develop streams of earned income to be desired, reducing their dependence on government and on gifts and increasing their effectiveness. In his influential 1999 book, *The Cathedral Within,* Bill Shore writes that nonprofits "forfeited the marketplace long ago, simply walked off the field . . . and chose instead to settle for the crumbs instead of the cake" (p. 205). He argues that non-profits should begin businesses that generate revenue as a way to gain independence from philanthropic giving and government funds. "Redistributing wealth is not going to be enough," Shore says. "Creating new [economic] wealth is the only course for nonprofits and community-based organizations struggling to meet social needs" (p. 208). Shore is the founder of the nonprofit Share Our Strength, an antihunger organization based in Washington, D.C. Consistent with his own advice, he also created Community Wealth Ventures, a for-profit subsidiary of Share Our Strength. Community Wealth Ventures earns revenue by advising nonprofits on how to start revenue-producing businesses and directs its profits to help support Share Our Strength's programs.

But others express concern that the increasing commercialization of the nonprofit sector may eventually lead some organizations to put profit ahead of their social missions. For example, Burton Weisbrod (2004), an economist who was a pioneer in studying the non-profit sector, cites the YMCA, which he says has "morphed into a health-and-fitness goliath" (p. 1, electronic version). Observing the YMCA's increasing presence in upscale neighbor-hoods, where it competes with for-profit health clubs, Weisbrod questions whether it has strayed from its traditional mission of serving low-income families and asks "whether it has become overly commercialized and whether it [even] deserves tax-exempt status" (p. 3, electronic version). He advocates policies to limit the commercial activity of nonprofits while creating stronger tax incentives to encourage traditional charitable and philan-thropic giving. Thus, the issue of commercialization is more than philosophical; it has impli-cations for the continued tax-exempt status of some nonprofits.

Commercialization and Tax Exemption

A companion to the common misunderstanding that nonprofit organizations cannot earn profits is the misunderstanding that nonprofits are *always* exempt from taxation. They are exempt from income taxation on revenues related to their social missions, but revenues from activities that are not related to the mission are subject to the *unrelated business income tax* (UBIT). An activity is unrelated and subject to this tax if it meets three requirements: (1) it is a trade or business, as defined by the IRS; (2) it is regularly carried on; and (3) it is not substantially related to the exempt purpose of the organization. The definition of "substantially related" is provided by the IRS (2005a), with characteristic clarity:

> To determine if a business activity is "substantially related" requires examining the relationship between the activities that generate income and the accomplishment of the organization's exempt purpose. Trade or business is related to exempt purposes, in the statutory sense, only when the conduct of the business activities

has causal relationship to achieving exempt purposes (other than through the production of income). The causal relationship must be substantial. The activities that generate the income must contribute importantly to accomplishing the organization's exempt purposes to be substantially related.

Activities carried out by volunteers; a trade or business carried out for what IRS calls the "convenience" of clients or members; and sales of donated merchandise, for example, in a thrift shop, are specifically excluded from UBIT. So, for example, universities are not taxed on revenue from dining halls or other food operations since these services are provided for the convenience of students (although it may surprise students to learn this)!

Most business activities undertaken by nonprofits are related to the mission, and the revenues generated are therefore not taxable. For example, a nonprofit that develops a business to employ individuals with disabilities is serving its mission of providing job training and rehabilitation, even though the services it provides may generate substantial revenue and even compete with the services provided by for-profit companies. But the line is not always clear. For example, one area of dispute has been gift shops operated by museums. If an art museum gift shop sells products that include reproductions of paintings in its exhibits, that could be related to its mission of educating and informing the public about art. But sales of products that are not related to the museum's collections might be regarded as unrelated and subject to the UBIT (IRS, 2005b).

One concern is that unrelated business activities not become a substantial part of the organization's activities. If they do—in general, if the amount of the nonprofit's time and resources devoted to the business activity exceeds that devoted to its mission, it is in danger of having its tax exemption revoked. The issue of related and unrelated income is far from settled and is often an area of dispute between nonprofits and the IRS. In subsectors where commercialization has advanced the most—for example, health services, the tax exemption of institutions is a topic of continuing political debate. In other words, as a nonprofit becomes more like a commercial enterprise, moving as it were from left to right across Dees et al.'s (2001) spectrum, there could come a point at which it will be deemed to have crossed over the line, ceasing to be a nonprofit at all.

Implications for Nonprofit Managers

What are the implications of increasing commercialization, the blurring of the sectors, and related policy debates for the practice of nonprofit management? Today's nonprofit sector requires that managers be somewhat hybrids themselves. They must combine a commitment to their organization's nonprofit mission with business skills, to manage the double bottom line. They must hold an appreciation for the nonprofit sector's unique history and traditions while also understanding how to succeed in a competitive marketplace. They must be able to adapt to the social and political forces affecting their organizations while also preserving the core values and defending the special status of their organizations. In other words, as we said in the Introduction to this book, nonprofit management requires a unique blend of skills, distinguishing it from management in government or the for-profit sector. And current trends suggest that the task will not become less challenging in the years ahead.

CHAPTER SUMMARY

America's nonprofit sector is large and diverse. Its roots lie in the ancient traditions of charity, philanthropy, and voluntarism; voluntary efforts were prominent in the nation's early days. But the sector's modern form is a product of 20th-century history and especially the period since the 1970s. Although *nonprofit organization* and *nonprofit sector* are the terms most commonly used, others have proposed a variety of alternative names for the sector.

The nonprofit sector is large and growing, including about 400,000 member-serving and about 1,200,000 public-serving organizations. Organizations may be placed in categories according to the tax-exempt classifications used by the IRS or the more elaborated NTEE, both of which determine categories based on organizations' principal activities. Most organizations registered with the IRS fall into two classifications. "Charitable nonprofits" are both exempt from taxation under Section 501 (c) (3) of the IRC and also eligible to receive tax-deductible gifts from individuals and other donors. "Social welfare organizations" are tax-exempt under Section 501 (c) (4), but gifts to them are not tax deductible, since they are not limited in their expenditures on lobbying activities.

Most nonprofit organizations are small, but in terms of revenues and employment the sector is dominated by five subsectors: health care, education and research, social and legal services, religion, and art and culture. The subsectors show significant differences in their sources of revenue and the extent to which their management has been professionalized.

Many nonprofits today are said to be hybrids. They are not purely philanthropic or purely commercial but fall somewhere on a spectrum between those two extreme cases. This is because they demonstrate a mixture of philanthropic and commercial motives, methods, and goals, and their relationships with their stakeholders demonstrate a mix of philanthropic and business characteristics. Many nonprofits have become more commercial at the same time as some businesses are expressing more concern about social goals. This blurring of the sectors pleases some and concerns others, who fear that nonprofits will drift away from their social missions. In this environment, nonprofit management requires a unique combination of commitment, knowledge, and skills.

NOTES

1. Beginning in 2008, small nonprofits that are not required to file Form 990 will nevertheless be required to file a brief Form 990-N, also known as the "e-postcard" (www.irs.gov, accessed December 5, 2007).

2. The terms *nonprofit* and *tax-exempt* are not strictly synonymous, since there are some for-profit entities—for example, certain partnerships—that are also not required to pay income tax and there are organizations that are required to pay taxes but do not distribute profits to owners (Hopkins, 2005, p. 30).

3. It is a fine but important distinction to understand that the IRS does not "grant" tax exemption to nonprofit organizations. If they meet appropriate criteria, they *are* tax-exempt under the law. The IRS merely "recognizes" that status conferred by the law (Hopkins, 2005).

4. Although we do not focus on member-serving organizations in this book, students who are interested will find a rich array of resources, including those available through the American Society of Association Executives (www.asaenet.org), a professional association comprising trade and professional association managers, based in Washington, D.C.

5. There is a distinction between churches, synagogues, and mosques and nonprofit organizations that are faith based but provide social services to their communities without regard to religious affiliation.

KEY TERMS AND CONCEPTS FROM CHAPTER 1

charitable choice

charitable nonprofits

charity

civil society

hybrid organization

Independent Sector

institutionally related foundations

member-serving organizations

National Taxonomy of Exempt Entities (NTEE)

nongovernmental organizations

operating foundations

philanthropy

private foundation

public charity

public-serving organizations

social enterprise

social welfare organizations

supporting organization

tax deductible

tax-exempt

voluntarism

unrelated business income tax

QUESTIONS FOR DISCUSSION

1. If you had $25 to give today to any nonprofit organization, which one would it be? Now, imagine that you are 75 years old and have $1,000,000 to give to an organization on your death—that is, through your will. Which one would it be? Do your answers reflect a difference between charity and philanthropy?

2. If you were the president of a private college or university, what things would you consider in making a decision on a possible tuition increase, which might enhance your bottom line but possibly work against your mission of providing educational opportunity?

3. Should gifts made by individuals to a nonprofit organization that receives the largest portion of its revenues from fees for services be fully tax deductible, partially tax deductible, or not deductible at all? Why or why not?

4. Suppose a nonprofit organization operates a business that is related to its mission, such that revenue is not subject to the UBIT, but it competes directly with a for-profit business nearby that must pay taxes. (Think of the nonprofit jazz club HR-57, which exists on the same street as for-profit bars and clubs.) Is that unfair competition with the for-profit businesses, and should the nonprofit be taxed just to level the playing field? Why or why not?

5. Is nonprofit management best taught in business schools; in schools of public affairs; or in some other school, department, or program of the university?

SUGGESTIONS FOR FURTHER READING RELATED TO CHAPTER 1

Books

Hammack, D. C. (1998). *Making the nonprofit sector in the United States*. Bloomington: Indiana University Press.

O'Neill, M. (2002). *Non profit nation: A new look at the third America*. San Francisco: Jossey-Bass.

Ott, J. S. (2001). *The nature of the nonprofit sector*. Boulder, CO: Westview Press.

Payton, R. L. (1988). *Philanthropy: Voluntary action for the public good*. New York: Macmillan.

Powell, W. W., & Steinberg, R. (2006). *The non-profit sector: A research handbook* (2nd ed.). New Haven, CT: Yale University Press.

Salamon, L. M. (1999). *America's nonprofit sector: A primer* (2nd ed.). New York: Foundation Center.

Salamon, L. M. (2002). *The state of nonprofit America*. Washington, DC: Brookings Institution.

Web Sites

Alliance for Nonprofit Management Web site, www.allianceonline.org

Council on Foundations, www.cof.org

Independent Sector, www.independentsector.org

Urban Institute Center on Nonprofits and Philanthropy, www.urban.org/content /PolicyCenters/NonprofitsandPhilanthropy/Overview.htm

Understanding the Nonprofit Sector and Nonprofit Organizations

In this chapter, we will discuss some theoretical views of the nonprofit sector and nonprofit organizations, as a foundation for consideration of more applied management topics in later chapters. We will first examine some macro theories advanced by scholars from various disciplines. These theories attempt to explain the nonprofit sector as a whole, addressing questions such as why the nonprofit sector exists at all in the United States; what role it plays in American society; and what relationship it has to the other two sectors, private business and government. In the second section of the chapter, we will consider some micro theories—that is, theories that attempt to explain nonprofit organizations as individual units. These will include concepts drawn from organizational theory that help explain why nonprofit organizations look and behave the way they do, how they make decisions, and how they are different from both public and for-profit organizations.

EXPLAINING THE NONPROFIT SECTOR

Theories that seek to explain America's nonprofit sector have been developed by economists, sociologists, historians, political scientists, psychologists, social psychologists, anthropologists, and scholars in other disciplines. There continues to be no unified theory to explain the existence of the nonprofit sector. Moreover, as we will discuss, some theories are at odds with others, and each theory has its advocates as well as critics.

Nonprofit Theory Across the Disciplines

Historians explain the existence of America's nonprofit sector as largely a result of historical forces and events. As noted in Chapter 1, the growth of America's nonprofit sector closely parallels the development of the nation itself. The nation was founded in rebellion against the authority of the British monarch, and skepticism toward government is deeply imbedded in American political attitudes. Moreover, many American towns and cities developed before local governments, and vital services often were provided by voluntary associations, including volunteer fire departments, libraries, schools, and hospitals. In the small towns of early America, people came together to meet common needs and provide for the poor, their voluntarism often reflecting religious convictions. Religion played an important role in colonial America, and missionary and charitable organizations were often founded by a religious congregation. The freedoms of speech, religion, assembly, and petition, enshrined in the First Amendment to the U.S. Constitution, also have created a hospitable environment for voluntary action throughout the nation's history, especially for organizations seeking social change. For example, the civil rights and women's rights movements focused public attention on injustices and helped create changes in social attitudes that paved the way for legislative action.

As the nation grew, movements such as urbanization, industrialization, and immigration increased the need for nonprofit organizations to serve the needs of a diverse population. The evolution of U.S. law further supported the growth of the nonprofit sector. The income tax was introduced in 1913, and Congress approved tax deductibility for gifts to certain nonprofits four years later (Ott, 2001, p. 144). Changes in public policy, including the expansion of government social programs in the 1960s and 1970s and their reduction and devolvement in the 1980s and 1990s, also have shaped today's nonprofit sector. In sum, historians explain today's nonprofit sector as a consequence of America's unique past, critical historical movements and events, and policies that tended to reinforce the sector's development and growth.

Theories advanced by sociologists, which focus on relationships between and among people in groups, also help explain the nonprofit sector. Sociologists' theories describe how involvement in nonprofits helps socialize individuals, reinforce norms and values, and develop "social capital," creating "interpersonal bonds of trust and cooperation and counteracting loneliness and isolation" (O'Neill, 2002, p. 42). Their theories emphasize "the roles of community networks of individuals, groups, and organizations; niches; and the importance of community elites and influentials for nonprofits" (Ott, 2001, p. 233). Sociologists discuss nonprofits as mediating structures, operating as buffers between individuals and the larger institutions of government and business. Berger and Neuhaus, in their prominent book *To Empower People: The Role of Mediating Structures in Public Policy* (1977), argued that in our complex society people need organizations like nonprofits to provide such interfaces. Their thinking was cited by some as one justification for the Reagan administration's efforts to devolve social programs to state and local governments and nonprofits during the 1980s.

Political scientists have looked at nonprofit organizations with respect to their role in supporting democratic traditions and in terms of power relationships between citizens and government. They have identified four major functions that nonprofits perform in relation to government:

1. *Accommodate diversity:* Nonprofits give voice to groups with differing values, beliefs, and practices that cannot be fully accommodated within government, with its obligation to treat all citizens the same.

2. *Undertake experimentation:* Nonprofits can undertake research and development (or "R&D") for social programs. In other words, nonprofits can begin new programs on

a smaller scale and undertake greater risk than government can with public funds. New programs developed by nonprofits that prove to be successful then may provide models and eventually be incorporated into larger government efforts.

3. *Provide freedom from bureaucracy:* Nonprofits may be able to respond more efficiently and quickly to new needs because they do not have the large bureaucracies that characterize government.

4. *Attention to minority needs:* Government's priorities must be consistent with those of the majority of voters. There may not be political support for programs to meet the needs of minority groups that do not possess sufficient political power. Nonprofits fill such gaps created by political realities (Douglas 1983, 1987).

Economists have made significant contributions to theories of the nonprofit sector, but as Ott (2001) notes, "Nonprofit organizations provide an interesting challenge for mainstream economic theory" (p. 181). Economists analyze the working of markets in terms of the variables of supply and demand and based on certain assumptions about human nature that nonprofits, at least on the surface of things, would seem to defy. How can we explain labor markets in which people work without compensation or the seemingly irrational act of giving away one's money?

The Failure Theories

Because some readers may be more familiar with the science of economics than others, let's define some terms before we discuss economic theories of the nonprofit sector. Some key concepts include *private goods, public goods, externalities*, and *free riders.*

By *goods*, economists mean what we conventionally think of as goods—that is, products that are *things*, but they also include services and intangible benefits, such as our enjoyment of a symphony, the knowledge we acquire through education, and the solace we may gain from participation in religious services.

Working on the principle of supply and demand, the market is an efficient mechanism for regulating the production and distribution of what are called private goods—that is, products or services that we buy and consume as individuals, with no significant impact on others. These would include, for example, the clothing and food that we buy and consume, as well as the services that we personally receive, such as haircuts or personal training sessions at a health club. With a private good, the person who pays also gains the full benefit of the good. Unless you choose to lend your friend your shirt or share your fries, enjoyment of the good is all yours, and society is not significantly affected by your consumption of it. The market works well for private goods, because we as consumers vote with our dollars. In other words, we buy the products we like and allow others to sit on the shelves; ultimately, the latter will disappear from the market. The market thus determines—very efficiently and effectively—what private goods are produced and who consumes them.

But some goods have what economists call externalities; very simply, their consumption affects other people, either negatively or positively. For example, your new barbeque grill may bring great pleasure to you and your cookout guests, but its smoke may annoy your neighbors. The smoke is a negative externality. On the other hand, if you beautify your yard, the plants you purchase and plant are private goods, but their consumption by you may create a positive externality for your neighbors—an improved neighborhood and perhaps enhanced property values.

Some goods create so many positive externalities that it is not possible to confine the benefits to an individual purchaser. For example, were you to assemble a private army to protect your property from foreign invaders, your neighbors' houses inevitably also would be protected from invasion. You would be paying the *full costs* of such protection, even though your neighbors would benefit as well. The same would be true if you were to hire a private contractor to pave your street—your neighbors also would benefit from a smoother ride but without paying for it. In other words, there would be a disconnect between the cost that you would incur and the portion of the benefit you would receive. Your neighbors might say "thanks," but you might perceive the situation as unfair.

In situations like that—the privately funded army or street paving—those who benefit without paying are known as *free riders*. They benefit from your expenditure at no cost to them—you are paying the fare, and they are just riding along for free! Who would be willing to spend his or her resources under such circumstances? Well, just about nobody, so the market is not a very good mechanism for ensuring that such goods will be produced at all. Therefore, when there is a potential problem with free riders, we as a society may decide that the good should be provided by government; in other words, we treat it as a public good. This is clearly a fairer way to provide public goods than leaving their production to the market. In this way, because everyone (or a large group of people) benefits, everyone is forced to pay for these goods through the tax system.

To sum it up, then, if the purchaser is able to capture all the externalities, it makes sense to have a product provided through the free market—to treat it as a private good. But if the externalities are so great that the good also will benefit many others who do not pay, the free riders, then the market is unlikely to provide it and it should be provided as a public good.

Market and Government Failure

One problem is that in some situations the market does not work effectively or efficiently. Economists call this *market failure* (Hansmann, 1987; Weisbrod, 1975, 1988). There are various reasons why the market may fail. For example, there may be a type of market failure that economists call *contract failure*, essentially a breakdown in the ideal or typical relationship between a buyer and a seller. This may occur when there is information asymmetry, meaning a situation in which the seller has more information about the product than does the purchaser, undermining the economic assumption that exchanges occur with complete knowledge on both sides of the deal.

Information asymmetry might be especially likely to occur in the case of complex or intangible products. For example, it is difficult for a person to judge the actual quality of the education or medical care he or she is receiving (Young, 2001a, p. 193). And, in some cases, the purchaser may actually be a different person from the one who is receiving the service—for example, parents who pay the tuition fees for their children's college education or children who pay for parents' nursing home care. In these instances, it may be difficult for the purchaser to obtain accurate information, even from the consumer, about the actual quality of the good or service being provided. The market also does not work well for people who are poor or belong to groups that face discrimination, since they may not have the resources with which to purchase what they need or may face other barriers.

In situations where the market does not work, government could step in to fill the gap left by the market. But government also can fail—there may be *government failure.* This is not meant to imply that government is incompetent but rather that there are political, structural, and systemic reasons that may prevent government from filling the gaps left by the private market.

Among those reasons is the fact that government must by its nature respond to the needs and demands of the majority. Weisbrod (1975, 1988), who is credited with introducing the "public goods theory" of nonprofits, discusses the concepts of "demand heterogeneity" and the "median voter." In the simplest terms, demand heterogeneity means that in a diverse society such as the United States, there may not be universal agreement about what goods and services government should provide. Some groups may want different kinds or different amounts of some goods. The "median voter," that is, the typical voter who comprises the largest single bloc, may not support some of the governmental activity that other groups may favor.

Government may be unable to provide services that some may desire but that are politically controversial—for example, family planning services for poor women. Or the problem may not yet be recognized as relevant to the majority—as, for example, AIDS in the early years of the pandemic in the early 1980s—and thus not command the attention of government.

Government also might fail to fill the gaps left by the private market because the time horizon of elected officials is often short; they need to focus on issues of current concern to the electorate and on policies that can show progress within their terms in office. They may not be able to find political support for undertaking solutions to problems or issues that require many years to come to fruition. For example, some people do not accept the idea of global warming, and others do not think much about it because its most serious implications seem far in the future. It is not a problem that the market can easily address, and while public awareness of the problem is growing, until quite recently there has not been a political consensus for strong government action.

Finally, government agencies are of necessity often large and bureaucratic; as a result, they may not have complete information, especially on local problems, and their size may make it difficult to undertake quick action. Their perceived bureaucracy also may inhibit individuals from interacting with them, thus limiting government's ability to meet needs and leaving gaps that are unaddressed by either the market or government. Who can fill such gaps?

Nonprofits as Gap Fillers

In the context of the failures theories, nonprofit organizations are essentially gap-fillers—they fill the gaps left by market failure and government failure, providing the goods and services that the other two sectors, for whatever reasons, could not.

For example, maybe the market has failed because of information asymmetry. Individuals just do not have complete information or lack the ability to understand or judge the quality of the good they seek to purchase. In such circumstances, they may choose to receive services from a nonprofit. Students may choose to enroll at a nonprofit (or state) university rather than a for-profit school. Children may prefer to entrust their parents' care to a church-sponsored nursing home rather than one operated by a for-profit company. They may do so because they believe that the nondistribution constraint removes the motive to exploit consumers, because they believe that nonprofit leaders are driven more by altruistic motivations than for-profit managers, or because they do not trust for-profit providers for some other reason. This thinking, known as the "trust theory" of nonprofits, has been developed over the past three decades by various scholars, including Hansmann (1987), who is often credited for it.

Nonprofits can compensate for the failings of government by jumping in to serve the needs of minority interests that government cannot serve, perhaps because such services do not hold the interest or concern of the political majority. In the early years of the AIDS pandemic in the United States, it was nonprofit organizations that served the needs of those who were infected, until there developed a widespread awareness of the threat posed to the general population and the problem became more visible on government's radar. In some developing countries, governments have yet to recognize the full implications of AIDS—or do not have the resources to respond to it adequately—and nonprofit organizations continue to play a leading role (U.S. Department of State Bureau of International Information Programs Web site, http://usinfo.state.gov/gi/Archive/2006/Jun/05-381621.html, accessed August 14, 2006).

As we have noted, sometimes government is simply too constrained by its size and complexity to respond quickly, especially in situations that may affect only a small group of people or a single community. For example, while the federal or state governments may respond to major disasters, nonprofit relief organizations like the Red Cross or Salvation Army may be more nimble in responding to the needs of victims in smaller, local disasters, such as an individual house fire or local flooding (Salamon, 2001, p. 164).

Nonprofit organizations also provide a buffer between individuals and large government agencies, which they may find difficult to access. For example, organizations that serve immigrants, the mentally ill, and the homeless help them to access government programs that may provide benefits—a task that some would find daunting on their own (Young, 2001b, p. 190).

In essence, the failure theories' explanation of the existence of nonprofits is parallel to the vocabulary issue we discussed in Chapter 1. Just as the term *nonprofit* connotes what such organizations are *not*, the failure theories explain their role by what others *do not do*; that is, nonprofits serve needs that the private market and government, for various reasons, do not meet. Although they enjoy wide support, the failure theories leave unanswered questions. How do we explain industries in which both nonprofits and government provide services (e.g., education)? Or in which nonprofits and for-profits compete side-by-side (e.g., in health care)? Moreover, some critics dismiss the failure theories as missing the unique and positive realities of nonprofit values, motivations, and contributions to society (Ott, 2001, p. 185). For example, Lohmann (1992), whose theory we will soon discuss, mentions activities such as worship, contemplation, help, inquiry, self-expression, and other purposes served by the nonprofit sector, arguing that "any theory of economics that reduces [such] goods to the basic categories of production, consumption, and exchange is reductionist and misleading" (p. 62).

Supply-Side Theories

Before we conclude our discussion of economic theories, it is important to consider other approaches that go beyond the failure theories and explain the existence of the nonprofit sector based on supply-side forces. In economics, a supply-side theory explains events based on the motivations of and incentives given to those who produce a good or a service rather than on the motivations of those who have the capability and desire to consume it—which constitute "demand." In other words, supply-side theories look at the push side of the market rather than the pull.

Supply-side nonprofit theorists observe that many nonprofits are, either currently or historically, outgrowths of religious congregations, motivated by faith rather than primarily economic incentives. Thus, we cannot explain them by market forces alone; rather, we need to consider what is known as the *entrepreneurship* theory of the nonprofit sector. This theory attributes the existence of nonprofit organizations to the vision and initiative of individuals who have created and built them. Such individuals are often motivated by religious zeal or strong secular values of idealism and social justice (Young, 1983; James, 1987; Rose-Ackerman, 1996).

The entrepreneurship theory is implicit in the writing of a number of contemporary authors who have gained attention in the 1990s and 2000s. For example, Dees et al. (2001) write that

> social entrepreneurs . . . are the reformers and revolutionaries of society today. They make fundamental changes in the way that things are done in the social sector. Their visions are bold. They seek out opportunities to improve society, and they take action. (p. 5)

The Ashoka Foundation, which provides support for promising social entrepreneurs around the world, extols the power of such individuals to lead fundamental change:

> Identifying and solving large-scale social problems requires a social entrepreneur because only the entrepreneur has the committed vision and inexhaustible determination to persist until they have transformed an entire system. The scholar comes to rest when he expresses an idea. The professional succeeds when she solves a client's problem. The manager calls it quits when he has enabled his organization to succeed. Social entrepreneurs go beyond the immediate problem to fundamentally change communities, societies, the world. (Ashoka Foundation, 2005)

Supply-side explanations complement the theories of market and government failure by defining nonprofits as more than gap fillers. They suggest that nonprofits exist not just to pick up the pieces left behind by the market and government but also as organizations different from business and government that are driven by vision and values.

Theories of Altruism and Giving

Some scholars offer theories to explain the nonprofit sector based on the motivations underlying altruism and philanthropic giving. We consider them at this point in this text because their perspective is similar to that of the supply-side economic theorists. That is, they focus not on those who consume the goods and services that nonprofits provide (the demand side) but rather on those who supply the funds to support the work of nonprofits. Theories related to altruistic behavior and giving predate the nonprofit theories of economists and continue to be a focus of scholars. They are drawn from the work of philosophers, theologians, and legal scholars as well as psychologists, social psychologists, and other social scientists.

The following are some of the questions raised by theorists who focus on charitable and philanthropic giving: Do people really make gifts based on altruism, or is philanthropy merely a tool used by the wealthy to exert control over society? And what influence do tax benefits play in the motivation of individuals to make gifts? In other words, is charitable and philanthropic giving always motivated by ideals, or do donors also expect to receive some benefits for themselves?

Kathleen Kelly, in her 1998 book, which includes a review of the research literature around these questions (pp. 44–45), joins those who conclude that donors have mixed motives (Jeavons, 1991; Martin, 1994, cited by Kelly, 1998, pp. 44–45; Payton, 1991; Van Til, 1988). These theorists find that altruism plays a role in giving, but so does self-interest. Kelly (1998) concludes that "donors hold interests both in self and in a common good" and that giving is a "social exchange," in which donors give money in exchange for positive feelings, influence, recognition, and tax benefits, among other rewards. Regarding the importance of tax incentives, Kelly argues that "the tax deductibility of gifts is vital to sustaining America's philanthropic tradition" (p. 48).

But in a controversial 2001 article, the sociologists Paul Schervish and John Havens deemphasize the importance of financial incentives to giving. Schervish and Havens describe a "new physics of philanthropy," arguing that donors are motivated by six "supply-side inclinations": (1) *hyperagency*, or "the enhanced capacity of wealthy individuals to establish or substantially control the conditions under which they and others live"; (2) *identification*, that is, a donor's empathy with the needs of others; (3) *association*, meaning donors' participation in activities that bring them into contact with people in need, leading them to identify with those individuals and their needs; (4) contemplation of their own *death*, guiding them perhaps to a desire to leave some legacy behind; (5) *gratitude* for the benefits they have received and a desire to give back to society; and (6) *tax aversion*, the desire to minimize their taxes through the deductions they earn for their charitable gifts.

Schervish and Havens (2001) argue that for these reasons, or some combination of them, individuals are "inclined" to be philanthropic. They do not need to be cajoled or scolded into giving, nor are self-interested motivations paramount. Although these authors acknowledge the desire to avoid taxes as one motivator for making gifts, they argue—and this is a controversial conclusion—that repeal of the estate tax "will not negatively affect charitable giving and may even prove to be a boon for philanthropy" (p. 234). This position is at odds with Kelly's (1998) and with the findings of most economists who have studied the relationship between taxes and giving. We will consider the question of donor motivations again in Chapter 10 of this volume.

Theory of the Commons: An Interdisciplinary Approach

Roger Lohmann's *The Commons*, published in 1992, offers an interdisciplinary theory of the nonprofit sector that offers a different perspective and introduces some new vocabulary with which to discuss the sector. Lohmann challenges the economists' failure theories directly.

Lohmann (1992) uses the term *commons* in various ways. In some contexts, *commons* refers to nonprofit organizations themselves. But used more abstractly, the commons comprises a "protected space for the collective expression of what people find most important in their lives" (Van Til, 1992, p. xi) or "an economic, political, and social space outside the market, households, and state in which associative communities create and reproduce social worlds" (Lohmann, 1992, p. 59).

Lohmann (1992) argues that common goods are a *third category*, alongside private goods (provided through the market) and public goods (provided by government). Nonprofits are not just making up for the failure of the market and government—they are not just gap fillers. Rather, they produce a distinctive third kind of good—common goods. How are common goods different from private and public goods? Unlike private goods, common goods cannot be consumed alone by an individual. But neither are they of interest or benefit to all people, like public goods. As Lohmann explains,

> One of the most powerful criticisms of the application of the public goods orientation to nonprofit or voluntary action is that most commons fail to fit the description of a public good. [For example,] church services, lodge meetings, food pantries, scientific meetings, amateur athletic events, and most other commons are available to some people (members and participants) without being available to all. Thus, they fail to meet the criterion of indivisibility, which is one of two defining characteristics of public goods.
>
> Yet many of the desired or preferred ends or objectives of common action are clearly not private goods either. They cannot be fully alienated and controlled exclusively by particular individuals without ceasing to be what they are. There is an undeniably other-oriented quality to any religious ritual, scientific finding, or artistic expression, for example. (p. 171)

Whereas a private good benefits only the individual who consumes it and a public good benefits all of society, common goods benefit (or are of interest to) all the members of the particular commons but possibly not those beyond. This helps explain how organizations that may hold entirely opposite positions or goals can coexist. The "good" of one common may be viewed as a "bad" by members of another common, but the existence of the commons foster social and political pluralism. In other words,

> no assumptions need to be made about the universal desirability of common goods. In most instances, it is sufficient that common goods are shared or held jointly by members of a particular commons, even in the face of indifference or hostility from others. (Lohmann, 1992, p. 18)

Lohmann (1992) cites the shortcomings of the failure theories. He acknowledges that economic theories are useful in explaining nonprofits that derive a substantial portion of their revenues from earned income—for example, "through ticket sales or fees charged for services, such as orchestras, opera companies, hospitals, nursing homes, and various types of social service agencies" (p. 175). But he argues, "Contemporary economists have largely ignored large portions of the commons" (p. 175).

Lohmann's work is widely admired. For example, Van Til (1992) calls it "original, robust, and powerful" and "the first definitive large-scale theory of the voluntary and nonprofit sector" (p. xii). But it is not universally accepted, and economists in particular take issue with Lohmann's (1992) assertion that their tools of analysis are unsuited to understanding nonprofit organizations. For example, Dollery and Wallis (2003) write, in a somewhat defensive tone, that "compared to sociological and other non-economic theories of the voluntary sector, economic theorizing represents a rather rare success story in the conceptual analysis of voluntary organizations" (p. 34). Indeed, while Lohmann's (1992) theory is persuasive with regard to many nonprofits, his concession that traditional economic theories *do* apply to nonprofits that rely substantially on earned income is a significant one, especially since earned income is the predominant source of revenue for the sector overall and for many of its largest organizations. His examples of commons include many organizations that would fit Salamon's (1999) member-serving category—for example, associations of bird watchers or car collectors and amateur athletic leagues—rather than the commercialized nonprofits that are an increasingly large component of the sector. But, like the supply-side economic theorists and those who identify altruistic motivations of donors, he succeeds in arguing that the failure theories do not provide a complete explanation for the nonprofit sector and in establishing the importance of shared values and purposes among those who participate in the sector's work.

Changing Definitions of Private, Public, and Common

Now that we have established the concepts of private, public, and common goods, how can they be applied to better understand today's nonprofit sector and explain some of the changes that we already have observed—for example, commercialization within the nonprofit sector and the shifting roles of government?

Clearly, if private goods benefit only their consumers, then they should be paid for by the individuals who use them. Public goods benefit everyone, and payment is thus compelled from all through the tax system. And common goods, because they are of interest and/or benefit only to members of the particular commons, should be funded by members of that particular commons. Most would agree on these simple rules. But there is often disagreement on the details and debate about whether certain goods should be considered private, public, or common. None will likely disagree that military defense is a public good to be provided by government or that a soft drink is a private good that should be paid for by the individual who consumes it. And most would agree that religious worship fits Lohmann's (1992) concept of a common good, that churches, synagogues, and mosques should be sustained by adherents of their respective faiths collectively rather than through appropriated public funds. But for other goods, there may be disagreement, and public attitudes may change over time.

For example, where should we place health care? In many nations, it is considered primarily a public good, to be provided to everyone through government programs. In the United States, health care has the characteristics of private, common, and public goods. Government programs support health care for some members of society, so we regard it at least in part as a public good. But nonprofit hospitals are supported in part through philanthropic gifts from members of the community they serve, as if they are common goods. Some analysts call for greater privatization of health care, in the belief that giving consumers more control will increase efficiency, reduce unnecessary treatment, and reduce costs. So some regard medical care as primarily a private good, at least in part.

Historically, K-12 education has been considered a public good in the United States, based on the belief that an educated citizenry is of benefit to all of society because it is essential to a successful democracy and a healthy economy. In early U.S. history, higher education was a private good. But beginning with the founding of the land grant universities in the mid 19th century and until recent decades, higher education was increasingly treated as a public good. State support of public universities, the establishment of community colleges, and federal assistance to colleges and universities and their students sought to make higher education more like K-12, accessible and affordable to anyone with the ability to succeed—like a public good. But in the past three decades, higher education has come to be considered more like a private good, with government support for higher education declining in many states and students and their families being expected to shoulder an increasing portion of the cost. In other words, the prevailing view has swung to the point that higher education is seen primarily as an investment made by an individual and his or her family, with the benefits accruing mostly to that individual in the form of higher income. "Lawmakers increasingly view higher education as a private good that should be supported by students and donors, rather than as a public good that deserves state support" (Selingo, 2003).

Most people today probably think of highways as a public good, but in the nation's early days, it was not uncommon for roads to be developed by private interests, and there have been recent proposals in some states to privatize some highways by charging tolls that would go to the private investors in the highway (Guerrero, 2005). And what are we to make of the Blue Ridge Parkway Foundation (www.brpfoundation.org), a "professional fundraising organization" established to help fund projects to improve a road owned and operated by the National Park Service? Are roads public, private, or common goods? When national parks that were previously free start to charge admission fees, it represents some movement of the good they provide from the public toward the private sphere. And when foundations are created to raise funds for the support of public parks, it begins to give them characteristics more like those of common goods. When a performing arts center that is primarily supported through audience fees and philanthropic gifts receives a government grant, it has moved from somewhere between private and common to a position that is some blend of private, common, and public. Again, we find that boundaries are not always clear, definitions are not always fixed, and thinking can change over time.

Lohmann (1992) suggests that public support for what are in reality common goods is often provided in response to "appeals by various leisure classes for tax-supported patronage of particular common goods valued by those leisure classes" (p. 187). He explains that such appeals are often based on the argument that there is an indirect benefit to society. For example, advocates for greater public support of higher education might argue that there is a benefit to all citizens in having well-educated leaders, although the students who attend universities may be the primary beneficiaries of the education they receive there. Similarly, arts patrons might advocate for public support of the arts because they provide an indirect benefit to society, not just to those who participate as their patrons. Lohmann disputes such arguments, saying that such claims are "demonstrably untrue, simply by virtue of the fact that many people never even attend artistic performances" (p. 186).

As attitudes of the public and its political leaders change over time, goods may come to be viewed as more public, more private, or more common—in varying combinations, and the roles of business, government, and nonprofits will evolve to reflect that new philosophical and political landscape. Lohmann's (1992) theory provides us with both the vocabulary and the concepts with which to consider some of the most fundamental political and public policy debates and to understand some of the tides of change affecting today's nonprofit sector.

EXPLAINING NONPROFIT ORGANIZATIONS

The theories we have been discussing so far in this chapter are macro theories—they attempt to explain why nonprofit organizations exist and what role they play in our society. We now will shift our discussion to micro theories, theories that look inside nonprofit organizations and attempt to explain why they behave the way they do and make the decisions they make—how we can understand them as *organizations*. This discussion will include a look at the characteristics of nonprofit organizations, a review of some concepts from the field of organizational theory, and principles related to the structure and culture of nonprofit organizations. There is a rich literature in the fields of organizational behavior and organizational theory, but historically, much of the theory has been generic, meaning that its originators apply it to all forms of organization, whether business, government, or nonprofit. Recent years have produced "a veritable wave" of theories addressing the distinctive features of nonprofit organizations, but as Ott (2001) says, "there is not, cannot be, and should not be a single theory of nonprofit organizations" (p. 269). Our discussion of theories is thus of necessity selective.[1]

Characteristics of Nonprofit Organizations

As we saw in Chapter 1, the nonprofit sector encompasses an array of organizations and institutions that are very different from one another. Is it possible, then, to identify some characteristics that are associated with what it means to be a "nonprofit?" In his 1999 book, *America's Nonprofit Sector: A Primer*, Lester Salamon identifies and discusses six qualities that characterize nonprofit organizations (pp. 10–11): They are *organized entities*, they are *private*, they are *non–profit distributing*, they are *self-governing*, they are *voluntary*, and they are of *public benefit*. Let's discuss these qualities one at a time.

Organized Entities

There are loose and informal groups of people who undertake voluntary efforts similar to the programs of nonprofits. But the organizations that we will consider in this book are generally chartered as *formal organizations*. Most are incorporated under state law and enjoy the same benefits as business corporations—that is, status as a legal person in and of itself, separate from the individuals who may control it.

Private

Although nonprofit organizations have a commitment to public service, they operate in the *private* sector rather than as agencies of government. Many receive government funds, and indeed, government funds make up the largest source of revenue for some. Some authors use the term *nonprofit agencies*, implying that they are essentially like units of government. But it is important to be clear that the control of nonprofit organizations lies outside the sphere of government, and they have considerable autonomy to set their own strategies, design their own programs, pursue revenues through multiple means, and select those who will benefit from their services.

A government agency, by contrast, is generally obligated to provide services to anyone who qualifies, or as Thomas Wolf (1999) describes it, they have "a requirement of equity" (p. 20). The requirement may be specifically defined—for example, people making below some level of annual income or people over a certain age. But the agency is required to provide services to anyone who meets those criteria, within the limits of resources appropriated to it. Nonprofit organizations may receive government funding that requires them to provide specific services to qualified individuals as a condition of accepting the funds. But, in general, they have both the liberty and the challenge of defining their own constituencies, deciding the services to be offered, and deciding which funding they will or will not accept.

Non–Profit Distributing

As we already have discussed, nonprofits, by definition, do not distribute any excess of revenues over expenditures to benefit individual owners. Any profit that a nonprofit organization generates must be reinvested in the organization itself rather than used to pay dividends to owners or investors. This requirement is indeed one of the primary criteria for being recognized as a nonprofit organization, and any violation of it could be a cause for IRS revoking recognition of the organization's nonprofit status. It is also required that compensation to employees of the organization be reasonable, so that managers are not being enriched as if they were in fact owners of the enterprise. Indeed, nonprofit executive compensation is an area of potential abuse that has received increasing attention from the Congress and the IRS in recent years. The standard of reasonableness does not mean that nonprofit executives must be paid low salaries, and indeed, in some fields, nonprofit salaries are comparable with salaries for similar jobs in the for-profit sector. It does require, however, that nonprofits justify the compensation paid to their executives, to ensure that they are receiving payment in exchange for the services they provide to the organization rather than a share of profits disguised as salary or benefits.

Self-Governing

Nonprofits are self-governing, another way of saying that they are not controlled either by the government or by individual owners. Control of the nonprofit lies with a board of directors or a board of trustees, a group of individuals who have overall responsibility for ensuring that the organization serves its nonprofit mission and uses funds in accordance with that mission and the law. The board also has responsibility for the overall welfare of the organization itself.

Voluntary

Although many nonprofits employ significant numbers of paid staff, they are rooted in the tradition of voluntarism. Most—although not all—members of nonprofit governing boards are volunteers, who serve without compensation. And many organizations also engage substantial numbers of service volunteers in delivering their programs. Even nonprofits that employ significant numbers of staff often had an earlier period in their histories when volunteers were the predominant workforce, and the values of inclusion and openness to varying opinions often remain important components of their cultures. Indeed, nonprofits can be somewhat unruly forums of debate about even basic questions of values, mission, and priorities.

Of Public Benefit

Nonprofits are privately controlled entities, but they exist to serve a social purpose that has been deemed to be of public benefit. The public benefit is obvious with regard to some organizations. For example, who would argue with the benefits of feeding the hungry, eliminating drunk driving, or fighting drug addiction? In other instances, however, definition of the greater good will vary between those who advocate the two opposite sides of a controversial issue. For example, there are organizations that hold prolife or prochoice positions. Some advocate prayer in public schools, while others emphasize the separation of church and state and oppose school prayer. Some citizens see environmental organizations as accomplishing important public benefits, while others may see them as extremist roadblocks to economic progress. All these organizations may be tax-exempt because they are deemed to be of public benefit. In such cases, the public benefit that all of them advance is the protection and encouragement of free and open debate, a value presumably shared by all sides of an issue in a democratic society.

A nonprofit's purpose is stated in broad terms in its charter and is elaborated in its mission statement. The mission statement is a guide to every action taken by the organization and, many argue, the principal standard against which its performance should be measured. Amending a charter is a complex process, but the mission of an organization is more easily changed. Indeed, consideration of the mission is usually among the first steps undertaken in an organization's planning process.

The mission is so central to all nonprofit organizations that they are said to be mission driven. The mission is their purpose and accomplishing it their overriding goal. This commitment to a mission is a fundamental difference between nonprofits and the for-profit sector and one of the reasons why nonprofit management is a distinctive professional field.

Government agencies also have missions, to which the individuals who work in them are often highly dedicated. But government agencies are ultimately controlled by elected officials, who must respond to the wishes of the majority. They can only support programs according to what is politically feasible—that is, those favored by a majority of the voters. This is not to disparage the practice of politics, or to imply that politicians do not have personal convictions, but merely to state the reality that if officials do not meet the expectations of the majority over time, they will be replaced by others whose programs are more reflective of the majority's mandate. Thus, political viability is in a sense an ultimate test as fundamental to the purposes of government as profit is to business (Wolf, 1999, p. 27).

Nonprofits stand somewhere between business and government. They are driven neither by the need to maximize profit nor by the need to meet the expectations or desires of a majority, but rather by achievement of the missions for which they exist. Like businesses, some nonprofits can and do generate profits. But, by definition, the generation of revenue is the *means to the end* of providing the public benefit envisioned in their charters and fulfilling the social purposes expressed in their mission statements.

The characteristics of nonprofit organizations identified by Salamon (1999) help explain *what* they are. Now let's look at some concepts and theories that go to the "why" of how nonprofit organizations look and behave as they do.

Nonprofits as Open Systems

To many people today, the word *bureaucracy* provokes negative images of a slow-moving, complex, unresponsive institution—perhaps a government agency like the motor vehicles department or even a large university. But in the early years of the 20th century, Max Weber advanced the idea of a bureaucracy as an ideal model. Characterized by rules and a formal hierarchy of positions, he thought a bureaucracy to be especially capable of efficiency and effectiveness. For decades after Weber's pioneering work, his concept of a bureaucracy remained central in organizational theory, and other scholars expanded on his work, studying issues such as the span of manager control, the roles of managers, and other questions based on his idea of organizations as machine-like entities. Later scholars, such as Barnard, Simon, Cyert and March, Lewin, Maslow, McGregor, Argyris, and others, began to chip away at Weber's principles by placing more emphasis on human needs, motivations, and incentives rather than on formal organizational structures, eventually leading to development of the "human relations school" of management (Rainey, 2003, pp. 32–40). But Weber's concept of a bureaucracy, operating with formal structures, rules, and machine-like precision, probably still comports with many people's image of how an organization works.

Theories based on Weber's concept of bureaucracy usually focus on *internal* dynamics and on the behaviors of individuals within the organization. Beginning in the 1960s and 1970s, however, thinking about organizations began to shift toward viewing them as systems and analyzing their ability to adapt to different circumstances, or contingencies, in the *external* environment facing them. A landmark book by Daniel Katz and Robert Kahn (1966) was a classic description of organizations as open systems that is still widely cited. Widely read books authored by Peter Senge (1990, 1994) describing "learning organizations" also were based on systems theory. This shift in attention from the internal mechanics of an organization's operation to studying the effects of pressures and constraints brought to bear on the organization by the social context in which it exists was a profound change.

The simplest system includes inputs, a transformative process that acts on the inputs—that is, changes or manipulates them in some way, and the outputs resulting from that process. Systems also include feedback loops. Feedback enables the system to adapt to changing circumstances—that is, to learn and alter its behavior accordingly. In their ability to learn and adapt, systems are less like machines and more like living organisms. Indeed, some theorists study systems using principles drawn from the study of living organisms. For example, population ecology is an approach taken by some sociologists to explain the birth and death of organizations. They analyze organizations in terms of population density—that is, the number of organizations occupying particular niches—and the competition for resources among them. Population ecologists see some organizations as being selected in a Darwinian competition for scarce resources. They tend to place less emphasis on the ability of organizations to survive by adapting to environmental changes than do some other theories—for example, the resource dependence model we will consider below (Aldrich, 1999).

Systems theorists make a distinction between closed and open systems. A system is closed or open depending on the extent to which it interacts with and is influenced by the environment in which it exists. A totally closed system would be one that is entirely self-sufficient and impervious to influences from its environment. It is difficult to conceive of an example of this extreme situation; no organization is insulated against all impact from outside. But some government agencies may be relatively closed. For example, those that provide essential services and have relatively assured appropriations may enjoy a high degree of autonomy in determining their own policies and procedures. A nonprofit that has a large endowment and thus can rely on investment earnings for all its operating support, not requiring revenue from donors, government, or fees for service, also might operate as a relatively closed system. This could describe foundations, for example, and indeed, foundations have been criticized in recent years for being insufficiently responsive to the world outside.

Most nonprofit organizations, however, are open systems. They are dependent on and interact frequently with their external environments. This is true because of their dependence on external resources, their social missions, and the involvement of volunteers at various levels of the organization.

As we have discussed, most nonprofit organizations have voluntary cultures. This has important implications for how they work. Individuals *choose* to be associated with a nonprofit. This is obviously true of service volunteers, people who perform the organization's work for no compensation and are free to stay or leave as they may prefer. But it is often true that even paid staff of nonprofits have a voluntary attitude, meaning that they are motivated as much by the nature of the work and the organization's mission as by the pay and often see themselves as performing a service. Even organizations that are highly commercialized or that rely primarily on government contracts have a "long history, deep traditions, and cultures steeped in voluntaristic values" (Ott, 2001, p. 289).

Most nonprofit governing boards are composed of volunteers, who may be drawn from constituencies served by the organization or from among its donors and who, in some cases, may have worked their way up through the ranks to join the board after having served as volunteers in delivering the organization's programs. The nonprofit board plays a boundary-spanning role; that is, its members are a part of the organization and represent the organization to the outside world, but they also are representatives of the outside world who bring the views and desires of the organization's stakeholders to bear on the organization and its management. The boundaries between "inside" and "outside" the organization may be fuzzy and permeable. Volunteers often work alongside paid staff, and communication flows back and forth across the formal boundaries of the organization. Volunteers providing the organization's services and also sitting on its governing board bring their own views and values to bear on the board's discussions, and since they are not bound by the constraints of paid employment, they can be forcefully outspoken. Thus, communications both within the organization and between the organization and its external environment often do not follow the paths and patterns of formal authority.

Because nonprofits serve a public purpose, are subsidized through the tax deductibility of gifts, and often serve as contractors to government in the delivery of public services, they are often subject to the scrutiny and opinions of government officials, the media, recipients of their services, and the general public. Unlike businesses, which have the relatively simple and clear goal of generating profits, nonprofits often have ambiguous goals, and there is generally lack of agreement on how achievement of the goals should be measured. This leaves plenty of room for debate and discussion, which are not easily contained within the organization's walls. In sum, most nonprofits are very open systems, interacting with their external constituencies and needing to adjust to changes in their environment all the time.

Resource Dependency

Expanding on the open systems theory, Pfeffer's and Salancik's (1978) resource dependency theory explains the behavior of organizations in terms of their dependence on external constituencies—for revenue, information, and other resources. Although the theory has been around for about 30 years, it is still widely cited and applied in research on nonprofit organizations.

According to this theory, we can understand the choices and behavior of organizations less by studying their internal structures and dynamics than by focusing on their interdependencies with external organizations and individuals who hold power over them by virtue of the resources they provide. For example, if a nonprofit receives most of its funding from government, the government will be able to impose its policies on that organization. An example of this can be seen in higher education, where government support was leveraged to require that colleges and universities make changes in their admissions policies favoring affirmative action and in their allocation of resources to provide equal support for men's and women's athletic programs (Pfeffer, 2003). An organization that is highly dependent on a single foundation or a major individual donor also loses some of its autonomy and must respond to the priorities or demands of those who provide it with needed resources.

Goal Displacement

One significant risk of resource dependency is what is called *goal displacement*—that is, actions taken by the nonprofit to alter its goals and activities to satisfy the contributor of funds. This sometimes occurs not as a result of overt demands by funders but in more subtle ways, when an organization expands its programs and activities into areas that may be appealing to donors or when it avoids activities that may alienate donors. For example, Karen Froelich (1999) looked at public broadcasting stations to see if their programming decisions were influenced by their need to raise funds from corporate donors. She found that "although respondents insisted that program content was not influenced by corporate support, they demonstrated the *opposite* via 'self censoring' behavior that continually pressures stations to provide programming more readily salable to corporations" (p. 256, italics added).

Resource Dependency and Performance Measurement

Resource dependency helps explain some recent trends and issues in the nonprofit sector, including efforts to make nonprofits more accountable for performance. Government funders, foundations, and federated funders, such as United Way, can impose performance standards on nonprofits that receive their support and establish the achievement of certain goals as conditions for future support. The extent to which organizations are constrained by such requirements depends on how important the resources of a particular funder are. For example, United Way has been a leader in advocating the use of outcomes measures as a method for evaluating nonprofit effectiveness (something we will explore further in Chapter 5). To the extent that individuals make unrestricted gifts to United Way, permitting it to allocate those funds to specific organizations, United Way holds considerable influence over those organizations and can require that they follow its approach to measuring effectiveness. However, to the extent that individuals designate their United Way gifts to specific organizations, or bypass United Way and make gifts directly to the organizations themselves, United Way loses the ability to influence those organizations. The trend toward designated gifts has made organizations less dependent on United Way and thus has reduced United Way's ability to influence their priorities and policies.

Internal Impact of Resource Dependency

An important insight from the resource dependence theory is that *external* resource dependencies also can affect power relationships and structures *within* the organization. As Pffefer (2003) explains, "The people, groups, or departments inside organizations that . . . manage important environmental dependencies, and help the organization obtain resources, [hold] more power as a result of their critical role" (p. xiii). Consider, for example, an organization that depends primarily on charitable gifts for the largest portion of its revenues. The person who raises such money—perhaps the chief executive or a fundraising professional—will hold power within the organization because he or she delivers so much of the revenue on which it depends. Requests for increases to the fundraising budget or perhaps a higher salary for the chief fundraising officer are likely to be favorably received. Alternatively, think about a commercialized nonprofit that derives most of its revenue from fees for services. Gifts may be less important to the organization, and hence its fundraisers may have less internal clout. For example, they may have a more difficult time gaining approval of increased budgets. Such an organization is more dependent on fee-paying consumers or clients than on donors, and internal power thus may lie more with those who are experts in marketing or customer relations.

How does dependence on government funds affect a nonprofit organization? Froelich (1999) argues that "the most pronounced effects of government funding involve changes in internal processes and ultimately in the structures of nonprofit organizations" (p. 6). For example, she points to studies showing that the government's "dense web" of regulations and required accounting and reporting have altered the internal structure of arts organizations. She calls government "the primary force driving out the technical experts in arts management in favor of professional arts administrators, many of whom know little about the art forms they are managing" (p. 261).

The influence of resource dependency on an organization's internal structure, processes, and culture is so great that over time nonprofits may indeed become more like those very organizations that are their principal sources of revenue. For example, nonprofits that are primarily government contractors may come to "look, think, feel, and act" much like a government agency (Ott, 2001, p. 357). In contrast, those that receive a high percentage of their revenues through fees-for-service and other business activities may come to exhibit the characteristics of entrepreneurial business firms.

Organizations Adapt to Resource Dependency

Organizations use a variety of strategies to try and maintain their autonomy—that is, to resist external pressure on their decision making. They may try to make changes to accommodate to the external demands, perhaps by undertaking internal reforms, or they may try to alter the environment in a way that ameliorates the demands (Pfeffer & Salancik, 1978). For example, when in 2004 the nonprofit sector was threatened with new federal legislation to curb perceived abuses, the organization Independent Sector responded both with proposals for self-regulation of the sector and with intensive lobbying efforts aimed at forestalling (or at least influencing) the proposed new federal legislation (Panel on the Nonprofit Sector, 2005).

Managing Resource Dependency

A hallmark of the resource dependence theory is the idea that "although organizations [are] . . . constrained by their situations and environments, [they have] opportunities to *do things* . . . to obtain, at least temporarily, more autonomy and the ability to pursue organizational interests" (Pfeffer, 2003, p. xii, italics added). In other words, organizations need not be helpless captives of their funding sources. They can make strategic choices that enable them to *manage* resource dependency in a way that maximizes their autonomy.

One way to reduce dependency and thus maintain more autonomy is to diversify the sources of revenue. For example, an organization that is highly dependent on gifts may decide to develop a revenue-producing business to reduce its reliance on donors. Or an organization that relies on the support of one government agency or foundation may focus on broadening its base of donors. The goal is to reduce dependence on any one source of revenue in order to achieve the autonomy needed to determine its own mission, programs, and measures of effectiveness.

Isomorphism

Resource dependency suggests that some nonprofits may become more like their primary funders. Other scholars see a tendency for organizations in the same field to become more like *each other* as a result of facing similar influences from their environments.

Called *isomorphism*, this concept is drawn from the work of organizational scholars who use institutional theory.

Like resource dependency and population ecology, institutional theory represents "a continuation and extension of . . . open systems conceptions" (Scott, 1995, p. xiv). It recognizes the importance of an organization's environment and emphasizes the constraints placed on it by rules, expectations, norms, and values. Institutional theory describes organizations' efforts to gain legitimacy by embracing the norms, values, beliefs, and mores prescribed by the environment in which they exist.

Walter Powell and Paul DiMaggio (1991) describe three types of isomorphism—*coercive isomorphism, mimetic isomorphism,* and *normative isomorphism,* and we can find examples of all three types at work in the nonprofit sector. Coercive isomorphism, as the term implies, is "forced" on organizations. This pressure might come, for example, from laws, government regulations, accrediting bodies, or accounting rules established by the Financial Accounting Standards Board. There also are several standards of nonprofit behavior that have been established by watchdog organizations, such as the Better Business Bureau's Wise Giving Alliance. Such standards do not have the force of law, but they can nevertheless be coercive, since the media attention given to organizations that do not meet them may have a negative impact on giving and other sources of support. In other words, nonprofit organizations, particularly in the same field, might tend to become more alike over time simply because they are *forced* to play by the same sets of rules.

Mimetic isomorphism refers to the tendency of organizations to mimic each other—that is, to look to the example of similar organizations for models to be adopted. Many nonprofit organizations today engage in benchmarking, a practice we will discuss more fully elsewhere in this book. "In benchmarking, an organization that has defined an opportunity for improved performance identifies another organization . . . that has achieved better results and conducts a systematic study of the other organization's achievements, practices, and processes" (Letts et al., 1999a, p. 86). Through this approach, organizations try to identify the best practices of other organizations they consider to be similar to them and thus learn ways to improve their own operations. It is not surprising that this leads eventually to different organizations in the same field doing things in much the same way.

Normative isomorphism arises when organizations are influenced by the same standards of professional practice. For example, doctors follow the same ethical codes, so some things will be done the same way in all hospitals. Social service organizations will reflect the norms of the social work profession. And university professors' similar understandings about academic freedom will affect the way in which all colleges and universities operate.

Explaining Nonprofit Organizational Structures

Isomorphism creates a tendency for organizations to become more alike. But we can observe that there are also often differences. For example, some organizations are relatively bureaucratic and centralized, with everyone following tightly prescribed policies and procedures sent down from the top. Others are more entrepreneurial and flexible, with decisions being made closer to the action in the field. What explains such differences?

As we already have discussed, some of the explanation lies with resource dependency. Structure is influenced by the organization's principal sources of support. For example, those that are dependent on just a few sources of support may operate with more centralized managements, to achieve consistent communication with funding sources and ensure compliance with funders' requirements. Those that have more broad-based public support may be more decentralized, to tap the involvement and support of larger numbers of volunteers and local donors.

But a nonprofit's structure also is influenced by other variables, including the *task environment* it faces. The task environment includes the nature of the goods or services it provides; the type of technology it uses; the degree of uncertainty it faces in its environment; the complexity of its environment; the dynamism or rate of change in its environment;

whether its units are tightly or loosely coupled, that is, in what time, proximity, and sequence they must interact in the process of producing the organization's product or service; and whether the interactions are complex or linear, that is "the extent to which interaction sequences in operations are well known, predictable, unambiguous, and recoverable among operational units" (Anheier, 2005, pp. 152–154). In simplest terms, how an organization is structured may depend in part on whether the work it does is straightforward, follows some clear set of procedures, and is predictable or whether it often faces complex, unique, and messy situations that cannot be well predicted in advance.

Let's consider an example that illustrates this idea. One of the nation's largest nonprofits, the American Red Cross, engages in two principal activities—blood services and disaster relief. It collects blood; processes and stores it; and provides it to hospitals and other medical facilities as needed. It also responds to natural disasters, providing immediate relief to victims in the form of food, shelter, and other help. The task environment is different for each of these activities. Handling the blood supply requires precision, and it needs to be done one way. Disasters are different. Of the more than 70,000 disasters to which the Red Cross responds annually, the majority are local, including incidents such as house fires, hazardous material spills, and transportation accidents. The timing and nature of events are unpredictable—each situation is different and requires a somewhat different, tailored response. Blood services and disasters present different task environments, and the Red Cross organizes itself differently for each of these activities.

In local disasters, most services are provided by local chapters, which operate in a relatively decentralized manner with the support of local donors and volunteers. In this area, there is relatively loose coupling between the national office and local chapters. Blood services were once more decentralized, but the Red Cross reorganized its blood services in the 1990s in the face of growing national concern about HIV infection. This reorganization created a more centralized structure and additional bureaucratic policies and procedures (www.redcross.org). In other words, the organizational structure changed when the nature of the task was changed by HIV. Following Hurricane Katrina in 2005, the Red Cross' disaster relief services also were reorganized, to reflect the new task environment presented by the seemingly more frequent incidence of catastrophic disasters affecting large geographic regions as well as the potential for terrorist incidents that have regional or national implications.

Organizational Culture

Any of us who has experience with organizations—as employees, volunteers, students, or in any other capacity—know that formal structures and written rules often do not fully account for "the way things work around here." There are unwritten rules of behavior that govern things such as what people wear (suits or jeans?), how people address each other (by first name or formal title?), whether personal phone calls and e-mails can be received during working hours or not, whether or not people who work together also socialize outside the office, and many other realities of day-to-day organizational life. These realities often are controlled not by formal policies but rather by organizational culture.

Scholars long have studied the subject of organizational culture, but the "topic [of culture] really came alive in the management literature" following the publication in the 1980s and 1990s of popular business books that emphasized the importance of culture in successful corporations (Rainey, 2003, p. 307). Peters and Waterman's book, *In Search of Excellence,* published in 1982, focused the attention of corporate managers on the idea of corporate culture and inspired additional research.

The lesson of Peters and Waterman (1982) was simple: Great companies that produce excellent results have core values that are widely shared; in other words, they have strong cultures. In their 1994 book, *Built to Last: Successful Habits of Visionary Companies*, James Collins and Jerry Porras identified several characteristics that were associated with successful business corporations. Like Peters and Waterman, they found that culture was important. Successful companies have core values that are widely understood and often codified; they undertake efforts to protect the core values; they have a shared understanding of "purpose" that goes beyond the maximization of profit; and they demonstrate strong, "cult-like" cultures that are often perpetuated through promotion from within (Collins & Porras, 1994).

Culture is a word that is frequently used in everyday conversation, and most people probably have a reasonably accurate understanding of what it means. But organizational scholars offer precise definitions. For example, Edgar Schein (1992) breaks culture down into three categories: (1) *artifacts and creations*—for example, logos, symbols, ceremonies, rituals, and words used in conversations; (2) *basic values*—the less observable understandings of "how things are done around here," for example, who communicates with whom within the organization and in what manner, what external relationships are important, and so forth; and (3) *basic assumptions*—for example, how people see things, their personal theories about human nature, and expectations about whether people in the organization should be entrepreneurial and aggressive or compliant and passive.

It may be an oversimplification to speak of an organization's culture, as if it is coherent and uniform throughout. Most organizations, except perhaps the smallest, will include various subcultures—that is groups of individuals "who share strong values about basic beliefs with some, but not all, of the other members of the organization" (Clegg, Kornberger, & Pitsis, 2005, p. 277). For example, executives may have different values and beliefs than do rank-and-file staff or volunteers. Staff members may have values derived from their professional cultures; for example, doctors and nurses working in hospitals may be influenced by professional norms not shared by professional hospital managers. The leadership and staff in the national headquarters of a nonprofit organization may see things quite differently from those who work in the local chapters. In hybrid organizations, like those we discussed in Chapter 1, there may be cultural differences between staff who provide mission-related services and those who are engaged in the revenue-producing business ventures of the organization.

Is there something that can be called "the nonprofit culture," some set of values and beliefs that runs commonly and consistently across the nonprofit sector? A number of authors assert that there is. We mentioned earlier in this chapter that many nonprofits, even those that may be largely dependent on earned income and paid staff, have a "long history, deep traditions, and cultures steeped in *voluntaristic values*" (Ott, 2001, p. 289; italics added). Christine Letts and colleagues (1999a) describes a "service culture" in nonprofits, stating that

> organizational issues hold little appeal for the several types of nonprofit employees who populate much of the sector. . . . many nonprofit employees develop a "just do it" attitude that places more value on service than on the analysis and measurement needed to improve organizational performance.

Letts et al. also observe a "cooperative [rather than competitive] nature" in nonprofit workplaces and nonprofit professionals who see their work as "artistry" that is diminished by performance measurement (pp. 33–34). Frumkin and Imber (2004) claim that

> many nonprofit employees, and even some donors and volunteers, are uncomfortable with the language and practices of business and may be skeptical of the values and motives of people trying to introduce business concepts . . . [and that] the sector overall . . . seems to have a bias towards small organizations, local autonomy, and consensus-driven decision making. (p. 70)

And Anheier (2005) states that "the organizational culture of nonprofit organizations encourages conflict avoidance rather than engagement" (p. 253).

That culture exists and is an important aspect of understanding organizations is well supported and resonates with our own experience as individuals. However, as we have discussed, the nonprofit sector is diverse and complex, so it may not be a simple matter to describe a universal nonprofit culture. In addition, the blurring of the for-profit, governmental, and nonprofit sectors may be changing the culture of at least some organizations. The working of isomorphism may not be constrained to organizations within the same sector. Nonprofit hospitals may become more like for-profit hospitals. Nonprofit museums may become more like for-profit entertainment venues. Human services organizations may become more like competitive service businesses. Nonprofits are adopting the methods and vocabulary of the marketplace, becoming more businesslike at the same time as some corporations are emphasizing missions, vision, and values and implementing more socially responsible policies. In essence, some nonprofits may be developing more corporate-like cultures, while some corporations are becoming more nonprofit-like in theirs. In this changing environment, it may be increasingly unrealistic to describe a distinctive nonprofit culture that is universally characteristic of all organizations across the entire sector.

CHAPTER SUMMARY

Scholars in various disciplines have developed theories to explain the nonprofit sector as a whole and the behavior of individual nonprofit organizations.

Theories drawn from economics surround the concepts of public goods and private goods, externalities, and free riders and explain nonprofits as gap fillers that compensate for the failures of the market and government. Other theories address the supply side and explain nonprofits in terms of social entrepreneurship; the contributions that nonprofits make to freedom, pluralism, and joint action; and motivations for altruism and giving.

Lohmann's (1992) interdisciplinary theory of the commons explains nonprofits as providers of common goods, a third category of goods alongside private and public. The definitions of what is private, public, or common may change over time, reflecting current philosophical and political trends.

Nonprofit organizations exhibit six characteristics: (1) they are organized entities, (2) they are private, (3) they are non–profit distributing, (4) they are self-governing, (5) they are voluntary, and (6) they are of public benefit. These characteristics have implications for how they behave as organizations. Their purposes are stated in their mission statements. The mission is so central to nonprofit organizations that they are said to be mission driven.

Organizational theorists discuss nonprofits as open systems that respond to the pressures and constraints presented by their environments. Their behavior reflects their resource dependency, and nonprofits face the risks of goal displacement and loss of autonomy if they are too dependent on one or a few sources of funding. Most attempt to manage resource dependency by diversifying the sources of support and remaining committed to their missions.

Isomorphism describes the tendency of organizations in the same field to become alike. This may result from external pressures, the inclination of organizations to adopt each other's practices, or the commonalities of professional codes practiced by the organization's staff members. The organizational structure of a nonprofit also may be determined by the task environments it faces.

An organization's culture, the informal rules about "the way things are done around here," has received increased emphasis in management literature over the past two decades. Some authors describe an identifiable nonprofit culture, but the much-noted blurring of sectors may be reducing the cultural differences, especially between nonprofits and business firms.

NOTE

1. There is a distinction between the terms *organizational behavior* and *organizational theory*, although most books on management blend the two fields and some consider organizational behavior to be the larger, encompassing field. Scholars of organizational behavior generally focus on the behavior of individuals or groups in organizations, often drawing on the disciplines of psychology and social psychology. Their interest is often in questions related to topics such as motivation, work satisfaction, and leadership. Organizational theory, which is usually based on sociology, is more concerned with the organization as a whole, considering topics such as organizational culture, environment, structure, and effectiveness (Rainey, 2003, p. 8).

KEY TERMS AND CONCEPTS FROM CHAPTER 2

bureaucracy	*mission driven*
contract failure	*open systems*
externalities	*organizational culture*
free riders	*population ecology*
goal displacement	*private goods*
government failure	*public goods*
information asymmetry	*resource dependency*
institutional theory	*supply-side theory*
isomorphism	*task environment*
market failure	*theory of the commons*

CASE 2.1

The Smithsonian Institution and the Catherine B. Reynolds Foundation

The Smithsonian Institution, an educational and research institution in Washington, D.C., is best known for its 19 museums and 7 research centers. It is an unusual hybrid of federal government agency and nonprofit institution. It was chartered by Congress as a charitable trust in 1846, in response to a bequest from the Englishman James Smithson, who left a gift to the United States of America to establish an institution "for the increase and diffusion of knowledge among men." But the Smithsonian is administered by the federal government, and courts have held that it is legally part of the federal government. More than two thirds of its workforce are employees of the federal government, while others supported by private funds are known as "trust fund employees." Although significant governance reforms were proposed in 2007, in 2000 the Smithsonian was governed by a 17-member Board of Regents, including officials of the federal government and private citizens. The Secretary of the Smithsonian is the paid chief executive, who is appointed by the Board of Regents.

Throughout most if its history, the Smithsonian relied on ample funding from the U.S. government. But beginning in the 1980s, federal funds failed to keep pace with the Smithsonian's needs. Faced with a change in its environment, the Smithsonian "didn't exactly turn on a dime," and battles over the influence of private donors over the content of exhibits led to subsequent "knock-down, drag-out funding fight[s]," centered in particular on one of the Smithsonian's most prominent components, the National Museum of American History (Thompson, 2002).

By 2000, federal funds were only sufficient to cover the Smithsonian's core budget, including salaries. Private funds needed to be raised for new exhibits, and some standing exhibits had become dated. Deferred maintenance on the Smithsonian's extensive physical facilities had allowed many to deteriorate. Recognizing the need for change, the Board of Regents reached outside the scientific and museum communities for a new Secretary, to someone who could bring business methods and private resources to bear on the Smithsonian's mounting problems. Lawrence Small, appointed by the Board of Regents as the new Secretary in 2000, came from a background in banking and finance rather than science or museum management. Small noted the deteriorating condition of the Smithsonian's facilities and the continuing decline in federal funds and committed himself to "a vision that involves two M's: modernization and money," with most of the money to come from more aggressive fundraising in the private sector (Thompson, 2002, p. 22).

Small had met Catherine B. Reynolds, a Washington-area entrepreneur who controlled a large foundation bearing her name. She shared Small's view that the National Museum of American History needed to be updated, and in May, 2001, she announced a gift of $38 million from her foundation to support a project on which she and Small had agreed: a 10,000-sq.-ft "hall of achievement" exhibit, intended to portray the lives of eminent Americans. Small and Reynolds had agreed that the selection of individuals to be portrayed would be determined by a special advisory committee of 15 people, with 10 being appointed by the Reynolds Foundation. *The Washington Post* reported that the contract between the Foundation and the Smithsonian provided that if the committee could not agree, the dispute would be resolved not by the curatorial staff but by the Secretary himself ("Museums and Money," 2001).

(Continued)

(Continued)

The museum's staff erupted in anger, writing directly to the Smithsonian Board of Regents saying that the obligations Small had made to the Reynolds Foundation "breach[ed] established standards of museum practice and professional ethics" (Thompson, 2002, p. 26). The story caught the attention of the news media, resulting in a flurry of stories representing the curators' views and a *New York Times* editorial asking "what is the curatorial rationale for a permanent exhibit that seems to open the door for commercial and corporate influence at one of the capital's keystone institutions" ("Museums and Money," 2001). The American Historical Association, including prominent historians among its members, joined the debate in support of the museum staff's views. Museum staff began to post "Dump Small" stickers in elevators, on bulletin boards, and on their own lapels (Sciolino, 2001b). A series of meetings were held between the curators and Ms. Reynolds to try and reach a common understanding, but they did not resolve the differences.

At least two issues were central to the controversy. The first was a difference in philosophy about the meaning of history and the purpose of museums. Historians and museum curators believed that the purpose of museums was to educate and that the study of history should not focus on the personal stories of "great" men and women. Rather, they argued that the teaching of history should focus on broad historical forces and movements, often portrayed in exhibits through their impact on the lives of everyday people. They believed that the purpose of a museum was to encourage people to think critically about history, not to inspire people personally. As one curator expressed it, "We are not a great man/great woman place. . . . This museum is about context, about putting people and events in place within the social fabric" (Thompson, 2002, p. 18). But Ms. Reynolds held a different view of history and the purpose of the museum's exhibits—it should be to inspire young people by portraying the lives of famous Americans and extolling the virtues of entrepreneurship in achieving success. "The foundation was created out of a very entrepreneurial business," Ms. Reynolds said, "and that is the spirit and culture we want to apply to the philanthropic world" (Sciolino, 2001a).

The second, and broader, issue was the question of who should control the content of museum exhibits—professional historians and museum curators, or donors. To what degree should private donors have a say in museum exhibits to be developed with the money they are voluntarily giving? One scholar asked, "Will the Smithsonian Institution actually allow private funders to rent space in a public museum for the expression of private and personal views?" (Thompson, 2002, p. 16). Scholars accused Small of "selling" the museum to wealthy donors, with jeopardizing the "integrity and authority" of professional curators, and with having "[pre-empted] the issue of control" by reaching an agreement with the Reynolds Foundation without adequate consultation with his own staff (Sciolino, 2001a).

Small responded saying that "government funding cannot do it all" and pointing out that the idea of private donors—who had something to say about how their money would be used—was not exactly new. After all, the Institution had been founded with James Smithson's gift! Small said, "We make no apologies for seeking private support to develop programs or facilities that the public wants and benefits from." He argued,

In all cases, we retain intellectual control while demonstrating to donors that their money can be spent productively and prudently. Does that mean we don't consult them? Of course we do. But the Smithsonian regents and staff control, without limitation or question, the Smithsonian activity. (Small, 2001, p. A25)

In February, 2002, Ms. Reynolds cancelled the bulk of her foundation's pledge to the Smithsonian, saying merely that she felt the exhibit would not adequately portray "the power of the individual" (Lewis, 2002). But important questions remained, for the Smithsonian and generally for other organizations. Like the Smithsonian, others have long relied on relatively assured sources of revenues, perhaps the government, a single foundation, or some other generous source. But many find themselves now needing to pursue new and more diversified sources of financial support. The questions that need to be addressed clearly go beyond the specific one raised by the Reynolds Foundation's gift to the Smithsonian, that of how history should be portrayed and who should decide. There are more generic questions: What tradeoffs are appropriate, realistic, and necessary for institutions and organizations striving to meet their financial needs and develop new sources of revenue while preserving their traditional missions and values? And how can CEOs meet expectations for their leadership in such a time of change?

Sources: Cash (2002), "Gifts That Can Warp a Museum" (2001), Lewis (2002), "Museums and Money" (2001), Sciolino (2001a, 2001b, 2001c), Small (2001), and Thompson (2002).

QUESTIONS FOR DISCUSSION

1. How are the concepts of open and closed systems reflected in the case of the Smithsonian Institution and the Catherine B. Reynolds Foundation?

2. How does the theory of resource dependency relate to the case of the Smithsonian Institution and the Catherine B. Reynolds Foundation?

3. What cultures were at play in the case of the Smithsonian Institution and the Catherine B. Reynolds Foundation, and how did the interplay of cultures influence the controversy and the outcome?

4. Should higher education be considered a private good, to be paid for by those who benefit from it? Or should it be considered a public good, available as a right to all citizens (like K-12 education)?

5. Most industrialized countries have much greater government participation in the provision of medical care than does the United States. In the United States, with the exception of older people and low-income people, medical care is generally considered a private good, to be paid for by patients or by their private insurance companies. What do you think explains this different approach taken in the United States?

6. If you needed to stay in the hospital, would you prefer to go to a nonprofit hospital or one managed by a for-profit company? Or would it not make any difference to you? Why?

SUGGESTIONS FOR FURTHER READING RELATED TO CHAPTER 2

Books/Articles

Anheier, H., & Ben-Ner, A. (2003). *The study of the nonprofit enterprise*. New York: Kluwer Academic.

Clegg, S., Kornberger, M., & Pitsis, T. (2005). *Managing and organizations: An introduction to theory and practice*. Thousand Oaks, CA: Sage.

Froelich, K. A. (1999). Diversification of revenue strategies: Evolving resource dependence in nonprofit organizations. *Nonprofit and Voluntary Sector Quarterly, 28*(3), 246–268.

Lohmann, R. A. (1992). *The Commons*. San Francisco: Jossey-Bass.

Ott, J. S. (2001). *The nature of the nonprofit sector*. Boulder, CO: Westview Press.

Powell, W. W., & Steinberg, R. (2006). *The non-profit sector: A research handbook* (2nd ed.). New Haven, CT: Yale University Press.

Steinberg, R. (2004). *The economics of nonprofit enterprises*. Northampton, MA: Edward Elgar.

Weisbrod, B. A. (1988). *The nonprofit economy*. Cambridge, MA: Harvard University Press.

PART II

Governing and Leading Nonprofit Organizations

CHAPTER 3

Nonprofit Governing Boards

The governing board of a nonprofit organization holds ultimate responsibility for ensuring that the organization serves its mission and for the overall welfare of the organization itself. And, as we discussed in Chapter 2, the board plays a critical boundary-spanning role in the open system of a nonprofit organization, connecting the nonprofit to its community and constituencies, often including important sources of financial support. Understanding the board's responsibilities and role and knowing how to work with the board is an essential skill of effective nonprofit managers, especially chief executive officers (CEOs). This chapter will discuss the nature and responsibilities of governing boards, some characteristics of boards that are effective, and some challenges faced by nonprofit boards today. It also will consider the important question of the relationship between the board and the organization's CEO. But before we get started, it is important to clarify some terminology.

The boards we are concerned with here are those that have a legal responsibility for governing their organizations—they are *governing boards*. Nonprofit organizations may have various groups that are called "boards" but that do not have such responsibilities—for example, advisory groups that may contribute their expertise to the organization and help raise funds but that do not hold any legal authority for its governance. Such boards often play an important role in the organization, but they are not governing boards and will not be the focus of this chapter.[1]

Nonprofit organizations may use different terms to identify their governing boards. Most nonprofits are chartered as corporations, and members of the governing board are directors of the corporation under the law. Thus, many organizations use the term *board of directors* to identify them. Educational, cultural, and medical institutions often use the term *board of trustees*. Other organizations may use the term *board of governors, governing council*, or something else to describe their governing boards. This book generally uses the generic term, *governing board*, except when discussing the board of a specific organization, in which case it maintains the name that organization uses.

In many cases, the person who heads the board is called the "president" of the organization, and the paid staff person who manages the organization is called the "director" or "executive director." Some nonprofits—for example, universities, hospitals, and major arts and cultural institutions—have adopted corporate terminology, calling the head of the board the "chair" and the paid executive the "president." Others have adopted another corporate term, *chief executive officer*, or just "CEO," to identify the top paid staff person. This chapter refers to the top board officer as the "chair" and the paid executive of the organization as the "CEO."

One more point before we begin our discussion. The previous two chapters have drawn primarily from the academic literature, but this chapter relies much more on the practitioner literature. A substantial literature on boards has been developed by practicing nonprofit managers and consultants who work with boards and CEOs. Most of it *describes* what boards do or *prescribes* practices that boards should follow. Although the body of academic research on nonprofit boards is growing, it is still "limited, exploratory, and diffuse" (Callen, Klein, & Tinkelman, 2003, p. 496). This chapter draws on some of that research where it is especially relevant, but the practitioner literature is the more extensive, and it is the largest source of citations in this discussion.

TYPES OF GOVERNING BOARDS

Nonprofit governing boards are not all the same. For one thing, they differ in the way their members are selected. This may have important implications for how they operate and what agendas, priorities, and pressures members may bring to their work on the board. Different types of boards also may interact differently with the organization's CEO. For anyone working in a nonprofit organization, especially as a CEO or other senior executive, understanding how individuals come to be sitting at the governing board table is essential to understanding and working successfully with the board. Working successfully with the board is critical not only to the executive's effectiveness. Since in most cases the CEO is appointed by and reports to the board, it is also essential to his or her professional survival.

Elected Boards

Some boards are *elected* by the membership of the organization. This is common in member-serving and social welfare organizations. The methods used to elect the governing board vary; for example, some elections are conducted by mail, and others are conducted at an annual meeting. Depending on the political and cultural environment within the organization, elections may be contested, and some individuals may, in effect, campaign for seats on the board. In other cases, a nominating committee of the existing board presents recommended candidates, who are often approved in a proforma vote by the membership. Some procedures are multistaged and complex. Consider, for example, the process followed by the American Psychological Association:

> As in all democratic systems, the ultimate power is in the hands of the voters, in this case, the members of APA. The members of APA exercise their power through direct vote and through the election of members to serve on the Council of Representatives. The primary constituencies from which the representatives are elected are the divisions, which are an integral part of the Association, and the state and provincial psychological associations, which are affiliates. The number of representatives to which each is entitled is determined by an

apportionment ballot in which members allocate votes among the constituencies according to their own priorities.

The Council of Representatives has broad authority to develop the internal and external policies of the Association, within the framework of the charter and the bylaws. It has full authority over the affairs and funds of the Association. The Council elects almost all elected positions: the Board of Directors, the treasurer, the recording secretary and the chief staff officer. But the president, who is directly elected by the entire membership, chairs both the Council and the Board of Directors. (American Psychological Association, 2005)

Having an elected board may result in uncertainty about who will govern the organization from one year to the next—the outcome of elections is not always assured, and this may present a challenge to the CEO. What the board expects of the CEO may change; alliances and factions on the board may develop and shift; and the board's values and priorities may be dynamic, as political and philosophical cross-currents among the membership find their way into the boardroom. The controversy that surrounded the election of the Sierra Club's board in 2004 provides an interesting illustration.

In 2004, anyone could join the Sierra Club with a $25 dues payment, and all members were eligible to vote in the election of the board. (That was an unusually low threshold for voting eligibility. Many organizations limit those eligible to vote to members who have been active for a period of time or use an intermediate body like the APA's Council of Representatives.) The Sierra Club's board included 15 members, and five seats were open for election in 2004. Individuals who were strong advocates for more restrictive U.S. immigration began to organize and encourage people sympathetic to their views to join the Sierra Club. Their goal was to have their sympathizers elect new board members who would change the Club's position on the immigration issue. Within three months, 30,000 people became new members of the Sierra Club, compared with only 22,000 the previous year. Some of these new members had been organized by the anti-immigration candidates who were, in effect, running for the board. The election became contentious. Some described the outsiders' efforts as a "hostile takeover" and accused them of pursuing "the greening of hate." Others portrayed their efforts as addressing needed reform in the Club's operation and claimed that their election would increase the Club's effectiveness (Greene, 2004).

The insurgents did not prevail, but the Sierra Club case illustrates the potentially tumultuous environment that may be created when governing boards are elected by an organization's membership. To be the CEO of such an organization requires a high tolerance for discussion, debate, and uncertainty. In addition, the membership terms of an elected board tend to be relatively brief, and turnover on the board may make it difficult for it to sustain its focus on long-range goals and plans. Doing so requires considerable repetition of presentations and discussions, to maintain consensus among the changing membership of the board. It may be difficult to motivate members of an elected board to make gifts or engage in fundraising, since the ability and inclination to do so have not been the criteria in their selection. The skills of board members may be uneven, since their personal popularity or their positions on certain issues may have been the considerations in their election. However, elections do help ensure that the board will be representative of the constituency the organization serves and that the organization and its executive will be responsive to members' views and priorities. Elected boards are less likely than the next type, self-perpetuating boards, to become stale, uninvolved, or homogeneous in their membership.

Self-Perpetuating Boards

Most charitable nonprofits have *self-perpetuating boards*. New members of a self-perpetuating board are selected by the existing members of the board, who identify and enlist individuals according to criteria established by the board itself. When a new nonprofit organization receives a charter, it must identify the original, founding members of the governing board. Those individuals then have the authority to develop bylaws, which specify the total number of members of the board. The original board members then may select others to join them, up to the maximum permitted under the bylaws (which, of course, the board retains the authority to change). As individuals leave the board or complete their terms of service, the remaining trustees select others to take their seats, and this cycle continues as long as the organization exists.

In contrast to a board elected by the membership, a self-perpetuating board creates a relatively stable situation for the organization and its CEO. Although the bylaws of many boards do limit the number of terms that members may serve, self-perpetuating boards tend to have longer terms than elected boards, and the board's membership changes more slowly. Thus, the board's policies and culture may reflect continuity, reinforced by the tendency of its members to select successors who generally share their values and views. Indeed, in some cases, strong or long-serving CEOs may gain significant influence in the selection of board members, in effect choosing their own bosses.

One advantage is that a self-perpetuating board can craft its own membership, selecting individuals specifically to bring needed skills or augment its strength in areas important to its work. Many boards maintain an inventory of the expertise and connections represented among their members and make a systematic effort to identify and recruit new members to fill any identifiable gaps. For example, if someone with financial expertise is needed, the board can seek out such an individual and recruit him or her to join the board in order to add those skills. A social service organization may try to find someone with professional social work experience, who can help the board evaluate program recommendations from its staff. If the organization desires to increase the amount of support it receives from corporations, the board can identify and recruit corporate executives who may be helpful in that regard.

But these advantages of the self-perpetuating board are accompanied by some potential weaknesses as well. One is that the board may come to be unrepresentative of the constituency or community the organization serves. If the existing members of the board do not recognize the importance of diversity, they may continue to select new members who are just like them, drawing on their own business and social circles to fill board openings. Over time, the organization could become out of touch and be unable to adapt sufficiently to changes in its environment. Another risk is that a self-perpetuating board may become too stable in its membership and too complacent. There have been cases in which self-perpetuating boards, without the scrutiny that comes from the broader constituency of the organization, have been too lax in their oversight of their CEOs or even the behavior of their fellow board members, with disastrous results for the organization.

Appointed and Hybrid Boards

A third way in which board members may be selected is through appointment by some authority outside the organization. This is the typical model for public organizations; for example, the boards of state universities are usually appointed by the governor of the state. Few nonprofits have totally appointed boards, but some do have some appointed members. This is sometimes the case in nonprofit organizations that are affiliated with a religious congregation, which may have board members appointed by a church authority. Colleges and universities may have board members appointed by an alumni association. Organizations that work closely with government may have some board seats held by individuals who are appointed by a governmental authority. Boards also may have some seats that are held ex-officio—that is, designated to be held by the individual who holds a certain office or position. For example, the head of the board of trustees of the Catholic University of America is the Archbishop of Baltimore, who serves ex-officio. The organization's CEO often holds a seat on the board in an ex-officio capacity, which may come with or without a vote.

Some boards are hybrids, with some members being elected, some appointed, some self-perpetuating, and some serving ex-officio. Until recent reforms, the Board of Governors of the American Red Cross was an especially complex hybrid including 50 members. Eight were appointed by the President of the United States (an appointed component); 12 were at-large members elected by the governors themselves (a self-perpetuating component); and 30 were elected by delegates representing Red Cross chapters and Blood Services regions across the country (an elected component). The President of the United States served as the honorary chair of the Board of Governors in an ex-officio capacity (www.redcross.org).

Hybrid boards may represent the best of both worlds, encompassing an elected component that helps keep the organization responsive to its constituencies; a self-perpetuating component that provides stability, continuity, and perhaps financial support; and an appointed component that ensures the organization's accountability to a parent organization or government. However, hybrid boards also can present challenges. For example, if elected, appointed, and self-perpetuating members hold different views or agendas, stalemate may result. Ex-officio members may not always feel a real commitment to the organization and its mission, having just landed on the board by virtue of some other position they hold. If this is the case, they may not fully participate in the work of the board or develop a full understanding of the organization and its work. Indeed, following criticisms of the American Red Cross's response to Hurricane Katrina in 2005 and the resignation of its then president Marsha Evans, some cited the structure of the board as an area of needed reform. After a long study, the Red Cross announced in October, 2006, that it was undertaking major changes to its board to strengthen the organization's governance. The planned

TABLE 3.1   Types of Governing Boards

Type of Board	Advantages	Disadvantages
Elected	Helps ensure that the organization and the CEO will be responsive to members' needs and priorities	Political division among the membership may create disagreement on the board Turnover on the board may make it difficult to sustain the board's focus on long-term goals and plans Skills of board members may be uneven, since personal popularity or positions on issues may influence election
Self-perpetuating	Can maintain continuity of culture, priorities, goals Can craft the board membership to gain needed skills Can select members who are helpful in fundraising	May become unrepresentative of the community or constituency May become too stable to respond to changes in the environment May become too passive and yield too much authority to the CEO
Hybrid (including appointed, self-perpetuating, ex-officio)	May combine the responsiveness of elected boards, the stability of self-perpetuating boards, and accountability to an appointing authority—for example, a sponsoring church	Different interests and loyalties of board members may lead to a stalemate Ex-officio members may not be fully committed to the organization

reforms would include reducing the membership from 50 to 20 and increasing the number of self-perpetuating members. Under the new structure, individuals appointed by the president would serve on an advisory committee rather than as regular members of the governing board (Schwinn, 2006b).

THE BOARD'S RESPONSIBILITIES

Now that we understand different types of boards and how their members come to sit at the table, exactly what are their responsibilities? And to whom are they accountable for meeting those responsibilities? The answers are not always simple.

As Bruce Hopkins (2003) describes it, nonprofit governing board members are "fiduciaries of the organization's resources and guardians of its mission" (p. 1). The board is accountable, that is, answerable, "for everything the organization does and how those things are accomplished" (Howe, 2002, p. 30). In the corporate world, it is clear to whom the directors are accountable and for what they are accountable. Members of the corporate board of directors are the agents of the owners (the principals), and their responsibility is to direct and monitor the activities of management in the interests of the owners. Those interests also are quite clear—the maximization of economic value, consistent with sustainability of the business and the values of the owners. There are, of course, boards in the public sector as well. Most of them also have an identifiable constituency whose interest they serve; for example, a city council is accountable to the citizens of the city, who elected them. But in the nonprofit sector, it is not always so clear to which owners the governing board is accountable.

Perhaps the owners of a member-serving organization are the members—it is primarily their interests that the organization exists to serve. But suppose the organization is a professional association that also sets standards for practice and certifies members of the profession. It may be primarily a member-serving organization, but doesn't the public—especially individuals served by members of the profession—also have some interest at stake? Who owns a charitable nonprofit, chartered to pursue a mission in the public interest? Are the owners the donors who support the organization through their philanthropy, the clients served by the organization, or perhaps the general public? If it is the general public, how can the board serve its interests when there may not be consensus about what the public interest means? Without the simple measure of results that the bottom line provides to business, by what standards should a nonprofit's effectiveness be evaluated, and who should determine those standards? Without clarity or agreement about who owns the organization, it is difficult to answer those questions. This creates an environment in which the board's responsibilities and role may be the subject of discussion and debate.

The Board's Legal Responsibilities

Some governing board responsibilities are unambiguous. They are defined by law. Most law affecting nonprofit boards is state law, enforced by state attorneys general and state courts. However, the federal government, and specifically the Internal Revenue Service (IRS), has gained increasing power in recent years, and current debate surrounds proposals to increase the federal role.

A landmark case in 1974 is often cited as providing the most definitive statement of nonprofit board responsibility. In that case, *Stern v. Lucy Webb Hayes National Training School for Deaconesses and Missionaries* (usually known as just "The Sibley Hospital Case"), parents of children who had been patients at the hospital alleged that members of the board had mismanaged the hospital's assets and had placed hospital funds in accounts at banks in which they had personal financial interests. The parents claimed that hospital charges were unnecessarily high because of actions by the board. Judge Gerhard Gessell found that the Sibley board members had not really benefited financially and that the hospital had not been disadvantaged by the board's practices—in other words, the parents lost, but in the process of stating his decision, Judge Gessell clarified the standards of legal responsibilities of nonprofit boards that are still applied. Those responsibilities are summarized as the concepts of *care, loyalty*, and *obedience*.

Care, Loyalty, Obedience

"Care" in this context means paying attention and exercising due diligence in monitoring the organization's finances and supervising the actions of its management. Board members who do not attend meetings, who sleep through meetings, who do not read board materials, or who vote without understanding the issues are guilty of a lack of care. Included within the concept of care is the requirement that members of the board act in a prudent manner in managing the organization's finances—for example, by ensuring that any endowment assets are invested in a diversified portfolio to minimize risks. This does not mean that the board will necessarily have violated its responsibilities should it make the wrong investment decisions and the organization's assets decline but merely that it should exercise common sense and not lose money as a result of recklessness, indifference, or failure to seek appropriate advice.

The duty of loyalty means that members of the board put the interests of the organization above their own personal financial interests or that of another organization with which they may also have a formal relationship. Individuals cannot use their position on a nonprofit board to enhance their own businesses or financial position. Closely related to the concept of loyalty is that of *conflict of interest*. A conflict of interest may arise, for example, when the board has to vote on whether to give a business contract to a company that may be owned in whole or in part by a member of the board itself or that perhaps may employ a board member's relative. Or a conflict could exist if the board is voting to enter some kind of partnership with another nonprofit and one of the members voting serves on both boards. Conflicts of interest are not unusual, especially in smaller communities, where there may not be much choice about which suppliers or contractors the nonprofit can use and where prominent business leaders who own those businesses may serve on multiple nonprofit boards. Conflicts of interest are not per se illegal, but it is important how the board deals with them. Well-managed boards have formal conflict of interest policies that describe the procedures to be followed. Such policies usually require that potential conflicts be disclosed and that the board independently determine that any business transaction that gives rise to the conflict is not disadvantageous to the organization.

A legal concept related to conflict of interest is that of *private inurement*. Anyone who is an insider, generally any board member or officer of the organization, cannot unreasonably benefit from the organization's funds. This is related to the nondistribution constraint that was previously discussed. Nonprofits cannot use their profits to benefit owners, nor can they pay unreasonable amounts to board members or executives, which might have the same effect as sharing the profits with them—that is, giving them financial benefits as if they were owners. For example, a board can pay its CEO a salary and other compensation that is reasonable in exchange for his or her services, but anything exceeding a reasonable amount may be illegal private inurement. And an organization can do business with a company owned by a board member, but only if the payment is appropriate for the goods and services received.

The duty of obedience requires that the board makes sure that the organization is complying with the law and, in addition, that any decisions or actions taken are consistent with the organization's mission and governing documents, including its charter. Following the law may seem a simple charge, but ensuring that the organization does not drift from its mission may require greater vigilance, especially if that drift may bring with it some unanticipated risks.

Intermediate Sanctions

In general, if a board member carries out his or her duties faithfully and prudently, he or she is unlikely to be found personally liable for any losses that the organization may incur. Just making a mistake, or even a bad decision, is not in itself a violation of the board's responsibilities, provided that one has met the standards of care, loyalty, and obedience in making it. However, the risks to individual board members are somewhat higher today than they were prior to 1996, when federal legislation was passed providing IRS with the authority to impose *intermediate sanctions*—that is, financial penalties to punish individuals who engage in or permit improper transactions.

Prior to the passage of intermediate sanctions, virtually the only weapon available to the IRS in dealing with a nonprofit board that violated its fiduciary responsibilities was to drop the atom bomb by revoking the organization's tax-exempt status. Facing an all-or-nothing situation and reluctant to take a drastic step that might essentially impose a death sentence on the organization, the IRS had few options. Intermediate sanctions provided a fly swatter alternative to the atom bomb by permitting the IRS to impose penalties on *individual* board members or officers who engage in an *excess benefit transaction,* meaning one in which "a person's level or type of compensation is deemed to be in excess of the value of the person's services" (Hopkins, 2005, p. 219). The intermediate sanctions legislation and the regulations that the IRS has issued pursuant to it are complex and beyond the scope of our discussion here, but the penalties can involve return of the excess benefit received as well as additional penalties. Because it made the possibility of IRS action more than a remote threat, the passage of intermediate sanctions was a wake-up call to nonprofit boards. Faced with a more realistic possibility of IRS action, which could involve financial costs to individual board members, many boards quickly adopted new or more stringent conflict-of-interest and disclosure policies and standards for reasonable compensation.

Sarbanes-Oxley Act

In the wake of corporate governance scandals in the early 2000s, including the demise of Enron and WorldCom, Congress passed the Sarbanes-Oxley Act in 2002. Sarbanes-Oxley placed new requirements on the governance of publicly traded for-profit corporations. Only *two* provisions of Sarbanes-Oxley apply as well to nonprofit organizations, those regarding the destruction of documents and protection for whistle-blowers. However, Sarbanes-Oxley served as another wake-up call for nonprofit boards, and larger nonprofits in particular have voluntarily adopted some or all of its provisions (Williams, 2006, p. 59). Independent Sector and BoardSource have recommended that nonprofits voluntarily adopt some provisions of Sarbanes-Oxley, including those prohibiting loans to board members or executives, requiring the CEO's approval of the organization's Form 990, and requiring the creation of separate audit committees of the board for those organizations having outside auditors. In addition, some state laws—for example, the California Nonprofit Integrity Act of 2004—have incorporated Sarbanes-Oxley-type requirements. Sarbanes-Oxley will be discussed again, in more detail, in a later chapter of this book.

The Board's Functional Responsibilities

The law primarily dictates the things nonprofit boards *cannot* do—fail to exercise care, place its own members' individual interests above those of the organization, or lead the organization in directions inconsistent with its mission and the law. But what is it exactly that boards should *do*?

A number of authors have offered lists of a board's functional responsibilities—that is, job descriptions that list the duties that boards should perform (see, e.g., Axelrod, 1994; Ingram, 2003; Nason, 1993). Most lists are similar on the principal activities in which the board should be engaged, although there are often differences among the experts with regard to the division of specific tasks between the board and the organization's CEO. The following responsibilities are common to most board job descriptions, although, as we will see later, some authors express contrary views.

Appoint, Support, and Evaluate the CEO

Although the CEO may serve as an ex-officio member of the board, he or she is generally appointed by the board and serves at the pleasure of the board, subject, of course, to any contractual terms that may be negotiated at the time of appointment. However, having appointed the CEO, the board also has a responsibility to support that individual. That includes acting as a sounding board for the CEO to discuss ideas and problems and also coming to his or her defense when pressures may arise from within or outside the organization. If the board's response to every criticism of the CEO's actions is to challenge him or her or take the side of the critic, the board will quickly undermine the CEO's ability to be effective and it is unlikely to attract or retain a strong executive. But the board also is responsible for setting expectations for the CEO, monitoring his or her performance against those expectations, and providing the executive with performance evaluations. Of course, if expectations are regularly not met, the board also has the responsibility of dismissing the CEO and beginning a search for his or her successor.

The relationship between the governing board and the CEO is complex, and it is a topic that generates its own considerable literature. The subject is of such importance that we will return to a more thorough discussion of it shortly.

Establish a Clear Institutional Mission and Purpose

Establishing the organization's mission is the responsibility of its board. Although the organization's charter states its purposes in broad terms, the board can and should periodically review its mission; indeed, doing so is often the first step in the process of strategic planning.

Approve the Organization's Programs

Although experts advise boards to avoid becoming involved in the details of management, most think that the board should approve the programs undertaken by the organization, to meet its responsibility for ensuring adherence to the mission and protecting the organization's financial viability. For example, the board of a liberal arts college would need to consider whether establishing a business school would be consistent with its mission, the implications for the college's financial resources, and the ability of the college to maintain its academic standards and reputation in light of such an expansion of its programs. The board of an organization serving dinner to the homeless would need to consider any extension of its activities to provide medical services or transitional housing. Because such decisions relate directly to the mission, which is the responsibility of the board, they cannot be delegated to the CEO or the staff.

Ensure Sound Financial Management and the Organization's Financial Stability

Protecting the organization's assets is, of course, central to the board's legal responsibility as fiduciary. Most boards approve annual budgets and receive regular reports of the organization's financial status. Many boards, especially since the passage of Sarbanes-Oxley, also have separate audit committees that meet with outside auditors of the organization's finances (Williams, 2006, p. 59).

Some authors claim that board members' responsibility to ensure the organization's fiscal soundness implies an obligation to provide their own gifts and actively engage in fundraising. Indeed, except perhaps for the debate about the appropriate relationship between the board and the CEO, no subject commands more ink, or more lung power, than the role of the board in giving and raising philanthropic funds. Of course, not all boards are expected to provide their personal financial support to the organizations they serve. Boards of member-serving organizations often have no significant responsibility for fundraising, since the largest portion of revenue may come from dues, subscriptions, or meeting fees. Organizations that are primarily or entirely dependent on revenue from government contracts and grants also may not place emphasis on the board's fundraising role. But in most charitable nonprofits, the board is expected to play a significant role in providing and soliciting philanthropic funds.

There are divergent views on whether board members should be required to give or raise a specific minimum amount, and the question raises some complicated issues. Some boards require a minimum personal gift from each board member. But if this requirement is substantial, it may make it more difficult to achieve appropriate diversity among the board membership without making exceptions to the policy for those who may bring important skills and qualities but do not possess financial capacity. But making such exceptions may introduce the perception that there are two classes of board members—those who give and those who don't. If that perception exists, those who cannot provide financial support may too readily defer to those who are known to be important sources of support to the organization. On the other hand, if the minimum is set so low that all board members can meet it, it can have the effect of converting an intended floor into a ceiling. In other words, some board members who have the financial ability to give more than the minimum may come to see the minimum as all that is expected of them, foreclosing the possibility of larger gifts. Such a situation leaves potential "money on the table" (Rosso, 1991, p. 139; Worth, 2005, p. 73).

Some boards do not set a minimum for personal giving by board members but adopt what is often called a *give-or-get policy*, requiring that each board member either give personally or solicit gifts from others to total the minimum amount. But this may also be a standard that some board members may find difficult to meet, especially if they are not involved in business or professional circles that provide access to wealth. And it raises the risk that board members may solicit gifts without coordination by the organization's staff, creating a potentially chaotic situation that could alienate donors. An alternative to setting minimums for board giving and getting is to simply establish the expectation that each board member will give and participate in fundraising proportionate to his or her capacity to do so. If that standard is firmly embedded in the culture of the board, then conscience and the judgment of peers may motivate the board to its peak fundraising performance without the risks inherent in defining specific minimum amounts. Whatever approach is taken by individual boards, the subject of the board's responsibility for giving and fundraising is on the agenda for discussion at many nonprofit organizations today (Worth, 2005).

Establish Standards for Organizational Performance and Hold the Organization Accountable

The board should define the standards by which an organization's effectiveness in achieving its mission is to be evaluated. Establishing standards to judge whether the organization is effectively employing the resources entrusted to it in pursuit of its mission is a fundamental aspect of the board's responsibility to those who provide financial support, to the society that grants the organization exemption from taxation, and to those whose needs its programs serve.

Some authors see the role of nonprofit boards as especially important because many nonprofits do not face the same market discipline that business firms do. As John Carver (1997) explains, "Without a market to summarize consumer judgment, [a nonprofit] organization literally does not know what its product is worth. . . . In the absence of a market test, *the board must perform that function*" (p. 7). Christine Letts and colleagues (1999a) elaborate on this point:

> Compared to their for-profit counterparts, nonprofit boards carry a much bigger burden in demanding and supporting performance . . . [In the for-profit world] both boards and management can use market feedback to assess how well they are performing: customers, investors, and creditors all make evaluations that eventually show up in the bottom line. . . . In contrast, the nonprofit board must often substitute for many of the feedback systems available in the marketplace. Nonprofit clients very often do not have a choice of providers, and are therefore unlikely to signal dissatisfaction by "voting with their feet." [Funders of nonprofits] may signal dissatisfaction by withdrawing their support,

but are much less likely to play the affirmative role of a shareholder activist or institutional investor. (p. 133)

For these reasons, Letts et al. (1999a) argue that "nonprofit boards are more vital [than for-profit boards] in ensuring performance and accountability."

THE BOARD AND THE CEO

The relationship between the governing board and the organization's CEO is the subject of an extensive literature, reflecting divergent views. The questions addressed in this literature go well beyond who does what. Rather, they include fundamental assumptions about the nature of nonprofit governance and leadership.

At the heart of the matter is the question of who leads the nonprofit organization. In some organizations, the CEO may be dominant, with the board playing a passive role. The CEO proposes and the board disposes, often with little discussion or debate. As noted before, the CEO may even come to influence the selection of board members, in effect choosing his or her own bosses. This situation could arise in any organization, but it is especially common in organizations led by their founders, a special case we will discuss further in Chapter 4.

The realities of many organizations may enable CEOs to gain the upper hand. Boards are composed of "part-time amateurs," while the organization's staff, including the CEO, are "full-time professionals" (Chait, Holland, & Taylor, 1999). In other words, the CEO may know more about the organization and its programs than do the lay trustees, especially if its programs involve highly technical services, and board members may be reluctant to show their ignorance by questioning. Large boards pose a special challenge in this regard. Individual board members may be unwilling to risk embarrassment by challenging a CEO's proposals in front of a large number of other board members or may assume that others on the board are well-informed and just go along with what appears to be a consensus. The CEO may control access to information about the organization, and indeed, the CEO may be the only one who knows what information actually exists. He or she may determine what information reaches the board and develop the agenda of matters that the board will even get to consider. In sum, it may be possible for a CEO to manipulate the board, orchestrate board meetings, and relegate the board to the role of a rubber stamp for his or her initiatives.

The danger in such a scenario is that the CEO could lead the board and the organization in directions that are inappropriate or risky and that the board may not be able to meet its responsibilities for ensuring adherence to mission, fiscal soundness, and optimum performance. But an alternative scenario in which the board micromanages the organization and usurps the authority of the CEO is no better. Such a board is likely to find it difficult to attract or retain a strong chief executive and may find itself making decisions about details outside its expertise. What most experts recommend is neither of these extreme scenarios but rather a partnership between the board and the CEO in the leadership of the organization.

There are, however, different views on exactly how this partnership should be constructed and operate.

Various authors have addressed the subject of the board-CEO relationship, and a comprehensive review would be beyond the scope of this chapter. But let's compare the thinking of three sets of authors who are widely cited and whose different approaches highlight the major issues. First, we will look at John Carver's (1990) "policy governance model," described in his book *Boards That Make a Difference* and in subsequent editions published in 1997 and 2006 (Carver, 2006). Carver draws a clear line between the board's responsibility for *policymaking* and the executive's responsibility for *implementation* and provides what he calls an "operating system" to ensure that the distinction is maintained. Next, we will review the concept of "governance as leadership," described by Richard Chait, William Ryan, and Barbara Taylor (2005) in their book of that title, which was sponsored by BoardSource and which BoardSource uses as the foundation for its advisory work with nonprofit boards. Chait et al. target Carver (2006), writing that "governing is too complicated to reduce to simple aphorisms, however seductive, like 'boards set policies which administrators implement'" (p. 5). Instead, they advocate a leadership role for the board that blurs the distinction between policy and implementation and focuses the attention of both boards and CEOs on "what matters most." And, finally, we will consider the research of Robert Herman and Dick Heimovics (2005), who argue that the most effective CEOs are those who accept the reality of their "psychological centrality" in the organization and provide "board-centered leadership," working to "develop, promote, and enable their boards' effective functioning" (p. 157).

Carver's Policy Governance Model

According to John Carver (2006), boards should be the leaders of the organization, "not by invading territory best left to management but by controlling the big picture, the long term, and the value laden" (p. 6). But his diagnosis of the prevailing reality is bleak. He observes boards mired in the trivial, largely reactive to staff initiatives, and absorbed in reviewing and rehashing actions the staff has already undertaken (pp. 19–20). Carver argues that board committees are often organized in a way that leads to this condition. Committee responsibilities often coincide with those of senior managers; for example, there may be committees on finance, fundraising, program evaluation, and other areas of the organization's operation overseen by professional staff. In many cases, the staff prepares materials for meetings of the relevant committee and influences what items the committee considers. This structure pulls the board's attention into the details of each of the management silos. Board members thus become either supermanagers or just advisors to the professional staff. This prevents them from staying focused on big-picture matters such as mission and goals. As Carver writes, "Our tradition of board work encourages boards to derive their agendas from staff-based divisions of work. This common board practice is tantamount to classifying a manager's functions on the basis of his or her secretary's job areas" (p. 46).

Carver (2006) calls for a clear distinction between the work of the board and that of the management staff and argues that the board should lead the organization, by focusing its attention on establishing *policies*. But this does not mean the kinds of policies that boards often discuss, such as personnel policies, which really reflect the work of management and are related to implementation rather than leadership of the organization. The board should make policies that reflect the board's values and the interests of the "moral owners" of the organization.

In Carver's (1997) model, boards lead by developing and maintaining policies in four areas:

1. *Ends to be achieved:* Ends policy statements describe what the organization is to achieve and "could be called results, impacts, goals, or outcomes as well as ends, each title having its own connotations" (p. 31). The broadest ends statement would be the organization's mission. More specific ends policies might address more detailed goals—for example, those related to products, consumers, and costs.

2. *Means to the ends:* In Carver's model, means statements are expressed in terms of "executive limitations"—that is, boundaries that the CEO may not cross in pursuing the ends established by the board. For example, the broadest statement of policy in this area might be that the CEO not violate the law. More detailed limitations might address more specific constraints, perhaps levels of cost and debt that may not be exceeded. Carver argues that by stating executive limitations in negative terms—that is, by prescribing what executives may *not* do, the board preserves maximum flexibility for the CEO. Subject to the constraints that the board has explicitly stipulated, the CEO is free to determine the best methods for achieving the ends that the board has established, without the board's inappropriate involvement in operations.

3. *Board-staff relationship:* Policy statements in this area clearly delineate the responsibilities of the board and the CEO, defining what decisions are delegated to the CEO and which ones are retained by the board. This category of statement also includes specific criteria for monitoring and evaluating the CEOs' performance. Carter argues that one benefit of such clarity is that it addresses the common concern about board members communicating directly with other staff within the organization or with other volunteers. "When the roles are clear, it is possible for anyone to talk with or elicit wisdom from anyone with no harmful effects on the 'chain of command'" (p. 118).

4. *Process of governance:* This fourth category of policy addresses the board's own role and operation, clarifying which owners it represents and defining its own "job process and products"—for example, the procedure through which new board members are elected (p. 33).

Meetings of a board practicing Carver's (1997) model would be driven by the need to develop and maintain its policy manual. When issues arise, the first question to be addressed would be to which category of policy the issue belongs, whose issue it is, and whether it is addressed by an existing policy. If not, a new policy needs to be adopted, eliciting discussion and debate. Carver argues that this approach steers boards away from the mundane, from show-and-tell presentations by staff, and from merely rubber-stamping the staff's recommendations. According to Carver, following the policy governance approach leads the board toward discussions focused on the long term and rooted in the board's values and perspectives (p. 181).

Chait, Ryan, and Taylor: Governance as Leadership

Now let's examine a different approach, the governance-as-leadership model proposed by Chait et al. (2005). The authors agree with many of Carver's criticisms of the way boards operate today. Boards are not leading their organizations. They are reactive to staff initiatives. They structure their work in a way that draws them into managerial details and routine technical work. Indeed, these authors argue, things are turned upside down. Boards are so mired in operational details that they are, in effect, _managing_ their organizations. Meanwhile, CEOs are articulating missions, beliefs, values, and cultures—in essence _leading_ their organizations and engaging in activities that "closely resemble conventional notions of _governing_" (p. 3, italics added). As the authors explain,

> In theory, if not in practice, boards of trustees are supposed to be the ultimate guardians of institutional ethos and organizational values. Boards are charged with setting the organization's agenda and priorities. . . . Boards are empowered to specify the most important problems and opportunities that management should pursue. If this logic holds, as we contend, then many nonprofit executives are not only leading their organizations, but . . . they are actually governing them as well. (p. 3)
>
> With sophisticated leaders at the helm of nonprofits, a substantial portion of the governance portfolio has moved to the executive suite. The residue remains in the boardroom. This surprise twist in the story line suggests that the real threat to nonprofit governance today may not be a board that micro*manages* but a board that micro*governs*, while blind to governance as leadership. (pp. 4–5)

But while their diagnosis of board problems is similar to Carver's (1997), Chait and his colleagues (2005) offer a quite different prescription. Instead of drawing sharp lines between policy and implementation, clearly dividing the role of the board and the CEO, they call for breaking down the barriers and focusing the attention of both the board and the CEO on the critical issues facing the organization. In other words, the question should not be "Is this an issue of policy or implementation?" Rather, the question should be "Is the issue at hand important or unimportant, central or peripheral?" (Taylor, Chait, & Holland, 1999, p. 62).

In their book, Chait et al. (2005) define a new model, which they call "governance as leadership," based on three "modes" of governance in which a board may be operating at any given time:

1. *The fiduciary mode:* When the board is operating in this mode, it is concerned with the "bedrock of governance," that is, with matters such as stewardship of tangible assets, faithfulness to mission, performance accountability, and obedience to law—in other words, generally addressing its legal responsibilities.

2. *The strategic mode:* When operating in the strategic mode, boards go beyond their basic fiduciary responsibilities and "create a strategic partnership with management," addressing matters such as the organization's long-term directions and goals.

3. *The generative mode:* A board in generative mode is engaged in generative thinking—that is, the creative, out-of-the-box thinking in which visionary leaders often engage. It relates to values and judgments, encompasses "sense making" (essentially, coming to understand things in new ways), and may result in insights that lead to paradigm shifts. The authors say that generative thinking is a necessary foundation for setting direction and goals and thus an essential activity of leadership.

Chait et al. (2005) observe that most boards work only in the fiduciary and strategic modes and therefore are not participating in leadership of the organization. But "when trustees work well in *all three* of these modes, the board achieves governance as leadership" (p. 7, italics added). Thus, rather than maintaining a clear distinction between what is the board's territory and what is the CEOs' territory, Chait et al. propose that boards and CEOs focus together on what matters most, moving together among the three modes as appropriate to address the issues at hand. Setting goals, and thus generative thinking, cannot be a task for the CEO or the board alone but rather must be a *shared* activity:

> Because we resolutely regard this [generative thinking] as shared work, we cannot offer what the board-improvement field so often promises trustees and executives: a set of bright lights that neatly divide the board's work (policy, strategy, and governance) from the staff's (administration, implementation, and management). It simply makes no sense to reserve generative work for boards when leaders are vital to the process, or to reserve for leaders work that belongs at the heart of governance. Generative work demands a fusion of thinking, not a division of labor. (p. 95)

Simply stated, Carver (1997) envisions the board and the CEO on opposite sides of the table, one clearly labeled "policy" and the other "implementation." Chait and his coauthors (2005) envision a three-sided table, with the board and the CEO sitting together on one side but moving around the table to the other sides, depending on the nature of the business to be considered at the time.

Which model is "right?" Does adoption of Carver's (1997) policy governance model improve board performance? Does Chait et al.'s (2005) governance-as-leadership approach? One 2003 study, by Patricia Nobbie and Jeffrey Brudney, compared organizations using the Carver (1997) model with others that had received training from BoardSource, and suggested mixed results. There were few differences, and those were generally not significant. The job satisfaction of CEOs working under the Carver model measured somewhat higher than that of the others, but the researchers found the difference to be statistically nonsignificant. One important conclusion of the study was that boards that had received training tended to perform better than those that had not been trained, regardless of which model had been used. Carver, with characteristic confidence, responds to the Nobbie and Brudney

(2003) study in the 2006 edition of his book, arguing that his model is superior and that the latter authors' choice of variables reflects an inaccurate understanding of its purpose.

Herman and Heimovics: Psychological Centrality and Board-Centered Leadership

In Carver's (1997) approach, boards lead their organizations. Chait et al. (2005) describe a model for leadership shared by the board and the chief executive. Robert Herman and Dick Heimovics (2005) provide a third perspective. Based on their research concerning effective nonprofit CEOs, they offer a pragmatic approach, concluding that CEOs should lead but that their leadership needs to be *board centered* and designed to support the board in meeting its governing responsibilities.

The *purposive-rational model* of organizations, based on Weber's theory of the bureaucracy, conceives of the board as the top of a hierarchy and the CEO as merely its agent. Indeed, Herman and Heimovics's (2005) review of the normative literature on nonprofit boards finds that most research has been based on that model and thus "has advanced a heroic ideal for nonprofit boards" (p. 155). However, they apply the *social-constructionist* model and explain that "official or intended goals, structures, and procedures may exist only on paper. Actual goals, structures, and procedures emerge and change as participants interact and socially construct the meaning of ongoing events" (p. 156). Regardless of what the organizational chart or the conventional view of organizations may suggest, Herman and Heimovics find that the reality in most organizations is that of *executive psychological centrality*. In other words, it is the CEO who is actually *seen as* responsible for the organization's success or failure. They interviewed CEOs, board chairs, and other staff members and found that *all* of them saw the chief executive as "centrally responsible for what happens," including both successful and unsuccessful events (p. 156). This does not imply that the CEO holds more formal authority than the board or that the CEO *is* indeed the central figure in the life of the organization. "Psychological centrality" means than he or she is *perceived as* responsible, even by members of the board.

If this is the reality, then what do Herman and Heimovics (2005) recommend that CEOs should do? They do not recommend that CEOs become autocrats or demote their boards to rubber stamps but rather that they take a leadership role to ensure "that boards fulfill their legal, organizational, and public roles" (p. 156). In exercising board-centered leadership, CEOs take responsibility for "supporting and facilitating the board's work." In doing so, they engage in six behaviors that Herman and Heimovics observed among the effective, board-centered executives they studied (p. 158):

1. Facilitating interaction in board relationships

2. Showing consideration and respect toward board members

3. Envisioning change and innovation for the organization with the board

4. Providing useful and helpful information to the board

5. Initiating and maintaining structure for the board

6. Promoting board accomplishments and productivity

Herman and Heimovics (2005) conclude that not only are the CEOs who have developed these board-centered leadership skills effective as CEOs, they also have hardworking, effective boards. "The board-centered executive is likely to be effective because he or she has grasped that the work of the board is critical in adapting to and affecting the constraints and opportunities in the environment" (p. 159).

NONPROFIT BOARD EFFECTIVENESS

"And so," students may be wondering at this point in the chapter, "what's the bottom line?" Are most nonprofit boards effective or not? What are the characteristics of effective boards? What is the right way to define the relationship between the board and the nonprofit CEO? What is indeed the best model for governance?

Critics of Board Performance

In answer to the question of how nonprofit boards are doing, there is no shortage of negative commentary. For example, Chait et al. (1999) reported that "after 10 years of research and dozens of engagements as consultants to nonprofit boards, we have reached a rather stark conclusion: effective governance by a board of trustees is a relatively rare and unnatural act" (p. 1). Carver (1997) essentially agrees, writing that "the problem is not that a group or an individual *occasionally* slips into poor practice, but that intelligent, caring individuals regularly exhibit procedures of governance that are deeply flawed" (p. 9).

Writing in the *Stanford Social Innovation Review*, Michael Klausner and Jonathon Small (2005) note little improvement since Chait et al.'s (1999) and Carver's (1997) observations of several years before. They reference a 2004 newspaper story that revealed financial mismanagement at the Beard Foundation and write, "In recent years, news reports like this one increasingly suggest that too many directors of nonprofit organizations are failing to govern" (Klausner & Small, 2005, p. 42). They cite the opinions of (unnamed) "commentators [who] suggest that each and every director should work harder and more effectively at governance" and conclude, "In our view, the commentators are right on the money" (Klausner & Small, 2005, p. 43).

Such criticisms cannot be ignored, but it may be prudent to question the evidence behind such sweeping statements. Most are based on experience rather than research. Some are reported by consultants who are called on to work with troubled boards and whose samples therefore may be somewhat self-selecting. Others, like Klausner and Small (2005), generalize from single anecdotes. Surely, instances of board corruption or mismanagement are to be deplored. But it is reasonable to question whether individual cases illustrate the systematic failure of nonprofit governance or merely reveal the frailties of particular boards and individuals, which are unfortunately all too often visible in business and government as well. However, it is equally reasonable to believe that the performance of boards and their members can be improved and to continue the search for best practices in nonprofit governance.

The Search for Best Practices

Various researchers have attempted to identify behaviors that are associated with effective nonprofit governing boards—that is, to identify those practices that, if followed, will lead to effective governance. In 2005, BoardSource assembled a panel of experts to address the question. Their consensus produced the following "twelve principles that power exceptional boards":

1. *Constructive partnership:* Exceptional boards govern in constructive partnership with the chief executive, recognizing that the effectiveness of the board and chief executive are interdependent.

2. *Mission driven:* Exceptional boards shape and uphold the mission, articulate a compelling vision, and ensure the congruence between decisions and core values.

3. *Strategic thinking:* Exceptional boards allocate time to what matters most and continuously engage in strategic thinking to hone the organization's direction.

4. *Culture of inquiry:* Exceptional boards institutionalize a culture of inquiry, mutual respect, and constructive debate that leads to sound and shared decision making.

5. *Independent-mindedness:* Exceptional boards are independent-minded. When making decisions, board members put the interests of the organization above all else.

6. *Ethos of transparency:* Exceptional boards promote an ethos of transparency by ensuring that donors, stakeholders, and interested members of the public have access to appropriate and accurate information regarding finances, operations, and results.

7. *Compliance with integrity:* Exceptional boards promote strong ethical values and disciplined compliance by establishing appropriate mechanisms for active oversight.

8. *Sustaining resources:* Exceptional boards link bold visions and ambitious plans to financial support, expertise, and networks of influence.

9. *Results-oriented:* Exceptional boards are results-oriented. They measure the organization's advancement toward its mission and evaluate the performance of major programs and services.

10. *Intentional board practices:* Exceptional boards intentionally structure themselves to fulfill essential governance duties and to support organizational priorities.

11. *Continuous learning:* Exceptional boards embrace the qualities of a continuous learning organization, evaluating their own performance and assessing the value they add to the organization.

12. *Revitalization:* Exceptional boards energize themselves through planned turnover, thoughtful recruitment, and inclusiveness. (Excerpted from BoardSource, 2005)

BoardSource's 12 principles of governance offer an attractive description of an exceptional board and reflect the consensus of a distinguished panel of experts assembled to develop them. But it is nevertheless primarily a compilation of practitioner wisdom rather than science. There remains a relative paucity of research on the subject of nonprofit board performance, and there is no single definition of board effectiveness. This is so in part because there is no single standard for defining the effectiveness of nonprofit organizations. As John Carver (2006) notes, the variables chosen for measurement in some research studies seem to imply

> that effectiveness in governance is to be judged by whether board members are more fulfilled, challenged, or involved; the CEO is happier or the board is less meddlesome; the board raises more funds; grant revenues are increased; committees are more active; or the board chair perceives the CEO to be meeting his or her objectives. (p. 337)

But the link between such variables and the effectiveness of boards—or organizations—remains elusive.

In a 2002 review of the literature on nonprofit effectiveness, Robert Herman and David Renz conclude that "[board] effectiveness is whatever significant stakeholders think it is, and there is no single objective reality." Calling the concept of best practices "somewhat of a holy grail," they advise nonprofit boards and CEOs to take a skeptical view of "one right way" prescriptions:

> Many sources that claim to offer "best practices" for NPO boards or management provide little or no basis for their assertions. *The evidence from our . . . study does not support the claim that particular board and management practices are automatically best or even good (that is, that using them leads to effective boards and organizations.* We prefer to talk in terms of "promising practices" to describe those approaches that warrant consideration.
>
> Not only is there no "silver bullet" (i.e., one practice that ensures board effectiveness)—there is no "silver arsenal." In the context of other research, we support the assertion that boards (perhaps with facilitative leadership from their chief executives) need to identify those processes that are most useful to them. Boards should not use a practice just because other boards, experts, or consultants say it is useful. They should ask some key questions: Does the practice fit this board's circumstances? Does the practice actually help the board reach good decisions? Does the practice contribute to the organization's success? (pp. 6–7)

Herman and Renz's (2002) caution should not be interpreted as saying that the literature on nonprofit governing boards has nothing to offer and should be disregarded. Rather, their conclusions are consistent with the philosophy expressed in the Introduction of this text: There is often no right answer, and the best way is often pragmatic and eclectic. This includes viewing a problem from multiple perspectives and drawing from various approaches selectively as the situation may dictate.

THE CHALLENGE OF NONPROFIT GOVERNANCE

Serving as a member of a nonprofit board today is an interesting and challenging assignment. Nonprofit boards are buffeted by strong cross-currents emanating from virtually all their constituencies. The forces of law, media scrutiny, and more demanding funders are pushing them to do a better job of governance. At the same time, the financial pressures facing many nonprofits in light of diminished government support, increased competition for philanthropy, and the rising needs and expectations of their clients are leading to greater emphasis on their responsibilities to serve as the organization's advocates, protectors, and fundraisers. As the brief review in this chapter reveals, the literature of nonprofit governance includes an abundance of advice, but some of it is inconsistent, even contradictory. Today's boards are being exhorted not only to raise money and promote the organization but also to be more aggressive in monitoring its performance. They are told to develop independent sources of information about the organization's operations but to stay focused on the big picture and not meddle in operations, to maintain a clear line between themselves and their CEO but not to forfeit their responsibility for leadership.

Nonprofit boards are expected to be Janus-like—that is, like the Roman god of doorways and arches, who was said to have two faces and be able to look outward and inward at the same time. Nonprofit organizations are open systems, with vaguely defined and often porous boundaries. The board is positioned on that boundary, between the organization and its external environment. From that position, the board is expected to look inward, fulfilling its fiduciary responsibilities on behalf of the membership or society. It is a kind of watchdog, responsible for ensuring that the organization is accountable for the resources entrusted to it, that those resources are used effectively in pursuit of its mission, and for representing the interests and viewpoints of the owners, whoever they may be.

But board members are also expected to be looking outward in order to meet their responsibilities to the organization itself and advance its interests. This is especially true for boards of charitable nonprofits, which may depend at least in part on philanthropic support. Because they are often leading citizens themselves, board members bring credibility to the organization in the broader community and authenticate its worthiness to receive support. They serve as its ambassadors and advocates, increasing its visibility and reputation within their own social and business circles. They protect the organization against inappropriate intrusions on its autonomy by government, donors, or other external forces. And they have a responsibility to ensure the organization's financial strength and sustainability, which many accomplish in part through giving or helping secure financial resources. These dual responsibilities—to society and to the organization itself, looking inward at the same time as looking outward—can sometimes be complex and competing. As Chait et al. (1999) explain,

> Boards constantly wrestle with when to be "product champions" and when to be studied neutrals—whether to stand and cheer like rabid partisans when the President of the United States delivers the State of the Union address or to remain seated and stone faced like the Supreme Court justices. (p. 3)

As Table 3.2 suggests, the complex responsibilities of boards may imply somewhat different ideal qualities in the individuals selected to serve, depending on which set of responsibilities are emphasized—a possible trade-off between what is often called "wisdom" (shorthand for the skills and judgment needed to govern well) and "wealth" (meaning the ability to give or obtain funds and other external resources). To fulfill their fiduciary responsibilities, boards must include individuals of integrity, and at least some will need to have specialized knowledge in finance and perhaps in professional fields related to the organization's programs and services. For example, a human services organization may need some board members with a background in social work, and it may be important that the boards of medical institutions include at least some members who understand medical terminology or the economics of health care. To properly represent the needs of the community and clients served by the organization, boards also need diverse memberships reflective of their constituencies, perhaps even including some who have been beneficiaries of the organization's programs—for example, former clients, patients, or students.

TABLE 3.2   The Board's Sometimes Competing Responsibilities

To society:	*To the organization:*
Accountability for resources and results	Advocacy and authenticity
Adherence to mission and law	Protection of autonomy
Representation of community needs	Fiscal stability and sustainability
Indicated board member qualities:	*Indicated board member qualities:*
Integrity	Stature
Expertise on programs and finances	Influence
Knowledge of community/clients	Wealth or access to wealth

But to advance its reputation, protect its interests, and secure funds, a nonprofit also needs board members who are individuals of stature in their communities, perhaps having influence with governmental officials or other regulators, and who have either the wealth to be significant donors or access to other individuals, foundations, or corporations that can provide financial support. John Pocock (1989) notes that "wealth and wisdom are not mutually exclusive [qualities of human beings]." He is, of course, correct that there may be *individual* candidates for governing board service who are possessed both of wisdom and of wealth—that is, who are equally well suited to meet their responsibilities for governing the organization and for serving as its external advocates and fundraisers. But not all individuals may be strong in all the requisite qualities. Boards attempting to craft their membership and faced with selecting a new member to fill an open seat may indeed face a dilemma regarding which qualities should be emphasized. Likewise, in deciding on which issues to focus its limited time and attention, a board may face either-or choices between the tasks associated with governing and those associated with advancing the organization, its interests, and its resources. Today's environment presents increasing pressures on boards to do all things better—to be better stewards and better fundraisers and to become more engaged with the organization's planning, programs, and effectiveness while also giving and raising more funds to support its work. The proper trade-offs between wealth and wisdom and how to balance the sometimes competing demands are questions causing discussion—and some anxiety—in many nonprofit boardrooms today.

CHAPTER SUMMARY

The governing board holds ultimate responsibility for the nonprofit organization. There are various types of boards, including those elected by the organization's membership; self-perpetuating boards; boards appointed by some outside authority; and hybrids, which may include elected, self-perpetuating, appointed, and ex-officio members. Each of these methods offers advantages but also introduces risks for the organization and the board.

The governing board's fiduciary responsibilities are defined in law and include the duty of care, the duty of loyalty, and the duty of obedience. Since the passage of intermediate sanctions in 1996 and the Sarbanes-Oxley Act in 2002, there has been increased scrutiny of nonprofit boards by the federal and state governments, the media, and other organizations. Under intermediate sanctions, nonprofit board members can face individual penalties for violating their fiduciary responsibilities, and many boards adopted new conflict-of-interest and disclosure policies in response to that legislation. Although Sarbanes-Oxley applies primarily to publicly traded corporations, many nonprofit organizations have voluntarily adopted some or all of its provisions, and some have been encompassed in legislation passed by states.

Functional responsibilities of boards have been defined in the literature and include appointing, supporting, and evaluating the CEO; establishing a clear institutional mission and purpose; approving the organization's programs to ensure consistency with its mission and financial prudence; ensuring sound management and financial stability; and establishing standards by which the organization's performance will be evaluated. Some view the board's responsibility to ensure the organization's financial stability and sustainability as implying an obligation on the part of board members to give from their personal resources and actively engage in fundraising. Some boards have policies requiring that members give or raise a minimum amount, but others rely on a culture that encourages members to participate as appropriate to their capacities.

The relationship between the governing board and the CEO is the subject of a substantial literature. In some organizations, especially those managed by a founder, the CEO may be a dominant figure, and the board may be largely reactive to the executive's initiatives. Most experts call for a partnership between the board and the CEO but differ on how that partnership should be designed. Three experts discussed in this chapter include John Carver (1997), whose policy governance model suggests a clear separation of roles, defined in policies established by the board related to ends, means, board-staff relationships, and governance process. Chait and colleagues (2005) propose a model they call governance-as-leadership, in which the lines between the responsibilities of the board and the CEO are broken down and both work together in focusing on the most critical issues and questions facing the organization. Leadership is shared, particularly when both engage in generative thinking. The research of Robert Herman and Dick Heimovics (2005) revealed that in reality both board members and the chief executive see the CEO as primarily responsible for the organization's success or failure, a condition they call "executive psychological centrality." They advise CEOs to accept that reality and practice board-centered leadership, not usurping the responsibilities of the board but rather supporting and facilitating its work.

In today's environment, there is considerable emphasis on the effectiveness of nonprofit governance. There are many criticisms, but there is a paucity of research to substantiate many of them. BoardSource and others have identified best practices of effective boards, but research by Herman and Renz (2002) suggests that there may be no one right way that works for every organization.

Nonprofit boards today face conflicting pressures. They are expected to do a more effective job of governing but also become more active in generating financial support for the organizations they serve. The appropriate trade-offs between the wealth and wisdom needed to meet these sometimes competing priorities are a matter of current discussion and debate in many nonprofit boardrooms.

NOTE

1. Some experts recommend that advisory groups not be called "boards" at all but rather "councils" or by some other term that does not imply legal responsibility for the organization.

KEY TERMS AND CONCEPTS FROM CHAPTER 3

board-centered leadership	*generative mode*
board of directors	*give-or-get policy*
board of trustees	*governance as leadership*
BoardSource	*governing boards*
conflict of interest	*intermediate sanctions*
duty of care	*policy governance model*
duty of loyalty	*private inurement*
duty of obedience	*purposive-rational model*
excess benefit transaction	*Sarbanes-Oxley Act*
executive psychological centrality	*self-perpetuating*
ex-officio	*social-constructionist model*
fiduciary mode	*strategic mode*

CASE 3.1

United Way of the National Capital Area

The United Way of the National Capital Area (UWNCA) is one of about 1,350 local United Way organizations, each of which is separately incorporated and governed by a board of volunteers from the community it serves. UWNCA serves the Washington, D.C., area, including the District of Columbia and its suburbs in Maryland and Virginia.

In 2002, the community was rocked by accusations that UWNCA's executive director, Oral Suer, had received as much as $1.6 million in improper payments, including nonreimbursed cash advances, encashment of vacation and sick leave that he had in fact taken, and reimbursement for travel and entertainment that were personal rather than related to United Way business. Those improper payments were alleged to have occurred over the period of 27 years that Mr. Suer was employed at the UWNCA (Wolverton, 2003b). *The Washington Post* also reported that UWNCA had withheld funds from charities, had excessive overhead costs, and had inflated its reported fundraising totals ("New Directors to Be Installed at United Way," 2002).

The UWNCA's board had 45 members, including prominent business leaders, attorneys, and accountants. One former employee of the organization told the *Chronicle of Philanthropy*, "This was definitely a 'clapper' board. They listened to staff members tell wonderful stories about how much money we were raising, and they applauded instead of asking tough questions" (Wolverton, 2003b). Others cited the organization's internal culture, which made it difficult for the board to meet its fiduciary responsibilities. One board member said that the board met only four times a year, a total of eight hours, and that the large board discouraged her from speaking. She said that she didn't have the phone numbers of the other board members, so she was unable to follow up with them after meetings. When she tried to obtain the numbers, a secretary at UWNCA told her that the numbers were confidential (Wolverton, 2003b).

Following the scandal at UWNCA, the national office of the United Way of America established new guidelines for the governance of local United Ways. UWNCA's board resigned, and a committee of community leaders was appointed to recruit a new board of 21 members. A new executive director was appointed to reform the organization and rebuild the community's trust.

Sources: "New Directors To Be Installed at United Way" (2002), Salmon (2002a, 2002b), Salmon and Whoriskey (2003), and Wolverton (2003b).

CASE 3.2

Robin Hood Foundation

The Robin Hood Foundation is a nonprofit that fights poverty in New York City. Its board includes prominent Wall Street hedge-fund managers as well as other well-known figures. An article by Donmoyer and Fitzgerald (2007) in the *Washington Post* raised questions about Robin Hood's "rainy-day fund," which had grown to $144.5 million from $20 million in a decade. The article noted that about half the fund was invested in hedge funds, managed by members of the Robin Hood board.

The article noted that there was nothing illegal about the arrangement. Robin Hood's executive director also pointed out that the managers are among the best and that the Foundation's investment returns had been excellent. The amount of management fees being paid were standard in the industry. He said that decisions on where to invest were made by a committee of Robin Hood's board and that the committee was not allowed to invest in funds managed by members of that committee. He also explained that the board members received fees for managing the Foundation's funds because their company policies did not allow them to charge different fees to different investors. The director of the Better Business Bureau's (BBB) New York Philanthropic Advisory Service said that Robin Hood met BBB's standards for charity accountability. (The BBB standards are discussed in Chapter 5 of this text.)

But some people raised questions about the role of Robin Hood board members in managing the organization's funds. Senator Charles Grassley, a member of the Senate Finance Committee, who is often critical of nonprofit organizations, said, "I don't remember Robin Hood keeping [management fees] as his cut." An official of the Kellogg Foundation described the situation as "flirting with self-dealing." The national president of the Better Business Bureau Wise Giving Alliance also raised questions: "You start to wonder what happens in the year that the hedge fund doesn't do well. Does the board have the power to fire the hedge-fund manager?"

Source: Based on Donmoyer and Fitzgerald (2007).

CASE 3.3

Bishop Estate

Hawaii's Bishop Estate is a charitable trust created through the will of Princess Bernice Pauahi Bishop, a descendant of King Kamehamena I, and has as its sole purpose supporting the Kamehamemaha Schools for children of native Hawaiian descent. It was reported in 1999 that the Estate was the largest landowner in Hawaii, and its assets were estimated at between $5 billion and $10 billion. According to the Princess's will, the trust was to be governed by five trustees, who would be appointed by the justices of Hawaii's Supreme Court (Greene, 1999).

(Continued)

(Continued)

In the 1990s, the IRS began investigating the trust and expressed its concern about the activities of the trustees. First, the IRS said that the trustees were receiving excessive compensation for their services, reported to be more than $1 million annually each. In addition, the IRS said that the trustees were using the Estate's funds to pay for personal expenses, that they were focused more on the Estate's commercial activities than on running the schools, and that they had improperly lobbied against passage of the intermediate sanctions legislation in 1996. The trustees defended their actions, arguing among other things that they deserved the compensation for their work in managing the trust's assets as well as the schools. The trustees had indeed been involved in the day-to-day management of the schools, which some said had caused problems and tension between the schools and the trustees.

The IRS threatened to terminate the Estate's tax exemption, which would have required the Estate to pay millions of dollars each year in federal taxes as well as state and county taxes, thus diminishing the benefit of its assets to the schools and the children. The IRS demanded changes that would include removal of the existing trustees, a new method for selecting trustees, revisions in trustee compensation, stronger internal financial controls, and external audits.

Reacting to the IRS criticism, in 1999 Judge Kevin Chang of the Hawaii court removed four of the five trustees and accepted the resignation of the fifth, saying that their "inaction and indifference" was "a breach of duty." The IRS decided to pursue intermediate sanctions against the removed trustees, making it one of the first cases under the law passed in 1996. In 2001, the former trustees announced that they had settled with the IRS, which did not disclose the details. The media reported that the State of Hawaii also had brought a case against the trustees, which also was settled, but the court records were sealed, so the final result could not be known (Schwinn, 2002).

Some saw the IRS's action as an encouraging example, showing that it would act to curb abuses. Others saw it as alarming for the nonprofit sector that the IRS would use its power to pressure a state court to remove nonprofit trustees (Greene, 1999).

Source: Greene (1999) and Schwinn (2002).

QUESTIONS FOR DISCUSSION

1. Which of the legal responsibilities of boards may not have been met by the board of the United Way of the National Capital Area? How might this scandal have been prevented?

2. What does the United Way case suggest about the relationship between the CEO and the board?

3. What are the issues in the case of the Robin Hood Foundation? Although they are legal, are the relationships between the board and the managers of the organization's finances appropriate? Why or why not? What safeguards would you introduce to assure the organization's donors that the board is behaving properly?

4. How is the case of the Bishop Estate different from that of the Robin Hood Foundation and the United Way of the National Capital Area?

5. Do you see any ways in which the recommendations of Carver (1997), Chait et al. (2005), and Herman and Heimovics (2005) might be relevant to the cases discussed in this chapter?

SUGGESTIONS FOR FURTHER READING RELATED TO CHAPTER 3

Books

Carver, J. (2006). *Boards that make a difference: A new design for leadership in nonprofit and public organizations* (3rd ed.). San Francisco: Jossey-Bass.

Chait, R. P., Ryan, W. R., & Taylor, B. E. (2005). *Governance as leadership: Reframing the work of nonprofit boards*. Hoboken, NJ: Wiley.

Ingram, R. T. (2003). *Ten basic responsibilities of nonprofit boards*. Washington, DC: BoardSource.

Worth, M. J. (2005). *Securing the future: A fund-raising guide for boards of independent colleges and universities*. Washington, DC: Association of Governing Boards of Universities and Colleges.

Web Sites

Association of Governing Boards of Universities and Colleges, www.agb.org

BoardSource, www.boardsource.org

CHAPTER 4

Executive Leadership

The Introduction to this text discussed why nonprofit management is a distinctive undertaking, different in important ways from management in the for-profit sector or in government. Among these differences were the need for nonprofits to integrate mission, the acquisition of resources, and strategy; the complex relationships among a nonprofit organization's stakeholders (including volunteers) that require negotiation and compromise and the need for executives to possess a high tolerance for ambiguity; and the need to manage a double bottom line of financial results and social impact.

These differences may not directly affect the work of everyone employed at a nonprofit organization. For example, there is no particular nonprofit way of processing bills or payments, programming computers, or maintaining physical facilities. Many who work in the nonprofit sector are engaged in such technical work that their skills may be readily transferable across the for-profit, nonprofit, and governmental sectors. Even those who provide the services of a nonprofit organization may not perform their functions in any unique way. For example, a doctor working in a nonprofit, for-profit, or government hospital will follow the same medical protocols; a counselor working with clients recovering from drug or alcohol addiction may use the same treatments whether working in a nonprofit organization or a state-managed entity; and teachers in private and public schools may teach a similar curriculum. Where the unique characteristics of nonprofit management come together with the greatest significance is in the position of the chief executive officer (CEO). It is a position requiring unique skills in both management and leadership, which this chapter explores. In this examination, we will draw on the theoretical literature of leadership as well as the practitioner literature produced by consultants, other experts, and nonprofit CEOs themselves.

THE CEO'S JOB

What do nonprofit chief executives actually do? In other words, what is the job description? Of course, because no two organizations are exactly the same, the CEO's job may vary widely from one to another. In some, fundraising may be an important expectation, while in others it is not. In organizations that have mostly paid professional staff, the skills required of a CEO may be different from those needed to lead an organization that relies on volunteers for a substantial portion of its workforce. And, as discussed in Chapter 3, the type of governing board with which the chief executive works may greatly influence the types of challenges that he or she may face. While recognizing these inevitable differences, Richard Moyers identified 10 basic responsibilities of the nonprofit chief executives in a 2005 publication from BoardSource* (Moyers, 2005):

1. *Commit to the mission:* The CEO must understand the mission, keep the mission prominently in mind when making decisions, and guard against mission drift.

2. *Lead the staff and manage the organization:* The CEO has direct responsibility for hiring, training, developing, and motivating the staff, developing an organizational structure that suits the organization's work, and ensuring that day-to-day operations and programs are effective and efficient.

3. *Exercise responsible financial stewardship:* While the governing board has overall responsibility for ensuring the organization's financial soundness, it is the chief executive who must manage its assets, revenues, and expenditures on a day-to-day basis and ensure that controls are in place to protect the organization against fraud or waste.

4. *Lead and manage fundraising:* The CEO's responsibility for fundraising will vary from one organization to another and is shared with the governing board. In charitable nonprofits, the CEO's direct engagement in fundraising, planning fundraising programs, and managing the fundraising staff may consume a substantial portion of his or her time and energy.

5. *Follow the highest ethical standards, ensure accountability, and comply with the law:* Again, the governing board may establish policies (remember Carver's executive limitations discussed in Chapter 3) that establish standards and procedures to ensure legal and ethical behavior. But it is the chief executive who needs to put these policies into practice in the organization's daily life and set an example through his or her own behavior.

6. *Engage the board in planning and lead implementation:* Planning for the organization's future is a shared responsibility of the board and the CEO, but the reality in many organizations requires that the chief executive take a significant role in initiating the planning effort, providing the resources for planning, and defining issues and questions for the board to deliberate.

7. *Develop future leadership:* In many organizations the CEO plays a role in developing the leadership of the board, both informally and often as a member of the board's nominating committee. There is also an increasing emphasis on the importance of the CEO's preparing for possible staff departures by developing a bench of qualified successors and, indeed, for preparing the way for a smooth transition when he or she may leave the chief executive's position.

8. *Build external relationships and serve as an advocate:* Some research considered later in this chapter emphasizes that effective chief executives are those who are externally oriented—who are constantly alert to opportunities and threats in the external environment and engaged in building external partnerships for their organization.

*Source: BoardSource (2005). *The source: Twelve principles of governance that power exceptional boards.* Washington, DC: Author. Used with permission.

9. *Ensure the quality and effectiveness of programs:* The board may set the standards by which the effectiveness of programs is to be evaluated, but the CEO must ensure that the right questions are asked and the right data collected so that a process of evaluation and continuous learning is a part of the organization's ongoing work.

10. *Support the board:* Just as the governing board has a responsibility to support its CEO, the CEO has a reciprocal responsibility to support the board. And, as we discussed in Chapter 3, research suggests that effective CEOs are ones who practice board-centered leadership.

Two realities are evident in Moyer's list of CEO responsibilities. One is the number of areas in which the chief executive shares responsibility with the governing board regarding mission, financial stewardship, fundraising, accountability, planning, performance standards, and the work of the board itself. This explains why the relationship between the CEO and the board is so complex and why so many experts have focused on delineating the CEO and board responsibilities in each area.

The second observation that emerges from a review of the CEO's responsibilities is that they involve both *managing* and *leading.* The CEO is responsible for ensuring that financial management systems are in place, for the hiring and evaluation of staff, and for monitoring the quality and effectiveness of programs. But chief executives are also expected to be external spokespersons for their organizations, able to articulate the mission and make a persuasive case for financial support; to be capable of motivating both paid staff and volunteers to high performance; and to hold a vision and strategy for the organization's future, which, working together with the board, they translate into a plan for the organization's advancement and growth. These latter tasks require something beyond management: They require that the CEO be a leader.

MANAGEMENT AND LEADERSHIP

Although people may use the words interchangeably, *leadership* and *management* are not the same thing. Management is generally concerned with day-to-day operations, with making things work. It emphasizes policies, procedures, rules, and processes. Management is transactional; the manager provides rewards in exchange for the work contributions of others or imposes sanctions (punishments) on those who do not meet the requirements of their assignments. A manager is often concerned primarily with maintaining a smooth operation, that is, keeping the machine running and avoiding breakdowns, rather than with change.

Leadership is more about purpose, vision, and direction—that is, more about the "where" and the "why" rather than the "how." In a widely quoted statement, Bennis and Nanus (1985) suggest a moral element to leadership: "Managers are people who do things right and leaders are people who do the right thing" (p. 221). Leadership is interactive; that is, it is a *process*, and it involves a *relationship* between the leader and the people who are led. There can be no leaders without followers, and both play a part in the process of leadership. Leaders are focused on change, and that change is not directionless; leadership involves moving people toward the achievement of some defined *goals.* Some of the differences between leaders and managers are summarized in Table 4.1.

TABLE 4.1	Managers and Leaders Compared

Managers	*Leaders*
Concerned with mastering routines	Concerned with vision and judgment
Adopt impersonal or passive attitudes toward goals	Active and visionary about the future
Excel in problem solving and work design	Seek out opportunities and take risks
Work with people in carefully controlled ways	Passionate about their work and likely to cause turbulence
See themselves as conservators or regulators	See themselves as agents of change

Source: Based on Denhardt, Denhardt, and Aristigueta (2002, p. 195).

Sometimes, leaders and managers are different people; indeed, some argue that the two roles require different personal qualities or skills rarely found in the same individual. Sometimes, one person may have the responsibility both for leading the organization and for managing its affairs—for example, the CEO of a small nonprofit. But the functions of leadership and management are different, and such people need to be able to switch from one role to the other as the needs of the organization and the occasion may dictate. Indeed, some argue that those who are founders of nonprofit organizations often exhibit strong qualities of leadership but may be unable to provide the management the organization needs as it grows, sometimes leading to the problem known as founder syndrome.

In larger organizations, CEOs sometimes play the leadership role and delegate management responsibilities to subordinates, including perhaps a chief operating officer. It is possible for a CEO to delegate management to others, but only the CEO can provide leadership to the entire organization. Leadership of the organization is not a responsibility that can be delegated.

All organizations need both leadership and management to be successful in the long run. It is conceivable that an organization—whether a for-profit business, a government agency, or a nonprofit organization—can survive for a time with only good management. But to thrive and grow, an organization also needs leaders who define vision, articulate direction, set goals, and influence others to achieve them together.

Nonprofit organizations especially need leadership. The reasons are rooted in their characteristics that we have discussed in earlier chapters. Corporations and government agencies generally have well-defined missions, straightforward measures of performance, and revenue that is derived from either appropriated funds or quid pro quo transactions with customers. In contrast, nonprofits are *values based* and *mission driven.* There is not always consensus about mission or about appropriate ways of measuring performance against the mission. Financial and other resources are often bestowed *voluntarily*. Leadership is essential to develop consensus about mission and performance and to articulate a vision that gains and holds the commitment of volunteer board members, service volunteers, donors, and others. This book includes a chapter on executive leadership simply because leadership is so central to the role of a nonprofit CEO. A lack of leadership by the CEO of a nonprofit organization will eventually, and inevitably, lead to drift, decline, and failure.

OVERVIEW OF LEADERSHIP THEORIES

If leadership is so critical, how can we understand it? Are leaders born or made? If they are made, what specific knowledge or skills do individuals need to acquire in order to be strong leaders? What is it that successful leaders actually do—in other words, are there specific behaviors that are associated with effective leadership? These are questions that long have been asked, and there is a substantial body of research that has sought to provide answers.

It is important to remember two points as we review some of the well-known leadership theories. First, most of them are generic; that is, theorists intend them to apply to leadership in all types of organizations, not just nonprofits. And, second, as in our earlier discussion of governing, there may be no one right theory of leadership that is applicable in every situation, at all times. Each of the theories we will discuss have their critics as well as their proponents.

Leadership theory has evolved over the decades. Among the earliest theories were the *trait theories,* which explain leadership in terms of the innate characteristics of individuals who are leaders. They are essentially "great man or woman" theories, which hold the qualities of leadership to be fundamental aspects of an individual's personality. In the past, some have looked to physical characteristics to explain why certain people are leaders; for example, physical height and resonance of speaking voice—essentially male qualities— were once considered intrinsic to leadership, although they would not explain Golda Meir, Indira Gandhi, or Mother Teresa! Other trait theorists have pointed more to elements of personality, character, or psychology. For example, in 1948, Stodgill studied leaders and found them to be better than the average person in terms of intelligence, alertness, insight, responsibility, initiative, persistence, self-confidence, and sociability. Since it is difficult for individuals to change their intelligence or personalities, trait theories imply that leaders are born, not made; that is, leadership is not something that can be taught or learned (Northouse, 2004, p. 16).

The trait theories, however, do not seem to provide the whole answer. Thus, in about the middle of the 20th century, theorists began to take a different approach, developing *skills theories* of leadership. Skills theories hold that it is not the innate qualities of individuals, such as physical appearance or even intelligence, that make them effective leaders. Rather, there are specific skills that effective leaders possess; in other words, effective leadership depends less on what the leaders are and more on what they are able to do. For example, in 1955, Daniel Katz (cited by Northouse, 2004, pp. 37–38) suggested that effective leadership depends on the leader possessing skills in three areas: *technical* (knowledge of the job, profession, or task), *human* (the ability to work with people), and *conceptual* (the ability to understand ideas and principles). A skills theory is the assumption underlying most leadership training or development programs.

Beginning in the 1950s, leadership researchers began to move beyond studying the traits and skills of individual leaders toward looking at what it is that leaders actually *do*—that is, they considered whether it was possible to identify specific *behaviors* associated with effective leadership. Among the most famous of leadership studies that followed this approach were those conducted at Ohio State University. These studies identified two basic types of leader behaviors: *task behaviors* (actions that relate to the work to be done) and *relationship behaviors* (actions that focus on the feelings of subordinates.) At about the same time, similar studies conducted at the University of Michigan identified essentially the same categories, which researchers there labeled *production orientation* and *employee orientation.*

The ways in which leaders mix task and relationship behaviors can define a leadership style. Among the theorists who analyzed leadership styles are Blake and Mouton, who in the 1980s developed their well-known *managerial grid.* This grid is based on different combinations of task and relationship behaviors and defines four styles. Organizations that are high on production (task) and low on relationships are said to have *authority-obedience management.* Essentially, they are dictatorships, although they may be productive. Those high on relationships and low on concern for production are described as having *country club management.* They may be great places to work, but they get little or nothing accomplished. Organizations that are low on both concern for people and production exhibit *impoverished management.* These would be dreadful places to work, and most people likely would not stay long in such an uninspiring environment. The ideal type, showing high concern for both people and production, is called *team management* (Rainey, 2003, p. 292). It is likely that most readers can imagine situations, or perhaps have even experienced ones, in which each of these styles is practiced.

It may seem obvious that what may be an effective leadership style in one situation may not be so under different circumstances. But the idea that effective leadership behavior might depend or be *contingent* on the situation was a new insight in leadership theory in the 1960s.[1] In this way of thinking, effective leadership would require matching the leader's style to the situation. Different situations might call for different combinations of task-oriented and relationship-oriented behaviors. But what defines a "situation?" Exactly what differences between situations are relevant to determining the right leadership style (Northouse, 2004, pp. 88–89)?

One of the best-known contingency theories is the one developed by Fiedler in 1967. According to Fiedler, the situation may be favorable or unfavorable to the leader, depending on three variables: *leader-member relations* (e.g., the degree of trust, cooperativeness, and friendliness between the leader and followers); the *task structure* (whether the job to be done is clear and specific or ambiguous and uncertain); and the *position power* of the leader (i.e., the formal position of authority the leader holds.) The most favorable situation is when all three variables are high, and the least favorable is when all three are low, but there can be moderately favorable situations that show some combination of favorable and unfavorable conditions. According to Fiedler's findings, task-oriented leaders do best when conditions are very favorable or very unfavorable, while relationship-oriented leaders do best in the intermediate circumstances (Rainey, 2003, pp. 292–293).

Contingency theories add a level of sophistication beyond the trait, skill, and behavior theories of leadership. They begin to explain why some styles of leadership may be successful in certain circumstances and not in others. Imagine, for example, a situation in which a nonprofit chief executive is facing the need to mobilize staff and volunteers to provide relief to victims of a natural disaster. The urgency of the situation makes everyone inclined to be cooperative. Let's also assume that the executive is trusted and well liked by the staff and volunteers. The task is clear and unambiguous: It is to provide food, clothing, and shelter to the victims as quickly as possible. These circumstances— cooperativeness, trust, a clear task, a leader with formal authority–would be a situation that Fiedler's model would define as favorable to the leader. A task-oriented style likely would be most effective. The important thing would be to get the job done, and there would be little need to concentrate on relationships among people, which are already good. But imagine a different situation, one in which an acting executive director has been on the job for just a few months while a search for a permanent director is proceeding. This person leads an environmental advocacy organization and is trying to mobilize volunteers to support critical environmental legislation by contacting their elected representatives. The task seems clear and specific. But the person's position power is weak because of the acting status, and he or she may not have been in the role long enough to have gained the trust and friendship of the staff and volunteers. In Fiedler's theory, this situation is intermediate in its favorableness to the leader, who likely would need to devote considerable attention to nurturing his or her relationships with the volunteers and staff to mobilize them to action; in other words, the leader would need to emphasize relationship behaviors more than task behaviors.

Although not a theory per se, one approach to leadership that has gained a following and spawned a number of books is that of *servant leadership*, advanced by Robert Greenleaf (1977). Greenleaf argues that leadership begins with the leader's values and commitments and that moral leaders are more concerned with serving others than with meeting their own self-interest. Servant leaders exhibit honesty, integrity, character, and spirit. Rather than trying to impose their will on others, they listen, empathize with others, and focus on relationships, approaching the position of leader as a type of stewardship of the organization, with the goal of social improvement (Denhardt et al., 2002, p. 195).

Transformational Leadership

A 1978 book by political scientist James MacGregor Burns, titled simply *Leadership,* had seminal influence on thinking about the topic and offers insights that may be of particular relevance to leadership in the nonprofit sector (Burns, 1978). First, Burns made a distinction between *transactional leadership* and *transformational leadership.* Transactional leadership is an exchange process, in which the leader exchanges rewards or punishments for the behaviors of others. If you come to work, you will get paid; if you don't you won't. If you miss work too often, you will be fired. Thus, transactional leadership is essentially like management. In contrast, transformational leadership, as the name implies, is leadership that *changes* people. According to Burns, transformational leadership inspires and enables people to grow, both morally and in terms of their levels of motivation. It empowers individuals to go beyond self-interest and pursue goals that are in the common interest. Transformational leaders accomplish this by developing a relationship with followers and tapping into their personal values in a way that matches them to the values of the organization. They motivate followers not based on rewards and punishments but by appealing to these shared values and ideals.

Let's consider a simple example that might illustrate transactional and transformational approaches. Tom is the CEO of a nonprofit organization that delivers meals to house-bound older people. He is addressing a meeting of his staff, and he is concerned that some have been showing up late for work, delaying the delivery of meals to clients. One way to approach the issue would be for Tom to say something like, "I've noticed that I am the first one here in the morning. Some of you don't show up for an hour later. As a result, some meals are being delivered late. If this continues, I will need to consider docking the pay of staff who report late and firing others if it continues. I will expect to see you all here at 6 a.m. tomorrow morning."

But, taking a different approach, Tom might say something like, "I am concerned. I know that some of our clients wait for their meals to be delivered and that in fact their contact with our volunteers may be the high point of their days. When I see that we are late in getting the meals out the door in the morning, I cannot help but worry about a lonely older person, perhaps a little hungry, who is left waiting because maybe we had other things to do that morning. I know you share my concern about that. I know our clients appreciate everything you can do to make sure we are meeting their needs—and on time—because they count on us."

Which approach is more likely to result in staff arriving earlier? The first is purely transactional: You do (or do not do) this and I will do (or not do) that. The transactional approach may be effective in the short run; after all, staff members rely on their paychecks. But the effects of Tom's speech may wear off in a few days unless he repeats it, and his threats are backed up. That will require his continuing intervention, possibly undermining his relationships with the staff over time. The second approach has tones of transformational leadership. It appeals to shared values rather than the promise or threat of consequences. It may move staff members to change their behaviors by affecting changes in their own heads and hearts. If accomplished, such change may be more lasting and powerful than the tools of a more transactional style.

Burns' book inspired work by other scholars, who adopted, expanded, and refined his ideas. One prominent leadership scholar, Bernard Bass (1985; Bass & Avolio, 1994) developed a more comprehensive model of transformational leadership. He differed slightly with Burns on some points. For one, Bass emphasized that transformational leaders also use transactional techniques. They do provide goals and rewards for reaching them. This is not a problem as long as they do not overemphasize these techniques, especially those that are negative. Rewards may be more consistent with transformational leadership than are punishments. In other words, there may be times when the hypothetical CEO Tom may find that some staff members do not respond adequately to his values-based approach and will indeed need to be subject to "transactions" (Rainey, 2003, pp. 304–305).

Most of the leadership theories considered in this chapter describe a leader's relationship with subordinates. What is significant about the concept of transformational leadership is that it also offers an approach to leading *organizations*—especially those that are values based and mission driven. A nonprofit chief executive must lead more than the members of his or her paid staff. Among others, the CEO must also at times lead donors, volunteers, and even members of the board.

Think back to the earlier example of Tom speaking to members of his staff. The transactional approach, using rewards and punishments to change behavior, might be effective with the staff, at least in the short run. But how could that approach be effective in motivating individuals to give or members of the board to increase their efforts in fundraising, or in inspiring volunteers to work longer and harder? Would not those goals be better accomplished by identifying how the values of those individuals coincide with those of the organization and appealing to those values in a way that the desired behavior is dictated from within their own hearts?

In a sequel to his best-selling book on companies *Good to Great,* Jim Collins (2001) observes how nonprofit leadership is unique and describes two types (or styles) of leadership that have similarities to Burns' transactional and transformational approaches. *Executive leadership* exists when the leader has the power to simply make decisions. *Legislative leadership* is a style that "relies more upon persuasion, political currency, and shared interests to create the conditions for the right decisions to happen" (Collins, 2005, p. 11). Nonprofit executives often do not have the formal power of corporate CEOs. They generally do not have the financial resources with which to offer significant monetary incentives. Indeed, some of their workforce is not paid at all, and even those who are may be motivated as much by their commitment to the mission as they are by their financial needs. Rather than lead through rewards and punishments, nonprofit executives must use the less raw, but considerable, power of ideas, persuasion, inspiration, and relationships to lead others—and their organizations—in the directions they wish them to pursue.

Charismatic Leadership

The idea of charisma is one that is familiar to most people. When asked to name someone who is a leader, people often will mention the names of political figures, such as Bill Clinton, Nelson Mandela, or Martin Luther King Jr. When asked what makes all these individuals unusual, some inevitably will use the term *charisma.*

The prominence of Burns' concept of transformational leadership has led to an increasing interest in *charismatic leadership*, which remains an active area of research today. Some debate whether transformational and charismatic leadership are the same, different, or overlapping concepts, but fine distinctions need not concern us here. They are, at the least, related.

There is debate about the nature of charisma. Is it based on personal characteristics of the leader—is it some kind of right stuff that some people just have and others do not? Or is charisma defined by behaviors that can be learned? Some argue that theories of charismatic leadership really represent a retreat to the earlier trait theories. But Bass and other scholars have identified specific behaviors that may cause followers to *attribute* the characteristics of charisma to the leader. In other words, a leader is someone who behaves in certain ways that cause others to see him or her as charismatic (Bryman, 1992, pp. 100–102).

What are some of the behaviors that may cause others to see the leader as charismatic? Here are some that researchers have identified (Rainey, 2003, p. 305):

- *The leader advocates a vision that is different from the status quo but still acceptable to followers.* Leadership is about change but not change so radical as to alienate potential followers. Martin Luther King Jr. advocated an end to segregation and racial discrimination. This represented a change from the status quo in America in the 1960s but also a change that King's followers, and eventually the entire nation, came to accept as morally compelling. Rather than call for violent revolution, King advocated nonviolent means, remaining within the boundaries of what his followers and sympathizers could find acceptable.
- *The leader acts in unconventional ways in pursuit of the vision.* King led boycotts and marches. Nelson Mandela spent 27 years in jail in protest against South Africa's inhuman system of apartheid. Neither brought about change by writing letters to the editor or by other, more conventional activities.
- *The leader engages in self-sacrifice and risk taking in pursuit of the vision.* Mandela sacrificed 27 years. Mother Teresa lived a life of poverty among the poor. King gave his life. The deep commitment of a leader, as evidenced by his or her willingness to sacrifice, even suffer, for the cause compels attention and confers a charismatic appeal.
- *The leader displays confidence in his or her own ideas and proposals.* Perhaps the undoing of Jimmy Carter as President of the United States was a speech he gave to the nation in which he acknowledged his own shortcomings as president and described the nation's mood as a "malaise." In contrast, Ronald Reagan's optimistic assertion that it was "morning in America" was an important factor in his defeating Carter for the presidency in 1980, although many opinion polls showed that a majority of Americans disagreed with his specific positions on issues. Charismatic leaders command our following, in part, simply because they appear so certain that their course is right.
- *The leader uses visioning and persuasive appeals to influence followers, rather than relying mainly on formal authority.* Martin Luther King Jr. never held public office. But the words "I have a dream" created a vision of a different America that inspired millions and changed the nation more dramatically than most Presidents of the United States have ever been able to do.
- *The leader uses the capacity to assess context and locate opportunities for novel strategies.* Charismatic leaders read the moment; that is, they can take the temperature of their times and followers and create opportunities to demonstrate their cause in dramatic and novel ways. In 1987, Ronald Reagan stood yards from the Berlin Wall and addressed himself to the then leader of the Soviet Union saying, "Mr. Gorbachev, tear down this wall!" It was a dramatic moment, which Reagan must have known would resonate with people on both sides of the wall at that point in history. Two years later, the wall was gone, not entirely as a result of Reagan's speech but rather as the culmination of historical forces that were

gathering strength. But Reagan understood the context and used the opportunity of his visit to the wall to dramatize the issue.

To the above list of behaviors of charismatic leaders, Fisher (1984) who writes about the use of charismatic leadership by college and university presidents, adds the idea of *social distance.* He suggests that to be perceived as charismatic, the leader cannot permit himself or herself to be too familiar. Consistent with the military's long-standing rule that officers don't fraternize with enlisted personnel, leaders may be friendly, but not too much so. They can be congenial but never silly. They can socialize with subordinates (or board members or donors) but never stay too long or drink too much. If charisma is something attributed to leaders, as psychologists suggest, it seems that we may prefer just a bit of mystery and to believe that they are just a little different from us.

Although they play an important part in contemporary leadership theory and research, the ideas of transformational leadership and charismatic leadership have their critics. Some raise academic issues, saying that charisma is too ill defined to measure or analyze. Some say the idea of charismatic leadership is really just a newer version of the "great man/great woman" theory of leadership. (Remember the issue from our case in Chapter 2 about the Smithsonian's National Museum of American History and the Catherine B. Reynolds Foundation?) Others raise substantive concerns about the risks of charismatic leadership to organizations: For example, the power of charismatic leadership may be abused, or an organization dependent on a charismatic leader may be vulnerable if that leader leaves, retires, or dies (Northouse, 2004, pp. 185–186).

THE EFFECTIVE NONPROFIT CEO

If leadership is so vital to the success of the nonprofit organization, what do we know about what makes an effective nonprofit CEO? We have discussed some major theories of leadership, but what evidence do we have of what actually works best in the nonprofit sector?

As with the topic of governing boards, much of the literature on nonprofit executive leadership is prescriptive. In other words, "It tells more about how to lead and much less about how leaders actually go about their business" (Dym & Hutson, 2005, p. 6). And, as is the case with governing boards, a significant portion of the literature on nonprofit leadership has been written by consultants or reflective practitioners and is practitioner oriented in its approach.

Empirical research focused specifically on nonprofit leadership is growing. But research on effective nonprofit leadership faces challenges. One problem is how to define effective nonprofit leadership; it is bound up with the larger issue of how to define an effective nonprofit organization. As in measuring the effectiveness of the nonprofit board, the idea of CEO effectiveness is also socially constructed, and the definition of what constitutes an effective nonprofit CEO may vary according to the perceptions of the organization's diverse constituencies.

Indeed, a common method that researchers have used for identifying effective nonprofit leaders is based on perceptions. Nonprofit executives or perhaps opinion leaders, such as foundation officers and academics, are asked to identify those CEOs whom they deem to be most successful or effective. The characteristics of these CEOs are then compared with those of another group of CEOs who were not named. But this method is problematic and raises the question of how the nominators are defining "effective." Those identified as effective may simply be the most visible or popular in their fields. Charismatic leaders may be favored over others since they are often highly visible and magnetic personalities. Or perhaps the executives identified by their colleagues as being effective were those who had been active as presenters at professional conferences or as authors, demonstrating perhaps their knowledge about nonprofit leadership, not necessarily bearing any relationship to their performance as leaders of their own organizations. Furthermore, it is not always clear whether survey or interview respondents are describing how things are, how they believe they should be, or how they think they should respond.

Many studies based on surveys of perceptions reflect what seem to be trait or skills theories of leadership. For example, nonprofit CEOs interviewed by Hudson identified openness and honesty as the most important qualities of effective nonprofit chief executives (Hudson, 2005, p. 157). In another study, nonprofit sector opinion leaders identified passion and commitment, vision, integrity, trust, and credibility (Light, 2002). Similar traits are also mentioned in the practitioner-oriented literature—integrity and trust (Pidgeon, 2004, p. 92), vision, initiative, openness, and responsiveness (Howe, 2004, pp. 4–5).

Some research studies and the practitioner literature have also identified skills associated with effective nonprofit leadership. They commonly identify interpersonal skills, communication skills, delegation skills, staff management skills, the ability to articulate and write a message, and the ability to raise funds (Howe, 2004; Light, 2002; Pidgeon, 2004). Many of the skills identified are, of course, generic and would seem to be useful to leaders in any organization. The skills unique to nonprofits (e.g., fundraising) are essentially technical, and others mentioned are more related to management than to leadership.

Some authors do describe behaviors of effective nonprofit CEOs, but most of this literature is prescriptive. It tells us what CEOs should *do* to be effective, and it often emphasizes areas on which the chief executive should focus his or her time and attention. Five areas are frequently mentioned, and these are discussed below.

Focus on Mission

The importance of staying focused on the mission is emphasized by almost all authors on the topic. The mission is the nonprofit's reason for existence, and the CEO should use it as a guide for every decision. As Frances Hesselbein, former CEO of the Girl Scouts, expresses it, "Mission is the star we steer by. Everything begins with mission, everything flows from mission" (quoted by Dees et al., 2001, p. 19). Many nonprofit boards include leaders from business, who may sometimes find it attractive to direct the organization toward activities that are financially lucrative but that may distract it from its primary mission. Staff may sometimes propose activities that would be "nice to do" but that may not advance the mission directly. The CEO can use the mission as a shield against such pressures from the staff or board, to explain, justify, and give coherence to his or her actions.

Focus on the Board

Many authors emphasize the importance of the CEO's relationship with the board. Chapter 3 discussed the research of Robert Herman and Dick Heimovics, who identified board-centered leadership as the behavior distinguishing effective CEOs from others (Herman & Heimovics, 1991, 2005). As they report their research findings:

> Analysis showed that executive leadership in relation to staff and in relation to the board are independent and distinct factors. Effective and comparison executives differed little in leadership with their staffs. The most important finding was that the effective executives provided significantly more leadership to their boards. (Herman & Heimovics, 2005, p. 157)

Focus on External Relationships

Effective nonprofit leaders are those who are not excessively focused on internal management. They are not obsessed with policies and procedures and the day-to-day activities of their subordinates. Rather, they "delegate much of the management of internal affairs and focus on the external" (Herman & Heimovics, 2005, p. 159). Practical strategies for enhancing external impact include developing an informal information network, including contacts in government, other nonprofits, foundations, and professional associations, to supplement hard data with soft information about emerging trends and practices in the field.

Fundraising is an important aspect of the external activity of many nonprofit CEOs, and indeed, its importance is growing as government support for many programs has been reduced. While the opinion leaders and nonprofit CEOs interviewed by Light (2002) mentioned fundraising as an important skill, it is surprising how seldom it is addressed in much of the nonprofit leadership literature.

Focus on Key Roles and Priorities

In their well-known work on leadership, Nanus and Dobbs (1999) address the question of where the nonprofit CEO needs to direct his or her attention. Their answer: almost everywhere. They define four quadrants in which the CEO may focus and operate at any given time—inside the organization, outside the organization, on present operations, and on future possibilities. They identify six roles defined by these four areas and argue that the effective CEO needs to be proficient in *all* of them. When the CEO combines an internal perspective with attention to present operations, he or she is acting in the role of "coach," guiding staff and others who are performing the organization's work. Looking inward but with a view to the future, the CEO is playing the role of "change agent." When CEOs are focused outside the organization but concerned with present operations, they are performing as "politicians" and as "fundraisers." And when CEOs are focused externally and looking to the future, they are performing as "visionaries" and "strategists."

Herman and Heimovics (2005) urge nonprofit CEOs to stay focused on key "goals or outcomes [that are] crucial"; that is, they advise nonprofit CEOs to "know your agenda"

(p. 160). A well-managed organization may have goals derived from a formal process of strategic planning, but effective executives have their own short list of priorities—a few key things they wish to accomplish. Those priorities may be drawn from the plan or be supplemental to it. Rather than scatter their attention and efforts across a broad list of goals, CEOs will be more successful if they can limit their priorities to a few critical initiatives that will define their leadership of the organization and focus their own attention and that of others on those items. Carlson and Donohoe, both former nonprofit executives and now consultants, agree, advising, "Don't let a list of priorities exceed five items, and three is better" (Carlson & Donohoe, 2003, p. 33).

Remembering that board members, donors, and even staff, may not be thinking about organizational goals all the time and that they face innumerable distractions in their own personal and professional lives, it is important for the CEO to keep the short-listed goals constantly in front of them and to ensure that they have the same information and perspective as the CEO, so that they will come to share his or her understanding of what the priorities are and why. For example, one university president regularly sends packages of clippings to his senior staff and the board, articles highlighting trends or issues that he thinks may have a bearing on decisions the university will eventually need to face. His purpose is to ensure that when the decisions come before the board, they will have read the same things as he has and will understand the context for his recommendations. Leaders also need to simplify the priorities and "lay a bread crumb trail" to key decisions through communications and small actions that lead the way to larger changes, as a way of preparing the board and others, such that when changes need to be made, they will not seem to come out of the blue. They will have prepared their constituents for change one step at a time (Herman & Heimovics, 2005, pp. 160–161).

Use the "Political Frame"

In their insightful and practical research on nonprofit executives, Herman and Heimovics (2005) find that the effective CEOs are distinguished from others by their use of a "political frame." Indeed, they say this is a finding of their research in which they have particular confidence. The concept of frames was developed by Bolman and Deal (2003). A frame is a perspective or a way of seeing and understanding things—like seeing the glass either half empty or half full.

By referring to nonprofit CEOs using a political frame, Herman and Heimovics (2005) do not mean that they see things in terms of partisan or elective politics but rather that they recognize the inevitable interplay among the organization's important constituencies. The political frame is a perspective through which the CEO sees and understands the environment in terms of the pressures brought by various constituencies that compete, bargain, and negotiate over the allocation of resources. Leaders using this frame will be sensitive to external forces that might affect the organization and, therefore, devote their time and effort to maintaining relationships and influencing various competing constituencies.

Right Person, Right Place, Right Time

In a book focused on leadership in the nonprofit sector, but with more generic applications as well, Dym and Hutson (2005) argue that nonprofit executive effectiveness results from having the right person in the right job at the right time; in other words, it is necessary to have a good fit between the leader and the needs of the organization at the time.

They propose an *alignment model* that seeks to integrate the major leadership theories, that is, to provide "an overarching conceptual framework that brings the theories together, or at least describes how the theories relate to one another" (Dym & Hutson, 2005, p. 36). The leader's fit with the organization involves traits as well as skills, leadership style as well as situation. In other words, there is no one right theory, but all have relevance in the context of the right time and place. Invoking many of the major leadership theories in one paragraph to describe their concepts of fit and alignment, they write,

> If one were to align a leader who is determined and communicates well and whose personality and behavior (style) fit well with the organizational culture, who understands how to structure the organization's future and light up the pathway to success, who communicates frequently with direct reports and makes staff followers feel supported and understood, and who holds high standards in a way that is sensitive to both individual and group psychological needs—if someone were to see such alignment, what would be witnessed is effective leadership." (p. 345)

Dym and Hutson (2005) provide an *alignment map* (see Table 4.2), summarizing the components on which they say alignment must be achieved. It encompasses the characteristics of the individual as well as characteristics of the organization and of the community or market that the organization serves. All three must be aligned to produce a perfect fit. Thus, for example, a charismatic leader with an extroverted personality might be a good fit for an advocacy organization that is working to gain public awareness and change public policy, but such an individual might not be a good fit as a director of a museum, university, or think tank, where a more collegial, participative style might be more readily accepted. An executive director who does not speak Spanish and has little understanding of Hispanic/Latino culture might not be a good fit as the executive director of an organization that serves primarily Hispanic/Latino clients. A leader who comes from the business world—or even from a different type of nonprofit organization—might find it difficult to be effective in a nonprofit organization that has an established culture different from that with which he or she is familiar. An organization that encourages self-empowerment among its clients would not be aligned with its mission if its own leadership behaved in autocratic ways. In other words, for a CEO to be effective, his or her traits, styles, skills, and values need to be in sync with the organization and its constituencies. Too much dissonance may diminish the CEO's ability to lead or even, in the case of a bad fit, result in his or her eventual departure.

According to Dym and Hutson (2005), alignment is a two-way process that involves the leader and the nonprofit itself: "Leaders must therefore align themselves to organizations by adapting themselves to the organization's structure, process, culture, and strategy—and by aligning the organization's to fit their style. Both processes are necessary for effective

TABLE 4.2   Dym and Hutson's Alignment Map

	Leader	*Organization*	*Comn*
Basic nature	Character and style	Organizational type	Patterns and norms
Underlying principles	Personal values	Organizational culture	Larger culture
Means available	Individual skills	Organizational resources	Economy and industry
Purpose and direction	Personal objectives	Mission and strategy	Community needs and market demands

Source: Dym and Hutson (2005, p. 93).

leadership" (p. 100). But, they advise, alignment should not be perfect and some tension is desirable. "A fit that is too perfect leads to stagnation. . . . Close but imperfect fit combines the smooth functioning we associate with efficiency and effectiveness with the flexible adjustment to change we associate with creativity" (p. 67).

FOUNDER SYNDROME

As Dym and Hutson discuss, one leadership style may be appropriate at one point in an organization's history and another at a different time. The idea that the organization's need for leadership might change over time derives from *life-cycle theories* of nonprofit organization development, which describe specific stages through which organizations naturally evolve.

For example, charismatic leaders are often seen leading an organization in its early stages, where the vision and inspiration of a committed founder drive volunteers and early-generation staff members to exceptional effort. However, as the organization matures, it may require a different kind of leader—one "who feels comfortable in and supported enough by the stable organization to begin to implement long-term growth projects" (Dym & Hutson, 2005, p. 89). In other words, as the organization grows, adds staff, develops systems, and expands its programs, there will be an increased need for professional management, and the charisma of the founder may no longer suffice. (We will discuss organization life cycles in more detail in Chapter 6.)

There are many examples of nonprofit organizations founded by visionary and charismatic individuals, who may become the first executive directors. The founder attracts and inspires dedicated and loyal volunteers, donors, and staff. The board may consist of individuals recruited by the founder, who generally acquiesce to his or her authority and charisma. But at some point, as the organization grows and its needs for professional management, formal systems, and a more deliberate approach increase, the founder may not possess the required management skills or may be unable to adjust his or her vision of the organization to the new reality. He or she may prefer the entrepreneurial culture of the early organization.

The founder is likely to have a deep dedication to the organization and the cause—it may be his or her life and he or she may expect staff to make similar personal sacrifices. Founders often have task-oriented styles and are described as "difficult" and "demanding" by their subordinates. Like a controlling parent, the founder may have become accustomed to making all the decisions and may resist any initiative from the board or staff to be more independent. That style may work in the early days when the staff and board comprise a small number of loyal followers who share the founder's enthusiasm, but it may become less tolerated as the organization comes to require a larger staff of technical specialists and professional managers. Passion no longer becomes an adequate substitute for rational decision making.

But the founder's psychological identification with the organization—after all, it's his or her baby—may make it impossible for him or her to accept a more democratic, team approach. The situation becomes more stressful as staff turnover increases, management errors begin to mount, systems spin out of control, and the board feels increasingly torn between its loyalty to the founder and its responsibility to the organization. The board may begin to add more outsiders, people who are not personally selected by the founder and who bring more professional skills. These outsiders have less loyalty to the founder, and the balance begins to shift, increasing tension between the founder/executive director and the board: The organization is suffering from what is commonly called *founder syndrome.*

The arrival of founder syndrome in the life of the organization poses a challenge, even a crisis. Eventually, some crisis or event may trigger an explosion, resulting in the dismissal of the founder. Board members and staff loyal to the founder may leave amid bitterness while others scramble to save the organization. Often the founder will be replaced by a professional manager, who then faces the challenge of rebuilding and developing new relationships. Or if the crisis is not resolved, the founder's departure may precipitate the organization's decline into turmoil and eventual death. Dym and Hutson portray the ugly scene:

> There is a declining certainty about the organization's original purpose. People wonder whether they were naïve to think they could accomplish so much in the first place. They question whether they can survive without being more realistic about their goals, their methods, and the people they trust. As doubt creeps in, people grow more conservative, more cautious. They see problems where before they mainly saw solutions. They begin to invest less of themselves—their hopes and dreams, their willingness to risk, and their time. Or they begin a somewhat frenzied and exhausting alternation of investing more and less. (Dym & Hutson, 2005, p. 118)

If the transition from the founder to a professional manager is traumatic and risky for the organization, following the founder also can be a challenging assignment for the new CEO. It may be that the board, perhaps feeling guilty over their dismissal of the founder as executive director, has allowed him or her to remain as a member of the board—an unfortunate decision that may provide a platform for the founder to criticize and undermine the new executive. In other cases, the founder may be retained as a consultant or perhaps in an honorific position to engage in fundraising and other external tasks. But, under these arrangements, unless the founder has exceptional wisdom and grace and the new executive shows unusual understanding and sensitivity, the situation is likely to remain volatile for some time, continuing to burden the organization and distract it from pursuit of its mission.

Of course, there are enlightened and wise founders, who recognize their own limitations and their organization's changing needs. In this situation, founder syndrome really does not exist, since there are many options for providing both the leadership and management that the organization requires. For example, the founder may take on more of an external role, delegating much of the day-to-day management to others, perhaps an associate director, chief operating officer, or executive vice president. But, in such a scenario, it is also essential for the founder to avoid end runs around the new operating officer by staff who may have been hired by the founder and instead support and reinforce the operating officer's authority and control.

EXECUTIVE TRANSITIONS

Every nonprofit will eventually face the need to replace its CEO. Sometimes the need is first recognized by the board, and the current CEO needs to be persuaded—or forced—to step down. As we have discussed, this can be especially difficult when the chief executive is a charismatic founder of the organization; but the involuntary departure of any CEO is always a difficult and potentially wrenching experience for an organization. In other situations, the CEO may initiate the change. This may occur for several reasons. The CEO may receive a better offer from another organization or perhaps just feel burned out and want a change of scene. For some CEOs, there comes a point when they feel that their major goals for the organization have been accomplished and that it is just time to move on to something new. This may occur at the completion of some major effort, for example, a successful fundraising campaign, or on reaching some milestone, such as 10 years of service (Weisman & Goldbaum, 2004, p. 11) There is a difference, of course, between an anticipated departure, such as retirement, and one that comes as a surprise, possibly because the CEO receives an unanticipated job offer that is just too good to turn down. In the first instance, the board may have time to prepare for the transition; in the second, some boards may be caught unprepared to make one of the most critical decisions they will ever face.

In business corporations, it is not unusual for chief executives to come up through the ranks. They are often individuals who have worked in the company for a long time, are steeped in its culture, and are knowledgeable about its products and markets. Indeed, as a corporate executive approaches retirement, it is not unusual for there to be an heir apparent, who has been groomed for the top position over years.

Boards work in the same way with regard to their own membership; bylaws often include limits on how long the board chair can serve, and thus, the transition in leadership is predictable and planned. There is often a vice chair of the board or even a chair elect, who is well prepared to take over the job in a smooth transition. But nonprofit CEOs are more often than not recruited from outside the organization. This is often because the organization is thinly staffed and tightly budgeted and cannot afford the luxury of a number-two executive with the capability to be the CEO (Wolf, 1999, p. 338). The lack of an internal candidate for the chief executive position might also exist if the organization is still led by a founder, who may not have provided others with the opportunity to learn and grow sufficiently to be prepared for leadership. Thus, non-profits may be faced with the need to appoint as CEO an individual who is a virtual stranger—not someone whom they have known or have had the opportunity to get to know in more junior positions before advancing him or her to the top office. In these circumstances, the selection of a new CEO may carry some risk that the wrong person will be selected, with potentially serious consequences for the effectiveness and stability of the organization.

There is a growing literature concerning executive transition planning, and a growing number of nonprofits are preparing for the eventuality even before the CEO's departure is foreseen or imminent. Internal preparation is a shared responsibility of the board and the CEO. If the organization is large enough to have staff members capable of eventually filling the CEO position, the CEO can intentionally prepare those individuals by including them in important meetings and decisions, providing them with opportunities for additional professional training, giving them assignments with responsibility that can help develop their leadership skills, and exposing them to the board so that they will know the board and the board will know them (Weisman & Goldbaum, 2004). This requires, of course, a confident CEO with a participative style of leadership and a genuine commitment to the organization even beyond his or her own tenure as its leader.

In small organizations, there may be no internal candidate believed capable of rising to the CEO position within any reasonable period of time. But, the CEO can still prepare for the possibility of a transition whether planned or unexpected, by developing systems, documenting policies and procedures, and sharing responsibility with others in a way that will make it possible for a successor, or perhaps an interim director, to maintain the organization's activities with minimum disruption. Boards are advised to ensure that such internal planning is occurring and also to remain aware of leaders in other similar organizations whom they might try to recruit should the need arise (Weisman & Goldbaum, 2004).

The need for transition planning goes well below the level of the CEO. Other staff members, for example, program directors or even key volunteers, may need to be replaced and there may not always be advanced warning. Again, communication, documentation, and cross-training of staff in the responsibilities of each other's jobs can minimize disruption during the period of transition after someone leaves the organization.

Most nonprofits continue to appoint their chief executives from outside and conduct searches to identify and select their new executive leaders. A full discussion of the search process is beyond the scope of this text, but many excellent resources are available, through BoardSource, CompassPoint (www.compasspoint.org), and other organizations, describing how to conduct an effective search. As competition for management talent has intensified, professional executive search firms also have come to play a larger role.

The search for a new CEO must be rooted in the organization's own understanding of itself—its mission, its values, its vision, and its goals. The process cannot be rushed, and it is often about far more than just finding someone qualified for the job. To define who may be the right person in the right place at the right time, the organization must have a clear understanding of its past, its purpose, its constituencies, and its aspirations.

CHAPTER SUMMARY

The position of CEO in a nonprofit organization is different from similar positions in government or the business sector, for reasons that relate to the distinctive nature of non-profit organizations themselves. While every organization, regardless of sector, requires capable management to be effective, nonprofits especially need CEOs who can exercise strong leadership. This is true because they are organizations based on values and driven by their missions, which mobilize commitment and support by appealing to a shared vision.

Theorists have defined leadership in terms of individual qualities, skills that leaders possess, and behaviors that successful leaders exhibit. However, contemporary theories recognize that effective leadership may be contingent or situational; that is, it may depend on the circumstances, including human relationships, the nature of the task, and the formal position of the executive.

James MacGregor Burns (1978) offered a definition of transactional leadership that sounds very much like management. The transactional leader rewards or punishes others in exchange for the work that they perform and emphasizes rules, policies, and procedures to ensure that things are done right. Burns introduced the concept of transformational leader-ship, in which the leader enables individuals to experience their own moral and motivational growth by appealing to values that they share with the organization. This text suggests that transformational leadership may be especially appropriate in organizations that often attract the participation of people motivated by commitment to their values-based missions. The concept of charismatic leadership is often observed in the founders of nonprofit organiza-tions. They are individuals who inspire others to extraordinary effort through the model of their own commitment and their articulation of a vision, among other behaviors.

Various scholars and practitioners have tried to define the effective nonprofit CEO. Some reflect trait theories or skills theories of leadership, while others have described the behav-iors of effective chief executives. The behaviors most often identified involve the CEO's focusing his or her attention on the mission, the board, external relationships, and a few key priorities while understanding the political reality of competition among constituencies for the organization's resources. A framework offered by Dym and Hutson (2005) seeks to integrate various leadership theories and describe how effective leadership arises when the individual, the organization, and its community or market are aligned—in other words, when the right person serves in the right place at the right time.

Some organizations will face a significant challenge when a founding CEO leaves the organization, either voluntarily or through a forced transition. Chief executive transitions in general have received greater attention in the recent literature of nonprofit management. Organizations and their boards are encouraged to prepare and plan for changes in execu-tive leadership and to base the search for a new CEO firmly in the organization's mission, values, vision, goals, and aspirations.

NOTE

1. Although somewhat different and often presented separately in other texts, *situational theories* and *contingency theories* of leadership have in common the idea that there is no one right style of leadership that can be successful in all organizations or under all circumstances. This book just uses the term *contingency theory* to encompass that concept.

KEY TERMS AND CONCEPTS FROM CHAPTER 4

alignment map

behavior and style theories

Blake and Mouton managerial grid

charismatic leadership

contingency theories

employee orientation

executive leadership

founder syndrome

leadership

legislative leadership

management

production orientation

relationship behaviors

skills theories

situational theories

succession planning

task behaviors

trait theories

transactional leadership

transition planning

transformational leadership

CASE 4.1

A Change in Leadership at Habitat for Humanity

Habitat for Humanity International is an ecumenical, faith-based nonprofit dedicated to eliminating substandard housing and homelessness. Habitat constructs houses with the assistance of volunteers and partner families, who then purchase the homes with affordable loans. It has built more than 200,000 homes housing more than 1,000,000 people in 3,000 communities around the world (Habitat for Humanity International, 2005). Habitat has been hailed as one of the most successful nonprofits of the past 30 years and "one of the most dramatic examples of social entrepreneurship . . . that blends commercial and social methods to generate much of the cash, labor, and materials needed to construct its programs" (Dees et al., 2001, p. 12).

Habitat was founded in 1976 by Millard Fuller, who led the organization as its CEO for many years. Fuller had acquired wealth before the age of 30 and then dedicated himself to a life of service. While he was the CEO of Habitat, Fuller accepted an annual salary of only $15,000, declined raises, and lived for 23 years in a modest house without air-conditioning (Bixler, 2005). Fuller was widely praised as a visionary, and his commitment attracted volunteers and donors to Habitat, including former President Jimmy Carter, who became one of the organization's most prominent advocates.

But by the early 2000s, issues began to arise between Mr. Fuller and Habitat's board. As Fuller approached 70 in 2004, he sought to extend his service as CEO until 2005, when Habitat would complete its 200,000th house. But the board began to plan for transition and appointed a former board chairman as Managing Director. Although Fuller retained the title of President and Chief Executive Officer, he was said to have complained that the board's decision forced him into a figurehead role (Pierce, 2004).

The board had received a specific complaint about an incident involving Fuller and a Habitat employee and conducted an investigation. Although the board found insufficient proof of wrongdoing, the process brought to the surface other issues that had been developing over a period of years (Jensen, 2005). One board member observed that a gradual change had occurred in the composition of the board, saying, "There was a movement to start engaging board members who had some 'juice'—people who were powerful in different fields and were well connected." The changing board became critical of Fuller for undertaking some projects without its approval (Pierce, 2004) and Fuller became critical of the board, saying, "I've always seen Habitat for Humanity as a movement. . . . There's a certain mentality on the board now that wants to change it into an organizational bureaucracy" (Jensen, 2005).

In January of 2005, the board fired Fuller and his wife, who also had held a position at Habitat, and appointed an interim CEO. The interim CEO explained the situation saying, "The strength of vision and ego that was so important for the beginning and initial growth of Habitat are not what we need today to provide the structure for what has become a large, far-flung operation" (Jewell, 2005, p. 24). Fuller spoke out against the board's action, saying trustees were not committed to the faith-based nature of Habitat and just wanted to replace him with a "high paid bean counter" (Jewell, 2005, p. 24).

Some Habitat for Humanity affiliates, volunteers, and donors spoke out in opposition to the board's action and in support of Fuller. Fuller created a new organization, which he called "Building Habitat," but he later changed its name to the Fuller Center for Housing after Habitat for Humanity filed suit alleging infringement of its trademark (Wilhelm, 2005). Habitat for Humanity undertook a search for a new CEO and eventually hired Jonathon Reckford, a former businessman with Goldman Sachs and Best Buy. Reckford met with Fuller. Afterward, Fuller said, "I was not prepared to like the guy, but I did" (Wilhelm, 2005).

Reckford committed the organization to continued growth but said that it needed to "build the platform" for that growth and determine the right organizational structure and ways of maximizing effectiveness (Wilhelm, 2005). Fuller continued to voice opinions about Habitat's directions. Reacting to the possibility that Habitat might move its headquarters to Atlanta from Americus, Georgia, where Fuller had founded it, he said, "I'm astounded they would even consider it."

Reflecting on the controversy that had surrounded the transition in leadership from Habitat's founder, one nonprofit scholar observed, "Habitat for Humanity is much bigger than one man, and that speaks of Mr. Fuller's success" (Minor, 2005).

Sources: Habitat for Humanity International (2005), Bixler (2005), Dees et al. (2001), Jensen (2005), Pierce (2004), Minor (2005), Wilhelm (2005), and Jewell (2005).

QUESTIONS FOR DISCUSSION

1. Which theory or theories seem to best describe the career of Millard Fuller at Habitat for Humanity? Of what is the story of his departure an example?

2. Are leaders born or made? Can anyone learn to be a leader, or does it require some innate qualities or characteristics of the individual?

3. Could one individual be a great leader in government, a corporation, or a nonprofit? Why or why not?

4. Is leadership necessarily moral? Was Hitler a leader even though he was evil?

5. Who are some contemporary leaders that you would identify as charismatic? How do they exhibit the behaviors of charismatic leaders identified in this chapter?

SUGGESTIONS FOR FURTHER READING RELATED TO CHAPTER 4

Books

Burns, J. M. (1978). *Leadership*. New York: HarperCollins.

Carlson, M., & Donohoe, M. (2003). *The executive director's survival guide: Thriving as a nonprofit leader.* San Francisco: Jossey-Bass.

Collins, J. (2005). *Good to great and the social sectors* [Monograph]. (www.jimcollins.com, www .amazon.com/s/ref = nb_ss_gw?url = search-alias % 3Daps&field-keywords = jim + collins)

Dym, B., & Hutson, H. (2005). *Leadership in nonprofit organizations.* Thousand Oaks, CA: Sage.

Nanus, B., & Dobbs, S. M. (1999). *Leaders who make a difference: Essential strategies for meeting the nonprofit challenge.* San Francisco: Jossey-Bass.

Northouse, P. G. (2007). *Leadership: Theory and practice* (4th ed.). Thousand Oaks, CA: Sage.

Weisman, C., & Goldbaum, R. I. (2004). *Losing your executive director without losing your way.* San Francisco: Jossey-Bass.

Web Sites

Center for Creative Leadership, www.ccl.org/leadership/index.aspx

Leader to Leader Institute, www.pfdf.org

PART III

Managing the Nonprofit Organization

Accountability and Performance Measurement

Nonprofit organizations enjoy considerable autonomy in defining their missions, setting their own goals, and crafting their own strategies for achieving those goals. They are private organizations. But they are granted charters to serve purposes that society has deemed to be of public benefit. The organizations are exempt from taxation, and donors are permitted deductions for gifts made to charitable nonprofits to further those purposes. Tax exemption and the tax deductibility of gifts represent foregone government revenue and therefore are regarded by many as a form of tax subsidy; in other words, to some extent, nonprofits are working with the public's money. That gives society an interest in ensuring that they are *accountable* for their use of the resources entrusted to them and that those resources are indeed being directed toward the pursuit of their social missions. But what exactly is society entitled to expect?

The question is a little like asking, "What is a good student?" Does one qualify just by attending all classes, turning in papers on time, and showing up for exams—that is, by not breaking any of the rules of the course? Or is a good student someone who studies hard and seeks help from the professor when something is not clear—in other words, someone who shows exemplary student behavior? Does being a good student require earning good grades? Do grades accurately reflect what a student may have gained from a course, or is it possible that a better measure would be to compare what he or she knew at the beginning of a course with what he or she knew at the end, maybe basing the label of "good student" on some measure of "value added"? As we will see in this chapter, similar questions arise when we consider ideas such as the accountability, effectiveness, and performance of nonprofit organizations.

DEFINING AND ENSURING ACCOUNTABILITY

To be accountable essentially means being required to answer, to take responsibility, for one's actions. But for what, and to whom, should nonprofit organizations be required to account?

Perhaps the narrowest concept of accountability would require merely following the law—for example, obeying the nondistribution requirement, avoiding conflicts of interest, treating staff without discrimination, and filing IRS (Internal Revenue Service) reports as required. But that might seem to be a minimal standard to expect. Perhaps we might look for something more—not just following the law but also going beyond the requirements of law to follow best practices in governing and managing the organization, in other words, doing the right things as well as not doing things that are wrong.

But does even a definition of accountability that expects nonprofits to do the right things really go far enough? For example, the board may meet regularly, the budget may be invariably balanced, the staff may be happy and motivated, and there may be a written strategic plan. But that does not ensure that clients are recovering, the symphony is achieving artistic excellence, or public attitudes on the environment are being changed. Thus, perhaps accountability needs to include more than just avoiding transgressions and exhibiting model behavior. It may need to encompass demonstrated effectiveness in achieving the purposes for which the nonprofit exists. That requires not only that the resources entrusted to the nonprofit not be misused but also that they be used to maximum benefit in pursuing the organization's mission. As we will see, however, this component of accountability turns out to be the most complex, since there is not always consensus on how results should be measured, or even on how they should be defined.

Concern about the accountability of nonprofit organizations has a long history. As early as 1918, the National Charities Information Bureau was created to educate the public about nonprofit organization behavior in order to reduce the incidence of charity fraud. But concern about accountability became heightened in the 1980s and 1990s. The widely publicized misuse of United Way funds by the then president, William Aramony, for which he was convicted and served jail time, shocked the nation. Again after September 11, 2001, accusations that some charity fundraising appeals were misleading and questions about the use of the funds given to help victims of the terrorist attacks further undermined the public's confidence in the integrity of the sector. The misdeeds of management at Enron, WorldCom, and Tyco exacerbated concern about corruption and fraud throughout American society. By the mid-2000s, the U.S. Congress had turned its attention from corporate scandals to the nonprofit sector, and the national spotlight was focused on the need to make nonprofits more accountable.

Mechanisms For Accountability

There are three principal mechanisms by which nonprofits are held accountable: the rule of *law*, *self-regulation*, and *transparency*—that is, holding nonprofit behavior up in clear view for donors, the media, and others to see. Let's take a look at what is currently in place in these three arenas.

Requirements of Law

Chapters 2 and 3 covered some of the legal requirements facing nonprofits, but let's review some key points. Nonprofits must comply with laws at both state and federal levels. State governments grant nonprofits their charters, and state attorneys general and state courts have the authority to take action against law-breaking nonprofits. This can include the removal of board members who violate their fiduciary responsibilities and possibly even revoking of the organization's charter. Most states also have laws regulating the behavior of nonprofits in specific areas—for example, requiring that they be registered in order to solicit gifts from the general public.

At the federal level, regulation of nonprofits is carried out primarily by the IRS's Division on Tax-Exempt and Government Entities. IRS has the authority to impose intermediate sanctions and to revoke an organization's tax exemption, eliminating its ability to raise tax-deductible gifts. Nonprofits that receive federal funds above certain amounts are also subject to additional rules with regard to their use of the federal dollars. Organizations with revenues greater than $25,000 (except religious congregations) are required to file an annual Form 990, 990-EZ, or 990-PF with the IRS. Form 990 provides a summary of an organization's financial and program data, and it is selectively audited by the IRS. In 2007, the IRS released for comment a draft of a revised Form 990 that would make it an even more effective vehicle for increased transparency. The proposed new Form 990 includes questions related to governance as well as finances and programs. Beginning in 2008, small nonprofits that are not required to file Form 990 will however be required to electronically file Form 990-N, also known as the *e-Postcard* (www.irs.gov).

In 2002, Congress passed the Sarbanes-Oxley Act, responding to corporate governance scandals. While Sarbanes-Oxley (or "SOX," as it is commonly called) pertains primarily to publicly traded corporations, two of its provisions—those regarding protection for whistleblowers and destruction of documents—also apply to nonprofit organizations. Some states, including California, have passed legislation directed at nonprofits that essentially incorporates Sarbanes-Oxley-type requirements (Nonprofit Integrity Act, 2004). Many nonprofits, especially larger organizations, have voluntarily adopted Sarbanes-Oxley provisions as a way to assure their donors that they are operating with high integrity, transparency, and sound governance. Even though most aspects of Sarbanes-Oxley do not apply to nonprofits, it has nevertheless established standards against which nonprofits are often judged today.

In 2004, concern about nonprofit accountability prompted the Finance Committee of the U.S. Senate to hold hearings and consider proposals for significantly increased regulation of the nonprofit sector at the national level. At the committee's request, Independent Sector formed a Panel on the Nonprofit Sector to develop recommendations. The Panel's report was presented to the Congress in June 2005; it suggested increased enforcement of existing state and federal law, increased reporting by nonprofits, and some additional legislation. But its emphasis was on the importance of maintaining the sector's independence and on its capacity for self-regulation (Independent Sector, 2005). The Panel on the Nonprofit Sector continued its work into 2007, focusing on the development of principles for good governance and ethical conduct. Students are encouraged to seek updated information to learn what changes may have occurred since this book was written.

While much of the legislation proposed in 2005 was not passed into law that year, there is likely to be continued debate and discussion about the need for more federal action, and the subject of nonprofit accountability is unlikely to disappear from the policy agenda. The Independent Sector Web site is an excellent resource on the status of public policy issues related to the sector. It also provides detailed information on the implications of Sarbanes-Oxley for the governance of nonprofit organizations (www.independentsector.org).

Self-Regulation: Standards and Accreditation

If the nonprofit sector would prefer not to be burdened by increased government regulation, then the alternative is to develop more effective mechanisms for self-regulation. There is a long history on which to draw, especially within the fields of education and health care. Educational and health care institutions long have been self-regulating through the process of *accreditation*. Schools and colleges are accredited through regional associations, through which the institutions establish voluntary standards. Individual institutions engage in self-studies according to a process defined by the accrediting body and are evaluated through intensive visits by teams from peer institutions. Professional schools within universities have separate accrediting mechanisms; for example, law schools are accredited by the American Bar Association and business schools by the Association to Advance Collegiate Schools of Business. Health care organizations, including hospitals, nursing homes, health care networks, and other service providers are accredited by the Joint Commission on Accreditation of Healthcare Organizations, itself a nonprofit organization.

Although educational accreditation is voluntary, accrediting bodies are recognized by the U.S. Department of Education, and accreditation is required in order to be eligible for certain government funds. Likewise, accreditation of health care organizations is voluntary, but the power of government creates a significant incentive, since status as an accredited health care provider is required in order to be eligible to receive certain government reimbursements, an essential source of revenue for many organizations.

In the broader nonprofit sector, the accreditation of organizations is a relatively recent concept, having its origins in the development of accountability standards and definitions of best practices by state associations of nonprofits and others. As one example, the Maryland Association of Nonprofit Organizations (2006) developed Standards for Excellence in nonprofit management that are well regarded and have become a model for other state associations across the country. The Maryland standards are based on 8 guiding principles and 54 standards related to these principles. The guiding principles are presented under the categories of mission and program, governing body, conflict of interest, human resources (including both volunteers and staff), financial and legal, openness (or transparency), fundraising, and public affairs and public policy (including public education and public policy advocacy). The standards essentially describe recommended best practices—that is, a set of guides for behavior that reflect a consensus about how a well-managed and accountable nonprofit should operate.

Like other state associations, Maryland offers a voluntary certification program to organizations that wish to demonstrate their adherence to its Standards for Excellence. Similar to the accreditation process in educational and health care institutions, the process requires that the organization complete a lengthy application, pay a fee, and be approved by a team of trained peer reviewers. Organizations that successfully complete the process are entitled to use of a Standards for Excellence Seal, a kind of "Good Housekeeping Seal" of approval, in their solicitations and other materials (Maryland Association of Nonprofit Organizations, 2006).

State nonprofit association standards are hardly the only ones available. Indeed, a compendium of standards, codes, and principles developed by Independent Sector encompasses over 100 sources. Not all include an accreditation or certification process. Most have few mechanisms for enforcement beyond the power of negative publicity, but many have gained wide visibility and are frequently cited. Independent Sector's compendium includes some standards intended to apply to all nonprofit organizations. Others have been developed specifically for organizations within a particular subsector, including education, health, and human services. There are also standards developed by organizations for internal use, to guide the actions of their own boards, staff, and volunteers. In addition, Independent Sector identifies standards or codes that apply to grantmaking foundations and that govern the behavior of individual professionals working within the nonprofit sector (e.g., fundraisers). Other standards specifically address fundraising and cause marketing practices and the rights of donors. And the list is not confined to the United States; it includes codes of conduct applicable to nonprofit organizations in Canada, Australia, Colombia, and the Czech Republic, among other nations (Independent Sector, 2006). For a nonprofit seeking guidance on what constitutes best practice, there is no shortage of resources; but the proliferation of standards also means that there remains no single definition of what constitutes an excellent organization.

Charity Watchdogs and Raters

Nonprofits may find it in their own best interest to voluntarily comply with some set of standards or codes of behavior and seek accreditation from a recognized organization. But there is an increasingly influential array of charity watchdog organizations or charity raters that proactively examine nonprofit organizations, applying their own standards, with or without the cooperation of the organizations they evaluate. They are an important force in creating increased transparency, but they are also often controversial.

For example, among the best known may be the ratings of colleges and universities and hospitals by popular magazines, notably *U.S. News & World Report*, which have been shown to influence students' choices about where to attend college and patients' decisions about where to receive medical care. Such ratings surely do not have the force of law, but they are powerful. A negative ranking poses a significant potential threat to an organization, since publicity may deter potential customers, chill giving, or even invite scrutiny from government.

One well-known charity rater that operates at the national level is the Better Business Bureau (BBB) Wise Giving Alliance. Formed in 2001 through a merger of the National Charities Information Bureau and the Better Business Bureau's Philanthropic Advisory Service, the Wise Giving Alliance focuses its attention on the largest nonprofits in the United States. The BBB undertakes investigations of an organization based on complaints or inquiries from the public (in the long-established tradition of consumers reporting businesses to the BBB.) While it does not rate organizations, it does report whether they meet or do not meet its various standards, which are included in Box 5.1.

(Text continues on page 124)

BOX 5.1   Better Business Bureau Wise Giving Alliance Standards for Charity Accountability

PREFACE

The BBB Wise Giving Alliance Standards for Charity Accountability were developed to assist donors in making sound giving decisions and to foster public confidence in charitable organizations. The standards seek to encourage fair and honest solicitation practices, to promote ethical conduct by charitable organizations and to advance support of philanthropy.

These standards replace the separate standards of the National Charities Information Bureau and the Council of Better Business Bureaus' Foundation and its Philanthropic Advisory Service that were in place at the time the organizations merged.

The Standards for Charity Accountability were developed with professional and technical assistance from representatives of small and large charitable organizations, the accounting profession, grant making foundations, corporate contributions officers, regulatory agencies, research organizations and the Better Business Bureau system. The BBB Wise Giving Alliance also commissioned significant independent research on donor expectations to ensure that the views of the general public were reflected in the standards.

The generous support of the Charles Stewart Mott Foundation, the Surdna Foundation, and Sony Corporation of America helped underwrite the development of these standards and related research.

Organizations that comply with these accountability standards have provided documentation that they meet basic standards:

- In how they govern their organization,
- In the ways they spend their money,
- In the truthfulness of their representations, and
- In their willingness to disclose basic information to the public.

These standards apply to publicly soliciting organizations that are tax exempt under section 501(c)(3) of the Internal Revenue Code and to other organizations conducting charitable solicitations. The standards are not intended to apply to private foundations, as they do not solicit contributions from the public.

The overarching principle of the BBB Wise Giving Alliance Standards for Charity Accountability is full disclosure to donors and potential donors at the time of solicitation and thereafter.

However, where indicated, the standards recommend ethical practices beyond the act of disclosure in order to ensure public confidence and encourage giving. As voluntary standards, they also go beyond the requirements of local, state, and federal laws and regulations.

In addition to the specific areas addressed in the standards, the BBB Wise Giving Alliance encourages charitable organizations to adopt the following management practices to further the cause of charitable accountability.

- Initiate a policy promoting pluralism and diversity within the organization's board, staff, and constituencies. While organizations vary widely in their ability to demonstrate pluralism and diversity, every organization should establish a policy, consistent with its mission statement, that fosters such inclusiveness.
- Ensure adherence to all applicable local, state, and federal laws and regulations including submission of financial information.
- Maintain an organizational adherence to the specific standards cited below. The BBB Wise Giving Alliance also encourages charities to maintain an organizational commitment to accountability that transcends specific standards and places a priority on openness and ethical behavior in the charity's programs and activities.

STANDARDS FOR CHARITABLE ACCOUNTABILITY

Governance and Oversight

The governing board has the ultimate oversight authority for any charitable organization. This section of the standards seeks to ensure that the volunteer board is active, independent and free of self-dealing. To meet these standards, the organization shall have:

1. A board of directors that provides adequate oversight of the charity's operations and its staff. Indication of adequate oversight includes, but is not limited to, regularly scheduled appraisals of the CEO's performance, evidence of disbursement controls such as board approval of the budget, fundraising practices, establishment of a conflict of interest policy, and establishment of accounting procedures sufficient to safeguard charity finances.

2. A board of directors with a minimum of five voting members.

3. A minimum of three evenly spaced meetings per year of the full governing body with a majority in attendance, with face-to-face participation. **A conference call of the full board can substitute for one of the three meetings of the governing body. For all meetings, alternative modes of participation are acceptable for those with physical disabilities.**

4. Not more than one or 10% (whichever is greater) directly or indirectly compensated person(s) serving as voting member(s) of the board. **Compensated members shall not serve as the board's chair or treasurer.**

5. No transaction(s) in which any board or staff members have material conflicting interests with the charity resulting from any relationship or business affiliation. **Factors that will be considered when concluding whether or not a related party transaction constitutes a conflict of interest and if such a conflict is material, include, but are not limited to: any arm's length procedures established by the charity; the size of the transaction relative to like expenses of the charity; whether the interested party participated in the board vote on the transaction; if competitive bids were sought and whether the transaction is one-time, recurring, or ongoing.**

(Continued)

(Continued)

Measuring Effectiveness

An organization should regularly assess its effectiveness in achieving its mission. This section seeks to ensure that an organization has defined, measurable goals and objectives in place and a defined process in place to evaluate the success and impact of its program(s) in fulfilling the goals and objectives of the organization and that also identifies ways to address any deficiencies. To meet these standards, a charitable organization shall:

6. Have a board policy of assessing, no less than every two years, the organization's performance and effectiveness and of determining future actions required to achieve its mission.

7. Submit to the organization's governing body, for its approval, a written report that outlines the results of the aforementioned performance and effectiveness assessment and recommendations for future actions.

FINANCES

This section of the standards seeks to ensure that the charity spends its funds honestly, prudently and in accordance with statements made in fundraising appeals. To meet these standards, the charitable organization shall:
Please note that standards 8 and 9 have different denominators.

8. Spend at least 65% of its total expenses on program activities.

Formula for Standard 8:

Total Program Service Expenses ÷ Total Expenses [should be at least 65%]

9. Spend no more than 35% of related contributions on fundraising. Related contributions include donations, legacies, and other gifts received as a result of fundraising efforts.

Formula for Standard 9:

Total Fundraising Expenses ÷ Total Related Contributions [should be no more than 35%]

10. Avoid accumulating funds that could be used for current program activities. **To meet this standard, the charity's unrestricted net assets available for use should not be more than three times the size of the past year's expenses or three times the size of the current year's budget, whichever is higher.**

An organization that does not meet Standards 8, 9 and/or 10 may provide evidence to demonstrate that its use of funds is reasonable. The higher fundraising and administrative costs of a newly created organization, donor restrictions on the use of funds, exceptional bequests, a stigma associated with a cause and environmental or political events beyond an organization's control are among factors which may result in expenditures that are reasonable although they do not meet the financial measures cited in these standards.

11. Make available to all, on request, complete annual financial statements prepared in accordance with generally accepted accounting principles. When total annual gross income exceeds $250,000, these statements should be audited in accordance with generally accepted auditing standards. For charities whose annual gross income is less than $250,000, a review by a certified

public accountant is sufficient to meet this standard. For charities whose annual gross income is less than $100,000, an internally produced, complete financial statement is sufficient to meet this standard.

12.   Include in the financial statements a breakdown of expenses (e.g., salaries, travel, postage, etc.) that shows what portion of these expenses was allocated to program, fundraising, and administrative activities. If the charity has more than one major program category, the schedule should provide a breakdown for each category.

13.   Accurately report the charity's expenses, including any joint cost allocations, in its financial statements. For example, audited or unaudited statements which inaccurately claim zero fundraising expenses or otherwise understate the amount a charity spends on fundraising, and/or overstate the amount it spends on programs will not meet this standard.

14.   Have a board-approved annual budget for its current fiscal year, outlining projected expenses for major program activities, fundraising, and administration.

FUNDRAISING AND INFORMATIONAL MATERIALS

A fundraising appeal is often the only contact a donor has with a charity and may be the sole impetus for giving. This section of the standards seeks to ensure that a charity's representations to the public are accurate, complete, and respectful. To meet these standards, the charitable organization shall:

15.   Have solicitations and informational materials, distributed by any means, that are accurate, truthful and not misleading, both in whole and in part. Appeals that omit a clear description of program(s) for which contributions are sought will not meet this standard.

A charity should also be able to substantiate that the timing and nature of its expenditures are in accordance with what is stated, expressed, or implied in the charity's solicitations.

16.   Have an annual report available to all, on request, that includes:

   a. the organization's mission statement,
   b. a summary of the past year's program service accomplishments,
   c. a roster of the officers and members of the board of directors, financial information that includes (i) total income in the past fiscal year, (ii) expenses in the same program, fundraising and administrative categories as in the financial statements, and (iii) ending net assets.

17.   Include on any charity websites that solicit contributions, the same information that is recommended for annual reports, as well as the mailing address of the charity and electronic access to its most recent IRS Form 990.

18.   Address privacy concerns of donors by

   a. providing in written appeals, at least annually, a means (e.g., such as a check off box) for both new and continuing donors to inform the charity if they do not want their name and address shared outside the organization, and

(Continued)

(Continued)

  b. providing a clear, prominent and easily accessible privacy policy on any of its websites that tells visitors (i) what information, if any, is being collected about them by the charity and how this information will be used, (ii) how to contact the charity to review personal information collected and request corrections, (iii) how to inform the charity (e.g., a check off box) that the visitor does not wish his/her personal information to be shared outside the organization, and (iv) what security measures the charity has in place to protect personal information.

19. Clearly disclose how the charity benefits from the sale of products or services (i.e., cause-related marketing) that state or imply that a charity will benefit from a consumer sale or transaction. Such promotions should disclose, at the point of solicitation:

  a. the actual or anticipated portion of the purchase price that will benefit the charity (e.g., 5 cents will be contributed to abc charity for every xyz company product sold),

  b. the duration of the campaign (e.g., the month of October),

  c. any maximum or guaranteed minimum contribution amount (e.g., up to a maximum of $200,000).

20. Respond promptly to and act on complaints brought to its attention by the BBB Wise Giving Alliance and/or local Better Business Bureaus about fundraising practices, privacy policy violations and/or other issues.

Source: BBB Wise Giving Alliance (2003). Copyright 2003, BBB Wise Giving Alliance.

Since the BBB has a long history and an established reputation as a watchdog that acts to protect consumers against unethical business practices, the Wise Giving Alliance standards for nonprofits are among the best known and most widely cited in the news media. For example, the Wise Giving Alliance made news in 2001, when it temporarily dropped the American Red Cross from its list of organizations meeting its standards, in the wake of controversy concerning the organization's post–9/11 fundraising. (Its approval was subsequently restored.) Beginning in 2003, the Wise Giving Alliance offered charities that meet its standards the use of a "BBB national charity seal" in their promotional and solicitation materials.

The BBB standards are based on best practices; that is, they prescribe what accountable nonprofits should *do* in the areas of governance and oversight, measuring effectiveness, finances, fundraising, and informational material. They require that organizations have a mechanism for measuring results that involves the governing board, but they do not prescribe the *specific* standards that organizations must apply. They require that organizations "have a board policy of assessing, no less than every two years, the organization's performance and effectiveness and of determining future actions required to achieve its mission." And the organization must submit "to [its] governing body, for its approval, a written report that outlines the results of the aforementioned performance and effectiveness assessment and recommendations for future actions" (BBB Wise Giving Alliance, 2003). But aside from a couple of key financial ratios, which we will discuss below, the BBB does not advocate specific methods for measuring effectiveness or performance.

Many nonprofit organizations have accepted the idea of best practices, adhere to one or other of the recommended standards, and have sought some type of accreditation or certification. In a 2005 study by Salamon and Geller, 65% of organizations surveyed were participating in some type of best-practice accreditation program and identified several benefits of doing so, including improved staff and board knowledge, improved accountability and governance, and enhanced staff attention to the organization's mission (pp. 10–11). It may be that in addition to the potential threat of negative publicity, the widespread acceptance of voluntary standards reflects, as Light (2000) suggests, institutional theory at work (p. 18). Enunciated standards become a part of the conventional wisdom of what constitutes ethical or sound practice and are increasingly adopted by organizations that seek recognition for being consistent with the norms of the subsector or profession within which they operate.

But the question remains, Does doing the rights things ensure that the organization is effective in accomplishing its mission? Is there some mechanism that automatically leads from best practices in governance and management to an effective organization? Light (2000), and others, conclude that the connection is tenuous:

> Even if one could develop hard measures of finance, mission, record keeping, and operations, [funders of nonprofits] would be hard pressed to demonstrate a link between any single measure and overall organizational effectiveness. There is no evidence, for example, that having a merit pay system for staff is related to organizational effectiveness, or that holding a strategic planning process is somehow going to improve outcomes. (p. 52)

MEASURING EFFECTIVENESS AND PERFORMANCE

If doing the right things does not guarantee that the organization is effective in achieving its mission, then we need some tools to evaluate results. But how should results be defined, and how should they be measured? There is no consensus answer, or even a consistent vocabulary among experts in the field. Some use the terms *organizational effectiveness* and *organizational performance* synonymously. But others draw distinctions—for example, measuring effectiveness more through perceptions and performance through more objective indicators. Others define performance as broader than effectiveness, with the latter reflecting achievement against mission and the former encompassing "other concepts such as efficiency, productivity, or quality" (Baruch & Ramalho, 2006, p. 41). For example, let's consider a software company. If its software works and meets the needs of customers, that may define an effective product and an effective company. But if the company loses money every year, the staff are miserable, and management is always just skirting the law, it would be hard to say it is a high-performing company. Being effective may be necessary to being high performing, but it not necessarily sufficient.

It is also important to distinguish between *effectiveness* and *efficiency*. As Kelly (1998) explains it, efficiency is "a measure of the proportion of resources used to produce outputs or attain inputs-cost ratios," whereas effectiveness "is measured by comparing the results achieved with the results sought." As Kelly further observes, "Although efficiency may help an organization be more effective, the two concepts are not interchangeable" (p. 428). Indeed, some argue that an emphasis on efficiency may in fact work against the effectiveness of organizations by discouraging investment in capacity, a topic that will be discussed in greater detail in the next chapter.

Another important distinction is between program effectiveness and the effectiveness or performance of an *organization*. *Program evaluation* is a method that many nonprofits use to determine whether specific programs are effective in achieving their goals and objectives. A program "is a set of resources and activities directed toward one or more common goals, typically under the direction of a single manager or management team." Program evaluation is "the systematic assessment of program results and, to the extent feasible, systematic assessment of the extent to which the program caused those results" (Newcomer, Hatry, & Wholey, 2004, p. xxxiii).

Organizational effectiveness looks at the broader question of whether the organization as a whole is effective in achieving its mission. Of course, for a small nonprofit with a single program, the distinction may not be very meaningful. For larger, more complex organizations with broad missions, the difference may be significant. For example, a university might have a very effective basketball team, one that frequently wins championships, but it may not be a very strong university overall. However, some argue that program outcome evaluations can be aggregated at the organizational level as a measure of the organization's overall effectiveness (Murray, 2004, p. 357). Again, evaluating the organization's overall *performance* could include factors in addition to its effectiveness, such as efficiency, financial results, and others.

Financial Ratios as Measures of Performance

In the business world, financial data and ratios are the principal way to measure a company's performance and strength. A company's earnings, earnings per share, stock price, and the ratio of stock price to earnings (the P:E ratio) are important variables that investors consider. Some have applied a similar approach to nonprofit organizations. One prominent rater, Charity Navigator, bases its ratings of nonprofit organizations exclusively on financial ratios that it obtains from Form 990s. Other raters also use financial ratios, either exclusively or in combination with other standards.

The advantages of using financial indicators are that the data are objective, readily available, and easily compared, across either the nonprofit sector or particular subsectors. But critics argue that they fail to account for the realities faced by many organizations, that they may be at best misleading, and that they are potentially destructive.

A 2004 study by the Urban Institute and Harvard's Hauser Institute (Fremont-Smith & Cordes, 2004) looked at 10 monitoring organizations that use financial ratios and found a variety of measures being applied, including variations of the following:

- The ratio of program expenses to contributed income
- The ratio of fundraising expenditures and private support received—that is, the cost of raising a dollar

- The percentage of total expenditure (or income received from contributions) on charitable programs or activities
- The percentage of total expenditure on fundraising and administration (overhead)
- Accumulated cash and asset reserves in relation to operating budget

Two of the most emphasized ratios are the cost of fundraising and the percentage of expenditures that go for overhead rather than for programs and services. The BBB standards do not in general emphasize financial ratios, but they require that an organization's spending on fundraising be no more than 35% of the funds raised. However, the BBB also permits an organization to offer a justification for higher ratios, an accommodation to individual realities that some raters do not make. The Maryland standards establish a 3:1 ratio for fundraising costs (i.e., expenditures should be no more than about 33% of gift revenue), and they also permit some flexibility:

> A nonprofit's fundraising costs should be reasonable over time. On average, over a five year period, a nonprofit should realize revenue from fundraising and other development activities that are at least three times the amount spent on conducting them. Organizations whose fundraising ratio is less than 3:1 should demonstrate that they are making steady progress toward achieving this goal, or should be able to justify why a 3:1 ratio is not appropriate for their organization. (Maryland Association of Nonprofit Organizations, 2006)

The percentage of total expenditures directed toward program-related activities, rather than overhead or fundraising, is viewed by some as a measure of an organization's efficiency in delivering its services. Too low a percentage may even be seen as a potential red flag, suggesting that management is deriving excessive compensation or other benefits from the organization or that fundraising has replaced mission as the organization's highest priority. For example, the BBB standards require that at least 65% of expenditures be devoted to programs but, again, allow that organizations not meeting that standard may provide an explanation.

Charity Navigator, which bases its ratings exclusively on financial ratios, does not establish an absolute standard for program expenditures or fundraising costs, but for the former, higher is better and for the latter, lower is better; that is, the higher the percentage spent on programs and the lower the percentage spent on fundraising, the more stars the organization will receive. Charity Navigator evaluates organizations on the basis of "organizational efficiency" and "organizational capacity," both defined in financial terms, using the indicators listed below. The seven categories of indicators are combined to calculate an overall numerical rating, which Charity Navigator then compares with the ratings of all the charities it surveys, charities with similar missions, and organizations in the same peer group as the one being rated.

Charity Navigator's indicators of organizational efficiency are as follows:

1. Fundraising Efficiency: Amount a charity spends to raise $1 (lower is better)

2. Fundraising Expenses: Percent of total functional expenses spent on fundraising. (lower is better)

3. Program Expenses: Percent of total functional expenses spent on programs and services. (higher is better)

4. Administration Expenses: Percent of total functional expenses spent on management and general purposes. (lower is better)

And indicators of organizational capacity are the following:

5 & 6. Primary Revenue Growth & Program Expenses Growth: Measures a charity's average annual growth of primary revenue or program expenses over its three to five most recent fiscal years. (higher is better)

7. Working Capital Ratio: Determines how long a charity could sustain its level of spending using only its net liquid assets, as reported on its most recently filed Form 990. (higher is better) (Charity Navigator, www.charitynavigator.org/index.cfm/bay/content.view/catid/2/cpid/182.htm, accessed February 21, 2006)

Indeed, organizations that spend too much on overhead or fundraising may be making inefficient use of donor funds or perhaps may be spending too lavishly on salaries and other overhead costs. Very high fundraising costs may suggest the possibility of inefficiency, or even unethical or fraudulent behavior. But, critics argue, rating organizations based on their overhead and fundraising costs may create perverse incentives. For example, this approach may simply encourage organizations to engage in creative accounting to allocate costs to programs rather than administration. Insisting on low fundraising costs also may place young organizations at a disadvantage. They often need to invest substantial amounts in developing a database of regular donors that will ultimately produce continuing revenue at lower costs. And low fundraising costs may not be realistic for an organization that advocates unpopular causes or lacks a constituency of major donors (Fremont-Smith & Cordes, 2004).

Others critics argue that "the fundraising efficiency standard is not a measure of efficiency at all. [Rather,] it documents the sunk costs associated with cultivating donors" ("The Pros and Cons of Financial Efficiency Standards," 2004, p. 3). In other words, looking at just this year's fundraising costs ignores the substantial amounts that the organization may have spent in earlier years to develop relationships with donors who now make larger gifts, lowering the per-dollar cost of fundraising today.

Some argue that high program-spending ratios are not a measure of organizational effectiveness, and indeed, they may even work against building effective organizations, by encouraging organizations to "value thrift over excellence." Trying to maintain a low ratio may cause an organization to invest too little in "good governance, planning, compliance and risk management, collection of data for service performance evaluations, and staff training" ("The Pros and Cons of Financial Efficiency Standards," 2004, p. 4).

Financial ratios do provide one perspective on the operations of an organization. But, despite the ease of their use, they may not present the complete picture. It may even be the case, as some critics charge, that "the undue emphasis on financial ratios diverts attention and resources from the development of more meaningful measures that address performance against mission and program objectives" ("The Pros and Cons of Financial Efficiency Standards," 2004, p. 4).

Measuring Against Peers

If simple financial measures applied to all nonprofit organizations are potentially misleading, perhaps a more accurate picture may be obtained from comparing data from organizations that are similar in their mission, size, location, and other characteristics. Comparing similar organizations is at the heart of *benchmarking*.

As Poister (2003) notes, the term *benchmarking* is often misused. Some organizations set goals for future years in their strategic plans and then measure their progress by looking at targets, which they call "benchmarks." But in its proper definition, benchmarking involves comparisons among organizations, either at the macro or at the micro (program or function) level (p. 238). Benchmarking involves collecting data from multiple organizations "in order to 'peg' the performance of a particular [organization] in relation to [those offering] comparable programs" (p. 238). For example, an organization might look at statistics on client outcomes across a group of organizations providing services to individuals with similar problems or compare its patterns of gift revenues with those of similar organizations. This macro approach, called *statistical benchmarking*, may be a useful technique in strategic planning and may help highlight strengths or weaknesses of the organization that require further analysis.

Another approach to benchmarking, what Poister (2003) calls *corporate benchmarking*, "compares the organization's practices with those of others doing similar things but who are deemed to be the best at doing it" (Murray, 2004, p. 361). A technique adopted from business, this type of benchmarking requires identifying best practices—that is, the most effective or efficient methods of performing specific functions—and seeing how the subject organization compares with the best. It is thus not really a tool for evaluating the whole organization, although some assume that "a thorough program of benchmarking will 'roll up' to provide a good indicator of how well the organization is doing overall" (Murray, 2004, p. 361).

Christine Letts, an advocate of benchmarking, argues that it "bridges the gap between great ideas and great performance" (Letts et al., 1999a, p. 86) and that the nonprofit culture of openness and sharing may make it a more feasible approach for them than for competitive businesses. But, like the use of financial ratios, benchmarking also has its critics. For one, it requires a larger investment of time and effort than comparing financial ratios, which are readily available from Form 990s. Second, there is no way to really know whether the practice being studied is related to an organization's overall effectiveness. For example, how does the amount of time required to process the payroll translate into a more effective organization? In addition, it is often difficult to identify the specific indicators on which the best practice is to be compared. For example, what number best indicates how many clients have "recovered" from an illness or addiction? It is also often difficult to identify which organizations can really be considered alike. For example, nonprofits in different cities may face very different funding environments and more or less favorable markets for volunteers and staff.

Benchmarking is a useful tool, but perhaps more for examining specific program or administrative functions than for evaluating the effectiveness or performance of an organization. Moreover, since the selection of like or peer organizations is often complicated by local factors, benchmarking may be better used as a tool for learning than for evaluating. If used (or perceived) as a technique for evaluating the performance of specific departments or staff, it also may come to be manipulated; that is, individuals may try to game the system by selecting peers that offer the most favorable comparisons.

Measuring Against Mission

Financial ratios and benchmark data may provide some insights on a nonprofit's performance, but mission is the heart of the matter. It is the very purpose for which a nonprofit exists. Thus, the most important indicators of effectiveness should be related to its success in accomplishing that mission. As Brian Gallagher, President of the United Way of America, expressed it in 2005,

> Financial accountability is just table stakes. You *have* to get that right first. But, ultimately, the American public should hold our sector accountable for delivering on our missions. . . . We should be asked to report concrete results that are tied directly to our missions, not just the level of activity we produce.

One obstacle to measuring success in accomplishing the mission is the loftiness and vagueness of many mission statements. For example, the mission of one organization serving the needs of older people is to enable them "to live with dignity and independence." One educational institution includes as a part of its mission "fostering a love of learning." But how are "dignity" or "love of learning" to be defined or measured? And if they are defined and measured and found to exist, how can the organization be sure that its programs are indeed what created them? In other words, what is the organization's _impact_ on the measured changes, since there are many factors that influence the lives of older people and students.

An instructive example is provided by the experience of The Nature Conservancy (TNC) in the 1990s. TNC was struggling with the question of how to measure its performance against its ambitious mission "to preserve the plants, animals, and natural communities that represent the diversity of life on Earth by protecting the lands and waters they need to survive." For 50 years, it had measured its success by looking at two figures that were readily available, the amount of money it raised and the quantity of land this money enabled it to protect—what became known as "bucks and acres." But these two measures really reflected the _means_ TNC was using, not the _ends_ it was committed to achieving. In other words, if the mission was ultimately to preserve biodiversity on Earth, how could TNC be sure that the means it was employing—the acquisition of money and land—was indeed having an impact on the achievement of that purpose? (Sawhill & Williamson, 2001).

Possibly a better measure of TNC's effectiveness in achieving its mission might have been to count the number of species existing on the planet each year—to measure biodiversity. But even if it were practical to take an annual global inventory, the number continues to decline every year, despite TNC's efforts, for reasons way beyond TNC's control. The impact of its programs is small compared with all the other forces affecting the survival of species on Earth. Indeed, using that figure as an indicator of effectiveness in achieving the mission would doom TNC's performance to be assessed as a continual failure because that figure inevitably declines. Moreover, it would be meaningless as a measure of TNC's own results.

After considering the problem, TNC adopted a family of measures, including the number of species existing on land it *controls*. Easier to count than all the species on the entire planet, and more reflective of TNC's own efforts, this intermediate number could provide a realistic and feasible proxy for the organization's impact on the Earth's overall biodiversity. This approach thus requires developing

> micro-level goals that, if achieved, would *imply* success on a grander scale; indicators of goal achievement that can be measured with a feasible level of effort, and that arguably are affected by the organization's efforts rather than other extraneous and uncontrollable factors. (Sawhill & Williamson, 2001, p. 23)

The challenge is greater for some organizations than for others. Let's consider an organization with the simple mission of "providing a hot meal every day to homeless people." It is hard to improve on a simple count of the number of meals served—and perhaps a measure of the food's temperature—as a way to measure effectiveness in delivering that straightforward and uncomplicated mission. But take a more complicated mission, say that of the American Cancer Society: "Eliminating cancer as a major health problem by preventing cancer, saving lives, and diminishing suffering from cancer, through research, education, advocacy, and service." (www.cancer.org, accessed February 11, 2006). Unfortunately, many variables affect the incidence of cancer and cancer death rates—individuals' life styles, environmental factors, and the availability of medical care, among others. Just measuring the national cancer rates, whether they are found to be increasing or declining, would not tell the American Cancer Society much about the effectiveness or ineffectiveness of its efforts. But research has demonstrated that screening and educational programs are effective in reducing cancer incidence and mortality; thus, the American Cancer Society can make a sound theoretical link between the effectiveness of its screening and educational programs, which can be more easily evaluated, and achievement of its larger mission, the prevention and eventual elimination of cancer (Sawhill & Williamson, 2001). Obviously, however, the validity of any microlevel indicator as a measure of effectiveness toward achievement of a broader mission depends on the soundness of the *logic model* behind it— that is, the chain of theoretical reasoning that explains exactly how the organization's efforts lead to the desired larger result.

Program Outcomes

The outcomes approach to measuring program effectiveness has gained wide acceptance through the efforts of United Way of America, which applies it in evaluating its supported organizations. It also has been adopted by many foundations and government agencies for measuring their grantees' effectiveness. It is a method for evaluating programs and may not address the effectiveness of the organization, although again, the distinction may be small for organizations that operate only a few or a single program.

The United Way outcomes model is illustrated in Table 5.1, which highlights the key variables: *inputs, activities, outputs*, and *outcomes*. Inputs are the resources dedicated to the program, including money, staff, volunteers, facilities, equipment, and supplies, as well as the constraints imposed by the external environment. Activities are what the program does—for example, tutoring children, feeding the homeless, or providing job training. Outputs are the direct products of the activities and are often relatively easy things to measure—for example, the number of children tutored, the number of homeless fed, and the number of individuals trained in employment skills. But measuring outputs does not make the connection to the program's goals, which are generally to change in some way the individuals it serves and to make a lasting difference in their lives. Outcomes are the changes that occur in the individuals as a result of their participation in the program—for example, new knowledge, expanded job skills, or a better position in life.

Outcomes may be measured immediately after the individual completes the program (initial outcomes); after a longer period has elapsed, say a few years (intermediate outcomes); and after an even longer period of time (long-term outcomes.) Thus, it may be found that students who participate in an after-school tutoring program improve their grades, but are they still succeeding academically two years later? Do they go on to complete college in larger numbers than students who do not participate in the program? Are they more likely to be employed a decade after their participation in the program? Obviously, measuring outcomes

TABLE 5.1	United Way Program Outcome Model		
Inputs	*Activities*	*Outputs*	*Outcomes*
Resources dedicated to or consumed by the program e.g. • money • staff and staff time • volunteers and volunteer time • facilities • equipment and supplies Constraints on the program e.g. • laws • regulations • funders requirements	What the program does with the inputs to fulfill its mission e.g. • feed and shelter homeless families • provide job training • educate the public about signs of child abuse • counsel pregnant women • create mentoring relationships for youth	The direct products of program activities e.g. • number of classes taught • number of counseling sessions conducted • number of educational materials distributed • number of hours of service delivered • number of participants served	Benefits for participants during and after program activities e.g. • new knowledge • increased skills • changed attitudes or values • modified behavior • improved condition • altered status

Source: United Way of America (1996).

over the longer term can require considerable effort and expense, perhaps involving the tracking of former clients and follow-up surveys. That can be difficult for organizations that serve clients who are highly mobile and difficult to reach—for example, homeless people.

But as mentioned earlier, monitoring outcomes is not the same as evaluating programs. In other words, it is one thing to establish that outcomes have occurred, but evaluating the program requires determining that these outcomes were in fact caused by the program (Kopczynski & Pritchard, 2004, p. 650). That requires developing a sound and plausible *logic model*—that is, a theoretical explanation of the links all the way through the process from inputs to outcomes. Figure 5.1 depicts the logic model of a program offering tutoring to at-risk teens. It shows how the organization believes the process works. To justify using school graduation rates as an outcome measure for its program, the organization would need to explain how the mentoring experience causes students to complete their homework and attend school more regularly and how homework and attendance affect graduation rates. Otherwise, the rate of students' graduation from high school cannot be a useful indicator of the tutoring program's outcome. One obvious problem in developing such logic models is trying to identify the external influences that can cause the outcome in addition to the activities associated with the program. This becomes more of an issue the higher up in the model one ascends. For example, students' grades and graduation rates may be positively affected by the tutoring program, but they also could be affected—either positively or negatively—by students' experiences at home or in the community where they live (Poister, 2003, p. 38).

The program outcome model offers a significant advantage over some other approaches to measuring effectiveness that we have discussed, since it does not suggest arbitrary standards but rather permits each organization to develop its own in relation to its mission. For instance, in our earlier example, TNC's bucks and acres were really *inputs* to its program. Shifting the focus from bucks and acres to biodiversity reflects outcomes thinking.

To emphasize again, however, the outcomes model overlooks other important aspects of organizational performance. For example, it is possible to conceive of an organization that is delivering effective programs but whose sustainability as an organization over the long run is imperiled by financial imbalances. It could also be possible to achieve positive program outcomes, but at a very high cost; in other words, the organization could be very inefficient. And measuring program outcomes does not tell us anything about the organization's ability to learn and adapt to change. In sum, the outcomes model measures the effectiveness of programs but cannot by itself provide a complete picture of organizational performance.

Balanced Scorecard

The balanced scorecard is a concept developed by Kaplan and Norton (1992) as a way for businesses to obtain, as the term suggests, a balanced perspective on performance by combining financial data with other considerations. It has since been adopted by some nonprofit organizations and government agencies as a way to combine financial ratios and other data in measuring organizational performance. The balanced scorecard looks at an organization from four perspectives:

1. *The financial perspective,* including financial performance indicators

2. *The customer perspective,* including measures of customer satisfaction

FIGURE 5.1   Logic Model of At-Risk Teen Mentoring Program

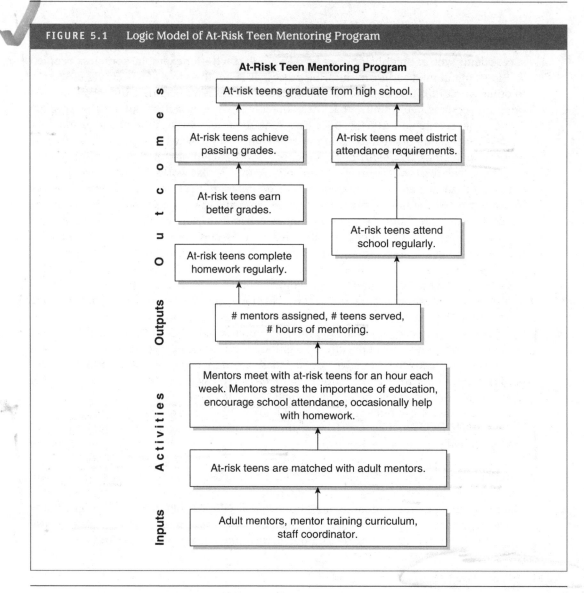

At-Risk Teen Mentoring Program

Source: United Way of America.

3. *The internal business perspective,* including measures of operational efficiency and quality

4. *The innovation and learning perspective,* including measures of the organization's ability to adapt to changes in the environment (Murray, 2004, p. 359)

Paton (2003) offers a variation of the balanced scorecard designed specifically for nonprofits, which he calls the *dashboard.* His model seeks to answer two fundamental questions: Does it work? In other words, "do the different activities, services, and programs achieve broadly the results intended?" (pp. 139–140). And is the organization well run? Paton notes that there may be a relationship between how well run an organization is and the effectiveness of the programs it delivers but that the two are separate matters and both need to be measured in order to obtain a complete picture of the organization's performance:

> A valuable and innovative service may be provided by an organization that is inefficiently administered, or even by one whose funds are being discretely embezzled; and a well administered organization with excellent morale may be delivering high quality programs to clients whose needs are slight compared to those of the client group originally envisaged. (p. 140)

Paton's (2003) dashboard thus looks at the organization from five perspectives, encompassing short-term, medium-term, and long-term measures:

1. *Current results:* Monthly checking against key targets—for example, a summary of achievements, a finance report, a marketing report

2. *Underlying performance:* Annual reviews of the appropriateness and cost-effectiveness of programs and support functions—for example, service outcomes, business outcomes, and external comparisons

3. *Risks:* Monitoring of the ways the organization may be put in jeopardy—for example, by a liquidity crisis, legal or procedural noncompliance, or a breakdown in key relationships

4. *Assets and capabilities:* Annual reviews of capacity to deliver future performance—for example, physical and financial assets, external reputation and relationships, expertise and process knowledge

5. *Change projects:* Regular reports on projects intended to bring about improvements in the organization that the board and the CEO are supervising directly (p. 142)

A number of variations on the balanced scorecard have been developed and are used, but this approach also has its critics. For example, Meyer (2002) notes that the balanced scorecard really measures very different things—for example, financial results and customer satisfaction, numbers that must be looked at alongside each other rather than combined. He suggests instead the idea of identifying correlations between measures. For example, do good financial results always go along with customer satisfaction? If so, there is no need to measure customer satisfaction directly, since it can be assumed from the financial results. Using this approach, he offers what he calls *activity-based profitability analysis* as a simpler alternative to balanced-scorecard approaches.

Social Return on Investment (SROI)

The concept of the double bottom line has been mentioned earlier in this text. It refers to the need for nonprofit managers to look to both their organization's financial performance as well as the social impact of its programs. In 1996, the Roberts Enterprise Foundation

(REDF), a venture philanthropy fund based in San Francisco, pioneered the concept of social return on investment (SROI) as a way to put a dollar figure on—that is, to monetize—the social value created by nonprofits. The idea was to add social return to financial return in order to generate a single number—in dollars—that could be used as an indicator of the organization's performance.

As a venture philanthropy fund, REDF approaches giving as a form of investing in a select group of nonprofits, called its portfolio organizations. And, like other investors, REDF seeks to measure the return on its investments. Financial return is easy to understand: If you invest $100,000 and receive $10,000 in income, that's a return of 10%. But how do we measure the less tangible social benefits created by a nonprofit's programs? SROI provides a method for measuring those social benefits in dollar terms so that they can be compared with expenditures to produce a single number as simple to understand as the rate of return on a philanthropic investment.

REDF's SROI methodology evolved from *cost-benefit analysis*, a technique drawn from applied economics and most often used to evaluate government programs. As Kee (2004) explains it,

> Cost-benefit analysis . . . attempts to assess a . . . program or project by determining whether societal welfare has or will increase (in the aggregate more people are better off) because of the program or project. Cost-benefit analysis can provide information on the full costs of the program and weigh those costs against the *dollar value of the benefits.* [italics added] The analyst can then calculate the net benefits (or costs) of the program or project, examine the ratio of benefits to costs, determine the rate of return on the . . . original investment, and compare the program's benefits and costs with those of other programs or proposed alternatives. (p. 524)

The advantage of this approach is that it produces a ratio that can be used to compare programs against programs. But putting a dollar value on social benefits—that is, monetizing them—can be a challenge. As an example, let's consider a program that offers job training, helping people move from welfare to work. The benefits may include the new income taxes paid by the people who become employed, savings through lower welfare costs, less need for homeless shelters, and perhaps savings in the cost of policing as fewer people are on the streets. These benefits can be given a dollar value and summed to find the SROI in the nonprofit's job-training programs. But that does not include, for example, the very real benefits of reduced fear and social tension resulting from the decrease in crime. Though real, that is hard to measure, especially in dollar terms. Moreover, costs are incurred to support the program today, but many of the benefits may not be realized until long in the future. For example, one benefit of an after-school tutoring program that helps young people complete high school may be their higher wages after graduation. That is, at least theoretically, easily stated in dollar terms. But increased education also may lead to healthier and happier lives through their lifetimes. That is harder to capture and harder to monetize (Kee, 2004, pp. 526–527).

Although SROI has been adopted by a number of organizations, especially social enterprises that worked with REDF and other venture philanthropy funds, REDF no longer uses

SROI as its sole measure of an organization's social performance. After experiencing methodological difficulties in requiring portfolio organizations to report data on a WebTrack system, REDF has now moved to a system it calls Ongoing Assessment of Social Impacts (OASIS), which collects and analyzes data on a range of measures, including

- quarterly aggregate information on the mission-related employees of each portfolio enterprise,
- social outcomes information on new hires,
- monthly income statement information,
- the first three measures in an SROI model,
- impact on overall effectiveness of portfolio member organizations,
- the cost-effectiveness of REDF's approach versus other similar approaches, and
- the relationship between specific employee social outcomes and the types of social purpose enterprises that employ these individuals (Tuan, 2004, p. 123).

While SROI, cost-benefit analysis, and REDF's OASIS system provide results that may be easy to interpret, their shortcomings include the practical limitations that many organizations face in collecting and analyzing complex data on an ongoing basis.

Blended Value

With the increasing focus by nonprofits on financial results and the growing corporate concern about social responsibility, many observers note a blurring of the nonprofit and for-profit sectors; in other words, they argue that nonprofits and business firms are becoming more alike and that it should therefore be possible to define some common measures of performance that could be applied to all organizations across the sectors. But this approach still faces a number of challenges.

Baruch and Ramalho (2006) analyzed a variety of scholarly articles, some reporting research on nonprofits and some research on for-profits. They found some common ground in the measures that those various studies used to measure organizational effectiveness. But, as they observed, "all measures seemed to correspond to broadly diffused concepts" (p. 58). In other words, organizations in different sectors can be compared using similar measurements, but only at a very high level and in very general terms. Corporations and nonprofits do have characteristics in common, since both are organizations. But limiting the study of effectiveness to their common characteristics may require a level of generalization that is simply not informative. For example, both dogs and cats might be evaluated by their effectiveness in winning their owners' hearts, as well as eating, drinking, and sleeping. But none of these qualities would be related to their effectiveness in catching mice or guarding a junkyard, tasks for which cats and dogs are generally superior, respectively.

One interesting approach to defining common measures across sectors is offered by the advocates of *blended value* ("Blended Value Map," 2006). In the past, corporations have worked to maximize *economic* value, while nonprofits have tried to maximize *social* value—that is, to increase SROI. But, the blended value theorists say, value should be thought about as having three components: economic value, social value, and environmental value. Both companies and nonprofits should be measured by how much of all three they create—in total. Thus, companies may create considerable economic value, but through socially responsible behavior they may also create some social value. For example, companies earn profits for their owners but also create jobs for the less well-off. Nonprofits may be high as creators of social value and lower than companies in creating economic value, but many now operate revenue-generating enterprises, and they may also earn profits and contribute to the economies of their communities. Both companies and nonprofits may affect the environment, in positive or negative ways. "The central premise of the blended value proposition is that value itself is a 'blend' of economic, environmental, and social factors, and that maximizing value requires taking all three elements into account" ("Blended Value Map," 2006). In other words, the blended value advocates call for "breaking down the silos" and developing a single measure to evaluate for-profits and nonprofits in terms of the total benefits, or value, that they create ("Blended Value Map," 2006).

Although the use of blended value to measure organizational performance across the nonprofit and business sectors is intellectually intriguing, there are several challenges to its wider acceptance. For one, there are some critics who challenge the very concept of corporate social responsibility, one of the silos across which blended value measures would be built (Doane, 2005), There are strong incentives for business corporations to maximize financial returns, including the ratings of financial analysts and the pressure of shareholders seeking to maximize the financial returns on their investments. And, of course, there remain the inherent difficulties of defining and measuring social impact in both sectors.

EFFECTIVENESS AND PERFORMANCE: THE STATE OF THE ART

We now have reviewed some of the more commonly discussed and applied approaches to nonprofit accountability and performance. In this section, we will look at some research that describes what organizations are actually doing, some of the benefits and potential pitfalls of performance measurement, and some of the current directions in which the field appears to be moving.

Research From the Field

Murray (2004) reports the results of a survey on the employment of performance measurement in various organizations, noting the limitation that most studies have been of individual cases and that few large-sample, comparative, longitudinal studies have been completed. One study of the latter type, conducted in Canada, included 1,965 nonprofit organizations and 322 funders of those organizations. It produced some interesting insights, including the following points:

- Forty-one percent of the funders said that they are requiring more performance data from their grantees.
- Over half of the funders did not provide their grantees with funds to cover the costs of the evaluations.
- Sixty percent of the funders said that they provide their grantees with advice on evaluation, but interestingly, only 38% of the grantees said that they had actually received any.

- Seventy-seven percent of the organizations had carried out some type of evaluation, but only 18% had focused on the performance of the organization as a whole (as opposed to program evaluation).
- Seventy-three percent of the organizations that had carried out evaluations said that they had measured outcomes, but many of them provided examples that were really output measures.
- Ninety-five percent of the nonprofits said that they were satisfied with the evaluations and had used the data in making decisions.
- Less that half of the funders had made any use of the evaluation data from their grantees, and 26% said that they did not have the capacity to review the information their grantees had provided (Murray, 2004, pp. 345).

The last point is interesting, indeed provocative, especially since funders have been a strong voice encouraging the greater use of performance measurement by their grantee organizations. As Murray (2004) recommends, additional research is needed to determine to what extent the emphasis on performance in today's nonprofit literature and discussion reflects real change and how much is rhetoric. Research also is needed to determine the extent to which measurement is actually influencing the management of organizations in positive ways.

Efforts to develop common performance indicators are continuing. For example, the Web site of the Urban Institute (www.urban.org) offers material on the Outcomes Indicator Project and is an excellent resource for students interested in following new developments in the field.

RISKS AND REWARDS

Nonprofits are being required to measure more and to reveal more about their finances, programs, and results. But nonprofit managers are confronted with both risks and potential rewards in sorting through the options and selecting the measures and methods that will meet both their own need for useful management information as well as the expectations of funders, watchdogs, and regulators.

One obvious concern is the proliferation of proposed standards and methods and the lack of even a vocabulary or process that is universally accepted or stable. As Baruch and Ramalho (2006) note, this leaves nonprofit practitioners and scholars vulnerable to "fads with doubtful empirical and theoretical foundations presenting themselves as simple recipes" (p. 59). Another concern is the amount of time and effort devoted to measuring effectiveness and whether indeed the effectiveness of organizations with limited capacity may be compromised by the effort required to compile, analyze, and report data. Some may eventually reach a condition of analysis paralysis, consumed with measurement to the preclusion of action. A related concern is expressed by Paton (2003) in his insightful concluding chapter. He sees a risk of developing "disconnected managerialism," a situation "where modern discourse and methods are conspicuous (and may even play well externally), but they do not impact the main work, except as noise and a burden" (p. 161). In other words, if nonprofit managers work to the numbers, there is the risk that the numbers will gain more importance than the important work their organizations are committed to performing:

> Performance improvement methods can be used in ways that gradually become burdensome, an end in themselves, irrelevant to the on-going work. They can become a focus of tension and distrust between managers, and professional and other staff who complain about "initiative overload," and "management speak." (p. 160)

In other words, too much emphasis on measuring performance may create a "Dilbert world," in which the passion and commitment of the professional staff and volunteers becomes replaced by caution, even skepticism, which might undermine the nonprofit culture and its traditional strengths.

Writing in the *Chronicle of Philanthropy*, Kennard King (2006) raises similar concerns about the risks to nonprofit values in an excessive focus on performance:

> When Americans want to preserve and promote values other than making a buck, they come together in nonprofit organizations. When they want to solve problems they see in society, they come together in nonprofit organizations. When they aspire to make the world a better place, they come together in nonprofit organizations. And that points to the real danger of the overzealous application of outcomes thinking: By undermining the value of our aspirations, we take away the purpose and meaning of the work of nonprofit organizations.

Failing to measure performance is the antithesis of managing and is unacceptable in the environment in which nonprofit organizations exist today. But practical good sense is required. It may be, as Paton (2003) suggests, that the appropriate position for nonprofit managers is a middle ground between ignoring the need for measuring effectiveness and making it the purpose of the organization. "In considerable measure they are obligated to support measurement and performance improvement—to object can easily appear self-serving and irrational." On the other hand, "they are fully entitled to have misgivings" (p. 164).

Managers may be tempted, and encouraged by their boards and funders, to embrace the performance jargon and techniques of the day. But in doing so, they may run the risks we already have identified—distraction from the work of the organization and the potential dissatisfaction of their staffs. But, as Paton (2003) notes,

> the alternative—to be negative and distrusting toward performance measurement [altogether]—would be a betrayal of management's role and responsibilities. Indeed, it can easily become so, slipping into a cynical, overly political attitude, in which the gulf between professional stance and private belief grows steadily wider and more uncomfortable. (p. 165)

The middle position, which Paton (2003) finds to be the "proper one," is to be "realistic about the range of possibilities," to engage constructively with measurement while being very alert to its limitations and misuse, and to approach the performance agenda positively while also being fully aware that every valid and useful method can also become an occasion for goal displacement by being pursued inappropriately or excessively. (p. 165)

CHAPTER SUMMARY

use in DISC?

There is an increasing demand that nonprofit organizations be accountable—that is, responsible for their actions. For some, this has a narrow meaning of following legal and ethical requirements; others include the requirement that nonprofits follow recommended best practices in governance and management. A still broader definition includes the responsibility to demonstrate that the organization is achieving results, that the resources entrusted to it are used not only ethically and legally but also efficiently and effectively.

Accountability is enforced by state and federal laws, but the nonprofit sector also has established methods for self-regulation. These include standards of best practice and programs through which nonprofits can gain accreditation or certification indicating their adherence to such standards. Charity watchdogs and raters, private organizations that evaluate nonprofits according to their own standards, also have influence because of the visibility their ratings command.

It is necessary to distinguish among program effectiveness, organizational effectiveness, and organizational performance. Effectiveness relates to achieving the mission, but performance is a broader concept that also includes financial results and other variables related to the overall organization. In evaluating effectiveness and performance, some emphasize financial ratios, including the percentage of expenditures devoted to programs rather than overall management and fundraising. But it is important to distinguish efficiency from effectiveness, with the latter related to accomplishment of the mission rather than merely minimizing costs. Some argue that an undue emphasis on efficiency could undermine effectiveness, by causing organizations not to invest in capacity, the subject of the next chapter.

Among other approaches to evaluating performance is benchmarking, which compares organizations with others with similar characteristics, but this may be a technique better suited to learning than to evaluation. An influential approach, advocated by the United Way, uses outcome measures. It may be more appropriate to evaluating the effectiveness of individual programs rather than organizations. This approach requires developing a logic model that links inputs to activities, to outputs, and to outcomes, the latter representing changes in the people who are served by the program. Outcomes may be measured immediately following completion of the program, over an intermediate term, or over the long term. Long-term measurement may be difficult and costly.

Other approaches to measuring performance, such as the balanced scorecard and the dashboard, seek to integrate internal and external variables to provide a comprehensive picture. Some venture philanthropists and scholars have adopted the tools of cost-benefit analysis and SROI to measure social impact. Others have developed concepts of value incorporating financial, social, and environmental impacts, which they would apply to both nonprofit and for-profit entities.

All methods of measuring nonprofit performance offer advantages as well as disadvantages. Nonprofit managers must be committed to measurement but should not become obsessed with measuring performance to the neglect of actual delivery of their missions.

KEY TERMS AND CONCEPTS FROM CHAPTER 5

accountability
accreditation
activity-based profitability model
balanced scorecard
blended value
charity raters
corporate benchmarking
cost-benefit analysis
dashboard
effectiveness

efficiency
e-Postcard
inputs
logic model
outcomes
outputs
performance
Sarbanes-Oxley Act
social return on investment (SROI)
statistical benchmarking

CASE 5.1

The Nature Conservancy

The Nature Conservancy (TNC) is one of the nation's largest nonprofit organizations. Founded in 1951, by 2004 it controlled more than $3 billion in assets and employed 3,200 staff in 528 offices located in every U.S. state and 30 other nations (Ottaway & Stephens, 2003).

TNC's mission is "to preserve the plants, animals, and natural communities that represent the diversity of life on Earth by protecting the lands and waters they need to survive." TNC purchases land itself, which it then preserves, and also operates a Conservation Buyers Program, which enables private individuals to purchase land, subject to conservation easements. By accepting an easement on the property, the buyer agrees to permanent limits on the scale and type of development that will be allowed, thus preserving at least a portion of the property in its natural condition. The program is consistent with TNC's philosophy of "compatible development," that is, the idea that some conservation is better than none and that through this practical approach TNC can leverage the resources of private individuals and companies to accomplish more conservation that it could working by itself.

Under the Conservation Buyer's Program, TNC buys land, then obtains the conservation easements. Because they limit what can be done with the land, the easements reduce the market value of the land. TNC then sells the land to the private buyer at the reduced price, and the buyer makes a gift to TNC for the difference.

In 2003, a series of three articles in the Washington Post written by Joe Stephens and David B. Ottaway (2003b, 2003c) leveled serious criticisms against TNC and its practices. The articles raised a number of issues, including TNC's relationship with corporations, the consistency of some of its entrepreneurial activities with its mission, and compensation and loans made to employees. The Conservation Buyer's Program received some of the strongest criticism.

The *Post* articles noted that conservation buyers had included individuals who were donors or active volunteer leaders of the organization, who appeared to have had an inside track on purchasing property. Property purchased by conservation buyers included beautiful wooded sites, on which some buyers were able to build homes despite the environmental easements. The authors suggested that while the transactions may have been legal, many of the owners gained valuable land for a discounted price and a deductible gift without really having to alter their plans for the land. As the *Post* authors describe one of the transactions

> On New York's Shelter Island, the Nature Conservancy three years ago bought an undeveloped, 10-acre tract overlooking its Mashomack Preserve, an oasis of hardwoods and tidal pools located just a stone's skip from the exclusive Hamptons. Cost to the charity: $2.1 million.
> Seven weeks after, it resold the land, with some development restrictions to [a former chair of the TNC regional chapter] and his wife. . . . Cost to the [buyers]: $500,000. (Stephens & Ottaway, 2003c, p. A01)

Like other conservation buyers, the couple in this transaction then made a $1.6 million gift to TNC, enabling it to recoup its cost of the land. The donors received a tax deduction for the gift. The *Post* authors cite tax experts who disagree on whether such deductions were legal, with a key issue being whether the donors had received a quid pro quo for the gift (Stephen & Ottaway, 2003c, p. A01). TNC assured the *Post* authors that the gifts were not tied to the land transactions, but the authors interviewed some donors who said they believed that they were.

TNC's then president, Steve McCormick, issued a sharp response to the series of articles within a week of their publication. He claimed that the articles had "painted a distorted picture" with its accusations and, while defending the Conservation Buyer's Program, announced that TNC would immediately suspend all new conservation buyer transactions (McCormick, 2003; Stephens & Ottaway, 2003a).

Following a yearlong review of its policies and practices, including the assistance of an outside panel, TNC announced in 2005 a wide range of changes, including restructuring of the TNC board, adoption of a number of principles from Sarbanes-Oxley, a strengthened audit function, and new conflict-of-interest policies. With regard to the Conservation Buyer's Program, the following new policies were implemented among others (TNC, 2005b):

- Transactions will no longer be undertaken with related parties (generally board members or employees), although such transactions are not prohibited by law.
- Transactions with major donors will be undertaken only following advance review against TNC's strengthened conflict-of-interest policies.
- The land will need to fall within a priority conservation site, established by scientists.
- The land will be offered for sale in a manner that provides an "open and equitable purchase opportunity to all potentially interested parties."
- TNC will obtain independent appraisals to ensure that it receives fair value for the land sold.

(Continued)

(Continued)

- When a gift is solicited in connection with a land sale, TNC "must document that fact and provide the buyer with a statement of the link between the gift and the sale."
- TNC will obtain community input on future use of the land.

The *Washington Post* series focused attention not only on the Conservation Buyer's Program but also on a range of TNC policies and practices. During the following year, while TNC was developing its own strengthened policies, the Finance Committee of the U.S. Senate conducted its own investigation and released a report in 2005 critical of some of TNC's practices, some of which already had been addressed in TNC's own reforms. The Senate Committee's review of TNC coincided with its consideration of broader legislation regulating the nonprofit sector and influenced its thinking about wider reforms (TNC, 2005a).

By 2006, the TNC Web site featured the Better Business Bureau Wise Giving Alliance seal, certifying its full compliance with the standards, and its positive ratings by Charity Navigator, the American Institute of Philanthropy, and other watchdog organizations.

In an analysis of the *Washington Post* series on TNC, the scholars Max Stephenson Jr. and Elisabeth Chaves (2006) state that the authors used a rhetorical style that "strongly directs the reader toward specific conclusions through inference and implication" (p. 350). The authors conclude that the series influenced the policies of the organization and the public policy debate on nonprofit accountability. They also provide an interesting perspective on TNC's response to the communication issues presented by the publication of the *Post* articles.

Sources: Ottaway and Stephens (2003); Stephens and Ottaway (2003a, 2003b, 2003c); McCormick (2003); TNC (2005b); and Stephenson and Chaves (2006).

QUESTIONS FOR DISCUSSION

1. Is the TNC case about accountability, effectiveness, or performance?

2. How does this case relate to the BBB Wise Giving Alliance Standards for Excellence?

3. What does the case illustrate about the media as a force for accountability?

4. In its rankings of colleges and universities, *U.S. News and World Report* uses a formula that includes the following variables:
   - Peer assessment (a survey regarding the institution's academic reputation)
   - Retention and graduation rates (e.g., percentage of freshmen who return and graduate)
   - Faculty resources (e.g., class size, student-faculty ratio)
   - Student selectivity (e.g., SAT scores and high school class rank of entering freshmen)
   - Financial resources (e.g., expenditures per student)

- Graduation rate performance (compares actual graduation rate with "predicted")
- Alumni giving rate (percentage of alumni who make a gift)

Do each of these indicators measure inputs, outputs, or outcomes? How relevant is each as a measure of performance against the typical university mission of teaching, research, and service?

5. Select a few organizations that are of interest to you. Look up their Form 990s on Guidestar and compare their fundraising costs with the total gifts they receive. Are their ratios similar or different? If they are different, can you think of explanations as to why that is true?

SUGGESTIONS FOR FURTHER READING RELATED TO CHAPTER 5

Books

Light, P. C. (2000). *Making nonprofits work: A report on the tides of nonprofit management reform.* Washington, DC: Brookings Institution.

Paton, R. (2003). *Managing and measuring social enterprises.* Thousand Oaks, CA: Sage.

Poister, T. H. (2003). *Measuring performance in public and nonprofit organizations.* San Francisco: Jossey-Bass.

Wholey, J. S., Hatry, H. P., & Newcomer, K. E. (Eds.). (2004). *Handbook of practical program evaluation* (2nd ed.). San Francisco: Jossey-Bass.

Web Sites

BBB Wise Giving Alliance, www.give.org; Maryland Association of Nonprofit Organizations, www.marylandnonprofits.org

Charity Navigator, www.charitynavigator.org; Guidestar, www.guidestar.org

Blended Value, www.blendedvalue.org

United Way, www.unitedway.org/outcomes; The Balanced Scorecard Institute, www.balancedscorecard.org

CHAPTER 6

Building Capacity
and Managing Change

Capacity building is everywhere! Hardly a day goes by in the life of a nonprofit CEO—or a professor of nonprofit management—without the mail bringing in an announcement of another workshop or conference focused on the topic of *capacity building*. Capacity building has become a significant industry, with numerous nonprofit and for-profit consultants and trainers offering services to assist organizations in undertaking it. This focus on capacity is largely a result of increased interest in the performance of nonprofits and the view of many that building the capacity of the organization is an important way to enhance it.

Exactly what is "capacity?" Paul Light (2004b) offers a succinct, but expansive, definition: Capacity is "everything an organization uses to achieve its mission, from desks and chairs to programs and people" (p. 15). What is "capacity building?" Letts et al. (1999a) call it simply a process to "develop, sustain, and improve [nonprofit] mission delivery." But these brief definitions are like saying that life encompasses everything that happens and that eating sustains it. They do not really offer enough for us to have an understanding of life or of food. That requires that we go inside the black box of capacity to look at its component parts and observe some specific activities that it comprises, topics that will be explored later in this chapter.

GROWING EMPHASIS ON CAPACITY

Despite the current emphasis on capacity building, the concept itself is not a new one. Organizational development is a discipline with a long history and its own substantial literature. But interest in nonprofit capacity building has exploded since the 1990s. As Christine Letts and her colleagues (1999a) describe it, there has been

> a fundamental redefinition of the challenge [confronting the nonprofit sector] from the most prevalent conception of the challenge, as one of expanding effective *programs*, to a new formulation of the challenge, as one of building effective *organizations* that can sustain and improve those programs. (p. 3)

Several widely read authors of the late 1990s observed weakness in nonprofits' capacity and laid the blame partly on patterns of foundation grantmaking (Letts et al., 1999a; Shore, 1999). Foundation giving historically has tended to support the development and delivery of nonprofits' programs rather than the building of organizations. Funders generally encourage organizations to keep overhead costs low, in order to maximize the resources spent on direct program services. In other words, they are pleased when nonprofits can demonstrate efficiency in their operations. But an emphasis on efficiency and low overhead may discourage expenditures undertaken to build the organization itself for the long haul. According to critics, this mindset has had several negative consequences. First, without building capacity, organizations cannot grow successful programs to a larger scale, thus limiting their impact. As Shore (1999) explains, "Even the best [programs] do not get to scale, do not reach more than a fraction of those who need their services, and often do not endure" (p. 88). Second, there is the toll that inadequate capacity takes on nonprofit staff and volunteers who struggle to deliver services with limited resources, possibly resulting in higher rates of staff turnover and burnout. As Light (2004b) describes the situation, "Nonprofits have been doing more with less for so long that many now border on doing everything with nothing" (p. 14). And, third, inadequate capacity may not support the effectiveness of programs or performance of the organization over the long run, possibly depriving clients of quality services and society of the benefits of sustained efforts in addressing problems. As Light (2004a) describes it,

> Many organizations can produce program success for a short period. All they need are extraordinary employees who are ready to work long hours, tolerate stress, and persevere despite organizational barriers. This is the picture of the small early-stage nonprofit—closely connected to its constituency and attractive to others as a result of its passion and accuracy of approach. The real trick for organizations is to sustain, improve, and build on this strength, producing progressively improving results over time. This is good management. (p. 38)

In the late 1990s, critiques like those offered by Letts et al. (1999a) and by Shore (1999) influenced the thinking of some newly wealthy entrepreneurs who had made fortunes in the dot-com boom and were turning their attention to philanthropy. Some adopted a new approach to giving that applied the methods of venture capitalist investing to philanthropy. They became identified as *venture philanthropists*, and the funds they established became known as *venture philanthropy funds*.

Today, some have shifted emphasis and terminology and describe their approach as *high-engagement grantmaking*. This style of philanthropy is characterized by the funder's involvement in building the organizations supported rather than just providing financial resources. Venture philanthropy funds (or high-engagement grantmakers) have evolved in somewhat different directions since the 1990s. Some focus their efforts on helping nonprofits develop revenue-generating businesses as a strategy for achieving sustainability, while others are concentrated on building capacity. In addition to providing direct assistance to their grantees, or *portfolio organizations*, they often engage consultants and other specialists to work with those organizations on capacity-building efforts.

Such funders approach their relationships with the nonprofit organizations they support in the same way they would approach the future of a company in which they might invest. In contrast to the traditional pattern of short-term program grants, venture philanthropists, or high-engagement grantmakers, provide sustained support over a period of years and work closely with the organization's management to develop strategy and capacity, with the goal of making the organization sustainable for the long run (Venture Philanthropy Partners Web site, http://venturephilanthropypartners.org, accessed April 27, 2007).

A number of traditional foundations have adopted some of the principles of high-engagement grantmaking, at least with some portion of their resources and especially with regard to organizations they already support with programmatic grants. Some notable examples include the Edna McConnell Clark Foundation, the Charles and Helen Schwab Foundation, and the Agnes and Eugene Meyer Foundation. Meyer's Management Assistance Program "provides grants to help Meyer grantees [organizations receiving program support from Meyer] strengthen their management and leadership [generally by hiring consultants] to help board and staff accomplish work that requires time, energy, and innovative thinking beyond everyday operations" (http://meyerfoundation.org, accessed May 7, 2007). Foundation grants to help nonprofits build capacity increased by 180% in the 1990s and by 2002 supported more than 350 organizational capacity-building programs. Grantmakers for Effective Organizations, an organization based in Washington, D.C., was founded in 1997 and provides a range of information and services related to foundations interested in supporting nonprofit capacity-building activities (Kibbe, 2004, pp. 1–2).

Another significant resource for capacity building is the associations of nonprofits in 41 states and the District of Columbia. These associations provide a variety of training programs for nonprofit managers as well as opportunities for collaboration and the exchange of ideas. The National Council of Nonprofit Associations, a network of state and regional associations, has advocated establishment of a federal government agency to support capacity building by small nonprofits in the same way that the Small Business Administration helps small business firms (www.ncna.org, accessed May 9, 2007).

There are also a number of free resources available to organizations that wish to undertake capacity-building activities. Nonprofit culture supports information sharing, and many are willing to make their materials and experiences known to colleagues who can learn from them. Jonathan Peizer, Chief Technology Officer of the Open Society Institute, has developed a searchable database of capacity-building resources that includes peer review of the various methods offered (www.capaciteria.org). This useful site includes information on capacity building in 10 broad categories, including finance, grants, personnel management, technology, legal matters, general management, facilities and facilities planning, marketing, volunteers, and public relations.

However, the availability of funds to support capacity building is still relatively modest compared with the total of philanthropic giving, and most capacity-building efforts are undertaken by nonprofit organizations using their own internal resources or with unrestricted operating funds obtained through traditional fundraising, earned income, or other methods (Light, 2004b).

UNDERSTANDING CAPACITY AND CAPACITY BUILDING

Now let's go inside the black box of capacity building to look at some of the details. It is no more meaningful to think about an organization's capacity as an indivisible quality than it is to think about a person's capacity in that way. For example, your capacity for study may be different from your capacity for athletics or for singing, so we would need to think about your *capacities* in the plural—that is, break capacity down into different categories or elements. Having done so, we could then consider what activities you might need to undertake in order to increase your capacity in areas that need improvement, perhaps some tutoring to improve your study skills, weight training to enhance your athletic prowess, and singing lessons. Fortunately, various authors have identified components of nonprofit organization capacity in much the same way, in categories. Although they offer somewhat different lists, there are many similarities in the elements they include.

Mike Hudson (2005) divides capacity into internal and external elements, writing that

> building organization capacity is about systematically investing in developing an organization's internal systems (for example, its people, processes, and infrastructure) and its external relationships (for example, with funders, partners, and volunteers) so that it can better realize its mission and achieve greater impact. (p. 1)

When the term *capacity* is used, some people may think primarily about the internal elements. That is understandable. For example, if we think about individuals' capacities—like studying, swimming, or singing—we are really talking about the skills or talents they possess. We are perhaps less inclined to think about their relationships with others as elements of their capacity as individuals. But, as discussed before, nonprofit organizations are open systems and resource dependent. Their relationships with the external world—including other nonprofits, the media, government, donors and other funders—are critical to their survival. Establishing and strengthening these relationships, thus, may be important aspects of capacity building, equal in importance to developing their internal structures, systems, and skills.

Internal and *external* are still two very broad categories. Dividing capacity up that way is like saying it's about "you and your friends." It still doesn't tell us too much about *you* or your various capacities. Paul Connolly and Carol Lukas (2002) offer a more comprehensive framework that helps deepen our understanding. The elements of capacity they identify include (1) the organization's mission, vision, and strategy; (2) its governance and leadership; (3) its ability to deliver programs and ensure the impact of its programs; (4) its strategic relationships—or in other words, the important external relationships that are critical sources of revenue or that may present constraints on the nonprofit's activities; and (5) its internal systems and management—its human resources, financial management systems, technology and information systems, facilities, plans for managing risk, programs for volunteer recruitment and management, and working relationships among its managers, staff, and volunteers.

Connolly and Lukas's (2002) list reminds us again that capacity encompasses almost everything a nonprofit organization has, does, knows, or is. Its definition is so comprehensive that it may seem difficult to distinguish capacity building from simply managing the organization. It may help look at some specific processes and activities that nonprofits actually undertake when they say they are engaged in building capacity.

CAPACITY BUILDING IN ACTION

An organization beginning a capacity-building initiative might use one of a number of tools that are available to evaluate its various capacities and identify areas of weakness that might need to be addressed. For example, the consulting firm McKinsey & Company offers a capacity assessment grid that nonprofit managers, staff, board members, and others can use to rate the organization's current status on each element of capacity, assigning a score of "1" where there is a clear need for increased capacity, a "2" when there is a basic level of capacity in place, a "3" if there is a moderate level of capacity in place, and a "4" if there is a high level of capacity in place on the element being evaluated (McKinsey & Company, 2001). When the instrument is completed by various people within the organization, the combined scores help identify areas in which there is consensus about the need for improvement.

Having identified areas of its capacity that need to be strengthened, exactly what actions might an organization undertake? There is a large toolbox available, with tools designed to address almost any need. Strategic planning is a capacity-building activity undertaken by many nonprofit organizations. Indeed, it offers a comprehensive approach that provides a good place to start in identifying elements of capacity that need to be addressed as part of an overall plan to achieve the organization's goals. Because strategic planning is an important subject, it will be explored in some detail in Chapter 7. Capacity building often includes efforts to strengthen the organization's leadership, including the governing board and the CEO. As discussed in Chapters 3 and 4, there are a variety of tools for assessing and improving the skills of boards and CEOs and for developing policies designed to improve their performance. Board development activities might include, for example, board self-assessments, retreats, and establishing a governance committee of the board to focus on the board's own responsibilities, structure, and operation. There are a number of ways in which organizations invest in their executive leadership. Participation in professional associations and activities enables CEOs to learn from the experiences of their peers. There are a wide variety of formal leadership training programs available. Some organizations support their CEOs by retaining an executive coach, a practitioner of a field that has grown into a distinguishable profession in recent years. Having a plan for executive transition is a recommended practice for well-managed nonprofit organizations, and the existence of such a plan is indeed an element of capacity (Kibbe, 2004; Light, 2004b).

Establishing a system for the regular evaluation of programs would add to an organization's program delivery capacity. Strengthening fundraising and partnerships, perhaps developing plans for earned-income ventures, improving facilities and systems, and enhancing staff and volunteer skills are all important purposes of capacity building. Undertaking a campaign, which will be discussed in Chapter 10, may be an important capacity-building activity that will provide the funds needed for improving physical facilities and strengthening the organization's financial base. Strengthening internal management systems and functions, including human resource management, volunteer programs, financial systems, and operating procedures and policies, is commonly included in capacity-building initiatives.

Paul Light's (2004b) book on capacity building makes a contribution to our understanding because it is based on a study of such activities *actually undertaken* by 318 nonprofits that he surveyed. Light divides capacity into four categories: internal structure, external relations, leadership, and management systems. Table 6.1 identifies these categories and some specific activities that the majority of organizations encompassed in his study had completed. They include many of the activities that already have been discussed, with some differences in how they are categorized.

TABLE 6.1	Capacities and Capacity-Building Activities

Capacity	*Capacity-Building Activities*
External relations	Improve collaboration with other nonprofits Conduct strategic planning Strengthen fundraising Improve media relations
Internal structure	Engage in team-building Add staff Undertake reorganization
Leadership	Undertake board development Delegate more responsibility Undertake leadership development
Management systems	Adopt new information technology Provide staff training Update accounting system Engage in program evaluation Engage in organizational assessment

Source: Based on Light (2004b, pp. 58–59).

A MODEL FOR CAPACITY BUILDING

We now have an understanding of the various elements of capacity and the broad array of activities that can be undertaken to enhance capacity in each area. But where do we start? How do the elements fit together, and where should an organization begin to address its capacity in a holistic way?

In work undertaken for Venture Philanthropy Partners, a prominent venture philanthropy fund, the consulting firm McKinsey & Company (2001) developed a comprehensive capacity framework that helps answer these questions. As depicted in Figure 6.1, McKinsey defines nonprofit capacity in a pyramid of seven essential elements. These elements include some of the items we saw from Connolly and Lukas (2002) and from Light (2004b), but their depiction in the framework of a pyramid implies relationships among them and suggests a process for capacity building. McKinsey & Company's (2001) pyramid also highlights the importance of an intangible but powerful force that affects every aspect of capacity and efforts to strengthen it—the organization's culture.

FIGURE 6.1   McKinsey & Company Capacity Framework

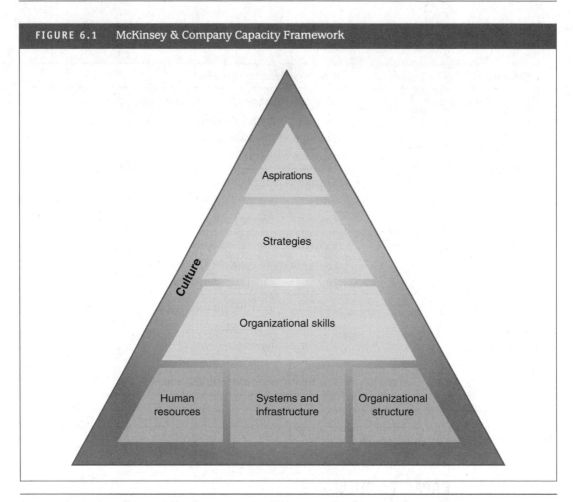

McKinsey & Company's (2001) model begins at the top with aspirations, which encompass what are generally called mission, vision, and values. At the next level of detail are the organization's strategies, and then its skills—that is, what it knows and can do. On the bottom of the pyramid are human resources, systems and infrastructure, and organizational structure. In the McKinsey pyramid, all six elements are surrounded by, or embedded within, a shell called "culture," which affects all the elements and provides the overall environment in which capacity-building efforts may be undertaken.

It may be tempting to initiate capacity building at the bottom of the pyramid, perhaps by completing an inventory of staff skills, analyzing organizational charts, and evaluating the suitability of information and accounting systems. Those are areas in which many organizations have some deficiencies, and they often affect the daily work of its staff, so there is a high awareness of them. They are concrete and specific and thus easier for people to get their heads around. But McKinsey & Company (2001) emphasize the importance of following a process that begins at the top of the pyramid and works down, stating that its capacity-building work with nonprofits has been most successful when larger questions of mission, vision, and values, and then strategies and organizational skills, are addressed before the work proceeds to the elements at the foundation of the pyramid:

> The act of resetting aspirations and strategy is often the first step in dramatically improving an organization's capacity. The nonprofits [among those McKinsey studied] that experienced the greatest gains in capacity were those that undertook a reassessment of their aspirations—their vision of what the organization was attempting to accomplish in the next phase of its development. (p. 15)

> Resetting aspirations alone is not sufficient in and of itself, however.

> A new aspiration or strategy can only be transformative if it is then used to align the other aspects of organizational capacity. If done thoroughly, this alignment process provides a tight institutional focus and a road map for the organization to use with both internal and external audiences, which help keep everyone on track during the long and difficult process of building capacity. (McKinsey & Company, 2001, p. 15)

Thus, capacity building may mean more than making modest enhancements to staff skills or management systems. In its most expansive conception, capacity building may represent disruptive transformational change that goes to the basic values and purposes of the organization.

CAPACITY AND ORGANIZATIONAL LIFE CYCLES

Let's look at two examples of capacity building in action, undertaken in two different organizations under very different circumstances. Wendy Kopp founded Teach for America in 1989, recruiting recent graduates from top colleges and universities to spend two years teaching in schools serving low-income students before beginning other careers. She attracted hundreds of talented young men and women to her cause, and her organization grew rapidly. But five years later, Teach for America was "on the verge of collapse" (Hauser, 2003). While Kopp's energy and charisma were sufficient to keep the organization running and growing for a time, its lack of organizational structure, management systems, and comprehensive fundraising strategies eventually left it in debt and struggling with problems of communications and morale (Hauser, 2003). After considering the possibility of closing, in 1995 the organization launched an effort to achieve stability. "They . . . implemented a plan to build a diverse and sustainable funding base, to concentrate on core activities, to introduce much-needed management processes, and to strengthen the [organization's] culture" (Hauser, 2003). By 2003, Teach for America had recovered and grown, with 3,400 corps members engaged in teaching more than 250,000 students (Hauser, 2003).

Rubicon Programs, a California-based organization that helps homeless and disadvantaged people gain independence and self-sufficiency, did not face a crisis like Teach for America. Rather, its goal in 1994 was to further develop its already successful programs and increase their impact. With support from the Roberts Enterprise Development Fund, Rubicon built a measurement system to track client outcomes. The new system made it possible not only to serve more clients and better match programs to their needs but also to accurately report outcomes to funders, and it "fundamentally reshaped the organization's performance culture" by making management and staff focus on social impact. By 2000, Rubicon had quadrupled its staff, achieved financial self-sufficiency, and increased the number of people served from 800 to 4,000 (McKinsey & Company, 2001, pp. 55–56).

Teach for America and Rubicon Programs offer examples of nonprofit organizations at different places in their histories, one struggling to survive and the other aspiring to greater scale and effectiveness. But both represent examples of capacity-building efforts that helped lead to stability, growth, and recognition for performance.

A number of authors have advanced life-cycle models describing how organizations grow, mature, and may eventually decline. Many are similar and include the same basic stages, identified by different terms (see, e.g., Adizes, 1999; Carlson & Donohoe, 2003; Stevens, 2001). Let's look at one life-cycle model of nonprofit organizations, developed by Judith Sharken Simon and summarized in Table 6.2.

TABLE 6.2   Life Stages of Nonprofits

Organizational Life Stage	Description of Organization
Stage I: Imagine and inspire	The organization has not yet been founded; it is still an idea or a dream. This stage is characterized by enthusiasm, energy, and creativity.
Stage II: Found and frame	The organization is created and begins to frame its program. There is still great enthusiasm and energy.
Stage III: Ground and grow	The organization is building its foundation and growing. There is an emphasis on accountability, but rapid growth can be challenging to management.
Stage IV: Produce and sustain	The organization is mature and stable. It may be on autopilot. There is the risk of becoming stale, and maintaining momentum is a concern.
Stage V: Review and renew	The organization revisits its mission and programs and undertakes change. Minor changes may take it back to Stage IV. Major changes may take it back to Stage II.

Source: Based on Simon (2001).

As Table 6.2 suggests, an organization begins as an idea, a dream, often in the mind of its founder. Once chartered as a formal organization, it still resonates with the enthusiasm of the founder and a small group of founding board or staff members, who work to frame its programs, establish some structure, and chart its direction for future growth. Like an adolescent, it may sometimes be chaotic, but raw energy and commitment drive it forward. Once a foundation has been established, the organization may grow as rapidly as an adolescent. It adds new programs, raises more funds, hires more staff, and becomes more systematic in its approach. It will place greater emphasis on measuring results and ensuring accountability as it approaches maturity. As for individuals, maturity has its risks. The organization may be stable, its programs churning along in an effective way, its systems operating so well that it runs almost on autopilot. But there is the risk of complacency, bureaucracy, stagnation, and decline.

Simon's (2001) concept of life stages is a more optimistic one than some models depict. The organization proceeds from an idea to existence as a mature organization and then has the capacity to renew itself and return to an earlier stage of growth. But not all scenarios may proceed so well. There are threats at every stage. A new organization may not have sufficient resources or skills to survive past its childhood. It may be unable to raise enough funds; attract enough volunteers or staff; or keep pace with the competition offered by older, more established organizations in its field. The organization's leadership may not be able to manage the period of rapid growth. For example, Chapter 4 discussed the risk of founder syndrome, in which a founding CEO is unable or unwilling to step aside while the organization's growth demands a different set of management skills. Systems and skills may lag behind the demands placed on them by expanding programs, and quality may deteriorate. Chaos may reign, and the organization may collapse during this period.

If the organization survives to the stage of maturity, it may be in danger of losing its edge. A mature organization may not have the energy and innovativeness of its early years. It may become a lumbering bureaucracy. Its staff may be going through the motions. It may not confront the need for change. It may be unprepared to respond to changes in its environment, to a loss of a key source of support, or to shifting patterns of community needs. If it does not move to the stage of "review and renew," it may stagnate, decline, and eventually expire (Simon, 2001).

This suggests that a focus on capacity is important at every stage of an organization's life but that the elements of capacity that are most relevant may be different in each stage. A young organization may need to be concerned primarily with honing its mission, developing its programs, securing funds, and ensuring accountability. A growing organization may need to devote attention to its management systems and organizational structure, in order to accommodate more complexity and greater scale. And a mature organization may need to return to its aspirations in order to renew the enthusiasm and energy of its earlier years, revive growth, and ensure its continued relevance and survival.

Indeed, in his study of 318 nonprofits, Paul Light (2004b) discovered that the types of capacity-building activities undertaken do vary according to the organization's size and age. He found that younger organizations are more likely than older ones to develop collaborations with other organizations and undertake organizational assessments but are less likely to focus their capacity building on media relations, reorganization, team building, leadership development, or the implementation of new information or personnel systems (p. 60). As Light describes the situation, "Younger organizations behave like the more agile, yet naïve organizations they are. They adopt capacity-building approaches that build their influence through collaboration and outcomes measurement but show less interest in media relations and new information technology, either because they do not recognize the need or do not have the funding (p. 60).

Older and larger organizations in Light's (2004b) study were more likely to "behave like weight-conscious organizations: They adopt capacity-building approaches designed to counter bureaucratic encrustation," including reorganization, team building, leadership development, changes in their personnel systems, staff training, and program evaluation. Strategic planning, a topic considered in the next chapter, also is more likely to be used by older and larger nonprofits than by younger and smaller ones and is an approach that may enable them to break out from a stage of maturity and potential stagnation to a period of renewed growth. Light offers his own life-cycle theory, which he calls the "spiral of sustainable excellence," and relates it to the need for the right capacity building at each stage:

> Imagine nonprofit life as a journey up and down a spiral. All organizations would start with a simple idea for some new program or service and then move up the spiral toward greater and greater impact. Also imagine five landings, or stops, along the climb: the organic phase of life in which they struggle to create a presence in their environment, the enterprising phase in which they seek to expand their size and scope, the intentional phase in which they try to focus themselves on what they do best, the robust phase in which they strengthen their organizational infrastructure to hedge against the unexpected, and the reflective phase in which they address longer-term issues of succession and legacy. (p. 136)

In Light's (2004b) model, nonprofits might move up the spiral at different rates, some quickly, some slowly, and many never reaching the top. Some might also descend the spiral at certain times. and some might occasionally go all the way down to "their organic roots from time to time to ask themselves again why they exist, whom they serve, and how they intend to make a difference" (p. 137). The type of capacity building needed would depend on where the organization is on this spiral:

> Some forms of capacity building are much more important for moving from the organic to the enterprising stage or for stopping the fall backward, while others are much more appropriate for the climb from intentional to robust. As such, successful capacity building depends in large part on picking the right improvement effort at the right time. (p. 138)

CAPACITY, CULTURE, AND CHANGE

Capacity building inevitably involves change. The changes may be relatively small ones and easily accommodated—for example, developing a new set of personnel policies or gift-processing procedures. Others may be somewhat more disruptive and challenging—for example, implementation of a new accounting system or reorganization of the staff. Some may be viewed as positive changes—for example, the hiring of additional fundraising staff or increased opportunities for staff to receive training. But transformational changes may strike at the heart of the organization, perhaps requiring a new board consensus about mission and values, challenging deeply rooted rituals of the staff, and perhaps even a change in executive leadership. Perhaps most unsettling of all, increasing capacity may demand a change in the *culture* of the organization.

Culture includes shared values, attitudes, feelings, beliefs, rituals, habits, codes of conduct, and other such characteristics of an organization—invisible rules that may support or hinder an initiative for change. McKinsey & Company (2001) call it the "invisible thread that runs throughout the entire subject of capacity building" (p. 63). Like McKinsey's framework, Barbara Kibbe's (2004) discussion of capacity building emphasizes the importance of a clear-cut mission, goals, and measurable objectives, and something else—what she calls "planfulness." An organization's planfulness is its "capacity to revisit the organization's mission, goals, and strategies on a regular basis to make sure they are fresh and appropriate to new opportunities, new challenges, and changes in the wider world." Planfulness thus implies "more than a one-time strategic planning project"; it is a way of life for the organization (p. 7).

Similar to Kibbe (2004), Letts et al. (1999a) also describe an aspect of an organization's capacity that is intangible. Letts and her colleagues describe three types of capacity an organization may possess: *program delivery capacity, program expansion capacity,* and *adaptive capacity.* They say that most nonprofit organizations are familiar with the first two, but it is "adaptive capacity that makes an organization not only efficient but also effective" (p. 20). As the term implies, program delivery capacity grows out of the organization's knowledge of a specific field—for example, education, the environment, public health (p. 20). Its capacities include the skills of its staff, who are recruited for their professional expertise. If this is the only capacity the organization possesses, "the organization is little more than a convenient venue where programs are implemented" (p. 20). As an organization expands its program, possibly to multiple sites, it needs to develop additional capacities, including payroll and financial systems, fundraising, and staff with supervisory skills. But, Letts and her coauthors argue, it is the third capacity—adaptive capacity—"that an organization needs to be sure it is delivering on its mission" (p. 21). This includes the ability to learn as an organization and identify ways to improve, to change in response to client needs, to create new and innovative programs, and to create an environment that is motivating to staff and volunteers (p. 23). Letts et al. draw on models developed in the business sector that they say can be adapted to build the capacity of nonprofits, and they emphasize the need to develop a "culture of performance."

In other words, capacity may involve more than what an organization *has*—its facilities, structure, and systems—and more than what it can *do*—the skills of its leaders, staff, and volunteers. It may be related as well to what the organization *is*—in other words, it may encompass intangible qualities such as orientation, commitment, and *culture* (Kibbe, 2004, p. 7).

Capacity building, or any effort to change the way in which an organization conducts its business, therefore must acknowledge the reality of existing culture and follow a process that seeks change in the context of it. In addition, new ways must be sufficiently embedded in the organization's culture to ensure their lasting impact.

There are a number of prominent *change theories* and models. Most include the idea of stages in the change process, including recognition of the need for change, building of support for change, identification of a new vision, and assurance that change becomes embedded in the organization's culture. One of the best-known experts on change, John Kotter (1996), describes eight common mistakes that leaders trying to implement change are prone to make and proposes a parallel eight-step change process to avoid them. Although Kotter's model is based on business corporations, it can be applied as well in the nonprofit setting.

According to Kotter (1996), efforts at transformational change in an organization often fail because leaders allow too much *complacency*; that is, they do not engender a sufficient sense of urgency about the need for change. For example, in a mature organization, decline may be gradual, and future threats may not be visible to most people. As long as the operating budget is balanced, there is no negative publicity or scandal, and staff positions seem secure, most people may be content to continue with business as usual and not be receptive to changes that would disrupt their worldviews or routines.

Leaders often fail to develop what Kotter (1996) calls a *powerful guiding coalition* in support of change. In other words, they too often try to drive the change alone without first developing a critical mass of allies—perhaps including key staff members, members of the board, and others—who share their commitment to the need for change. Leaders sometimes underestimate the power of *vision*. They try to bring about change through a series of actions—incremental changes, perhaps small modifications to procedures, reorganizations of staff, or incremental enhancements to fundraising or communications programs. These are steps along the way that may appear unconnected to those who do not see or understand the larger vision toward which they are intended to lead. Leaders may try to operate behind the scenes, without adequately painting the picture of what the future will be like. In that case, they are unlikely to build the steam necessary to propel real and lasting change in the organization. The inertia of current culture and practice may be just too strong to overcome with an incremental approach.

Too often, change leaders *undercommunicate* the vision, perhaps relying on routine communication vehicles, such as newsletters, annual reports, and other publications. They may assume that everyone in the organization carefully reads and considers such publications—or takes them seriously—and is thus sufficiently aware of the plan for change and shares the leader's commitment to it, when in fact this may not be true.

Kotter (1996) says that leaders may fail because they do not create *short-term wins*—that is, set intermediate goals that can be achieved and reassure followers that the ultimate longer-term changes can be successfully reached. Summarizing lessons from their experience in working with nonprofit clients on capacity building, McKinsey & Company (2001) conclude,

> You must have patience. . . . Almost everything about capacity building . . . takes longer and is more complicated than one would expect. Building capacity can feel like a never-ending process because improvements in one area or practice have a way of placing unexpected new demands on other areas, which in turn trigger new needs. There are few quick fixes when it comes to building capacity. (p. 15)

Setting some achievable short-term goals and celebrating their attainment can be an essential tactic to retain the commitment of staff and volunteers to a long-term change process and prevent frustration and inertia from bringing it to a halt midstream.

But there is also the risk of *declaring victory too soon*. Change may have occurred on the surface, but leaders err when they do not stay with the program long enough for the changes to "sink down deeply into the [organization's] culture" (Kotter, 1996, p. 13). Only by *anchoring the changes* in the organization's culture can the leader pursuing change ensure that the board and successive generations of management will also adhere to new ways of doing things. As Kotter (1996) explains,

> Smart people miss the mark here when they are insensitive to cultural issues. Economically oriented finance people and analytically oriented engineers can find the topic of social norms and values too soft for their tastes. So, they ignore culture—at their peril. (p. 15)

Kotter (1996) offers an eight-step change process that avoids each of the potential mistakes (p. 21). To ensure that the momentum for change is not overwhelmed by the inertia of existing culture and practices and to ensure that the change is real and permanent, the leader should follow the steps sequentially, not moving on to the next until the previous has been solidly accomplished:

- Establish a sense of urgency
- Create a guiding coalition
- Develop a vision and strategy
- Communicate the change vision
- Empower broad-based action
- Generate short-term wins
- Consolidate gains and produce more change
- Anchor new approaches in the culture

What is the essential ingredient of successful change? Kotter (1996) argues that it requires 70% to 90% leadership and just 10% to 30% the skills of management. "Leadership defines what the future should look like, aligns people with that vision, and inspires them to make it happen despite the obstacles" (p. 26). But leadership may be in short supply when an organization needs it to drive essential change. Kotter describes a life-cycle theory of business firms that is reminiscent of the nonprofit life cycles we discussed earlier. Companies start as entrepreneurial businesses, then grow and achieve a position of market dominance. As size and dominance increase, control becomes most important, and management predominates over leadership. But that can produce a bureaucratic, inward orientation that causes managers to become complacent about performance. The situation requires change, but the forces of complacency and inertia make change difficult, requiring "sacrifice, dedication, and creativity." These cannot be engendered through coercion but instead require "leadership, leadership, and more leadership" (p. 31).

DOES CAPACITY BUILDING WORK?

Now we come to the bottom-line question: Does capacity building really have an impact on an organization's effectiveness or performance? A positive answer may seem intuitive. How could improved governance, strengthened leadership, better systems and facilities, more highly trained staff, and an adaptive culture *not* lead to the more effective delivery of programs and a better-performing organization? Indeed, most experts agree with intuition, arguing that capacity and effectiveness are "inextricably linked" (www.vppartners.org/report2004.html, accessed, May 5, 2008). But solid evidence of the link has proven to be elusive. One of the problems, of course, is in defining effectiveness or performance for a nonprofit organization. As discussed in Chapter 5, there are different views on how effectiveness or performance should be defined, and there is not always agreement on how effectiveness or performance should be measured even among those who may agree on the definition. If we have difficulty defining it and measuring it, how can we be certain that capacity building increases it?

In his book, Paul Light (2004b) concludes that greater capacity *does* lead to increased effectiveness and proposes a logic model to explain the implications of the link: Greater capacity leads to increased effectiveness, he argues, which increases public confidence, which in turn results in more discretionary giving and volunteering. Light's solution to diminished public confidence in nonprofits is thus to invest more in building their capacity, thereby increasing their effectiveness and changing the public's perceptions. But his evidence of the initial link, between capacity and effectiveness, is based on the perceptions of nonprofit employees who participated in his study. He acknowledges that "perceptions are always affected by self-interest" but nevertheless concludes that "given the lack of objective data for measuring nonprofit capacity and effectiveness, perceptions will have to do for now." Additionally,

> the evidence presented here [in the report of his study] is strong enough to make the case that capacity matters to the effectiveness of nonprofit organizations, which is more than enough to justify further analysis of whether and how capacity-building efforts work. (p. 15)

Light (2004b) may be right that perceptions will need to do for now. And intuition may be a sufficient justification for continued investment in nonprofit capacity. But, nevertheless, prudent managers will give careful consideration to the costs and benefits associated with any particular initiative. And it is essential to evaluate the impact of completed capacity-building efforts. The Alliance for Nonprofit Management and others have provided guides for such evaluation, and some are included in the suggested readings at the end of this chapter.

Few will disagree with Light's (2004b) call for additional analysis. But given the larger issue of how to define and measure effectiveness, questions of whether, how, and how much capacity-building efforts affect the performance of nonprofit organizations likely will continue to be raised.

CHAPTER SUMMARY

A nonprofit organization's capacity includes all of the resources it uses to pursue its mission. Capacity building means efforts that are undertaken to strengthen the organization in order to make it more effective in achieving its mission. Capacity includes an organization's internal systems, such as people, processes, and infrastructure, as well as its external relationships with funders, partners, volunteers, and others. Many observers have argued that historically nonprofits focused on delivering services rather than building the organization and that the funding practices of foundations and others reinforced that inclination by failing to provide support for capacity building. These critiques have led to a growing interest in capacity building and some increased funding to support it, although most such efforts are funded through organizations' internal resources.

An organization's capacity is not an indivisible quality; rather, there are various elements of capacity—or capacities—that it might concentrate on strengthening. Some authors divide these elements into internal and external, while others have developed more comprehensive taxonomies. For example, Paul Light (2004b) divides capacity into four categories: external relations, internal structure, leadership, and management systems. Instruments are available to assist organizations in identifying elements of capacity that need to be strengthened and the type of capacity-building initiatives that should be undertaken. These could include board development leadership training for the CEO, training for staff members, or the use of consultants to improve management systems and procedures, among many others.

Some theorists describe life cycles of nonprofit organizations. Beginning as a dream, they are founded and pass through a period of growth, eventually reaching maturity. They then may enter a period of renewal, in which they are redefined and reenergized, returning to a period of additional growth, although some that do not change may decline and expire. The type of capacity building that is needed will differ at various stages; for example, young organizations may need to focus on building systems and accountability, while mature organizations may need to revisit their missions and values. Some experts, including the consulting firm McKinsey & Company (2001), advise that capacity building is most likely to succeed if it begins with mission, vision, and values and then proceeds to more detailed considerations of staff, systems, and structure.

An organization's efforts to build capacity are affected by its prevailing culture, which is also given an important role in theories of change. The prominent change theorist John Kotter (1996) recommends a process of change that culminates in new practices becoming anchored in the organization's culture and argues that this final step is necessary to ensure that the change is permanent. Kotter also emphasizes the need for leadership as a catalyst for organizational change.

Whether capacity building increases organizational effectiveness remains a debated question. While Light (2004b) and others assert that it does, there remain disagreements about the appropriate definition of effectiveness and the indicators that should be used to measure it. This lack of consensus makes it difficult to prove the link between capacity building and improved organizational performance. Capacity-building initiatives should be preceded by an analysis of expected costs and benefits and followed by a thorough evaluation of their impact on the organization's effectiveness and performance.

KEY TERMS AND CONCEPTS FROM CHAPTER 6

adaptive capacity   *life cycle*
capacity   *organizational change*
capacity building   *program delivery capacity*
change theories   *program expansion capacity*
high-engagement grantmaking   *venture philanthropy*
life stages

CASE 6.1

Change at the Girl Scouts of America

When Kathy Cloninger arrived as CEO of the Girl Scouts of America in 2003, she joined an organization with a long and distinguished history but one better known for its cookie sales than for its programs to develop girls as future leaders. Founded in 1912 by Juliette Gordon Low with an original troop of 18, the organization had grown to include 2.7 million girl members and nearly 1 million adult volunteers. Although it was a stable and respected organization, the Girls Scouts nevertheless had developed an image as "musty and uncool" and faced several significant challenges (LaBarre, 2006).

First, membership in Girl Scout troops had declined over the previous five years, and there were reasons to be concerned about the future. Social trends, including more mothers having careers, were making it more difficult to attract volunteers. A greater range of available activities for girls was presenting increased competition for their time, attention, and participation. Registration for individual programs and events across the country had increased significantly in recent years, but Cloninger determined that the delivery of programs was fragmented and that the quality of the experience being provided to girls and volunteers was uneven across the country.

Some of the challenges were rooted in the Girl Scouts's organizational structure. The national office, based in New York, provided service to the local councils, and overall policy and direction were established by a national council of about 2,000 elected delegates, who met every three years. But local Girl Scout councils were relatively autonomous, and they had their own operating budgets, boards, and staff. Given the decentralized culture of the organization, the relationship between the national office and local councils was sometimes uneasy, with some local councils resistant to centralized direction or control.

In this model, population trends were creating disparities at the local level, with some councils able to fund innovative programs and others struggling to serve their dwindling memberships with inadequate resources. There were 312 councils. Sixty were on the brink of failure. The largest 20% were serving 50% of the membership, and the smallest 20% were serving just 5% of the members.

Cloninger determined that incremental changes would not be sufficient and that the 90-year-old organization needed transformation. The last major reorganization of the Girl Scouts had occurred in the 1950s. It was a top-down process that met resistance from local councils and required 20 years to complete (Hrywna, 2007). Cloninger knew that it would need to be done differently this time.

She began by creating a 26-person core strategy team, including not just individuals from the national office but a diverse group encompassing staff, volunteers and board leaders, and CEOs of local councils. This core group was given six months, from June to December 2004, to draft a new mission statement and identify strategic priorities. This led to the creation of six "gap teams," so called because their charge was to help in "bridging the gap between Girl Scouts today and Girl Scouts of the future." With even more diverse and broadly representative membership than the core strategy team, the gap teams were to focus on key areas with specific assignments:

Program model and pathways: Build the best integrated personal/leadership development model that defines activities and outcomes, differentiated by age level, for girls 5 to 17 and offers flexible pathways for participation.

Volunteerism: Develop a nimble state-of-the-art model of volunteerism that mobilizes a diverse cadre of volunteers committed to the Girl Scout mission.

Brand: Transform the Girl Scout image into a compelling, contemporary brand.

Funding: Substantially increase contributed income.

Governance and organizational structure: Create an efficient and effective organizational structure and democratic governance system.

Culture: Lead the transformation of our culture, which is a key component of the broader transformation of Girl Scouting (Girl Scouts Web site, http://girlscouts.org/strategy/gap_team.asp, accessed April 11, 2007).

The gap teams were given a firm deadline. Their work had to be completed by the time of the Girl Scouts' 50th convention in October 2005. Demographers were retained to support the work of the gap teams by developing data to show population trends and reveal the disparities among councils in different areas. Cloninger launched a massive communications effort, meeting with council CEOs, visiting troops, and setting up Web sites to report on progress. When the national convention arrived, delegates were given multiple opportunities to provide their input on the plan. Six "strategy cafes" permitted focused discussion with each of the gap teams, and a large open discussion was held on the question of governance. When the time came for a vote, the new mission statement and strategy were approved by an overwhelming majority.

Then the hard work began. Cloninger created a process to restructure the headquarters staff. She continued intensive communication and a participative approach, asking staff for their suggestions on a new structure and revised job descriptions. The realignment of local councils was an even more sensitive matter. The plan was to reduce 312 councils to just over 100 "high-performance" councils. This would require mergers, a reduction in CEO positions, and a loss of autonomy for some small councils. A pilot program including 37 "early adopters" was initiated, and as of January, 2007, the process was continuing with the expectation that the realignment would be completed nationwide by 2009 (Hrywna, 2007).

What will be the results of the change? Cloninger emphasizes that the transformation of the Girl Scouts is about much more than the realignment of councils. "There will be cost savings," Cloninger

(Continued)

(Continued)

says, "but we did not go into it because of financial issues or troubles. We went in thinking about what structure would give us capacity." She adds, "We're developing a very girl-driven model, rewriting programs, really putting our program out there in a whole new arena packaged around leadership" (quoted in Hrywna, 2007, p. 2). The realignment of councils is "just one of many pieces" of the organization's transformation. Linda Foreman, the national secretary of the national board, makes the same point—reorganization was just one of several strategic priorities, but it was the change that needed to be undertaken in order to gain the capacity to achieve other goals:

"This was a very complex . . . learning process that ended up with five priorities," she explains. "But when looking at volunteerism, brand, funding, and program, it became clear we probably needed to address the structural piece first. Realignment in my mind is about positioning ourselves to be able to deliver on all the rest of it." (Hrywna, 2007, p. 4)

Reflecting on the process of change, Cloninger speaks frankly:

"It's very messy. It can't but impact the culture and some people leave and new people are coming in, so it's pretty chaotic. But you can't get sidetracked by angst over the fact that things aren't perfect. This isn't a two-year plan with a finish line—it's a transforming strategy. It's going to be hard and we'll make mistakes, but we're in it for the long haul." (LaBarre, 2006, p. 50)

Sources: LaBarre (2006), Hrywna (2007), and Girl Scouts Web site (www.girlscouts.org/strategy, accessed April 11, 2007).

QUESTIONS FOR DISCUSSION

1. At what point in its organizational life cycle did Kathy Cloninger join the Girl Scouts? What might have happened if the organization did not go through a transformation?

2. How do the six strategic priorities identified by the Girl Scouts fit into the capacity elements identified in Table 6.1 (Light, 2004b)?

3. Does the change process at the Girl Scouts follow Kotter's model? Knowing that the process was not yet finished as of the writing of this book, in 2007, what steps in Kotter's process were yet to be completed?

4. Did Cloninger's approach follow the McKinsey capacity-building model?

5. How was Cloninger's approach to change influenced by the culture of the Girl Scouts organization?

SUGGESTIONS FOR FURTHER READING RELATED TO CHAPTER 6

Books

Connolly, P., & Lukas, C. (2002). *Strengthening nonprofit performance: A funder's guide to capacity building*. Saint Paul, MN: Amherst H. Wilder Foundation/Grantmakers for Effective Organizations.

Grantmakers for Effective Organizations. (2004). Funding effectiveness: Lessons in building nonprofit capacity. San Francisco: Jossey-Bass.

Hudson, M. (2005). *Managing at the leading edge*. San Francisco: Jossey-Bass.

Light, P. C. (2004). *Sustaining nonprofit performance: The case for capacity building and the evidence to support it*. Washington, DC: Brookings Institution.

Linnell, D. (2003). *Evaluation of capacity building: Lessons from the field*. Washington, DC: Alliance for Nonprofit Management.

McKinsey & Company. (2001). *Effective capacity building in nonprofit organizations*. Washington, DC: Venture Philanthropy Partners. Retrieved April 24, 2007, from http://venturephilanthropy partners.org/learning/reports/capacity/capacity.html

Simon, J. S. (2001). *The 5 stages of nonprofit organizations*. St. Paul, MN: Amherst H. Wilder Foundation.

Web Sites

Alliance for Nonprofit Management, www.allianceonline.org

Amherst Wilder Foundation, www.wilder.org

Capaciteria (a searchable database of capacity-building resources), www.capaciteria.org

Grantmakers for Effective Organizations, www.geofunders.org

New Profit, Inc., www.newprofit.com

Venture Philanthropy Partners, http://venturephilanthropypartners.org

CHAPTER 7

Strategic Planning and Strategic Management

As discussed in Chapter 6, strategic planning may be an important vehicle for capacity building, especially for well-established nonprofits that have moved beyond their earliest life stage. Many nonprofit organizations are founded by charismatic leaders, whose personal vision and energy inspire the commitment of staff and volunteers and drive the organization's growth in its early years. However, as the organization becomes larger, with more staff, bigger budgets, and more complex operations, passion and intuition may no longer be sufficient. A more rational approach to management and decision making becomes essential to ensure the organization's continued viability and effectiveness. This chapter will discuss *strategic planning*, the broader concept of *strategic management*, and other tools that nonprofit organizations can use to make rational decisions about their programs and resources.

UNDERSTANDING STRATEGY

Concepts like strategic planning and strategic management may seem intimidating at first—they sound complicated, technical, and perhaps like something that requires highly specialized training to conduct. But let's start with a simpler concept—that of *strategy*.

In 1967, Herb Kelleher, a Texas lawyer, and Rollin King, one of his clients, were sitting in a restaurant. On the back of a napkin, Kelleher drew a triangle, labeling the points Dallas, Houston, and San Antonio. He had an idea. Instead of flying passengers into a major hub airport and then redistributing them back out to smaller cities, like the major airlines, what if an airline flew directly between the smaller cities? And what if that airline offered no frills, like food service or reserved seats, saving costs? Short flights, lower costs, lower fares? Although he had not written a strategic plan, Kelleher had a winning strategy simple enough to be sketched on the back of a napkin—and Southwest Airlines was born!

In 1989, Robert Egger was managing nightclubs in Washington, D.C. His fiancé persuaded him to join her in a volunteer program that passed out food to the city's homeless from trucks that toured the city's streets and parks. He began to think about the tons of food that were wasted every day by restaurants, hotels, and caterers throughout Washington. He put these two insights together and founded DC Central Kitchen. The Kitchen collects surplus food, processes and repackages it, and today provides more than 4,000 meals a day to shelters and other facilities throughout the area. Like Kelleher, Egger didn't start out with a strategic plan, but he had a winning strategy.

Management scholars and consultants have offered many definitions of strategy and there is no agreement either on exactly what it is or how to develop it. It may involve a plan, that is, a written document, or it may be more intangible, perhaps no more than an idea or an approach to reaching a goal. Strategy is focused on the long term not on the day-to-day or, as Allison and Kaye (2005) write, "It is concerned with the longer-term course that the ship is steering, not with the waves" (p. 12). Developing strategy does not necessarily require any formal process or result in any written document at all. It does require creativity and a different way of seeing reality.

Kevin Kearns (2000) identifies three approaches to formulating strategy for an organization. The first is the *visioning approach*. This approach begins with the leader's vision and then works backward to determine "what strategies, tactic, actions, and resources are needed to achieve it" (pp. 31, 41). A charismatic leader knows what he or she wants to accomplish and the staff scramble to make it happen. This approach has its advantages and may be the best way to go in a new or young organization or one facing a crisis, situations in which, as we will discuss later, formal strategic planning may not be useful or appropriate. The visioning approach also may create an entrepreneurial "do it now" culture, one that can be very inspirational and motivating, and produces an opportunistic and flexible organization that can move quickly to seize new opportunities that may arise. But it may be risky as well. The leader's vision may not always be 20/20. Relying on the leader's vision may leave the organization open to external threats that the optimistic leader just can't or doesn't see but that are real. It is an approach to formulating strategy, but it may become increasingly inadequate as the organization grows and becomes more complex—in other words, as it gains more to lose.

Another approach to developing strategy that Kearns (2000) describes is the *incremental approach*. Strategy evolves out of experience as the organization goes along, one decision at a time, buffeted by bargaining and the push-and-pull of its constituencies. Basically, it muddles along. This may be a realistic way to go given the complexity of many nonprofits' environments, and it does produce an organization that is flexible and open to new opportunities. But it may also produce an organization that keeps moving to who knows where. It is not strategic planning and, indeed, some would question whether an organization operating this way has a strategy at all (p. 44).

The third approach to developing strategy is what Kearns (2000) calls the *analytical approach*, one in which "you use logic and in-depth analysis to improve the strategic fit between your organization and its environment." This approach is what most people have in mind when they say *strategic planning* (p. 32).

STRATEGIC PLANNING AND STRATEGIC MANAGEMENT

Strategic planning is more than a strategy—it is a *process* that produces a *product*—a strategic plan—that puts meat on the strategy and points the way to implementing it. John Bryson (2004), one of the most widely cited authors on strategic planning, defines it as "a disciplined effort to produce fundamental decisions and actions that shape and guide what an organization (or other entity) is, what it does, and why it exists" (p. 6). While Bryson emphasizes the need to achieve clarity about the organization's mission and set priorities, Allison and Kaye (2005) point to the value of the strategic planning process in building _consensus_ about the priorities that are identified: "Strategic planning is a systematic process through which an organization agrees on–and builds commitment among key stakeholders to–priorities that are essential to its mission and are responsive to the environment" (p. 1).

Strategic planning is a process that begins with where the organization is, defines some new place where it wants to be, and develops a plan to get there, all in the context of its mission and values and the realities of the environment in which it operates. It is a practice that began in the corporate world and has been adopted by government and the nonprofit sector. Today, most nonprofit organizations except the newest and smallest engage in some form of strategic planning—both because they find it an effective tool and because many funders, including foundations, regard it as an essential badge of a well-managed organization.

Indeed, strategic planning offers many benefits. It forces the organization to think about its mission and values, to confront basic questions about what it is, what it does, and where it wants to go. It requires that the organization look beyond itself to the environment around it and see itself in the context of broader trends and forces, including the society, economy, and competitors. It provides a basis for rational decision making, rather than guesswork or intuition. But strategic planning is not a panacea for all ills, and it is not appropriate for every organization in all circumstances. It may not be a useful thing to undertake in a new organization, especially one guided by a charismatic, visionary leader. In such a situation, it might be a wasted exercise, since the leader will do whatever he or she intends to do regardless of what others may think or what plan may be devised. Indeed, any attempt at planning is sure to fail unless the leader supports it from the start. Strategic planning may not make sense for an organization that is in a state of crisis. What's the point of taking time to debate the mission or scan the environment when the roof is caving in, the creditors are at the door, or the executive director has just resigned and the staff is scrambling to keep things afloat until a new CEO can be found?

Strategic planning cannot become the purpose of the organization, which is to say, it cannot become an all-consuming activity. Inevitably, when strategic planning is mentioned, some people will resist, perhaps groan, based on previous negative experiences—the long meetings spent debating every word in the mission statement, the weekend retreats filled with team-building exercises—the weeks and months go by and a 200-page report is produced. The report then goes on the shelf and life goes on as before. Properly conducted, strategic planning should not consume everybody's time. Bryson (2004) suggests that it should take no more than 10% of any key decision maker's time during the year and even that may be more than most organizations will require (p. 14). But neither is strategic planning a one-shot, over-and-done exercise. Planning cannot be about just putting a report on the shelf. It needs to be a continuous part of the organization's way of operating, and the plan itself needs to be a living document that is revisited and adjusted in light of experience and the changing environment.

Strategic planning is not a substitute for leadership. Unfortunately, some organizations try to make it so. Perhaps confused and out of ideas, board members or managers may think, "What we need is a strategic plan." They hire a consultant, go through a series of meetings and retreats, and end up with a document that is as lifeless and unimaginative as the paper it is printed on. Planning may provide a roadmap for implementing a vision, but it is not the vision, and it can only succeed if it is used as a tool of leadership. In the early 1980s, when Jack Welch became the CEO of General Electric, he all but eliminated staff in the planning department, believing that they had become aloof from the real business and were driven by data rather than instincts about what consumers want.

Strategic planning is not to be confused with what is sometimes called *long-range planning*, a term that was more commonly used in the past. Long-range planning really involves projecting trends and data into the future—that is, estimating what is *going to happen* based on certain assumptions. In contrast, strategic planning is goal oriented and action oriented—its purpose is to change the future rather than merely predict it. Nor is a strategic plan, the same as a business plan. Most business plans are developed for specific programs or initiatives to be undertaken by the organization, rather than the whole organization. Business plans build on the decisions made in strategic planning, but they are more focused on implementation and financial elements, typically including detailed projections for revenue and expenses over at least three years. Strategic planning is also not the same as *operational planning,* which as the term suggests, relates to the short-term decision making necessary to implementation of the strategic plan. In some organizations, the strategic plan and the operational plan are separate documents, although many nonprofits combine them in one (Rogers, Finley, & Galloway, 2001). Most significantly, to repeat, a strategic plan is not synonymous with strategy! Mintzberg (1996) calls the belief that the two equate "the planning school's grand fallacy," observing that "establishing a plan will not ensure the creation of a strategy" (p. 141).

Strategic management is a concept that has gained popularity in the business world and that has been applied to government and the nonprofit sector in numerous books and business school courses in the past decade. It is a broader concept than strategic planning, although the strategic plan is the center of this approach.

As Koteen (1997) acknowledges, the term *strategic management* "does not possess an exact, universally accepted definition" (p. 25), but he offers at least a description:

> Strategic management emphasizes an ongoing process that integrates strategic planning with other management systems . . . [it] seeks to use and merge all necessary approaches and resources to reach strategic goals . . . it embraces the entire set of managerial decisions and actions that determine the long-run performance of an organization. (p. 21)

In other words, strategic management is a holistic approach to managing the organization based on the strategic plan that includes the entire cycle of strategy formulation, strategy implementation, and strategy evaluation. The goals of the strategic plan drive decisions on managerial matters such as program design, budgeting, organizational structure, human resources development, and evaluation. The goals of the strategic plan provide "guidelines to direct resources and talent into the highest priority activity" (Koteen, 1997, p. 27). Strategic management links strategy and implementation.

THE STRATEGIC PLANNING PROCESS

There are eight basic approaches to strategic planning, all developed in the business environment and with varying applicability to nonprofit organizations. The *Harvard Policy Model,* developed at the Harvard Business School by various scholars over a period of decades is the most commonly cited and is the inspiration for several well-known variations (Bryson, 2001, p. 132). We will not explore all these models in this text, but students will find detailed descriptions and comparisons, including discussion of the strengths and weaknesses of each approach, in some of the readings recommended at the end of this chapter. In practice, most strategic planning models are a hybrid of the various approaches, which is appropriate because the planning process needs to be tailored to fit each specific situation (Bryson, 2001, p. 138). In this chapter, we will describe a generic model to discuss the typical steps in strategic planning and will draw concepts and tools from various approaches without going into detail about their roots.

A basic strategic planning model is depicted in Figure 7.1 and includes the steps common to many models.

- Plan to plan—that is, determine the process, the players, and their roles.
- Clarify the organization's mission, values, and vision.
- Assess the situation—that is, scan the external environment and the organization's internal realities.
- Develop strategies, goals, and objectives.
- Complete the written plan.
- Develop implementation plans.
- Execute the plan.

Planning to Plan

It is important to have a plan for planning, that is, to identify what process will be used, who will participate, and what information will be needed to inform the planning. There needs to be agreement among the participants, on points such as the purpose of the effort; the preferred steps in the process; the form and timing of reports that will be issued; the role, functions, and membership of any group or committee empowered to oversee the effort; the role, functions, and membership of the strategic planning team; the commitment of the resources necessary for proceeding with the effort; and any important limitations or boundaries for the effort (Bryson, 2004, p. 35).

Some organizations may use an outside consultant to guide their strategic planning process; others may prefer to manage it themselves. Some may plan an off-site retreat at some point in the process—perhaps a day or weekend in which the participants devote extensive time to discussion of strategies without the normal interruptions of daily business. Up-front time spent planning for the planning will be well spent if it avoids misunderstandings or wasted motion during the planning process itself.

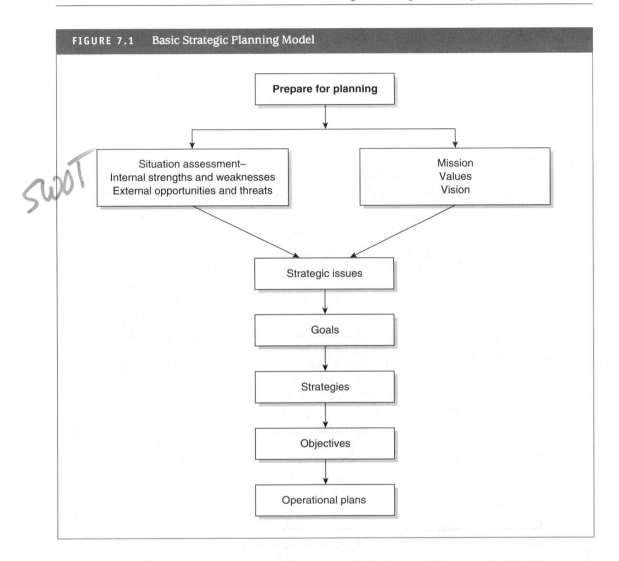

FIGURE 7.1   Basic Strategic Planning Model

Defining Mission, Values, and Vision

Effective planning begins with consensus about basics—mission, values, and vision. Discussion on these basics often can take considerable time and some pragmatic individuals, eager to jump into identifying issues and goals, may find the exercise frustrating. But experience has shown that neglecting to create a solid foundation for planning by achieving consensus on the basics of mission, vision, and values will likely lead to a breakdown in planning at some later stage.

Mission

As we have discussed before, mission is everything for a nonprofit organization—it is the reason the organization exists, and it must be the starting point for its planning. James Phills (2005) speaks eloquently to the point:

> Mission is the psychological and emotional logic that drives an organization. It is the reason why people get up in the morning and go to work in a nonprofit . . . Mission [defines] the social value that the organization creates. The key feature of social value—whether it is spiritual, moral, societal, aesthetic, intellectual, or environmental—is that it transcends economic value. Thus, it is inextricably linked to fundamental human values, which are the basis for intrinsic worth or importance. (p. 22)

It is important to distinguish mission from *mandates*. Mandates are things that the organization is *required* to do, perhaps by its charter or law. For example, a college may have a charter that requires it to enroll only women students. The American Red Cross has mandated services that it is required to provide to the government under its Congressional charter. Organizations have more control over their missions than their mandates, but in general, nonprofit organizations have fewer mandates than do public agencies and thus have considerable freedom to design their own futures.

We might think that an organization's mission should be relatively unchanging. Indeed, a performing arts organization is not likely to one day alter its mission statement to address environmental issues or the welfare of animals. But there are often shifts that require a rethinking, or at least a restatement of the mission. For example, you may recall Miriam's Kitchen, the Washington-based organization serving homeless people, that was discussed in Chapter 1. Miriam's began as a breakfast program, and its mission was once simply to provide a healthy meal each day to homeless men and women. But as its programs evolved, it began to offer case management services to its breakfast clients, after-breakfast arts programs, and expanded medical care. Eventually, it purchased a house that offered transitional housing and began to engage in more advocacy on behalf of the homeless community. The scope of its activities had changed, and it became essential to consider a broader mission statement that enveloped all the organization's activities. Its mission evolved from providing breakfast to "addressing the causes and consequences of homelessness" (www.miriams kitchen.org). This broader statement of mission encompassed what it was actually now doing but did not represent a complete departure from its original purposes.

Saying that the mission can change is not to suggest that organizations should simply expand their programs and then change their mission statements to fit. Rather, programs and missions often will evolve as the organization grows and expands its capabilities. Considering that the mission is related to the question of "What business are we in?" Sometimes an organization's current understanding of the answer to that question is too narrow either to allow for growth or even for survival.

There are different philosophies about mission statements. Some argue for fairly simple statements, while others argue that the mission statement should say not only what the organization does but how it does it. Box 7.1 provides a sampling of mission statements that reflect the latter approach. There is always a trade-off between keeping the mission statement sufficiently broad and keeping it focused—there is a risk in going to extremes in either direction. Too narrow a mission statement may be too constraining, making it impossible for the organization to grow or expand without going beyond its mission. But a statement that is too broad may become meaningless and open the door to *mission creep,* in other words, a gradual evolution away from the organization's purposes into ancillary activities that may eventually result in an organization that is very unfocused.

BOX 7.1   Mission Statements

Boston Symphony Orchestra Mission Statement

Our mission is to foster and maintain an organization dedicated to the making of music consonant with the highest aspirations of the musical art, creating performance and providing educational and training programs at the highest level of excellence (www.volunteermatch.org/orgs/org10207.html, accessed January 16, 2006).

American Cancer Society Mission Statement

The American Cancer Society is the nationwide community-based voluntary health organization dedicated to eliminating cancer as a major health problem by preventing cancer, saving lives, and diminishing suffering from cancer, through research, education, advocacy, and service (www.cancer.org/docroot/AA/content/AA_1_1_ACS_Mission_Statements.asp, accessed January 16, 2006).

City Year Mission Statement

City Year's mission is to build democracy through citizen service, civic leadership and social entrepreneurship. City Year seeks to unite ever-greater numbers of citizens to share a common experience – service. It is on this common ground that City Year inspires the active citizenship vital to a strong and vibrant democracy (City Year Annual Report, 2004, www.cityyear.org/search.aspx?searchtext=mission%20statement, accessed May 5, 2008).

Values

Values are those principles that the organization holds most important. For example, does an organization serving the homeless value access—making it easy for any homeless person to obtain services—or is it most concerned with serving just those who have the best chance of improving their lives? Does an arts organization most value the artistic quality of its work or the diversity of its audience? Some organizations include beliefs as a part of their values statements. For example, the values statement of the Higher Achievement Program, shown in Box 7.2, is really a mixture of statements about beliefs (how things work) as well as about values (what's important).

BOX 7.2   Values and Vision Statements
Higher Achievement Program, Inc.

Values

Talent is everywhere—in every community.

Intellectual capacities are built through effort.

Opportunities matter.

Vision

Higher Achievement shares a vision of Washington, D.C., as a city where all children can access the resources and opportunities that enable them to *elect* their educational futures.

Source: Higher Achievement, Inc. Web site (www.higherachievement.org/index.html, accessed January 9, 2006).

Vision

A successful organization will be one in which as many constituents as possible share a vision of the future. Developing a statement to describe that shared vision is an important step in the planning process. Some vision statements describe the future of the organization itself. For example, Miriam's Kitchen expresses its vision that "by 2010, Miriam's Kitchen will be the preeminent agency serving people who are chronically homeless in the District of Columbia" (Miriam's Kitchen, Draft Strategic Plan, January 16, 2006). But other vision statements paint a picture of the world that the organization is striving to shape. For example, Higher Achievement's vision, shown in Box 7.2, describes a future for children in Washington, D.C.

Some experts suggest that developing a vision statement should come later in the strategic planning process, believing that planners need to go through other phases of the planning process before they are able to do so (Bryson, 2004). But many models call for developing the vision along with the mission and values as an early step in planning. Taken together, the statements about mission, values, and vision establish a kind of preamble to the strategic plan and establish the tone for the planning exercise.

Assessing the Situation

As discussed in Chapter 2, nonprofits are open systems, that is, the boundaries between the organization and its environment often blur, and changes or pressures originating in the environment will have a profound impact on what the organization is able to do and how it needs to go about doing it.

Strategic planners need to collect information in two arenas—within the organization and outside. There are various methods available for analyzing external and internal conditions, but the most commonly used is the SWOT analysis—a method that comes from the Harvard Policy Model mentioned earlier. In this approach, the organization itself is surveyed to identify *strengths* (S) and *weaknesses* (W) and the external environment is examined to discern *opportunities* (O) and *threats* (T). The purpose of the exercise is to develop a matching between the organization's strengths and weaknesses and the opportunities and threats in the environment in order to identify strategic issues that need to be addressed.

Strengths and weaknesses of the organization may be analyzed in terms of assets or competencies. That is, what resources does it have or lack and what does it do well or poorly? As a result of this analysis, it will identify its *core competencies,* that is, "the organization's strongest abilities, most effective strategies and actions, or best resources (broadly conceived), on which it can draw routinely to perform well" (Bryson, 2004, p. 42). Its weaknesses might also be viewed in terms of resources that are lacking or the organization's ability to perform in certain areas. For example, identified weaknesses might include inadequate facilities, insufficient staff, poor fundraising performance, or a chronic inability to meet performance objectives.

The external scan, to identify opportunities and threats, might encompass things such as demographic trends; trends in philanthropy, grantmaking, or government funding; a *stakeholder analysis,* to identify the characteristics, values, perceptions, expectations, and concerns of stakeholders, including clients or customers, donors, and relevant government officials; and an analysis of the positions and programs of competitors or partners offering similar services.

It is essential to focus on factors that are relevant to the organization, in other words, to be somewhat selective. For example, there may be national trends that are affecting performing arts organizations, but are all of them relevant to an opera company in Chicago? Do national birth rates really provide useful insight for an organization that serves children in a city with a large and growing immigrant population? Not being selective in looking at the environment can cause the process to just bog down and overwhelm the planners with too much information.

Kearns (2000, pp. 54–55) suggests delimiting the environmental scan by looking at three categories of organizations—organizations that offer related programs and services, organizations that offer similar programs and services, and organizations that offer substitutable programs and services. So, for example, an organization that is involved in addictions counseling would need to be alert to trends affecting hospitals, government agencies that fund addiction counseling programs, and homeless services organizations that may be sources of referrals. Organizations that offer similar programs or services in other markets or locations may be relevant, too. An addictions counseling program in Boston should examine trends affecting similar organizations in Baltimore and Los Angeles, since they may also face similar situations. And even a nonprofit needs to scan what is happening with regard to its competitors. For example, a YMCA/YWCA needs to be aware of trends in health club memberships and the expansion of for-profit health clubs in its community. Some may resist the idea of competition among nonprofit organizations, but it is a reality that many, if not most, need to address in their planning.

Table 7.1 shows the hypothetical results of a simple SWOT analysis that might be conducted by the board of a performing arts organization. Some obvious issues fall out of an examination of its strengths, weakness, opportunities, and threats. The organization has strengths, including a good reputation for quality performances and a capable artistic director. It seems possible that it has the potential for growth, due to the gentrification of the downtown area by college educated people, offering the potential for larger audiences. But lack of any staff dedicated to marketing is an obstacle to capitalizing on that opportunity, as is its small and outdated facility. Threats to the organization include the possibility that its one principal donor might lose interest or perhaps suffer reversals that would make continued support impossible, the possibility that it may become difficult to attract performers to work in the old and outdated facility, and competition from other performing arts organizations that may have better facilities and a stronger base of financial support.

Identifying Strategic Issues

Drawing on the information available from the environmental scan and guided by the organization's own mission, values, and vision, the next step in strategic planning is to identify the key *strategic issues* facing the organization. Strategic issues are "the fundamental policy questions or critical challenges facing the organization's mandates, mission and values, product or service level and mix, clients, users or payers, cost, financing, structure, processes, and management" (Bryson, 2004, p. 42). Strategic issues often are framed as questions. For example, the performing arts organization used as an example in Table 7.1 might ask, "How can we prepare for the possible loss of our principal donor?" or "How can we provide the quality of facilities that our performers require?"

In other words, the strategic issues are areas in which the organization needs to take action. This could mean taking defensive action to protect against threats or it might mean developing new initiatives to grow, expand, or improve. In the case of the performing arts organization just discussed, it would appear that its facility is an issue, as is its capacity for fundraising and marketing. Both relate to potential threats confronting the organization as well as to the opportunities it faces. Strategic issues may be identified by considering the

TABLE 7.1	SWOT Analysis for a Performing Arts Organization
The Organization (Internal)	*The Environment (External)*

Strengths
  Reputation for quality performances
  Capable artistic director
  Good location near downtown
	Opportunities
	  More college-educated people living downtown
	  New restaurants opening nearby
	  City's plan to develop an arts district

Weaknesses
  Facility too small and outdated
  No staff dedicated to marketing or fundraising
  Overdependence on one major donor
	Threats
	  Competition from other organizations
	  Loss of key major donor
	  Performers don't wish to work in old facility

consequences of not addressing them, which generally will involve either some undesirable result or a missed opportunity.

Identifying strategic issues requires setting priorities, that is, determining the urgent issues that need to be addressed and also those that can be deferred or ignored altogether. Bryson (2004) categorizes strategic issues into four types:

1. Developmental issues that go to the heart of the organization's vision and goals, involving "a fundamental change in products or services, customers or clients, service distribution channels, sources of revenue, identity or image," or some other fundamental change

2. Issues that require no organizational action at present but that must be continuously monitored

3. Issues that are on the horizon and likely to require some action in the future and perhaps some action now

4. Issues that require an immediate response and therefore cannot be handled in a routine way (p. 44)

Setting Goals

Goals are, as the term implies, something that the organization will strive to reach or accomplish with respect to the strategic issues that it has identified. In the context of strategic planning, they are sometimes called *strategic goals* or *strategic directions*. Koteen (1997) divides goals into three types: those addressed to *program* thrusts, that is, those that go to services that the organization provides; those addressed to *institutional concerns*, matters that need to be addressed to build a more effective organization (i.e., capacity building); and, *financial goals*, which of course, have to do with resources (p. 126).

Goal statements are stated in broad terms and do not need to be quantifiable. They generally use action verbs—words such as increase, improve, strengthen, expand, develop, encourage, initiate. For example, the goals derived from the strategic planning effort at Kalamazoo College are shown in Box 7.3. The college's goal statements do not say what the college intends to do to achieve them nor does it include any numbers. They are statements of direction, but they do not, for example, explain how internationalism will be integrated into the curriculum or how an environment supporting faculty's excellence will be created.

Strategies and Initiatives

Once goals have been established, the planners next need to determine strategies to achieve them. Developing strategies is, of course, the heart of the strategic planning process. This is when the organization determines what it will do to address the strategic issues that it has identified as a result of its SWOT analysis.

Various scholars have identified core or generic strategies that organizations might follow. For example, Kearns (2000) identifies four strategies: growth, retrenchment, stability, and collaboration. These would seem to be virtually exhaustive of possible strategies in the broadest sense, but strategic planners need to develop more specific strategies with respect

---

BOX 7.3   Kalamazoo College Goals

- Develop a campus culture and climate in which internationalism, multiculturalism, and diversity flourish as integral components of a holistic, integrated educational experience.
- Create a strong sense of community among faculty, administration, staff, and students and an enduring sense of connection to the institution among alumnae and alumni.
- Attain an optimal student enrollment representing broad domestic and international diversity.
- Develop resources and an environment in which faculty excel in their teaching and research while serving the College effectively and participating as citizens of the College community.
- Use information technology to enhance and support scholarship of students and faculty.
- Raise and maintain the College's facilities to a level that complements the quality of the academic program.
- Support an ongoing culture of planning and assessment as systemic activities of the College.

Source: www.kzoo.edu/pres/plan/plan.htm, accessed January 16, 2006.

---

to programs, activities, and the goals that they have identified. Strategies may include developing new initiatives, expanding current programs, or decreasing or even eliminating others. One technique for making such decisions is offered by portfolio analysis, which will be considered in the next section of this chapter.

A review of nonprofit strategic plans shows that organizations take a variety of approaches to presenting their strategies. Some discuss only new programs and activities, calling them *strategic initiatives*. Others include a comprehensive description of their programs and activities, linking each to the goals. For example, Box 7.4 shows the strategies described by Carpenter's Shelter, a Virginia organization serving homeless families. Note the references to the environmental scan that preceded it, significant findings of which are incorporated in the statement of each program that the organization proposes to undertake.

BOX 7.4   Carpenter's Shelter "Strategies"

Nine strategies were developed to enable Carpenter's Shelter to address these needs and better serve the homeless. These strategies involve the revision and expansion of existing services as well as the initiation of new programs. They are as follows:

1. *Aftercare:* According to a 1999 study by the Interagency Council for the Homeless, 34% of those currently homeless have been homeless three or more times. To respond to this recidivism, Carpenter's will implement an aftercare program designed to maintain a continuum of care after clients leave the shelter. Continued case management, including ongoing coordination with other service providers, will be established.

2. *Life skills and job readiness:* Finding a job is the top need reported by adult homeless clients. Carpenter's will respond to this need by developing a monitored job readiness program at the Shelter. This will be coupled with a life skills program designed to ensure that both residents and David's Place members are able to function in the community to the best of their abilities.

3. *Children's programs and family enrichment:* Children form nearly one third of the Alexandria shelter population, and yet their special needs can go unnoticed as emphasis is placed on helping parents reestablish their lives. Carpenter's has developed a plan to meet the developmental needs of each child within the context of a family enrichment program. Each child entering the shelter will be given a comprehensive assessment and a plan will be prepared to address the child's developmental needs. Tutoring and enrichment programs will also be expanded.

4. *David's place services:* Carpenter's daytime drop-in facility offers unsheltered homeless men and women access to showers, washing machines, secure lockers, computers, and other resources in a safe environment. Initiating evening and weekend hours, and implementing life skills and job readiness programs will expand these critical services.

5. *Substance abuse and mental health services:* A poll of Carpenter's Shelter residents revealed that many believed substance abuses to be the main cause of homelessness. Mental health issues are also a characteristic of many in the homeless community. Carpenter's plans to expand services devoted to these problems for both shelter residents and David's Place members. Collaboration with mental health and substance abuse service providers in the community will also be expanded.

6. *Serving the multicultural community:* To respond to the growing needs of the Hispanic and immigrant communities in Alexandria, Carpenter's will take steps to eliminate cultural barriers in our services. These will include increasing awareness in the multicultural community of the services provided by the shelter, hiring a bilingual staff member, and expanding collaboration with the various cultural communities of Alexandria.

7. *Transitional housing:* A recent study by the Alexandria Homeless Services Coordinating Committee reported that only half of the needed transitional housing units currently exist. More research is necessary to determine Carpenter's future role in transitional housing. Ultimately, Carpenter's goal is to help ensure that residents have adequate housing options on leaving the shelter.

8. *Service coordination:* Carpenter's Shelter plans to reduce recidivism through increased cooperation with other local service providers and government agencies. Enhanced coordination of services will help ensure that homeless individuals will not be "recycled" through various programs but, instead, will benefit from an effective continuum of care. Carpenter's will also explore possible collaboration with other shelters to develop more specialized care programs.

9. *Advocacy:* As Northern Virginia's largest homeless shelter, Carpenter's has the ability to advocate for homeless issues and increase community awareness. Carpenter's will take a more active role in encouraging the community and government at local, regional, and state levels to do more to address the needs of the homeless. Furthermore, Carpenter's will advocate for those homeless populations that are sometimes overlooked, such as the elderly and those needing medical attention.

Source: Carpenter's Shelter Web site (www.carpentersshelter.org/vision.htm, accessed January 10, 2006).

Objectives

Objectives are specific, quantified targets that represent steps toward accomplishing the goals. Objectives are often stated in the form of "Increase (something) from (some number) to (another number) by (deadline)." The statement could, of course, also use "decrease," "reduce," or some other verb that implies a change in the value used to define the objective. This form is useful in communicating not only what the objective is but how ambitious it is—it enables any reader of the plan to see exactly what rate of change is anticipated and the date by which it is to be achieved. For example, in the case of a college, objectives might include, "Increase the percentage of minority students from 10% to 15% within three years" or "Increase the number of students volunteering in community nonprofits from 200 to 300 by 2012." For new activities, objectives need to be stated differently, and in some cases, a numeric objective may not be appropriate—just accomplishing something may constitute achievement of the goal, although a deadline should be included. For example, a college might have an objective, "Design and offer a new writing course for freshmen by the fall of 2010." A performing arts organization might set a goal to "retain an architect and develop plans for expansion and modernization of our building, to be presented to the board by the fall meeting of 2012." There need not be a one-to-one correspondence between objectives and goals—that is, achievement of an objective might well address more than one goal.

Quantifiable objectives create the bridge from strategy to implementation by setting specific targets to be achieved. Operational plans then can be developed to spell out in detail exactly what will be done, when, and by whom in order to achieve the objectives in the strategic plan.

Writing the Strategic Plan

Strategic plans are, almost by definition, written documents. The written plan records the decisions reached and the goals and objectives to be pursued. Usually, it is best if one or two people do the actual writing, but the draft is often used to stimulate wider discussion throughout the organization and its constituencies. Eventually, the governing board should take formal action to adopt the plan as the organization's policy.

The length of the written plan varies. Some plans may be no more than a few pages, summarizing mission, values, vision, core strategies, a list of programs and objectives. Others may run 50 pages or more and include appendices with supporting data. As an alternative to a narrative document, some organizations use a columnar format showing the relationships among strategies, goals, and objectives (Allison & Kaye, 2005, p. 259). Some plans provide year-to-year objectives for the next three to five years. But this may assume an unrealistic ability to forecast in detail and it may be preferable to state objectives to be accomplished over the entire period of the plan, combined with a detailed operating plan for the first year (p. 262).

Once the written plan has been completed, it is important to use it as a tool for communication throughout the organization. One of the benefits of strategic planning is that it helps build wide consensus and common understanding about mission, values, vision, goals, and strategies. That benefit is sacrificed if it remains a document available only to a select few in management.

Developing Operational Plans

Once the strategic plan is in place, there remains the job of developing a detailed operational plan—that is, a plan for implementation. This will include identifying specific tasks to be completed, establishing a timeline for their completion, assigning responsibility for each task, identifying the resources that will be needed—human and financial, determining the right organizational structure, identifying what information systems will be required, defining measures by which the completion or success will be determined, and other operational details. As we have said, some organizations combine the strategic and operational plans in one document, but developing them requires separate processes, usually with different individuals involved. Whereas board members and representatives of other constituencies may be involved in developing the strategic plan, the detailed work of producing an operational plan generally needs to be done primarily by the staff.

IDENTIFYING STRATEGIC ISSUES AND DEVELOPING STRATEGIES

As noted above, strategic planning is a tool developed in the business world that many non-profits have adapted to their unique environment. There are additional tools that have been adapted from business that can be usefully applied in the two steps that are at the heart of the strategic planning process—the identification of strategic issues and the development of strategies to address them. Because these concepts were developed in the business sector, the vocabulary they use—terms such as "competitive advantage"—may sometimes seem strange in the nonprofit sector. But with appropriate adjustments in terminology, many of the concepts can be useful in nonprofit strategic planning.

Portfolio Analysis

One useful tool is *portfolio analysis,* a technique used by business firms to determine if their various programs and services are in sync with their missions and strategies. "Portfolio" in this context means not a collection of investments in stocks and bonds, as most people might understand the term, but rather the array of programs and services that an organization operates. Portfolio analysis places various programs, service, or products into categories—the cells or boxes of a matrix based on some set of variables considered to be relevant.

Perhaps, the best known version of portfolio analysis is the Growth-Share Matrix developed by the Boston Consulting Group. It is used to evaluate company products or services based on the rate of growth in a particular market and the share of the total market that their products and services represent (Kearns, 2000, p. 113). In its original form, this is not a model that is of much value to nonprofits, which may be concerned about the growth of markets (read "growth in need for services"), but are generally less concerned with their market share. But others have developed variations that do offer a better fit to the nonprofit environment and provide useful tools in the strategic planning process.

Kevin Kearns (2000) provides a portfolio analysis matrix that offers a good way for non-profits to identify strategic issues. As shown in Table 7.2, this approach uses a grid that highlights intersections of the organization's strengths and weaknesses with the opportunities and threats facing it from the environment. Let's look at how it might work from the perspective of a hypothetical medical center located in the downtown area of a major city.

In the upper left (northwest) quadrant opportunities presented by the environment coincide with areas of strength for the organization. The population of the city is growing older, increasing the incidence of cardiovascular disease and the need for related medical services. (Remember that in the vocabulary of SWOT, a growing need for services is an "opportunity" for the organization that provides them, however perverse that may sometimes seem. It may help the organization think about it as an "opportunity to be of service.") The medical center always has had a reputation for excellence in cardiology and cardiac surgery, so an opportunity presented by the environment coincides with a strength of the hospital. The strategic issue is, "How can we leverage our strong programs in cardiology and cardiac surgery to meet the growing need (opportunity)?" Strategies to be considered might include things such as expanding facilities, recruiting new physicians with a specialty in cardiology or cardiac surgery, or other initiatives.

In the lower left (southwest) quadrant, there is an opportunity presented by the environment, but it is in an area in which the organization is relatively weak. With the city's aging population—the baby boomers are starting to turn 60—there is a growing market for cosmetic surgery. But our medical center has never been a leader in this area—other

TABLE 7.2	Strategic Issue Grid: Urban Medical Center	
	Opportunities (Growing Need for Services)	*Threats*
Strengths	**Strategic issues** How can we leverage our strong programs in cardiology and cardiac surgery to meet the growing need (opportunity)?	**Strategic issues** How can we mobilize to avert the threat from suburban hospitals to our strong birthing program or at least minimize their negative impact?
Weaknesses	**Strategic issues** Should we invest in our cosmetic surgery services to meet the growing need? Should we seek a partner in this area? Should we phase out cosmetic surgery?	**Strategic issues** How can we minimize the damage to our rehabilitation program from the new specialized hospital across town? Should we phase out our weak rehabilitation program?

Source: Based on Kearns (2000, p. 130).

medical centers in the city have always been stronger than we are in this field. The strategic issues are as follows: Should we invest in our cosmetic surgery program to meet the growing need, in other words, to seize the opportunity of a growing market in this field? Should we seek a partnership to compensate for our weakness in this field, perhaps some type of marketing relationship with one of the health club chains in the area? Or, should we phase out our cosmetic surgery services and concentrate our efforts in areas where we are strong, for example, in cardiology and cardiac surgery?

The upper right (northeast) quadrant of the grid includes a threat that will potentially affect an area in which the organization is strong. Our medical center has always been well-known as an excellent place for women to give birth—it's been a great strength for us over the years. But there are fewer young families living in the city—many are moving to the suburbs. Suburban hospitals have built new birthing facilities closer to where young families live and threaten to take much of this business away from us. We can't abandon this area of care. It's one of our strengths, we already have significant investment in this area, and if we leave the field, we will be giving up a significant amount of revenue. The strategic issues are as follows: How can we mobilize our strong birthing program to avert the threat or at least to minimize its negative impact? The planners might consider ideas such as developing a new, more modern birthing center or perhaps installing more state-of-the-art technology or offering specialized services that will attract suburban women to continue coming downtown to have their babies.

The bottom right (southeast) quadrant of the grid portrays a situation in which the organization faces a threat in an area where it is relatively weak. Our medical center has never been strong in providing rehabilitation services—and now a new specialized rehabilitation hospital has opened across town, posing a serious threat. The strategic issue is, "How can we minimize the damage from this threat—maybe by cutting our rehabilitation program back to the minimum and reducing costs?" Or, "Should we just close down this weak program altogether and refocus our efforts on areas in which we have greater strength?"

Grids such as the one developed by Kearns (2000), thus, provide a useful tool for organizations to identify the strategic issues facing their organizations. Again, Kearns's approach helps identify the questions but leaves the answers up to the judgment and creativity of the planners who best know the specific circumstances of their organization's situation. That is a realistic approach, but other models prescribe more specific strategies to fit various scenarios. Let's take a look at a well-known one of those—MacMillan's Competitive Strategies Matrix.

MacMillan's Strategies Matrix

A portfolio analysis model development by MacMillan (1983) adds complexity to the one we just saw and goes beyond the identification of strategic issues to suggest strategies the organization might pursue. MacMillan's model looks at each of the organization's programs or services according to three criteria:

1. The organization's *competitive position* with regard to the program, which might be *strong* or *weak*: Again, competition may not be a comfortable concept for many nonprofits—it is a concept drawn from the business world. But another way to

interpret this is to think about whether the organization can claim superiority over other organizations in its ability to deliver the program. In other words, does the organization have resources, skills, advantages of location, or other advantages that make it the best organization—or potentially the best—to provide this program or service?

2. The *attractiveness* of the program to the organization, which might be *high* or *low*: In other words, to what extent does the organization really want to offer this program or service. This assessment would be based on a variety of criteria, including its fit with the mission, its potential for attracting resources to support the program, and others.

3. The extent of *alternative coverage*, that is, similar services offered by other organizations, which might be *high* or *low*: In the business world, this really means, "Are there many competitors in this market?" But a nonprofit may look at it as the question of whether there are other options available to people who need the service.

Because there are three variables to be considered, each of which may be high or low, a matrix depicting this model is three dimensional rather than a rectangle. In other words, it has width, length, and height. The space is divided up into eight cells, or eight scenarios, that exist with regard to each program considered. MacMillan (1983) suggests a strategy for each scenario.

Three dimensions are a difficult image to visualize or depict, so to simplify our understanding, Table 7.3 just summarizes the eight scenarios. It also shows the strategy recommended by MacMillan (1983) for each, using terms taken from the business vocabulary. But the table also includes a description of each situation in ordinary language—that is, in the words that a group of nonprofit planners might actually use in their conversations.

The weakness in MacMillan's (1983) matrix is that it is so prescriptive; that is, it suggests a cookie-cutter strategy to fit every combination of criteria. In reality, every organization faces a complex array of considerations unique to it. Despite this shortcoming, though, it does provide nonprofits with a way of recognizing patterns that may help clarify thinking. As Kearns (2000) observes, if an organization finds that all its programs fall into Scenarios 1 to 4, that is, encompassing just those that are highly attractive, that may suggest that it is drifting away from addressing the most hardcore social problems in favor of those that are the most lucrative, perhaps in terms of paying customers or the ease of raising gifts. That might cause some concern about its adherence to mission. On the other hand, if all its programs fall into scenarios 5 to 8—scenarios in which the programs are relatively unattractive—perhaps because they are tangential to the mission or difficult to support in the long term—Kearns speculates that the organization may just be responding to the availability of short-term funding for some programs, running the risk that it will be stuck with them if the funding evaporates (p. 126). MacMillan (1983) recommends that an organization try to build a balanced portfolio of programs in which it has a strong competitive position, in other words, where it is able to achieve high quality compared with other organizations (Scenarios 1, 2, 5, and 6), including some that are attractive and some that are not. In simplest terms, the portfolio may include some moneymakers, which help subsidize others that lose money but are at the heart

TABLE 7.3 MacMillan Scenarios

Scenario #	Competitive Position	Program Attractiveness	Alternative Coverage	Suggested Strategy (MacMillan)	The Situation in Ordinary Language
1	Strong	High	High	Aggressive competition	We're the best at this, or we easily can be, and we really want to do it. There are a lot of other organizations offering the same thing, but we're going to compete head-on and try to persuade them to yield this program to us.
2	Strong	High	Low	Aggressive growth	We're the best at this or we easily can be. We really want to do it. And, there is almost nobody else doing it. It's an open road—let's invest in this program and grow it quickly before others start to compete with us.
3	Weak	High	High	Aggressive divestment	We would really like to continue offering this program, but we are just not good at it and probably never will be. There are a lot of others doing it who are a lot better than we are. Let's just get out and let them have it.
4	Weak	High	Low	Build strength or sell out	We would really like to do this, and there are few others who do. But let's be realistic, we just aren't very good at it. We either need to invest in this program to make it good or find some other organization that can do it better and is willing to take it on.

(Continued)

TABLE 7.3 (Continued)

Scenario #	Competitive Position	Program Attractiveness	Alternative Coverage	Suggested Strategy (MacMillan)	The Situation in Ordinary Language
5	Strong	Low	High	Build up best competitor	We're the best at doing this, but it is just not attractive to us to do it any longer. We don't want to let people down who rely on this program, but there are other organizations that do the same thing. Let's talk to the next best organization and help them take this over from us.
6	Strong	Low	Low	Soul of the agency	We are the best and almost the only organization doing this. We're really known for it. It's not that attractive to us in many ways—for one thing, we lose money on it. But a lot of people depend on us and have nowhere else to go. We just have to find a way to keep it going.
7	Weak	Low	High	Orderly divestment	This is just not an attractive program for us, and we're not that good at it either. A lot of other organizations offer the same thing. No rush, but let's gradually direct people elsewhere and phase this program out.
8	Weak	Low	Low	Joint venture	We're not very good at this, and we really don't want to do it. Some people need the program, but not that many. We're stuck with it for now, but let's see if we can find another organization that's willing to help us in this area, so we can focus on our higher priorities.

Source: Based on MacMillan (1983).

of the organization's mission (the "soul of the agency" programs). Applying MacMillan's thinking, an organization would achieve such an ideal balance of programs by

- giving up programs to other organizations that can do them better, even if they may be attractive financially and in other ways,
- encouraging other organizations to abandon programs in which it has a clear advantage and can operate with greater quality and efficiency, and
- making sure that all its programs are consistent with its mission and strategy.

Achieving such balance may produce not only an ideal mix of programs for an organization but also an effective allocation of resources in the nonprofit sector collectively. Thus, despite the sometimes uncomfortable vocabulary of strategic planning, portfolio analysis, and other business concepts, they do offer nonprofits useful tools that can help them clarify thinking, engage in rational decision making, and strengthen their effectiveness in pursuit of their social missions.

CHAPTER SUMMARY

Strategy is an abstract concept that may simply mean a direction or new, innovative approach to getting from one place to another. It may arise from a leader's vision, incrementally from smaller decisions the organization makes one at a time, or from a formal analytical approach such as strategic planning.

Strategic planning is a process that many nonprofit organizations have adopted from the business world. It is a useful tool for organizations in designing their futures, but may not be appropriate in every situation. Strategic management is a broader concept that links the goals of the strategic plan to decisions on managerial matters such as program design, budgeting, organizational structure, human resources development, and evaluation.

There are many different models for strategic planning and most practice a hybrid of different approaches. One well-known version is the Harvard Policy Model on which many alternative models are based. Most start with clarification of the organization's mandates, mission, values, and vision. The opportunities and threats presented by the external environment are compared with the organization's internal strengths and weaknesses in order to identify strategic issues that need to be addressed (the SWOT analysis). The SWOT analysis helps define strategic issues or questions on which the planners need to focus. Broad goals are then established; strategies, programs, and activities are developed to achieve them; and measurable objectives are set to measure progress toward the goals. Operational plans are written to set specific timetables and accountability for the achievement of the objectives according to the plan.

With appropriate modifications in vocabulary, tools that businesses use to analyze their competitive environment may be adapted to help nonprofits identify strategic issues. Portfolio analysis models developed by Kearns (2000), MacMillan (1983), and others suggest generic strategies under various scenarios defined by the organization's strengths or competitive position, the desirability of the program, and the extent to which other organizations are providing coverage.

KEY TERMS AND CONCEPTS FROM CHAPTER 7

core competencies   *stakeholder analysis*
goals   *strategic issues*
Harvard Policy Model   *strategic management*
mission   *strategic planning*
mission creep   *strategy*
objectives   *SWOT analysis*
operational planning   *values*
portfolio analysis   *vision*

QUESTIONS FOR DISCUSSION

1. One organization that students will all have some knowledge about is their own college or university. What are the strengths, weaknesses, opportunities, and threats that you see facing your college or university? What strategic issues do you suggest for your institution?

2. Suppose a nonprofit organization's strategy requires that it phase out a program on which few people rely, but those people are vulnerable and no good substitute exists. How might the organization proceed with its plan in an ethical and humane manner?

3. Is competition among nonprofit organizations an acceptable concept or is it contrary to the values of the sector?

4. What similarities do you see between strategic planning as described in this chapter and models for capacity building that were discussed in Chapter 6?

5. Does the case of the Girl Scouts, presented in Chapter 6, reveal use of strategic planning techniques?

SUGGESTIONS FOR FURTHER READING RELATED TO CHAPTER 7

Books

Allison, M., & Kaye, J. (2005). *Strategic planning for nonprofit organizations* (2nd ed.). Hoboken, NJ: Wiley.

Bryson, J. M. (2004). *Strategic planning for public and nonprofit organizations* (3rd ed.). San Francisco: Wiley.

Kearns, K. P. (2000). *Private sector strategies for social sector success.* San Francisco: Jossey-Bass.

Mintzberg, H. (1994). *The rise and fall of strategic planning.* New York: Free Press.

Oster, S. M. (1995). *Strategic management for nonprofit organizations.* New York: Oxford University Press.

Managing Paid Staff and Service Volunteers

Chapter 4 discussed how nonprofit chief executives provide leadership to their organizations. Some of the theories considered there also help inform how managers lead the individuals who work with and for them, including the organization's staff and volunteers. This chapter takes a closer look at some theories that help explain the motivations of staff and volunteers and specific practices based on those theories that experts recommend to ensure a productive workforce.

It is important to distinguish between volunteers who serve as members of a nonprofit's governing board and volunteers who help provide its programs and services—for example, individuals who prepare food for the homeless or ill, tutor children, bring relief to the victims of disasters, or guide Boy Scout and Girl Scout troops and other youth organizations as unpaid leaders. The latter, sometimes termed *service volunteers*, are the focus of this chapter.

The discussion in this chapter blends theory and the recommendations of practitioner-oriented authors, addressing questions such as the following: What does management theory and research tell us about human motivation, especially in the workplace? Are nonprofit staff members motivated in the same way as those who work in for-profit environments, or are there differences that need to be understood? Are there differences in the motivations of paid staff and volunteers? What practices should nonprofit managers use to organize and direct staff members and volunteers in ways consistent with their motivations and needs and that also will lead to optimum performance?

AN OVERVIEW OF MANAGEMENT THEORIES

Management theory is not static. Theories are advanced and sometimes gain wide acceptance for a period of years. As scholars test them through research, they may find that the theories do not provide adequate explanations. Some theories thus pass into the dustbin of academic history. But often some of their principles are taken forward and incorporated into new theories. Other theories, even though challenged by research, have an intuitive appeal for managers and take hold in the conventional wisdom, despite evidence of their shortcomings. If there were one accepted approach to management, perhaps there would be need for only one management book, but a survey of any bookshelf will reveal that such is not the situation. In other words, management theory remains unsettled territory, although many theories, both old and new, offer at least some insights that may inform practice. This chapter discusses just a few theories relevant to the topic of staff and volunteer management. Students should recognize in advance that almost all of them have critics as well as adherents.

One influential management theorist of the early 20th century was Frederick W. Taylor, whose approach, developed in industrial settings, became known as *scientific management*. Taylor saw organizations operating much like machines and emphasized procedures and systems rather than human motivations and relationships. Much of his research involved time-and-motion studies in factories, with the purpose of increasing efficiency—in other words, finding ways to have people operate more like machines. Taylor's views were controversial even at the time, and they were later overtaken by entirely new approaches.

A series of experiments conducted in the 1920s at the Hawthorne plant of the Western Electric Company had a profound influence on thinking about management. Among other findings, the experiments suggested that the mere attention of supervisors had an influence on the performance of workers. That suggested that social and psychological factors might be important in creating a more productive workforce. Although the Hawthorne experiments have been controversial right from the beginning, they provided "pathbreaking illustrations of the influence of social and psychological factors on work behavior" (Rainey, 2003, p. 32). Management theory continues to evolve, but it has not returned to the era of Taylor, in which humans were viewed as cogs in the industrial machine. The shift in attention from the rules and mechanics of the workplace to an emphasis on human motivations and attitudes was a permanent change in our understanding and perspective. It is reflected in most contemporary work.

UNDERSTANDING HUMAN MOTIVATIONS

Theories about human motivation are of practical importance. Every manager holds some theory about motivation, even if implicitly. What a manager may believe about human nature will dictate how he or she interacts with people, seeks to motivate them, and addresses disappointments with their performance. Many people have known great bosses, who inspired loyalty and created a pleasant, productive working environment, and perhaps also screamer bosses, whose demands, rants, and insults created a dysfunctional workplace. Such differences may in fact reflect the psychology of the manager and his or her own needs, but they likely also reflect the manager's theory of how other people operate. It is thus important for a manager to hold some explicit theory of human motivation, rather than just an implicit home-grown theory, perhaps developed through his or her own life experiences.

On of the most influential of motivation theorists was Abraham Maslow, who developed his principal concepts in the 1940s and 1950s. Although it has been challenged by some scholars, Maslow's theory (1954) had an important influence on later thinking and has been the foundation for later work. For example, Burns's (1978) concept of transformational leadership, which we discussed in Chapter 4, draws substantially on Maslow's (1954) *hierarchy of needs*.

As the term *hierarchy* implies, Maslow's theory (1954) states that human needs progress from those at lower levels to those at higher levels as the lower-level needs are met. Human beings strive to meet their lower-level needs before addressing those in higher categories. In the lowest category—that is, at the bottom of the hierarchy—are basic physiological needs. Any student who has tried to study while hungry will readily recognize that it is difficult to focus on higher pursuits until more immediate needs are addressed. Some things must come first. But once the basics such as food, drink, and shelter are met, people can turn their attention to meeting their higher-level needs. The next steps up the hierarchy include safety needs, social needs, self-esteem needs, and, finally, self-actualization needs. So once human beings have met their physiological needs, they may focus on safety. (A hungry person would take risks to obtain food or drink; in other words, those basic needs would outweigh the desire for safety.) Once individuals feel safe, they are then able to focus on meeting their needs for the camaraderie and affection of others and on meeting needs that satisfy their own egos and build their self-esteem. At the top of the hierarchy, self-actualization encompasses the need for self-fulfillment and achievement commensurate with one's ultimate capacity. People motivated at this level are the self-starters so often described in job advertisements. They are in essence freed to pursue their goals for fulfillment and achievement by having met lower-level needs.

Another way to understand Maslow's hierarchy (1954) is to think about how people might descend to lower-level needs under certain adverse circumstances. For example, someone engaged in fulfilling his or her ego and self-actualization needs might retreat to address lower-level needs if faced with a threat to safety or nourishment. For example, a person in fear of losing his or her job may not be thinking much about taking art classes to expand his or her creativity; that person's attention probably will be focused on the essential need to remain employed. But someone who feels safe in his or her employment and life may be able to reach farther up the hierarchy to address such higher-level needs.

How does this play out in the workplace? Maslow's theory (1954) helps us understand that human beings have their own psychological needs that they bring to the workplace from other aspects of their lives. They may be highly motivated to address whatever needs they have, regardless of what practices the manager may follow. That insight is an essential one for any realistic manager to grasp.

Another influential theorist, who wrote in the 1960s, was Douglas McGregor. McGregor (1960) is known for his definitions of *Theory X* and *Theory Y*. Theory X, which McGregor saw reflected in management practices in most industrial organizations, is based on the assumption that workers are lazy, resistant to change, and not concerned with the organization's needs. It is basically a negative view of human nature and might be used to justify an approach something like Taylor's scientific management. Someone who subscribes to Theory Y, on the other hand, views employees as capable of self-motivation and self-direction. A manager holding that theory of human behavior would be inclined to give individuals more self-control, decentralize responsibility, and seek to unleash human potential. If a manager subscribes to Theory Y, he or she might be more inclined toward the transformational approach to leadership, which was discussed in Chapter 4.

David McClelland, also writing in the 1960s, explained that it is not only workers who have needs that affect their behavior on the workplace. Managers have their own psychological needs, too, which influence how they behave with regard to their subordinates. McClelland (1961) identified three principal needs of managers: the need for achievement, the need for power over others, and the need for affiliation or good relationships with others. McClelland's theories stimulated a large body of follow-up research and the development of instruments to measure managers' needs. Its standing today is mixed, with some still supporting it and others criticizing it harshly (Rainey, 2003, p. 255). But, like Maslow (1954), McClelland (1961) helped us recognize that managers, like all human beings, do not come to the workplace as empty canisters; they come with their own psychological needs and may behave at work in a way that helps address them.

Katharine Cook Briggs and her daughter Isabel Briggs Myers made an important contribution to management by developing a tool known as the Myers-Briggs type indicator, which is widely used in the workplace today. Myers-Briggs and other similar instruments are used to reveal *personality style*, which "refers to the manner in which individuals gather and process information" (Denhardt et al., 2002). Based on the theories of the psychologist Carl Jung, personality tests like Myers-Briggs are used to provide individuals with insights about their own perspectives and preferences, which may help them understand their own behavior and that of others with whom they work. Perhaps the best-known distinction made by Myers-Briggs is that between introverts and extroverts, although it measures personality in many additional dimensions.

Like most theories, those of Frederick Herzberg, first described in the late 1960s, have been challenged by other researchers. However, his findings are still widely cited and have implications for the management of nonprofit staff and volunteers that are interesting to consider. Herzberg conducted studies in which he claimed to identify two sets of factors that influence motivation. He called them *motivators* and *hygiene factors*, also sometimes called *satisfiers* and *dissatisfiers*. Table 8.1 shows both sets of factors. According to Herzberg (1968), there is a big difference between them. The *absence* of hygiene factors can lead to dissatisfaction, but they cannot be used in a positive way to *motivate* people. Only the motivators can do that. This implies that managers should design work to reduce dissatisifers and increase motivators in the environment of the workplace.

TABLE 8.1   Herzberg's Motivators (Satisfiers) and Hygiene Factors (Dissatisfiers)

Motivators (Satisfiers) (Related to the job and to motivation)	Hygiene Factors (Dissatisfiers) (Related to the environment)
Achievement	Company policies and administration
Recognition	Relations with supervisor
The work itself	Interpersonal relations with coworkers
Advancement	Working conditions
Growth	Compensation
Responsibility	Status and security

Source: Adapted from Herzberg (1968).

To understand Herzberg's theory (1968), students may find it useful to think about their own work or volunteer experience and what they found to be satisfying or intolerable in specific cases. Looking at the right-hand column of Table 8.1, dissatisfaction with a job can be caused by the frustrations that derive from company policy or administration—for example, the mindless bureaucracy reflected in Dilbert cartoons. Dissatisfaction may arise from poor interpersonal relationships with a supervisor or peer or from physical working conditions that do not provide safety and security. (Remember Maslow's [1954] hierarchy!) A tyrannical or incompetent boss, petty colleagues, or an unclean and unsafe work environment are reasons that might cause most people to go home discouraged and start looking for alternative employment. Students will note that compensation—that is, salary, benefits, and other financial rewards—appears on the list of dissatisfiers and not as a motivator. Let's return to that interesting point in a moment.

Take a look at the left-hand side of Table 8.1, a list of Herzberg's (1968) motivators. People who participated in his studies described the factors that motivated them at work to include achievement and recognition, opportunities for advancement, opportunities for greater responsibility and personal growth, and the inherent rewards of certain types of work. For example, tutoring children might be an inherently rewarding activity, as opposed to, let's say, slaughtering pigs. If that work is also carried out in an environment that provides the other motivators, the job may prove very satisfying, unless some dissatisfiers from the right-hand column get in the way. If the dissatisfiers are present at significant levels, even rewarding work may not be enough to compensate for the aggravation, and people may become unmotivated and perhaps inclined to look for other places to spend their working hours.

What about money? It may seem counterintuitive to many people that salary appears in Herzberg's theory (1968) not as a motivator but rather as a potential dissatisfier. After all, do not many companies, and an increasing number of nonprofits, offer financial incentives to encourage higher performance? That practice suggests an underlying theory that people are motivated in a positive way by the opportunity to make a greater income. But then how do we explain the fact that many nonprofit staff members work for less income than they could earn in the for-profit sector and yet are highly motivated in their jobs? Or that volunteers work for no financial compensation at all?

If the wage is so low that it isn't livable or if an employee feels that he or she is not paid what his or her effort is worth, that may be a source of dissatisfaction. If the employee believes that others, within the organization or elsewhere, are being paid more for the same work, that sense of unfairness may be *dissatisfying*. But ensuring that salaries are fair, and at least sufficient, may be more important than the level of compensation per se. Sufficient and fair may be enough to remove money as a cause of dissatisfaction. If Herzberg (1968) is right, as long as those standards are met, more money may not produce greater motivation. Motivation comes from the factors on the left-hand side of Table 8.1.

Again, it is important to recognize that many scholars have challenged Herzberg's (1968) findings. But his theory seems consistent with what we observe in many nonprofit organizations, so it has some intuitive appeal. Even though paid staff often are paid less than their counterparts in the for-profit world and volunteers are, by definition, unpaid in financial terms, many will find their work very rewarding if Herzberg's motivators are present. Since they do not expect to receive the same salaries that are paid in some for-profit companies, they are not dissatisfied by their nonprofit incomes so long as they are at least adequate and perceived as fair. This perspective has many implications for management practice. If managers can design jobs and create working environments in a way that provides their staff and volunteers with opportunities for achievement, recognition, advancement, and growth and if the nature of the work is inherently rewarding, staff and volunteers may be highly motivated even within the limits of nonprofits' financial constraints.

Joslyn (2002) reports on a study of nonprofit workers conducted by the Princeton Survey Research Associates and supervised by the Brookings Institution (p. 1). This study provides further insight on the motivations of nonprofit staff members that are consistent with Herzberg's theory (1968). The study found that nonprofit workers are indeed driven by mission rather than money. Only 16% of nonprofit staff surveyed said that they come to work for their pay, compared with 31% of federal employees and 47% of for-profit employees. More than 70% of nonprofit workers reported that they were satisfied with their pay. Other sources of satisfaction reported were flexibility, collaborative decision making, and being treated as well-rounded human beings rather than just workers. Most sources of dissatisfaction reported were related to ineffective supervision, overwork and burnout, or inadequate resources with which to work. The positives and the negatives sound much like Herzberg's two sets of factors (Joslyn, 2002).

It could even be argued that nonprofits have an advantage over for-profit companies in motivating their workforces. Their sometimes limited financial resources do not prevent them from eliminating most of the potential dissatisifers or increasing most of the Herzberg (1968) motivators. In addition, many offer work that is inherently rewarding because it is tied to a social purpose and the improvement or enrichment of human lives, something that some, but not all, for-profit companies can offer. If nonprofit managers keep their staff and volunteers focused on the nonprofit's mission, they may keep them highly motivated.

There are many additional theories of motivation that this chapter does not discuss in detail. Students with an interest in this area should explore them in some of the resources suggested for additional reading. An important group of theories go under the rubric of *expectancy theory*. These theories describe how individuals make decisions based on their expectations about the likely outcomes. They do things that they believe have a high probability of a good outcome and avoid actions that they expect to lead to bad outcomes. Some theorists (e.g., Vroom, 1964) have devised algebraic formulas to describe this type of decision-making process. Other theories have been based on the research of B. F. Skinner, whose experiments measured the response of animals to stimuli. In basic terms, Skinner's (1953) principle of *operant conditioning* explains that we repeat behaviors that are rewarded and tend not to repeat those that are not. Important contributions to understanding also have come from social learning theory, as developed by Albert Bandura (1978) and others, and goal-setting theory, identified with the work of the psychologist Edwin Locke. (2000). Much recent work has been devoted to attempts to integrate earlier theories. Some say that motivation theory is currently in a state of disarray, providing at best insights that offer partial explanations (Rainey, 2003, p. 268). However, most theories offer some useful insights that may help guide managers and increase their understanding of staff and volunteers.

APPLYING THEORIES TO THE NONPROFIT WORKFORCE

As noted at various points earlier in this book, the literature of nonprofit management includes both theory and the prescriptions of practitioner-oriented authors. This book attempts to integrate both perspectives. Now that we have reviewed some of the theoretical literature on human motivation, let's look at one attempt to translate that theory into specific recommended practices in managing the nonprofit workforce.

In their book *Managing Human Behavior in Public and Nonprofit Organizations*, Robert Denhardt et al. (2002) review the motivation literature and offer nine suggested "ways of acting," which they found to reflect commonalities of the various theoretical approaches. The following paragraphs discuss each of their recommendations and how they may relate to the various theories discussed above.

Managers should be reflective and proactive about their own motivation. McClelland (1961) and others theorists have suggested that the manager's own needs and motivations affect how he or she interacts with and communicates with colleagues and subordinates. This would imply that self-knowledge and understanding are essential for any individual who aspires to be an effective manager of others.

Managers should be aware that what motivates them is not necessarily what will motivate others. This advice is supported by several theories and reflects the simple but important understanding that people are not all alike. As Maslow (1954) and other theorists suggest, they bring their own needs to the workplace, which may reflect circumstances in their personal lives, their cultural backgrounds, or perhaps their preferred communication styles, reflecting their personality styles.

Managers should have realistic expectations about the extent to which they can influence the motivation of others. Again, Maslow (1954) and others theories explain, people come to the workplace already motivated. They are motivated to meet whatever psychological needs they may already have. The manager may not be able to influence those motivations very much. It may be more productive to assign people to jobs that enable them to meet their existing needs or perhaps redesign jobs to make them a better fit with the natural inclinations of those who hold them. Of course, if individuals' needs and motivations simply do not align with the goals of the organization, it may be best to suggest that they find employment in a more suitable environment. Too much effort to change the individuals may be frustrating and fruitless.

Managers should participate in setting clear and challenging goals. As Herzberg (1968) discovered, the opportunity for achievement is a motivator for most individuals. But achievement requires that there are clear goals by which it is defined. Otherwise, effort finds no emotional reward, or a situation may evolve in which individuals feel that even "enough" is not sufficient to please their supervisors. The manager thus should establish goals in a participative manner so that the staff member accepts them as his or her own, provide regular feedback on progress, and grant recognition when the goals are reached.

As Letts et al. (1999a) observe, managers often face two challenges: getting the job done and keeping the staff satisfied. But they state, "Organizing jobs so employees can achieve and see results does both: It advances the organization's mission and motivates people in the process" (p. 108).

Managers should think about the salience of various rewards. Again, individuals are motivated differently. They have different values. And what they will find rewarding may be different in each case. A manager needs to listen, determine what each member of the staff finds important, and provide rewards consistent with that insight. Some may thrive on recognition—for example, being named "staff member of the week." Others may value the opportunity for flexible hours or to earn additional free time through outstanding performance. As Denhardt and colleagues (2002) emphasize, and as the Hawthorne experiments suggested so many years ago, the interest and attention of the manager may itself be a reward that will reinforce high performance for some members of the staff.

Managers should be honest with people about what rewards are possible and what rewards are not. As expectancy theory describes, individuals may be motivated not only by the value of rewards but by the probability that they can be obtained. A manager who is unrealistic in promising increased compensation, increased responsibility, community recognition, or some other reward for achievement of goals may buy some short-term motivation. But over time, such a manager will lose credibility and the power to influence the behavior of his or her staff.

Managers should treat people equitably and fairly. People in a workplace have a sense of what is equitable, in terms of effort, compensation, status, and other matters. As Herzberg's (1968) theory suggests, inequities in salary paid to individuals who perform similar work or put forth comparable effort may create more dissatisfaction than compensation that is modest in absolute terms. Of course, no person should be treated unfairly for reasons of his or her race, nationality, gender, religion, lifestyle, disability, political perspective, or other personal characteristics or preferences. To do so is morally wrong and generally illegal. And it is just poor management, likely to result in a dysfunctional, dissatisfied, and unproductive workforce that will not build a high-performing organization.

Effective nonprofit organizations today go beyond the requirements of law and embrace diversity as an organizational value, seeking to draw the strength that comes from bringing together people of different perspectives, experiences, cultures, and backgrounds. In our complex society, any organization that does not incorporate such diversity will quickly lose touch with its community and constituency and, by excluding important talent, weaken its ability to serve its mission and achieve its goals.

Managers should make the work satisfying and meaningful. Motivation arises not only from the characteristics of people but also from the nature of the work they are given to perform. As Herzberg (1968) observed, some work is intrinsically motivating. But routine tasks may become monotonous and dissatisfying. Even interesting work may become less interesting if it is unchanging over time. Good managers provide their staff members with opportunities to grow personally and professionally, to take on new challenges, and to develop new skills in a variety of areas. This may be accomplished by rotating assignments or redesigning jobs, by providing training, and by providing opportunities for advancement from within the organization. Those who are employed in nonprofits are usually motivated by the impact of their work on the lives of clients. As Denhardt and colleagues (2002) suggest, it is good management practice to provide staff with as much exposure to clients as possible, enabling them to see firsthand the outcomes of their efforts (p. 173).

Managers should think about the life stages of the people they work with and offer appropriate support. There are various life-stage theories that describe the needs and motivations of people in various periods and positions. Those theories do have many critics. But they suggest that understanding the issues facing individuals in their personal lives may provide the manager with a useful perspective that is of benefit both to the individual and to the organization. It is also an approach that creates a humane environment consistent with the values of most nonprofit organizations.

MANAGING VOLUNTEERS

The discussion in the previous section of this chapter was focused primarily on the management of nonprofit staff members. Let's now shift our discussion to look at some principles that apply specifically to managing service volunteers.

Effective management of volunteers is an important topic because volunteers are a major component of the workforce of many nonprofits. Independent Sector (2001) estimates that in 2001, 44% of adults, nearly 84 million Americans, engaged in some volunteer activity. That would be equivalent to an additional 9 million full-time nonprofit employees.

Young adults, aged 35 to 54, are the most likely to volunteer, with more than 31% percent doing so in 2006 compared with only 18% of people in their early twenties. In general, women are more likely to be volunteers than men, and this is true across all age groups, educational levels, and other characteristics (Bureau of Labor Statistics, 2008).

The service of volunteers is of enormous economic importance to nonprofit organizations and to society. Independent Sector (2008) estimates that each hour of volunteer time contributed to nonprofits in 2007 was worth $19.51; that is an average of what organizations would have needed to pay to obtain similar services from paid staff, not an inconsequential sum. It is important to note, however, that individuals cannot claim a tax deduction for the value of their volunteered time. A nonprofit organization can cite the value of volunteer services in its communications, to demonstrate wide community support or for purposes of recognizing volunteers like donors. However, there are limitations on how that value can be used on nonprofit financial statements. According to rules established by the Financial Accounting Standards Board (1993), the value of volunteer work can be used on financial statements, in grant proposals, and in other formal ways only if the volunteers are providing specialized services for which the nonprofit would otherwise have paid. That might include, for example, services of accountants, architects, doctors, and similar professionals.

As O'Neill (2002) observes, "Nonprofits differ greatly with regard to the role of volunteers." Most nonprofits are small, all-volunteer efforts. Many nonprofits with paid staff also rely heavily on volunteers. Others, such as research institutes, universities, and private foundations, use few volunteers (p. 31). Recent decades have seen the increased professionalization of nonprofit management, with paid staff replacing volunteers in some organizations, especially the largest and most commercialized. Today, volunteers often work alongside paid staff, and volunteer management has itself become a specialty of professional nonprofit management.

There are different types of volunteers, characterized by the pattern of their participation, the extent of their commitment, and their motivations. For example, Sunney Shin and

Brian Kleiner (2003) identify three types. One is what Shin and Kleiner call the *spot volunteer*, whose participation is casual and episodic. For example, an individual may respond to a call for volunteers to help clean up a park or a hiking trail—it is a one-day commitment and there is likely enough work to occupy as many people as show up. The effort may not need to be repeated again, at least for some period of time, and there is no special skill required to participate.

A second type is the *regular volunteer*, who makes a commitment to the activity and gains a sense of gratification and accomplishment from the work. Such volunteer assignments may have the formality of regular paid jobs; there may be job descriptions, clear statements of responsibilities, and specific skills required to perform the work. Continuity may be important; for example, those who participate in tutoring programs need to be present in every session in order to develop relationships and gain the trust of the children. In other situations, dependability is essential; for example, volunteer fire departments or disaster relief organizations cannot rely on whoever may choose to show up on a given occasion.

The third type of volunteer that Shin and Kleiner (2003) identify is someone who is pressured to volunteer, perhaps by an employer, a peer group, or an educational requirement. Many corporations encourage their employees to engage in community service activities, as a strategy both for gaining goodwill for the company and for building camaraderie among the workforce. Many states require that high school students complete a volunteer experience as a graduation requirement, and of course, courts often assign first-time offenders of minor crimes to community service as a form of restitution. Although some may regard mandatory voluntarism, or even that performed under pressure, as an oxymoron, some speculate that the requirement of voluntary service for young people may be helpful in introducing them to the concept, perhaps beginning a commitment that they will continue throughout their lives.

Motivations of Volunteers

We need to consider the motivations of volunteers in two ways: first, what motivates people to become volunteers in the first place and, second, what factors motivate them to perform at a high level and continue in their volunteer roles?

Why do people volunteer in the first place? Since individuals have varied needs, there are a variety of reasons. Some, probably most, at least in part, are motivated by the mission of the nonprofit and by their personal values. They may volunteer because they have the desire to give something back to society, to improve the lives of others, or to advance some activity or cause that they believe to be important to the future. Others may undertake voluntary service, at least in part, to meet personal needs and desires. This may include making new friends, perhaps meeting potential mates or business contacts; learning new skills; improving their resumes; alleviating boredom; or a host of other reasons. The fact that people may be motivated by a combination of altruism and personal needs does not diminish the value of their efforts or make them less admirable. But it is essential for the nonprofit manager to understand these sometimes mixed and complex motivations in order to create an experience that will attract and retain the volunteer workforce.

A considerable body of research on volunteers suggests that the factors leading to motivation and satisfaction are very similar to those for paid staff. For example, studies have found that volunteers are motivated by a desire to serve the mission; that volunteers who remain with the organization are those who experience positive relationships with other volunteers; that those who continue to serve are those who find the nature of the work itself rewarding; and that volunteers value opportunities to learn new skills through their voluntary service. Volunteers who have participated in studies assign importance to factors such as clearly defined responsibilities, a reasonable work schedule, and competent supervision, all consistent with the motivation theories we have previously discussed. This suggests that a list of recommended practices for managing volunteers will include many points similar to those outlined above for the management of staff (McCurley, 2004).

Volunteer Management Practices

There is an extensive literature on the management of volunteers. Indeed, volunteer management has become a recognized subspecialty of nonprofit management, the practitioners of which have their own professional associations, conferences, and journals. The list of suggested readings at the end of this chapter provides a small sample of the many publications and Web sites that offer summaries of research on voluntarism and the management of volunteer programs.

There is much commonality among the recommendations of experts on managing an effective volunteer program. Most include some or all of the following points (see, e.g., McCurley & Lynch, 2006).

Nonprofits should assess the need for volunteers and develop volunteer job descriptions. Before an organization launches a program for the use of regular volunteers, it needs to determine why volunteers are needed. If volunteers are to serve episodically (e.g., a group is going to the woods for one day to clean up trash and repair hiking trails), there may not be a need for much formality in defining volunteer jobs—a supervisor can just assign those who show up to the tasks that need to be done. But if the organization needs volunteers to play an ongoing role as a part of its workforce, then volunteer jobs need to be designed and defined with some precision in order to establish clear expectations and ensure that the volunteer's work is related to program needs. Having formal job descriptions also helps communicate to volunteers that they are accepting a significant responsibility and that their assignment involves doing real work that is central to the program of the nonprofit.

Job descriptions do not need to be complex or extensive but should carefully state the type of work, skills needed, and expectations of volunteers. For example, the job description for a volunteer hotline advocate at the Denver Center for Crime Victims, shown in Box 8.1, lists the specific tasks that the volunteer will perform and the qualifications required for the position, as well as the organization's commitment to provide training and compensation in the form of nonfinancial benefits.

BOX 8.1   The Denver Center for Crime Victims

Volunteer Job Description

Job Title: Volunteer Hotline Advocate

Purpose: Hotline advocates are trained to staff DCCV's 24-hour Hotline and offer emotional support, information and referrals to crime victims in the Denver area. Hotline advocates connect clients with appropriate resources.

Reports To: Director of Training and Volunteer Services

Responsibilities:

1. Staff the hotline for a minimum of one four-hour shift per week; day and evening shifts available.

2. Assess immediate victim needs and provide referrals and follow-up services.

3. Document contacts and contributions to statistical reports.

4. Work cooperatively with Denver-area service providers.

5. Attend quarterly in-service training and support meetings.

6. Provide advocacy and support for clients.

7. Any other related duties as assigned.

Qualifications: 18 years of age or older; ability to work shifts; possess open, nonjudgmental attitude toward victims/survivors of crime; good communication skills; ability to work well with wide range of people.

Special Requirements: Complete initial training; six-month commitment to program; background records check.

Benefits: Advocates will be provided with in-depth and ongoing training in the dynamics of victimization and will gain direct experience in providing support to people in need. Participation will enhance the community responsiveness to rights of victims and survivors of crime. College and other academic internships available.

DCCV is an equal opportunity employer. As such, reasonable accommodations for persons with disabilities will be made in compliance with the Americans with Disabilities Act (ADA).

Source: The Denver Center for Crime Victims Web site (www.denvervictims.org/volunteerdescription.htm, accessed April 17, 2007). Used with permission of The Denver Center for Crime Victims.

Nonprofits should develop formal volunteer policies. Volunteers may be unpaid, but they are a part of the organization's workforce. Indeed, they often work alongside of paid staff in delivering its services. There should be formal policies that spell out the expectations, rules, and standards by which volunteers will be evaluated and, if necessary, terminated. The policies should spell out the relationship between volunteers and any paid staff by whom they are supervised or whom they may supervise. Organizations have personnel policies to govern their relationship with paid staff; not having such policies for volunteers might imply that they are not as essential as staff and set the stage for misunderstandings, conflict between volunteers and staff members, or even legal problems.

Having formal volunteer policies is also an important element of risk management for the organization. This is especially important in settings where volunteers will have direct contact with clients or access to confidential client information, or in which clients are particularly vulnerable or potentially volatile. For example, McLean Hospital, which treats people suffering from psychiatric illnesses, presents an especially sensitive environment. Its volunteer guidelines, shown in Box 8.2, are appropriately extensive and detailed. New volunteers should be given a copy of the policies and should sign a statement acknowledging that they have read them. And, most organizations should carry liability insurance, to protect both organizational assets and volunteers.

BOX 8.2   Guidelines for Volunteers

McLean Hospital

A Harvard University Affliliate

GUIDELINES FOR VOLUNTEERS

1. Volunteers have the responsibility to protect each patient's right to privacy. Therefore, information of a medical and psychiatric nature, as well as identifying data, such as name, address and telephone number, is strictly confidential, and may not be shared with any person or agency other than authorized McLean Hospital personnel. In response to inquiries made by people other than McLean staff and volunteers, volunteers shall neither confirm nor deny that a person is a patient at the hospital, nor provide any other information about the patient.

2. Volunteers shall not remove written material of a clinical nature, or copies of such material, from the hospital; nor shall they take photographs, tape recordings or any action that may infringe on the patient's right to privacy and dignity. Volunteers shall not have access to patients' records with the exception of specially approved volunteers.

3. Volunteers shall not write books or articles based on clinical experiences at the hospital. Volunteers must receive prior approval from both the Coordinator of Volunteers and supervisory staff before starting a journal or writing a paper based on their clinical experience.

4. Volunteers have the responsibility to treat all patients with respect, with an awareness of their dignity as persons and to observe their civil rights at all times.

5. Volunteers have the responsibility to seek out staff to talk about any situation that they encounter wherein they have questions concerning what is physically or emotionally safe for the patients, or for themselves, or which raises legal issues. Volunteers shall not handle discipline problems, nor shall they assist in any restraining procedures.

(Continued)

(Continued)

6. Volunteers shall avoid physical contact with patients unless a patient wants to shake hands or contact is required as part of an approved activity, such as pushing a patient on a swing.

7. Volunteers may participate with patients only as assigned by staff. They shall not see patients outside of the hospital, or after discharge, without prior approval from staff. Volunteers shall not give their telephone numbers or addresses to patients without permission from staff.

8. Volunteers have the responsibility to make sure patients have the proper authorization to participate in various activities.

9. Volunteers shall not drive patients in their cars, nor shall they leave the grounds with a patient.

10. Volunteers may accompany staff and patients on outings. As a general rule volunteers pay for their own expenses.

11. Volunteers have the responsibility to use discretion in disclosing information about themselves to patients. They shall not discuss their personal problems or their experiences with drugs, sex, therapy, and illness.

12. Volunteers have the responsibility to support the patients' treatment program by encouraging patients to discuss their clinical concerns with staff. Volunteers shall not agree to a patient's request to keep a secret. Experiences during a volunteer period should be discussed with staff afterwards to enhance volunteer-patient interactions.

13. Volunteers have the responsibility to support the staff and the policies and procedures of McLean Hospital.

14. Volunteers have the responsibility to refer patient or family member's complaints to departmental supervisory staff, or the Director of Social Work, to help ensure patient satisfaction.

15. Volunteers are expected to come regularly and promptly for the times they have agreed to work. On arrival, the volunteer should check in with staff to receive pertinent information and instructions.

16. Volunteers have the responsibility to be groomed and dressed appropriately, bearing in mind they are role models.

17. Volunteers shall not accept gifts from patients unless the gift has no appreciable monetary value and staff approves.

18. Volunteers are not assigned keys.

19. Volunteers have the responsibility to know the McLean Hospital emergency number for their own safety as well as the safety of the patients.

20. Volunteers have the responsibility to learn the hospital Fire Rules. If volunteers see/smell smoke or fire, they must immediately take the appropriate steps for responding.

21. Volunteers have the responsibility to learn and abide by the policies and procedures regarding hazardous materials.

22. Volunteers have the responsibility to know the infection control policies/procedures for Volunteer Services.

Source: McLean Hospital Web site (www.mclean.harvard.edu/employment/volunteer/vg.php, accessed April 17, 2007). Used with permission of the McLean Hospital.

Nonprofits should provide a sufficient budget and personnel to manage the volunteer program. Volunteers may be unpaid, but they do not come free. Without adequate resources, such as books, computers, tools, transportation, supervision, or whatever their work may require, volunteers are no more likely than staff to be successful. Depending on the scope of the volunteer program, it may be important to have a full-time member of the paid staff to manage the organization's overall relationship with volunteers. This does not imply that volunteers necessarily report to the volunteer manager with regard to their specific assignments but that the manager maintains an overall view of volunteers' involvement and performance. It is also important that all members of the paid staff who work with volunteers, including perhaps program or unit directors, are provided with training on the special considerations in managing them.

Nonprofits should recruit and hire volunteers as if they were employees. Some organizations may be in such need of volunteers that they may be tempted to accept anyone who may indicate an interest. But doing so may provide only a short-run gain and, indeed, is likely to be an approach that neither meets the organization's needs nor provides a satisfying experience for the volunteers. A well-managed program is likely to attract, at least over time, sufficient interest to permit selectivity in the hiring of volunteers.

Gaining the ability to be selective in choosing volunteers offers the organization at least two advantages. First, it can select people with the right skills to meet its needs and those who are likely to remain committed to their volunteer responsibilities. Second, the organization may be able to craft its volunteer program in order to include groups from prospective donor companies, religious congregations, or other groups with which it wishes to establish closer relationships. A volunteer program thus can become not only a vehicle for delivering the organization's programs but also an instrument of its fundraising, communications, and community relations efforts. A selective volunteer program requires that prospective volunteers complete an application and undergo an interview process. Background checks may also be required by law or by considerations of risk management.

Nonprofits should provide orientation and training to volunteers. Volunteer orientation should include an introduction to the organization that includes not only practical operational matters but also a discussion of its mission, values, and culture. It should clarify the relationship between volunteers and paid staff and the expectations of each. Depending on the nature of the volunteer's work, training may include working with another, more experienced volunteer for a period or a more formal program designed to develop specific skills.

Volunteer managers should set clear goals, evaluate performance, and recognize achievement. As discussed previously, people are motivated by clear goals, the explication of a clear path to their achievement, and recognition for having succeeded in reaching them. Since volunteers are not compensated financially, their achievement of goals and recognition may be their primary rewards. This suggests that volunteer job performance should be evaluated, which, of course, implies that volunteers could be terminated as well, the same as paid staff. Some organizations may find that a difficult decision to reach because they are in need of volunteers and feel they cannot afford to let one go. Or perhaps the culture of the organization may not encompass individual performance standards, at least not for volunteers. It also can be problematic if volunteers are also donors—even board members, whose termination might bring additional consequences. However, such concerns should be balanced against the need to maintain the overall quality and reputation of the program, the importance of achieving quality in service delivery, and the negative consequences for the morale of both staff and other volunteers of continuing someone whose work or attitude does not make a positive contribution. Of course, evaluation should be a two-way street. Volunteers should be given opportunities to provide feedback on the quality of their experience, including the conditions, supervision, and resources with which they work.

In summary, many experts suggest that, in most respects, volunteers should be managed with many of the same practices that apply to paid staff. To be sure, volunteers are entitled to respect and gratitude. Their impact is much the same as that of donors of financial gifts, and they are a precious asset that nonprofits need to nurture and cultivate. However, for all these reasons, they also deserve a structured and professional approach that maintains high expectations and stays focused on achievement of the organization's mission and goals.

How are nonprofit organizations doing in following recommended practices? A 2004 study by the Urban Institute found a mixed pattern, as shown in Table 8.2. While more than 60% of organizations had adopted each of the practices to some degree, of the nine practices studied, only supervision and communication with volunteers had been adopted to a large degree by the majority of nonprofits examined. There were, as might be expected, variations depending on the characteristics of the organization, including its size, the level of volunteer involvement, the relative predominance of volunteer roles, and the subsector or industry in which it operates. For example, organizations in the health care industry and larger nonprofits were more likely to have adopted the recommended practices, while small ones and those using episodic volunteers were less likely to have done so (Hager & Brudney, 2004).

It is perhaps because of the absence of sound management practices that many nonprofits experience high volunteer burnout and turnover. For example, a study conducted by the Corporation for National and Community Service, the federal agency that administers AmeriCorps, Senior Corps, and other programs, found that one third of individuals who volunteered in 2005 did not continue their activity in 2006 (Michaels, 2007). The turnover represents significant lost investment in volunteer training and experience. If nonprofits were to devote additional resources to volunteer management programs, those expenditures could be more than offset by the saving of costs in recruitment of volunteers and additional paid staff. More widespread adoption of recommended management practices thus could have a financial benefit as well as an impact on the effectiveness of nonprofit programs and services.

CHAPTER SUMMARY

Early management theories were often developed in industrial settings and portrayed human beings as part of a production machine, whose performance could be increased by focusing on procedures and rules. Since at least the Hawthorne experiments of the 1920s, theorists have focused on human psychology and motivation, emphasizing the influence of human needs and feelings on behavior in the workplace. Theories are often advanced, gain wide acceptance, and are subsequently discredited through further research. But most

TABLE 8.2	Volunteer Management Practices by Nonprofits		

Recommended Practice	Percentage of Organizations That Have Adopted to a Large Degree	Percentage of Organizations That Have Adopted to Some Degree
Regular supervision and communication with volunteers	67	30
Liability coverage or insurance protection for volunteers	46	26
Regular collection of information on volunteer numbers and hours	45	32
Screening procedures to identify suitable volunteers	45	42
Written policies and job descriptions for volunteer involvement	44	37
Recognition activities, such as award ceremonies for volunteers	35	47
Annual measurement of the impacts of volunteers	30	32
Training and professional development opportunities for volunteers	25	49
Training for paid staff in working with volunteers	19	46

Source: Hager, Mark A. and Jeffrey L. Brudney (2004). *Volunteer Management Practices and Retention of Volunteers.* Washington, DC: Urban Institute. Used with permission of the Urban Institute.

offer some principles that are adopted in new approaches or that gain continued acceptance by practitioners.

One theory, advanced by Frederick Herzberg (1968), suggests that there are two sets of factors present in the workplace. One set of factors, including intrinsically rewarding work and opportunities for achievement, recognition, and advancement, serve to motivate workers. Another set of factors, related to the work environment and including supervision, working conditions, and compensation, may be dissatisfiers but are not in themselves motivating. Managers should try to reduce or eliminate dissatisfiers and increase motivators. These principles may apply to the motivation of volunteers as well as paid staff members. Other theories, including those of Maslow (1954), McClelland (1961), and Myers and Briggs

(Denhardt et al., 2002), suggest that individuals bring their own personal needs and styles into the workplace. This may require that managers design jobs to reflect the existing motivations of their staff and volunteers.

Based on motivation theory, some recommended practices for managers of paid staff include being reflective about their own needs and motivations; being aware that what motivates the manager may not necessarily be what will motivate others; holding realistic expectations about the extent to which a manager can influence the motivation of others; participating in setting clear and challenging goals; thinking about the salience of various rewards to individuals who have different needs; being honest with people about what rewards are possible and what rewards are not; treating people equitably and fairly; making the work satisfying and meaningful; and, considering the implications of life stages and of personal life events for the individuals they manage. Fostering workplace diversity, encompassing characteristics such as race, gender, nationality, religion, lifestyle, and others, is not only the right thing to do but also is an essential element of sound management. Effective nonprofits embrace diversity as a strength, recognizing that combining individuals of different backgrounds, perspectives, values, and views adds to the organization's capacity for high performance.

Volunteers are the only workforce for many organizations and constitute an important component of the workforce for many others, including those that employ paid staff. Individuals may be motivated to volunteer by altruism and concern for others, by their own needs, or by some combination of factors. In the workplace, they are usually affected by many of the same principles of motivation as paid staff. Some recommended practices for managing volunteers include assessing the need for volunteers and developing volunteer job descriptions; developing formal volunteer policies; providing a sufficient budget and personnel to manage the volunteer program; recruiting and hiring volunteers as if they were employees; providing orientation and training; and, setting clear goals, evaluating performance, and recognizing achievement.

Following these practices may be especially important if volunteers provide regular service in the organization's programs, but it may be less essential with regard to episodic volunteers who just participate occasionally. Many nonprofit organizations do not yet follow most of these recommended practices, although those that are larger or work in certain industries, such as health care, are more likely to be doing so. Volunteer management has become an identified subspecialty of nonprofit management, and its practitioners have access to professional associations, publications, and training to improve their skills.

KEY TERMS AND CONCEPTS FROM CHAPTER 8

dissatisfiers
Hawthorne experiments
hierarchy of needs
hygiene factors
motivation
motivators
Myers-Briggs
operant conditioning

expectancy theory
regular volunteers
satisfiers
scientific management
spot volunteers
Theory X and Theory Y
volunteer management

CASES FOR DISCUSSION

In each of the cases described below,

Which theories of motivation might be most relevant to the situations described?

What recommended practices for the management of staff or volunteers may not have been followed in each of these cases?

What psychological needs may each staff person or volunteer be trying to meet?

What does the manager's behavior in each case suggest about his or her psychological needs?

What might the manager in each case have done differently at an earlier point in the relationship to have avoided the current problem?

CASE 8.1

Getta Grant

Getta Grant is Director of Development at a medium-sized nonprofit that provides a range of services to adolescents from disadvantaged urban communities. She reports to the Executive Director. The organization receives some government funding, but is also reliant on foundations and individual donors. Getta's responsibilities include staying informed about foundation interests and giving patterns and working with the organization's three program directors to identify foundations that may be prospects for support of their programs and projects. She drafts letters of inquiry and, where appropriate, meets with foundation officers and writes proposals. Getta has been with the organization for five years and was hired by the previous Executive Director, who always gave her "excellent" (the highest rating) on her annual performance reviews. The current Executive Director has been in her job less than a year. She inherited Getta from her predecessor. When she had just arrived, it was already time for Getta's annual evaluation. The new Executive Director read a couple of proposals Getta had written, thought they were good, and continued her "excellent" rating without much further thought. Getta seemed pleased to have her high rating continued.

When Getta writes something, it is generally of high quality. But over the past year, the Executive Director has become unhappy with the amount of work Getta produces and with her inability to meet deadlines. Since her last review, Getta has produced only a handful of letters and two proposals. The Executive Director gave her positive feedback on that work, which was indeed good, thinking that would motivate her to work harder and faster. But Getta has continued to produce relatively few proposals, and in some cases, they have taken so long that she missed foundation deadlines. She is coming up soon for her second evaluation with the Executive Director, who is now quite frustrated with her performance.

The Executive Director met with Getta recently and explained that she is unhappy. She warned Getta that her next performance evaluation may not be so positive this year. Getta seemed shocked. "But you said my proposals are good," she protested, "and you gave me an 'excellent' rating last year!" Since that meeting, Getta has missed several of days of work, calling in sick or saying she was "working at home." And the Executive Director has seen almost no additional work.

CASE 8.2

Rita Writer

Rita Writer is a member of the communications and marketing staff at a large environmental non-profit. She has various responsibilities, including writing press releases, articles for the quarterly magazine, and copy for brochures that are produced for fundraising and other purposes. Rita had previously worked as a marketing specialist in the alumni relations office of a local college and came with outstanding references. When she accepted her new job, she said she wanted to make the change so that she would have more opportunity to write, since her job in alumni relations also included responsibility for attending events and required considerable travel.

Rita now has been in her current job for about three months. She produces an adequate volume of writing, but it is consistently full of glaring errors. Her manager, the Vice President for Communications and Marketing, sometimes sends the work back to Rita for revisions. But most times the Vice President just edits the work himself, not wanting to confront Rita and thinking that it is faster for him to take on the task. He has not said anything to Rita, but he is becoming increasingly unhappy with her performance. He is concerned that firing her would make him unpopular among the other staff, so he is reluctant to do so. But he is wondering what he can do to increase Rita's contribution to the organization.

One of Rita's colleagues mentioned to the Vice President that Rita spends a lot of time on the phone talking to people in chapter offices around the country. In addition, the organization sponsors a number of public events, including lectures on environmental issues that are followed by receptions. Although she is not required to do so, Rita attends many of them on her work time and always stays for the reception, mingling with the guests. One of her colleagues said sarcastically to the Vice President, "Rita just seems to prefer socializing to doing her job."

CASE 8.3

Bob the Builder

Bob is a volunteer at an organization that provides services to older people in the community, enabling them to keep on living in their own homes. Older clients are matched with volunteers, who agree to visit with them at least once a week to assist them with matters such as paying bills, performing light housework or yard work, and similar tasks. When their homes need modest upkeep or repairs, such as painting, volunteers with appropriate skills are assigned as a team to complete the job. The organization's Director of Volunteers recruits volunteers with needed skills, assigning them to clients and projects and ensuring quality in the work they perform.

Bob was a building contractor and has recently retired. He has been a longtime but occasional volunteer. His wife, Mary, is a member of the board of directors, and Bob and Mary have been regular contributors to the annual fundraising campaign. A few months ago, Bob approached the Director of Volunteers and said that he now will have more time and would like to do more work with the organization. Delighted at the offer, especially in light of his professional skills, the Director assigned him to supervise several home repair project teams.

Recently, however, she became concerned when she heard from another volunteer that Bob was going way beyond the scope of the projects assigned. In one case, the project team was sent to do some painting for a homeowner, but Bob had performed some electrical wiring in the woman's house. In another case, he replaced some plumbing. The Director became concerned about the risks in that type of work and the potential liability to the organization should something go wrong. In addition, she is now receiving complaints from other volunteers who have worked with Bob. One volunteer has told her that Bob treats other volunteers as if they were members of the crew of his former construction company. And he doesn't treat them well. He assigns them work and then criticizes them for not doing it fast enough or well enough. Some of the volunteers have said that they will not work with him again.

The Director of Volunteers met with the Executive Director and discussed her concerns about Bob. The Executive Director was somewhat dismissive, saying she thinks Bob is a great asset to the organization. "After all," she said. "He's a professional builder. We are fortunate to have someone with his skills involved." She then added, "Anyway, it's difficult to do anything about it with Mary serving on the board."

SUGGESTIONS FOR FURTHER READING RELATED TO CHAPTER 8

Books/Reports/Articles

Corporation for National and Community Service. (2007). *Volunteering in America: 2007 State trends and rankings in civic life*. Washington, DC: Author. (http://nationalservice.gov/pdf/VIA/VIA_summary report.pdf)

Denhardt, R. B., Denhardt, J. V., & Aristigueta, M. P. (2002). *Managing human behavior in public and nonprofit organizations*. Thousand Oaks, CA: Sage.

Kotter, J. P. (2001). What leaders really do. *Harvard Business Review, December,* 85.

Macduff, N. (2005). Principles of training for volunteers and employees. In R. D. Herman & Associates (Eds.), *Jossey-Bass handbook of nonprofit management* (2nd ed., pp. 703–730). San Francisco: Jossey-Bass.

McCurley, S. (2005). Keeping the community involved: Recruiting and retaining volunteers. In R. D. Herman & Associates (Eds.), *Jossey-Bass handbook of nonprofit management* (2nd ed., pp. 587–622). San Francisco: Jossey-Bass.

Watson, M. R., & Abzug, R. (2005). Finding the ones you want, keeping the ones you find: Recruitment and retention in nonprofit organizations. In R. D. Herman & Associates (Eds.), *Jossey-Bass handbook of nonprofit management* (2nd ed., pp. 623–659). San Francisco: Jossey-Bass.

Web Sites

Corporation for National and Community Service, www.nationalservice.org

Independent Sector, www.independentsector.org

Points of Light Foundation, www.pointsoflight.org

CHAPTER 9

Marketing and Communications

At their monthly meeting, members of the Siwash College faculty were informed by the college's president that "we are enhancing our communication with prospective students in order to increase applications, especially from highly-qualified students." The news was greeted with enthusiasm. "We really need to get the word out," said one professor. "We have excellent programs that nobody knows about." Another professor added, "Communication is a general problem here; some of our own colleagues don't know how strong many of our departments are. I'm pleased to hear that the administration will be doing something about it."

A month later, the college's vice president for communications presented a follow-up report to the faculty. In her comments, she said things a little differently:

> We are really investing significantly in our marketing and, in fact, we are bringing in a team of marketing consultants to help us position the college and differentiate our brand and we will be hiring more recruiters on our own staff.

One professor immediately came to his feet, saying, "Wait a minute. Are you saying we are going to market the college like a brand of soda? We have a good reputation now and that will just tarnish it by making us look desperate." Another added,

> I agree. We attract students now because of the quality of our academic programs. If we want more and better students to apply, the money should be spent on academic resources, like the library, science labs, and computer technology. Those are the things that will attract the kind of students we want.

A third member of the faculty joined the conversation, saying,

> It concerns me that we are going for the hard sell. We don't need Madison Avenue types out representing us, exaggerating and misleading students into coming to Siwash. That wouldn't be fair to the students and could cause people to question our integrity.

While the concerns of the Siwash College faculty may not be completely unfounded, they may also reflect an incomplete understanding of "marketing." Although marketing principles are widely applied in many nonprofit organizations, misunderstanding of the concept is still not uncommon, and some individuals have a viscerally negative reaction to the use of marketing's vocabulary in organizations that are based on values and driven by missions. In part, the comments and concerns of the Siwash College faculty may reflect the shadows of earlier approaches to marketing in the business sector that remain prominent in some people's understanding of the concept.

When marketing first came on the business scene around the beginning of the 20th century, it reflected a *product mindset*. In other words, the prevailing view was "that to be an effective marketer, you simply had to 'build a better mousetrap,' and, in effect, customers would beat a pathway to your door" (Andreasen & Kotler, 2003, p. 40). That was essentially what Henry Ford did by inventing the Model T, and it may be the view of the Siwash faculty, who think it sufficient to improve the college's educational programs, assuming that prospective students will inevitably discover them and apply in greater numbers.

But the product mindset became obsolete in business in about the mid-20th century. It became increasingly clear that simply making a better product would not provide assurance that customers would buy it. An increasingly competitive economic environment led to a new approach to marketing in the business world, one reflecting a *sales mindset* (Andreasen & Kotler, 2003). The goal for a company or an organization with a sales mindset is to *convince* customers that they should buy the company's product rather than buy nothing or buy what a competitor is offering. With the adoption of this marketing perspective by American business in the 20th century, advertising became a major industry, and the hard sell became the preferred tactic of businesses trying to survive in a competitive environment.

> Salesmanship became a byword of successful marketing . . . the denizens of Madison Avenue achieved a central role in American folklore. Willy Loman and 'the Man in the Gray Flannel Suit' became important symbols of the new business culture. (Andreasen & Kotler, 2003, p. 41)

For many people, marketing is still synonymous with sales, and like some members of the Siwash faculty, they see it as something possibly inconsistent with the values and the culture of the nonprofit sector.

Both the product and the sales mindsets belong to an earlier period of American business history, and they are not the starting point for marketing today. Both mindsets would lead an organization to begin the marketing process *inside* its own walls, with the goal it wishes to achieve—more sales of the product or service, resulting in more revenue for the organization. When the sales mindset was predominant, messages were pushed out through advertising and other means of communication with the hope that they would fall on receptive ears But marketing today begins from the outside; that is, it reflects a *customer mindset*. This approach requires that

> the organization systematically study customers' needs, wants, perceptions, preferences, and satisfaction, using surveys, focus groups, and other means . . . [and that] *the organization . . . constantly act on this information to improve its offerings to meet its customers' needs better*. [italics added] (Andreasen & Kotler, 2003, p. 42)

Successful marketing is thus an interaction between the needs of customers and the services or products the organization produces. Unlike the sales model, which tries to persuade the customer that he or she wants what the organization has to offer, marketing implies that the organization develops its product to be responsive to what the customer needs and wants.[1] Of course, businesses do so readily. If consumers want larger cars, the auto makers will produce them. If consumers shift their priorities to saving oil and preserving the environment, auto makers will respond to that change by producing more fuel-efficient vehicles. If the product or service is well matched with what people really want, it will still be necessary to let potential customers know of its existence and the benefits it provides—there is still a need for advertising and communication, but there will be little need to persuade (or sell) individuals on the desirability of purchasing it.

Of course, even this more up-to-date understanding of marketing may still give pause to the faculty of Siwash College and to others who work in nonprofit organizations. How responsive should a nonprofit be to the expressed desires of its clients or customers? Should a college's curriculum be designed to encompass only what students say they wish to know, or should it reflect what the faculty believe to be the essential elements of a sound education? If a performing arts center is not attracting symphony audiences of sufficient size, should it abandon Beethoven in favor of presenting rock concerts? If patients express displeasure about having their blood tested, should hospitals skip that procedure in order to gain more customer satisfaction? Should a museum abandon its mission to preserve antiquities and educate museum patrons in order to provide entertainment along the lines of Disneyworld?

Stated at the extreme, all these ideas are obviously inappropriate, indeed ridiculous. A nonprofit organization cannot abandon its mission or act contrary to its values merely to increase sales of its product or service. To do so would be inconsistent with the essence of its nonprofit character and status. Marketing must serve the mission and not become the driver of the nonprofit organization's program. As Andreasen and Kotler (2003) write,

> Marketing is . . . a *means* to achieve the *organization's* goal. It is a tool—really a process and set of tools wrapped in a philosophy—for helping the organization do what *it* wants to do. Using marketing and being customer-oriented should *never* be thought of as goals; they are ways to achieve goals. (p. 57)

However, nonprofits cannot ignore the reality that they operate in a competitive environment, even if they do not compete directly against each other. A homeless shelter may not compete with another for clients, but two may compete for gifts from local corporations, foundations, and individuals. Organizations that advocate a cause or social goal may compete against others that advocate opposing positions; they compete in a marketplace of ideas, attitudes, and beliefs. Even those that may advocate noncontroversial ideas, like wearing seat belts and stopping smoking, still compete against complacency and habit and for attention amidst the distraction of all the other messages with which people are bombarded every day, what communication theory calls "noise."

Of course, many nonprofits do offer products and services for a fee, and they may compete against each other as well as against for-profit companies and public organizations engaged in similar activities. For example, two colleges may compete for students, and two theaters may compete for audiences. Even without such direct competition, organizations face *generic competition* from alternative uses of individuals' time and money. People can only be in one place or another at a time. Attending the museum, especially if the museum charges an admission fee, competes with going to the theater, attending the movies, or staying home on the sofa watching TV. The museum must offer something that will motivate people to spend their time, and perhaps their money, to visit the museum rather than engage in such alternative activities. Marketing is a strategy for competition, whether for resources, convictions, or customers, and thus marketing principles may prove useful for every nonprofit, regardless of its mission.

MARKETING TO CHANGE BEHAVIOR

Marketing and communications are terms often combined in the titles of individuals or offices—for example, the "Director of Communications and Marketing" or the "Office of Marketing and Communications." But the concepts are distinct. Communication, in the simplest of definitions, is the transmission or exchange of information. As a discipline, *communications* is more complex, encompassing an understanding of the principles by which information is transmitted and received—that is, "how messages are encoded, transmitted, screened, decoded, stored, retrieved, and acted on" (Gainer & Moyer, 2005, p. 303), as well as the various technologies employed, for example, print and electronic media. But communications is not synonymous with marketing; it may be undertaken with multiple goals. *Marketing* is a *process* that may encompass communications, but with a very specific purpose: "to influence the behavior of someone else" As Andreasen and Kotler (2003) explain,

> Marketing's objectives are not *ultimately* either to educate or to change values or attitudes. It may seek to do so as a *means* of influencing behavior. . . . If someone has a final goal of imparting information or knowledge, that person is in the education profession, not marketing. Further, if someone has a final goal of changing attitudes or values, that person may be described as a propagandist or lobbyist, or perhaps an artist, but not a marketer. While marketing may use the tools of the educator or the propagandist, its critical distinguishing feature is that its ultimate goal is to influence behavior (either changing it or keeping it the same in the face of other pressures). (p. 39)

If marketing is understood as a process undertaken with the goal of influencing behavior, then, again, its tools are relevant and useful to every nonprofit organization, whatever its mission. The goal may be to influence donors to give; volunteers to serve; and citizens to vote, wear seat belts, or eat less fat; or to attract customers or clients who will purchase the products and services the nonprofit offers. Despite its universal relevance, however, marketing has gained its widest acceptance and application by nonprofits for whom earned income, specifically fees for services, constitute a substantial portion of total revenues. For private colleges, tuition generally provides the largest share of income. Hospitals and other health-care institutions derive most of their revenue from charges for care provided, whether paid by patients or by private or public insurers who pay on their behalf. Many performing arts organizations rely substantially on ticket sales as well as gifts and other sources of income, and admission fees are an increasingly important source of income for museums. It is in such organizations that marketing finds its fullest application. Our discussion of marketing in the balance of this chapter will emphasize examples of marketing by nonprofits to attract clients or customers to their programs and activities and to retain them. We will discuss fundraising and advocacy in more detail later in this book and will revisit some marketing principles in those contexts at those points.

THE MARKETING MIX

Marketing implies an interaction between the customer and the organization. It begins with research to identify the needs and wants of potential customers or clients, which informs the development of the products or services to be offered. A simple description of the marketing process that is often stated says "Find a need and fill it." That implies a malleable marketer, one who will create almost any product or service for which there is a demand. This simple understanding of course may raise difficult issues for nonprofit organizations that are driven by the missions and values that are at the heart of their existence. It is obvious that any organization hoping to exchange its services for payment cannot be oblivious to the desires of its potential consumers. A college with great programs but no students eventually will close, and one that does not introduce new programs to address emerging new fields and industries will not keep pace with others that are more innovative. But it is necessary and appropriate that nonprofits sometimes push back against the market to preserve their core values in pursuit of their missions. Fortunately, there is a middle choice between rigidity and complete capitulation to the market; a nonprofit can change its *marketing mix* in response to information about what customers, clients, or donors need and want, while remaining faithful to its core purposes. By doing so, it can *differentiate* its product from that offered by others, *position* itself in a unique *market niche,* and gain a *competitive advantage* over others.

To illustrate the ideas of the marketing mix, differentiation, and market niche, let's start with a familiar example from the for-profit world—Starbucks. The campus on which this author works is in an urban setting; there are many places to buy coffee, including the student union, street vendors, and other restaurants and delis in the neighborhood. For many years, there was a large study room located in the front of the undergraduate library that was accessible through a door directly from the street—24 hours a day. It was rarely used at any time of the day or night. A few years ago the university decided to lease the space to Starbucks, which converted it to one of its ubiquitous coffee stores. The Starbucks is always busy; indeed, students, faculty, and staff sometimes stand in lines extending out the door to pay a higher price for Starbucks coffee than they would need to pay for coffee at other nearby locations. And, in the space formerly occupied by an underused study room, students now spend time studying—at Starbucks! How has Starbucks differentiated itself from the other coffee sellers in the neighborhood? What is it that people receive in exchange for their money when they patronize Starbucks, and how is that different from what others are offering? Obviously, it's the coffee, which is pretty good, but it's also the atmosphere of the store, the convenience of its location, the comfortable chairs and laid-back atmosphere—the fact that Starbucks lets you stay for a long time and offers wireless Internet access for those who wish to use their laptops. It's also the familiarity and instant recognition of the Starbucks logo, that lets you know exactly what to expect inside and something that's indescribably just "cool" about buying coffee with complex-sounding names in sizes other than "small, medium, and large." In other words, there are more variables involved than just the core product, or service, that is being sold by any business. The four key variables—*product, place, promotion, and price*—are called the *4-Ps* of marketing. Various combinations of these variables are called the *marketing mix*.

Product

The product, generally the good or service being offered, seems like the simplest variable to understand. In the nonprofit sector, it's education, health care, counseling, tutoring, food, or whatever programs the organization may operate. Products have both tangible and intangible qualities, like the consumption of Starbucks coffee. Education offers a clear example. There is little basis on which to conclude that an Ivy League education is always superior to that offered at other colleges and universities across the country, and indeed, other institutions may be stronger than any of the Ivy League schools in some fields. Why would a student be willing to pay more at an Ivy League university than perhaps at a local college or state university that may provide an equally good education? Because the prestige of holding an Ivy League degree is itself an intangible quality of the product. An Ivy League degree may instantly convey intellectual distinction because those universities are known to be selective in admissions. Membership in the alumni association of such a university may bring influential contacts and open important doors throughout life. And it happens that most Ivy League campuses are also attractive ones that provide an intellectually stimulating environment outside as well as inside the classroom. In other words, the product is not just the education itself, it's also the experiences and intangible benefits that may go along with it.

Intangibles may also be a part of the product in health care. For example, a hospital that provides a pleasant, modern environment may be preferred to one with a run-down facility that nevertheless provides excellent medical treatment. If the doctors and the nurses are nice and take the time to explain medical conditions to their patients, they are offering a different product from another hospital that follows exactly the same medical protocols but in which the staff are more distant or abrupt. A nonprofit that provides services to homeless individuals without significant barriers—that is, helps anyone without preconditions to receiving service—is offering a different product than one that is more difficult to access, although both may offer food, counseling, and housing of basically the same quality.

Think back on the meeting of the Siwash College faculty with which this chapter began. Their concern that the academic program be centered on educational values and not be shaped entirely to suit the expressed desires of high school students is understandable. But the college's product is not just its curriculum. The product also includes the quality of its facilities, the teaching skill of its professors, the closeness of relationships that professors form with their students, the quality of student activities offered, and many other aspects of the student experience that go beyond the classroom. These are qualities of the product that can be enhanced in response to student wants and needs without compromising the college's commitment to its educational mission or values.

Place

The location at which the product or service is available is an important variable in the marketing mix. A program operated in a location that is convenient for clients is a different product from the same program offered in a remote place beyond easy reach. A college located in a small rural town offers a different experience from one located in the suburbs of a big city, although it may offer an identical curriculum. A concert hall located on a bus line offers something different from one located in the distant suburbs accessible only by car. Some programs need to be taken to where the clients are. For example, many colleges offer off-campus courses for working adults; symphony orchestras located in cities undertake run-outs to smaller towns in their regions; major museums place exhibits on tour across the country; and hospitals send vans offering mammograms into neighborhoods in which many women do not have easy access to health care. The decision about place involves consideration of both the physical and the virtual worlds. An attractive and interactive Web site may be as much a part of the overall product as services provided in a physical location.

Promotion

In the minds of some, marketing may be virtually synonymous with *promotion*, which is the visible activity that everybody can see—the announcements, advertisements, brochures, and other efforts undertaken to gain visibility and notice for the organization's products. Marketing is not synonymous with promotion, but promotion is part of the marketing mix. Clients and customers cannot partake of products or services if they do not know of their existence or what they comprise. But to whom should the nonprofit's programs and services be promoted? A simple answer might be "to the public," but that would require a foolishly expensive effort, since most of the public are likely to have no interest in or need for the organization's offerings. The need to keep promotion cost-effective requires focusing communication on segments of the public most likely to respond. This *segmentation* is based on research and may employ sophisticated tools developed in the business sector and increasingly adopted by many nonprofits as well.

Market Segmentation

For an organization's promotion to be cost-effective, it needs to identify its *target market* or markets, which will be a subset of the larger general population. Some of this may seem intuitive. For example, a college likely will focus its promotion of undergraduate programs on high school students and their parents. A symphony orchestra may limit its mailing of concert announcements to people who live in higher-income areas, who can afford the cost of the tickets. A medical clinic that provides screenings for HIV might target its communication to neighborhoods with low-income or younger single people rather than areas with primarily families and older residents. But variables used for segmentation are often more sophisticated than these somewhat obvious examples suggest.

Objective measures include *demographic variables*, for example, age, gender, race or ethnicity, and income, and *geography*, that is, where people may live, work, or travel. The examples we described above reflect simple segmentation along these lines. Markets also may be segmented according to *behavioral measures*—in other words, patterns of past behavior that divide people into identifiable groups. For example, people who have never attended the theater constitute a segment different from those who attend occasionally, which is yet different from the group of people who are season ticket holders. A theater would design its strategy to communicate with these different segments of its market in different ways, perhaps offering varied prices or emphasizing unique aspects of the theater-going experience to each.

Some of the most sophisticated methods of segmentation involve *psychographics*. Psychographic measures combine demographic data with knowledge about individuals' *lifestyles*, defined by their activities, interests, and opinions (Andreasen & Kotler, 2003; Sargeant, 2005). Market researchers group individuals according to various lifestyles that are associated with certain behaviors, attitudes, or likes and dislikes. For example, we might assume that a young single person who lives with roommates, rides a motorcycle, and holds politically radical views may have different tastes in music than a couple with two young children and an SUV who live in the suburbs and have liberal views or a retired couple with a politically conservative orientation who live in a condo and travel only by public transportation. Individuals' lifestyles often predict not only the type of music they prefer but also the political and social causes they may favor, the kinds of artistic events they may attend, and the types of nonprofits they may support. Their patterns of behavior can help identify them as part of the target market for a particular product or service. For example, in one study undertaken in selected cities, Andreasen and Belk were able to identify six lifestyle groups, which they labeled Passive Homebodies, Active Sports Enthusiasts, Inner-Directed Self Sufficients, Active Homebodies, Culture Patrons, and Social Actives. People in the Culture Patron lifestyle were more likely than others to attend the theater or the symphony, while those in the Social Active lifestyle were more likely to attend only the symphony (cited in Andreasen & Kotler, 2003, p. 158). That kind of insight would be useful to a performing arts center in selecting those segments to which it would promote specific performances, ensuring that marketing dollars were used most efficiently. In other words, segmentation enables the nonprofit to target its promotion like a rifle shot, rather than scattering it like buckshot, at greater total expense and with the result that much of it is wasted on those who are unlikely to attend its programs or feel a need to use its services.

The smallest conceivable market segment is, of course, the individual, and the most sophisticated for-profit marketers have become adept at targeting their messages to one person at a time. Think, for example, about your experience with amazon.com. Amazon remembers what you purchased before and suggests new titles that may be in line with your demonstrated interests—it segments based on your past behavior. Knowing your interests in reading and in music, it lets you know what other products are being purchased by other people who are reading the same books or listening to the same music as you; this may reflect its assumptions about your lifestyle. Your interests and preferences are also revealed through your use of Google searches and the Web sites that you visit, which may be tracked by cookies placed on your computer's hard drive. Online advertising then is targeted to match the profile you have provided of yourself through your past behavior, defining the characteristics of a very precise market segment that includes just you! Among nonprofits, segmentation at this level is beginning to be applied in Internet fundraising.

Price

Pricing can be an especially sensitive issue for nonprofit organizations. Some provide their services to clients without charge; others have missions suggesting that prices should be kept as low as possible to encourage participation.

There are essentially four methods for establishing the price at which a product or service will be offered. One approach is *cost-oriented pricing,* in which the price charged to the customer or client is set to cover what it costs the organization to produce or provide it. A popular method is to set prices to produce a break-even situation for the organization overall. This method may seem the most appropriate for a nonprofit organization, which does not have the purpose of maximizing its profits. But it is important to ensure that the price reflects the direct costs of providing the service as well as the overhead needed to run the organization. Indeed, as we discussed in Chapter 6, earned income, including fees for service, may be a principal source of funds for capacity building, and a price set to break even might need to encompass the costs of such enhancements. Using the break-even method often will mean that different organizations charge about the same, since their costs are likely to be similar. This method is widely used in the nonprofit sector because of its "administrative simplicity, competitive harmony, and social fairness" (Andreasen & Kotler, 2003, p. 385).

Another way to establish prices is to look at the organization's competitors, perhaps in order to charge a bit less or provide a somewhat better product than others are offering at the same price. As discussed before, even if a nonprofit does not compete directly with another, it must take generic competition into account in establishing its prices. For example, a theater needs to consider how its ticket price compares not only with that of other theaters, but also with the cost of going to the movies instead. The price and the product interact. What does the theater experience offer to justify spending the price of a ticket rather than just staying home and watching TV? Does the product need to be more than just a play; for example, can a higher ticket price be justified and obtained if the experience includes a backstage reception attended by the cast of the play?

A third way of establishing prices is the *value-based* approach (Andreasen & Kotler, 2003, p. 385). This approach takes into consideration what may be the perceived value of the product or service to the customer, which may not be closely related to the costs of production. Indeed, some consumers may equate higher price with quality, for example, in buying wine or automobiles. A $30 bottle of wine may not be demonstrably better than a $10 bottle of wine, and it likely did not require three times as many grapes to make it. But buyers who are not wine experts may prefer to pay more believing that the price will equate to quality—or at least that their dinner guests will believe so. Is a Lexus a much better car than a Toyota? Possibly it is, although both will go about the same speed and arrive at a destination with equal dependability. But there is some psychological value to the buyer in owning a car that comes with more prestige, based at least in part on its higher price. A controversial example of value-based pricing involves the tuition policies of many colleges and universities. Some critics have charged that some higher-education institutions have intentionally increased their tuitions to create the image that they are elite, since that will be attractive to some students and their families.

Price Discrimination

Price discrimination sounds like something unethical, immoral, or even illegal, but it is an essential element of marketing strategy. It does not mean charging people different prices based on their race or ethnicity, gender, religion, or similar characteristics. Rather, it means charging people different prices based on the market segment to which they belong, based on objective variables.

Nonprofits may undertake price discrimination to cover the actual higher costs of serving a particular segment. For example, a college may charge more for on-campus courses than those offered off-campus, to cover the additional costs of providing library support and other services to students who come onto the campus. Price discrimination may also be used as a way to match the price to the perceived value of the experience. For example, concert halls charge more for close seats than for seats in the balcony, although the music may sound much the same from either location. A third reason to charge different prices might be to shift utilization. Theaters often charge less for matinees than for evening performances as a way to fill the hall at a time when it might otherwise be empty. Price discrimination also can help maximize a nonprofit's revenues by pricing the most desirable products or services at a high point that some may be willing and able to pay (Andreasen & Kotler, 2003, p. 386). An interesting example of that is provided by the Bolshoi Theater.

One of the world's most renowned ballet companies, the Bolshoi was heavily subsidized by the government of the former U.S.S.R. But with the fall of communism, it faced two challenges. One was to pay its artists at competitive rates, since they were now free to perform elsewhere in the world for potentially higher compensation. The other challenge was to replace reduced government support with other sources of revenue.

Under the communist system, the Bolshoi's best seats always had been reserved for artists, high-ranking government officials, and other VIPS, but in fact they often had not been used by those people. Instead, the tickets were sold to scalpers, who became known as "pillar people" because they often waited for possible customers while lurking behind the pillars in the lobby. Because the seats for which they had tickets were desirable, the scalpers could sell them for a profit and had done so for many years. Facing a new need to generate revenue on the introduction of a market economy, and freed from the constraints of the previous system, the Bolshoi revised its pricing policies to capture the higher value of those better seats for itself and put the pillar people out of business. It introduced price discrimination, charging varied prices for seats depending on their perceived desirability. The result was an increase in its ticket revenue of 82% in the first month. At the same time, it lowered the prices for less desirable seats, making them more accessible for students and others without wealth (Klintsov & Löhneysen, 2001).

BUILDING THE BRAND

Remember that competition requires an organization, nonprofit or for-profit, to differentiate its products or services from those of others. One strategy for doing so is building a recognizable *brand* and a positive image for that brand. When we think about a brand, what most readily comes to mind are commercial products, such as soda, cars, or clothing, and names like Coke or Pepsi, Honda or Toyota, Gap, or Benetton. But nonprofits have brands as well.

The American Marketing Association (2007) defines *brand* as "a name, term, design, symbol, or any other feature that identifies one seller's good or service as distinct from those of other sellers." Many brands are instantly recognizable, for example, the Nike swoosh. It doesn't even require a word for people to identify it with the company and its products. Some nonprofit logos are equally well-known worldwide—for example, the Red Cross's red cross and WWF's (formerly the World Wildlife Fund) panda.

The brand is shorthand for a collection of perceived qualities of the organization or its products, known as *brand attributes*. A brand may evoke feelings, attitudes, memories, and other intangibles that we associate with the name or symbol. "Coke" may bring to mind a refreshing break on a summer day. "Disney" may evoke memories of a childhood trip with one's family. And, depending on one's age, either "Chevy" or "Toyota" may evoke a sense of confidence, quality, and durability. "Greenpeace" or "Doctors Without Borders" likely stimulate very different images—and feelings—from "Harvard" or "MoMA" (the Museum of Modern Art in New York City). An individual's reaction to a brand may, of course, be quite different from that of others, depending upon their own values and their perception of the values of the organization. A brand is a promise, and the term *brand promise* describes the expectations that you have about what you will receive when you buy a specific product or service. For example, when you walk into Starbucks, you expect the coffee to be good and the atmosphere to be comfortable and welcoming; those are experiences that Starbucks has promised you by placing its logo over the door (Sargeant, 2005).

Establishing a strong and positive image for a brand brings many benefits to an organization. Think back to the aftermath of Hurricane Katrina in 2005. Horrified by the scenes unfolding on their television screens, many Americans went to their computers to make a gift to help those displaced by the storm. They were most likely to go to the Web sites of organizations with known brands—the Red Cross, the Salvation Army, and Habitat for Humanity—both because their brands were well-known and because donors attributed to them the qualities of competence and trust. Of course, a brand image can be fragile, and if an organization fails to deliver on the implied promise of its brand, the negative effect on its support can be both immediate and long lasting. When in 2002 the CEO of the United Way of the National Capital Area, serving the Washington, D.C., region, was forced to resign amid allegations of his misuse of donor funds, ripples battered the United Way brand across the country. The national office and local United Ways in other cities rushed to reassure their donors that the problems were limited to the National Capital chapter and to institute additional controls and safeguards so as to reestablish the credibility of the United Way brand. The CEO of United Way of America, the national umbrella organization, expressed the problem in this way: "To a United Way—to a nonprofit—trust is everything. [The National Capital Chapter] need[s] to do everything that has to be done to address the issues, create aggressive long-term resolutions to them, do it transparently, do it quickly—and that's the way you build trust back" (Lipman & Williams, 2002).

A positive brand image has value—monetary value, called *brand equity*. For example, if another company were to buy Nike, a part of the purchase price would reflect the value of the swoosh, which the buyer would expect to continue, stimulating sales and thereby increasing future revenue. When, in the 1990s, Nike was criticized for allegedly employing people in sweatshop conditions, the value of the brand, and thus the company, was at least temporarily suppressed. A company that finds its brand so degraded can be expected to undertake aggressive action, not necessarily to change its products or services but to resuscitate the value of its brand. Although nonprofit organizations are not bought or sold like corporations, their brands also have value. Its brand value is among the assets that a nonprofit brings to the table when it negotiates a partnership with a for-profit company, which will be discussed further in Chapter 11.

INTEGRATED COMMUNICATIONS AND MARKETING

Building a positive and consistent brand image requires that an organization integrate its marketing and communications efforts—in other words, that it ensures "that all the communications [it] generates represent a coherent whole" (Sargeant, 2005, p. 140). This requires that the messages and the values that they reflect permeate every aspect of the organization's work. If, for example, the organization desires to create an image of itself as "caring," its logo may include fuzzy small animals; but its staff also must treat clients in a caring manner, answer the phone in a responsive tone, and create an internal culture consistent with the external image the organization seeks to build. As Sargeant (2005) expresses it, the organization needs to "live the brand" in everything it does (p. 140). The brand and its image are unlikely to settle too far from the reality of what the organization actually does or what it really is.

In an integrated approach, communications with various constituencies and stakeholders, both internally and externally, must be consistent. As mentioned before, the constituencies of a nonprofit are often overlapping and interlaced. Remember the idea of open systems from back in Chapter 2? Staff talk to clients and to volunteers, who may also be donors, who may communicate their attitudes to their family, friends, and neighbors in the broader community. Although the organization may have high-quality publications and may skillfully manage its communications with the news media, these are unlikely to outweigh the word-of-mouth information and impressions communicated by those who have first-hand knowledge about the organization.

The way a message is received has as much to do with the predilections of the receiver as with the intentions of the sender. The receiver will interpret the message in the context of his or her own values, culture, and preformed attitudes about the organization. And established views may be difficult to change. For example, if a woman who has been a loyal donor to the local humane society hears rumors that animals are being mistreated, she may respond in one of four ways. She may practice denial, that is, persuade herself that the rumors just can't be true. Or she may search for disconfirmation of the rumors, perhaps calling the director of the shelter hoping that he will tell her they are not correct. She may minimize the problem, rationalizing that perhaps there have been a few cases of mistreatment but that surely they are not part of a consistent pattern and the stories have just been exaggerated by people who, for some reason, have it in for the humane society. Or she may accept the rumors as true and change her beliefs, discontinuing her financial support (Andreasen & Kotler, 2003). Human beings tend to resist changing their beliefs, whether positive or negative; thus, a minimum goal of communication is to continually reinforce the positive attitudes that your friends may hold, positively affect those of individuals who have been previously indifferent, and do nothing to further strengthen the negative attitudes of those who may already hold them. Just as for an individual, a tarnished reputation for an organization may be difficult to repair.

The source of information is a critical variable in its credibility. People are more inclined to believe what they hear from other individuals than what they read in the newspaper or hear on television. This is especially the case if the individual who provides the information is someone close to them, whom they trust, or close to the organization and thus presumed to know the real truth. This is one of the reasons why members of nonprofit boards, who are generally respected citizens in their communities, are so important as advocates for the organization's goals.

The most credible sources of information are family members, closely followed by friends and associates. Professionals like clergy, doctors, and counselors rank right after friends as credible sources of information. Newspapers, direct mail, and the Internet come next. The mass media, including radio and TV, have the least credibility as sources of information, although, interestingly, positive publicity from a mass media source is often highly prized by organizations that wish to improve their image (Bonk, Griggs & Tynes, 1999, p. 13). The most credible medium of communication is word-of-mouth. One research study, reported in 2007, found that 53% of Americans were inclined to accept the credibility of what they were told by friends and family and that 51% are likely to pass along the information they received by word-of-mouth to others (Hall, 2006). Positive coverage in the news media is thus unlikely to outweigh the comments of an unhappy staff member to a client or of a disgruntled volunteer to his or her neighbor. Consistency of message—and of behavior—is thus essential to establishing and maintaining the organization's positive brand image.

DEVELOPING THE PLAN

To be effective, a nonprofit's marketing and communication efforts must be more than a collection of random, sporadic activities—an occasional press release, a brochure updated every few years, and a few speeches by the executive director to schools or community groups. *Strategic marketing* and *strategic communications* require, by definition, "a plan, a method, or a series of maneuvers, for obtaining a specific goal or result" (Bonk et al., 1999, p. 3). The goals must be rooted in the organization's mission and values; the plan must be focused on achievement of those goals; and the plan must include a mechanism for measuring progress against the goals and providing feedback to adjust the plan as experience requires.

Various experts have developed templates or guides for developing a communications or marketing plan. They follow somewhat different formats and use varied terminology but include many of the same elements. Let's look at two examples: (1) a practical guide for developing a *communications plan*, offered by Bonk et al. (1999), and (2) a more elaborated and more theoretical format for *marketing planning*, devised by Sargeant (2005). Bonk et al. divide communications planning into three broad areas: (1) the overall goals to be achieved, (2) the specific elements of the communications plan, and (3) the ongoing communications activities through which the plan will be implemented. Their framework is illustrated in Box 9.1. Sargeant's model for developing a marketing plan is shown in Box 9.2.

BOX 9.1 Strategic Communications Planning Guide

Overall goals

Identify goals and outcomes

Develop vision and mission statement

Integrate values

Elements of the communication plan

Identify target audiences

Conduct research

Develop messages

Produce materials

Assess resources

Write the work plan

Ongoing communications activities

Ensure positive media coverage

Secure editorial endorsements and columnist support

Identify and train spokespeople

Build media partnerships

Be mindful of internal communications

Consider advertising

Develop crisis control and backlash plan

Conduct evaluations

Source: Bonk et al. (1999). Used with permission of John Wiley & Sons, Inc.

BOX 9.2 Marketing Planning Process

Mission statement

Organizational objectives

Marketing audit

(a) PEEST analysis

Political

Economic

Environmental

Socio-cultural

Technological

(b) Market analysis

(c) Competitor analysis

(d) Analysis of publics

(e) Analysis of own organization

SWOT Analysis

Marketing Objectives

Key Marketing Strategies

Tactical Marketing Mix

Product/service

Price

Place

Promotion

People

Process

Physical evidence

Budget

Scheduling

Monitoring and control

Source: Sargeant (2005, p. 52). Used with permission of Oxford University Press.

Theoreti (handwritten)

Students likely will see some differences between the Bonk and Sargeant models. Remember that Bonk and colleagues (1999) are describing a process for developing a *communications* plan. Their framework thus includes specific communications vehicles and tools, such as media relations, the printed and electronic materials, and advertising. It involves research to identify target audiences and develop appropriate messages, but it does not focus on the organization's products or services themselves. In other words, their process results in a plan that pushes information outward from the organization, to achieve whatever goals the organization has established for its communications program. Those may involve influencing the behavior of donors, clients, customers, and other constituencies, or communication may be intended for other purposes. The communications plan does not encompass detailed analysis of the organization or the design of its products.

Sargeant offers a process for developing a *marketing* plan. It includes a comprehensive environmental scan encompassing relevant political, economic, environmental, sociocultural, and technological conditions and trends (the PEEST analysis). It encompasses a market and competitor analysis, and a SWOT analysis, which students will recall from Chapter 7. It includes determination of a marketing mix, marketing strategies and objectives, and implementation plans.

These two models reflect the difference between communications and marketing, but there are similarities in the two models as well. Both begin with the organization's mission and goals; both proceed from research to implementation tactics; and both provide for evaluation, monitoring, and control to ensure the achievement of strategic goals.

You may see some parallels between Sargeant's model for marketing planning and the process of strategic planning discussed in Chapter 7. Indeed, some enthusiastic advocates have suggested that a marketing orientation should replace a strategic planning approach for some nonprofit organizations. Writing in 2000, with regard to higher education institutions, Roger L. Williams asserted that "strategic planning efforts have been ineffective because of fear of hard decisions, passive-aggressive behavior at the institutional level, fuzzy goals and unrealistic objectives, and because they try to be 'all things to all people.'" Marketing, Williams argues, is in contrast integrated, grounded in reality, constituency oriented, and survey and perception driven; it pays attention to relationships and offers an easier way to measure progress. He concludes that it is time to adopt a new paradigm, writing "Death to strategic planning; long live marketing" (pp. 63–64).

THE BOTTOM LINE

This discussion of marketing and communications concludes with the same question that has been raised in previous chapters: Does it work? In other words, what impact does adoption of a marketing approach have on the performance of nonprofit organizations? By now, readers who have progressed through this book from the beginning will recognize the issues associated with the question—the complexity of defining what constitutes nonprofit organizational performance and how to measure it once defined.

It is, of course, relatively easy to establish the link between marketing and performance in a for-profit company. Indeed, most research on the link between marketing and performance has been focused on the business sector. A number of studies have identified a relationship between market orientation and financial outcomes such as return on investment (Gainer & Moyer, 2005, p. 280; Shoham, Ruvio, Vigoda-Gadot, & Schwabsky, 2006). Similar methods may be suitable to studying marketing by nonprofits that also provide services in a competitive environment, such as health care. For many nonprofits, however, assessing the benefits of marketing also requires measuring its effect on donors, clients, and the advancement of causes or ideas, outcomes that may be less easily quantified.

The findings of several studies suggest that nonprofit organizations that hold a market orientation, perhaps better defined as a "social orientation," do attain greater financial support and client satisfaction than those that do not (Gainer & Moyer, 2005, p. 280). But as Shoham et al. (2006) acknowledge in a report on their investigations in this area, "New measures of [nonprofit organization] performance are needed and should guide future research" (p. 470).

CHAPTER SUMMARY

Marketing principles have been widely adopted in the nonprofit sector, especially by organizations that derive substantial revenue from fees for service. However, some remain concerned that marketing may not be appropriate to nonprofit values and cultures. This may reflect, in part, an understanding of marketing that is a throwback to earlier mindsets about the concept, especially the idea that marketing is equivalent to sales.

Contemporary marketing follows a customer mindset. That requires that "the organization systematically study customers' needs, wants, perceptions, preferences, and satisfaction . . . and act on this information to improve its offerings to meet its customers' needs better" (Andreasen & Kotler, 2003, p. 42). This implies that the organization's programs and services need to be adapted to meet identified customer desires; but this should not be taken as a reason for a nonprofit to abandon its mission or central values. Rather, marketing should be used as a tool for pursuing the mission and achieving mission-related goals.

The marketing mix includes four variables (called the 4-Ps of marketing): product, place, price, and promotion. Organizations can adjust the marketing mix to differentiate themselves from others and position themselves in a unique market niche, gaining an advantage over other organizations or alternative activities with which they may compete. Nonprofits may compete directly with other organizations, nonprofit or for-profit, but also face generic competition from all alternative uses for individuals' time and money.

Products have tangible and intangible qualities, including the prestige associated with a degree from a well-known university or the environment in which coffee is consumed. Place, or location, determines access to a program or service and is a critical variable in the marketing mix. Some products and services need to be taken to where the customers are—for example, vans that provide mobile medical care. Prices for products and services may be set to provide a break-even result for the nonprofit, to compete with what others are charging or to reflect the perceived value of the product or service to the customer. Sophisticated marketers practice price discrimination, charging different prices to different segments of their target market. Price discrimination may be intended to match differences in product value, e.g., seats closer to or farther from the theater stage; to shift utilization from peak to nonpeak periods; or to maximize revenue by charging the highest prices that some consumers are willing to pay.

Brand is defined as "a name, term, design, symbol, or any other feature that identifies one seller's good or service as distinct from those of other sellers" (American Marketing Association, 2007) . Individuals attribute qualities to a brand and organizations work to establish a positive brand image, which may help attract both clients and donors. A positive brand has a monetary value, called brand equity, which may form the basis of some partnerships between nonprofits and for-profit companies.

Communications and marketing must be integrated; that is, their goals must permeate all aspects of the organization, with consistent messages being delivered to various constituencies. This is especially important in nonprofits because their borders are porous and members of various constituencies, including staff, volunteers, and donors, may communicate with each other. Individuals attribute greater credibility to information they receive through word-of-mouth than to what they read or see in the public media, especially if the source is someone close to them or with inside knowledge of the organization.

Effective communication and marketing programs are more than collections of random activities; they are guided by a plan. There are many models for planning, but most begin with the organization's mission and goals, require analysis of target markets or audiences, and include evaluation to ensure that the program's goals are being achieved. Marketing is a process that seeks to influence the behavior of individuals. Communication may be a tool of marketing or may be undertaken for other purposes. If the ultimate goal of communication is to provide information or change attitudes, then it does not fit the definition of marketing.

Some enthusiastic advocates suggest that a marketing orientation should replace strategic planning as the approach of some nonprofit organizations. Research suggests that nonprofits that adopt a market orientation or a societal orientation do achieve greater financial support and client satisfaction. But establishing a link between marketing and organizational performance remains bedeviled by the difficulty of defining and measuring performance in ways that have universal acceptance.

NOTE

1. If a product or service is provided for a fee, then the relevant variable is what the customer *wants*, not what he or she may need. For example, a person may need more exercise, and his or her doctor may even recommend it. That person should join a health club. But unless the person also wants more exercise, his or her need is irrelevant from a marketing perspective because he or she will not be willing to spend money on health club dues.

KEY TERMS AND CONCEPTS FROM CHAPTER 9

4-Ps of marketing
brand
brand attributes
brand equity
communication
communications

competitive advantage
competitive rates
cost-oriented pricing
customer mindset
demographic variables
differentiation

integrated communications/integrated
marketing
marketing
marketing mix
market niche
position
place
price
price discrimination

product
product mindset
promotion
psychographics
sales mindset
segmentation
strategic communications/marketing
target market/target audience
value-based pricing

CASE 9.1

AARP

AARP is one of the nation's largest nonprofit organizations, with more than 35 million members, all of whom are over the age of 50 years. Its purposes include promoting independence, dignity, and purpose for older persons; enhancing the quality of life of older persons; and encouraging older people "to serve, not to be served." It pursues those purposes by informing its members and the public on issues important to older people; advocating on legislative, consumer, and legal issues; promoting community service by older people; and offering a wide range of special products and services to its members, including insurance plans and discounts on travel and various other products (AARP Web site, www.aarp.org, accessed May 23, 2007).

What is today known as AARP was founded in 1958 by Dr. Ethel Percy Andrus and for most of its history was known as the "American Association of Retired Persons." For most of that time, the name accurately reflected the status of most of its members. But in 1998, it needed to respond to powerful demographic trends. The baby boomer generation, with some 78 million people, was aging, with its oldest members entering their fifties. They were the future market for the association's programs, but their lives were different from those of earlier generations. People were living longer and working longer. The baby boomers were in apparent denial about their own aging—remember, this was the generation that in the 1960s had invented the phrase "Don't trust anybody over 30." If the association was going to continue growing, it would need to attract this rising and somewhat different generation of Americans.

Beginning in 1998, AARP undertook extensive research into the attitudes of baby boomers toward the organization, and the findings were reason for concern. Many baby boomers were attracted to AARP's products and services, but as the organization's president summarized the situation, "Boomers right now think of AARP as more for their parents [than for them]" (Lipke, 2000, p. D37). Armed with the insights of market research, the organization went about changing itself to become more attractive to the growing hoard of aging baby boomer Americans.

For one thing, the "American Association of Retired Persons" became just AARP, much as Kentucky Fried Chicken had become KFC and the American Telephone and Telegraph Company had changed to

(Continued)

(Continued)

simply AT&T. In other words, the word *retired* was retired, since it no longer applied to the actual working status of most of the organization's prospective members. But the name change was not all. AARP introduced a new magazine targeting baby boomers and divided its existing magazine, *Modern Maturity*, into two editions—one for people who are retired and one for people who are still working (Lipke, 2000). It launched a $100 million advertising campaign to announce its rebranding and to promote its various products and services. It launched a new Internet service aimed at issues faced by baby boomers. In 2006, it was developing additional new products aimed at the baby boom generation, including podcasts and an "audio logo" like the well-known sound of "Intel inside" (Elliott, 2006).

The stakes were high, and AARP set ambitious goals for increasing its membership by capturing a larger share of the baby boomers who were reaching the age of eligibility (Lipke, 2000). By 2006, it had reached 36.5 million members, including 44% of all Americans over 50 (Nelson, 2006).

Sources: AARP Web site, Nelson (2006), Lipke (2000), and Elliott (2006).

CASE 9.2

Randolph College

Randolph-Macon Women's College, located in Lynchburg, Virginia, was founded in 1893 and until 2007 was a college for women. The College had a distinguished history, producing notable graduates including the Nobel Prize winner Pearl Buck. But by 2003, the college's board of trustees faced a serious situation. The college was discounting tuition by 60% and spending more than the usual amount from its endowment, while enrollment had stagnated well below the level of 1,000 students, which the board considered the minimum for financial stability. A marketing research firm identified several problems, including the college's rural location and the fact that only 3% of college-age young women would even consider attending a single-sex institution (Pulley, 2007).

The board feared for the survival of the college and launched a strategic planning process. In the fall of 2006, the board released the strategic plan, which called for the college to become a coeducational institution. Men would be admitted for the fall, 2007, semester. The institution's name would be changed to Randolph College.

Announcement of the board's decision elicited a strong reaction from some of the college's alumnae. Opponents of the change organized themselves under the name "Preserve Educational Choice, Inc." and set up a Web site to solicit contributions and disseminate information arguing against the change. The group distributed a paper titled "20 Reasons Why You Should Change Your Vote," trying to persuade the board to reverse its decision (Preserve Educational Choice, 2007).

The college responded with its own paper, disputing the group's arguments (Randolph College, 2007). College leaders launched a national tour to meet with alumni to explain their reasons for the decision; but some remained angry and threatened to withhold future gifts.

In an article in *Currents*, John Pulley (2007) analyzed communication failures surrounding the issue. Some alumnae said that the college had led them to believe things were going well, announcing successful campaigns and other good news that did not prepare them for a radical new plan. Some felt that they were misled by a 2005 letter from the chair of the college's board suggesting that coeducation was just one of the many options being considered and that it was not likely to happen. Some alumnae said that they had received e-mails asking for suggestions of a new name for the college before they had even been informed of the board's decision to turn it coed. Others said that the college had disseminated enough information throughout the process but had not given alumnae opportunities to engage in real conversation about what the board was considering. The acting president of the college explained, "We tried to let people know what was happening as it was happening. In retrospect, we probably should have employed a specific public relations effort" (Pulley, 2007).

Sources: Randolph College (2007), Preserve Educational Choice (2007), Pulley (2007), and Ashburn (2006).

QUESTIONS FOR DISCUSSION

1. What similarities (and differences) do you see between Sargeant's model for developing marketing strategy and the strategic planning model discussed in Chapter 7?

2. How might the tools of portfolio analysis reviewed in Chapter 7 be applied in developing a marketing strategy?

3. Which principles from this chapter are illustrated by the case of AARP?

4. Is the case of Randolph College primarily about communication or about marketing? How are principles of each illustrated in this case?

5. Below is a list of some well-known nonprofit organizations and a list of attributes. Look at each nonprofit and identify up to three attributes that you would use to describe your impression of the organization. Don't think too long, just write down the first three words that come to mind when you read the organization's name. When you are done, consider these questions:

   How do your results compare with those of your classmates?

   What do the results suggest about attributes of the brand in each case?

   Why do you think each organization has the image that it does, either positive or negative?

American Red Cross	___,___,___	a) innovative
		b) well-managed
Salvation Army	___,___,___	c) caring
		d) greedy
Nature Conservancy	___,___,___	e) unresponsive
		f) dependable

(Continued)

Greenpeace	___,___,___	g) high quality
		h) patriotic ✓
Boy Scouts	___,___,___	i) untrustworthy
		j) cold-hearted
National Geographic Society	___,___,___	k) friendly
		1) radical
City Year	___,___,___	m) exciting
		n) prestigious ✓
United Way of America	___,___,___	o) courageous ✓
Boys and Girls Clubs	___,___,___	
Doctors Without Borders	___,___,___	
Habitat for Humanity	___,___,___	
Children's Defense Fund	___,___,___	
Boston Symphony Orchestra	___,___,___	
Yale University	___,___,___	

SUGGESTIONS FOR FURTHER READING RELATED TO CHAPTER 9

Books/Journals

Andreasen, A.R., & Kotler, P. (2003). *Strategic marketing for nonprofit organizations* (6th ed.). Upper Saddle River, NJ: Prentice Hall.

Bonk, K., Griggs, H., & Tynes, E. (2007). *Strategic communications for nonprofits*. San Francisco: Jossey-Bass.

Hart, T., Greenfield, J. M., & Johnston, M. (2005). *Nonprofit internet strategies: Best practices for marketing, communications, and fundraising success*. Hoboken, NJ: Wiley.

International Journal of Nonprofit and Voluntary Sector Marketing. Hoboken, NJ: Wiley (www3 .interscience.wiley.com/cgi-bin/jabout/110481870/ProductInformation.html).

McLeish, B. J. (1995). *Successful marketing strategies for nonprofit organizations*. New York: Wiley.

Sargeant, A. (2005). *Marketing management for nonprofit organizations* (2nd ed.). Oxford, UK: Oxford University Press.

Web Sites

American Marketing Association, www.marketingpower.com

Council for Advancement and Support of Education, www.case.org

Public Relations Society of America, www.prsa.org

PART IV

Obtaining and Managing Resources

Philanthropic Fundraising

Fundraising is synonymous with nonprofit organizations in the minds of many people. They may associate it with the flood of solicitation letters that fill their mailboxes around the holiday season, some enclosing address labels, book markers, or other items from a charitable organization. Or they may think of the charity golf tournament, tennis tournament, or some other event in which they participate. Or, perhaps, they may think about the annual phone call they receive from a student at their college or university, or a former classmate, asking for a gift to the institution's annual fund. Indeed, charitable or philanthropic giving is an important source of revenue for many nonprofits, although just how important varies considerably among subsectors.

For example, gifts provide just 4% of total revenues for health services organizations, which receive most of their revenue from government or private payments for services provided. In contrast, most religious organizations and many human services organizations almost entirely depend on giving. Educational institutions and civic, social, and fraternal organizations are in the middle, receiving 13% and 35% of their revenues from gifts, respectively (Weitzman et al., 2002, p. 99). But even for large institutions with substantial revenue from other sources, such as hospitals and universities, private gifts sometimes have an impact disproportionate to their share of total revenues because they address organizational priorities rather than supporting specific programs or services. For example, unrestricted giving may help support core operations or capacity building; new facilities may require a combination of fundraising and borrowing; new initiatives that do not yet attract paying customers or grants may be financed through discretionary dollars available to the CEO from endowment income or private gifts.

Although philanthropy in some form is common around the world, organized fundraising and philanthropy on a massive scale is still primarily an American phenomenon. And massive it is. In 2006, an estimated $295.02 billion was given to nonprofit organizations by foundations, corporations, and individuals. When philanthropy is mentioned, some people think about corporate giving or perhaps the large national foundations, such as the Gates Foundation or the Ford Foundation. But private individuals are overwhelmingly the largest sources of giving, accounting for more than $222 billion of the 2006 total. The largest portion of giving by individuals is directed to religion, which accounts for nearly 33% of the total each year; however, even when religious giving is excluded, individuals still account for much more than either corporations or foundations in their impact on U.S. philanthropy.

In 2006, foundations gave 12.4% and corporations accounted for just 4.3% of the total (Center on Philanthropy at Indiana University, 2007).

Where does the money go? Next to religion, which receives 33% of the total, the largest recipient of philanthropy is education, accounting for nearly 14% of the total, followed by human services (10%). Giving to create or enlarge foundations accounts for another 10% of the total, followed by gifts to public and society benefit organizations (7.3%), and health (6.9%). Although they are important causes for many people, the environment and animals and the arts, culture, and humanities receive relatively small shares of the philanthropic pie, each accounting for 5% or less of total giving. An important and growing component of philanthropy is bequests—that is, gifts made by individuals through their wills or other estate planning vehicles. Bequest accounted for almost 8% of total giving in 2006. With the aging of the population and the growing wealth of older people, giving through bequests is expected to grow substantially in the coming decades (Center on Philanthropy at Indiana University, 2007, pp. 15–16).

DEFINITIONS AND DISTINCTIONS

When the planes hit the World Trade Center towers on September 11, 2001, millions of Americans went to their computers or reached for their checkbooks to give more than $2 billion to help the victims and their families. Four years later, when Hurricane Katrina hit the Gulf Coast, the response was again immediate and overwhelming, totaling more than $3.3 billion in gifts to organizations providing relief and support for rebuilding (Lipman, 2006). Just a year after Katrina, investor Warren Buffet rocked the philanthropy community when he announced that he would give the bulk of his fortune, an estimated $37 billion, to five charitable foundations, including $31 billion to the foundation established by his friends and fellow billionaires, Bill and Melinda Gates. The gift made Buffet one of the largest donors in the U.S. history (Perry & Wilhelm, 2006). These gifts demonstrate the scale and impact of giving in the United States, but they also illustrate two different approaches to giving—one focused on immediate needs and the other taking a more long-term, strategic perspective.

In Chapter 2, this text made a distinction between *charity* and *philanthropy* as two types of voluntary giving. Charity includes gifts to meet immediate human needs, for example, to provide food to those who are starving or shelter to those dislocated as a result of natural disaster—such as the post–September 11 and post-Katrina outpouring of generosity. It is often impulsive and always driven by human compassion. Philanthropy is giving to strengthen the infrastructure of society, that is, to develop institutions that serve human needs or enhance human development over the long run. The objects of philanthropy often include hospitals, universities, museums, and arts organizations—institutions with missions that are perpetually relevant across generations, but which do not have the same urgency as immediate human suffering. Some philanthropic gifts, such as Warren Buffet's, also go to create or expand foundations, most of which are established to last forever or a long time, tackling long-term problems and issues. Philanthropic gifts are made carefully and thoughtfully, often as the culmination of a long-standing relationship with an institution. Emotion plays an important role in the decision to make philanthropic gifts, certainly for individual donors, but many also reflect a highly rational analysis that makes giving a form of investing in society and its important institutions. In practice, many people use the terms *charity* and *philanthropy* as if they were synonymous or use "philanthropy" as the broader concept, encompassing all voluntary giving. But the distinction is important, and it is useful for nonprofit organizations to be mindful of how their donors may think about their giving in these different ways.

Before proceeding further, it is important also to clarify some other common terms that have somewhat different meanings but are sometimes used interchangeably in everyday conversation. *Fundraising* is an activity undertaken with the goal of eliciting charitable or philanthropic giving. Fundraising is related to philanthropy as preaching is to faith, that is, one is intended to inspire the other, with no guarantee of success because the response lies within the power of the respondent to determine. In the simplest understanding, fundraising means "asking for a gift," although, as we will soon discuss, it is really a process in which asking for, or *soliciting,* a gift is but one step in a more complicated process.

Many organizations have an office known as the *development office.* Staff who work in that office may be called "development officers" and have titles such as "Director of Development." If asked what they do, they are likely to respond that they are engaged in fundraising. The two terms, *fundraising* and *development,* represent somewhat different concepts, although the difference is not always maintained in common usage. *Development* is a term that originated in the 1920s at Northwestern University (Worth, 1993, p. 6). The university had completed a fundraising campaign to build a new campus. When the campaign was completed, they determined that fundraising should be an ongoing, organized effort to continually improve and *develop* the institution, rather than a sporadic activity undertaken now and then to meet a specific need. The university created a new department to manage this ongoing effort and called it the office of "development," meaning "institutional development." Although fundraising and development became interchangeable over time, the latter is properly understood as a more comprehensive approach to the long-term growth of an organization or institution. As Worth explains,

> Fundraising is but one aspect of a complex process involving the institution, its hopes and goals, and the aspirations of its benefactors. Fundraising is episodic; development is continuous. Fundraising is focused on a particular objective or set of goals; development is a generic and long-term commitment to the financial and physical growth of the institution. Successful fundraising requires a specific set of interpersonal and communication skills; development requires a broader understanding of the institution and its mission as well as patience, judgment, and sensitivity in building relationships over the long haul. A "fundraiser" is an individual skillful in soliciting gifts; a "development officer" may be a fundraiser, but he or she is also a strategist and manager of the entire development process. (Worth, 1993, pp. 7–8)

By the mid-1970s, however, the terms *fundraising* and *development* had become so interchangeable in use that when the Council for Advancement and Support of Education (CASE) was established in 1975, it adopted the new term of *institutional advancement* to describe the activities performed by its members. Institutional advancement, or just advancement, encompasses not only fundraising or development but also the related activities of communications, marketing, and other programs for constituent relations. In other words, institutional advancement has a meaning similar to the original concept of development—a long-term and broad-based program to build an organization or institution. In the decades since CASE's founding, "advancement" has been widely adopted by colleges and universities and also has gained currency in nonprofit organizations more broadly. Ironically, it also has come to be used synonymously with fundraising by many people, so that some organizations now have an advancement office, employing staff members who describe their responsibilities as "fundraising."

MOTIVATIONS FOR GIVING

The question of what motivates donors is of obvious practical interest to nonprofit managers in determining which of their needs may be met through philanthropy and in designing their fundraising programs. But donor motivation is also a topic that has generated a substantial body of research. Let's look at motivation from the perspective of the three principal sources of giving—corporations, foundations, and individuals. Although they are the largest source of gifts, we discuss individuals last because their motivation is the most complex of these three types of donors.

Understanding Corporate Philanthropy

Corporations make philanthropic gifts both directly and through foundations that some have established as separate nonprofit entities. Using a foundation offers advantages over direct giving by the corporation, including the ability to add resources to the foundation in highly profitable years and then sustain a relatively even level of giving in years when the business may not be as profitable. Corporations make cash gifts and also gifts of products, known as *gifts-in-kind,* which indeed account for about one third of corporate philanthropy (Center on Philanthropy at Indiana University, 2007). But corporations also support nonprofits through a variety of partnerships, which as the term implies, offer benefits to both the nonprofit and the business. These partnerships are sometimes complex and represent a growing component of nonprofit revenue. Although they provide financial benefit to many nonprofit organizations, they are not "philanthropy," since the company expects a financial return as well as a benefit to the nonprofit partner.

Corporate philanthropy is a relatively recent phenomenon. Indeed, prior to the case of *A.P. Smith Mfg. Co. v Barlow* in 1953 (cited in Rosso, 2003, p. 178), the courts imposed restrictions on corporate giving that did not directly benefit the interests of shareholders or employees of the firm. This landmark case opened the door to the concept of *enlightened self-interest,* that is, the idea that companies could make gifts that might not have a direct or immediate benefit to the bottom line but that would generally help maintain a healthy society in which to do business.

Corporate giving generally increased during the decades of the 1960s, 1970s, and 1980s and its purposes often reflected the interests and affiliations of the senior executives and directors of the company. However, during the 1980s and with increasing momentum during the 1990s, corporate giving became professionalized. Many companies created committees to make decisions about where to direct the corporation's giving or created separate foundations to undertake philanthropy in the company's name.

Since the mid-1980s, corporate giving has increasingly reflected an approach known as *strategic philanthropy*—that is, giving according to a plan that relates the corporation's philanthropy to its overall strategic and business goals. Giving is viewed as an investment and is subject to evaluation based on how much return it produces—that is, the extent to which it enhances the corporation's competitiveness. For example, a corporation might target its giving in communities where it plans to develop new facilities or to specific groups of people who are likely to be customers of its products. The various corporate-nonprofit partnerships, which will be discussed in Chapter 11, have evolved from the strategic philanthropy approach (Yankey, 1996).

Today, the line between corporate philanthropy and marketing has become blurred as has the line between fundraising and negotiating business relationships. Indeed, in 2004 the Association of Fundraising Professionals (AFP) amended its code of professional ethics, which had long required that fundraisers not accept compensation based on a percentage of gifts, to include a similar prohibition with regard to the solicitation of corporate partnership arrangements (Hall, 2005).

To understand the motivation for corporate giving, a nonprofit needs to understand the company's business plans and goals, on which its program of philanthropy is likely to be based. This is not to imply that corporations give in a way that is detrimental to the interests of nonprofits or society or that their motivations should be viewed as invidious. Nevertheless, the realities do suggest that nonprofits begin their search for corporate dollars not in terms of their own needs but rather with a view to how there can be a mutual benefit to the nonprofit's welfare and the interests of the corporation from which it seeks support.

Foundation Giving

It is not difficult to understand the motivations for giving by foundations. Very simply, that is what they exist to do; indeed, it is what they are required to do as a condition of their tax-exempt status. Foundations are required to expend a minimum of an amount equivalent to 5% of the value of their invested assets each year, either for grants or operating expenses. The questions of whether the 5% payout is sufficient and how much of their operating expenses foundations should be permitted to include within that 5% have been topics of policy debate in Congress in recent years (Wolverton, 2003a).

Foundations are created by corporations, individuals, or families, and their activities generally reflect the interests of the founders. Of the more than 60,000 foundations chartered in the United States, more than half, about 33,000, are *family foundations,* controlled primarily by members of a single family, often as a vehicle for pursuing their personal giving interests (Foundation Center Web site, http://foundationcenter.org/gainknowledge/research/pdf/key_facts_fam.pdf, accessed January 23, 2007). Family foundations often evolve as they grow, becoming *independent foundations* that employ professional staff and develop formal programs and guidelines that make explicit their interests and priorities. Many have geographic and other restrictions on their giving and have well-defined areas of interest and grant programs through which they provide support, as illustrated by the example of the MacArthur Foundation, shown in Box 10.1. It is usually fruitless to approach an independent foundation for support if it does not operate programs related to the organization's activities or has policies that exclude the organization from consideration.

BOX 10.1   Programs of the John D. and Catherine T. MacArthur Foundation

The Foundation makes grants and loans through four programs.

The Program on Global Security and Sustainability focuses on international issues, including human rights and international justice, peace and security, conservation and sustainable development, higher education, migration, and population and reproductive health. MacArthur grantees work in 65 countries, and the Foundation has offices in India, Mexico, Nigeria, and Russia.

The Program on Human and Community Development addresses issues in the United States that include community and economic development; housing, with a focus on the preservation of affordable rental housing; juvenile justice reform; and education, with an emerging interest in how digital media impact learning.

The General Program supports public interest media, including public radio, television, and the production of independent documentary film. Grants are also made to arts and cultural institutions in the Chicago area and for special initiatives, currently including intellectual property rights in a digital environment.

The MacArthur Fellows Program awards five-year, unrestricted fellowships to individuals across all ages and fields who show exceptional merit and promise of continued creative work. It is limited to U.S. citizens and other residents of the United States.

Source: MacArthur Foundation Web site (www.macfound.org/site/c.lkLXJ8MQKrH/b.860781/k.D616/Overview.htm). Used with permission of the MacArthur Foundation.

Other types of foundations include *operating foundations* that support their own programs and generally do not make grants to other organizations, for example, Colonial Williamsburg in Virginia and Longwood Gardens in Pennsylvania. And, as discussed earlier in this book, some public charities use the term *foundation* in their names, although they both raise money and distribute it, usually to a single organization or a defined community. Operating foundations usually are not good fundraising prospects for other nonprofits, nor are most foundations that are public charities, although some community foundations have discretionary funds that may be available to nonprofit organizations in their areas.

Motivations of Individual Donors

As illustrated by the spontaneous response to 9/11 and Katrina, the motivations of individual donors are often more complex and less calculated than those of corporations or foundations. Individual donors have been the focus of a substantial number of research studies. Most have examined characteristics that distinguish donors from nondonors and have identified statistical relationships between giving and certain characteristics, for example, age, gender, income level, and geographic location. Fewer have explored the more complex question of donor motivation, that is, to answer the question of *why* they give.

Traditionally, the literature has been divided between those who attribute giving to altruism, that is, those who say that individuals are driven by nature to help others and improve the human condition, and those who say that individuals give to obtain some benefit for themselves, perhaps recognition, social position, or control. Although dated, a comprehensive review of the research on these questions is provided by Kathleen Kelly, who reaches the conclusion that individual donor motivations are complex and mixed, with donors having interests both in the common good and in the benefits that may come from being philanthropic (Kelly, 1998, p. 44).

Although methodologically flawed, a 1994 study by Russ Prince and Karen File identified seven motivational types that some fundraising practitioners find to be intuitively attractive. According to Prince and File (1994), the largest group of donors, 26%, are "communitarians," motivated by the belief that giving makes good sense in terms of a better community for their businesses and lives. Another 21% are the "devout," who give because of their religious beliefs. The third largest group is the 15% that Prince and File call "investors." They are donors who are particularly concerned with the tax and estate benefits of giving and will be interested to know exactly what result will be accomplished with their support. "Socialites," 10.8% of donors, give because it provides opportunities for social interactions; they are often people who will attend charity events. The "altruists," the selfless donors who may give without any desire for recognition, comprise another 9%. "Repayers," who give based on gratitude for benefits they have received, are 10.2%. The final category, the "dynasts," are people who give because it is a family tradition; they constitute another 8.3% of donors (Prince & File, 1994). Different types of donors gravitate toward various nonprofit subsectors; for example, the devout tend to support religion, the socialites give to arts organizations, and repayers often direct their support to universities and hospitals that may have influenced their or their family members' lives.

In the early 2000s, Paul Schervish and John Havens, of the Social Welfare Research Institute at Boston College, studied social-psychological factors influencing the giving of wealthy individuals and identified several "dispositions" or "inclinations" that motivate individuals to engage in significant philanthropy. These inclinations include "hyperagency," the ability to make history and affect the conditions under which people live; "identification," the unity of self-regard and regard for others; and consideration of income and estate tax benefits. The authors de-emphasize the impact of tax incentives, arguing that their data suggest that as wealth increases, individuals gain a preference for leaving their estates to charity rather than to heirs. They speculate that removal of estate taxes thus would result in more money becoming available for bequests to nonprofit organizations (Schervish & Havens, 2001).

The influence of tax incentives on giving is controversial. Although most economists' studies have found a relationship between changes in tax rates and giving the following year, some fundraising practitioners and some scholars argue that other motivations are predominant and that changes in tax laws would not negatively affect giving totals (Kelly, 1998). For example, in a 2006 study conducted by the Indiana University Center on Philanthropy, a sample of high net worth households, 52% responded that their giving would not decrease if they received no income tax deductions for their gifts, 38% said that their giving would decrease somewhat, and only 7% said that it would decrease dramatically (Beatty, 2006). But such studies are flawed because they ask people to say what they would do under certain hypothetical circumstances rather than analyzing data reflecting actual past behavior. People are often inclined to give what they think to be the right or appropriate answer, which may or may not predict what their behavior would be under the hypothetical circumstances described. For example, when asked if we would wait for a red light in the middle of the night when the police are not in sight, most of us probably would answer "yes." But what some might actually do could differ from this appropriate response to the question.

The mathematics of giving and taxes suggests that tax rates may influence the amount that individuals are *able* to give, regardless of what their desire to give may be. For example, assume that an individual in a 35% income tax bracket makes a gift of $1,000 that is tax deductible. Because of the deduction, the donor's income is reduced by $1,000, which reduces his or her income tax bill by $350 below what it would otherwise have been (35% of $1,000). That makes the out-of-pocket or actual cost of the $1,000 gift $650, since there is a *tax saving* of $350. Now, assume that the donor's tax rate has been reduced to 10%. The $1,000 gift now saves $100 in taxes, making its out-of-pocket cost $900. Although it may seem perverse, a lower tax rate increases the cost of a gift. Depending on donors' overall financial position, this could have the effect of making it more difficult for them to give as much as they otherwise might have been able to provide, regardless of how highly motivated they might be to give.

The preponderance of research suggests that the motivations of most individual donors are mixed, including some combination of altruism and self interest, and that tax policies have an impact on the amount that individuals are able to give, whether during their lifetimes or through their estates on their death. But both questions are likely to remain controversial and the focus of future research.

With the increasing diversity of the American population, a number of studies in recent years have examined the particular giving traditions and patterns of various groups, including women, African Americans, and Hispanic Latinos. The topic is of increasing interest to many nonprofits, as greater wealth is being accumulated by women and members of minority groups. Students will find additional reading on this topic suggested at the end of this chapter.

THE FUNDRAISING PROCESS

Some people may think of fundraising as synonymous with asking for money, but it is indeed a process with identifiable stages and steps. Without following the process, fundraising is random and not really very different from standing on a corner with a tin cup, hoping that some passerby will drop a few coins. That is not an approach that is likely to generate the substantial and continuing support needed to sustain an organization.

The fundraising process is depicted in Figure 10.1 and includes six basic steps. Once an organization has identified its needs for financial support and developed a case to justify its goals, it must identify the prospects most likely to give. A process of cultivation develops a relationship between the organization and the prospect and, at the appropriate point in the relationship, the prospect is asked for a gift. The gift is acknowledged and the donor is recognized. The organization then works to properly steward the gift, keeping the donor engaged and informed of what it has accomplished with the support provided. The process is sometimes described as a cycle because effective fundraising programs seek to develop a base of donors who continue to give on a regular basis and continues to cultivate relationships with those donors, leading to additional, and it is hoped increased, support in the future. Let's walk through each step in the process in greater detail.

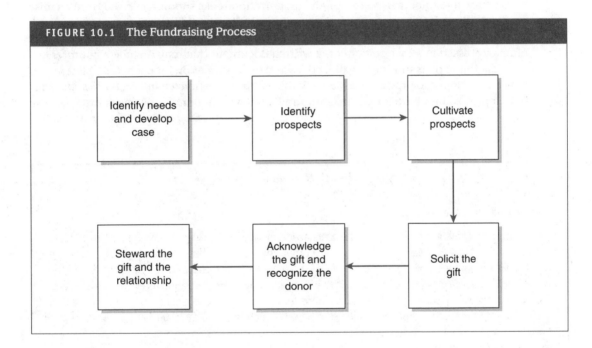

FIGURE 10.1 The Fundraising Process

Identifying Needs and Developing the Case

Fundraising without a purpose is unlikely to elicit support. As Thomas Broce writes, "Donors give gifts to meet objectives, not simply to give money away" (Broce, 1974, p. 19). This reality requires that an organization base its fundraising on identified needs related to achievement of its mission and rooted in a plan for its future growth and improvement. Strategic planning is often the first step in setting the organization's vision and goals for the future, which then can be translated into specific fundraising objectives with a rationale for why the support will enhance its ability to achieve its social mission.

The organization must develop a *case for support,* or a rationale for giving, that goes beyond its own needs and links its goals to broader social and human purposes. An organization's leaders may be convinced of its worthiness and the importance of its financial needs. But in a competitive philanthropic marketplace, they must make the case for how support for its purposes will bring a greater benefit than a gift to another organization or cause. For example, Box 10.2 shows a summary of the case for the hypothetical Siwash College that is based entirely on what its faculty and students may perceive to be important to them and entirely on the institution's self-interest. The needs may be real, but this statement is unlikely to inspire many donors to sacrifice in order to address them. In contrast, the second case explains Siwash's need for philanthropy in relation to social justice and economic prosperity, helping place its needs in a broader context and appeal to the values and emotions of potential donors.

The case for support is the reason the organization seeks support, derived from its mission and values—it is the answer to the questions, "Why should I give to this organization?" and "Why is this cause more important than others that also ask for my support?" It is often expressed in a case statement, a written document that may include a comprehensive discussion of its fundraising objectives and the justification for each. Case statements may be developed to provide a resource within the organization (*an internal case statement*) or as a printed brochure for use in communicating with donor prospects (*an external case*

BOX 10.2   The Case for Support

Siwash College Case #1

The College's enrollment has increased in the past decade, resulting in crowded classrooms and inadequate office space for the faculty. Colleges are competing for the best students with offers of scholarship support. We now have fallen behind our competitors in the quality of our facilities and the amount of financial aid that we can provide. We are losing many of the best students to other institutions. For this reason, we are seeking $10 million in funds for new campus construction and scholarships that we will offer to the students from our region who have the highest SAT (Scholastic Aptitude Test) scores.

Siwash College Case #2

The United States always has been a nation of economic opportunity. Today, as we face great challenges from global economic competition, the talents of too many young men and women are undeveloped because they lack the financial means to attend college. College tuition has risen dramatically and financial aid has not kept pace. This is unjust and threatens America's future economic prosperity. Educational opportunity always has been fundamental to the mission and values of Siwash College. The Board of Trustees has established a plan to maintain our tradition by expanding enrollment and providing additional scholarship support for worthy young men and women of our region. To that end, we seek $10 million in support to expand our facilities and increase scholarship support to more promising and worthy students.

statement). But the product known as the case statement should not be confused with the idea of the case. An organization that rushes to produce a glossy brochure without careful thought about the essence of its case is unlikely to successfully address the motivations of donors, whether corporations, foundations, or individuals.

Identifying Prospects

Just as an individual seeking a marriage partner likely would not do well by calling people at random from the phone directory or by proposing to strangers on the street, an organization seeking gift support needs to focus on *prospects* who offer a better than random chance of giving. Otherwise, its time and fundraising resources will be allocated inefficiently and ineffectively. The identification of prospects begins by limiting the search to those who have the financial *ability* or *capacity* to give; obviously, an individual or company in bankruptcy or a foundation that has already allocated all its resources would not be worthy of further attention. But making a list of successful companies and wealthy individuals still does not provide likely prospects for a particular nonprofit; it would be a large list and include many who are remote or already deeply committed to other causes. It would be like making a list of marriage prospects that included every single person in the world; they might have the ability to consider marriage, but it would still be a fruitless task to send proposals to all of them. The list would need to be culled by some additional criteria. For example, it might help limit the search to people with whom the marriage seeker already has some connection—maybe school mates, individuals who attend the same church, or friends of friends. And, being single does not automatically imply a desire to be married, so it would be wise to limit the list of prospects to those who may have indicated some interest in changing their matrimonial status. (It is instructive to observe that online dating sites do provide tools for screening a large pool of people in order to identify those with the ability and desire to marry and who have some interests in common with the searcher—the matching is not random.)

Like marriage prospects, the most likely prospects for charitable gifts will be those who have not only the *ability* to give but also some *linkage* to the organization and some determinable *interest* in the organization or the area of activity in which it is engaged (Seiler, 2003, p. 28). Identifying such individuals, foundations, and corporations is a task often performed by professionals engaged in *prospect research*, a specialty increasingly in demand by nonprofit organizations with sophisticated fundraising programs. Prospect researchers have a variety of tools and techniques, including a growing array of electronic databases, to help narrow the list to those with the greatest likelihood of making a gift to their organizations.

Financial ability may be easily determined for foundations, on which information is readily available in published sources. Corporations may be somewhat less easily assessed, but some indication of ability to give may be assumed from revenue and profits. Individuals present more of a challenge. Although public information can help determine income and wealth, for example, real estate values, much wealth will be less visible.

Linkage to the organization may occur in a variety of ways. Volunteers, graduates, former patients or their families have obvious connections to the organization that have served them. But other types of nonprofits may need to build their network of prospects in a pattern similar to concentric circles, beginning with those who are already part of its inner circle of friends and donors, then moving outward to less connected members of the community. The organization's governing board is its principal link to the outside world and, absent an easily identifiable constituency of potential donors with direct linkage, the board's efforts in identifying and engaging prospects among their own business and social contacts may be important.

Interest may be relatively easy to determine for a foundation, if it provides a clear statement of its priorities. Some corporations that have formal giving programs offer similar clarity about their interests, while in other cases interest may be presumed because the company's business activities bear a close relationship to the work of the nonprofit. For example, a home builder or a mortgage lender may have an interest in the issues of homelessness and affordable housing, and companies that manufacture products for use by women are often among the most prominent contributors to nonprofits that address women's issues or diseases. For individual prospects, interest may be revealed by past gifts to the organization or perhaps gifts to another organization addressing similar issues or needs, but often an individual's interest can be determined with confidence only through personal contact and discussion.

Cultivating Prospects

To invoke again the metaphor of courtship, most people would not consider proposing marriage on the first date. The odds of such a proposal gaining a positive response are increased if some time and effort have been devoted to cultivating a relationship, perhaps involving smaller steps such as dinner and flowers. A nonprofit cultivating a prospective donor likewise will increase the chances of gaining support if it devotes some time and attention to *cultivating* a relationship before moving to solicit a gift. The larger the amount of the gift to be solicited, the greater the investment that will need to be made in cultivation of the relationship in advance of asking.

In fundraising for small gifts, solicitation may not require significant cultivation; for example, very little cultivation precedes broad-based solicitations by mail, phone, or Internet. However, fundraising for major gifts involves developing and executing a series of planned initiatives expected to *move* an individual toward a closer relationship with the organization, leading to support. Major gift fundraisers manage and track such activity through what are known as *moves management* systems.

Soliciting the Gift

Nonprofit fundraisers have an array of techniques available for soliciting gifts, and a full discussion is beyond the scope of this chapter. The Fund-Raising School, associated with the Center on Philanthropy at Indiana University, introduced the concept of a "ladder of effectiveness," which arrays solicitation methods from the least to the most effective (Rosso & Associates, 2003, p. 82). Box 10.3 provides a summary of some commonly used methods arranged to indicate their position on that ladder, that is, from those that are generally least effective to those that are usually most effective. In general, the more personal the contact the better it is. Personal solicitations and mail or phone solicitations that include a message tailored to the individual being asked are more effective than communications that are very impersonal, such as broad-based mailings and telemarketing calls. But the selection of methods employed by a nonprofit depends on several considerations.

BOX 10.3   Common Solicitation Methods
(From most to least effective)

1. Personal solicitation (face-to-face)

   Team of two
   One person

2. Personal letter (on personal stationary)

   With telephone follow up
   Without telephone follow up

3. Personal phone call

   With letter follow up
   Without letter follow up

4. Personalized letter or e-mail

5. Telephone solicitation (Phonathon using volunteer callers)

6. Impersonal letters, direct mail, e-mail

7. Impersonal telephone (telemarketing)

8. Fundraising benefit, special events

9. Media, advertising, website

Source: Adapted from Rosso and Associates (2003, p. 82). Used with permission of John Wiley & Sons, Inc.

First, the method used must be appropriate to the level and type of support that the organization needs. Soliciting by direct mail or by phone may be appropriate to secure a large number of relatively small gifts on a recurring basis to support the current operating budget. But major gifts to address capital or endowment needs will require personal contact and time for a full discussion of the organization's plans and the purpose that will be achieved through the gift. If the gift being solicited is for the organization's endowment, the personal contact with the prospective donor may need to be prolonged, in order to fully explore the individual's desires about his or her legacy to society after his or her lifetime.

A related consideration is the cost-benefit of the method selected. Personal solicitation, by fundraising staff or volunteers, is generally more effective than solicitation by phone or mail, but it may also require a substantial commitment of time by the CEO, a development officer, and perhaps a volunteer, and it may also involve costs for travel. It is to be reserved for the most promising prospects for the largest gifts. Personalized letters are generally more effective than impersonal, "Dear Friend" letters, but also require more labor or more sophisticated technology to produce. The expected better returns always need to be balanced against the costs of a particular method.

And, third, an organization needs to consider what resources are available to it at particular points in its organizational life cycle. For example, a nonprofit that has little visibility, no clear donor constituency, and a fundraising program that is just beginning, may find special events to be a useful method for engaging new people, increasing its visibility in the community, and raising some funds. Fundraising or benefit events are not an especially effective way of raising money and the costs of producing them may in fact consume much or all the gross revenues. But if they can be used as a strategy for developing a new group of interested friends who may later be solicited for gifts through more effective methods, including mail, phone, and personal contact, then they may play a useful role in a comprehensive fundraising strategy.

On the other hand, a young organization, perhaps with a somewhat uncertain future, would be unlikely to attract significant bequests for its endowment. Many people would question whether it would use such gifts effectively or whether it provides a lasting purpose for their philanthropy. However, a well-established nonprofit that continues to raise funds through events and does not solicit larger gifts is not maximizing its long-term revenue potential. In other words, the methods used to raise funds, and the purpose for which they are raised, must match the realities of an organization's financial needs and philanthropic market; or, as architects say, form should follow function.

One of the most rapidly growing methods of solicitation is the Internet and Web. Solicitations may be sent by e-mail and provide a link to the organization's Web site, which allows the donor to give using a credit card or electronic funds transfer. Electronic solicitations offer many of the same advantages as direct mail, but messages can be even more personalized and costs can be very low. However, as with all methods, there are disadvantages as well, including the increasing use of spam filters and the ease with which prospective donors can delete a message from their crowded inbox without opening it. Many organizations make effective use of e-mail to stay in touch with current and past donors and even to discuss or negotiate the terms of a major gift. But such gifts will generally require some other form of contact, usually in person, with e-mail being used as a device to continue and conclude an ongoing discussion.

Acknowledging and Recognizing Donors

Well-managed development offices acknowledge gifts promptly and most tailor the acknowledgement to the level of the gift or status of the donor. For example, donors of gifts above a certain level may receive a letter from the CEO, others may receive a letter from the Director of Development, and small gifts may be acknowledged only with a preprinted receipt. Donors are required to have a formal receipt in order to deduct cash gifts of $250 or more and additional rules apply to the substantiation of the value of gifts-in-kind.

Recognition of donors may include listing their names in an annual report, including them in special recognition societies according to the level of the gift, and displaying their names on plaques or wall displays. Larger gifts may be recognized through the naming of facilities or endowment funds. While some donors may request anonymity, most appreciate tasteful and appropriate recognition, which itself becomes a part of the process of cultivation for the next gift.

Stewarding the Gift and the Relationship

The stewardship of past donors is an activity that has received more attention in most development offices in recent years. Experience suggests that past donors are the best prospects for future gifts, and it is therefore important to continue building their relationship with the organization after a gift has been made. The concept of stewardship can have two meanings. The most common usage encompasses the activities that the organization undertakes to keep the donor informed and engaged. These may include recognition, sending reports about the impact of the gift, and developing events to strengthen donors' involvement and knowledge about the organization's activities. It is essentially the cultivation of current and past donors with an eye toward future support. The second meaning of stewardship is more substantial, relating to the organization's responsibility to manage the gift according to the donor's intention, that is, to keep faith with the donor. This is especially important with gifts made to endowment, which are invested in perpetuity to produce income supporting current programs. Many organizations have developed regular written reports to endowment donors, informing them of the fund's financial performance as well as the activities undertaken with the income it produces. In addition, recent legal cases involving claims by donors or their heirs that gifts are not being used as originally intended have caused nonprofit organizations to exercise greater care in documenting the mutual understandings of the donor and the organization in formal, written *gift agreements.*

The fundraising process described above applies equally whether the prospect or donor is a corporation, foundation, individual, or some other type. Although corporate and foundation philanthropy may be more professionalized and giving decisions may be made more objectively than they are by individuals, it is still essential to identify likely prospects based on linkage, ability, and interest; to cultivate the prospect's interest; to solicit the gift in the appropriate manner at the appropriate time; to acknowledge the gift and recognize the donor; and to steward the gift and the relationship with the donor for the long run.

However, individual donors are different from corporations and foundations in at least two important ways. First, corporate and foundation giving patterns may change over time as their strategies are redefined. They are less likely than individuals to develop an emotional connection to an organization and become regular, long-term donors. Indeed, while the individuals working in a corporation or a foundation may have personal feelings about the organizations they support, the corporation or foundation itself is not a living thing capable of such relationships. Corporations and foundations, thus, support an organization so long as its activities are consistent with their goals—there is inevitably a quid pro quo element to their giving—and many limit their support to specific programs or activities and do not provide unrestricted gifts that can be used to meet general operating expenses, undertake capacity building, or address other organizational goals. Second, corporations and foundations are not mortal. Unlike individuals, they do not consider their giving over the course of an expected lifetime; they do not write wills or plan for the disposition of their estates. Understanding the giving behavior of individuals, thus, requires analysis of how they view their philanthropy at various points in their lives and how they develop giving relationships with favored nonprofits over time.

INDIVIDUAL DONOR LIFE CYCLES

The fundraising pyramid is a classic depiction of how individuals are believed to develop their giving relationship with an organization. It is a standard element of fundraising training and has been a part of fundraising theory for many decades. Depicted in Figure 10.2, the pyramid is broader at the base and narrows as the level of gift increases going toward the top, because a smaller number of donors will ascend to each successively higher level. The organization's *total constituency*; that is, its database of prospects, contains the largest number and is thus the widest part of the pyramid. Some, but not all prospects, will provide gifts to its *annual fund*—that is, gifts to support current operating needs. Of those who do support the annual fund, some, but not all, may respond to special needs of the organization by making a *major gift*. The definition of a major gift will vary among organizations, depending on the overall levels of support they receive, but such gifts typically are at least in five figures or more and are often pledged to be paid over a period of three to five years. Major gifts often come from the individual's assets rather than current income and many are paid using securities, real estate, or other marketable assets. Some, but only a few, of those who make major gifts will eventually make a *principal gift* to the organization. The term *principal gift* has entered the fundraising vocabulary only within the past two decades. Like major gifts, principal gifts are defined by their size—they are large major gifts. These are the transformative gifts that have a significant impact on the organization, and they may total in the millions of dollars.

David Dunlop, a thoughtful fundraising practitioner with Cornell University for many decades, defines three types of gifts that people make, and they generally correspond with the annual, major, and principal gifts depicted in the fundraising pyramid. In Dunlop's terminology, *regular gifts* are the ones that people make on a recurring basis, usually to support the annual fund. Dunlop's *special gifts* are those that individual donors make to meet some nonrecurring need of the organization, for example, a capital project or perhaps a campaign to increase the organization's endowment assets. They are *stretch gifts*, meaning that giving them requires some real sacrifice on the part of the donor. Some individuals who make regular gifts and periodically stretch to make special gifts will develop a lifelong relationship with a nonprofit organization, making it the beneficiary of their *ultimate gift*. In Dunlop's definition, an ultimate gift is not necessarily the individual's last gift, but rather "the largest gift that the person is ultimately capable of making" (Dunlop, 1993, p. 98). Some individuals make their ultimate or largest gift while living; others make their ultimate gift in the form of a bequest or other charitable provision that takes effect on their death. It is not unusual for ultimate gifts to be made to endowment, usually to large nonprofits such as universities and museums or to establish or enhance a foundation created by the donor.

FIGURE 10.2   The Fundraising Pyramid

Note: The terms *regular*, *special*, and *ultimate gifts* were introduced by Dunlop (1993).

Although the fundraising pyramid has been used for a long time to show how individual donors develop their relationships with favored organizations and as an analytical tool to describe the outlines of an organization's donor constituency, some recent literature has questioned whether its principles still apply. Observers have identified a type of *new philanthropist,* including many young entrepreneurs who acquired wealth quickly in technology industries. They tend to approach giving like investing, preferring to fund organizations that are engaged in cutting-edge approaches rather than traditional programs. They wish to be actively involved in an organization rather than be a passive donor. They may select organizations based on their demonstrated performance rather than on the basis of traditional loyalties. As Lilya Wagner observes, "These donors challenge the donor development process . . . since many make major gifts as their first gifts to organizations" (Wagner, 2003, p. 217). To the extent that there is a new generation of philanthropists whose behavior is markedly different from that of previous donors, the traditional fundraising pyramid may have less validity. However, many of the new donors are also relatively young people; what has changed is that wealth is now held by individuals at earlier ages than in the past. Whether their giving behavior will become more traditional as they age is a question to which there is yet no answer.

Another criticism of the fundraising pyramid is that it describes a situation most applicable to large nonprofit institutions, such as universities, and that it is less relevant for smaller nonprofits. Colleges and universities have natural lifelong relationships with their graduates and most have sufficient financial stability that they can patiently nurture relationships leading to ultimate gifts. For many nonprofits in urgent need of increased support to balance current budgets, the distant promise of an ultimate gift may seem unworthy of too much time and effort today. But as Dunlop emphasizes, most organizations have at least a few close friends and donors with whom it should be cultivating long-term relationships with the hope that they will eventually produce the level of giving that can be transformative.

Planned Giving

A rapidly growing component of philanthropy includes gifts that are made in connection with individuals' financial or estate planning, known as *planned gifts.* Many major gifts today do involve the use of sophisticated financial instruments, and planned giving has become a major subfield within the fundraising profession. Experienced planned giving officers, or *gift planners* as some are called, are highly sought by all types of nonprofit organizations. The aging of the U.S. population and the increasing wealth held by older people suggests that this form of giving will grow in importance in coming decades.

The simplest form of a planned gift is a *bequest,* merely a statement in an individual's will or living trust dictating that on his or her death some amount or portion of his or her estate is to be given to a charitable organization. Other planned gifts, for example, those using *charitable remainder trusts* and *charitable gift annuities,* are arrangements that provide for the donor or another beneficiary to receive lifetime income, with the charitable organization not gaining full use of the donated assets until after the death of the donor or the last income recipient. Such gifts provide a tax deduction for some portion of the gift, but not for the full amount, since the donor has a retained life income interest attributable to the noncharitable portion of the payment. In addition to qualifying for income tax deductions, donors may avoid or defer capital gains taxes on appreciated assets used to make a planned gift and, since the donated assets are removed from the donor's estate, there may be an estate tax saving as well. As in our earlier example, these tax benefits reduce the out-of-pocket cost of the gift, making the rate of income received by the donor sometimes an attractive feature. Planned giving is a complex topic and a full discussion is beyond the scope of this text, but additional reading is recommended at the end of this chapter for those who wish to pursue a more in-depth understanding.

CAMPAIGNS

Fundraising campaigns have been a part of the nonprofit landscape since the early years of the 20th century, when the campaign method was developed by fundraisers for the YMCA. The model was later adopted by higher education institutions and subsequently by most other nonprofit organizations. Historically, campaigns were known as *capital campaigns* and were usually undertaken specifically to construct new physical facilities. Over the past three decades, however, many campaigns have become comprehensive, including within their goals not only funds for facilities but also endowment, operating funds, and support for programs. At any given time in most communities today, there will be highly publicized campaigns underway by multiple organizations, seeking funds for all these purposes. And, the dollar goals are often substantial to be achieved typically between five and seven years.

What distinguishes a campaign from just ordinary fundraising? First, a campaign is intensive, ranking among the highest priorities of the organization and usually commanding a significant amount of time and energy from the CEO, board members, fundraising staff, and others. This intensity is created by two essential characteristics of a campaign—an announced dollar goal and deadline. A campaign has defined objectives, that is, specific purposes for which the funds are being raised that are spelled out in campaign literature. The solicitation of gifts to a campaign follows the principle of *sequential fundraising,* in which prospects are solicited in a planned sequence beginning with those closest to the organization and the most promising prospects, proceeding later to those who are less related or who are deemed to have less financial potential. This process helps raise the sights of prospective donors by offering the example of those who have already made impressive financial commitments. And, finally, solicitations in a campaign request a specific amount, which has been deemed realistic for the particular donor. Donors are rated according to their capacity to give and solicited, in the appropriate order, for a gift at that level. Without meeting these essential conditions, a fundraising effort is not really a campaign. Thus, fundraising that aims to raise "as much as possible" or "as soon as possible" is, by definition, not a campaign, because it does not proceed against a specific goal that it intends to reach within a defined period of time. Solicitations that ask people to give as much as they can represent a "collection," but not a campaign, which seeks specific gifts from donors deemed capable of making them (Dove, 2000).

Campaigns proceed in phases, as depicted in Figure 10.3. They are rooted in the organization's strategic planning, which defines goals and directions and financial needs. Planning for a campaign itself is a process that may encompass months or years and includes the identification of prospects, enlistment of volunteer leaders, and the hiring of fundraising staff. In order to maximize the solicitation of significant early gifts, and their impact on the sights of donors in later phases, a campaign is not announced to the public until a significant portion of its total goal has been raised as part of a *nucleus fund* during what is known as the campaign's *quiet period or quiet phase.* A formal kickoff of the campaign usually includes announcement of the overall goal, celebration of the amount already raised toward it as part of the nucleus fund, and recognition of nucleus fund donors. The kickoff is intended to establish momentum, generate good feelings, demonstrate that the campaign is likely to be successful, and inspire prospects who have not yet given to set their sights in relationship to what the nucleus fund donors already have done.

Following the kickoff, the campaign is in its *public phase.* Efforts to bring visibility to the campaign and its goals often become a significant component of the organization's communication efforts for the duration of the campaign. Planning for today's campaigns includes marketing and communication goals that are nearly as important to the organization as the financial goals addressed by the campaign. They have become tools for positioning organizations and, indeed, some campaign goals, especially in higher education, are often set at least in part to make a statement about the institution's relative rank and prestige, rather than reflecting exclusively its considered financial needs.

An important tool in planning and managing a campaign is the *gift range table,* also known as the *gift standards chart.* An example, based on a campaign goal of $250 million, is provided in Table 10.1. The table reflects the proportional giving necessary to achieve the

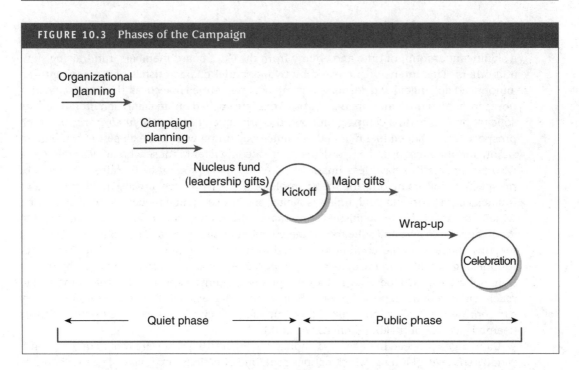

FIGURE 10.3 Phases of the Campaign

campaign's overall goal, starting with a lead gift that is at least 10% of the goal and then doubling the number of gifts needed at each successive lower dollar level. The ratios used to construct the table have been developed through experience in many campaigns over the past century and often reflect the pattern of giving to a campaign when studied retrospectively. In recent years, however, some campaigns have diverged from these historic patterns, with an increasingly large percentage of the total coming from a decreasing number of very large gifts at the top of the chart.

The gift range table is useful in projecting how many gifts will be needed to obtain a specified goal. Using the industry standard that four prospects are required to produce every closed gift, it also provides a way to assess if the organization has developed a donor constituency sufficient to support a proposed campaign goal. It may also be useful in demonstrating to the early donors to the nucleus fund, often including board members, why their gifts need to be exceptional, in order to meet the requirements at the upper ranges of the table and set the standards for others who will ultimately be asked to support the campaign.

MANAGING FUNDRAISING PROGRAMS

Fundraising programs today are sophisticated undertakings, even at modestly sized nonprofit organizations. In larger institutions, the staff of a development office may include dozens or even hundreds of professionals in various specialties, including annual giving, corporate and foundation relations, major gifts, and *advancement services*.

| TABLE 10.1 | Gift Range Table for Campaign With Goal of $250 Million | | | | |

Gift Range (in $)	Number of Gifts Required	Number of Prospects Required	Total of Gifts in This Range (in $)	Cumulative Total (in $)	Cumulative Percentage of Goal
25,000,000	1	4	25,000,000	25,000,000	10
10,000,000	3	12	30,000,000	55,000,000	22
5,000,000	6	24	30,000,000	85,000,000	34
2,500,000	12	48	30,000,000	115,000,000	46
1,000,000	27	108	27,000,000	142,000,000	57
500,000	52	208	26,000,000	168,000,000	68
250,000	100	400	25,000,000	193,000,000	77
100,000	180	720	18,000,000	211,000,000	84
50,000	300	1,200	15,000,000	226,000,000	90
25,000	560	2,240	14,000,000	240,000,000	96
Less than 25,000	Many	Many	10,000,000	250,000,000	100
Totals	1,241+	4,964+	250,000,000	—	—

Advancement Services

Advancement services has emerged as an important subspecialty in the field, encompassing all the back office operations such as gift recording and acknowledgement, prospect research, and information systems management. Most nonprofit organizations use one of the commercially available software packages that are comprehensive in their capabilities to maintain donor information and gift records as well as track cultivation and solicitation activity and evaluate the productivity and effectiveness of specific initiatives or fundraising staff.

As mentioned earlier, the growing availability of information on the Web has revolutionized the field of prospect research. Databases of corporate and foundation giving programs enable researchers to identify promising prospects quickly. The giving capacity of individual prospects can be evaluated using a number of sophisticated electronic screening tools that will also identify known relationships of prospects, for example, to members of the organization's board. However, the costs of such screening can be high for many small nonprofits, and there is still much insight and information to be obtained through the more traditional method of having prospects screened by peers. Individuals in the same business community, the same church, or in the same graduating class may have a good sense of the financial capability and interests of their peers and are often willing to rate their capacity in a setting that provides confidentiality.

Prospect Management

In sophisticated fundraising programs, relationships with donors and prospects are not developed casually or randomly. Contacts are planned, scheduled, and tracked, and a member of the development office staff is assigned as the *prospect manager* with responsibility for moving the relationship forward. A strategy is developed for each major prospect, and *contact reports* entered into the fundraising information system document every interaction and make it possible for a fundraising manager to monitor the movement of prospects through the fundraising cycle.

In large organizations, especially those with multiple units and decentralized fundraising, policies requiring prior clearance of contacts with donors are essential. For example, this situation is common in universities, where alumni may hold degrees from more than one school and be viewed as prospects for giving to all of them. Multiple contacts by different units of the organization may be irritating to donors and create the impression than the organization is poorly managed or inept. And there is always the risk of a preemptive smaller gift that disrupts a careful plan that might have led to a more significant commitment.

Fundraising Efficiency and Effectiveness

The costs of fundraising are a topic that receives considerable discussion and that has been the focus of various studies. As discussed in Chapter 5, some charity watchdog organizations have established guidelines suggesting that fundraising costs should not exceed about one third of the total funds contributed. The Supreme Court has held that government may not set a maximum level of fundraising expenditure because doing so would be an abridgement of free speech rights under the U.S. Constitution, but the public availability of Form 990 and other financial information has made organizations sensitive to the appearance of high costs in the eyes of their donors as well as the watchdog raters.

Some people say that setting limits on fundraising cost is unfair to organizations that are new or controversial and therefore must expend more effort, and more money, in order to meet their needs for gift support. In addition, it can sometimes be difficult to determine the true total costs of fundraising by an organization. Some portion of the time and effort of a CEO may be devoted to cultivating and soliciting gifts, but it is not always easy to identify that portion exactly, since some activities may involve donors but may also have other purposes. For example, is the CEO's time spent with a board member who is also a donor to be considered fundraising activity or is it related to broader governance of the organization? Printed materials and mail solicitations may include both a solicitation as well as other information, which may be considered educational or informative and thus an activity related to the organization's mission rather than fundraising. Accounting rules describe how the costs of such mailings and materials are to be allocated between fundraising and mission-related purposes, but some nonprofits may not be clear about exactly how such costs should be apportioned.

Historically, the ratio most commonly used to evaluate the efficiency of fundraising is *cost-per-dollar-raised,* that is, the amount of expenditure on fundraising divided by the total gifts received—it is a cost-benefit ratio stated in dollar terms. For example, if an organization spends $50,000 on fundraising and receives $500,000 in gifts as a result, its cost would be 10-cents-per-dollar-raised. If the same expenditure brought in $1,000,000, its relative cost would be half as much, just 5-cents-per-dollar-raised. But, some argue, this ratio is an inappropriate measure for at least two reasons. First, it is a negative way of looking at fundraising—as an expense rather than as an investment. For example, if an organization spends even 50 cents to raise a dollar, which would be considered a relatively high cost, that would still represent a 100% return on its original investment. There are few investments in which it is possible to double one's money and a 100% return would be considered very good performance by a manager of an investment portfolio.

The second related objection is that cost-per-dollar-raised measures fundraising efficiency, but it says nothing about fundraising effectiveness. For example, if one organization spends $50,000 to raise $500,000, its cost is just 10-cents-per-dollar and its net revenue is $450,000. Suppose another organization spends twice as much, $100,000, and its efforts result in gifts totaling $600,000. Its relative cost is much higher than the first organization—almost 17-cents-per-dollar. Its fundraising is less *efficient*. But its net revenue of $500,000 is higher than that of the first organization and its fundraising is thus more *effective*.

It would be a rational approach for a nonprofit to keep increasing its spending on fundraising until the marginal revenue generated is equal to the marginal cost of the increased effort. In other words, if the second organization in our example increased its fundraising budget from $100,000 to $200,000 and as a result its gift revenue increased from $600,000 to $700,001, its net revenue would be $1 higher than before, and perhaps the increased expenditure would make sense. But if the organization increased expenditure of $100,000 produced total revenues of exactly $700,000, it would gain nothing in net revenue from the additional effort. Logic would suggest that additional efforts above that would not be useful and could even result in a reduction of net revenues gained. But the situation may not be that simple. For example, if the organization is relatively new, or if its strategy is to acquire new donors in order to increase its base for future fundraising, it might be willing to spend more for no additional net revenue, or even less, if in the long run it has developed relationships with more donors who continue to give on a regular basis.

Attention to the costs, and results, of fundraising are commanding more attention by nonprofit managers as well as charity watchdogs and donors. Fundraising expenditures are being viewed as a form of investment and are expected to produce a suitable rate of return. Initiatives to collect more comparative data that will reveal the effectiveness of nonprofit fundraising are underway, including a survey launched in 2007 by the AFP and the Center on Nonprofits and Philanthropy at the Urban Institute. The survey will compare nonprofits' fundraising based on changes year-to-year and the sponsors intend to expand it in the future to gather more detailed information useful to managing fundraising programs (AFP Web site, www.afpnet.org/ka/ka-3.cfm?content_item_id = 23835&folder_id = 2326, accessed January 23, 2007.).

Staff Performance and Accountability

An important question, especially in larger development offices with staff who are specialized in the area of major gifts fundraising, is how to evaluate the performance of individual fundraising professionals.

Perhaps, the simplest measure would be the amount of money each staff member raises, but that approach creates a number of issues. First, most major gifts do not result from the efforts of a single individual. As we have described, a donor's relationship with an organization may develop over a long period of time, perhaps exceeding the tenure of any single member of the staff. There are many key players in building such relationships, including perhaps the CEO and volunteers, including members of the board. It is usually not easy to identify exactly who is responsible for the receipt of a major gift; indeed, the individual who solicits the gift may have played a relatively minor role.

A second problem with using dollars raised to evaluate the performance of a development staff member is that it might create incentives that would lead to inappropriate behavior. That is not to suggest that the fundraiser would necessarily engage in unethical or immoral behavior with regard to a donor, but it is possible that a development staff member who knows he or she will be evaluated on the basis of gifts secured will, even if unconsciously, short circuit the process in a way that is disadvantageous to the organization. For example, a fundraiser with such an incentive might direct his or her efforts toward soliciting gifts from prospects who are known to be ready to give, rather than cultivation of prospects who may not be ready yet but whose long-term capacity to give is much higher. The staff person might neglect stewardship of past donors who are still making payments on long-term pledges, and who have a high likelihood of giving again, while pursuing new donors to hit some dollar target on which his or her own performance will be evaluated. And, of course, there could be instances in which a development staff member under pressure to maximize gift revenue would indeed mislead a donor or exaggerate the benefits of a gift under a reward system that values only gifts closed. For these reasons, some organizations evaluate the performance of fundraising staff primarily on the activity they complete, for example, the number of visits made and the number of proposals submitted, rather than the dollars they raise in the short run. Others use formulas that combine credit for such activity as well as the value of gifts closed.

Again, while it is an issue mostly in larger fundraising operations, the best method for evaluating and rewarding professional staff is a topic of current discussion and debate. Some development staff are paid incentive-based compensation, including bonuses, which may reward activity (e.g., the number of donor visits completed) exceeding some predefined objectives. Such programs need to be carefully designed to ensure that the fundraising staff are not being paid a commission—that is, a percentage of the gifts they raise. Basing staff compensation on a percentage of gifts raised is unethical behavior, explicitly prohibited by the ethical codes of the AFP and other professional organizations in the field. The practice would raise concerns not only about the possibility of incentivizing misbehavior by fundraisers, but it goes to the heart of the philanthropic relationships and the assumption of trust and mutual commitment to a cause or organization that donors assume to be present when they discuss a gift with the organization's representative.

ETHICS AND PROFESSIONAL STANDARDS

The question of compensation for fundraising staff is just one area of potential ethical challenge always present in the complex relationships among organizations, their donors, and the individuals who solicit funds on the organization's behalf. Most ethical questions that arise in fundraising can be placed into one of four principal categories.

First, some issues involve the behavior of the staff person who is interacting with the donor. They would include making misleading or dishonest representations, for example, exaggerating the organization's effectiveness, lying about how the gift will be used, or making unreasonable or unrealistic promises to the donor about recognition or the financial benefits of giving. It is also unethical for a nonprofit staff member who is managing a relationship with a donor to attempt to use that relationship for his or her personal benefit or gain or to engage in behavior toward the donor that would be morally repugnant, for example, sexual harassment.

A second category of ethical issues that may confront nonprofit organizations relate to the donor rather than the staff member. For example, what if the organization has reason to believe that the donated funds were illegally obtained? Should a nonprofit accept gifts from a company that makes products it knows to be harmful? What about the question of accepting a gift from a donor who has been convicted of a white collar crime or who simply has an unsavory reputation that might reflect badly on the organization were the gift to receive publicity? There have been a number of examples of such dilemmas posed by gifts from business people who were later involved in corporate corruption scandals, after a building or program had been named to recognize a past gift. Should the organization remove the name? By whose judgment should such decisions be made and what are the limits of the organization's responsibility—and right—to investigate and judge the character of donors who may offer them support?

A third, and sometimes less obvious ethical question, is presented by restricted gifts. In other words, under what circumstances should an organization refuse to accept a gift that may require it to undertake new programs and perhaps incur additional expense that it had not anticipated? What if the new program is not entirely consistent with the organization's mission or would require a redefinition of its mission? For example, if an organization concerned with young children were offered a gift to begin a new program to help prevent high school students from dropping out, it would need to consider whether expanding its mission in that way would jeopardize its focus on its primary mission, what additional costs the new efforts might create in the future, and whether such expansion might endanger the organization's overall health and other sources of support. It might not be an easy decision to make if the offered gift were very substantial and, especially, if the donor were an important local businessperson or even a member of the organization's board. The risk to the relationship in turning down the gift would need to be weighed against the potential risk to the organization if it were accepted with the conditions that accompany it.

Another subcategory of questions arise with gifts that come with conditions that might give the donor inappropriate control. For example, most colleges will accept scholarship gifts that require recipients to be enrolled in certain academic programs; that raises few problems unless, for example, the college thinks it unlikely it will be able to recruit many students meeting the conditions. But there are limits to how much influence a donor can be allowed to have in the process of selecting specific scholarship recipients. Allowing the donor to select the recipient of the scholarships would not only present an ethical concern but, indeed, could invalidate the tax deductibility of the donor's gift, making it legally a gift to the scholarship recipient individually rather than to the college, university, or school.

A fourth category of ethical concern that has increased with the growing sophistication of prospect research involves maintaining appropriate safeguards to protect the privacy of donors and prospects. The development offices of many organizations may include information obtained from public sources about individuals' financial wealth and income, real estate holdings, and even family situations. It is legal to obtain such data. But some would argue, when it is assembled to create a donor profile, its wide distribution may be an inappropriate invasion of privacy. In addition, development office files may include information gained from reports written by staff members who have visited the donor over the years or heard second-hand from others who know the donor. Maintaining such information in the files of the fundraising office runs the risk that the donor, and the organization, could be embarrassed if it were inappropriately or inadvertently disclosed to another person.

The *Association of Fundraising Professionals Code of Ethical Principles and Principles of Professional Conduct* cover many of the major issues that nonprofits and members of their staff may encounter in raising philanthropic funds. But possible situations are so varied that no code can substitute for continuing ethical awareness and the application of good judgment by nonprofit managers who value the interests of their organizations and their missions above all else (see Box 10.4).

BOX 10.4   AFP Code of Ethical Principles and Standards

Ethical principles Adopted 1964; amended September 2007

The Association of Fundraising Professionals (AFP) exists to foster the development and growth of fundraising professionals and the profession, to promote high ethical behavior in the fundraising profession and to preserve and enhance philanthropy and volunteerism. Members of AFP are motivated by an inner drive to improve the quality of life through the causes they serve. They serve the ideal of philanthropy, are committed to the preservation and enhancement of volunteerism; and hold stewardship of these concepts as the overriding direction of their professional life. They recognize their responsibility to ensure that needed resources are vigorously and ethically sought and that the intent of the donor is honestly fulfilled. To these ends, AFP members, both individual and business, embrace certain values that they strive to uphold in performing their responsibilities for generating philanthropic support. AFP business members strive to promote and protect the work and mission of their client organizations.

AFP members both individual and business aspire to:

- practice their profession with integrity, honesty, truthfulness and adherence to the absolute obligation to safeguard the public trust
- act according to the highest goals and visions of their organizations, professions, clients and consciences

- put philanthropic mission above personal gain;
- inspire others through their own sense of dedication and high purpose
- improve their professional knowledge and skills, so that their performance will better serve others
- demonstrate concern for the interests and well-being of individuals affected by their actions
- value the privacy, freedom of choice and interests of all those affected by their actions
- foster cultural diversity and pluralistic values and treat all people with dignity and respect
- affirm, through personal giving, a commitment to philanthropy and its role in society
- adhere to the spirit as well as the letter of all applicable laws and regulations
- advocate within their organizations adherence to all applicable laws and regulations
- avoid even the appearance of any criminal offense or professional misconduct
- bring credit to the fundraising profession by their public demeanor
- encourage colleagues to embrace and practice these ethical principles and standards
- be aware of the codes of ethics promulgated by other professional organizations that serve philanthropy

Ethical standards

Furthermore, while striving to act according to the above values, AFP members, both individual and business, agree to abide (and to ensure, to the best of their ability, that all members of their staff abide) by the AFP standards. Violation of the standards may subject the member to disciplinary sanctions, including expulsion, as provided in the AFP Ethics Enforcement Procedures.

Member obligations

1. Members shall not engage in activities that harm the members' organizations, clients or profession.

2. Members shall not engage in activities that conflict with their fiduciary, ethical and legal obligations to their organizations, clients or profession.

3. Members shall effectively disclose all potential and actual conflicts of interest; such disclosure does not preclude or imply ethical impropriety.

4. Members shall not exploit any relationship with a donor, prospect, volunteer, client or employee for the benefit of the members or the members' organizations.

5. Members shall comply with all applicable local, state, provincial and federal civil and criminal laws.

6. Members recognize their individual boundaries of competence and are forthcoming and truthful about their professional experience and qualifications and will represent their achievements accurately and without exaggeration.

7. Members shall present and supply products and/or services honestly and without misrepresentation and will clearly identify the details of those products, such as availability of the products

(Continued)

(*Continued*)

and/or services and other factors that may affect the suitability of the products and/or services for donors, clients, or nonprofit organizations.

8. Members shall establish the nature and purpose of any contractual relationship at the outset and will be responsive and available to organizations and their employing organizations before, during, and after any sale of materials and/or services. Members will comply with all fair and reasonable obligations created by the contract.

9. Members shall refrain from knowingly infringing the intellectual property rights of other parties at all times. Members shall address and rectify any inadvertent infringement that may occur.

10. Members shall protect the confidentiality of all privileged information relating to the provider/client relationships.

11. Members shall refrain from any activity designed to disparage competitors untruthfully.

Solicitation and use of philanthropic funds

12. Members shall take care to ensure that all solicitation and communication materials are accurate and correctly reflect their organizations' mission and use of solicited funds.

13. Members shall take care to ensure that donors receive informed, accurate, and ethical advice about the value and tax implications of contributions.

14. Members shall take care to ensure that contributions are used in accordance with donors' intentions.

15. Members shall take care to ensure proper stewardship of all revenue sources, including timely reports on the use and management of such funds.

16. Members shall obtain explicit consent by donors before altering the conditions of financial transactions.

Presentation of information

17. Members shall not disclose privileged or confidential information to unauthorized parties.

18. Members shall adhere to the principle that all donor and prospect information created by, or on behalf of, an organization or a client is the property of that organization or client and shall not be transferred or utilized except on behalf of that organization or client.

19. Members shall give donors and clients the opportunity to have their names removed from lists that are sold to, rented to, or exchanged with other organizations.

20. Members shall, when stating fundraising results, use accurate and consistent accounting methods that conform to the appropriate guidelines adopted by the American Institute of Certified Public Accountants (AICPA)* for the type of organization involved. (*In countries outside of the United States, comparable authority should be utilized.)

Compensation and contracts

21. Members shall not accept compensation or enter into a contract that is based on a percentage of contributions; nor shall members accept finder's fees or contingent fees. Business members must refrain from receiving compensation from third parties derived from products or services for a client without disclosing that third-party compensation to the client (for example, volume rebates from vendors to business members).

22. Members may accept performance-based compensation, such as bonuses, provided such bonuses are in accord with prevailing practices within the members' own organizations and are not based on a percentage of contributions.

23. Members shall neither offer nor accept payments or special considerations for the purpose of influencing the selection of products or services.

24. Members shall not pay finder's fees, commissions, or percentage compensation based on contributions, and shall take care to discourage their organizations from making such payments.

25. Any member receiving funds on behalf of a donor or client must meet the legal requirements for the disbursement of those funds. Any interest or income earned on the funds should be fully disclosed.

Source: Used with permission of the Association of Fundraising Professionals.

CHAPTER SUMMARY

Gifts are a significant component of revenue for many nonprofit organizations, although patterns vary widely among subsectors. Gifts comprise a small percentage of revenue for health care institutions, which derive most of their revenue from fees for service. At the other end of the spectrum, gifts are almost the only source of income for religious congregations and many human services nonprofits. Organized fundraising is rapidly becoming more common across the world, but it is still most highly developed in the United States. The term *fundraising* is often used synonymously with the term *development* or *advancement*, but the latter is properly understood to encompass a more comprehensive approach to institution building that encompasses other external relations functions.

It is important to distinguish between charity, that is, giving to address current human needs, and philanthropy, which seeks to establish or strengthen institutions that address society's needs on a long-term basis. Charity is sometimes impulsive and is emotionally driven; philanthropy is often more thoughtful and deliberate.

The motivation to give is quite different among corporations, foundations, and individual donors. Corporate philanthropy generally seeks to advance the corporation's business interests while also accomplishing some social benefit. Corporate support of nonprofits encompasses philanthropy and also various partnerships, which will be discussed in the next chapter. Foundations exist to make gifts and are required by law to do so. There are various types of foundations, some of which may be prospects for support of nonprofit organizations and others that operate their own programs and generally do not provide grants to others.

Most individual donors are likely to be less organized and rational in their giving than are corporations or foundations. A considerable body of research exists on the motivations of individual donors. Findings generally suggest that individuals are motivated by altruism, a desire to pay back for benefits that they have received, desires for social advancement and recognition, as well as other reasons. The influence of tax incentives on giving by individuals is a subject of debate among economists and other experts.

Fundraising is a process that begins with the organization identifying its own needs and developing a case for support; identifying prospects who have linkage, interest, and the ability to give; cultivation of relationships with those prospects; solicitation of the gift; acknowledgement and recognition of the gift and donor; and stewardship to continue the relationship and prepare for continued support from past donors. Development of the case, or the rationale for why the organization deserves support, is a critical step. A strong case is larger than the organization, that is, it starts with the social needs that the organization's programs address and then becomes more specific in describing how needed funds will enhance the organization's ability to address those broader needs.

The fundraising pyramid depicts how many donors evolve in their giving relationship with an organization, beginning as regular annual donors and possibly advancing to become major donors and eventually donors of ultimate gifts. Organizations often build their fundraising programs in accordance with the pyramid, beginning with solicitations for annual gifts and then developing major gift and planned gift programs as their constituency is ready. Planned giving is a growing area of fundraising and philanthropy that encompasses giving through wills as well as a variety of other financial instruments.

Campaigns are intensive fundraising efforts that seek to raise a specific amount by a specified deadline for specific purposes, or campaign objectives. Campaigns proceed in phases, and it is important that the model be followed to ensure success in achieving the goal. The gift range table depicts the pattern of giving necessary to achieve a dollar goal and is a useful tool in planning and managing a campaign.

Advancement services, encompassing the back-office operations of fundraising, has become an important subspecialty of the field. This area includes prospect research, gift accounting, and the maintenance of fundraising information systems and records.

Questions about the efficiency and effectiveness of fundraising are often discussed and debated. The most commonly used ratio of fundraising cost to dollars raised may be unfair to younger, smaller organizations and does not reveal the effectiveness of a fundraising program in maximizing net revenue. Discussion also surrounds the compensation of fundraising staff, some of whom receive financial incentives for performance. Compensation based on a percentage of gifts secured is considered unethical in the field.

Fundraising often raises ethical issues, including among others those related to the behavior of fundraisers themselves, the reputation of the donor or the source of that individual's wealth, the impact of restricted gifts on the mission of the organization, and concerns about donor privacy and the use of information resulting from prospect research. AFP and other organizations have established ethics codes that are widely followed by practitioners.

NOTE

1. Students will note various styles used for the term *fundraising*. Some use it as one word (*fundraising*). Others, for example, the *New York Times,* hyphenate the term in all cases (*fund-raising*). Others, including the Associated Press stylebook, use two words, unhyphenated when used as a noun and hyphenated when used as an adjective, for example, "we engaged in fund raising" (noun); "we applied fund-raising techniques" (adjective). This text uses the single word (*fundraising*) for both adjectives and nouns, which is the style endorsed by the Association of Fund Raising Professionals. However, any one of these approaches is correct, so long as it is applied consistently.

KEY TERMS AND CONCEPTS FROM CHAPTER 10

advancement

advancement services

Association of Fundraising
*   Professionals*

bequest

campaign

case for support

case statement

charitable gift annuity

charitable remainder trust

Charity

Contact reports

cost-per-dollar-raised

cultivation

development

enlightened self-interest

family foundations

fundraising

fundraising pyramid

gift range table/gift standards chart

gifts-in-kind

identification of prospects

institutional advancement

internal case statement

kickoff

linkage, ability, interest

major gifts

nucleus fund

out-of-pocket cost

philanthropy

planned giving

prospect

prospect management

prospect research

quiet phase

regular gifts

soliciting

special gifts

stewardship

strategic philanthropy

FUNDRAISING ETHICAL CASES

1. In the following cases, do the ethical issues involve behavior of a fundraiser; conditions placed on the gift and/or the impact of the gift on the organization's mission and resources; characteristics or personal reputation of the donor; or concerns about privacy?

2. How would you handle the issues raised by each case?

Case #1

A generous gift is offered by a donor who has been convicted of a white-collar crime. Do you accept it? What if he has served his sentence? Does the purpose of the gift make a difference? What if it is to support cancer research? To establish a free medical clinic for children in a disadvantaged neighborhood? To endow a chair at a business school?

Case #2

A donor wants to give an art collection to the art gallery at which you are employed. Her requirement is that the gallery be set up just like her home and that she be able to use it for private events on request. Do you accept?

Case #3

In private conversation, a fundraiser is told that a prospect's husband is terminally ill and the family has financial problems, despite appearances. Do you record that in the database? A volunteer is about to solicit that prospect for a major gift. Do you reveal this information to the volunteer?

Case #4

A donor is considering a major gift to a center on competitiveness at your institution, a public policy "think tank." He is a corporate executive and you know that he is a strong proponent of tariff protection for U.S. companies. A leading proponent of free trade is about to be appointed as a senior fellow in your research center and you know, but it hasn't been publicly announced. Do you tell the donor about the impending appointment?

Case #5

A donor you had cultivated dies and in her will she leaves you a watch you had once admired as a personal gift to you. Do you accept it? What if she leaves you $5,000? What if it's $5 million?

Case #6

A donor pledges $1 million payable over 5 years to name a room in a new building. Another donor pledges $1 million to name the identical room next door but says he can only pay it over 10 years. Do you accept the second gift and name the room? If so, what do you tell the first donor?

Case #7

An elderly donor says that she wants to change her will, leaving everything to your organization. This will cut out her daughter from whom she is estranged. The daughter, whom you know, is disabled. Do you encourage the donor? Do you tell the daughter what is going on?

Case #8

Divorce records are public and may reveal a person's assets. Should a prospect researcher look at them? Put a copy in the donor's file?

SUGGESTIONS FOR FURTHER READING RELATED TO CHAPTER 10

Books

Dove, K. E. (2000). *Conducting a successful capital campaign* (2nd ed.). San Francisco: Jossey-Bass.

Frumkin, P. (2007). *Strategic giving: The art and science of philanthropy.* Chicago/London: University of Chicago Press.

Rosso, H. A., & Associates. (2003). *Achieving excellence in fund raising* (E. R. Tempel, Ed., 2nd ed.). San Francisco: Jossey-Bass.

Worth, M. J. (2002). *New strategies for educational fund raising.* Westport, CT: Praeger/American Council on Education.

Web Sites

Association of Fundraising Professionals, www.afpnet.org

Association for Healthcare Philanthropy, www.ahp.org

Council for Advancement and Support of Education, www.case.org

Center for Philanthropy at Indiana University, www.philanthropy.iupui.edu

CHAPTER 11

Nonprofit Enterprise

This chapter discusses efforts by nonprofit organizations to increase and diversify their sources of revenue by engaging in various relationships with business corporations and by undertaking their own business ventures. Such activities are often discussed under the rubric of *earned income*, that is, income from payment for goods or services that the nonprofit has provided, rather than *contributed income* (gifts). As mentioned earlier in this book, *most* revenue to the nonprofit sector overall is earned income. Gifts comprise just 4% of revenue in health care, 13% in education, 20% in social and legal services, and 44% in arts and cultural institutions (Weitzman et al., 2002). Many organizations also receive a significant portion of their revenue from government, but most government funds are not gifts or grants. They are payment for services that the nonprofit has provided and for which the government is paying on behalf of the clients served. Obvious examples include government reimbursements paid to health care institutions under the Medicare and Medicaid programs and scholarship funds paid to a college or university to be applied to a student's tuition bill. Both are earned income to the recipient organizations, since they pay for services the organization provided to specific patients or students, respectively.

Thus, although it has been the focus of an explosion in literature and discussion in the past decade, earned income is not something new for many nonprofit organizations. Indeed, much of the discussion in Chapter 9 concerned the use of marketing principles to increase earned income from nonprofits' core mission-related activities, such as providing education, health care, and artistic performances. In this chapter, we will consider two specific sources of earned income: partnerships with business corporations, and business ventures undertaken by nonprofits themselves.

The vocabulary in this area remains unsettled. Some terms that are widely used include *social enterprise, affirmative business, nonprofit business venture*, and *earned-income ventures* (Oster, Massarsky, & Beinhacker, 2004, p. xviii). Community Wealth Ventures (CWV), a consulting firm that works with nonprofits to increase earned income, uses the term *community wealth* to mean "resources generated through profitable enterprises to promote social change, e.g., business ventures, cause-related marketing, partnerships and licensing." *Community wealth* is a term coined by Billy Shore, the founder of Share Our Strength and CWV. In this book, we use the term *nonprofit enterprise* to mean the activities that CWV describes: business ventures undertaken by nonprofits and a variety of nonprofit-corporate partnerships, including licensing, sponsorships, and cause-related marketing. Figure 11.1 depicts the various elements of nonprofit enterprise fitting our definition.

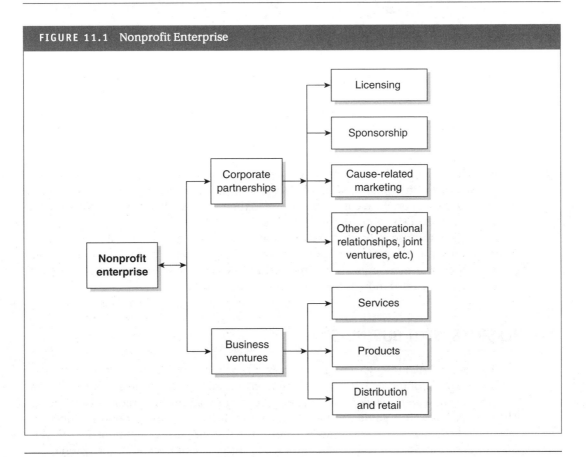

FIGURE 11.1   Nonprofit Enterprise

Source: Adapted from Community Wealth Ventures (2001, p. 7). Used with permission of Community Wealth Ventures.

WHY NONPROFIT ENTERPRISE?

Why would a nonprofit want to engage in nonprofit enterprise, and why has interest in this area increased? Primarily because there is increased competition for revenue, resulting from some of the changes of the past two decades that were discussed in Chapter 2 of this book. Government funding for social programs generally has declined. Some government funding has shifted to a voucher approach that has given potential clients choices about where to obtain services, introducing competition into the nonprofit marketplace. Government increasingly has outsourced the provision of services based on competitive contracts, forcing nonprofits to go head-to-head with each other as well as with for-profit firms. Philanthropic giving has increased with the improvement of the general economy but has remained relatively constant as a percentage of gross domestic product, while the number of nonprofits and their needs has continued to grow in real terms. In addition, nonprofits have sought to diversify their sources of revenue, in order to protect themselves from the vicissitudes of shifting political priorities that affect government support and the economic cycles that determine charitable giving.

But it's not all about money. Many nonprofits have found that engaging in nonprofit enterprise helps them advance their missions. For example, organizations that offer recovery and job-training programs have opened their own businesses, providing catering and food service, maintenance services, and retail stores that employ their clients as well as generate income to support their core programs. Others have found that starting a business has forced the entire organization to become more focused and to sharpen its goals and management skills in all aspects of its work. Partnerships with corporations offer not only the opportunity for new revenue but also the increased visibility that may come from the company's promotion of the partnership, benefiting the nonprofit's efforts to raise traditional charitable support. Such relationships also have given nonprofits access to new volunteers and to the management skills and resources of corporate partners. In sum, many nonprofits have found that nonprofit enterprise improves their balance sheets as well as their effectiveness in achieving their charitable missions.

Nonprofit enterprise offers downside risks as well as potential benefits. It is not for every organization, nor is it a panacea for the nonprofit sector. Indeed, nonprofit enterprise, which some view as synonymous with commercialization, has vociferous critics. Some of the issues will be discussed more fully at the end of this chapter.

PARTNERSHIPS WITH BUSINESS

Let's begin our journey through the topic of nonprofit enterprise with the top half of Figure 11.1—the various types of relationships nonprofits may establish with corporate partners. First, let's be clear what we are talking about when we refer to nonprofit-corporate *partnerships*. The term *partnership* is sometimes used rather loosely. For example, nonprofit donor lists may include the names of "corporate partners," but they are really corporate *donors,* since the company has not received much in return for its payment beyond its inclusion on the list. A true partnership is not a one-directional transaction; rather, it is a relationship that advances the goals of *both* parties, an arrangement in which both sides receive specific benefits related to their goals. If a corporation gives money to a nonprofit based on altruism or a general sense of corporate responsibility without receiving any specific benefit beyond perhaps the modest recognition given to all donors, that is an example of corporate philanthropy but not a partnership.

Chapter 10 described some history of corporate philanthropy, including the emergence of strategic philanthropy in the 1980s. Strategic philanthropy is an approach that aligns the corporation's giving with its competitive strategy as a business. In strategic philanthropy, the effectiveness of corporate giving is measured by its impact on achieving the company's business goals, ultimately by the bottom line of profitability. The emergence of this approach to philanthropy sets the stage for the development of corporate-nonprofit partnerships on a major scale starting in the 1980s and continuing today.

The watershed event for nonprofit-corporate partnerships came in 1983, when American Express supported renovation of the Statue of Liberty by offering to contribute a penny to the campaign each time a consumer used his or her American Express credit card. Use of the card increased by 28% during the campaign. Other companies took notice, and corporate-nonprofit partnerships took off (Independent Sector, 2004).

Corporate philanthropy remains an important force. Companies gave almost $14 billion in 2005, including cash and gifts-in-kind of company products (Center on Philanthropy at Indiana University, 2006). But partnerships are the area of growth in corporate support of nonprofit organizations and causes. Our review in this chapter will encompass a few of the most common relationships—licensing agreements, sponsorships, cause-related marketing, and operational relationships. Let's run through brief descriptions of each and look at some examples.

Licensing

If students buy T-shirts or coffee mugs with the name and logo of their college on it, they probably do not think that the college manufactured the garment, but they may not know by what arrangement the school's logo is displayed. It is likely to be an example of a *licensing agreement* between the college and the manufacturer of the sweatshirt.

A licensing agreement is a contract that permits a for-profit company to use the non-profit's name and/or logo on its products in return for a royalty payment to the nonprofit. The benefit to the nonprofit is the revenue it gains from the royalty and the increased visibility of its name. For the company, having the nonprofit's logo on its products will presumably attract purchases from individuals who are affiliated with the nonprofit or who prefer the product over others because of the perceived benefit to the nonprofit cause. But there is also something more subtle at work. By using the nonprofit's name or logo on its product, the company gains some of the attributes of the nonprofit's brand; that is, the company may come to be seen as more "caring," more "green," or more concerned about specific groups of people by virtue of its association with the positive qualities that people attribute to its non-profit partner. In effect, when it enters a licensing agreement, a nonprofit leverages some of its brand equity into a stream of income in the form of royalties from the corporation.

Many licensing agreements bring few risks. For example, there is probably little that can go wrong by having a college's logo on a sweatshirt. Neckties with the logo of Save the Children or the Nature Conservancy on them probably arouse little controversy and entail no significant risk to the nonprofit's reputation, unless perhaps the wearer were to choke on one, an unlikely event. But some licensing is more controversial, especially agreements that place nonprofit logos on products that relate to food, health, or the environment. The concern is that the presence of the logo implies the nonprofit's endorsement of the product; that is, the appearance of the name implies that the nonprofit is certifying the product's benefits, which may or may not be the case. In some instances, as, for example, the American Heart Association's food certification program, the products presumably have been screened and found to comply with the association's criteria (American Heart Association Web site, www.americanheart.org/presenter.jhtml?identifier = 2115, accessed May 27, 2007). However, in other instances, the appearance of the logo means only that the company has provided a payment to the nonprofit. It does not ensure that the nonprofit has investigated the product or guarantees its consistency with the organization's values. This could be easy for consumers to misunderstand. One well-known licensing fiasco occurred in 1997, when the American Medical Association (AMA) licensed its name to be used on home medical products manufactured by Sunbeam Corporation. The endorsement implied that the AMA had established the effectiveness of the products, but it had not done so. There was public criticism and an outcry by doctors, who are the members of AMA. AMA was forced to end the relationship with Sunbeam, paying the company almost $10 million in a lawsuit settlement. Not surprisingly, some AMA employees also lost their jobs (Sagawa & Segal, 2000, p. 124). The Nature Conservancy was the focus of similar criticism in 2003 when investigative reporters for the *Washington Post* charged that many of the products on which the Conservancy's logo appeared were not more environmentally friendly than those of their competitors (Stephens & Ottaway, 2003d).

Sponsorships

In a licensing agreement, a corporation pays for use of a nonprofit's name or logo on its products. In a sponsorship, the company pays for the use of its name or logo in connection with the nonprofit's products or events. We are all familiar with corporate sponsorships; they would be hard to miss. They are represented by the corporate logos on the scoreboards in many university stadiums and arenas, on the T-shirts worn by participants in events like the Race for the Cure, and almost everywhere at the Olympic games.

Sponsorship is not the same as advertising. Advertising communicates more information and describes the virtues of the company's products. Sponsorship is limited to exposure of the company's name or logo. It is intended to enhance the company's overall visibility and image, not to promote the sale of specific products. Corporations sponsor events such as charity walks, runs, and rides, or athletic competitions. Some also sponsor organizations, entitling them to visibility and recognition across a broad range of programs, products, and communications. Some sponsor facilities, such as athletic arenas and concerts halls, which may be named for the corporation. The facility may be named in perpetuity to recognize a corporate *gift*, but many are named only for the term of a sponsorship contract under which the company makes annual payments to the organization or institution operating the facility. Again, sponsorship does not include detailed descriptions of the company's products, and the payment to the nonprofit is tied to opportunities for visibility and exposure, not directly to sales.

Like licensing of its own name and logo, corporate sponsorships offer nonprofits the benefits of added revenue and increased visibility through the company's promotion of the relationship. Since they do not imply as strongly the nonprofit's endorsement of the company's products, the risk to the nonprofit's reputation may be somewhat less. But there are still reasons for caution. One consideration, of course, is the consistency of the corporation and its products with the mission and values of the nonprofit organization. It would be unlikely for an athletic event to accept sponsorship from a tobacco company or an organization serving children to be visibly associated with a company that sells alcohol. But some cases are closer calls, and it is wise to review sponsorship opportunities against a predetermined list of criteria reflecting the judgment of the organization's board.

Cause-Related Marketing

Some writers use *cause-related marketing* broadly to encompass virtually all relationships in which a nonprofit's and a corporation's identities are combined, including licensing and sponsorships. This text uses the term in a more specific way to mean an arrangement under which the company contributes either a fixed amount for each sale of a product or a specified percentage of its sales of a product to the nonprofit, usually in connection with a short-term promotion. Unlike sponsorships and licensing arrangements, the nonprofit's revenue from the relationship is *transaction based*; that is, it is directly related to the volume or amount of sales of the company's products. Let's look at a few examples:

- Home Depot gave $1.25 to KaBOOM!, a nonprofit that builds playgrounds, for every Racing Roadster Car Swing sold between January 1 and December 31, 2006 (www.kaboom.org, accessed May 28, 2007).
- The Intercontinental Hotel Group, which includes Holiday Inn Express, gave 9% of the room rate to Reading Is Fundamental, a children's literacy organization, if the reservation was made through RIF's Web site (www.rif.org/about/promotions/, accessed May 28, 2007).
- As part of its "Cook for the Cure" promotion featuring pink kitchen appliances, KitchenAid promised to give $50 for each purchase during 2007 to the Susan G. Komen Breast Cancer Foundation (www.kitchenaid.com, accessed May 27, 2007).

Cause-related marketing ties the nonprofit's income directly to the number or amount of total sales made by the corporate partner and thus represents a true partnership in which the interests of both partners are aligned. The corporation may find the relationship beneficial both as a strategy for increasing sales and as a way to improve its image and attract a new customer base, perhaps among the members of a specific market segment. In one often cited 2004 study, 86% of consumers surveyed said that they would switch brands if the favored brand were associated with a charitable cause (www.coneinc.com/Pages/pr_30 .html#Promotions, accessed May 28, 2007).[1]

For the nonprofit, the marketing relationship may generate not only additional revenue but also increased visibility. Promotions of the relationship often feature the logos of both the nonprofit and the corporate partner, and a comprehensive campaign may include advertising, in-store displays, and exposure in other media.

Cause-related marketing relationships are governed by a contract between the nonprofit and the corporate partner. Among other matters, the contract usually spells out how much is to be paid (e.g., a fixed amount per sale or a percentage); the length of time for which the promotion will be in effect; the maximum sum (if any) that the corporate partner will give; and rights of approval that each partner retains with regard to ad copy, use of its logo, and related concerns. One important question is whether and how the terms of the contract will be clearly disclosed to consumers. Promotions that include statements such as "a portion of your purchase will be given to charity" are inadequate, since they do not disclose what portion, whether the promotion covers only certain dates, or whether the total contribution by the company is capped at some maximum amount, as many are. In sum, such a statement does not assure an individual consumer that his or her own purchase will result in a payment to the nonprofit.

Standard 19 of the Better Business Bureau Wise Giving Alliance Standards of Excellence addresses these potential issues, requiring that nonprofit organizations clearly disclose how the charity benefits from the sale of products or services (i.e., cause-related marketing) that state or imply that a charity will benefit from a consumer sale or transaction. Such promotions should disclose, at the point of solicitation:

a. the actual or anticipated portion of the purchase price that will benefit the charity (e.g., 5 cents will be contributed to abc charity for every xyz company product sold),

b. the duration of the campaign (e.g., the month of October),

c. any maximum or guaranteed minimum contribution amount (e.g., up to a maximum of $200,000). (BBB Wise Giving Alliance, 2003)

One difficulty is that Standard 19 applies to the conduct of the nonprofit organization. It requires that when a nonprofit enters a cause-related marketing contract, the contract it negotiates with the corporation should include the disclosure requirements as a provision binding on both parties. Many contracts will give the nonprofit the right to approve any advertising copy or other materials using its name or logo in connection with the promotion. Reputable corporations will, of course, agree and act accordingly. However, there are still examples in which the details of such arrangements are not clearly stated at the point of sale, and ensuring adherence to Standard 19 may be difficult for some nonprofits, which may be reluctant to challenge the practices of their corporate partners too aggressively.

Operational Relationships

The relationships we have been considering so far all involve the blending of nonprofit and corporate identities in some manner. The nonprofit's principle contribution to the partnership is its name, recognition, and reputation, for which the corporation is willing to pay in order to enhance its own visibility, image, and sales. Such relationships are in large part an exchange of intangibles. But some nonprofit-corporate relationships bring the nonprofit into the heart of the company's business operations by "acting as a supplier, improving training or recruitment services, offering benefits for employees, or serving as a test site for new products" (Sagawa & Segal, 2000, p. 23). Let's get a sense of such relationships by looking at some examples:

- Pioneer Human Services in Seattle is a nonprofit that provides rehabilitation and employment services for individuals who are ex-offenders or in recovery from alcohol or drug addiction. Pioneer has a long-standing relationship with Boeing, under which it manufactures parts for Boeing aircraft (Sagawa & Segal, 2000, pp. 154–162).
- Greyston Bakery in Brooklyn, New York, is the exclusive provider of brownies for Ben and Jerry's, producing over 20,000 pounds of ice cream mix-ins each day. Profits from the bakery support the Greyston Foundation, which engages in community development initiatives, including low-income housing, child care, health services, and technology education (www.greystonbakery.com, accessed June 3, 2007).

- Goodwill Industries International, Inc., through its independent local chapters, provides training for individuals who are disadvantaged and/or have disabilities. The nonprofit has contracts with businesses to provide temporary workers in document management, assembly, mailing, custodial work, groundskeeping, and other fields (www.goodwill.org, accessed May 29, 2007).

A significant number of operational relationships involve nonprofits that provide employment or training programs, as in the Pioneer, Greyston, and Goodwill examples. The nonprofits provide services and resources that corporations need for their business operations, but they also provide opportunities for companies to achieve a social benefit with resources that are outside their philanthropic or marketing budgets. By directing some portion of their payroll or purchasing dollars to a nonprofit serving people with needs, companies gain a kind of double impact: They advance a social purpose while also meeting their own core operational needs.

Joint ventures are another type of operational relationship between nonprofits and for-profit companies. As the term suggests, they are new initiatives undertaken jointly by the two entities. A joint venture may involve a specific activity or the creation of a new entity jointly owned by the two partners. Here are two examples:

1. In 2002, the University of Chicago Hospitals and Health Systems and Vanguard Health Systems, a for-profit health care company, created a joint venture to acquire Weiss Memorial Hospital on Chicago's north side (www.uchospitals.edu/news/2002/20020423-uchvhs.html, accessed May 29, 2007).

2. In 2001, the National Geographic Society and the Fox Entertainment Group formed a joint venture to expand the National Geographic Channel globally (www.nationalgeographic.com/tv/press/990505.html, accessed May 29, 2007).

Entering a joint venture with a for-profit company can provide a nonprofit access to capital that it might find otherwise impossible to raise and access to management and technical skills that it does not possess. But there are risks, including possible distraction from the nonprofit's mission, potential financial losses, damage to the nonprofit's image and reputation through actions of the for-profit partner or the joint venture, and a multitude of legal hurdles. The IRS requires that the joint venture serve a charitable purpose and that the nonprofit be free to act exclusively to pursue its own purposes without benefit to the for-profit coventurers (Simon, Dale & Chisolm, 2006, p. 291). The law regarding joint ventures is complex and beyond the scope of this text.

PUTTING PARTNERSHIPS TOGETHER

Successful partnerships have a logic to them, and a nonprofit seeking a corporate sponsor needs to think in terms of the company's interests and goals. For example, it makes sense for Home Depot to help KaBOOM build playgrounds. It sells building materials; its employees know something about construction; it has stores in many locations and an interest in maintaining good relationships with the communities from which it attracts both employees and customers. The relationship is a good fit. It makes sense for Fannie Mae, a financial services company focused on mortgages, to partner with nonprofits working for affordable housing and against homelessness. It is logical that KitchenAid would support the fight against breast cancer, since many of its customers are women. Calphalon, a maker of cookware, is a partner with Share Our Strength, an antihunger nonprofit that also works with chefs across the country in its Taste of the Nation events (Sagawa & Segal, 2000, pp. 114–115). That makes sense. But it would not be logical, or even appropriate, for a tobacco company or a brewer to partner with an organization serving children, nor would it make obvious sense for a company that manufactures widgets to be a partner with a nonprofit concerned with homelessness. Indeed, companies that do business primarily with other companies, for example, as suppliers of parts or back-office services, are less likely to engage in a partnership with a nonprofit than are those that sell directly to consumers. There is less need for them to establish their brand in their target markets or to provide incentives to individual consumers to select their brand over others.

Successful partnerships are not automatic. Sagawa and Segal (2000) identify five obstacles that can get in the way. First, nonprofits and corporations often speak a "different language" (p. 181). They use different jargon with nuances that may complicate communication across sector lines. They may have different cultures; for example, corporations may be accustomed to top-down decision making, while nonprofits need to build consensus before acting. The different status of the two partners may be an issue; after all, the corporation has the money the nonprofit needs, and they may expect greater deference than the nonprofit anticipates providing (p. 180). The two parties may hold different world views. Nonprofits leaders may be skeptical about business motives, and business people may not hold nonprofit management in high regard. Finally, the two organizations have different bottom lines; the nonprofit is mission driven while the corporation, whatever the level of social consciousness it may hold, exists to generate profit and wealth for its owners. To identify and avoid such potential hazards, nonprofits are advised to enter partnerships with an understanding of themselves and their own needs, to seek out potential corporate partners consistent with their values, to engage in discussion and with due diligence to explore the possibility of a relationship, and to test it with small steps before expanding it to a wider engagement (p. 181).

Partnerships have become attractive to corporations, some of whom eagerly seek relationships with nonprofits that provide a good fit with their strategic goals. Some engage for-profit marketing firms to identify organizations and negotiate the partnership agreement. This suggests the need for careful judgment on the part of organizations that are approached, to ensure that potential partnerships offer both the promise of financial reward and an appropriate fit with the organization's mission, values, and image. The Web site of Independent Sector includes sample guidelines that can be used to screen for appropriate relationships, created by some major national nonprofits and associations that recommend policies for organizations in particular sectors, such as museums (Independent Sector, 2004).

NONPROFIT BUSINESS VENTURES

Let's now shift our attention to the bottom half of Figure 11.1 and consider some strategies and tools available to nonprofit organizations that wish to explore the idea of starting their own revenue-generating business ventures. It is an idea that many have considered and implemented; but again, a note of caution is appropriate. Dees (2004) warns, "It would be a mistake to think that nonprofit business ventures are always beneficial" (cited in Oster et al., 2004, p. 4). Oster et al. (2004) agree that "earning income from commercial ventures is often no easier than generating donations. The failure rate for small businesses (for-profit as well as nonprofit) is extraordinarily high" (p. xviii). Thankfully, there are some well-established methods of analysis that an organization can use to evaluate both the risks and rewards of a business venture; we will consider some of them in this chapter and students will find abundant additional resources in some of the books and Web sites suggested for further reading.

As Figure 11.1 depicts, nonprofits operate businesses engaged in three principal activities: services, manufacturing, and distribution or retail. Some are very familiar and have been around for a long time. For example, many of us have shopped in retail stores operated by Goodwill or the Salvation Army. Most museums and hospitals operate gift shops and restaurants. Colleges and universities also have bookstores and restaurants, and some have created for-profit subsidiaries engaged in research or online education. But the range and variety of nonprofit businesses across the country is reflected in many examples of creative and unusual enterprises. Some examples will help us get the picture:

- DC Central Kitchen prepares meals for shelters and other institutions serving the homeless in Washington, D.C. It employs homeless men and women in its kitchen and offers training programs in the culinary arts to prepare them for careers in the food service industry. Fresh Start Catering was launched in 1996 as an outgrowth of the training programs. It is a full-service catering business that serves clients in the public and for-profit sector as well as nonprofits. "All of the proceeds from Fresh Start provide support for the Kitchen's charitable programs, thus creating an on-going, repetitive cycle of training, support and mutual reliance" (www.dccentralkitchen.org/program.php?id = 6, accessed May 30, 2007).
- Triangle Residential Options for Substance Abusers (TROSA), located in North Carolina, helps recovering drug and alcohol abusers change their addictive behaviors. Residents receive food, clothing, and therapy for free for two years but are required to work in one of TROSA's seven businesses, engaged in moving, brick masonry, catering, commercial and residential painting, lawn maintenance, picture framing, and retail sales (Community Wealth Ventures, 2003, p. 87).
- CompuMentor is a San Francisco nonprofit founded in 1987 to help other nonprofits develop technology systems to serve their missions. CompuMentor started an enterprise called TechSoup Stock, a Web-based service that distributes donated and discounted technology products, services, and support to nonprofits across the United States at the lowest possible cost. TechSoup Stock works with leading technology companies such as Microsoft, Cisco Systems, Symantec, and Intuit to donate or steeply discount their products especially for the nonprofit sector. TechSoup earns income by charging a low administrative fee for each item distributed and uses the profit to support the mission of CompuMentor (www.compumentor.org/default.html, accessed May 30, 2007; http://mba.yale.edu/news_events/cms/articles/1772.shtml, accessed May 12, 2008).

- The Caroline Center in Baltimore provides job training programs for low-income women. It launched Caroline Center Upholstery, a business "that provides high quality custom retail upholstery services including antiques for residential and commercial customers in the Baltimore metropolitan area" (Caroline Center Web site, www.caroline-center.org).
- Homeboyz Interactive is a Milwaukee nonprofit founded in 1996 with the goal of reducing gang violence by preparing young people for careers in information technology. It started a consulting business, called "hbi consulting," to work with major corporations and government agencies in designing and developing Web applications. The business provides employment opportunities to young people in the training program, often opens doors for jobs in the corporate sector when they have completed the program, and generates profits that are all used to support Homeboyz Interactive's mission programs in training and rehabilitation (Community Wealth Ventures, 2003, pp. 79–80).
- First Book, headquartered in Washington, D.C., is a nonprofit that promotes children's literacy by giving children from low-income families the opportunity to read and own their first new books. First Book Marketplace, its business venture, sells new, high-quality children's books at low cost to organizations serving disadvantaged children. First Book Marketplace acquires large quantities of books at deep discounts from its publishing partners and sells them to organizations at prices lower than they could obtain on their own. First Book Marketplace makes a small profit, which it uses to support First Book's core literacy programs (First Book Web site, www.firstbook.org, accessed May 30, 2007).
- Share Our Strength, an antihunger nonprofit, has developed extensive partnerships with corporations, including American Express, Barnes & Noble, Calphalon Cookware, Tyson Foods, and Evian. In 1997, it created a subsidiary for-profit consulting firm, Community Wealth Ventures, to work with other nonprofits in developing corporate partnerships and business ventures (www.communitywealth.org, accessed May 31, 2007).

IDENTIFYING BUSINESS OPPORTUNITIES

How does a nonprofit organization that wishes to establish a business enterprise get started? It will not surprise students who have read previous chapters on capacity, strategic planning, and marketing that the first steps involve looking both outward to the marketplace and inward to the organization itself. Planning for a successful business enterprise requires that the organization know itself as well as the environment surrounding it.

There are three fundamental questions that the organization needs to answer to narrow down its search for business ideas (Community Wealth Ventures, 2001, p. 6). First, does the organization possess marketable assets? In other words, is there anything it *has*, anything it *does*, or anything it *knows* that others may find valuable and worth paying for? Are there assets that might be *leveraged* to provide a source of revenue? Second, is there a market opportunity waiting to be seized? Is there some unmet need that consumers would be willing to pay to have met? Answering this question may require use some of the tools we have discussed earlier, including market research and portfolio analysis, as well as some imagination. The third fundamental question relates to the capacity of the organization to undertake a new enterprise. Does it have the staffing, the skills, the access to financial resources, and a culture that will support entrepreneurial activity? As we have said before, nonprofit enterprise is not for every organization, and it makes no sense to stretch an already struggling staff to explore something that is just beyond the organization's capacity to even consider. In other words, organizations need to be realistic.

Figure 11.2 illustrates some types of assets that a nonprofit might possess and that could have value in the marketplace. Some assets may seem obvious—for example, space. Many museums rent their attractive spaces for special events, and some have opened restaurants. Underutilized space might be leased to a commercial retailer, like Starbuck's on a university campus; or perhaps unused offices could be rented for use by other nonprofits. But relationships and access to a constituency may be assets that can be leveraged, too. In the examples of nonprofit businesses we listed above, both CompuMentor and First Book leveraged their relationships with networks of other nonprofits, assets that made it possible for them to negotiate favorable financial arrangements with for-profit suppliers whose access to those markets was not as well established. The Caroline Center and DC Central Kitchen used what they knew how to do—reupholster and cook—as the basis of new business ventures. Homeboyz Interactive took something they knew, how to design Web sites, and put it together with the previously underutilized asset of young people with skills and in search of careers. Share Our Strength leveraged its expertise in nonprofit enterprise to create a consulting practice helping other nonprofits with nonprofit enterprise.

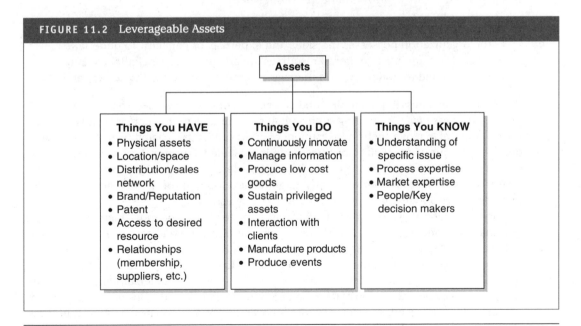

FIGURE 11.2 Leverageable Assets

Assets

Things You HAVE	**Things You DO**	**Things You KNOW**
• Physical assets	• Continuously innovate	• Understanding of specific issue
• Location/space	• Manage information	• Process expertise
• Distribution/sales network	• Procuce low cost goods	• Market expertise
• Brand/Reputation	• Sustain privileged assets	• People/Key decision makers
• Patent	• Interaction with clients	
• Access to desired resource	• Manufacture products	
• Relationships (membership, suppliers, etc.)	• Produce events	

Source: From Community Wealth Ventures (2001, p. 14).

FEASIBILITY ANALYSIS AND BUSINESS PLANNING

Having completed the process described in the previous section and identified some assets that might be leveraged into business ventures, a nonprofit may proceed to analyze the feasibility of a selected set of ideas. A feasibility analysis uses many of the tools we have described previously in this text; it looks both to the market and to the organization's own capacities (Community Wealth Ventures, 2004). The external variables that need to be considered include

- the overall size of the market for the product or service that the nonprofit plans to provide;
- the outlook for the industry in which it will be engaged—for example, whether it is expanding or contracting;
- competitive factors, including the study of others offering the same or competing goods and services, as well as generic competition for the same consumer dollars;
- the ease of entry—that is, how much investment will be required to break in; for example, starting a coffee shop may be relatively easy to do, but setting up a factory to manufacture complicated electronics would be a more daunting challenge; and
- profitability—whether this is a business in which it is possible to make money or whether it is, like many restaurants and retail stores, an enterprise that is likely to have a very small profit margin if any at all.

Looking at itself, the organization needs to ask whether

- the venture fits with its mission;
- the organization possesses the skills and expertise, or capacity, to undertake it;
- its facilities and other material resources are adequate to the challenge; and
- it is prepared to undertake and manage the risk associated with the new activity.

Of the few business opportunities studied in detail, one may be selected for development of a full *business plan*. Developing such a plan is a time-consuming endeavor, and it would not be practical to make such an investment of effort unless the feasibility analysis has produced an encouraging result. A business plan is a detailed, comprehensive document that encompasses elements of strategic, marketing, business, and operational plans. A business plan is an essential tool both internally, to guide development of the business, and externally, as a sales document for enlisting donors or investors.

Business plans may follow somewhat different formats, but most include the same essential components. Box 11.1 provides a typical outline for a business plan and its major sections. Most begin with an executive summary that gives a thorough but succinct overview of the major points made in the following sections of the plan. A potential investor or donor should be able to read the executive summary and have a basic understanding of what the venture entails. Another section of the plan describes the nature of the business and the products or services it intends to offer, provides an overview of the industry in which it plans to operate, and summarizes the strategic plan. A section on management and organization includes the organizational structure and the backgrounds of key staff and board members.

BOX 11.1   Elements of a Typical Business Plan

1. Executive summary

2. Description of the business

3. Management, organizational structure, key personnel

4. Market analysis and marketing plan

5. Description of products and services

6. Operational plan

7. Financial assumptions

8. Detailed financial plan

9. Uncertainties and risks

10. Plan for growth or exit

Source: Adapted from Dees et al. (2001) and Massarsky (1988).

One key question that needs to be addressed is how the business venture will be related to the nonprofit itself. Will it operate within the organization, perhaps just as a separate department? Or will it be organized as a subsidiary with a separate board and management structure? If a separate entity, will it be organized as a nonprofit or as a for-profit corporation? All these alternatives have pros and cons, and a full discussion is beyond our scope in this chapter, but they need to be addressed explicitly in developing the business plan.

The plan needs to include a detailed market analysis. What data have been identified, perhaps during the feasibility study process, to ensure that there is a demand for the products or services to be offered? Who are the competitors, and what will be the competitive advantage of the proposed new venture? The 4-Ps of marketing, which readers will remember from Chapter 9, need to be addressed in this section of the business plan.

The products and services should be described in detail. If the business is a retail store, exactly where will the store be located, how will it be designed, and what types of goods will it carry? If the business involves manufacturing or distribution, what technologies will be used? How will customer satisfaction be measured, and how will the quality of the product be controlled?

To set the stage for the financial plan, a section is devoted to summarizing the assumptions on which financial projections are based. Those may include, for example, assumptions about the economy, about demographics, or about growth in a particular market or industry. Careful business plans will include a *sensitivity analysis* that shows how projected results will vary if the assumptions are wrong by some percentage. For example, if sales are 10% less than forecast or inflation is two points higher than expected, how will the changes in those assumptions affect the venture's bottom line?

The financial section of the plan shows proforma income statements, proforma cash flows, and proforma balance sheets, usually projected for the first three years. Putting this section of the business plan together is essentially like writing the entries of income and revenue, by date, in your checkbook—hypothetically looking out into the future. As a result of this exercise, the business planner should be able to project a point at which the business reaches a break-even position and then, hopefully, begins to earn a profit.

Although some business plan outlines may arrange sections in a different order, closing sections usually discuss potential risks and the precautions that the business is taking to protect against them. For example, risk management may include carrying sufficient insurance or operating the business venture as a subsidiary organization so as to protect the parent from liabilities it may incur. An exit strategy may be one aspect of risk management; in other words, if the business is not viable and needs to shut down, how will that be accomplished in an orderly way while minimizing risks and losses?

The previous paragraphs have provided a very brief discussion of business plans, but it is a large topic. Students will find many books devoted to the subject, and software packages are available to guide the writing of such a plan. For three years, from 2002 to 2005, the Yale School of Management, the Goldman-Sachs Foundation, and the Pew Charitable Trusts conducted a national nonprofit business plan competition and made samples of winners available on its Web site. Although the competition ended in 2005, the Web site was still available as of this writing and provided full text of some excellent, award-winning plans, the source of some examples that have been cited in this book (http://mba.yale.edu/news_events/cms/articles/1772.shtml, accessed May 12, 2008). A new organization, called SocialReturns, Inc., was established to continue the competition under different auspices; as of the writing of this chapter the organization maintained a Web site (http://social-returns.org) but had not yet launched the new program. Other sources listed at the end of this chapter, including the National Center on Nonprofit Enterprise Web site, also provide useful information and materials.

NONPROFIT ENTERPRISE ISSUES AND DECISIONS

Readers will recall from the Introduction to this book that the growth of nonprofit enterprise, what some call the "commercial transformation of the nonprofit sector" (Weisbrod, 1988), has elicited debate. Some have reacted negatively to specific cases of nonprofit enterprise that they found to be inappropriate, while others have expressed more generic concerns about the threat that commercialization may pose to the nonprofit sector and society.

Sorting Out the Issues

Let's look at two cases from the museum world, each of which created a swirl of controversy, and try to sort out the issues that they raised. In 2006, the Smithsonian Institution and Showtime Networks created a joint venture, Smithsonian Networks, to produce documentaries using the museum's archives and artifacts. The agreement provides Showtime with semi-exclusive rights to some museum resources. Although an investigation by the Government Accountability Office (GAO) found that the arrangement did not hamper researchers' access to the museum's materials, there was an outcry of criticism from curators, historians, and the documentary filmmaking community (Trescott, 2006). Critics raised objections not only to the terms of the arrangement itself but also to the fact that as a business contract, some of its provisions would be kept confidential. The *Washington Post* editors weighed in:

> The Smithsonian argues that the filmmakers in question make money out of their work: Why can't the Smithsonian do so, too? Of course it can . . . , but it must be under different rules from a purely private body. As a quasi-public institution that receives taxpayers' money, the Smithsonian is obligated to reveal the details of its business deals to the public. It is also obligated not to make deals that restrict public access. Charging larger fees when its collections are to be used for commercial purposes may be acceptable; writing complex, secret rules about who can use them and who cannot is clearly wrong ("The Nation's Attic," 2006).

In 2004, the Boston Museum of Art agreed to lend 21 Monet masterworks to the Bellagio Casino in Las Vegas. The Bellagio paid the museum a fee of 1-million dollars for its use of the pieces from the museum's collection (Edgers, 2004). Critics, including art historians, raised pointed questions: "Is the MFA's art available to the highest bidder?" "Should priceless works of art be displayed in the vicinity of "slot machines and . . . blackjack tables?" (Edgers, 2004).

Both cases raise legitimate issues. For example, should collections, or information, or performances, or other products or services owned or produced by nonprofit organizations be available only to individuals or companies who can pay for them, or does an institution's nonprofit status, especially if the institution also receives public funds, require it to serve a broader public interest? If so, what is the appropriate balance between that interest and the nonprofit's inescapable need for revenue? How can a nonprofit organization engaged in a contractual relationship with a for-profit entity meet its own responsibilities for transparency and disclosure while respecting the need of its partner to protect business secrets? But some criticisms also reflect entrenched traditions and perspectives. Some may find it inherently offensive to see Monets in a casino, or a Starbuck's on a university campus, or a corporate logo on the entrance to a music hall. But unless the corporate interest affects what is shown, what is taught, or what is played, such concerns may be more a matter of personal values than a threat to the organization's mission. Perceptions do, of course, matter, especially if they may erode confidence in the nonprofit or create the impression that it no longer needs other sources of support, such as philanthropic giving. But the issues are often separable, and it is those that relate to the mission that require the most thoughtful and careful consideration.

Evaluating Opportunities Against Mission

Leaving aside for the moment those who do not favor nonprofit enterprise at all, opinions on the appropriate relationship of the activity to the mission surround two poles. Some argue that nonprofits should consider only ventures that are aligned with their missions and should not undertake activities intended solely to produce additional revenue. For example, those who hold this view would consider it suitable for a nonprofit group that trains its clients in culinary skills to start a restaurant business to provide a quality work experience for its graduates, but would look askance at an environmental organization that opened a restaurant. (Hochberg, 2002, p. 35)

Others take a different view, arguing that nonprofits should look exclusively at whether a business venture is financially profitable. Since the profits are plowed back to support mission-related programs, maximizing revenue from the business ultimately helps deliver more and better services to clients, thus serving the mission. In addition, some say, even successful business ventures that are not related to the mission may create a halo effect that brings other benefits to the nonprofit, including greater visibility and the ability to attract and retain capable staff (Hochberg, 2002). But the question may require more shades of gray than these two positions encompass.

The economist Dennis Young (2006) provides a useful framework for decision making, which is illustrated by Table 11.1. Young's model helps in thinking through the risks and rewards of possible business ventures. As the diagram suggests, a profitable venture opportunity is worth exploring if it also supports the mission or if its impact on the mission is neutral. The former would seem to offer the best of all possible worlds. In the latter case, nothing really is lost, and additional revenue may be gained. However, an activity that could be profitable but that threatens the mission surely would require the most exacting of scrutiny. If it offered the possibility of a huge gain in revenue that would make it possible to greatly expand mission-related programs, with considerable benefit to the organization's clients, then a nonprofit might consider it, making adjustments to manage the mission risk.

What about a partnership or business venture that would just break even financially? If it enhances the mission, then it makes sense to explore it. It may be an opportunity to expand mission programs and services, totally supported by new revenue. If the new venture would just break even while having no impact on the mission, it might seem to be nothing more than a potential distraction that has little to offer. It would best be avoided unless it could be tweaked in some way to either produce more profit or better serve the mission. A break-even business that threatens the mission offers nothing, except for those who may

TABLE 11.1   Evaluating Partnership Opportunities

	Mission-enhancing	Mission-neutral	Mission-threatening
Profitable	**undertake** (fine tune)	**undertake** (fine tune)	**scrutinize** (adjust)
Break-even	**undertake** (fine tune)	**avoid** (or redesign)	**avoid** (or redesign)
Loss-creating	**consider** (adjust)	**avoid** (or redesign)	**avoid** (or redesign)

Source: Young (2006).

be feeling masochistic. Undertaking a business that loses money while either having no impact on the mission or actually threatening it may appeal only to nonprofit managers who are, indeed, professionally suicidal. Unless such possibilities can be redesigned to overcome their shortcomings, they are most certainly best avoided.

Finally, there is the possibility of a nonprofit enterprise partnership or business venture that actually generates a financial loss but contributes in some way to advancing the mission. A nonprofit might consider engaging in that activity, but it would need to be thought about carefully. The benefits and costs of the proposed venture would need to be weighed against those of alternative activities that might also serve the mission equally or better, at the same or less cost.

Risks to Society?

In recent years, the criticisms and alarms about commercialization in the nonprofit sector have attained considerable volume and have appeared in prominent, respected venues. An article in the *Harvard Business Review* (Foster & Bradach, 2005) argued against encouraging nonprofits to pursue "the holy grail of earned income," saying that "sending social-service agencies down that path jeopardizes those who benefit from their programs—and it harms society itself, which depends for its well-being on a vibrant and mission-driven nonprofit sector" (p. 100). Just months before, the economist Burton Weisbrod had argued in the *Stanford Social Innovation Review* that Congress should discourage nonprofits from undertaking business ventures and instead should increase the tax incentives to donors for philanthropy (Weisbrod, 2004). Eikenberry and Kluver (2004), in the *Public Administration Review,* made the case that

> though marketization may be beneficial for the short-term survival needs of nonprofit organizations, it may have negative long-term consequences. Marketization may harm democracy and citizenship because of its impact on non-profit organizations' ability to create and maintain a strong civil society. (p. 132)

Some proponents of nonprofit enterprise write in an evangelical voice. While most offer the obligatory caveat that nonprofit enterprise is not for everyone, it is often parenthetical in an otherwise enthusiastic presentation. Some imply that nonprofit enterprise is altogether preferable to nonprofits' dependence on philanthropy and government support and, indeed, offer it as a source of revenue that will free nonprofit managers from thinking about money so as to focus more on delivery of their programs and as a way to make organizations sustainable. But they sometimes minimize the fact that running a business can be no less demanding of effort and attention than traditional fundraising or grantsmanship and that sustainability of a business enterprise itself is far from guaranteed.

Some critics of nonprofit enterprise are also extreme in their alarms. For one, their writing implies that the nonprofit sector is synonymous with social service agencies, not acknowledging that many nonprofits, including colleges, schools, performing arts groups, health care institutions, and many others, long have generated earned income as a major portion of their revenue without apparent abandonment of their missions or the loss of philanthropic support. Nor do the critics always acknowledge that as many as 90% of nonprofit business ventures conducted by nonprofits that do provide human and social services are "directly or closely related to their missions" (Hochberg & Wise, 2005). These include Girl Scout cookie sales and Goodwill and Salvation Army thrift shops—entities that have long been significant components of their organizations' revenue without inflicting apparent harm. Some critics also do not sufficiently acknowledge the substantial dependence of many nonprofits on government support and the implications of changed policies that have forced them into competitive situations. Nonprofits' responses are sometimes portrayed as capitulation to the market rather than accommodation to the realities that public policy has thrust on them. It is reasonable to ask if their clients and society would be better served were the nonprofits forced from existence by rigid adherence to traditional methods of revenue generation. Increased incentives to philanthropy do not offer a realistic alternative to meeting nonprofits' financial needs, for a variety of reasons that go beyond the scope of this discussion. And, it must be acknowledged, even small nonprofits are increasingly dependent on major gifts from a relatively small number of donors, a situation that presents no less of a threat to their autonomy than their partnerships with the for-profit sector.

As at previous points in this text, the author recommends a balanced perspective. Nonprofit enterprise offers one way for nonprofits to obtain revenue and to diversify sources, managing the risks inherent in reliance on philanthropy and government alone. It will be a more appropriate and useful strategy for some organizations than for others. Some may rely entirely on earned income, but for most it is one component of a diversified funding base, together with philanthropy, government funds, and earned income from core mission programs. Indeed, some nonprofit organizations that long have been reliant on earned income are increasing their efforts to obtain philanthropic support, with the goal of creating a more balanced revenue profile.

Opportunities for nonprofit enterprise always need to be evaluated against their impact on achievement of the mission. Those that threaten it generally should be avoided. Others may serve both financial and mission goals. Some may provide income to advance the mission from activities that bear no relationship to it but also do it no harm. Leaving aside the tax implications of unrelated business income, which we discussed earlier in this text, that is really no different in its ultimate effect from investing endowment funds in the stock of companies and using the dividends to support charitable purposes, a practice in which many nonprofits engage without arousing much complaint.

It is ultimately the responsibility of the nonprofit's board to establish, after thoughtful reflection and discussion, policies and guidelines, rooted in the organization's mission and values, against which such decisions will be made. Those policies should take into consideration mission-related, financial, and public relations risks; they need to be in place before the organization enters into new partnerships or ventures, and not put together as a response once the editorialists are at the door.

CHAPTER SUMMARY

Although nonprofits in some sectors long have derived a major portion of their revenue from earned income, that is, fees for goods and services they provide, there has been an increased emphasis on such activities in recent decades. Terminology varies in the literature of the field, but this book adopts the term *nonprofit enterprise* to encompass a variety of partnerships between nonprofits and corporations and business ventures undertaken by nonprofit organizations themselves. Nonprofits engage in such activities to increase and diversify sources of revenue and to advance their missions and gain other benefits. Nonprofit enterprise is not synonymous with being a social entrepreneur.

This chapter discussed four types of relationships between nonprofits and corporations that are among the most common. *Licensing agreements* permit a company to use a nonprofit name or logo on its products in exchange for a royalty paid to the nonprofit. *Sponsorships* are arrangements by which a corporation contributes to support an event, facility, or organization in exchange for the prominent association of its name or logo. It is not the same as advertising because it does not include descriptions or depictions of the company's products. Some authors use the term *cause-related marketing* more broadly, but in this book it refers to partnerships in which a nonprofit is paid a fixed amount per sale or a percentage of total sales of a company's product, usually in connection with a short-term promotion. This type of relationship became popular following a very successful arrangement in 1983 whereby American Express made a payment to the Statue of Liberty campaign each time its credit card was used.

Some nonprofits have operational relationships with companies, often as suppliers or sources of workers. Others have entered joint ventures with corporations; that is, they have become partners in the ownership and operation of a new business. Successful nonprofit-corporate partnerships are built on commonality of values and interests. There is usually a logical connection between the company's products or target markets and the mission and programs of the nonprofit.

Some nonprofits have launched their own business ventures; most provide services, manufacture products, or are in the fields of retail or distribution. Some examples include DC Central Kitchen, which established a catering business based on the use of its kitchen facilities and the employment of homeless people enrolled in its culinary training program, and Homeboyz Interactive in Milwaukee, which provides training in IT skills to young people from low-income neighborhoods and sells Web services to companies and agencies.

Nonprofits begin to identify business opportunities by inventorying their assets—things they have, things they do, or things they know. Assets may be tangible, such as space, or may include relationships with particular constituencies, knowledge of specific cultures, or the organization's reputation and brand. Once it has identified assets that might be used to produce earned income, the organization analyzes the feasibility of using a select few of them. The feasibility analysis looks both inside the organization, to ensure that it has the capacity to undertake the venture, and outside, to gain knowledge of market demand and competitors.

Development of a full business plan is an intensive and time-consuming effort and likely will be undertaken only for the most promising of business opportunities that have been identified. There are many formats for a business plan, but most include an executive summary, a description of the business, a market analysis and marketing plan, a description of the products and services to be offered, an operational plan, clarification of financial assumptions, a detailed financial plan and projection of cash flow for at least the first three years, a summary of uncertainty and risks and plans to manage them, and a plan for growth or exit from the business.

Nonprofit enterprise has generated some controversy. Some critics raise legitimate issues about the impact of commercialization on nonprofits' commitment to mission. Others reflect traditional views of what are appropriate activities and revenue sources for nonprofit organizations. Dennis Young (2006; see Table 11.1) offers a framework for evaluating nonprofit enterprise opportunities that may be profitable, break-even, or money losing, each in terms of whether it advances the mission, is mission-neutral, or mission-threatening. Ventures that threaten the mission usually should be avoided.

Some see commercialization of the nonprofit sector as a threat to democracy and civil society. Both advocates and critics of nonprofit enterprise are sometimes too extreme in their arguments. This book advocates a balanced perspective, in which nonprofit-corporate partnerships and nonprofit business ventures offer one way to increase and diversify revenues. A well-managed nonprofit seeks a balanced portfolio of revenue streams, from earned income, philanthropy, and possibly government sources. Nonprofit boards have a responsibility to develop policies and guidelines to ensure that nonprofit enterprise is consistent with their organizations' missions and values and that financial and public relations risks also are weighed with the mission as paramount.

NOTE

1. The study was conducted by Cone, a for-profit marketing firm that arranges cause-marketing relationships between corporations and nonprofits.

KEY TERMS AND CONCEPTS FROM CHAPTER 11

business plan
cause-related marketing
commercialization
community wealth
contributed income
earned income
feasibility analysis
joint ventures

leveragable assets
licensing
nonprofit business ventures
nonprofit enterprise
sensitivity analysis
social enterprise
sponsorship

QUESTIONS FOR DISCUSSION

1. In each of the following cases, what was the asset that the organization leveraged to create a source of earned income? Was that asset something it had, something it did, something it knew, or some combination of those?

   • The Guthrie Theater and the Children's Theater Company in Minneapolis had a collection of costumes. They created a business to rent the costumes to schools, theaters, companies, and individuals across the country at reasonable rates.

- Nation's Capital Child and Family Development operated a large kitchen to provide food for its twenty-five sites. It created a business to cater food to other child care and elder care providers and to offer technical support to other organizations in the operation of their own kitchens.
- Dakota Area Resources and Transportation for Seniors maintained its own fleet of vehicles, which it used to transport seniors. It began a business offering maintenance services to other nonprofits that owned their own vehicles.

Source: Examples are drawn from the Yale School of Management/Goldman Sachs Foundation Partnership's national business plan competition 2002–2005.

2. Some well-known nonprofit-corporate partnerships are listed below. In each case, what do you think is the logic behind the relationship, in other words, why does this relationship make sense? What may be the principal benefits that each party receives as a result of the partnership? Do you see any possible issues related to each of these relationships?

   - Neutrogena sells sunscreen with the American Cancer Society logo.
   - Microsoft has created technology centers at Boys & Girls Club locations.
   - Nike created its 10/2 brand of clothing with $1 from the sale of each product going to the Lance Armstrong Foundation to fight cancer.
   - Chefs around the nation contribute their time to the Taste of the Nation, an event that supports Share Our Strength, an antihunger nonprofit. Other sponsors of the event include Jenn-Air, a subsidiary of Maytag, a kitchen appliance manufacturer.
   - Christmas in April is a nonprofit that renovates homes for the elderly and disabled. Home Depot has provided the organization with training for its volunteers, assistance from Home Depot employees, and lines of credit for merchandise at its stores, as well as cash gifts.
   - In 1993, after Denny's was charged with racial discrimination in one of its restaurants, new management adopted a zero-tolerance policy on racial discrimination throughout the company. Shortly afterward, it established a partnership with Save the Children, a nonprofit that helps children throughout the world with health and nutrition programs, emergency relief, and economic development (Sagawa & Segal, 2000, pp. 72–75).

3. Some well-attended exhibits at art museums have included collections of automobiles, motorcycles, and photographs of Madonna. Are these appropriate subjects for exhibition in a nonprofit art museum? Why or why not? Do they put the museum's mission at risk—in the short term or long term? Why or why not?

SUGGESTIONS FOR FURTHER READING RELATED TO CHAPTER 11

Books

Community Wealth Ventures. (2001). *The community wealth seekers guide*. Washington, DC: Author. (www.communitywealth.com/resources_tools.htm)

Community Wealth Ventures. (2003). *Powering social change: Lessons on community wealth generation for nonprofit sustainability*. Washington, DC: Author.

Oster, S. M., Massarsky, C. W., & Beinhacker, S. L. (Eds.). (2004). *Generating and sustaining nonprofit earned income*. San Francisco: Jossey-Bass.

Sagawa, S., & Segal, E. (2000). *Common interest, common good: Creating value through businesses and social sector partnerships*. Cambridge, MA: Harvard Business School Press.

Wymer, W. W., Jr., & Samu, S. (Eds.). (2003). *Nonprofit and business sector collaboration*. Binghamton, NY: Best Business Books.

Web Sites

Community Wealth Ventures, www.communitywealth.org

National Center for Nonprofit Enterprise, www.nationalcne.org

Financial Management

As emphasized before, nonprofit organizations do not measure their success exclusively or primarily by their financial results but rather by outcomes related to their missions or by a double bottom line that considers both financial and program results. That being the case, however, it is the reality that many boards and CEOs pay particular attention to their organizations' financial condition. Without adequate and well-managed resources, achievement of the mission is jeopardized, and the very survival of the organization may be threatened.

It is realistic to acknowledge that an organization may be of mediocre effectiveness in achieving mission goals and still continues on for a long time without facing a crisis. But budget deficits or the erosion of financial assets are likely to gain the focused attention of the board and CEO and require immediate action. Many nonprofit board members are drawn from the business community and may be more familiar, or more comfortable, with financial concepts than with the professional fields of the organization's staff, so they often focus their attention on the budget and financial statements. In addition, conservation of the nonprofit's assets is an essential part of the board's fiduciary responsibility, and any signs of trouble are likely to be addressed urgently. Few events can so quickly place a nonprofit CEO's tenure in jeopardy as an operating deficit, financial mismanagement, or a bad audit report. In sum, financial skills are necessary, even if not sufficient, to effective nonprofit management.

This chapter considers some basic concepts in nonprofit accounting and financial management. Some readers may have had prior courses or experience in accounting and will be familiar with many of the points. However, for others, this chapter may be an introduction to unfamiliar territory. Those who have a background in accounting in the for-profit or government sectors are encouraged to read with a particular eye to the ways in which nonprofit accounting is different.

Before getting into the discussion, it may be useful to clarify a few terms, especially the differences among *bookkeeping, accounting*, and *financial management*. Bookkeeping refers to the methods and systems by which financial transactions are recorded, either by hand or on a computer. This chapter does not discuss nonprofit bookkeeping, but some manuals are suggested as additional reading for those who may wish to know more. Accounting encompasses the rules by which financial transactions are classified and reported. There are two types of accounting. *Financial accounting* "deals with the financial information published for use by parties outside the organization." *Managerial accounting* "deals with information that is useful to an organization's managers," but it is not required to be made available to others. For example, a banker considering a loan to a nonprofit would need to see financial accounting statements but might not be concerned about how much it costs per client to run each of the organization's programs. The latter, however, might be important information for a CEO to have when planning budget allocations (Anthony & Young, 2005, p. 466).

Financial management relies on accounting statements for data, but it "focuses on the *meaning* of those figures" (Anthony & Young, 2005, p. 487). Financial management usually involves the analysis of various financial ratios that may provide indicators of trends and the organization's financial health. Thus, the key in bookkeeping is accuracy; in accounting, consistency, and following the rules; and in financial management, making judgments and establishing policies to guide the organization's financial life.

OVERVIEW OF NONPROFIT AND PERSONAL FINANCES

Organizational finance may be unfamiliar to some individuals, but most of us have at least some understanding of how we manage our own assets and accounts. Thus, let's begin by looking at the types of funds that nonprofits manage and how they are like—or unlike—an individual's personal finances (Table 12.1). It will be necessary to oversimplify some ideas initially, but some complications will be introduced later on in our discussion.

A nonprofit's operating funds are much like those each of us manages in his or her checking account. In general, payments received are intended to be spent within the same period to pay current bills. Expenses may be limited by a budget, although both individuals and organizations also have the ability to borrow funds to meet current obligations, with obvious risks in both cases. Operating income, that is, the funds that flow into your checkbook or the nonprofit's operating accounts, may be unrestricted or restricted. Fees that nonprofits receive for services provided, gifts from donors who do not designate a specific use, and revenue from nonprofit enterprise is usually unrestricted, which means it may be used to meet any legitimate expense, including, for example, the salaries of staff, rent and

TABLE 12.1   Nonprofit Organization and Individual Funds

Nonprofit Funds	Personal Funds
Endowment (permanent or pure)	Not comparable
Endowment (board-designated)	Retirement funds
Operating reserves	Savings account
Operating funds—restricted	Checking account (e.g., birthday gift)
Operating funds—unrestricted	Checking account (e.g., salary)

utility bills, or capacity-building activities. A person's salary is generally unrestricted, too, that is, nobody tells you how to spend the money as long as the purpose is legal.

But suppose your grandmother gives you a check for your birthday, directing that you use the money to buy a new overcoat for the winter. You might deposit her check in your checking account, but you would need to somehow keep that money separate, at least in your mind, because it has been restricted to a specific use. Nonprofits also receive payments that are designated for particular purposes and likewise need to ensure that they are spent accordingly. Your responsibility to follow your grandmother's direction may be only a moral obligation, while nonprofits are required to adhere to the purposes attached to restricted funds. (Of course, both you and the nonprofit may also have the concern that a donor, or grandmother, could decide not to give again if the money is not properly applied.)

A nonprofit's operating funds that are *temporarily restricted* could represent, for example, an advance payment on a grant or contract to cover some service that it has not yet performed. The organization has not yet incurred the expenses that the payment was intended to cover, and the money must be set aside until it has. The funds are restricted until such time as the work has been completed and the revenue actually earned. Or it may have received a gift that is to be used for the purchase of a new item of equipment. The money is restricted until the item is purchased; it cannot be used for something else, just as you cannot use the money from your grandmother for a new iPod.

Most of us count on our weekly or monthly income to cover our expenses but recognize that something could go wrong. An unexpected car repair bill could arise that was not in the budget. Summer jobs may turn out to be in short supply this year, eliminating some of the additional income you had anticipated earning toward fall semester expenses. Knowing these risks, we might accumulate some money in a savings account, something we can turn to for the proverbial "rainy day." Organizations also establish rainy day funds, or *operating reserves*, to be available under similar circumstances. The existence of such reserves, often equivalent to six months or one year of the operating budget, is one hallmark of a soundly managed organization. Like your personal savings, operating reserves are generally invested in very secure, short-term instruments such as bank certificates of deposit or money market funds. As with your personal savings, there may be the hope that reserves will not need to be touched, but it is important that they be preserved and kept liquid in case they are needed.

The analogy between individual and organizational funds breaks down a little when we talk about endowment, for one reason in particular—individuals are mortal, but organizations and institutions are not necessarily so! Many *endowments* are funds that are not intended to be spent—ever. The investment income that they generate may be expended for current operating expenses, but the principal is preserved *in perpetuity*. No individual has a need for funds of such a long-term nature.

There are two basic categories of endowment funds: *board-designated endowment* (also called *quasi endowment*) and *permanent endowment* (also called *pure endowment*).[1] Board-designated endowment includes, as the term suggests, money that the organization's board has decided to invest as endowment; for example, maybe the organization has run an operating surplus for awhile and has accumulated more operating reserves than it really needs. The money is not earning much interest in the safe bank account where it is being kept, and it seems unlikely that the organization will need to draw on its reserves, at least not all of them, for the foreseeable future. The board decides that some of that excess should be invested and preserved over the long term to provide additional income to support or enhance the organization's programs in future years. Its purpose might be to build up an independent source of annual income as a way to diversify revenue sources, enable the organization to sustain and enhance its programs, and gain more independence from traditional funding sources. Because its time horizon is long, and it does not foresee needing to tap the principal, the board likely would invest those funds in stocks, bonds, real estate, and other classes of assets, willing to ride out short-term fluctuations in order to gain greater investment returns over the long haul.

Since it was the board's decision to place funds into board-designated or quasi endowment, the board has the authority to withdraw the money from that type of endowment if it determines that to be necessary or desirable. But that is not a decision that the board is going to make lightly. Just as you would not be quick to cash out your IRA (individual retirement account) to pay for lunch, a board's decision to take funds out of board-designated endowment is not one that it would make except to meet some special need, for example, to build a badly needed new facility or some similar purpose that represents a major and long-lasting improvement.[2] Again, these are not the same as reserves and should not be regarded as such; they are investments for the long term.

With permanent or pure endowment, the board has limited or no flexibility. These are funds given by donors who specified that the principal be retained and be invested *in perpetuity*, meaning forever. They are *permanently restricted*. Donors may also have designated that annual income generated through the investment of endowment principal be used for certain purposes, for example, to provide scholarships to students or to maintain a chair for a violinist in the symphony orchestra. Under most circumstances, the board does not have the legal authority to invade the original principal of the gift or to use the income for purposes not consistent with the donor's direction without first obtaining the donor's approval or, with strong justification, permission from a court of law.[3]

In looking at your personal finances, the closest thing that you may have to endowment funds are the resources you or your employer have placed into retirement accounts, perhaps a 401 (k), a 403 (b), or an IRA. These assets are not intended to be spent today or anytime soon and, indeed, the law may place significant barriers to your gaining access to the money now. They are like board-designated or quasi endowment; you might be able to withdraw the funds, but that is not your intention or plan, except under highly unusual circumstances. Obviously, there is a big difference between your retirement funds and a nonprofit's permanent endowment, since you probably intend to spend your retirement funds eventually to support yourself once you reach an older age and end your career. A nonprofit's permanent endowment is intended *never* to be spent. There is nothing quite comparable to "in perpetuity" for an individual.

In addition to financial assets, organizations—and individuals—have *physical assets*. Like an individual or a family, nonprofits own buildings, vehicles, equipment, and other *things*. (Physical assets are not depicted in Table 12.1.) Physical assets are quite different from money. For one thing, they are generally *illiquid*, meaning that they are not easy to sell. It is also often difficult to know exactly how much they are worth. For these reasons, they do not serve the same purpose as operating funds or reserves. They also are not the same as endowment because they generally do not generate income that might be used to meet current expenses. It could be possible, of course, to sell the car or the house if needed to pay bills, but that would reflect a relatively dire and undesirable situation both for an individual or an organization.

Before looking at nonprofit financial statements, let's consider how two additional principles of accounting may be understood both in terms of an organization's or an individual's finances: the distinction between the *cash basis* of accounting and the *accrual basis* of accounting and the concept of *cash flow.* Using the cash basis, financial transactions are recorded only when money changes hands. This is the way many of us handle our checking accounts; we add to the balance when we make a deposit and subtract when we withdraw funds. But using a cash basis can provide a misleading picture of one's actual financial situation; for example, it ignores the purchases that have been placed on a credit card. The amount of those purchases may not yet have hit your checking account, but they should be subtracted from its balance—at least in your mind—to gain an accurate sense of where you stand. The credit card is an *account payable*. On the other hand, let's say you have sold something on eBay and are awaiting the payment to clear your PayPal account. The money is not reflected in your checking account balance, but you can plan your expenses in anticipation of receiving it, since it is on the way. It is an *account receivable,* and it needs to be taken into account in assessing your current position.

A nonprofit organization faces similar situations. For example, it may have sent bills to clients for services that it has provided or it may have pledges from donors that have not yet been received. Those are accounts receivable and need to be taken into consideration along with the cash it has in the bank, since they represent money that it has earned or is entitled to receive. Alternatively, a nonprofit may receive payment on a grant or contract for services that it is going to provide in the future. It has received the cash but it hasn't yet *earned* it; it has future expenses to which it is obligated as a result of the terms of the grant or contract. It cannot look at that cash as money available to pay for salaries, rent, or the electric bill. The cash basis of accounting thus presents some drawbacks. As Zietlow, Hankin, and Seidner (2007) explain,

> In cash basis accounting, revenues are recorded when cash comes in and expenses are recorded when cash is expended. The problem is that revenues and expenditures are not properly matched during the year. This mismatch becomes serious whenever your organization has significant dollar amount of payables, receivables, inventories, or depreciable assets. (p. 171)

Accounting on an accrual basis takes into account the money that a nonprofit has earned and is entitled to receive, as well as obligations for expenditures that it has not yet incurred. It thus presents a much more accurate portrayal of its actual situation than cash basis accounting and, indeed, is mandated for external financial reporting.

But the accrual basis of accounting also may lead to a misleading picture. For example, suppose your friend has a wealthy aunt who has promised to leave him her entire large estate when she dies. He may think of himself as wealthy already; he has mentally recorded his inheritance as a receivable. But every time you are out together, he needs to borrow money from you to pay for dinner. He is thinking on an accrual basis, but unfortunately, he does not have sufficient *cash flow* right now to meet his living needs. A nonprofit organization could be in the same situation. For example, it may have landed some lucrative contracts, but it has not yet received payment. Using the accrual basis of accounting, the anticipated payment shows up as revenue on its financial reports. But it may not have cash on hand in the bank to meet this month's rent or payroll. For these reasons, organizations—and individuals—also need to track cash flow. We will see more about how they do this in the next section of this chapter.

NONPROFIT FINANCIAL STATEMENTS

Again, accounting is about following the rules. For nonprofit organizations, rules are established by the Financial Accounting Standards Board (FASB), which most people pronounce as "Faz-bee." The standards most relevant to nonprofit organizations are No. 93 ("Accounting for Depreciation"), No. 95 ("Statement of Cash Flows"), No. 116 ("Accounting for Contributions Received and Contributions Made"), No. 117 ("Financial Statements of Not-for-Profit Organizations"), and No. 124 ("Accounting for Certain Investments Held by Not-for-Profit Organizations") (Anthony & Young, 2005, p. 469). We will not go into detail on all these in this discussion, but there will be occasions to refer in particular to the Statement of Financial Accounting Standards (SFAS) No. 116 and SFAS No. 117. These standards required significant changes in nonprofit accounting when they were implemented in 1995 and have implications not only for how nonprofits keep track of their finances but also for their relationships with donors.

Tables 12.2, 12.3, 12.4, and 12.5, respectively, provide examples of four financial statements that many nonprofit organizations prepare: (1) *statement of financial position* (sometimes called the *balance sheet*), (2) *statement of activities* (sometimes called the *income statement*), (3) *statement of cash flows*, and (4) *statement of functional expenses*. Space does not permit a line-by-line discussion of the statements. Let's just look at a few key items, especially those that illustrate unique features of nonprofit accounting.

The examples in this chapter are the 2006 financial statements of the Michigan Nonprofit Association (MNA). The MNA is itself a nonprofit organization that works to enhance other nonprofits in the State of Michigan. Its financial statements have been taken directly from its Web site (www.mnaonline.org/index.asp, accessed June 6, 2007). Much of the same data found in an organization's financial statements are also provided in its Form 990, which is filed with the Internal Revenue Service (IRS) and easily accessed through services such as Guidestar. Although the examples do not include them, the *Notes to Financial Statements* are an integral part of an organization's overall financial statements and are often illuminating of some important details.

Statement of Financial Position

The statement of financial position (sometimes called the balance sheet) provides a snapshot of the organization at a point in time, usually the end of a fiscal year. It summarizes its *assets*, that is, "the items that the organization possesses, with which it carries out its programs and service," and its *liabilities*, the "amounts of borrowed money, or debt, that the

(Text continues on page 299)

TABLE 12.2   Statement of Financial Position

MICHIGAN NONPROFIT ASSOCIATION

Statement of Financial Position

June 30, 2006

	Unrestricted	Temporarily Restricted	Total	2005 Comparative Total
Assets				
Cash and equivalents	$111,807	$761,812	$873,619	$334,087
Accounts receivable	45,437	-	45,437	89,871
Grants & pledges receivable	24,212	1,112,500	1,136,712	-
Prepaid expenses	28,425	-	28,425	6,979
Furniture and Equipment:				
Furniture and office equipment	154,340	-	154,340	124,781
Less accumulated depreciation	111,808	-	111,808	94,332
Net Furniture and Equipment	42,532	-	42,532	30,449
Total Assets	$252,413	$1,874,312	$2,126,725	$461,386
Liabilities and Net Assets				
Liabilities:				
Accounts payable	$130,643	-	$130,643	$124,279
Accrued payroll and vacation payable	33,742	-	33,742	35,003
Deferred revenue	6,550	-	6,550	28,750
Capital leases payable	21,566	-	21,566	-
Total Liabilities	192,501	-	192,501	188,032
Net Assets:				
Unrestricted	59,912	-	59,912	78,158
Temporarily restricted	-	1,874,312	1,874,312	195,196
Total Net Assets	59,912	1,874,312	1,934,224	273,354
Total Liabilities and Net Assets	$252,413	$1,874,312	$2,126,725	$461,386

Source: Michigan Nonprofit Association Web site (www.mnaonline.org/index.asp, accessed June 6, 2007). Used with permission of the Michigan Nonprofit Association (www.mnaonline.org).

TABLE 12.3 Statement of Financial Position

MICHIGAN NONPROFIT ASSOCIATION

Statement of Activities

Year ended June 30, 2006

	Unrestricted	Temporarily Restricted	Total	2005 Comparative Total
Contributions, Revenues, and Gains:				
Grant allocations	-	$2,439,023	$2,439,023	$588,680
Contributions	9,705	-	9,705	8,222
In-kind contributions	100,520	-	100,520	100,520
Membership dues	-	179,367	179,367	167,534
Program fees, consulting, and sponsorship	418,638	-	418,638	478,649
Investment income	10,714	-	10,714	1,822
Miscellaneous income	13,880	-	13,880	13,070
Net assets released from restrictions:				
Time restrictions expired	165,692	(165,692)	-	-
Program restrictions satisfied	773,582	(773,582)	-	-
Total Contributions, Revenues and Gains	1,492,731	1,679,116	3,171,847	1,358,497
Expenses:				
Program Services:				
Educational Services	539,152	-	539,152	386,328
Public Policy	293,271	-	293,271	218,403
Nonprofit Outreach	394,229	-	394,229	327,197
Volunteerism	114,625	-	114,625	155,106
Total Program Services	1,341,277	-	1,341,277	1,087,034
Supporting Services:				
Administration	105,691	-	105,691	140,345
Fundraising	64,009	-	64,009	86,769
Total Supporting Services	169.700	-	169,700	227,114
Total Expenses	1,510,977	-	1,510,977	1,314,148
Increase (decrease) in net assets	(18,246)	1,679,116	1,660,870	44,349
Net Assets, beginning of period	78,158	195,196	273,354	229,005
Net Assets, end of period	$59,912	$1,874,312	$1,934,224	$273,354

Source: Michigan Nonprofit Association Web site (www.mnaonline.org/index.asp, accessed June 6, 2007).

TABLE 12.4   Statement of Cash Flows

MICHIGAN NONPROFIT ASSOCIATION

Statement of Cash Flows

Year ended June 30, 2006

	2006	2005 Comparative Total
Cash flows from operating activities:		
Increase (decrease) in net assets	$1,666,870	$44,349
Adjustments to reconcile increase in net assets to net cash provided by operating activities:		
Depreciation	17,476	12,776
(Increase) decrease in operating assets:		
Accounts receivable	44,434	7,612
Grants receivable	(1,136,712)	40,000
Prepaid expenses	(21,446)	11,168
Increase (decrease) in operating liabilities:		
Accounts payable	6,364	103,536
Account payroll and vacation	(1,261)	6,690
Deferred revenue	(22,200)	19,350
Net cash provided by operating activities	547,525	245,481
Cash flows from investing activities		
Purchase of fixed assets	(29,559)	(2,140)
Cash flows from financing activities:		
Lease contracts executed	29,559	-
Payment on capital lease payable	(7,993)	-
Net cash provided by financing activities	21,566	-
Net increase (decrease) in cash	539,532	243,341
Cash and equivalents, beginning of period	334,087	90,746
Cash and equivalents, end of period	$873,619	$334,087

Source: Michigan Nonprofit Association Web site (www.mnaonline.org/index.asp, accessed June 6, 2007).

TABLE 12.5 Statement of Functional Expenses

MICHIGAN NONPROFIT ASSOCIATION
Statement of Functional Expenses
Year ended June 30, 2006

| | Program Services | | | | | Supporting Services | | | | 2005 |
Expenses:	Educational Services	Public Policy	Nonprofit Outreach	Volunteerism	Total	Administration	Fundraising	Total	Total	Comparative Total
Compensation	$232,609	$128,138	$159,739	$62,548	$583,034	$53,853	$35,071	$88,924	$671,958	$595,519
Pension plan contributions	16,000	9,602	12,488	4,516	42,606	3,888	2,532	6,420	49,026	45,013
Other employee benefits	17,974	15,174	22,931	7,660	63,739	6,596	4,295	10,891	74,630	75,042
Payroll taxes	18,475	10,140	12,276	4,639	45,530	3,994	2,601	6,595	52,125	46,493
Accounting fees	1,536	1,132	1,985	1,351	6,004	1,163	758	1,921	7,925	7,530
Legal fees	1,687	-	240	-	1,927	-	-	-	1,927	-
Supplies	8,194	977	2,229	846	12,246	729	474	1,203	13,449	18,186
Telephone	389	800	2,555	274	4,018	236	153	389	4,407	2,980
Postage and shipping	14,189	4,293	11,325	417	30,224	354	230	584	30,808	25,996
Occupancy	11,870	9,117	15,351	10,448	46,786	8,996	5,858	14,854	61,640	61,580
Equipment rental & maintenance	11,632	6,872	12,830	7,851	39,185	6,760	4,402	11,162	50,347	11,644
Printing & publications	26,795	9,467	54,555	1,251	92,068	988	643	1,631	93,699	88,933
Travel	16,564	10,235	5,379	2,480	34,658	2,099	1,367	3,466	38,124	21,994
Conferences & meetings	105,666	14,191	1,334	761	121,952	625	407	1,032	122,984	141,923
Contract services	43,438	26,621	67,861	2,772	140,692	2,387	1,554	3,941	144,633	126,325
Organization dues	3,190	1,537	2,545	1,488	8,760	1,281	834	2,115	10,875	7,195
Staff/Board development	4,577	4,070	3,998	2,186	14,831	1,644	1,070	2,714	17,545	9,195
Program grants	120	38,277	-	-	38,397	1,000	-	1,000	39,397	8,240
Miscellaneous	862	131	230	157	1,380	6,533	89	6,622	8,002	7,584
Total expenses before depreciation	535,767	290,774	389,851	111,645	1,328,037	103,126	62,338	165,464	1,493,501	1,301,372
Depreciation expense	3,385	2,497	4,378	2,980	13,240	2,565	1,671	4,236	17,476	12,776
	$539,152	$293,271	$394,229	$114,625	$1,341,277	$105,691	$64,009	$169,700	$1,510,977	$1,314,148

See accompanying notes to financial statements.

Source: Michigan Nonprofit Association Web site (www.mnaonline.org/index.asp, accessed June 6, 2007).

organization has used to finance some of those assets" (Zietlow et al., 2007, p. 172). To put it in personal terms again, your personal assets may include your bank accounts, the book value of your car, and the market value of your house. They need to be offset by your liabilities, for example, the balances on your car loan, mortgage, and credit cards. The difference is your personal net worth. In a for-profit company, the difference is called *equity*; it represents the value of the owners' interest in the firm. For a nonprofit, there is no ownership interest, so the difference between assets and liabilities is simply defined as *net assets.* The way balance sheets are constructed, assets always equal the sum of liabilities and net assets; if these totals do not agree, there is something wrong with the numbers.

The MNA's balance sheet reflects some of the accounting principles discussed before. For example, net assets are divided into those that are unrestricted and those that are temporarily restricted. It shows no permanently restricted assets; thus, we can assume that the MNA does not have any endowment that donors have designated for permanent investment. (Board-designated endowment is treated as unrestricted under the accounting rules, since the board could, if it wished, spend the money.)

The MNA shows an asset called "grants and pledges receivable." This reflects the accrual basis of accounting. These assets are payments that MNA has earned or that have been committed to it, but it has not yet received the cash. SFAS 116, which was mentioned above, requires that under certain circumstances nonprofits show pledges as assets, even if they have not received payment of the gift. That was a controversial requirement when introduced in the 1990s and caused some organizations to reconsider how pledges were written and documented. It was one of the factors that have led to more formal relationships between nonprofits and their donors over the past decade.

A liability worth noting on the MNA's SFP is "accrued payroll and vacation payable." When staff members earn vacation, the organization also accrues a financial liability, since it will eventually be required to pay for the time. This accounting requirement is why some organizations have use-it-or-lose-it policies that require employees to take earned vacation days within a certain period of time or lose the days. Such policies generally are established not because employers are stingy but rather because they do not wish to carry too much accrued vacation time on their balance sheets, which adversely affects its financial position.

Statement of Activities

Now, let's go to Table 12.3. The balance sheet, or statement of financial position, is a *snapshot* of the organization's finances taken at a point in time. But the statement of activities shown in Table 12.3 is more like a motion picture that shows the flow of revenues and expenses of the organization, and the resulting changes in net assets, *over* a period of time, generally a year. Accordingly, some nonprofit organizations call this the "statement of revenues, expenses, and changes in net assets." For a business, this statement would be the same as its "profit and loss" or "P&L" statement (Zietlow et al., 2007, p. 179).

Remember that revenues are not necessarily the same as "income" or cash. For example, pledges are shown as revenue, the same as cash gifts. Although the MNA statement of activities does not reflect any, the standards permit nonprofits' financial statements to show as revenue the value of some contributed services, that is, the value of volunteers' time. But this is only true if the services are ones for which the organization would otherwise have paid. This generally includes professional services by individuals who are architects, carpenters, doctors, lawyers, and the like, but it does not service volunteers who work in the organization's mission programs (McMillan, 2003a, p. 135).

It is to be noted that in 2006, the MNA received grant allocations that are temporarily restricted. This means that they are intended to cover expenses that the organization has not yet incurred; perhaps the work is scheduled for sometime in the next year. At the same time, some funds have been "released from restrictions" this year, either because a time restriction expired or because the organization provided the services for which funds received earlier were intended to cover. The payments may have been received last year, but they show up as revenue for this year because the activity that they supported was completed this year.

Looking at the expenses portion of the statement, we can see that they are divided into categories: expenses that were related to programs services and those that paid for "supporting services," including administration and fundraising. In Table 12.5, the MNA's statement of functional expenses breaks out each of the budget lines—for example, compensation, supplies, and postage—across those functional categories. A similar break out is provided on the Form 990 and is used to calculate the ratios that some charity raters, such as Charity Navigator, use to evaluate nonprofits.

Statement of Cash Flows

Table 12.4 is MNA's statement of cash flows for 2006. As discussed above, the statement of activities does not give the whole picture because of the accrual basis of accounting it reflects. For that reason, SFAS 117 requires that nonprofits also produce a statement of cash flows to show cash inflows and inflows over the year, enabling us to see how the cash amount changed from one year to the next. There are two methods of presenting cash flow, direct and indirect, but this chapter does not go into those details (McMillan, 2003a, p. 124).

Look again at the MNA's SFP in Table 12.2 and the total of "cash and equivalents" reported on the first line under "assets"—$873.619.[4] Now look at the bottom line of the statement of cash flows in Table 12.4—it's the same number. What the statement of cash flows does is walk us through exactly how the cash changed from the beginning to the end of 2006. Cash flow may occur through operating activities, investing activities, or financing activities. Think again about your own checkbook. Cash might flow in from your paycheck. You may have sold your car, a physical asset, and placed the proceeds in the same account. Or you may have borrowed money from the bank, and they deposited the amount of the loan directly into your checking account. All those transactions comprise your cash flow, but again, tracking just the flow of cash into and out of your checking account would not provide a complete picture of your financial position; that requires looking at the cash flow in relationship to the other financial statements discussed above.

Before leaving the discussion of financial statements, there is one additional concept that is important to understand—*depreciation*. The concept of depreciation, and the way it is handled in financial accounting, is sometimes difficult for individuals to quite grasp in terms of their personal financial life. The most familiar experience that most of us have with depreciation is the decline in the book value of our cars. Your new car may lose much of its value as soon as it is driven from the dealer's showroom. If you keep it long enough, it will continue to decline until it is ready for the junk yard and is worth next to zero. You may not feel that decline as an expense as it occurs, since it is not coming out of your pocket or checkbook each day, but clearly your personal net worth is less when the car gets old than it was when the car was new. Thus, the car's depreciation is a real expense in terms of its effect on your total net worth, even though it may not affect your cash flow.

Let's say a nonprofit organization owns physical assets, including cars, buildings, and equipment. Those assets have a value and that value is reflected on its balance sheet. But they are assets that will be used up or wear out over some period of time, so their value declines with every passing month or year. That decline must be accounted for as an *expense*, even though it does not involve an actual outlay of money. Take a look at MNA's statement of functional expenses in Table 12.5; the amount of depreciation of its assets in 2006 is shown on the next to bottom line, totaling $17,476. But it is an accounting expense rather than a real outlay of cash, so an adjustment needs to be made to provide a clear picture of MNA's cash flow. Look at Table 12.4, the statement of cash flows. The $17,476 has been added back in on the second line to make the necessary adjustment; otherwise, it would understate the amount of cash generated by operations during the year (Zietlow et al., 2007, p. 182).

USING FINANCIAL RATIOS

Now that we have examined some basic accounting principles and looked at the financial statements that many nonprofits produce, what do we make of the data? How can we interpret the financial data and use it to make decision about the financial management of the organization?

The concept of financial rations was introduced back in Chapter 5, which discussed some ratios that external observers use to evaluate the performance of nonprofit organizations. Readers may recall from Chapter 5 that a 2004 study by the Urban Institute and Harvard's Hauser Institute (Fremont-Smith & Cordes, 2004) looked at 10 charity watchdog organizations that use financial ratios and found a variety of measures being applied, including variations of the following:

- The ratio of program expenses to contributed income
- The ratio of fundraising expenditures and private support received—that is, the cost of raising a dollar
- The percentage of total expenses (or income received from contributions) spent on charitable programs or activities
- The percentage of total expenses spent on fundraising and administration (overhead)
- Accumulated cash and asset reserves in relation to operating budget

Most of these ratios measure an organization's efficiency rather than its effectiveness. They may be of interest to the organization's board and management, but taken alone, they may not provide an appropriate way to rate or rank nonprofits.

There are a number of ratios that can be calculated from the data provided on an organization's financial statements or similar data obtained from the Form 990. The ratios that are most commonly tracked by managers are those that measure *profitability, liquidity, asset management,* and *long-term solvency* (Anthony & Young, 2005, p. 488). This chapter does not go into detail on the calculation of ratios but rather will focus on explaining the concepts that they are intended to measure and their significance to assessing the financial health of a nonprofit organization. One comprehensive list is provided by Anthony and Young (2005) in an appendix to their chapter on financial management in the *Jossey-Bass Handbook on Nonprofit Leadership and Management,* second edition. The ratios are defined in mathematical formulas, and there are also good summary descriptions of what they mean (pp. 501–510).

Although the term *profitability* may seem out of place in the nonprofit setting, it is just describing the change in net assets on the statement of activities, in other words, it considers whether the organization had an operating surplus, broke even, or operated at a loss. Liquidity relates to the organization's use of cash.

Remember from the earlier discussion the example of your friend who thinks himself wealthy because he anticipates an inheritance but who lacks the cash to pay for dinner. To avoid being in a similar bind, an organization needs to manage its cash flows effectively in order to be sufficiently liquid, that is, possessed of sufficient cash at the right times to meet its obligations as they come due. An analysis of cash management would address areas such as accounts receivable, accounts payable, and inventory maintained. For example, if clients are slow to pay bills for service, the organization will need to keep more cash on hand to pay its own bills as they come due. If the collection process could be made more efficient, it would need to maintain less of a cash balance and that money then could be put to work in other productive ways. Vendors need to be paid on time, but management of the process could reduce the amount of unproductive cash needing to be kept on hand. To use another example from personal financial life, there may not be a need to keep money sitting in your checking account on the 15th of the month if the rent is not due until the 1st, and you know you will be receiving a paycheck in the meantime. Tracking when revenues come in and bill payments are due is a way to stretch dollars farther and gain more leverage from your personal cash flow.

Another issue for organizations is management of inventories. If too much money is tied up in inventories, it may leave too little liquidity to meet cash obligations as they arise. For example, if a food program spends all its cash to fill up its freezers with a six-month supply of food, then it may be in a bind to pay its staff or other expenses. Developing a more efficient system for food purchases that could reduce the amount of inventory kept in the freezer could provide for more liquidity to meet other obligations or to be put toward more effective purposes.

Management of fixed assets requires looking at how efficiently they are being used; for example, how much revenue is being generated through the use of buildings and equipment? The condition of assets needs to be tracked and adequate funds earmarked for replacement or repair. That is a way to avoid unexpected expenses for which there may not be funds readily at hand from current revenue.

Assessing long-term solvency, that is, evaluating whether the organization is financially strong or in jeopardy, requires looking at the right-hand side of the statement of financial position, the liabilities, as well as the revenue and expenses shown on the statement of activities. One big issue is the amount of debt, specifically the relationship between assets and liabilities. Borrowing funds may be a good thing; it provides the organization with a way to leverage its assets and support a larger program of services than it could just with current revenue. But obviously, debt also increases risks and requires careful management of cash flow to ensure that debt payments can be made as due (Anthony & Young, p. 492).

Which are the most important financial ratios to watch and manage? Zietlow et al. (2007) make the case that for most nonprofit organizations, liquidity—"the ability of the organization to augment its future cash flows"—is the biggest problem. Many nonprofits depend on contributions and giving may fluctuate from year to year. An unforeseen event, such as the loss of a key donor or perhaps a decline in allocations from United Way, can leave a nonprofit in a cash crunch, stretched to meet its own obligations. Some pledges, which are reflected on the financial statements as assets, may in fact not be paid and estimates of how much may be uncollectible may not be based on reliable information. If the organization depends on earned income, it faces business risks; if a college's enrollment turns down, a concert attracts fewer than expected attendees, or a blizzard reduces attendance at a major fundraising event, revenue may turn out to be much different from what the budget anticipates. Nonprofits that rely on contracts may face similar problems; for example, costs may exceed what was projected and exceed the revenue that the contract provides. Some clients may be slow to pay. The only options may then include obtaining short-term financing from banks or other lenders, making emergency appeals to donors, tapping into reserves or even quasi endowment, delaying payments to vendors, and reducing costs by cutting staff or their compensation. Zietlow and colleagues (2007) argue that such problems are "endemic to the nonprofit sector [and that liquidity] is one of the most important yet least studied areas in the management of nonprofits." Zietlow et al. criticize the charity watchdogs, such as the BBB Wise Giving Alliance and others, who set a maximum that organizations should keep in reserves (p. 23). The view of the charity raters is that excess funds held in reserves should instead be used to support current programs and services. But Zietlow and colleagues argue, "[While] these policy guidelines may be appropriate for commercial nonprofits, [they] will severely limit the management style of small donative religious organizations" (p. 24). Drawing on data from a study that Zietlow conducted in 2002 to 2004, these authors suggest a model that nonprofits can use to determining the appropriate level of liquidity to maintain (pp. 28–43).

MANAGING ENDOWMENT FUNDS

As noted above, most nonprofit organizations do not have significant endowments; most are held by large institutions such as colleges and universities, health organizations and medical institutions, museums, and major arts centers. The largest is the endowment of Harvard University, which totaled nearly $30 billion in 2006. Other institutions with substantial endowment in 2006 included the Shriner's Hospital for Children, with $8.6 billion, the Metropolitan Museum of Art, with $2.6 billion, and the Nature Conservancy, with $922 million. But building endowment has become a priority for nonprofits across the sector in recent years and by 2006 even some social services organizations had accumulated impressive amounts; for example, Covenant House held an endowment of $25.5 million and America's Second Harvest had more than $9 million in endowment assets (DiMento, 2007). The trend is exemplified by World Vision, an organization that provides relief for children around the world. For philo-sophical and religious reasons, World Vision did not seek endowment before 2006. But that year, it accepted a gift of $3 million to start an endowment and began actively promoting endowment gifts, with the goal of reaching $50 million within a few years (Blum, 2006).

As discussed above, some endowment is created by the nonprofit's board from internal resources, perhaps excess operating surpluses accumulated over several years. Although board-designated endowment could be expended at the board's discretion, it is intended for long-term use and would generally be managed according to the same policies applied to permanent endowment created through donor-designated gifts. Term endowments, which are established for a period of years, after which the funds may be spent, might be invested and managed dif-ferently, depending on the date or their anticipated termination. The discussion of endowment management here applies to funds that the organization intends, or must, hold for investment in perpetuity, using only the annual income earned from investments to support its operating needs. There are two key concepts related to the management of endowment funds. One is the *total return* approach to investing endowment assets and the other is the *spending limit* that determines how much will be available from endowment for expenditure each year.

In earlier decades, a large portion of endowment assets were invested in secure, inter-est-paying instruments, such as bonds and bank certificates of deposit. The drawbacks of this approach became evident in the high inflation economy of the 1970s, since the fixed amount of interest income became increasingly inadequate to support the activities for which the endowment was intended. Over the long term, investments in stocks produce higher overall returns and keep pace with inflation, but stocks also often pay dividends that provide less current income than bonds. Institutions found a way around this dilemma by adopting the total return approach to investing endowments, combined with a spending limit to determine how much could be used each year.

The approach is to invest in a portfolio that includes stocks, cash, bonds, real estate, and other classes of assets, providing for the *long-term* growth of the principal. The investment strategy is to maximize total return, that is, the total of interest, dividends, and appreciation in the value of stocks and other assets. Each year, some percentage of the total market value of the endowment is withdrawn from the endowment fund and transferred to operating funds for expenditure that year. Any additional investment returns are reinvested in the principal, enabling it to grow.[5]

The spending limit is established by the board and can be varied from year to year as eco-nomic conditions change. The goal is to provide enough payout each year to meet the needs of current programs, while also allowing the value of the endowment principal to grow to keep pace with inflation and provide more income to sustain programs in future years. The latter is not only important to maintain the benefit of the endowment to the organization; it is also essential in order to keep faith with the intention of a donor who wished to sup-port some activity in perpetuity.

Let's take a look at a simple example in Table 12.6 to see how this approach might work over a period of five years. Assume a donor has made a gift of $500,000 for the purpose of endowing "full tuition scholarships" to students in perpetuity. Tuition is now $25,000, but the assumption in this example is that it will increase by an average of 5% each year.

Assume also that the original gift is invested in a portfolio of securities that will earn an average of 10% each year, in some combination of interest, dividends, and appreciation. This may be relatively high in terms of actual experience, but the round number will simplify our example. The first year the $500,000 endowment earns $50,000. The college could spend $50,000 to award two full-tuition scholarships that year. But the problem with that approach would start to become obvious in the second year. The endowment would still be just $500,000, it would again earn $50,000, no longer enough for two full-tuition scholarships at the higher tuition rate. Instead, if the college awards one $25,000 scholarship the first year (equivalent to the 5% payout rate that the board has established), and reinvests the additional $25,000 back into the endowment, the principal of the endowment now becomes $525,000. If it follows that practice every year—spend 5% and reinvest 5%—look what happens as we go down the table to year number five. Because the endowment principal has been increased, the 5% available for spending also has increased, sufficiently to cover the ever-higher cost of tuition. Continuing out forever in the future, if all the assumptions hold, there will always be sufficient income from this endowment to provide a full-tuition scholarship, which was the intention of the donor. Now, if the market has a bad year, it may not earn 10%, but in some years it may do better than 10%, averaging out over the long haul. Tuition may increase more than expected, or less. The board can adjust the spending limit as well as the investment portfolio to accommodate these trends as they emerge. Properly executed, this approach enables the organization to count on ever-increasing income from its endowment and to keep faith *in real terms* with the intention of its endowment donors.

TABLE 12.6   Hypothetical Endowment Fund

Year	Tuition ($)	Endowment return 10% ($)	Spendable 5% ($)	Reinvest 5% ($)	Endowment principal ($)
Gift					500,000
1	25,000	50,000	25,000	25,000	525,000
2	26,250	52,500	26,250	26,250	551,250
3	27,563	55,125	27,563	27,563	578,813
4	28,941	57,881	28,941	28,941	607,754
5	30,388	60,775	30,388	30,388	638,142

The management of nonprofit endowments is governed by state law and most have adopted a version of the Uniform Management of Institutional Funds Act (UMIFA). UMIFA is a recommended law developed by National Conference of Commissioners on Uniform

State Laws, an organization that advises states on how they can adopt laws that will be consistent. One problem that arose under UMIFA in the early 2000s is the requirement that the organization could never spend the original principal of the endowment gift. Some donors had made gifts in 2000 or 2001, believing that endowment income would start to be spent in the next year or so. But the stock market declined precipitously and the value of some endowment shrank below the amount of the original gift. Under UMIFA, the organization could make no payout because it was not permitted to spend any portion of the original principal from the gift. This led to the dismay of some donors who had hoped to see some immediate benefits from their gifts. Reforms to UMIFA were under consideration at the time of this writing, to address this and other problems. Students should check Web sites such as that of the Council on Foundations to be sure where the current law stands at the time of their reading (www.cof.org).

DEVELOPING AND MANAGING THE BUDGET

A nonprofit organization's financial statements are important documents both to individuals inside and outside the organization. But on a month-to-month or day-to-day basis, for most people working in the organization, the budget and reports related to the budget are the guides to action. A full discussion of budgeting is beyond the scope of this text, but this section will summarize some of the more important principles and concepts.

Most nonprofit organizations have three separate budgets: an *operating budget*, a *capital budget*, and a *cash budget*. As their names suggest, one tracks all revenues and expenditures; another concerns the purchase or disposal of long-term physical assets, such as buildings and equipment; and the third tracks the flow of cash during the year, whether related to operating or capital activities. As Maddox (1999) correctly observes, "Most people think of the operating budget when they think of a budget (if they do at all)." Our discussion in this section focuses generally on principles that relate to developing and managing the operating budget, although some are relevant to the others as well (p. 60).

A budget is a political as well as a financial document. Some say that the budget reveals an organization's "real strategy," despite what may be written in the strategic plan or other documents (Maddox, 1999, p. 12) because the budget is a tangible expression of what the organization's real priorities are. It reflects not only considered plans but also the push and pull of political forces within the leadership of the organization. Readers may recall the idea of nonprofit leaders' political frame, an idea described by Herman and Heimovics and discussed in Chapter 4. Managers may be guided by a strategic plan, but various departments, programs, or purposes are in competition for the organization's limited resources and the outcome of that competition may be important in determining where funds are actually allocated.

Budgets invariably create incentives and disincentives that will affect the behavior of managers and staff. For example, some organizations have a use-it-or-lose-it approach to annual budgets. If a department has not expended its budgeted funds by the end of the fiscal year, the remaining funds do not carry over to be available to the department the following year. The organization's top budget managers may be counting on unexpended funds in some department budgets to cover overspending by others or as a reserve of sorts to cover unanticipated expenses of the general organization. But savvy managers often work to ensure that no unspent money remains, rushing to place orders for supplies and new computers before the fiscal year ends. The use-it-or-lose-it policy, thus, may turn out to create a perverse incentive that results in needless spending.

The way in which budgets are structured, whether on an organizational or center basis, also affects incentives. For example, a university may develop a budget that treats tuition from all students as revenue to the institution as a whole. Individual colleges, schools, and programs then are given an expense budget on which they need to operate, and the dean or director of each is responsible for not exceeding the budgeted amount. The individual units thus are viewed as *cost centers*, and their managers may have little incentive beyond controlling costs. Alternatively, some universities treat each unit as a *profit center*. The school or college keeps the revenue it generates, from which it meets its own direct costs and makes some contribution to cover general institutional costs and services provided to the unit by the overall organization, for example, its share of expenses related to utilities and information systems technology. This approach may create considerable incentive for unit heads to be entrepreneurial and undertake new efforts to increase revenue. However, the trade-off may be that the central administration has less control and a reduced ability to reallocate funds across units, either to address institutional priorities or to cross-subsidize less profitable programs through the surpluses of others.

Another consideration is whether budgets are developed incrementally or allow for redistribution. A common and simple way to develop next year's budget is just to add some percentage to last year's budget or to the amounts actually expended, maybe one percentage for salary increases and another for other expenses. If the allocation is based on funds expended, then it will, of course, exacerbate the tendency of units to make sure they spend all of last year's budgeted amount before the year ends. If they do not, they take, in effect, a double hit; they lose the unexpended funds at the end of the year and also receive a reduced allocation for the year that follows. Other budgeting systems allow for considerable redistribution from one year to the next. One benefit of having a strategic plan with specific goals and objectives is that it can serve to justify such redistribution over time in order to pursue strategic priorities. If the plan has been developed in a participative process, with buy-in from all parts of the organization, it may help mitigate the inevitable political pressures that come to bear on annual budgeting. Another process, perhaps to be seen as the extreme of the redistribution spectrum, is the zero-based approach. All programs and departments start at zero at the beginning of each year's budget process and need to justify their budgets from the ground up. But this approach has a number of disadvantages, including the amount of time and effort required to prepare justifications and the potential for management competition and negative staff morale (McMillan, 2003b, p. 114).

A fundamental idea in budgeting is to recognize the difference between controllable and uncontrollable expenses and to hold managers accountable accordingly. Individual departments or programs may be credited with or charged with revenues and expenditures attributable to them, but a manager can only be held responsible for line items under his or her control. For example, a manager may be able to control salaries, travel, and the use of outside consultants, but he or she may not be able to control, at the department or program level, items such as fringe benefits, rent, heat, or electricity. Monthly budget reports typically show—for each line item—the amount budgeted for the year, the amount and percentage of the annual budget for that item expended year-to-date, and a comparison with the amount spent the previous year to the same date. Such reports enable managers to note significant variations from the budget and make mid-year corrections as needed.

FINANCIAL POLICIES AND CONTROLS

As discussed in Chapter 5, recent years have included increased demands for accountability throughout American society, resulting in legislation such as Sarbanes-Oxley and laws in several states that apply similar requirements to nonprofit organizations. In this environment, it is essential for well-managed nonprofits to have policies to guide the management and reporting of their financial affairs. Good judgment and intentions are no longer sufficient; explicit policies are required.

Organizations have internal policies, developed by management and often adopted by the governing board. Other policies are external; they are required of organizations by law or by their funders. For example, nonprofits that receive federal funds are obligated to a complex hierarchy of requirements imposed by federal agencies.

Like laws, policies may be *prescriptive* or *restrictive*, that is, they can state what must be done or they can limit or place boundaries on the actions that be taken under certain circumstances. Zietlow and colleagues (2007) agree with John Carver, whose views were discussed in Chapter 3, that "the prescriptive approach to policy is doomed to failure" (p. 145). It is just impossible to predict all future circumstances; it is undesirable to unduly limit the flexibility of managers; and enforcement is difficult with the prescriptive approach. For example, society can make laws that prohibit people from driving too fast, driving after consuming alcohol, or driving without seat belts. But a law that required "safe driving" would be unenforceable because it encompasses too wide a range of possible behaviors. Zietlow and colleagues identify three basic categories of financial policies that nonprofit organizations should have: *accountability and regulatory compliance policies, financial and financial management policies,* and *data integrity policies.*

Accountability and regulatory compliance policies encompass matters such as filing Form 990s, avoiding conflicts of interest, and meeting other requirements of behavior and/or disclosure required by law. Financial and financial management policies are established by the governing board. They may identify allowable ranges for specific financial indicators or ratios, for example, liquidity, debt, or assets held in the endowment fund. They may also encompass procedures for purchasing, risk management, internal financial controls, fundraising, and other areas of activity. The third category, data integrity policies, involves privacy, confidentiality, records retention, the separation of duties, data backup, and other such concerns (Zietlow et al., 2007, pp. 146–154).

Internal controls have become increasingly a focus of attention in the wake of several scandals of malfeasance by nonprofit executives, and some nonprofits have adopted internal control policies similar to those required of public corporations by Sarbanes-Oxley. One fundamental principle of internal control requires that duties of individuals be separated so that no one person handles an entire transaction from beginning to end. For example, it is common to have policies that require that the person who enters donor gifts is different from the person who deposits the funds; that the person who reconciles the checking account monthly is different from the person who signs the checks; and that payments to vendors be made only with an invoice approved by someone other than the person who sends the payment.

As Zietlow and colleagues (2007) observe, "Depending on the nature of your organization and the specific policy, internal or external noncompliance can range from fraud to poor business management, from felony to raised eyebrows" (p. 138). Ensuring that such policies are in place and followed is a fundamental aspect of responsibility for nonprofit managers and boards.

CHAPTER SUMMARY

Financial management goes to the heart of the board's fiduciary responsibility, and any problems involving budgets or assets are likely to demand immediate attention from the board and the nonprofit CEO. Bookkeeping involves the entry of financial transactions on the organization's records; accounting encompasses the rules by which transactions are allocated and reported; and financial management requires making judgments based on data in financial statements, relationships among that data, and financial management policies of the organization.

Although the terminology of nonprofit accounting is precise and can be unclear to those without a financial background, the basic concepts have analogs in the personal finances of individuals. For example, operating funds are similar to a personal checking account and operating reserves are like savings. A nonprofit may have board-designated endowment, which is like an individual's retirement funds—it is intended for investment over the long run, but the board can withdraw the funds with good reason. Permanent endowment must be invested in perpetuity because donors have placed that requirement on their endowment gifts. The nonprofit can withdraw the principal from an endowment only with agreement of the donor or a court. Individuals do not have a component of their personal finances that can be compared with permanent endowment, since they are mortal and do not hold funds in perpetuity.

There are two basic methods of accounting, the cash basis and the accrual basis. Very small organizations that do not have accounts receivable or payable may use the cash method, but most use the accrual method, which is required for external financial reports. In accrual basis accounting, revenues and expenses are recorded as they are earned or as obligations are incurred, not necessarily when the cash is received or paid out. Thus, reports based on the accrual method may provide a better picture of the organization's real financial picture than ones based on the cash basis. However, it is also necessary to look at cash flows to get a complete sense of the organization's financial position.

There are four financial statements that many nonprofits produce for external purposes. The statement of financial position provides a snapshot of the organization's assets, liabilities, and net assets at a point in time, usually the end of its fiscal year. Net assets are equivalent to equity in a company or an individual's net worth.

The statement of activities shows revenues, expenditures, and changes in net assets over a period of time, usually a fiscal year. In a business, this would be the profit-and-loss statement. Revenues include receivables and noncash income, including, under some circumstances, the value of time contributed by volunteers who provide professional services.

Expenses may be allocated among programs and supporting services, including general management and fundraising. A statement of functional expenses shows the allocation of expenses among those categories in more detail. The functional statement is required for some nonprofits and similar data are provided on Form 990, which requires the allocation of expenses among these categories.

The statement of cash flows reveals cash transactions from operations, financing, or investing activities and the changes in cash balances over the period of the report, generally one year. Depreciation of the value of physical assets is an expense that is shown on the statement of activities. It must be added back in on the statement of cash flows to provide an accurate picture. The Notes to Financial Statements often provide important details and should be read in conjunction with the statements.

Financial ratios provide an important tool of financial management, although they are not a sufficient basis on which to rate nonprofit organizational performance. Commonly used ratios include those related to profitability, liquidity, asset management, and long-term solvency. According to some experts, liquidity is an endemic problem for nonprofit organizations. Cash management strategies may include speeding up the receipt of payments, managing the timing of expenses, reducing inventories, and obtaining a line of credit to cover temporary cash needs. Analytical models are available to determine the appropriate target for liquidity.

The largest endowment funds are held by major institutions, such as universities, but in recent years, many types of nonprofits have worked to establish or build endowments. Most endowments are invested under the total-return concept. The board of the organization sets a spending limit, which is a percentage of the endowment's market value each year (or of an average over a period of months or years). That amount is spent to support programs, and any additional investment gain is reinvested in the principal of the endowment. The payout may come from interest, dividends, or the appreciation in value of equities. That approach enables the principal and the income to grow over the years to match the higher future costs of activities that the endowment is intended to support.

Most nonprofits have three budgets: an operating budget, a capital budget, and a cash budget. The operating budget usually commands the most attention. The budget is a political document that reflects not only plans but the competition for resources within the organization. How budgets are constructed creates important incentives and disincentives that affect managers' behavior. One important consideration is whether budgets are maintained on an organizational or center basis and whether departments and programs are treated as cost centers or profit centers. Some budgeting methods simply add a percentage increment to previous years' budgeted or expended amounts, while others provide greater opportunity for the redistribution of funds across programs or units. Some expenses, such as salaries, are controllable. Others, such as fringe benefits, are less so. Unit managers should be accountable for expenses that are within their control.

Accountability in the current environment requires that nonprofits have explicit policies in three areas: accountability and regulatory compliance policies, financial and financial management policies, and data integrity policies. Ensuring that such policies are in place is a fundamental aspect of the governing board's responsibility.

NOTES

1. There are some endowments called *term endowments* that can be spent after a period of time passes. They are temporarily restricted. We do not consider them in this discussion.

2. Because the board does have the power to withdraw money from a quasi endowment, accounting rules require that such funds are treated as unrestricted in financial statements.

3. Some property owned by a nonprofit may also be considered permanently restricted, like endowment. For example, this would be true of a work of art that a donor gave with the condition that the nonprofit not sell it.

4. Cash equivalents are short-term investments, such as money market funds, that are almost as liquid as cash.

5. Most apply the spending limit to a percentage of a moving average of market value in order to smooth out changes from year-to-year; our simplified example in Table 12.6 does not reflect that practice.

KEY TERMS AND CONCEPTS FROM CHAPTER 12

accountability and regulatory compliance policies
accounting
accounts payable
accounts receivable
accrual basis of accounting
asset management
bookkeeping
capital budget
cash basis of accounting
cash budget
cash flow
cost center
data integrity policies
endowment (board designated and permanent)
financial accounting
financial and financial management policies
financial management

in perpetuity
liquidity
managerial accounting
operating budget
operating reserves
permanently restricted
prescriptive policies
profitability
profit center
restrictive policies
solvency
spending limit
statement of activities
statement of cash flows
statement of financial position
temporarily restricted
total return
Uniform Management of Institutional Funds Act (UMIFA)
unrestricted

QUESTIONS FOR DISCUSSION

1. Some people argue that nonprofit organizations should not have endowments at all. One of their arguments goes something such as the following. Putting money aside in endowment means depriving today's generation of the benefit of those

resources to benefit future generations, who will receive services supported by income from the endowment. But there are many people in great need of services today. Why are tomorrow's needy more deserving than today's? The funds should be spent now to meet current needs. Let future generations of donors support the needs of people in the future. Since the economy is growing, giving will increase over time and there should be enough philanthropy to meet those future needs. It is thus especially unjust to provide for the future at the expense of people alive today, who live in less affluent times. Do you agree? Why or why not? What arguments would you make on the other side of this issue? Would your view be different with regard to different types of nonprofits, for example, homeless shelters, universities, museums, environmental organizations?

2. Look up the Form 990 of a nonprofit organization that interests you. (It is likely available on Guidestar at www.guidestar.org.) Go through the financial data and develop your own analysis of the organization's finances. Questions you might think about include the following: Does it appear to have diversified sources of revenue? How vulnerable or unpredictable are these sources likely to be? What were its major categories of expenses for the year shown? What unforeseen expenses could arise? What kinds of assets does it hold? Does it have debt? What produced its cash flow for the year shown? Does it have endowment or other permanently restricted assets?

3. The following items were reported in the *Chronicle of Philanthropy*. In each case, what types of controls that might have prevented the incident if either were not in place or did not work?

- A former grants administrator at the Rockefeller Foundation has been found guilty of stealing more than $400,000 from the grantmaker by defrauding its employee matching-gift program over a seven-year period ("Former Rockefeller Executive Found Guilty of Stealing $400,000," 2007).

- The American Civil Liberties Union has generated a major controversy within its ranks by conducting undisclosed research on donors and potential donors. The situation has already sparked an investigation by the New York State attorney general that could have serious implications not only for the civil liberties group but also for many other charities unless the organizations move quickly to reassure donors that protecting their privacy is paramount ("New York Opens Inquiry on Donor Privacy," 2005).

- Eighteen months after the Milwaukee Public Museum, one of the largest natural history museums in the country, shocked the city by revealing that it was in a financial crisis, one of its top executives appears to be the only one to face criminal charges in the museum's near collapse. [The chief financial officer], who left his job . . . after [the] problems became public, was charged by Milwaukee's district attorney with using money from the endowment to cover operating expenses as the museum sank into a financial crisis, and lying about his actions in board meetings to hold on to his job, according to criminal charges filed this month. He did not profit personally from his actions, according to the complaint ("Former Financial Officer Faces Charges in Museum Debt Crisis," 2006).

SUGGESTIONS FOR FURTHER READING RELATED TO CHAPTER 12

Books

Gross, M. J., Jr., McCarthy, J. H., & Shelmon, N. (2005). *Financial and accounting guide for not-for-profit organizations* (7th ed.). Hoboken, NJ: Wiley.

Ruppel, W. (2002). *Not-for-profit accounting made easy.* Hoboken, NJ: Wiley.

Schneider, W. A., Robert, A. D., Benoit, M. S., & Associates (2005). *The practical guide to managing nonprofit assets.* Hoboken, NJ: Wiley.

Zietlow, J., Hankin, J. A., & Seidner, A. (2007). *Financial management for nonprofit organizations.* Hoboken, NJ: Wiley.

Web Sites

Financial Accounting Standards Board Web site, www.fasb.org

Nonprofit Finance Fund Web site, www.nonprofitfinancefund.org

PART V

Special Topics

Collaborations and Mergers

The number of nonprofit organizations has grown rapidly in the past decade. For example, the total number of nonprofits providing services related to children, youth, and families more than tripled, growing from 21,393 to 79,713 in the seven years between 1999 and 2006. In addition, there has been significant growth in the number of organizations established to protect animals, to improve the environment, or to serve other constituencies (Kirkpatrick, 2007, p. 43). These trends have prompted some to ask if there are too many nonprofits competing for the same limited funds, with too few having the capacity to grow to scale or effectively meet the needs of society or their clients. Some have called for more collaboration among organizations, so as to reduce the duplication of services, and for mergers to create larger, stronger organizations with the capacity to make a greater impact.

Many of the calls for consolidation have come from leaders of foundations and other funding agencies, such as United Way, which describe themselves as besieged with multiple requests for support by nonprofits providing similar services. As expressed by Robert Egger, the founder and CEO of DC Central Kitchen and author of the 2004 book *Begging for Change*, "If you talk to somebody from a large corporate foundation, in their view it's like the *Dawn of the Dead*: 'Where do they keep coming from?'" (Gose, 2005).

Proponents of consolidation argue that it is necessary to reduce the duplication of services, make more efficient use of resources, and increase the sector's overall impact and influence. Some foundations have, in fact, provided grants to support collaborative initiatives and mergers. But while foundation leaders have been in the forefront of calls for consolidation, some people say they are also part of the problem, because they prefer to support new initiatives rather than provide ongoing, core support. Critics also cite cases in which foundations have responded to mergers by reducing their grants—using the merger as an "exit strategy"—rather than by providing adequate support to the combined entity (Gammal, 2007, p. 51).

As with other issues we have considered in this book, opinions on consolidation vary. Concern over the competition for resources is, of course, intertwined with concern over the implications of fragmentation and duplication of services for nonprofit clients. For example, Kirkpatrick (2007) recounts the case of a woman seeking services for her family who encountered a "tangle of organizations" in her community. "'Every agency you work with has its own mission and philosophy and every agency pushes its programs on you,' the woman reported. 'I know a lot of them are fighting for their survival, and every referral they make to another agency or program potentially costs them in grant dollars. But, this is my family we're talking about'" (p. 43). However, those who are less enthusiastic about consolidation suggest that small organizations may stay in closer touch with the needs of their communities and are likely to provide more personal service than their larger, more bureaucratic counterparts (Gose, 2005). And some argue that competition in the nonprofit sector is as beneficial as in others, "providing checks and balances and protecting vulnerable populations from being exploited" (Gammal, 2007, p. 50).

REASONS TO COLLABORATE OR MERGE

Collaborations and mergers among nonprofit organizations may offer benefits to society, nonprofit clients, and the sector as a whole; but what are the potential gains for the organizations themselves? In other words, what might motivate an organization to seek a relationship with another?

Most authors describe *drivers* that may be external or internal, with the latter including financial, managerial, and programmatic considerations (Yankey & Willen, 2005, p. 255). External drivers arise from changes in the environment. They might include, for example, increased competition for clients or resources; shifting priorities or demands of private or government funders (who may require collaboration or merger as a condition of continued support); or political changes that could adversely affect a group of organizations, making it advantageous for them to work together to protect their interests. Internal drivers arise from conditions within an organization. Internal drivers could be financial. Collaboration or merger may enable organizations to reduce overhead costs, increase purchasing power, or perhaps gain better access to loans. Managerial considerations drive some relationships. For example, an organization may be able to gain access to specialized talent by working with a partner. Merging to create a larger organization may make it possible to recruit a more experienced CEO and to pay a more competitive salary. Drivers that are programmatic in nature relate to organizations' ability to enhance or expand their services through collaboration or merger; in other words, they relate to delivery of the mission (Yankey & Willen, 2005, p. 256).

In one study of 190 organizations, 83% mentioned the opportunity to improve efficiency as a reason for collaborating, and 47% mentioned problems with increasing overhead costs. By sharing costly overhead or support functions with another organization, a nonprofit may be able to reduce its overhead and direct more of its resources toward its strategic goals. In the same study, 60% mentioned increased competition in fundraising as a reason to collaborate, and 30% mentioned pressure from funders to do so (United Way of Greater Milwaukee et al., 2004, p. 20). Other formal research studies on collaboration have focused on identifying relevant organizational characteristics and environmental variables and how they influence the choices that organizations make among the various forms of collaboration, which we will discuss below. One research conclusion is that nonprofits with more diversified sources of revenue may be less inclined to collaborate or merge. This may be in part because they are better able to resist pressure from government and private funders to do so (Guo & Acar, 2005).

McCormick (2001) explains an organization's proclivity to merge in terms of three driving forces—liability, viability, and survivability. Regarding liability, he offers the example of an environmental organization that had acquired land in order to preserve it but found itself burdened with debt it could not manage. Its solution was to merge with a larger organization with a similar mission that could absorb that liability. Although it ceased to exist as an independent organization, its mission of preserving the land was achieved. Another situation that may encourage collaboration or merger is the diminished viability of an organization, which McCormick defines as "a condition in which your organization may be alive, but [is] not having a positive impact on its mission" (p. 9). Such an organization may be characterized by stagnant fundraising, high staff turnover, and perhaps a gradual erosion of financial position. An organization may decline to the point that its very survivability becomes questionable. That could result from significant financial problems, scandal or controversy, or a change in the environment that makes the mission no longer relevant—for example, discovery of a cure for the disease that the organization existed to combat. It may be forced to merge whatever assets remain with those of another, stronger nonprofit as the only alternative to closure. As McCormick notes, the position at which an organization stands along the continuum—liability, viability, survivability—determines its bargaining power in entering any collaboration or merger it may seek (p. 11).

Although collaboration and mergers are widely advocated and there is a substantial prescriptive literature on the subject, there are no reliable data on how many such relationships have been undertaken. An article by Gose (2005) in the *Chronicle of Philanthropy* asserted that "mergers [among nonprofits] have been relatively rare," although it offered no evidence. A study undertaken by the Stanford Project on the Evolution of Nonprofits looked at 200 organizations in the San Francisco Bay Area and found that just 8.5% had undertaken mergers or program acquisitions since the 1970s (Gammal, 2007, p. 48).

A CONTINUUM OF COLLABORATION

There is a multitude of words that are used to describe relationships between and among nonprofits. Although they have specific definitions, they are often used interchangeably. For example, many people call any relationship in which two organizations are working together a "partnership," although a partnership implies legal obligations that make it distinct from less formal arrangements. The terms *restructuring* and *strategic restructuring* also are widely used to describe the development of relationships that involve considerable integration of the participating organizations (Yankey & Willen, 2005). Box 13.1 summarizes definitions offered by Haider for some of the most common relationships. To keep things simple, this chapter uses *collaboration* as a generic term to encompass any relationship in which two or more independent organizations work together toward common objectives and *merger* to mean an action in which one or more organizations are combined into one corporate entity, involving a change in control, usually to a new or combined board (Haider, 2007, p. 54). As McCormick (2001, p. 2) notes, there are two types of mergers. There are *intermergers*, which combine two nonprofits that were previously legally separate, and *intramergers*, which combine units within a single corporate entity—for example, the consolidation of local chapters of a national organization. Students will recall an example of the latter from the case of the Girl Scouts presented in Chapter 6.

Box 13.1   Terms of Collaboration

Although the terms for nonprofit partnerships are often used interchangeably, they mean different things. Here are a few of these terms and their definitions.

Collaboration: A generic term for groups or organizations working together

Affiliation: The lowest level of collaboration, which involves meetings, letterhead, and possibly paying a fee to join

Alliance: A collaboration that involves some changes in operations or responsibilities, but not changes in control or structure; also called a network or a coalition

Integrated service network: An alliance of organizations that offer complementary services

Service organization: An alliance that shares operations such as legal, audit, and billing services

Partnerships: Two or more organizations that are legally bound to each other

Federation: An alliance of local affiliates that are united by a central headquarters; affiliates share a mission, a brand and a program model, but are legally independent of one another and of the headquarters

Consortium: Similar to a federation, but members are more independent of each other and of the headquarters

Franchise: Like a federation, but usually applied to commercial organizations

Merger: Combining two or more organizations into one; involves change of control

---

Source: From Haider (2007, p. 54).

Various authors have offered typologies of collaboration that define a continuum of relationships (Guo & Acar, 2005, p. 341). Sometimes, but not always, one thing may lead to another, just as dating may lead to engagement and eventually to marriage. For example, two organizations might begin to cooperate informally, perhaps by sharing information and referring clients to each other. Things might progress to more formal collaboration, perhaps sharing office space or developing some joint programs. Eventually, they may proceed to merge, giving up their separate identities to operate as a single, larger organization. And, as with individuals, some relationships work out and some do not, for a variety of reasons.

EXPLORING COLLABORATION AND MERGERS

Let's look at a few examples to gain a sense of the nature of the relationships that some nonprofits have developed and see how they fit on the collaboration continuum described above. We will start with some examples of success and then look at two in which the effort was deemed a failure:

- Two environmental organizations, the River Revitalization Foundation and Friends of Milwaukee's Rivers, were both operating from inadequate space, so they decided to pursue the idea of sharing larger quarters. Their efforts eventually led to the renovation of a facility to create space for eight environmental organizations. Although the organizations remain independent, the sharing of space provides financial benefits as well as an office environment that has improved employee morale (United Way of Greater Milwaukee et al., 2004, p. 13).

- When a county hospital closed in Milwaukee, many low-income patients lost their source of dental care. They began to visit other clinics, which were soon overloaded. The Madre Angela Dental Clinic was established as a new entity to meet the need. It is a collaborative effort of three hospitals in Milwaukee, Marquette University, several local nonprofits, and volunteers. An advisory board of representatives from participating organizations oversees the clinic, and the role of each is spelled out in written agreements (United Way of Greater Milwaukee et al., 2004, p. 17).

- The Cancer Wellness Center, Wellness House, Cancer Support Center, and Wellness Place are four independent nonprofits in the Chicago area that provide support to breast cancer patients. They are sufficiently far apart that they do not compete for patients; but they had been competing for corporate and foundation support, and each of them lacked sufficient visibility to gain referrals of patients from the area's major hospitals. They began cooperating to increase their combined visibility, then after a decade created a consortium to present themselves to the public as a single entity. Finally, they created a fifth nonprofit, the Cancer Health Alliance of Metropolitan Chicago, that promotes and helps support all four organizations (Haider, 2007, p. 52).

- In 2000, Second Harvest and Foodchain, competitors in hunger relief, decided to merge under the name America's Second Harvest. Deborah Legg, who became president of the merged organization, pointed to the benefits, including the ability of the larger organization to secure gifts from national corporations and the consolidation of administrative functions such as fundraising, finance, and public relations. By 2007, America's Second Harvest was the nation's largest hunger-relief organization, serving a network of 200 food banks in all 50 states (America's Second Harvest Web site, www.secondharvest.org/about_us, accessed June 19, 2007; Marchetti, 2000).

The four examples above illustrate different points along the collaboration continuum: eight organizations sharing space while remaining independent, several organizations collaborating to offer a new service, four organizations creating a fifth to pursue shared goals, and two organizations becoming one. Each step across the spectrum entails a reduction in the autonomy of individual organizations and increasing entanglements among them; in other words, some organizations are living together as roommates, others are doing things together as partners, and some are getting married.

Each of the above examples is one of success, but not all efforts turn out so well. Let's look at two that did not and then consider some of the obstacles and pitfalls that can prevent or complicate such undertakings.

- In 1999, 25 prominent child, youth, and family organizations created the National Call to Action, a collaborative effort to eliminate child abuse by 2020. The relationship started well, but "conflicts over trust and turf ultimately undercut the process" (Kirkpatrick, 2007, p. 46).

- In 1997, the health systems of Stanford University and the University of California at San Francisco faced an increasingly competitive situation in the health care industry, and both were experiencing massive losses. The universities decided to merge their health systems in order to "fortify their shaky finances" and gain a competitive advantage. Two years later, facing mounting debt and an $86 million budget shortfall, the merger was dissolved (Mangan, 1999).

OBSTACLES TO COLLABORATION

What differentiates successful from unsuccessful relationships between and among nonprofit organizations? What are some of the obstacles that need to be overcome and pitfalls to be avoided? What are some conditions that may favor a successful relationship? Let's look at some of the variables that are involved.

Motivations

As discussed earlier in this book on multiple occasions, there is a fundamental difference between for-profit and nonprofit entities. The primary purpose of a business corporation is to increase the wealth of the owners. The primary purpose of a nonprofit is to achieve its social mission. The shareholders of a corporation thus have a clear interest in the organization, focused on its long-term financial performance. They will evaluate potential partnerships and mergers based on their expected impact on the bottom line. Although some corporate mergers, for example, that of AOL and Time-Warner, turned out to be colossal mistakes, such failures often reflect miscalculations about the future of the business rather than confusion or disagreement about purposes or goals.

The stakeholders of a nonprofit do not have a financial interest in the organization and thus evaluate potential relationships by different, more complex criteria. Volunteers and staff may highly value the social relationships surrounding their involvement with the organization and see a potential collaboration or merger with another entity as uncomfortably disruptive. Since they do not have a personal financial stake in the decision, volunteers, including members of the governing board, "have little incentive to push for changes that could be wrenching in their short-term effects on programs and employees, [even if they may be] sound for the [organization in the] long term" (Wolf, 1999, p. 327). Both volunteers and staff are usually very committed to the mission and may place less importance on the potential financial or competitive advantages to be gained through collaboration. And, as McCormick (2001) explains, "Mission is an emotional issue. Nonprofit mission statements are about service and attention to causes, not like their for-profit counterparts, whose mission statements talk about financial security and market leadership" (p. 6).

Culture

Earlier chapters of this book have discussed the importance of culture. An organization's culture is usually a strong force, and the integration of two or more cultures can be a complex undertaking. In commenting on the failure of the Stanford/UCSF merger, discussed above, the president of Stanford cited, among other reasons, different cultures that made it difficult to integrate the medical departments, perhaps reflecting Stanford's tradition as a private university and UCSF's as a campus of the public University of California (Mangan, 1999). Gammal describes a merger between the Davis Center and Community Counseling, two organizations that also faced culture clashes. Davis had practiced a "holistic social welfare model." Counselors met clients off-site and worked to help families deal with a wide range of issues, not just psychological ones. But Community Counseling had a "traditional psychotherapeutic model," in which patients came to the office for counseling by psychologists holding Ph.D. degrees. After the merger, the Davis people expected the Community Counseling staff to go out to meet clients, which they resented, while the Community Counseling staff were concerned about patient confidentiality and the qualifications of some Davis staff. The merger ultimately survived, but only after most of the original counselors had left and the organization had spent over $100,000 on staff training and development (Gammal, 2007, p. 50).

Language is closely related to culture. For example, the very word *merger* may carry negative connotations in the nonprofit sector because of its association with the highly publicized consequences of corporate mergers. Influenced by what they hear or read about mergers in the commercial sector, people may tend to focus on what may be lost in a merger—the organization's identity, social relationships, possibly even jobs. Interestingly, a report published by the Chapin Hall Center for Children does not use the word *merger* but rather *integration*, which may carry more positive connotations for people working in the nonprofit sector (Kohm, La Piana, & Gowdy, 2003, p. 1).

Egos

Kirkpatrick (2007) quotes the words of one nonprofit executive: "'For all the cause-related work we do,' she says, 'there's a great deal of ego involved in "my way" of solving the problem'" (p. 46). Egos may be a problem especially if one or more of the organizations is led by a founder, whose personal identity may be bound up with that of the organization he or she leads. But as the words of the executive quoted above suggest, the issue may be more than a matter of personal pride. Even nonprofits that pursue similar missions may practice different philosophies or methodologies that they believe to be right and to which volunteers and staff may be strongly committed. For CEOs conditioned by a competitive environment, it may be psychologically difficult to approach any relationship without instinctively protecting the interests of their own organization. For example, in describing the failure of the National Call to Action, one observer recounted that things were going well until "the heads of the [collaborating] national organizations waltzed in." "All they wanted to know was 'What's in it for me?' 'How much money do I get?' 'How much money will this take away from my bottom line?'" (p. 46).

Costs

Collaborations and mergers may increase efficiency in the long run, but developing formal relationships also may require the investment of substantial resources. There are the time and opportunity costs of internal analyses and meetings between the potential collaborators.

There may be additional legal and accounting fees and other out-of-pocket expenses. If a merger is undertaken, there will be costs involved in the integration of management and information systems, the development of new printed materials, possibly relocation to new facilities, and continued staff development to meld the merged organization together. Full integration may take three years or more and cost more than anticipated (Gammal, 2007, p. 48). If the relationship does not work out, exit costs also can be high; for example, unraveling the merger between the Stanford and UCSF health systems was estimated to cost "tens of millions of dollars" on top of the costs that already had been experienced in putting the merger together (Mangan, 1999). And, although both organizations should engage in side-by-side analysis and due diligence before combining, there have been cases in which unforeseen or undiscovered liabilities or problems came back to haunt the new organization after the merger (Yankey & Willen, 2005, p. 263).

CONDITIONS FOR SUCCESS

Despite the obstacles, successful collaboration and mergers do occur. What are the conditions under which successful relationships are most likely to evolve? The prescriptive literature offers consistency on several points.

Driven by Mission

Relationships undertaken primarily to advance the mission are more likely to be successful than those undertaken solely for financial reasons or as a response to pressure from funders. Or, as Gammal (2007) expresses it, "in the nonprofit sector, as in the world of human courtship, money is not the right reason to merge. But mission may be" (p. 51). In the cases summarized above, neither the Milwaukee environmental and medical organizations nor the Chicago area cancer centers were driven primarily by financial considerations. There were financial benefits to be gained through their relationships, but all were driven by the opportunity to expand their services in pursuit of their missions. Only the Stanford/UCSF merger was driven primarily by financial problems, which were exacerbated rather than solved.

Commitment From Top Leadership

If the egos of CEOs and board members can be obstacles to successful collaboration, their commitment to the effort is a necessary condition for success. Indeed, in a study by the consulting firm La Piana Associates, organizations that had been involved in successful restructuring identified the fact that the relationship was initiated by a key staff or board member as critical. Board encouragement and support and positive board-executive relations in both organizations were also found to be essential (United Way of Milwaukee et al., 2004, p. 20).

One sensitive issue in a merger is the configuration of leadership in the merged entity. This will involve board leadership positions, the CEO, and managers at other levels. Some board members may have served in anticipation of ascending to leadership positions in the future, a route that now may be blocked by the integration of boards. Unless the board as a whole strongly supports the new relationship, such personal ambitions can become stumbling blocks. Staff will have loyalties to their CEOs or other managers and may undermine the relationship if they perceive that their leaders feel reluctant or skeptical about the change (McCormick, 2001, pp. 48–49).

Trust

As in human relationships, successful collaboration between or among nonprofit organizations must be built on a foundation of trust. An atmosphere of trust helps "lower the barriers between individuals and organizations, foster the growth of possible relationships, discourage hidden agendas, and promote good-faith negotiations" (Yankey & Willen, 2005, p. 270). The absence of trust is likely to bring all the obstacles to successful collaboration up to maximum strength. It will exacerbate fears about the impact of collaboration or merger on individual positions and careers and cause some to question the shared commitment to mission. Open communication is, of course, the concomitant of trust. This includes the sharing of objective data and disclosure of liabilities or problems that could surface in later phases of the relationship. Trust may be greater between organizations that have had a previous relationship with one another, that have had successful collaborations with others, that are part of the same professional or information network, and that have linkages at the level of the governing board (Guo & Acar, 2005, p. 348).

Relatedness

McCormick (2001) says that "mergers appear to work better when the parties involved can find an initial connection built on some tangible relationship" in one of four categories of relatedness: mission, constituency, organization or structure, and geography (p. 21). Although his principles apply to mergers, they could apply as well to any level of collaboration.

Creating a relationship may make sense if two or more organizations have compatible missions and may be illogical if the missions are very different. For example, it might be difficult for an organization focused on women's health to merge with one concerned with men's health; their expertise would likely be related to different diseases, and their funding sources would likely be ones with a particular interest in one gender or the other. But a health organization seeking to extend its programs into schools might find it useful to collaborate or merge with an educational organization (McCormick, 2001, p. 23).

Two organizations that operate in similar ways might find it advantageous and natural to work together. For example, two nonprofits that both raise funds primarily through direct mail might find it beneficial to combine lists or mail operations. In South Carolina, a group of nonprofits that were all raising funds through golf tournaments found that they were dividing up the population of golfers and combined their tournaments into one that, with higher fees, produced more revenue than their individual efforts combined (McCormick, 2001, p. 24).

Organizations that serve the same or similar constituencies may have rather obvious opportunities to combine efforts; but, as McCormick (2001) emphasizes, constituency relatedness needs to be considered in broad terms. Thus, two advocacy organizations that lobby the same individuals or agencies may find it beneficial to combine efforts, since "in seeking political clout, bigger is definitely better" (p. 25). So, for example, two nonprofits that lobby for environmental legislation, each having 1 million members, might get more attention from the Congress by presenting themselves under one banner representing 2 million member voters.

Geographic proximity may suggest the potential for collaboration or merger, perhaps eliminating confusion among clients or donors. Such relationships also may be a strategy by which a nonprofit can extend its reach into new markets, perhaps contiguous cities, towns, or regions (McCormick, 2001, p. 25). In sum, collaborations and mergers that have a natural logic to them are more likely to succeed than those that are forced or contrived.

Process

Research indicates that successful nonprofit collaboration requires sufficient time to develop and that following the right process is critical. Indeed, "the process through which the [relationship] is developed and operationalized has a significant impact on the likelihood of its success" (Yankey & Willen, 2005, p. 269).

Various scholars have described a process for the development of relationships through stages. While their vocabulary differs, most identify the following steps:

- Self-examination on the part of at least one organization [sometimes conducted in connection with a strategic planning process]
- A decision to explore the possibility of collaboration
- Identification of potential partners, perhaps using the four criteria of relatedness discussed above
- Initial contacts between representatives of the organizations, perhaps limited to the CEOs or selected board members initially
- Efforts to assess the degree of mutual interest
- A *side-by-side analysis* ("a multi-faceted analysis of the potential partner's background, current situation, and future potential," Yankey & Willen, 2005, p. 263)
- Negotiation and the development of agreements.
- Implementation (Adapted from Yankey & Willen, 2005, pp. 262–265)

As Gammal (2007) concludes in reporting research by the Stanford Project on the Evolution of Nonprofits,

Our findings suggest that nonprofits need to . . . budget a lot more time and get to know each other a lot better before walking down the aisle. Otherwise, they may face the fates of many couples who rush to the altar: unhappy marriages or costly divorces. (p. 47)

COLLABORATION AND MERGERS WITHIN NATIONAL NONPROFITS

The discussion in this chapter so far has focused on collaboration or merger between or among independent nonprofit organizations; but many of the same principles apply to collaborations between or among divisions or chapters of national nonprofit organizations or to intramergers—that is, the consolidation of chapters or units within a larger nonprofit.

National nonprofits with local chapters follow one of two principal organizational forms, which will affect the ease or difficulty with which collaborations and mergers may be undertaken. Some exist as a single corporation under one charter; chapters are essentially local branches or offices of the national organization. For example, the American Red Cross is a single organization governed by a single national board, and local chapters are accountable to the national office. Some governing authority has been delegated to local boards, but chapter assets are owned by the national organization and chapter executives ultimately report through channels to the national president. Other nonprofits are federations; local chapters have separate charters and are governed by independent boards. They may be required to follow prescribed policies and practices developed by the national office for the right to use the organization's name and logo, and they may pay dues to the national office in exchange for services provided to the chapters; but they also have considerable autonomy. This is the structure of a number of national disease-related organizations—for example, the Crohn's and Colitis Foundation, the American Lung Association, and the Arthritis Foundation. It is also the structure of some human services and environmental organizations, including Goodwill Industries.

While national nonprofits that operate under a single corporate charter have the formal authority to bring about collaboration and mergers among their chapters, there nevertheless are obstacles similar to those complicating such efforts among independent organizations. Issues about turf, ego, culture, and the allocation of resources are still relevant. One successful example is provided by the Girl Scouts case presented in Chapter 6, which some readers may find useful to review again at this point. Other cases provide examples of the challenges inherent in bringing together even disparate parts of a single organization with a tradition of operating with relative autonomy.

As mentioned earlier in this book, the American Red Cross received criticism for its response to Hurricane Katrina in 2005. Some individuals argued that the organization's reliance on local chapters, of which some were in rural areas with very limited resources, was no longer an adequate structure with which to respond to major disasters that could affect an entire region of the country. In response, the Red Cross's national governing board approved in May 2006 a major reorganization that would create a "hub and spoke" system with "hundreds of smaller chapters [being moved] under the purview of the 200 largest chapters," with the larger chapters assuming responsibility for the smaller chapters' administrative expenses. In effect, what was proposed was "a de facto form of merger of a number of Red Cross chapters" (Salmon, 2006).

The initiative provoked controversy among chapter leaders, some of whom walked out of the board meeting at which it was approved. Some executives of chapters that would gain responsibility questioned how they would be able to manage their own chapters while also providing oversight for others. Some chapters in wealthier communities resisted taking on the financial liabilities of those in less affluent communities. Some smaller chapters resisted the loss of their autonomy and cited the importance of maintaining a local base of financial support (Salmon, 2006).

As discussed in Chapter 10, individuals may be more inclined to support organizations with which they are involved and that have impact that they can observe in their own lives. For a national organization endeavoring to consolidate its local or regional chapters, the challenge is to gain the efficiency and effectiveness that consolidation may offer, while preserving the willingness of local volunteers and donors to participate and continue providing financial and other forms of support.

Organizations that are federations of independent local chapters may face even more difficult challenges in bringing about collaboration or mergers. As a first step, several federations have successfully established consolidated, centralized fundraising databases to be used by all chapters. For example, the Crohn's and Colitis Foundation, the Nature Conservancy, the Arthritis Foundation, and others have implemented such systems in recent years (Wallace, 2005).

A centralized database typically includes a complete profile of a donor's interactions with any part of the organization. Records of giving or volunteering are combined with the products of prospect research concerning the donor's interests and financial capacity. This comprehensive information supports a more coordinated approach to relationships with the donor that are likely to maximize that organization's or person's giving across the organization.

Policies on the sharing of revenue between national and local offices can help create incentives for cooperation and make the system work to the best advantage of all component entities. Nevertheless, such efforts often meet with resistance.

Local chapters may be concerned that the national office will encroach on their traditional donors or alienate them through excessively aggressive contacts. Some in the national office may be concerned about sharing information on major donor prospects with their local colleagues based on a presumption that they are not as skilled in fundraising. Others may be concerned that the centralization of donor records will be a first step toward greater control by the national office that will eventually undermine their autonomy in other areas (Wallace, 2005).

Mergers of chapters within a federated organization are, of course, not intramergers but rather intermergers, since the local organizations have independent charters. Lacking the authority to impose mergers, the national office may face significant resistance that is difficult to overcome. For example, several affiliates of the American Lung Association severed their ties with the national organization in 2007 over their displeasure with a plan to consolidate 78 state and local affiliates into 11 regional organizations. Some adopted new names to be free of control by the national association (Schwinn, 2007).

Pressures for nonprofits to collaborate and merge are not likely to abate in the future. Continued encouragement from funders, increased competition for resources, and the nation's focus on performance and accountability are likely to make independence less tenable for smaller and decentralized organizations and to increase the potential benefits to be gained through collaboration. However, as cases discussed in this chapter illustrate, there is also a need to ensure that relationships between and among organizations are well considered and that mission remains paramount. Those driven *exclusively* by financial considerations may find that the human and financial costs ultimately exceed the gains and that missions may be diluted or lost, to the detriment of the organizations and society.

CHAPTER SUMMARY

The number of nonprofits has increased in recent decades. In view of this, some have called for more collaboration among organizations to eliminate duplication of services and for mergers to reduce the number of competing nonprofits. Funders, including government bodies and foundations, have been visible among those calling for consolidation in the sector. However, some observers argue that funders have contributed to the problem and that small nonprofits may better provide more personal attention to clients.

Nonprofits may be driven to merge by external or internal drivers. External drivers may include pressure from funders, competition for resources, or the threat of regulation. Internal drivers include financial, managerial, and programmatic considerations.

There are no reliable data on the number of collaborations or mergers that have occurred, but collaboration is likely more common than merger.

Terminology in this area is unsettled. This book uses *collaboration* to encompass any relationship in which two or more organizations are working together toward common goals and *merger* to mean a combining of two or more organizations that includes a change in legal control. There are also *intramergers*, which are consolidations of chapters or units within a single legal entity. Collaboration is a continuum of relationships; it may include informal cooperation, such as sharing information and referring clients, or more formal relationships, in which the organizations are legally committed to each other, as in joint programs or joint ventures.

Obstacles to collaboration and merger include the distinctive motivations of nonprofit entities; organizational cultures that may be resistant to change; the egos of the individuals involved, especially founders; and the costs, in time and money, of the study, planning, and negotiations required. Successful collaborations and mergers are driven primarily by mission, rather than just financial benefits. Other conditions needed for success include support from the board and CEO, an appropriate process, trust, and relatedness. Relatedness means that there is a logic to the relationship based on mission, constituency, organization or structure, or geography. Various authors have described the process for considering collaboration or merger; although they use different terms, most include stages in which the organization examines itself, identifies potential partners, begins preliminary discussions with other organizations, conducts a side-by-side analysis of the two organizations, negotiates terms of the relationship, and implements the arrangement.

Some nonprofits have a single corporate charter, and local chapters are branches or offices of the national organization. In other cases, local chapters are independently chartered and pay dues to the national office for use of the charity's name and any services the national office may provide. For organizations that operate under a single charter, the merger of chapters, which are intramergers, nevertheless may face many of the same challenges as intermergers among independent nonprofits. It may be even more difficult to consolidate independent organizations that are part of a federation. A number of national organizations have established integrated, centralized databases for fundraising, but even this collaboration has sometimes met with resistance from local chapters that fear losing their relationships with donors to the national office.

Pressures to collaborate and merge are unlikely to abate as nonprofits face an increasingly competitive environment and there is a nationwide focus on performance and accountability. It is important that mission remain paramount and that such relationships not be based entirely on potential financial gains.

KEY TERMS AND CONCEPTS FROM CHAPTER 13

affiliation	*intramerger*
alliance	*intermerger*
collaboration	*integrated service network*
consortium	*merger*
drivers	*partnership*
federation	*restructuring*
franchise	*service organization*

QUESTIONS FOR DISCUSSION

1. How are McCormick's four categories of relatedness illustrated in the cases of the Milwaukee environmental organizations, the Milwaukee dental clinic, the Chicago cancer organizations, and the Second Harvest merger?

2. Review the principles of major gifts fundraising discussed in Chapter 10. How might a centralized database facilitate the practice of those principles?

3. In deciding whether to recognize the tax-exempt status of a new nonprofit, should the Internal Revenue Service consider whether or not it will duplicate the services of other, existing organizations in its community? Why or why not?

SUGGESTIONS FOR FURTHER READING RELATED TO CHAPTER 13

Books

La Piana, D., & Hyman, V. (2000). *The nonprofit mergers workbook: The leader's guide to considering, negotiating, and executing a merger.* St. Paul, MN: Amherst H. Wilder Foundation.

McCormick, D. H. (2001). *Nonprofit mergers: The power of successful partnerships.* Gaithersburg, MD: Aspen.

Web Sites

LaPiana Associates, Inc., www.lapiana.org

Stanford Project on the Evolution of Nonprofits (SPEN), www.gsb.stanford.edu/ csi/research/ spen.html

Advocacy and Lobbying

Within the lifetime of many people alive today, African American children were taught in schools segregated by law. Women could legally be denied jobs, barred from entire professions, and paid less than men simply because of their gender. Gay people were regularly fired from their jobs if their sexual orientation became known. People with physical disabilities were unable to access many public buildings, limiting their opportunities for employment and life experiences. Companies dumped raw sewage and industrial wastes into rivers with impunity. Highways were lined with ugly billboards and trash thrown from cars by un-seat-belted motorists. People could smoke in offices and other public places, and driving while drunk often was punishable by no more than a minor fine, even if it resulted in death. There remain many injustices, threats to the environment, diseases to be cured, and other problems to be solved. But over decades, new laws have been enacted to correct many of the intolerable situations mentioned above.

In virtually every instance, nonprofit organizations played an essential role by bringing the issue to the public's attention, influencing attitudes and building support for change, and lobbying for new laws. Indeed, nonprofits have been in the forefront of every important social change from the beginning of the nation. They have been the principal advocates for people who are disadvantaged or disenfranchised and for causes that initially concern only a minority of people. Nonprofits often have identified and given visibility to emerging issues and problems that ultimately became the focus of national attention and action.

Nonprofits may be found on every side of any issue, and they reflect all shades of opinion. There are organizations that advocate prolife positions and others that are prochoice. There are nonprofits that work to advance religious values and others that strive to protect the separation of Church and State. There are those whose mission is to promote sound government and there are those who seek to limit government's size and power. There are nonprofits that work toward economic and employment growth and others with a mission to preserve and protect the environment, historic structures, animals, and communities from the effects of commercial development. The public interest that is served by such diversity is the preservation of an uninhibited marketplace of ideas, allowing the free exchange of information and discussion that is believed to lead ultimately to sound public policy. Nonprofit advocacy and lobbying is thus a fundamental pillar of a democratic society.

However, various authors observe that most nonprofits do not engage in advocacy or lobbying. For example, Eisenberg observed in 2007 that "fewer than two percent of nonprofit organizations choose to exercise their legal right to influence legislation or lobby," and Smucker, writing in 2005, lamented that "many charities view lobbying as irrelevant to their mission, inappropriate, or even illegal" (p. 231). Research by Child and Grønbjerg (2007) also found that many nonprofits are ambivalent about advocacy and that only a relatively small number devote substantial resources to such efforts.

There are various reasons why so few nonprofits engage in lobbying. One obvious reason is that many lack the staff or resources, especially given the many demands of managing core service programs. Not surprisingly, larger national nonprofits are more likely to be directly involved in advocacy and lobbying than are smaller, local organizations, and such activity is more common among organizations in fields that are significantly regulated, such as health care (Child & Grønbjerg, 2007). Although small nonprofits may not conduct much lobbying on their own, they may belong to an association or coalition that represents their interests and issues at the state or national level. Such coalitions exist to serve specific groups of nonprofits, for example, higher education institutions, health care providers, and organizations concerned with homelessness.

Although research has indicated that nonprofits actually increase lobbying as government becomes a more predominant source of their revenue, concern about alienating government foundation funders is a barrier for some ("Executive Summary: Overview of Findings of Strengthening Nonprofit Advocacy Project," 2002). Nonprofits that are dependent on gifts from individuals also may be reluctant to take a position on issues that affect the organization but on which their donors hold different opinions. One interesting example occurred in 2003, when President George W. Bush recommended a permanent repeal of the estate tax. Although it was widely believed that a repeal would have a negative impact on charitable giving, some nonprofits were slow to oppose it. Some charged that their reluctance was based on the fact that many of their board members were affluent individuals who would be personally affected by the repeal and who thus supported the President's proposal.

One common conclusion about why nonprofits do not lobby more is that many nonprofit executives are simply unclear about what the law allows. They may decide to err on the side of caution by keeping their distance from the legislative process. As Berry, the director of a 2003 study, concluded, "Nonprofit organizations are excessively worried about losing their charity status. And that reflects a mis-understanding of how the law is enforced."

BASIC DISTINCTIONS

Let's start by clarifying three basic concepts and terms: *advocacy, lobbying,* and *political campaign activity.* Advocacy includes action taken in support of a cause or an idea. It may include, for example, providing education, distributing information, or holding events to dramatize an issue or the effects of a problem on people or a community. Advocacy is a basic right of every individual and organization and may be practiced without limit; it is an exercise of free speech protected by the U.S. Constitution (Hopkins, 2005, p. 226). Lobbying goes beyond advocacy—it is action taken to support or oppose specific legislation at the national, state, or local level. This could include, for example, contacting a Member of Congress, a state legislator, or a city councilperson to request his or her sponsorship or vote in favor or against a specific bill. It does not include contacting members of the executive branch, unless that individual is in a position to influence legislation.

Political campaign activity is action taken in support or opposition to specific candidates for office, including the publication or distribution of statements or printed materials. It does not include, however, conducting nonpartisan activities such as get-out-the-vote efforts or sponsoring a candidate debate or forum (Independent Sector, 2007). But the line may sometimes seem fuzzy, and there have been some controversial cases in recent years surrounding the involvement of nonprofits in political campaigns. We will come back to that issue for further discussion later in this chapter.

There is sometimes understandable confusion between what is advocacy and what is lobbying: Indeed, the former encompasses the latter. As Smucker (2005) explains, "Lobbying always includes advocacy but advocacy does not necessarily include lobbying" (p. 232).

For example, the marches, protests, and sit-ins of the civil rights movement were advocacy for equal rights, but they were not lobbying since they were not actions undertaken with the purpose of supporting or opposing any specific item of legislation. Once the Civil Rights Act of 1964 was up for consideration in Congress, many individuals and organizations contacted their elected representatives to urge a favorable vote. That activity was lobbying. The law defines lobbying quite precisely, including the identification of specific activities it does and does not include.

OVERVIEW OF LOBBYING LAW

As discussed in Chapter 1 of this book, organizations are tax-exempt under various sections of the IRS Code. Some of them, including 501 (c) (4) social welfare organizations, are permitted to engage in lobbying essentially without restriction (Hopkins, 2005, p. 226). As we also discussed earlier, some 501 (c) (3) organizations work with related 501 (c) (4) organizations: The Sierra Club was presented as an example in Chapter 1. Since space is limited and the law is complex, this chapter focuses on advocacy and lobbying by *charitable nonprofits,* that is, the 501 (c) (3) organizations that are both tax-exempt and eligible to receive tax-deductible contributions. Charitable nonprofits, including public charities and private foundations, face limitations on their lobbying activity and are prohibited from participating in political campaigns or endorsing or opposing candidates.

The reason that charitable nonprofits face restrictions on lobbying is directly related to the tax deductibility of gifts, which is viewed as a form of public subsidy given to the organization. In other words, the foregone tax revenue is regarded as public money. The purpose of the subsidy is to support an organization's charitable activities, and the law requires that its resources be used to pursue those purposes as its primary activity. Any lobbying it conducts must be "insubstantial" in relationship to its overall efforts to achieve its charitable mission (Hopkins, 2005, p. 226). But what is the meaning of *substantial* and *insubstantial,* and exactly what constitutes lobbying activity?

Prior to 1976, the meanings of *insubstantial* and *substantial* were unclear. IRS never defined the term and looked at each situation on a case-by-case basis. One of the problems was that the *substantial-part test* looked not only at how much a nonprofit spent on lobbying activity but also at how much time and effort was devoted to the activity. Some courts held that nonprofits were safe if they spent less than 5% on lobbying, but other courts said such an arbitrary standard was not appropriate. Thus, like a child whose parents just say "Don't wander too far," many nonprofits were unsure exactly how far they could safely go, that is, how much lobbying the IRS might find to be a substantial part of their activities. Some were inhibited from engaging in lobbying at all for fear of losing their tax-exempt status by crossing the fuzzy line.

In 1976, Congress passed Public Law 94–455 (the 1976 Lobby Law), which sought to clarify the situation. It took the IRS 14 years, until 1990, to issue sections 4911 and 501 of the Internal Revenue Code, describing how the law would be implemented. Since then, nonprofits have two options.

Option I: Substantial-Part Test

The first option is to continue to be covered by the substantial part test, essentially the same imprecise standard that applied before 1976. This may be a reasonable option for an organization that does not engage in lobbying or that does very little. If it is careful to differentiate lobbying from advocacy, it may find that it spends too little time or money on actual lobbying to be concerned about it. For example, the National Alliance to End Homelessness (2006) reports that many organizations affiliated with it chose to follow this standard. But this still leaves things vague and may not be a good choice for an organization that intends to engage in lobbying on a regular basis.

Option II: 501 (h) Expenditure Test

The second option, provided by the 1976 Lobby Law and subsequent IRS regulations, is for the nonprofit to file Form 5768 with the IRS, electing to be covered by the specific expenditure guidelines under Section 501 (h) of the Internal Revenue Code. Selecting this option offers a number of advantages. First, the limits do not consider the amount of time or effort devoted to lobbying—they are based entirely on how much the organization *spends* on lobbying activity, as a percentage of its total budget.[1] The standard is thus exact, and an organization can easily determine whether it is within or is approaching the limit. Second, it means that lobbying that does not involve expenditure is not limited at all. For example, if a volunteer calls on a Congressperson or a local legislator, that effort does not count unless the organization spends money to support it. If the organization reimburses the volunteer for his or her cab ride to the meeting, that expense would need to be included in its lobbying expense, but the volunteer's time would not. The 501 (h) option also presents fewer risks for nonprofits and their staff than does the substantial-part test. Nonprofits that may exceed the spending limits will not lose their tax exemption unless they exceed them by at least 150% averaged over a four-year period. And there are no penalties imposed on individual managers of an organization that exceeds the limit (see Table 14.1; Independent Sector, 2007; Minnesota Council on Nonprofits, 2006).

The spending limits are stated as a percentage of the nonprofit's total expenditures (on exempt activities), on a sliding scale depending on the size of the organization. There is an important distinction between the limit for *direct lobbying* and for *grassroots lobbying*. Direct

TABLE 14.1   Summary of Substantial-Part Test Compared With 501 (h) Election

	Nonprofit That Takes the 501(h) Election	*Nonprofit Subject to the "Substantial-Part" Test*
What's considered lobbying?	Clear definitions with specific exclusions for public policy activities that are not considered lobbying and therefore not subject to the spending limits	Not defined and no activities specifically excluded—therefore, a nonelecting nonprofit would need to track and account for all public policy activities
Spending limits	Generous and clear—20% of first $500,000 of "exempt purpose expenditures" with decreasing percentages up to a $1 million cap	Subjective and arbitrary—lobbying cannot be "substantial," but no established limits, and *substantial* is not defined
What's counted	Only count dollars spent—not volunteer and other cost-free activities	Count volunteer time as well as dollars spent
Record keeping and reporting	Document all lobbying expenses; report numbers only on annual Form 990A	Document all lobbying activities and expenses; provide detailed descriptions of the legislative activity and a classified schedule of the expenses paid or incurred on the annual Form 990A
Penalties for exceeding limits	Organization assessed a 25% excise tax on excess over limits in a year; no specific liability for officers/directors	Organization assessed a 5% excise tax on all lobbying expenses if "substantial lobbying" results in revocation; officers/directors subject to 5% if "substantial lobbying" deemed willful or unreasonably authorized
Revocation of tax exemption	Occurs only if lobbying exceeds 150% of limits generally averaged over four years	Could happen if "substantial lobbying" occurs in a single year
Risk of IRS audit	No greater risk of audit	No greater risk of audit

Source: Center for Lobbying in the Public Interest (2007).

lobbying includes any communication the organization has "with legislators or government officials who participate in the formulation of legislation or with its own members with regard to specific legislation and that expresses a view on it" (Minnesota Council on Nonprofits, 2006; Smucker, 2005, p. 240). Thus, it does not include communication with officials of the executive branch of government or communication that just provides information without expressing an opinion for or against the legislation. Grassroots lobbying refers to "any attempt to influence legislation by affecting the opinion of the general public" and that asks individuals to take action (Minnesota Council on Nonprofits, 2006; Smucker, 2005, p. 240). If the communication does not include a call to action, that is, does not ask people to do something to support or oppose the legislation, then it is not lobbying. The *general public* includes any individuals who are not members of the organization, but *members* is broadly defined. It includes donors to the organization as well as those who may be members in the formal sense of someone who pays dues in order to belong. Thus, if a nonprofit sends an e-mail to its donors urging them to contact their Congresspersons to support or oppose a bill, that expenditure comes under the limit for direct lobbying. But if it takes out an ad in the newspaper or hands out flyers on the corner urging members of the general public to do the same, that is grassroots lobbying, and any money expended in such an effort comes under a different, lower limit. (Again, if the communication does not specifically ask individuals to take action, it does not count as lobbying.)

There are other activities that also do not count as lobbying. For example, if the legislature asks the nonprofit for advice on a bill, responding to that request does not count. *Self-defense activity* does not count as lobbying. In other words, if the city council is about to pass an ordinance that would adversely affect the nonprofit, it may contact council members to oppose the legislation without having any expense involved count against its lobbying limit. However, pressing for legislation to support programs in the nonprofit's field, for example, a college lobbying for more scholarships, is not considered self-defense, and it would count as lobbying. Policy research organizations, such as the Brookings Institution or the American Enterprise Institute, may prepare reports that are nonpartisan and objective, and they will not count as lobbying efforts even if they recommend a specific course of action. Indeed, a nonprofit can discuss the need for legislation on some issue *generally* without it being considered lobbying, as long as it is not urging action on a *specific* bill. Thus, for example, a nonprofit concerned with child welfare may advocate stricter laws to protect children, and environmental organizations may generally call for better protection of wilderness areas; that is not lobbying unless it is directed at a specific item under consideration by the legislature (Smucker, 2005, pp. 242–243). In sum, the 1976 Lobby Law is quite generous in permitting nonprofit organizations to engage in lobbying. This is especially true if the distinction between what is lobbying and what is advocacy is carefully maintained since expenditures on the latter do not count against the limits at all.

Table 14.2 summarizes the expenditure limits on direct and grassroots lobbying for nonprofits of various sizes. An organization may spend only one fourth as much on grassroots lobbying as on direct lobbying, and there is an overall cap of $1 million. For example, if a nonprofit spent the maximum of $1 million on all of its lobbying and $250,000 of that was spent on grassroots efforts, it could spend the remaining $750,000 on direct lobbying (Minnesota Council on Nonprofits, 2006). The overall cap of $1 million would be encountered by a nonprofit with a budget of $17 million or more, but keep in mind that lobbying activity does not count against the limit if it does not involve the expenditure of money by the nonprofit. This limit is thus not that restrictive in terms of the amount of activity it allows.

Charitable nonprofits must report their lobbying expenses on Form 990. In addition, organizations that employ professional lobbyists and spend more than $24,500 on lobbying at the federal level must meet the requirements of the Lobbying Disclosure Act. This requires that they register and report their lobbying expenditures to Congress on a semi-annual basis (Independent Sector, 2007).

The rules discussed so far apply to nonprofits that are public charities. Private foundations face stricter limitations. They may not endorse or oppose legislation in communications with legislators or the general public if the communication includes a call to action. However, like public charities, they may provide technical advice to a legislature if asked to do so, provide nonpartisan analyses and studies, and lobby in self-defense. Like public charities, foundations are barred from participating in political campaigns. They can support nonpartisan activities such as candidate forums and get-out-the-vote drives, but they face strict regulation of their participation in voter registration drives (Independent Sector, 2007).

What if a private foundation makes grants to a nonprofit that comes under the more generous rules applied to public charities? Well, to start with, the foundation would not be permitted to *designate* a grant to support lobbying. That would be just an obvious end-run around the restrictions on its activity. But if the foundation provides unrestricted operating support to a public charity, there is nothing to prevent that organization from spending the money on lobbying activity. If a foundation makes a grant to support a nonprofit's program that has lobbying as one component of it, the lobbying is acceptable, but it must be paid for using funds from some other source, not with the foundation's grant funds

TABLE 14.2   Limits on Lobbying Expenditures

Total Expenditures on Exempt Purposes	Total Limit on Lobbying Expenditures	Limit on Expenditures for Grassroots Lobbying (25% of Total)
Up to $500,000	20% of exempt-purpose expenditures	5% of exempt-purpose expenditures
$500,000 to $1 million	$100,000 plus 15% of excess over $500,000	$25,000 plus 3.75% of excess over $500,000
$1 million to $1.5 million	$175,000 plus 10% of excess over $1 million	$43,750 plus 2.5% of excess over $1 million
$1.5 million to $17 million	$225,000 plus 5% of excess over $1.5 million	$56,250 plus 1.25% of excess over $1.5 million
Over $17 million	$1 million (overall maximum)	$250,000 (overall maximum)

Source: Center for Lobbying in the Public Interest (2007).

(Independent Sector, 2007). Since community foundations are public charities rather than private foundations, they can engage in lobbying up to the 501 (h) limits and can make grants to support lobbying by other nonprofits although such grants would count against the community foundation's own lobbying limit.

In addition to the basic provisions we have discussed in this chapter, nonprofits also must comply with various laws related to lobbying practice, which include, for example, restrictions on the participation of elected officials in charity events and on the way in which lobbyists can interact with legislators and their staff. In January, 2007, the 100th Congress amended House Rule 25 (called the *gift rule*), placing stricter limits on what gifts or privately supported travel members of the House of Representatives can accept from lobbyists. But the law is in a state of flux, and students with an interest in more details should check contemporary sources. The Web site of Independent Sector (www.independentsector.org) provides timely updates on recent legislation and policy actions and should be consulted for the latest information. Other Web sites listed as resources at the end of this chapter also track and report on recent changes in law with regard to lobbying, campaign finance, and other relevant areas.

Political Campaign Activity

Charitable nonprofits—including public charities and private foundations—are prohibited from engaging in campaigns and from endorsing candidates, either implicitly or explicitly. They may not coordinate their activities with those of a candidate or a campaign, contribute money or time to working for a candidate, or contribute the use of their facilities for a candidate or campaign (Independent Sector, 2007). But there have been some controversial cases that have highlighted the fine line between what is permissible advocacy and what is illegal involvement in electoral politics.

In the 2004 elections and again in 2006, the Internal Revenue Service (IRS) investigated activity by churches that allegedly had held events featuring a political candidate, distributed voter education guides that were favorable to a particular candidate, or engaged in other such activities (Schwinn, 2006a, 2006c). In one celebrated case, the IRS investigated the NAACP (National Association for the Advancement of Colored People) based on allegations that its president's remarks opposing the war in Iraq implied opposition to President Bush's re-election and thus violated the prohibition on political activity. Following a two-year investigation, it concluded that no violation had occurred (Jensen, 2006). Some expressed concern that the IRS's enforcement activity was inhibiting nonprofits, including churches, from legitimate advocacy activity, and others charged that the investigations were politically motivated (Jensen, 2006).

In June, 2007, the IRS released a Revenue Ruling (2007—41) to clarify the criteria by which it would determine what is and what is not illegal campaign involvement. The ruling included 21 hypothetical examples of activity and a discussion of why each does or does not constitute a violation of the law. But the area remains one of sometimes heated controversy. As the 2008 elections approached, some called for changing the law to permit nonprofits to become involved in partisan politics, while others argued that doing so would "set a dangerous precedent and cause nonprofit groups to lose one of their most important qualities—their independence from government and elected officials" (Egger, 2007; Eisenberg, 2007).

IMPLEMENTING AN ADVOCACY PROGRAM

Now that we have explored basic concepts and reviewed the law governing nonprofit advocacy, let's turn our attention to the practice of advocacy and lobbying. There is an extensive practitioner literature on lobbying; indeed, a 2007 search of amazon.com for *lobbying* identified over 46,000 results. However, various authors have developed manuals that offer guidance specifically to nonprofit organizations and take into consideration the unique requirements that apply to them. Some are listed as suggested additional reading at the end of this chapter. In addition, Web sites listed in this chapter also provide practical suggestions and guides, as well as links to other resources. Since the law changes from time to time, the Web sites are usually the best source of information. However, the techniques or tactics of lobbying are more consistent over time, and even some relatively dated but classic sources provide guidance that is still sound. That includes, for example, Bob Smucker's *Nonprofit Lobbying Guide* (Smucker, 1999), published in 1999 and still available in full text at the time of this writing at the Web sites of Independent Sector (www.independentsector.org) and the Center for Lobbying in the Public Interest (www.clpi.org), of which Smucker was a founder.

Various sources that advise nonprofits on developing an advocacy and lobbying effort offer many common points, including the following:

- Determine the reason for lobbying and how it advances the nonprofit's mission. *For a social welfare organization that exists for the purpose of changing public policy, the connection to the mission is obvious. A charitable nonprofit will need to consider how lobbying may advance its programs or the welfare of the constituents it serves and make strategic decisions about the emphasis to be given to lobbying in relationship to its service programs.*
- Understand the legislative process. *To lobby effectively, the organization needs to understand how legislation is considered, at the local, state, or national level— wherever its lobbying efforts will be focused. This includes knowledge of which committees play important roles and the stages in the process at which a lobbyist's intervention may be most helpful or persuasive.*
- Identify the sources of funds to be used for lobbying. *As discussed above, there are restrictions on the use of government or foundation funds, but unrestricted revenues from gifts, grants, or earned income may be used to fund a lobbying effort.*
- Undertake research to develop an understanding of the public policy issues related to the organization's mission and to obtain data needed to make the case with legislators. *Such information is available from, among others, policy research organizations, national charitable organizations with established public policy programs, and coalitions concerned with issues in particular areas. Approaching a legislator with facts is not only important to persuasion but may indeed be providing a real service to the legislator, whose time and staff may not be sufficient to undertake the depth of research that an interested nonprofit may offer.*
- Develop an infrastructure to support the lobbying program. *For an ongoing effort, this may require hiring staff or working with a professional lobbying firm, but smaller efforts may be managed by an existing staff member as a part-time*

assignment. An information system may be needed to track the progress of legislation and calls or visits with legislators. Managing a lobbying program has many of the same requirements as fundraising management since it involves developing and maintaining relationships, and undertaking contacts, in a systematic manner.

- *Inventory existing relationships and identify decision makers. A nonprofit may have many existing relationships in its community, through staff, members of the board, or other friends, who may in turn know key decision makers in the relevant legislature. They may be effective ambassadors who can be armed with information to deliver the nonprofit's messages to those decision makers, or they may help open the door to communications and visits by the nonprofit's CEO.*

- *Use a strategic mix of tactics. Direct lobbying with legislators may be the centerpiece of a lobbying program, but such efforts are more effective if they are used in conjunction with grassroots lobbying to influence and mobilize the community's opinions and with a media relations program to gain wider visibility for the issues. The latter may include developing relationships with reporters who may have an interest in writing articles about the issue as well as paid advertising, op-eds, and letters to the editor written by the nonprofit's CEO or volunteers. Walks, runs, marches, and demonstrations also are available tactics for drawing attention to a cause (Center for Lobbying in the Public Interest, 2007; Hessenius, 2007).*

The tools used for lobbying vary depending on whether the effort is grassroots or direct lobbying. Grassroots lobbying engages many of the principles and techniques of marketing that were discussed in Chapter 9. Direct lobbying also may use those tools as well as personal visits with legislators and their staff members. Both approaches use various communications vehicles, including letters, phone calls, faxes, petitions, and e-mails. The Internet offers great advantages to nonprofits in developing coalitions and constituencies as well as for contacting legislators. However, because e-mails are so easy to send and thus can arrive in volume, some legislative staff have come to ignore them or to prevail on organizations to cease such efforts. Ironically, because e-mail has become so common and voluminous, the old technology of regular mail sometimes may be more effective. A letter, especially if written by a constituent of the legislator, signifies that the individual cares enough to have taken the time to write, rather than tap out a quick e-mail or text message. Letters from clients of a nonprofit also may have an impact on the legislator and even gain the attention of the news media. However, form letters that make it obvious they have been solicited by the nonprofit or a professional lobbyist have less credibility than those that appear to genuinely express the views of an individual (Hessenius, 2007, pp. 164–166). As in fundraising, there is no tool more powerful than the personal visit by an individual or group of individuals to a legislator or a member of his or her staff who is in a position to influence what information and data the legislator receives.

TRENDS AND ISSUES

For nonprofits that are social welfare organizations, advocacy and lobbying are, of course, the essence of the mission. But despite the encouragement of some authors and organizations that promote more lobbying by charitable nonprofits—advocacy advocates, as it were—many remain understandably cautious. And nonprofit advocacy is likely to remain somewhat controversial.

Although the law allows considerable latitude for nonprofits to engage in advocacy and lobbying, there have been periodic efforts to constrain them further. One notable example was the *Istook Amendment*, introduced in 1995 by Representative Ernest Istook. The amendment would have restricted lobbying by nonprofits that receive federal funds, even with regard to their use of nonfederal funds. Although it did not pass into law, the amendment reflected a line of thinking that has been manifested in other such attempts, at both the federal and state levels (Grønbjerg and Salamon, 2002, pp. 464–465).

In 2006, the professional Washington lobbyist Jack Abramoff pleaded guilty to various felony counts growing out of his activities. Among other abuses, Abramoff had created nonprofit organizations, including one called the Capital Athletic Foundation, which he had used largely to pay for such things as golf trips for legislators and to influence the awarding of government contracts to his corporate clients (Cohen, 2006). His activities reflected not so much abuses by the nonprofit sector itself as abuses of nonprofit tax law by an individual with personal and political motives. Nevertheless, the episode connected the words *abuse, lobbyist,* and *nonprofit* in one story line and negatively affected public attitudes about the sector. In the politically charged and polarized environment of the 2000s, nonprofits are likely to face continued scrutiny and skepticism with regard to their lobbying activity.

As mentioned earlier in this chapter, some observers have called for increased involvement by nonprofits in electoral politics. For example, Hessenius writes that "nonprofits have traditionally played 'softball,' and now need to graduate to playing 'hardball' if they want to succeed" (p. 12). He accuses nonprofits of being naive in believing that making a credible case based on evidence is sufficient to obtain legislative action, when in reality "for the most part, decisions are made as a balance between competing interests, with no 'right' or 'wrong' position, and almost always in consideration of the *political* realities impacting the chances for election or reelection" (p. 7).

Although charitable nonprofits cannot engage directly in campaign activity or make contributions to candidates, Hessenius outlines a strategy for their becoming involved. He recommends that charitable nonprofits create *political action committees* and *527 funds,* tax exempt organizations that can endorse and support political candidates. He also advocates that the legal restrictions on 501 (c) (3) political involvement be changed to follow the same rules that currently apply to corporations (Hessenius, 2007).

Others regard such recommendations with alarm. For example, writing in the *Chronicle of Philanthropy,* Pablo Eisenberg offers a strong warning:

> Charities and foundations intelligently realize that staying away from direct political involvement is the price they must pay for continuing to be exempt from taxation and supported by tax-deductible gifts.
>
> Taxpayers will not tolerate subsidizing contributions to charities that are involved in partisan political activities, nor will Congress permit nonprofit groups to overstep the boundaries it has drawn to separate charities from political activity. The politicization of nonprofit organizations would be political suicide. (Eisenberg, 2007)

As Eisenberg notes, existing law provides charitable nonprofits with considerable freedom to influence public policy, while evidence suggests that relatively few attempt to do so. The need may not be for fewer restrictions but rather for nonprofits to more fully use the opportunities that already exist, provided, of course, that they have determined lobbying to be a useful strategy in pursuit of their charitable missions. For charitable nonprofits to go beyond allowable lobbying to endorse and oppose political candidates, even through the use of related organizations permitted to do so, could introduce real risk. The nonprofit sector could lose its special status in the attitudes of the public, leading perhaps eventually to the loss of its favored position under tax law.

CHAPTER SUMMARY

Advocacy by nonprofits has played an important role in the most significant social changes throughout the nation's history, including the civil rights movement, the expansion of women's freedom, and the environment. Nonprofits advocate on every side of every issue, and their advocacy and lobbying is thus a fundamental pillar of a democratic society. However, various studies have found that only a small percentage of charitable nonprofits engage in advocacy or lobbying. Some are hesitant to do so for various reasons, including lack of staff and resources, concern about alienating private or government funders, and misunderstanding of what the law permits them to do without jeopardizing their nonprofit status.

Advocacy includes action taken in support of a cause or an idea. It may include, for example, providing education, distributing information, or holding events to dramatize an issue or the effects of a problem on people or a community. Advocacy is a basic right of every individual and organization and may be practiced without limit—it is an exercise of free speech protected by the U.S. Constitution. Lobbying goes beyond advocacy—it is action taken to support or oppose specific legislation at the national, state, or local level. Advocacy is the larger concept, which encompasses lobbying.

Some nonprofits—for example, 501 (c) (4) social welfare organizations—are permitted to lobby without limitation but are not eligible to receive tax-deductible gifts. Because they can receive such gifts, which are a form of public subsidy, charitable nonprofits exempt under Section 501 (c) (3) face limitations on their lobbying activity. There are two standards under which a charitable nonprofit can determine the amount of permissible lobbying. The substantial-part test was the standard that existed prior to the 1976 Lobby Law, and organizations can still choose to be subject to it. However, *substantial part* applies to both time and expenditures, and it is not precisely defined.

The other option is to elect the expenditure test provided under Section 501 (h) of the Internal Revenue Code. That section establishes a specific percentage of total qualified expenditures that nonprofits of various sizes can spend on lobbying, with an overall cap of $1 million. This option also distinguishes between direct lobbying and grassroots. A lower limit applies to grassroots activities that attempt to influence the public's attitudes and that include a call to action in support of or opposition to specific legislation. It also identifies specific activities—for example, self–defense—that do not count as lobbying. The expenditure test does not consider activities of volunteers or other efforts that do not involve expenditures. It is thus relatively generous in the amount of lobbying that it permits nonprofits to undertake.

Private foundations are not permitted to lobby or to make grants to other nonprofits designated for support of lobbying. Foundation grants to public charities that are unrestricted operating support may be used for lobbying by the charity within its allowable limit. Since community foundations are public charities, they may make grants to other nonprofits for lobbying purposes, but they count against the foundation's lobbying limit.

Charitable nonprofits may not participate in political campaigns or endorse candidates. There have been recent cases in which the IRS investigated reports that churches and other nonprofits may have violated this prohibition, and some violators were punished by having their tax exempt status removed. The line can be a fuzzy one in situations where one candidate is closely identified with a particular position that a nonprofit opposes.

There are many guides to the practice of lobbying. Most practitioner guides emphasize linking the activity to the nonprofit's mission; understanding the legislative process; identifying sources of permissible funds to support lobbying; developing an infrastructure of staff and systems to support the lobbying effort; conducting research to identify public policy issues and gathering facts needed to make the organization's case; conducting an inventory of friends and identifying their relationships with key legislators; and developing a strategic mix of tactics to be employed. Some tools include letters, e-mails, media coverage, events, and personal visits with legislators and their staff members.

Although nonprofits have considerable freedom to engage in advocacy and lobbying, there have been attempts in recent years to impose more restrictions. Recent scandals involving the abuse of tax exemption by professional lobbyists have affected public attitudes. Nonprofits' advocacy and lobbying are likely to remain under scrutiny. Some call for removing the restrictions that prohibit nonprofits from participating in electoral politics, but others warn that doing so would undermine public support for tax exemption and result in harmful politicization of the sector.

NOTE

1. Specifically, its expenditures on exempt activity, which excludes fundraising and certain administrative expenses.

KEY TERMS AND CONCEPTS FROM CHAPTER 14

501 (h) election   *Istook Amendment*
527 funds   *lobbying*
advocacy   *political campaign activity*
direct lobbying   *political action committees (PACs)*
gift rule   *self-defense activity*
grassroots lobbying   *substantial-part test*

QUESTIONS FOR DISCUSSION

1. Although it is legal, as discussed in this chapter, some people feel that lobbying by charitable nonprofits is inappropriate and runs the risk of tarnishing the sector's image, possibly leading to reduced philanthropic support. Do you agree, or do you disagree? Why?

2. In 2004, the Boston Foundation and other nonprofits made gifts to help sponsor the National Democratic Convention, which was held in that city. The Foundation explained that its intention was to advance economic development in the city, that its funds would not be used for political activities, and that the convention would create work for "the working poor, immigrants, and minorities . . . that historically are of special concern to the foundation." It said it would have done the same for the National Republican Convention and had no political motivation. But some criticized the Foundation's actions, saying that it set a bad precedent by getting too close to politics and that the money might better have been spent on other programs to benefit the community. Do you agree, or do you disagree? Why? (Based on Eisenberg, 2003)

3. Should the law be changed to permit charitable nonprofits to endorse or oppose political candidates and provide financial support to political campaigns? Why or why not?

4. The Internal Revenue Code states as follows:

    Organizations that are exempt from income tax under section 501 (a) of the Internal Revenue Code as organizations described in section 501 (c) (3) may not participate in, or intervene in (including the publishing or distributing of statements), any political campaign on behalf of (or in opposition to) any candidate for public office.

    Each of the following hypothetical cases is based on examples from IRS Revenue Ruling 2007—41, released June 18, 2007. In each case, do you think the organization described violated the law? You can check your answer against the IRS's opinion by looking at Revenue Ruling 2007—41 on the IRS Web site (www.irs.gov/irb/2007-25_irb/ar09.html).

    *   *Organization B, a 501 (c) (3) organization that promotes community involvement, sets up a booth at the state fair where citizens can register to vote. The signs and banners in and around the booth give only the name of the organization, the date of the next upcoming statewide election, and notice of the opportunity to register. No reference to any candidate or political party is made by the volunteers staffing the booth or in the materials available at the booth, other than the official voter registration forms that allow registrants to select a party affiliation.*

    *   *Organization C is a 501 (c) (3) organization that educates the public on environmental issues. Candidate G is running for the state legislature, and an important element of her platform is challenging the environmental policies of*

the incumbent. Shortly before the election, Organization C sets up a telephone bank to call registered voters in the district in which Candidate G is seeking election. In the phone conversations, Organization C's caller tells the voter about the importance of environmental issues and asks questions about the voter's views on these issues. If the voter appears to agree with the incumbent's position, Organization C's representative thanks the voter and ends the call. If the voter appears to agree with Candidate G's position, then the caller reminds the voter about the upcoming election, stresses the importance of voting in the election, and offers to provide transportation to the polls.

- *Mr. D is the board chair of Organization M, a 501 (c) (3) nonprofit that educates the public on conservation issues. During a regular meeting of the organization shortly before the election, Mr. D spoke on a number of issues, including the importance of voting in the upcoming election, and concluded by saying, "It is important that you all do your duty in the election and vote for Candidate W."*

- *Ms. E is president of Society N, a historical society that is a 501 (c) (3) organization. In the month prior to the election, President E invites the three Congressional candidates for the district in which Society N is located to address the members, one each at a regular meeting held on three consecutive weeks. Each candidate is given an equal opportunity to address and field questions on a wide variety of topics from the members. Society N's publicity announcing the dates for each of the candidate's speeches and President E's introduction of each candidate include no comments on their qualifications or any indication of a preference for any candidate.*

- *Minister F is the minister of Church Q, a 501 (c) (3) nonprofit. The Sunday before the November election, Minister F invites Senate Candidate X to preach to her congregation during worship services. During his remarks, Candidate X states, "I am asking not only for your votes but for your enthusiasm and dedication, for your willingness to go the extra mile to get a very large turnout on Tuesday." Minister F invites no other candidate to address her congregation during the senatorial campaign.*

SUGGESTIONS FOR FURTHER READING RELATED TO CHAPTER 14

Books

Avner, M. (2001). *The lobbying and advocacy handbook for nonprofit organizations: Shaping public policy at the state and local level.* Saint Paul, MN: Amherst H. Wilder Foundation.

Boris, E. T., & Steuerle, C. E. (Eds.). (2006). *Nonprofits and government: Collaboration and conflict* (2nd ed.). Washington, DC: Urban Institute Press.

Hessenius, B. (2007). *Hardball lobbying for nonprofits: Real advocacy for nonprofits in the new century.* New York: Palgrave/Macmillan.

Richan, W. C. (2006). *Lobbying for social change.* New York: Haworth Press.

Smucker, B. (1999). *The nonprofit lobbying guide* (2nd ed.). Washington, DC: Independent Sector. (Full text available at www.independentsector.org)

Web Sites

Center for Lobbying in the Public Interest, www.clpi.org

Independent Sector, www.independentsector.org

Internal Revenue Service, www.irs.gov

MB Watch, http://ombwatch.org

NPAction, www.npaction.org

Urban Institute, http://urban.org

The International Perspective

$\mathbf{A}$ century ago, an increasing number of people were employed in industrial settings, including factories and mines, but most people still lived and worked on farms or in small communities. Travel was expensive, and communication was slow. The Wright Brothers' first flight had just occurred in 1903, and the majority of American homes would not have electricity until 1930. Television, the Internet, and space travel were still decades in the future.

Events in other parts of the world had little impact on most Americans' lives and, indeed, seldom intruded on their thinking, which was focused on the communities in which they lived and worked. Philanthropy included giving to one's church and an occasional campaign to build a new fire house, hospital, or school. The greatest threats to human health included common diseases for which there were yet no cures: The life expectancy for Americans at birth was less than 50 years (www.healthsentinel.com/graphs.php?id = 41&event = graphs_print_list_item, accessed July 16, 2007).

Over the past 100 years the pace and magnitude of change have been staggering. Consider just three events that illustrate the realities of the world now:

- In December 26, 2004, a massive tsunami struck South Asia, killing over 200,000 people and leaving millions of others endangered. The response was immediate and worldwide. More than 40 organizations, including the Red Cross, Catholic Relief Services, and Save the Children, moved into action, some to provide immediate relief and others to provide longer-term assistance for rebuilding. Individuals, foundations, and corporations in the United States alone gave over $3 billion to support such efforts. Individual donors, about 25% of all American households, provided $2.8 billion of the total, in gifts averaging $50 each, many of them made online (www.philanthropy.com/premium/articles/v19/i06/ 06002801.htm, accessed July 13, 2007).

- On May 28, 2007, health authorities ordered an American man to be isolated to prevent the spread of a form of tuberculosis that was believed to be resistant to medication. The Center for Disease Control rushed to find people with whom he had been in contact as he flew from Atlanta to Paris on Air France and then on Czech Air from Prague to Montreal before he drove back to New York and was returned to Atlanta on a CDC plane (www.reuters.com/article/wtMostRead/idUSN2934397420070529, accessed July 13, 2007).

• On July 8, 2007 (not coincidentally 7-8-07), Boeing unveiled its new 787 Dreamliner, a state-of-the-art airplane expected to be in flight by 2008. Hundreds of planes had already been ordered by airlines across the world, but Boeing's customers were not the only international aspect to the announcement. Although the plane would be assembled in the United States, Boeing announced that it would be built with parts from 43 suppliers, located in 135 sites around the world (www.boeing.com/commercial/787family/background.html, accessed July 13, 2007).

Today, the greatest threats facing humanity, including disease, terrorism, climate change, and natural disasters, are ones that cannot be confined within national boundaries nor isolated by the oceans that separate the continents. Instant communications and frequent travel transmit ideas, images, news, even diseases, as rapidly as people a century ago could cross the town squares of their small communities. At the same time, the greatest opportunities for technological and economic advancement lie in cooperative efforts that engage people, and minds, across the globe. Philanthropy, once primarily an American phenomenon, now flows in significant amounts across the world, and a gift requires only the click of a mouse to complete. While the nonprofit sector in the United States remains the largest and philanthropy on a large scale remains predominantly an American phenomenon, similar organizations are increasing in number and importance in many nations and on a global basis and are increasingly turning to fundraising in the American style.

Why has the world become smaller? And why have nonprofit organizations come to play an important role on the world stage? The answer lies in advances in communication technology as well as changes in political, cultural, and economic realities. One reason was the end of the Cold War and the spread of a democratic and capitalist philosophy across the globe. This change removed political barriers to economic interaction and to nonprofit organizations, which had often been viewed as threats by repressive governments. The establishment of free-trade areas and organizations in the 1990s, including the World Trade Organization, the European Union, and the North American Free Trade Agreement, led to greater economic integration across national boundaries (Thomas, 2002, p. 4). At the same time, the movement to devolution of government services and outsourcing to the private sector that has occurred in the United States has also been seen in other nations, which have sought to lower tax rates in order to encourage economic and business growth. As in the United States, private organizations have been called on to replace services previously provided through government programs and to seek financial support from the private sector, leading to the growth of fundraising as a worldwide profession. This new philosophy also has been reflected in the management of international aid programs, with governments preferring to deliver assistance through private organizations rather than directly (Anheier & Themudo, 2005, p. 115).

Among the most powerful forces for change has been technology. The development of the Internet, the Web, satellite communications, and fiber optic cable has made global communication instantaneous. It has driven international economic competition in a "flat" world, in which national borders prevent no barrier to entry into the mainstream of business life (Friedman, 2006). And it has been raising the awareness of people in developed nations about the needs of others on the planet, stimulating unprecedented global responses to humanitarian needs.

The pace of globalization appears to be accelerating, presenting all of American society with significant challenges. Those who will live their lives—and manage nonprofit organizations—in the balance of the 21st century will need to understand, accept, and be prepared to work with different mindsets and different skills than have ever been required before.

DEFINITIONS AND SCOPE OF INTERNATIONAL ORGANIZATIONS

As within the nonprofit sector in the United States, the terminology used to discuss organizations across the world is inconsistent and often confusing. The term *nonprofit organization* is not widely used in the international environment, although there are organizations in many countries that fit the definitions of *nonprofit* that were considered in Chapter 1. Although the term has different meanings in different parts of the world, what we call a nonprofit in the United States is elsewhere most commonly referred to as a *nongovernmental organization* (or NGO). The term has its origins in the United Nations system, and, indeed, the UN has formal consultative relationships with many such organizations engaged in economic development activity (UN Web site, www.un.org/issues/civilsociety/partnerships. asp, accessed July 16, 2007).

There are NGOs that engage in activities within one country that are similar to U.S. nonprofits in their essential characteristics, although they vary widely in the legal frameworks within which they exist, the sources of their funding, and especially their relationships with government. Some organizations are indeed operated by government and are known by the acronym GONGOs—*government-operated nongovernmental organizations*. There is no concept quite like the "nonprofit sector" in most parts of the world. Some scholars refer to the collection of such organizations as the "civil society sector" (Salamon & Sokolowski, 2004, p. 11).

The best-known NGOs are the *international nongovernmental organizations* (or INGOs). They are organizations that have activities not confined to a single country. They "make significant operating expenditures across national borders and do not identify themselves as domestic actors" [within one nation] (Anheier & Themudo, 2005, p. 102). They are sometimes said to be *transnational* because, as the term implies, they "organize . . . in pursuit of goals and purposes that transcend the boundaries of national territories and state jurisdictions" (Boli, 2006) Until recent decades, most INGOs were based in the United States or Western Europe, but they are now more diffused around the world (Anheier & Themudo, 2005). INGOs include the large brand name organizations that most people know, including, for example, the Red Cross, Oxfam, Friends of the Earth, Greenpeace, Amnesty International, CARE International, Save the Children, and CARE.

Some INGOs were created as global organizations from the beginning. For example, CIVICUS, an international alliance that works to strengthen civil society around the world, was founded in 1993 with a multinational board—it was global from the beginning both in its purposes and governance (Koenig, 2004, p. 124). Other INGOs are organizations that started out in one country and then over time developed into international or global organizations, following one of various paths. Some grew by opening offices or branches in other countries— that is, they *internationalized*, while others are federations or alliances of nationally based nonprofits that have banded together to pursue a common mission or cause.

Koenig (2004) describes a continuum along which some nonprofits have evolved. They start as local organizations with local interests. Then they begin to develop an international awareness, perhaps including international topics in their conferences and published materials. They may then move along to develop some international programs, possibly hosting conferences attended by people from around the world or publishing materials in various languages. At this point along the continuum, they have started to become *international organizations*. At a later point in their evolution, such organizations may begin to admit international members, open offices or form chapters in other countries, and enter alliances or partnerships with organizations in other nations. Finally, some ultimately may evolve into *global organizations* "with members, programs, or operations in many different regions around the world and having a multinational board of directors or other decision-making group" (Koenig, 2004, p. 5).

It is important to clarify and emphasize the distinction between organizations that are *international* and those that are *global,* especially since the terms are sometimes used interchangeably. An international organization is somewhere along Koenig's continuum: It may have some programs in other countries, but it is governed within and maintains a focus on its home country. A global organization is one that has activities throughout the world and that probably has a governance structure that places decision making in the hands of individuals from multiple countries. Today, most American national nonprofits are at least international. The large brand name INGOs are global organizations.

INGOs have grown in number, especially within recent decades. The *Yearbook of International Organizations*, published by the Union of International Associations, shows that the number of such organizations increased from fewer than 10,000 in 1981 to more than 25,000 in 2000 (Boli, 2006, p. 334). The INGOs are often large and visible, but it is a more complex challenge to track NGOs within various countries around the world. There is no single source of comprehensive data, although research interest has increased in recent years. One of the most ambitious efforts, begun in 1991, is the Johns Hopkins Comparative Nonprofit Sector Project, a collaborative investigation led by Lester Salamon at Johns Hopkins and including 150 researchers across the world. By 2004, the project had produced "52 books, more than 250 published articles, and hundreds of working papers, country reports, and presentations" (Salamon & Sokolowski, 2004, p. xxi). The first phase of work examined NGOs in 22 countries in Europe, Asia, North America, and Latin America, with later research adding data on organizations in an additional 14 countries in Africa, the Middle East, and South Asia. In addition to collecting and analyzing an abundance of data on the characteristics, revenues, and activities of such organizations, the project developed an *International Classification of Nonprofit Organizations*, which identifies 12 categories of organizations based on their activities, and a *global civil society index* to summarize data and "gauge the progress of civil society development among countries" (Salamon & Sokolowski, p. 4).

Like nonprofits in the United States, NGOs in other nations engage in a variety of activities. According to the Johns Hopkins project research, the largest number provide services, including education and social services. Another significant percentage are engaged in what Salamon and Sokolowski call "expressive functions," including arts, culture, recreation, and professional associations. Others are advocacy organizations that bring social and human problems to public attention and work for change—for example, to protect human rights, preserve the environment, and other goals (Salamon & Sokolowski, 2004).

The World Bank divides INGOs into two basic types: *operational NGOs* and *advocacy INGOs*. Advocacy INGOs are organizations that promote a cause or issue on a multinational basis. In the World Bank's definition, operational INGOs are those whose primary purpose is to design and implement economic development projects. However, the mission of other INGOs that also operate programs, for example the Red Cross, is to provide immediate and short-term relief from human suffering, rather than support economic or infrastructure development over the long run. The latter distinction is analogous to the differences between charity and philanthropy that we discussed earlier in this book. Many development INGOs working in partnership with the UN and the World Bank, are focused on accomplishment of the *UN Millennium Development Goals*, adopted by world leaders in 2000. They include specific targets for the reduction of poverty, disease, illiteracy, environmental degradation, and discrimination against women to be achieved by 2015 (United Nations, 2000). Most efforts in pursuit of these goals are funded by governments, although, as we will discuss below, philanthropy has begun to play a larger role.

INTERNATIONAL PHILANTHROPY AND FUNDRAISING

In this section, we will consider patterns of international philanthropy, which predominantly consists of gifts and grants from American and Western European donors to support organizations or activities affecting other regions. We will also look at the growth of organized fundraising efforts by NGOs around the world, which are increasingly adopting and adapting techniques developed by nonprofits in the United States.

As measured by the Center for Philanthropy at Indiana University and reported by the Giving USA Foundation, American philanthropy directed to international programs and purposes grew at an average annual rate of 16.3% between 1987 and 2006 and totaled an estimated $11.34 billion in 2006. The 2006 amount represented a decline over the 2005 total, the first in many years, and reflected the unusual upsurge of gifts in 2005 in response to the 2004 South Asia tsunami (Center on Philanthropy at Indiana University, 2007). The estimates are likely understated. For example, they do not include funds spent on international activities by U.S.-based nonprofits in fields such as education, health care, arts and culture, youth development, and religion, which are reported in other categories; they do not capture all foundation and corporate giving; and they do not include gifts that individuals made to organizations based in other countries that are not chartered in the United States. Unless the recipient organization is registered in the United States, the donor cannot claim a tax deduction for the gift. Some organizations headquartered abroad establish U.S.-based nonprofits, often called a "foundation" or "friends-of" in order to qualify to receive deductible gifts from U.S. citizens. Gifts to those organizations could be captured in the Giving USA totals, but gifts that Americans make directly to organizations abroad could not be, since the estimates are based on tax data.

Giving USA data also do not include the substantial payments made by recent immigrants to the United States who send funds directly to their home countries to support either families or projects. Since 2006, the Hudson Institute has published an *Index of Global Philanthropy*, in which it does estimate such payments, which are called *remittances* rather than gifts. Hudson reports a total of $61.7 billion in such payments from immigrant

U.S. residents in 2005, with the largest portion going to countries in Latin America (Hudson Institute, 2007, p. 23). Hudson's index also estimates international giving by corporations, foundations, and individuals in European nations, but the data are more difficult to track, in part because not all countries grant a tax deduction for charitable giving. Hudson's totals may be overstated since they are used to support the argument that private giving is preferable to and more efficient than government aid.

Global poverty and health have become the focus of a growing number of substantial gifts. The largest U.S. foundation, the Bill and Melinda Gates Foundation, is primarily concerned with global health and gave more than $1.3 billion for international programs in 2005. Warren Buffet's pledge of $31 billion to the Gates Foundation will, of course, increase the foundation's contributions to its international programs in the years ahead (Perry & Wilhelm, 2006). Other high-profile donors also have turned their attention to global concerns. For example, in 2006, David Rockefeller announced a bequest of $225 million to address poverty, health care, sustainable development, and other purposes; George Soros gave $50 million to the Millennium Villages program to reduce poverty in Africa; various donors gave a total of $2.1 billion to the William J. Clinton Foundation, focused on global needs; and Bono began a cause-related marketing effort, called "RED" to raise grassroots support to fight AIDS (Center on Philanthropy at Indiana University, 2007, pp. 177–178).

Dr. Muhammed Yunus, the founder of Grameen Bank, received the Nobel Peace Prize in 2006, drawing attention to the role of microcredit as a strategy for reducing poverty. Microfinance institutions provide small loans to entrepreneurs in developing countries who could otherwise not qualify for credit, helping them to start and sustain businesses. The microfinance approach has attracted an increasing number of philanthropic investments, including $103 million given in 2005 by Pierre and Pam Omidyar, the founders of EBay, $14.97 million from the Gates Foundation in 2006, and more than $1 million in computers given by the Chinese computer firm Lenovo in 2006 (Center on Philanthropy at Indiana University, 2007, pp. 176–177).

Global Fundraising

At the same time that international giving from the United States has increased, NGOs in many parts of the world have been required to pursue new sources of revenue. For example, governments in many nations have reduced funding for higher-education institutions, forcing them to institute or increase tuition charges and to look to U.S.-style fundraising for their future growth. Nonprofits in other fields, facing limited resources and growing needs, also have adopted and adapted the techniques of organized fundraising.

Fundraising and philanthropy face obstacles in many nations. First, philanthropy requires the presence of surplus income or wealth, which does not exist within many nations. It is illogical to assume that a country in which most individuals are desperately poor will be able to generate a level of giving that can sustain the growth of local organizations sufficient to have an impact on the country's overwhelming problems, and the competition for international giving is difficult for small organizations without internationally recognized brand names. Second, while most religions and cultures include expectations of altruistic behavior beyond one's family, not all cultures support organized fundraising or voluntarism on the U.S. model (Wagner, 2005). For example, in some cultures, it would be deemed inappropriate to ask another for funds to support an organization of whose board the solicitor served. In other countries, for example states of the former Soviet Union, the idea of prospect research might find a negative reaction, seeming too much like the files that the KGB maintained on its citizens (Wagner, 2005, p. 10).

In addition to cultural barriers, few national tax systems include benefits for giving as generous as those available to donors in the United States. Some Western European countries, including the United Kingdom and France, have greatly increased incentives for charitable giving in recent years, and as of 2007 the European Union (EU) was discussing the possibility of a uniform system. But some EU countries, including Austria, Sweden, and Finland, offer no tax deductions for giving at all (Hudson Institute, 2007, p. 29).

There are also technical obstacles to the implementation of U.S.-style fundraising techniques; for example, telephone and mail systems may not support sophisticated telemarketing or direct mail solicitation, and some countries have low rates of connectivity to the Internet. However, the Internet has greatly increased the ability of NGOs to reach potential donors on a global basis at minimal cost. Although obstacles remain, there have been recent examples of highly successful U.S.-style campaigns in other nations, and a tradition of philanthropy appears to be developing in some nations. For example, the Univerisidad de Monterrey in Mexico launched its first campaign in 1995 and by 2000 had raised $27.5 million against a $25 million goal. Sixty percent of the gifts were secured from donors who had never made such gifts before (Wagner & Galindo, 2004, p. 15).

As discussed in previous chapters, fundraising as a professional field has emerged in the United States primarily over the past 30 years and more recently internationally. Fundraising professional associations, like the Association of Fundraising Professionals in the United States, have developed in a number of countries, and some have relationships with AFP and the Fund Raising School, part of the Center on Philanthropy at Indiana University. The Mexican Center for Philanthropy (Centro Mexicano para la Filatropía) was founded in 1988 and provides fundraising courses, conducts research, and fosters voluntary service. AFP chapters were established in Mexico City in 1993, in Puerto Rico in 1999, and in Monterrey and Baja California in 2001. Similar organizations also were established in Argentina and Brazil during the 1990s (Viesca-Sada, 2004; Yoffe & Brunetti, 2004). The Council for Advancement and Support of Education opened a London office in 1994, and by 2007, its membership included more than 200 higher-education institutions in the United Kingdom, Ireland, and continental Europe. A Singapore office was opened in 2007 (www.case.org, accessed July 16, 2007).

INTERNATIONAL NONPROFIT GOVERNANCE AND MANAGEMENT

Managing an international or global organization combines the complexities of nonprofit management that have been discussed throughout this book with the additional challenges of working across legal systems, languages, cultures, and geographic distances. Indeed, a full discussion of international NGO management could easily follow the same sequence of chapters as that of this book and identify unique considerations of international management related to virtually every topic—governance, leadership, accountability, staff and volunteer management, fundraising, communications and marketing, and so forth. Many of the pressures facing nonprofit organizations in the United States—including growing needs for services amidst declining government support, calls for strengthened governance and accountability, and the need to balance commitment to mission with competition for resources—are all present in the international environment. Thus, with globalization, "international managers [both in business and NGOs] face an external environment more complex, more dynamic, more uncertain, and more competitive than ever before" (Thomas, 2002, p. 10). Space does not permit a full discussion of all these topics in this chapter, but let's consider briefly some issues related to managing across cultures, governance structure for international and global organizations, and models for organizational structure in the global environment.

Managing Across Cultures

NGO managers must accommodate to national and regional differences in legal systems, political environments, and culture. Among the three, Thomas argues, culture is uniquely important for three reasons. First, "the economic, legal, and political characteristics of a country are a manifestation of a nation's culture." Second, while the legal and political characteristics of nations are explicit and observable, culture is often invisible, especially to those who have grown up in different environments. "The influence of culture is difficult to detect and managers therefore often overlook it" (Thomas, 2002, p. 19). Finally, the practice of management often focuses on interpersonal relationships—with staff, volunteers, donors, and others—and it is in such interactions that cultural differences may be most manifest. It affects such ordinary events as how individuals greet each other, how directions are communicated, and other everyday interactions. It involves both language and customs regarding physical space, body language, and other subtle differences. An understanding of culture and its implications is essential to any manager expecting to work in the international environment, which, as discussed above, likely includes most nonprofit managers of the future.

There is an extensive theoretical literature on culture and its implications for international management, but a full discussion is beyond the scope of this chapter. One useful book is Thomas's *Essentials of International Management: A Cross-Cultural Perspective* (2002), which combines a review of theory with a discussion of how it relates to the roles of a manager in decision making, negotiating, communicating, providing leadership, and directing multicultural work groups and teams. Thomas also reviews and evaluates cross-cultural management studies and provides practical advice to those considering international management assignments. While the book is focused on business managers, its emphasis on culture makes it relevant to managers of NGOs.

Governing International and Global Organizations

In addition to the generic issues of nonprofit governance and organization that have been discussed earlier in this text, working across different legal and political systems, cultures, languages, and physical distances presents unique challenges. For example, as a U.S.-based nonprofit begins to internationalize and seek board members from other countries, it will be adding members who may not fully understand the fiduciary responsibilities of governing boards under U.S. law or the expectations of board members in American nonprofits, which may be quite different from those in their home countries. This suggests the importance of additional orientation and training for international members of such boards (Koenig, 2004).

As the organization moves along the continuum described earlier in this chapter, evolving from an international to a global organization, its governance structure will need to reflect its evolving nature. Table 15.1 summarizes three common governance models and the advantages and disadvantages of each (Koenig, 2004, pp. 101–102).

TABLE 15.1   Common Models for International Governance

Structure	Advantage/s	Disadvantage/s
Provide a seat for a representative from each region served by the organization	Ensures geographical representation	Board may become large as the organization expands. Does not ensure that representatives will primarily serve the interests of the entire organization.
Provide for a specific number of members or percentage of the board to be international, without specifying regions	Ensures some international representation Limits the size of the board Does not imply that international members represent regional interests	May not ensure representation of all regions served by the organization
Open elections, with a nominating committee mindful of the need for geographic diversity	Limits size of the board. Makes it possible to craft the board based on skills rather than geographic origins Focuses the board on the organization as an integrated global entity rather than on regional interests	Relies on the membership or a nominating committee to achieve a diverse board and does not ensure it.

Source: Based on Koenig (2004, pp. 101–102).

As Table 15.1 shows, one way to achieve international representation is to adopt bylaws that provide for a seat on the governing board for individuals representing each of the regions served by the organization. This might be an approach taken by an organization that is internationalizing: For example, a European seat might be created when it opens a European chapter of affiliates with a Europe-based partner, then a seat for a Latin American representative might be created as its programs expand into that region, and so forth. But as the organization continues to expand around the world, two problems may arise. First, the regional representatives may see their role as advocating the interests of the region they represent, rather than focusing on the overall welfare of the entire organization. As programs expand and seats for a larger number of regional representatives are added, the board may become unmanageably large and fragmented. It could become a forum in which regional representatives vie for favorable treatment of their regions, with a diminishing portion of the board focused on building an integrated organization.

In the second model, an internationalizing organization might decide to add some number of international members to its board, for example identifying three seats on an 11-person board to be held by individuals from abroad but without specifying particular regions to be represented (Koenig, 2004). This approach keeps the board at a manageable size and does provide for an international perspective. In addition, since the international members are elected or appointed at-large, they may not be as inclined to view their role as advocating regional interests. However, as the organization's programs expand around the world, this approach does not assure that the perspectives and views of all its constituencies will be represented at the board table.

The third approach is one that Koenig (2004) describes as the "most common" in organizations that have adopted "a greater global mindset throughout the organization . . . because it puts a premium on an integrated organization" (p. 102). In this model, board members are enlisted from around the world, based on the organization's needs for various skills, perspectives, and experiences. The board membership can thus be crafted to meet the organization's leadership needs at various times. In this approach, the organization's needs would be held paramount and the board's goal would be to enlist the best members from wherever they may be around the world. Gaining representation of various regions would be, of course, also a consideration, but the nominating committee and the board would not be constrained by such requirements in selecting people who bring desired qualities. The downside is, of course, that this approach does not assure that the perspectives of all regions will be reflected on the board.

Structuring International NGOs

Some issues related to the organizational structure of nonprofits in the United States, including relationships between national offices and chapters and the tradeoffs between centralized and decentralized management, were discussed earlier in this book. Such issues and challenges become exacerbated as the organization expands internationally.

As mentioned above, some NGOs have come into existence as global organizations; the example offered was CIVICUS, an international alliance that works to strengthen civil society around the world, founded in 1993 with a multinational board. But others have evolved from local to international organizations by establishing chapters or clubs abroad, maintaining a close relationship with headquarters. One example of this approach is Make-A-Wish Foundation International. With its headquarters in Arizona, Make-A-Wish International had 27 chapters around the world by 2002, each sharing "core values and policies and guidelines [that] outline the responsibilities of the local group and MAWF International." "The international goals include establishing basic principles to ensure that the highest standards of ethics and conduct are uniformly followed and adhered to by affiliated charities that are members of the Make-A-Wish family throughout the world" (Koenig, 2004, p. 98).

An alternative is to maintain relatively autonomous national organizations that are affiliated but do not receive direction from a headquarters. One example is Sister Cities International (SCI), which facilitates educational and other exchanges to promote cultural understanding, social development, and economic growth. SCI is a U.S. national organization that certifies relationships between U.S. cities and others abroad, which maintain their own independent organizations (Koenig, 2004, p. 99).

Some organizations have evolved a hybrid model, combining chapters linked to headquarters and affiliations with independent organizations abroad that share similar purposes. When AFP began to expand internationally, there were already some existing organizations in some other countries. In nations where no such organization existed, new AFP chapters were established with a close relationship to headquarters in the United States. However, wishing to preserve its good relationships with existing organizations and not be viewed as a competitor, AFP chose to develop strategic alliances with them. The first three alliances were formed in 2002 and 2003 with the Institute of Fundraising in the United Kingdom, the Fundraising Institute of Australia, and the Fundraising Institute of New Zealand. Members of these national organizations can select to join AFP and vice versa. Linked through the Web, members of both partners can access each other's members, databases, publications, and other information resources (Koenig, 2004, p. 101).

As in national nonprofits within the United States, achieving the proper balance between centralize control and local autonomy in an international organization requires careful calibration. Historically, many NGOs had centralized structures that were pushed out to chapters as they were established, but as growth extends into more geographically remote regions and diverse national and cultural settings, there is a trend toward greater autonomy for regional chapters or affiliates. The challenge is to determine what policies and what functions need to be retained centrally in order to maintain ethical standards, quality of programs, and adherence to a common mission, and which decisions can be left to local organizations. For example, Oxfam International is a confederation of national groups that was created in its present form in the mid-1990s. At the international level, the groups work together in advocacy, program harmonization, and emergency response. Local affiliates are responsible for allocating resources and managing their own programs (Koenig, 2004, p. 125).

Regarding the balance between centralization and decentralization, Koenig (2004) offers three pragmatic standards:

- The more parts of the world in which an organization has interactions or activities, the more it will want to determine which practices need to be standardized among its local entities or partners and which can vary or be locally determined.
- The larger an organization's international presence is, the more flexible it should be in looking at options for its operations.
- Organizations that want to grow internationally and develop sustainable structures are willing to review their progress in relation to their organizational goals and make modifications as needed (p. 126).

It is ironic that in a period of time when increasing calls for accountability may suggest tighter centralized controls and when concern about image and control of the message also would dictate more uniform standards, the realities of communications technology and internationalization pull in the opposite direction. Access to the Internet provides local organizations with control over messages seen around the world, and the need to adapt to widely diverse laws, cultures, and economic realities increases the benefits of a decentralized approach.

Questions about centralization and decentralization are, of course, familiar ones even in national nonprofits within the United States. But working across legal, cultural, and language differences and considerable geographic distances makes them even more complex and delicate in the international environment, placing a premium on communication, flexibility, and a tolerance for ambiguity. In the nonprofit world, as in business, "conventional organizational forms are giving way to networks of less hierarchical relationships and cooperative strategic alliances with other [organizations]" (Thomas, 2002, p. 5). Managing such enterprises is likely to be a challenging task for "control freaks" or those who do not possess or acquire communication skills, trust in others, and sophisticated cultural understanding. For nonprofit managers of the 21st century, developing such skills and qualities is essential to effective leadership.

CHAPTER SUMMARY

Unlike a century ago, when most people lived in rural areas or small communities and had little awareness of events in other parts of the world, we now live in a globalized society. Technological, economic, political, and cultural changes have created a world in which the greatest threats and the most promising opportunities require cooperation among nations and people from all parts of the world. Nonprofit organizations are playing an increasing role in global affairs and in efforts to address such problems as poverty and health. Those who live their lives and manage nonprofit organizations in the balance of the 21st century need to understand, accept, and be prepared to work with different mindsets and different skills than have ever been required before.

As within the nonprofit sector in the United States, the terminology used to discuss organizations across the world is inconsistent and often confusing. In most parts of the world, such organizations are known as nongovernmental organizations (NGOs) rather than nonprofits. NGOs that work within a single nation vary widely in the legal frameworks within which they exist, the sources of their funding, and especially their relationships with government. The best-known NGOs are the *international nongovernmental organization* (or INGOs). They are organizations that have activities not confined to a single country and that usually reflect a global approach to governance.

Some INGOs were created as global organizations from the beginning, while others were national nonprofits that became internationalized by opening chapters abroad or forming alliances with organizations abroad that pursue similar missions or causes. Local nonprofits may evolve along a continuum from being local to being internationalized to being global in perspective and operation.

INGOs have grown in number, especially within recent decades. The *Yearbook of International Organizations*, published by the Union of International Associations, shows that the number of such organizations increased from fewer than 10,000 in 1981 to more than 25,000 in 2000. Although there is no single source of comprehensive data on NGOs around the world, one of the most ambitious research efforts was the Johns Hopkins Comparative Nonprofit Sector Project, which developed the International Classification of Nonprofit Organizations and a global civil society index.

NGOs in other nations engage in a variety of activities, including educational and social services, arts, culture, recreation, and professional activities. Others are advocacy organizations that bring social and human problems to public attention and work for change. The World Bank divides INGOs into two basic types: operational NGOs and advocacy INGOs. Operational NGOs of interest to the Bank are those engaged in economic development. However, other NGOs are limited to providing temporary relief, for example, to victims of disasters or wars.

International philanthropy, especially that flowing from the United States and Western Europe to the rest of the world, has grown rapidly in recent years. American philanthropy directed to international programs and purposes grew at an average annual rate of 16.3% between 1987 and 2006 and totaled an estimated $11.34 billion in 2006. That total does not include private remittances that recent immigrants to the United States send to support families or causes in their home countries, which may total additional billions. Some of the largest U.S. foundations, including the Gates Foundation, are focused on global health and poverty and on achievement of the UN's Millennium Development Goals. Some significant gifts have supported the growth of microfinance, a strategy for reducing poverty by providing small loans to entrepreneurs in developing countries who could otherwise not qualify for credit, helping them to start and sustain businesses.

Fundraising and philanthropy as known in the United States face obstacles in many countries, including culture, tax laws, and technical issues. However, NGOs are adopting and adapting U.S.-style fundraising, and there have been some notable successes as a culture of philanthropy is developing around the world. Fundraising is emerging as a worldwide profession, through efforts by the Association of Fundraising Professionals, the Center on Philanthropy at Indiana University, the Council for Advancement and Support of Education, and professional associations that have been established in other nations.

Managing an international or global organization combines the complexities of nonprofit management that have been discussed throughout this book with the additional challenges of working across legal systems, languages, cultures, and geographic distances. Culture may be the most important variable since the economic, legal, and political characteristics of a country reflect its culture; culture is invisible and may be overlooked by managers; and much of managers' work involves personal interactions with people, in which cultural differences may be highly relevant.

As organizations evolve from local or national to international and global in scope, they need to adapt their governance structures to accommodate board members from various parts of the world. There are various models for doing so, each of which offers advantages and disadvantages. Another question that arises as a nonprofit begins to operate in various regions is how centralized or decentralized its policies and operations should be, that is, which matters need to be determined by headquarters and which can be left to local groups. The trend appears to be toward greater decentralization, and that presents challenges in terms of accountability and communication of an integrated message.

Managing nonprofit organizations or NGOs in the international environment requires skills in communication, flexibility, and a tolerance for ambiguity. Managers of the 21st century need to possess or develop these qualities in order to be effective leaders.

KEY TERMS AND CONCEPTS FROM CHAPTER 15

advocacy organizations
global civil society index
global organizations
government-operated nongovernmental
  organizations (GONGOs)
International Classification of
  Nonprofit Organizations
international nongovernmental
  organization (INGOs)

internationalized nonprofits
nongovernmental
  organization (NGO)
operational NGOs
remittances
transnational organizations
UN Millennium Development Goals

QUESTIONS FOR DISCUSSION

1. Thinking back on the discussion of Chapter 10 about the importance of developing a case for philanthropic support, how do you think an organization's case might need to be tailored to cultural differences? In other words, do you think people around the world are motivated by similar values and emotions or not?

2. If you had the financial capacity to be a significant philanthropist, would you focus your giving on reducing world poverty or on addressing social problems in the United States? Explain.

3. Should governments be the principal sources of assistance for economic development and poverty reduction, or should philanthropy play the leading role? What are the advantages and disadvantages of each type of action? What should be the relationship between private and government efforts? Explain.

SUGGESTIONS FOR FURTHER READING RELATED TO CHAPTER 15

Books/Articles

Boli, J. (2006). International nongovernmental organizations. In W. W. Powell & R. Steinberg (Eds.), *The non-profit sector: A research handbook* (2nd ed., pp. 333–354). New Haven, CT: Yale University Press.

Brinkerhoff, J. M., Smith, S. C., & Teegan, H. (Eds.). (2007). *NGOs and the millennium development goals: Citizen action to reduce poverty*. New York: Palgrave Macmillan.

Friedman, T. L. (2006). *The world is flat: The globalized world in the twenty-first century*. London: Penguin Books.

Koenig, B. L. (2004). *Going global for the greater good: Succeeding as a nonprofit in the international community*. San Francisco: Jossey-Bass.

Salamon, L. M., Sokolowski, S. W., & Associates. (2004). *Global civil society: Dimensions of the nonprofit sector* (Vol. 2). Bloomfield, CT: Kumarian Press.

Thomas, D. C. (2002). *Essentials of international management*. Thousand Oaks, CA: Sage.

Wagner, L., & Galindo, J. A. (Eds.). (2004). *Global perspectives on fundraising* (New Directions for Philanthropic Fundraising, No. 46). San Francisco: Jossey-Bass.

Web Sites

InterAction (American Council for Voluntary International Action), www.interaction.org

Idealist.org, www.idealist.org

International Society for Third Sector Research, www.istr.org

The Johns Hopkins Center for Civil Society Studies, www.jhu.edu/ ~ ccss

Union of International Associations, www.uia.be

Conclusion

Readers who have persisted through this entire text hopefully will have learned many things. Even those who may have had some prior experience working in a nonprofit organization may have found some new theory, some new concept, or some new data that added to their existing body of knowledge or understanding. Those for whom this book has been an initiation into the subject will have learned even more. But some may be wondering, "So exactly what have we learned?" "What, indeed, is the right way to manage a nonprofit organization?" "Is there a future for nonprofit management as a distinct profession?" "And, if so, what qualities, skills, and perspectives are needed to pursue a career in the field during the decades ahead?"

This book has no simple answers to offer. The nonprofit sector is so diverse that no specific approach can be equally effective in all organizations. Some of the skills needed to manage a university may be quite different from those required to manage an international nongovernmental organization or a community-based nonprofit serving the disadvantaged citizens of one particular city. Indeed, at the outset of this project, some of the author's friends advised him that the diversity of the nonprofit sector would render the task of writing a broadly useful book about nonprofit management far too challenging. Rather, they suggested, there should be a series of books on nonprofit management, each focused on a particular type of organization, such as universities, hospitals, arts institutions, human services organizations, and others. Of course, many such specialized books already exist.

The rationale for this book rests instead on the management commonalities we have discussed earlier, which are to be found in all types of nonprofits. These include the need to balance mission and money—to measure success by a double bottom line—and the need to manage relationships with multiple constituents who may hold competing or conflicting views of what the organization should be and do, and who are both free and motivated to express them. There is also a political dimension to the job. Thus, two constants of nonprofit management would be a highly nuanced leadership ability and—even for the more commercialized nonprofits—the deep underlying commitment to mission that differentiates good managers of nonprofits from good managers in organizations guided by the pursuit of wealth or constrained by the limits of political feasibility.

It remains true that such wide variation among organizations, and the rapid pace with which the sector is changing suggest that there can be no one right way to manage a nonprofit that students can learn today and then apply throughout their careers. Rather, as it has been said at various points in the book, successful management in this sector and in this period of history requires an approach that is pragmatic, eclectic, and flexible. Successful managers select the tools and approaches that best fit the circumstances and needs of their organizations, ever mindful of the overriding and immutable centrality of the mission. That may suggest the application of commercial methods or the exercise of charismatic leadership to inspire philanthropy. It may call for a strategic management approach or for creating an entrepreneurial culture. It may require seeking government funds or working to develop earned income or philanthropy to diversify support and preserve greater autonomy. Or it may require doing all these things—and others—at the same time.

While contemporary concerns such as accountability and compliance, effectiveness and performance, capacity and strategic management, earned income, and collaborations and mergers are all important, it is also essential not to become too committed to the management fads or buzzwords of the day. Of course, no manager can ignore current legal, social, and financial pressures, deny the realities of competition, or pretend that organizations can be managed as they may have been in some earlier period of time. Rather, students and future nonprofit managers need to maintain both openness to new ideas and a healthy skepticism about those that are offered as one-right-way prescriptions.

In his conclusion to the 2005 edition of the *Jossey-Bass Handbook of Nonprofit Leadership and Management*, its editor Robert Herman asks the question, whether nonprofit management as a distinct profession will continue to exist in the future. He concludes that it will, because the nonprofit sector will continue to exist. Herman (2005) bases this optimistic prediction on the supply-side theories about "the motives and desires of those who actually take the time and effort to create and sustain an organization" (p. 733).

But Herman's (2005) tone is one of cautious optimism rather than conviction. He emphasizes commercialism as a threat that could turn nonprofits into nothing more than businesses and government contractors, requiring nothing distinctive from their managers and causing some to question whether they should continue to exist in nonprofit form at all (pp. 733–734).

It is, as Yogi Berra is reported to have said, difficult to make predictions, especially about the future. But this author's view is that the nonprofit sector is likely to survive and thrive in the decades ahead, providing unprecedented opportunities for professional managers, volunteer leaders, and philanthropists alike.

Commercialism in the nonprofit sector is not new. It has existed in education and the arts for decades, yet most institutions in those fields continue to exhibit cultures and qualities that affirm their not-for-profit identities. Of course, most authors who express concern about commercialism are primarily focused on the human and social services organizations, which constitute the largest number of organizations in the sector. Critical observers worry that some of those organizations have become almost exclusively government contractors and that many philanthropists have come to see their support of them as a form of investment requiring a measurable return, transplanting the culture of capital markets into the nonprofit arena. Such concerns are not without foundation, but they may sometimes overshadow more promising developments and trends.

New nonprofit organizations continue to be created every day. Indeed, one of the joys of teaching nonprofit management at a university is the opportunity to interact with students who are not only aspiring social entrepreneurs, savvy in the methods of the marketplace, but also driven by compassion, conscience, and commitment to a social mission. There is no reason to believe that their numbers will diminish; indeed, their numbers may be growing in response to increasing awareness of the social, economic, and environmental problems that will occupy future generations of people worldwide. The energy of these young people will continue to add new nonprofit organizations to the mix and to drive renewal of existing ones—redefining the sector over and over again.

Nor are most philanthropists entirely consumed by a focus on the financial bottom line. To be sure, many expect and demand that their resources be used efficiently and effectively; but in all cases their involvement is driven by a passion for a cause, not by the desire to make a profit. Genuine philanthropists are motivated by emotion, however rational their methods. It is still true, as Seymour (1966) wrote in his classic book on fundraising, that "the heart has to prompt the mind to go where logic points the way" (p. 29). Social entrepreneurs and contemporary philanthropists may apply the tools and techniques of business to their endeavors, but their motivations still relate to the social missions of the organizations they support.

It is certain that nonprofit managers of the future will need to be able to implement business judgments and methods in their work. Skills in marketing, financial management, strategic planning, and other business techniques will become ever more essential, and students are strongly encouraged to pursue knowledge in these and other areas far beyond the brief introduction that this book provides. But also essential will be the ability to envision and to inspire, as well as the qualities of effective leadership that can only derive from deep personal commitment. Nonprofit management is likely to remain a distinct field because the nonprofit sector is likely to remain distinctive. It reflects the noble impulses and humane instincts that are the best elements of human nature and that cannot be fulfilled or expressed as fully anywhere else.

References

Adizes, I. (1999). *Managing corporate lifecycles*. Paramus, NJ: Prentice Hall.

Aldrich, H. E. (1999). *Organizations evolving*. Thousand Oaks, CA: Sage.

Allison, M., & Kaye, J. (2005). *Strategic planning for nonprofit organizations*. Hoboken, NJ: Wiley.

American Marketing Association. (2007). *Dictionary of marketing terms*. Retrieved May 22, 2007, from www.marketingpower.com/mg-dictionary-view329.php

American Psychological Association. (2005). *APA's organizational and governance structure*. Retrieved November 25, 2005, from www.apa.org/about/structure.html

Andreasen, A. R., & Kotler, P. (2003). *Strategic marketing for nonprofit organizations* (6th ed.). Upper Saddle River, NJ: Prentice Hall.

Anheier, H. K. (2005). *Nonprofit organizations: Theory, management, policy*. New York: Routledge.

Anheier, H. K., & Themudo, N. (2005). The internationalization of the nonprofit sector. In R. Herman & Associates (Eds.), *The Jossey-Bass handbook of nonprofit leadership and management* (2nd ed., pp. 102–127). San Francisco: Jossey-Bass.

Anthony, R. N., & Young, D. W. (2005). Financial accounting and financial management. In R. D. Herman & Associates (Eds.), *The Jossey-Bass handbook of nonprofit leadership and management* (2nd ed., pp. 466–512). San Francisco: Jossey-Bass.

Ashburn, E. (2006). VA Women's College will admit men. *Chronicle of Higher Education, 53*(5), A39.

Ashoka Foundation. (2005). *What is a social entrepreneur?* Retrieved October 24, 2005, from www.ashoka.org/fellows/social_entrepreneur.cfm

Axelrod, N. R. (1994). Board leadership and board development. In R. D. Herman & Associates (Eds.), *The Jossey-Bass handbook of nonprofit leadership and management* (1st ed., pp. 119–136). San Francisco: Jossey-Bass.

Bandura, A. (1978). *Social learning theory*. Upper Saddle River, NJ: Prentice Hall.

Baruch, Y., & Ramalho, N. (2006, March). Communalities and distinctions in the measurement of organizational performance and effectiveness across for-profit and nonprofit sectors. *Nonprofit and Voluntary Sector Quarterly, 35*(1), 39–61.

Bass, B. M. (1985). *Leadership and performance beyond expectations*. New York: Free Press.

Bass, B. M., & Avolio, B. J. (Eds.). (1994). *Improving organizational effectiveness through transformational leadership*. Thousand Oaks, CA: Sage.

Beatty, S. (2006, October 26). Survey finds giving by wealthy largely immune to tax changes. *Wall Street Journal, 248*(99), D3.

BBB Wise Giving Alliance. (2003). *Standards for charity accountability*. Retrieved May 28, 2007, from www.give.org/standards/newcbbbstds.asp

Bennis, W. G., & Nanus, B. (1985). *Leaders: The strategy for taking charge*. New York: Harper & Row.

Berger, P. L., & Neuhaus, J. (1977). *To empower people: The role of mediating structures in public policy*. Washington, DC: American Enterprise for Public Policy Research.

Berry, J. M. (2003, November 27). Nonprofit groups shouldn't be afraid to lobby. *Chronicle of Philanthropy, 16*(4), 33. Retrieved July 10, 2007, from www.philanthropy.com

Bixler, M. (2005, April 16), Habitat founder forms rival group. *Atlanta Journal-Constitution,* A1.

Blended value map. (2006). Retrieved February 21, 2006, from www.blendedvalue.org

Block, S. R. (2001). A history of the discipline. In J. S. Ott (Ed.), *The nature of the nonprofit sector* (pp. 97–111). Boulder, CO: Westview Press.

Blum, D. E. (2006, June 2). Cautiously, world vision creates an endowment. *Chronicle of Philanthropy, 18*(16), B17. Retrieved June 9, 2007, from www.philanthropy.com

BoardSource. (2005). *The source: Twelve principles of governance that power exceptional boards.* Washington, DC: Author. Retrieved April 29, 2008, from www.boardsource.org/files/thesource.pdf

Boli, J. (2006). International nongovernmental organizations. In W. W. Powell & R. Steinberg (Eds.), *The non-profit sector: A research handbook* (2nd ed., pp. 333–354). New Haven, CT: Yale University Press.

Bolman, L. G., & Deal, T. E. (2003). *Reframing organizations: Artistry, choice, and organizations* (3rd ed.). San Francisco: Jossey-Bass.

Bonk, K., Griggs, H., & Tynes, E. (1999). *The Jossey-Bass guide to strategic communications for nonprofits.* San Francisco: Jossey-Bass.

Broce, T. E. (1974). *Fund raising: The guide to raising money from private sources.* Norman: University of Oklahoma Press.

Bryman, A. (1992). *Charisma and leadership in organizations.* London: Sage.

Bryson, J. (2001). Strategic planning. In J. S. Ott (Ed.), *Understanding nonprofit organizations: Governance, leadership, and management* (pp. 131–141). Boulder, CO: Westview Press.

Bryson, J. M. (2004). *Strategic planning for public and nonprofit organizations* (3rd ed.). San Francisco: Wiley.

Bureau of Labor Statistics. (2008). *Volunteering in the United States, 2007.* Retrieved April 16, 2007, from www.bls.gov/news.release/pdf/volun.pdf

Burns, J. M. (1978). *Leadership.* New York: HarperCollins.

Callen, J. L., Klein, A., & Tinkelman, D. (2003, December). Board composition, committees, and organizational efficiency: The case of nonprofits. *Nonprofit and Voluntary Sector Quarterly, 32*(4), 493–520.

Carlson, M., & Donohoe, M. (2003). *The executive director's survival guide: Thriving as a nonprofit leader.* San Francisco: Jossey-Bass.

Carver, J. (1997). *Boards that make a difference: A new design for leadership in nonprofit and public organizations* (2nd ed.). San Francisco: Jossey-Bass.

Carver, J. (2006). *Boards that make a difference: A new design for leadership in nonprofit and public organizations* (3rd ed.). San Francisco: Jossey-Bass.

Cash, S. (2002, April). Smithsonian $35m gift. *Art in America, 90*(4), 33.

Center for Lobbying in the Public Interest. (2007). *Make a difference for your cause: strategies for nonprofit engagement in legislative advocacy.* Washington, DC: Author. Retrieved July 5, 2007, from www.clip.org

Center on Philanthropy at Indiana University. (2005). *Giving USA: The annual report on philanthropy for the year 2004.* Glenview, IL: Giving USA Foundation.

Center on Philanthropy at Indiana University. (2006). *Giving USA: The annual report on philanthropy for the year 2005.* Glenview, IL: Giving USA Foundation.

Center on Philanthropy at Indiana University. (2007). *Giving USA: The annual report on philanthropy for the year 2006.* Glenview, IL: Giving USA Foundation.

Chait, R. P., Holland, T. P., & Taylor, B. E. (1996). *Improving the performance of governing boards.* Phoenix, AZ: Oryx Press.

Chait, R. P., Holland, T. P., &. Taylor, B. E. (1999). The new work of the nonprofit board. In *Harvard business review on nonprofits* (pp. 53–75). Boston: Harvard Business School Press. (Reprinted from *Harvard Business Review, September/October,* 1996)

Chait, R. P., Ryan, W. P., & Taylor, B. E. (2005). *Governance as leadership: Reframing the work of nonprofit boards.* Hoboken, NJ: BoardSource/Wiley.

Child, C. D., & Grønbjerg, K. A. (2007, March). Nonprofit advocacy organizations: Their characteristics and activities. *Social Science Quarterly, 88*(1), 259–281.

Clegg, S., Kornberger, M., & Pitsis, T. (2005). *Managing and organizations: An introduction to theory and practice.* Thousand Oaks, CA: Sage.

Cohen, R. (2006, January 26). How to prevent politicians from misusing charities. *Chronicle of Philanthropy, 18*(7), 35–36. Retrieved July 6, 2007, from www.philanthropy.com

Collins, J. (2005). *Good to great and the social sectors* [Monograph]. (www.jimcollins.com, www .amazon.com/s/ref = nb_ss_gw?url = search-alias % 3Daps&field-keywords = jim + collins)

Collins, J. C. (2001). *Good to great.* New York: HarperCollins.

Collins, J. C., & Porras, J. L. (1994). *Built to last: Successful habits of visionary companies.* New York: Harper Business.

Commission on Private Philanthropy and Public Needs. (1975). *Giving in America: Toward a stronger voluntary sector.* Washington, DC: Author.

Community Wealth Ventures. (2001). *The community wealth seekers guide.* Washington, DC: Author. (www.communitywealth.com/resources_tools.htm)

Community Wealth Ventures. (2003). *Powering social change: Lessons on community wealth generation for nonprofit sustainability.* Washington, DC: Author.

Community Wealth Ventures. (2004). *Evaluating a social enterprise opportunity.* Washington, DC: Author.

Connolly, P., & Lukas, C. (2002). *Strengthening nonprofit performance: A funder's guide to capacity building* (Wilder Foundation with the Grantmakers for Effective Organizations). Saint Paul, MN: Amherst H. Wilder Foundation

Dees, J. G. (1998). Enterprising nonprofits. In *Harvard business review on nonprofits* (pp. 135–166). Boston: Harvard Business School Press. (Reprinted from *Harvard Business Review, January/February,* 1998)

Dees, J. G., Emerson, J., & Economy, P. (2001). *Enterprising nonprofits: A toolkit for social entrepreneurs.* New York: Wiley.

Denhardt, R. B., Denhardt, J. V., & Aristigueta, M. P. (2002). *Managing human behavior in public and nonprofit organizations.* Thousand Oaks, CA: Sage.

DiMento, M. (2007, May 31). Key results of the chronicle's annual survey and how it was compiled. *Chronicle of Philanthropy, 19*(16), 12–13. Retrieved June 11, 2007, from www.philanthropy.com/ premium/articles/v19/i16/16001201.htm

Doane, D. (2005). The myth of CSR. *Stanford Social Innovation Review, Fall,* 23–29. Retrieved May 12, 2008, from www.ssireview.org/pdf/2005FA_Feature_Doane.pdf

Dollery, B. E., & Wallis, J. L. (2003). *The political economy of the voluntary sector.* Northampton, MA: Edward Elgar.

Donmoyer, R. J., & Fitzgerald, A. (2007, July 22). Taking from the rich, giving to the board. *The Washington Post,* p. F07.

Douglas, J. (1983). *Why charity? The case for a third sector.* Beverly Hills, CA: Sage.

Douglas, J. (1987). Political theories of nonprofit organization. In W. W. Powell (Ed.), *The nonprofit sector: A research handbook* (pp. 43–54). New Haven, CT: Yale University Press.

Dove, K. E. (2000). *Conducting a successful capital campaign* (2nd ed.). San Francisco: Jossey-Bass.

Drucker, P. (1990). *Managing the nonprofit organization: Principles and practices.* New York: HarperCollins.

Dunlop, D. (1993). Major gift programs. In M. J. Worth (Ed.), *Educational fund raising: Principles and practice* (pp. 97–116). Washington, DC/Phoenix, AZ: American Council on Education/Oryx Press.

Dym, B., & Hutson, H. (2005). *Leadership in nonprofit organizations.* Thousand Oaks, CA: Sage.

Edgers, G. (2004, January 25). MFA's monets: Dicey deal? *Boston Globe,* A1.

Egger, R. (2004). *Begging for change.* New York: HarperCollins.

Egger, R. (2007, May 31). Charities must challenge politicians. *Chronicle of Philanthropy, 19*(16), 59–60. Retrieved June 28, 2007, from www.philanthropy.com

Eikenberry, A. M., & Kluver, J. D. (2004, March/April). The marketization of the nonprofit sector: Civil society at risk? *Public Administration Review, 64*(2), 132.

Eisenberg, P. (2003, February 6). Why foundation grants shouldn't mix with politics. *Chronicle of Philanthropy, 15*(8), 37. Retrieved June 29, 2007, from www.philanthropy.com

Eisenberg, P. (2007, June 28). Charities should remain nonpolitical. *Chronicle of Philanthropy, 19*(18), 53.

Elliott, S. (2006, June 5). Seeking a distinctive sound for people of a certain age. *New York Times, 155*(53601), p. C7.

Executive summary: Overview of findings of strengthening nonprofit advocacy project. (2002). Retrieved July 2, 2007, from OMB Web site: www.ombwatch.org/article/articleview/769/1/101

Financial Accounting Standards Board. (1993). *Statement of financial accounting standards, no. 116.* Retrieved April 16, 2007, from www.fasb.org/pdf/fas116.pdf

Fisher, J. L. (1984). *Power of the presidency.* New York: American Council on Education/Macmillan.

Foster, W., & Bradach, J. (2005, February). Should nonprofits seek profits? *Harvard Business Review, 83*(2), 92–100.

Fremont-Smith, M. R., & Cordes, J. (2004). *What the ratings revolution means for charities.* Washington, DC: Urban Institute.

Friedman, T. L. (2006). *The world is flat: The globalized world in the twenty-first century.* London: Penguin Books.

Froelich, K. A. (1999, September). Diversification of revenue strategies: Evolving resource dependence in nonprofit organizations [Electronic version]. *Nonprofit and Voluntary Sector Quarterly, 28*(3), 246–268.

Frumkin, P., & Imber, J. B. (2004). *In search of the nonprofit sector.* New Brunswick, NJ/London: Transaction.

Gainer, B., & Moyer, M. S. (2005). "Marketing for nonprofit managers." In R. D. Herman & Associates (Eds.), *The Jossey-Bass handbook of nonprofit leadership and management* (pp. 277–309). San Francisco: Jossey-Bass.

Gallagher, B. (2005, April 5). *Testimony of United Way of America's Brian Gallagher before U.S. Senate Committee on finance.* Retrieved May 13, 2008, from www.senate.gov/ ~ finance/hearings/testimony/2005test/bgtest040505.pdf

Gammal, D. L. (2007, Summer). Before you say "I do." *Stanford Social Innovation Review, 5*(3), 47–51.

Gamwell, F. I. (1984). *Beyond preference: Liberal theories of independent association.* Chicago: University of Chicago Press.

Gifts that can warp a museum [Editorial]. (2001, May 31). *New York Times*, p. 26.

Gose, B., (2005, January 6). America's charity explosion. *Chronicle of Philanthropy, 17*(6), 6–9. Retrieved September 12, 2005, from www.philanthropy.com

Greene, S. G. (1999, May 20). Trustees ousted in Hawaii. *Chronicle of Philanthropy, 11*(15), 30.

Greene, S. G. (2004, April 15). Hostile takeover or rescue? *Chronicle of Philanthropy, 13*(13), 24–27. Retrieved November 25, 2005, from www.philanthropy.com

Greenleaf, R. K. (1977). *Servant leadership: A journey into the nature of legitimate power and greatness.* Ramsey, NJ: Paulist Press.

Grønbjerg, K. A., & Salamon, L. M. (2002). Devolution, marketization, and the changing shape of government-nonprofit relations. In L. M. Salamon (Ed.), *The state of nonprofit America* (pp. 447–470). Washington, DC: Brookings Institution.

Guerrero, T. (2005, September 19). Toll proposal for Virginia highways draws criticism. *Transport Topics, September*(3657), 12.

Guo, C., & Acar, M. (2005, September). Understanding collaboration among nonprofit organizations: Combining resource dependency, institutional, and network perspectives. *Nonprofit and Voluntary Sector Quarterly, 34*(3), 340–353.

Habitat for Humanity International. (2005). *Habitat for humanity fact sheet.* Retrieved December 27, 2005, from www.habitat.org/how/factsheet.aspx

Hager, M. A., & Brudney, J. L. (2004). *Volunteer management practices and retention of volunteers.* Washington, DC: Urban Institute.

Haider, D. (2007, Summer). Uniting for survival. *Stanford Social Innovation Review, 5*(3), 52–55.

Hall, H. (2005, January 6). Fund-raising association clarifies stand on fees. *Chronicle of Philanthropy, 17*(6), 47. Retrieved December 15, 2006, from www.philanthropy.com/premium/articles/v17/i06/06004704.htm

Hall, H. (2006, July 20). Nonprofit-marketing experts outline hot trends, discuss challenges. *Chronicle of Philanthropy, 18*(19), 29.

Hammack, D. C. (1998). *Making the nonprofit sector in the United States.* Bloomington: Indiana University Press.

Hansmann, H. (1987). Economic theories of nonprofit organization. In W. W. Powell (Ed.), *The nonprofit sector: A research handbook* (pp. 27–42). New Haven, CT: Yale University Press.

Harvard Business Review. (1999). *Harvard business review on nonprofits.* Boston: Harvard Business School Press.

Hauser, J. (2003). Organizational lessons for nonprofits. *McKinsey Quarterly, 2003*(2), 52–59. Retrieved June 20, 2003, from www.mckinseyquarterly.com

Herman, R. D. (2005). Conclusion. In R. D. Herman & Associates (Eds.), *The Jossey-Bass handbook of nonprofit leadership and management* (2nd ed., pp. 731–736). San Francisco: Jossey-Bass.

Herman, R. D., & Heimovics, D. (1991). *Executive leadership in nonprofit organizations.* San Francisco: Jossey-Bass.

Herman, R. D., & Heimovics, D. (2005). Executive leadership. In R. D. Herman & Associates (Eds.). *The Jossey-Bass handbook of nonprofit leadership and management* (2nd ed., pp. 153–170). San Francisco: Jossey-Bass.

Herman, R. D., & Renz, D. O. (2002). *Nonprofit organizational effectiveness: Practical implications of research on an elusive concept* (Occasional paper.) Kansas City: University of Missouri-Kansas City Henry W. Bloch School of Business and Public Administration.

Herzberg, F. (1968). One more time: How do you motivate employees? *Harvard Business Review, 46,* 36–44.

Hessenius, B. (2007). *Hardball lobbying for nonprofits: Real advocacy for nonprofits in the new century.* New York: Palgrave/Macmillan.

Hochberg, E. (2002, August 8). Business ventures go beyond the bottom line. *Chronicle of Philanthropy, 14*(20), 35.

Hochberg, E., & Wise, A. (2005, March 3). Don't give up on charity-run businesses. *Chronicle of Philanthropy, 17*(10), 49–50.

Hopkins, B. R. (2003). *Legal responsibilities of nonprofit boards.* Washington, DC: BoardSource.

Hopkins, B. R. (2005). *Nonprofit law made easy.* Hoboken, NJ: Wiley.

Howe, F. (2002). Nonprofit accountability: The board's fiduciary responsibility. In V. Futter (Ed.), *Nonprofit governance and management* (pp. 29–38). Chicago: American Bar Association and American Society of Corporate Secretaries.

Howe, F. (2004). *The nonprofit leadership team: Building the board-executive director relationship.* San Francisco: Wiley.

Hrywna, M. (2007, January 2). Extreme makeover: Girl scouts shrink councils. *The Non Profit Times.* Retrieved April 11, 2007, from www.nptimes.com/07Jan/npt-070101-3.html

The Hudson Institute. (2007). *Index of global philanthropy*. Washington, DC: Author. Retrieved July 18, 2007, from http://gpr.hudson.org/files/publications/IndexGlobalPhilanthropy2007.pdf

Hudson, M. (2005). *Managing at the leading edge*. San Francisco: Jossey-Bass.

Independent Sector. (2001). *Giving and volunteering in the United States, 2001*. Retrieved April 16, 2007, from www.independentsector.org/programs/research/GV01main.html

Independent Sector. (2004). *Types of partnerships*. Retrieved May 27, 2007, from www.independent sector.org/mission_market/partnerships.htm

Independent Sector. (2005). *Panel on the nonprofit sector: Strengthening transparency, governance, accountability of charitable organizations* (A final report to Congress and the nonprofit sector). Washington, DC: Author.

Independent sector. (2006). *Accountability: Who's doing what*. Retrieved February 21, 2006, from www.independentsector.org/issues/accountability/standardsd2.html

Independent Sector. (2007). *Nonprofit advocacy and lobbying*. Retrieved June 13, 2007, from http://independentsector.org (updated June 5, 2007)

Independent Sector. (2008). *Value of volunteer time*. Retrieved May 7, 2008, from www.independent sector.org/programs/research/volunteer_time.html

Ingram, R. T. (2003). *Ten basic responsibilities of nonprofit boards*. Washington, DC: National Center for Nonprofit Boards (now BoardSource).

Internal Revenue Service. (2005a). *"Substantially related" defined*. Retrieved May 13, 2008, from www.irs.gov/charities/article/0,,id = 158843,00.html

Internal Revenue Service. (2005b). *U. Museum retailing: UBIT issues*. Retrieved September 22, 2005, from www.irs.gov/pub/irs-tege/eotopicu79.pdf

James, E. (1987). The nonprofit sector in comparative perspective. In W. W. Powell (Ed.), *The nonprofit sector: A research handbook* (pp. 397–415). New Haven, CT: Yale University Press.

Jeavons, T. H. (1991). A historical and moral analysis of religious fund raising. In D. F. Burlingame & L. J. Hulse (Eds.), *Taking fund raising seriously: Advancing the profession and practice of raising money* (pp. 53–72). San Francisco: Jossey-Bass.

Jensen, B. (2005, February 17). Housing group fires its founder. *Chronicle of Philanthropy, 17*(9), 26.

Jensen, B. (2006, September 14). Two-year investigation did little to clarify how charities can influence public policy, critics say. *Chronicle of Philanthropy, 18*(23), 13. Retrieved July 2, 2007, from www.philanthropy.com

Jewell, J. (2005). New times, new leaders. *Christianity Today, 49*(4), 24.

Joslyn, H. (2002, October 17). Driven by mission. *Chronicle of Philanthropy, 15*(1), 19.

Joslyn, H. (2004, January 8). Young people fuel demand for nonprofit study. *Chronicle of Philanthropy, 16*(6), 6–10. Retrieved May 15, 2005, from http://philanthropy.com/free/articles/v16/i06/ 06000901.htm

Kaplan, R. S., & Norton, D. (1992). Using the balanced scorecard as a strategic management system. *Harvard Business Review, 70*(1), 71–79.

Katz, D., & Kahn, R. L. (1966). *The social psychology of organizations*. New York: Wiley.

Kearns, K. P. (2000). *Private sector strategies for social sector success*. San Francisco: Jossey-Bass.

Kee, J. E. (2004). Cost-effectiveness and cost-benefit analysis. In J. S. Wholey, H. P. Hatry, & K. E. Newcomer (Eds.), *Handbook of practical program evaluation* (2nd ed., pp. 506–542). San Francisco: Jossey-Bass.

Kelly, K. S. (1998). *Effective fund-raising management*. Mahwah, NJ: Lawrence Erlbaum.

Kibbe, B. D. (2004). Investing in nonprofit capacity. In Grantmakers for Effective Organizations (Eds.), *Funding effectiveness: Lessons in building nonprofit capacity* (chap. 1). San Francisco: Wiley.

King, K. T. (2006, April 6). The limits of usefulness. *Chronicle of Philanthropy, 18*(12), 63–65.

Kirkpatrick, K. T. (2007, Summer). Go ahead: Pop the question. *Stanford Social Innovation Review, 5*(3), 3–46.

Klausner, M., & Small, J. (2005, Spring). Failing to govern? *Stanford Social Innovation Review, 3*(1), 43–49.

Klintsov, V., & von Löhneysen, E. (2001). Shall we dance? *McKinsey Quarterly, 2001*(4, Special Ed.), 6–9. Retrieved May 16, 2007, from www.mckinseyquarterly.com/article_print.aspx?L2 = 33&L3 = 95&ar = 1105

Koenig, B. L. (2004). *Going global for the greater good: Succeeding as a nonprofit in the international community.* San Francisco: Jossey-Bass.

Kohm, A., La Piana, D., & Gowdy, H. (2003). *Strategic restructuring: Findings from a study of integrations and alliances among nonprofit social sector and cultural organizations in the United States.* Chicago: Chapin Hall Center for Children.

Kopczynski, M. E., & Pritchard, K. (2004). The use of evaluation by nonprofit organizations, In J. S. Wholey, H. P. Hatry, & K. E. Newcomer (Eds.), *Handbook of practical program evaluation* (pp. 649–669). San Francisco: Jossey-Bass.

Koteen, J. (1997). *Strategic management in public and nonprofit organizations.* Westport, CT: Praeger.

Kotter, J. P. (1996). *Leading change.* Boston: Harvard Business School Press.

LaBarre, P. (2006, November/December). How do you transform a 95-year-old organization? Ask the girls. *The Merrill Lynch Leadership Magazine, November/December,* 44–50.

Letts, C. W., Ryan, W. P., & Grossman, A. (1999a). *High performance nonprofit organizations: Managing upstream for greater impact.* New York: Wiley.

Letts, C. W., Ryan, W. P., & Grossman, A. (1999b). Virtuous capital: What foundations can learn from venture capitalists. In *Harvard Business Review on Nonprofits* (pp. 91–110). Boston: Harvard Business School Press. (Reprinted from *Harvard Business Review, March/April,* 1997)

Lewis, N. (2002, February 21). Controversy over Donor's role causes Smithsonian to lose $36.5 million. *Chronicle of Philanthropy, 14*(9), 16.

Light, P. C. (2000). *Making nonprofits work: A report on the tides of nonprofit management reform.* Washington, DC: Brookings Institution.

Light, P. C. (2002). *Pathways to nonprofit excellence.* Washington, DC: Brookings Institution.

Light, P. C. (2004a). Capacity building and the national infrastructure to support it. *Nonprofit Quarterly, Spring,* 36–41.

Light, P. C. (2004b). *Sustaining nonprofit performance: The case for capacity building and the evidence to support it.* Washington, DC: Brookings Institution.

Lipke, D. J. (2000, September). Fountain of youth: AARP woos reluctant boomers with a high-priced makeover. *American Demographics, 22*(9), 37–39.

Lipman, H. (2006, August 17). A record fundraising feat. *Chronicle of Philanthropy, 18*(21), 2. Retrieved December 15, 2006, from www.philanthropy.com/premium/articles/v18/i21/21002201.htm

Lipman, H., & Williams, G. (2002, August 8). D.C. United Way's troubles cause concern elsewhere. *Chronicle of Philanthropy, 14*(20), 30.

Locke, E. A. (2000). Motivation by goal setting. In R. T. Golembiewski (Ed.), *Handbook of organizational behavior* (2nd ed., pp. 43–56). New York: Marcel Dekker.

Lohmann, R. A. (1992). *The commons.* San Francisco: Jossey-Bass.

MacMillan, I. C. (1983). Competitive strategies for nonprofit organizations. *Advances in Strategic Management, 1,* 61–82.

Maddox, D. (1999). *Budgeting for not-for-profit organizations.* Hoboken, NJ: Wiley.

Mangan, K. S. (1999, November 12). Stanford's health system ends merger with University of California at San Francisco. *Chronicle of Higher Education, 46*(12), A43. Retrieved June 18, 2007, from www.chronicle.com

Marchetti, D. (2000, May 4). Two food charities join forces in one of biggest non-profit mergers. *Chronicle of Philanthropy, 12*(14), 33. Retrieved June 18, 2007, from www.philanthropy.com

Maryland Association of Nonprofit Organizations. (2006). *Standards for excellence.* Retrieved February 10, 2006, from www.marylandnonprofits.org/html/standards/principles.asp

Maslow, A. H. (1954). *Motivation and personality.* New York: Harper.

Massarsky, C. W. (1988). How to build a business plan. In E. Skloot (Ed.), *Business planning for nonprofit enterprises*. New York: The Foundation Center.

McClelland, D. C. (1961). *The achieving society*. New York: Free Press.

McCormick, D. H. (2001). *Nonprofit mergers: The power of successful partnerships*. Gaithersburg, MD: Aspen.

McCormick, S. (2003, May 13). Balancing the story. *The Washington Post*, p. A19.

McCurley, S. (2004). Keeping the community involved: Recruiting and retaining volunteers. In R. Herman & Associates (Eds.), *The Jossey-Bass handbook of nonprofit leadership and management* (pp. 587–622). San Francisco: Jossey-Bass.

McCurley, S., & Lynch, R. (2006). *Volunteer management: Mobilizing all the resources in the community* (2nd ed.). Kemptville, ON: Johnstone Training and Consultation (available online at www.jtcinc.ca)

McGregor, D. (1960). *The human side of enterprise*. New York: McGraw-Hill.

McKinsey & Company. (2001). *Effective capacity building in nonprofit organizations*. Washington, DC: Venture Philanthropy Partners.

McMillan, E. J. (2003a). *Not-for-profit accounting, tax, and reporting requirements*. Hoboken, NJ: Wiley.

McMillan, E. J. (2003b). *Not-for-profit budgeting and financial management*. Hoboken, NJ: Wiley.

Meyer, M. W. (2002). *Rethinking performance measures: Beyond the balanced scorecard*. Cambridge, UK: Cambridge University Press.

Michaels, M. (2007, April 16). High turnover among adult volunteers, report finds. *Chronicle of Philanthropy*. Retrieved April 17, 2007, from www.philanthropy.com/free/update/2007/04/2007041601.htm

Miller-Millesen, J. L. (2003). Understanding the behavior of nonprofit boards of directors: A theory-based approach. *Nonprofit and Voluntary Sector Quarterly, 32*(4), 521–547.

Minnesota Council on Nonprofits. (2006). *Nonprofit lobbying and the law*. Retrieved June 28, 2007, from www.mncn.org (updated February 6, 2006)

Minor, E. (2005, February 3). Habitat for humanity volunteers urge reinstatement of founder and president. *Associated Press Report*. Retrieved December 23, 2005, from web.lexis-nexis.com.proxygw.wrlc.org/universe/document?_m = 3549a37e35924f6b

Mintzberg, H. (1996). The rise and fall of strategic planning. In J. L. Pierce & J. W. Newstrom (Eds.), *The manager's bookshelf* (pp. 137–142). New York: HarperCollins.

Mirabella, R. M. (2004). *Nonprofit management education: Current offerings in university-based programs*. Retrieved April 18, 2005, from http://tltc.shu.edu/npo (last updated March 30, 2004)

Mirabella, R. M., & Wish, N. B. (2000, May/June). The "Best Place" debate: A comparison of graduate education programs for nonprofit managers. *Public Administration Review, 60*(3), 219–229.

Moyers, R. L. (2005). *The nonprofit chief executive's ten basic responsibilities*. Washington, DC: BoardSource.

Murray, V. (2004). Evaluating the effectiveness of nonprofit organizations. In R. D. Herman & Associates (Eds.), *The Jossey-Bass handbook of nonprofit leadership and management* (2nd ed., pp. 345–370). San Francisco: Jossey-Bass.

Museums and money [Editorial]. (2001, May 31). *The Washington Post*, p. A24.

Nanus, B., & Dobbs, S. M. (1999). *Leaders who make a difference: Essential strategies for meeting the nonprofit challenge*. San Francisco: Jossey-Bass.

Nason, J. W. (1993). Responsibilities of the governing board. In R. T. Ingram & Associates (Eds.), *Governing independent colleges and universities* (p. 17). San Francisco: Jossey-Bass.

National Alliance to End Homelessness. (2006). *Determining lobbying limits for nonprofit organizations*. Washington, DC: Author. Retrieved June 29, 2007, from www.endhomelessness.org/content/article/detail/1436

National Association of Schools of Public Affairs and Administration. (2001). *Guidelines for graduate professional education in nonprofit organizations, management and leadership*. Retrieved May 25, 2001, from the NASPAA Web site, www.naspaa.org/guidelines/guide_npft.htm

The nation's attic: Secret contracts, soaring salaries—they don't belong at the Smithsonian [Editorial]. (2006, April 24). *The Washington Post,* p. A16.

The Nature Conservancy. (2005a, June 7). *Review of Senate Finance Committee Staff Report on The Nature Conservancy*. Retrieved March 2, 2006, from http://nature.org/pressroom/press/press1954 .html

The Nature Conservancy. (2005b). *Summary of actions taken to strengthen governance, policies, and procedures*. Retrieved March 2, 2006, from http://nature.org/aboutus/files/strengthened_governance_en.pdf

Nelson, T. C. (2006). What we've learned at AARP. *Vital Speeches of the Day, September,* 626–632.

Newcomer, K. E., Hatry, H. P., & Wholey, J. S. (2004). Meeting the need for practical evaluation approaches: An introduction. In J. S. Wholey, H. P. Hatry, & K. E. Newcomer (Eds.), *Handbook of practical program evaluation* (2nd ed., p. xxxiii). San Francisco: Jossey-Bass.

New directors to be installed at United Way: Area trustees dissolve board in bid to restore confidence. (2002, October 4). *The Washington Post,* p. B01.

Nobbie, P. D., & Brudney, J. L. (2003, December). Testing the implementation, board performance, and organizational effectiveness of the policy governance model in nonprofit boards of directors. *Nonprofit and Voluntary Sector Quarterly, 32*(4), 571–595.

Nonprofit Academic Centers Council. (2004). *Curricular guidelines for graduate study in philanthropy, the nonprofit sector, and nonprofit leadership*. Cleveland, OH: Author.

Nonprofit Integrity Act. (2004). Retrieved February 5, 2006, from http://ag.ca.gov/charities/publications/nonprofit_integrity_act_nov04.pdf

Northouse, P. G. (2004). *Leadership: Theory and practice*. Thousand Oaks, CA: Sage.

O'Neill, M. (2002). *Non profit nation: A new look at the third America*. San Francisco: Jossey-Bass.

Oster, S. M. (1995). *Strategic management for nonprofit organizations*. New York: Oxford University Press.

Oster, S. M., Massarsky, C. W., & Beinhacker, S. L. (Eds.). (2004). *Generating and sustaining nonprofit earned income*. San Francisco: Jossey-Bass.

Ott, J. S. (2001). *The nature of the nonprofit sector*. Boulder, CO: Westview Press.

Ottaway, D. B., & Stephens, J. (2003, May 4). Nonprofit land bank amasses billions. *The Washington Post,* p. A01.

Panel on the nonprofit sector (Convened by Independent Sector). (2005). *Strengthening transparency governance accountability of charitable organizations: Final report to Congress and the nonprofit sector*. Washington, DC: Independent Sector.

Paton, R. (2003). *Managing and measuring social enterprises*. Thousand Oaks, CA: Sage.

Payton, R. L. (1988). *Philanthropy: Voluntary action for the public good*. New York: Macmillan.

Payton, R. L. (1991). Foreword. In H. A. Rosso & Associates (Eds.), *Achieving excellence in fund raising: A comprehensive guide to principles, strategies, and methods* (pp. xiii–xv). San Francisco: Jossey-Bass.

Perry, S., & Wilhelm, I. (2006, July 20). Contribution to history. *Chronicle of Philanthropy, 18*(19), 6. Retrieved December 15, 2006, from www.philanthropy.com/premium/articles/v18/i19/19000601 .htm

Peters, T. J., & Waterman, R. H. (1982). *In search of excellence*. New York: Harper & Row.

Pfeffer, J. (2003). Introduction to the classic edition. In *External control of organizations: A resource dependence perspective* (Classic ed.). Palo Alto, CA: Stanford University Press.

Pfeffer, J., & Salancik, G. R. (1978). *The external control of organizations: A resource dependence perspective*. New York: Harper & Row.

Phills, J. A., Jr. (2005). *Integrating mission and strategy for nonprofit organizations*. New York: Oxford University Press.

Pidgeon, W. P., Jr. (2004). *The not-for-profit CEO: How to attain and retain the corner office*. Hoboken, NJ: Wiley.

Pierce, J. (2004). Habitat founder and board disagree on his retirement date. *Christian Century, 121*(20), 15.

Pocock, J. (1989). *Fund-raising leadership: A guide for college and university boards*. Washington, DC: Association of Governing Boards of Universities and Colleges.

Poister, T. H. (2003). *Measuring performance in public and nonprofit organizations.* San Francisco: Jossey-Bass.

Powell, W. W., & DiMaggio, P. J. (1991). *The new institutionalism in organizational analysis.* Chicago: University of Chicago Press.

Preserve Educational Choice. (2007). *20 Reasons why you should change your vote.* Retrieved May 24, 2007, from www.preserveeducationalchoice.org

Prince, R. A., & File, K. M. (1994). *The seven faces of philanthropy.* San Francisco: Jossey-Bass.

The pros and cons of financial efficiency standards (Brief No. 5). (2004, August). Washington, DC/Indianapolis: Urban Institute/Indiana University Center on Philanthropy.

Pulley, J. (2007, February). Hell hath no fury. *Currents.* Retrieved May 22, 2007, from www.case.org

Putnam, R. (1995, January). Bowling alone: America's declining social capital. *Journal of Democracy, 6*(1), 65–78.

Rainey, H. G. (2003). *Understanding and managing public organizations* (3rd ed.). San Francisco: Jossey-Bass.

Randolph College. (2007). *Strategic Plan: Response to "20 Reasons."* Retrieved May 13, 2008, from http://web.randolphcollege.edu/strategicplan/20reasons_response.asp

Rogers, G., Finley, D. S., & Galloway, J. R. (2001). *Strategic planning in social service organizations.* Toronto, Ontario, Canada: Canadian Scholars' Press.

Rogers, J. L. (2006, April 16). Foundations are burning out charity CEOs. *Chronicle of Philanthropy, 18*(10), 45–46.

Rose-Ackerman, S. (1996). Altruism, nonprofits and economic theory. *Journal of Economic Literature, 34,* 701–728.

Rosso, H. A., & Associates. (1991). *Achieving excellence in fund raising.* San Francisco: Jossey-Bass.

Rosso, H. A., & Associates, & Tempel, E. R. (Ed.). (2003). *Achieving excellence in fund raising* (2nd ed.). San Francisco: Jossey-Bass.

Sagawa, S., & Segal, E. (2000). *Common interest, common good: Creating value through business and social sector partnerships.* Cambridge, MA: Harvard Business School Press.

Salamon, L. M. (1999). *America's nonprofit sector: A primer* (2nd ed.). New York: Foundation Center.

Salamon, L. M. (2001). What is the nonprofit sector and why do we need it? In J. S. Ott (Ed.), *The nature of the nonprofit sector* (pp. 162–166). Boulder, CO: Westview Press.

Salamon, L. M. (2002). *The state of nonprofit America.* Washington, DC: Brookings Institution.

Salamon, L. M., & Geller, S. L. (2005). *Nonprofit governance and accountability* (The Johns Hopkins Nonprofit Listening Post Project Communique No. 4). Baltimore: Johns Hopkins University Center for Civil Society Studies/Institute for Policy Studies.

Salamon, L. M., Sokolowski, S. W., & Associates. (2004). *Global civil society: Dimensions of the nonprofit sector* (Vol. 2). Bloomfield, CT: Kumarian Press.

Salmon, J. L. (2002a, September 28). United Way to delay severance deal. *The Washington Post,* p. B01.

Salmon, J. L. (2002b, October 19). Nominees sought for United Way: All-New board to oversee charity. *The Washington Post,* p. B01.

Salmon, J. L. (2006, June 27). Chapter overhaul adds to Red Cross turmoil. *The Washington Post,* p. A27.

Salmon, J. L., & Whoriskey, P. (2003, August 12). Audit excoriates United Way leadership. *The Washington Post,* p. A01.

Sander, T. H., & Putnam, R. D. (2005, September 10). September 11 as civics lesson. *The Washington Post,* p. A23.

Sargeant, A. (2005). *Marketing management for nonprofit organizations.* New York: Oxford University Press.

Sawhill, J., & Williamson, D. (2001). Measuring what matters most in nonprofits. *McKinsey Quarterly, 2001*(2), 16–25.

Schein, E. H. (1992). *Organizational culture and leadership: A dynamic view* (2nd ed.). San Francisco: Jossey-Bass.

Schervish, P. G., & Havens, J. J. (2001). The new physics of philanthropy: The supply-side vectors of charitable giving—Part 2: The spiritual side of the supply-side. *CASE International Journal of Educational Advancement, 2*(3), 221–241.

Schwinn, E. (2002, November 14). How '96 law on financial abuses has been applied by IRS in four cases. *Chronicle of Philanthropy, 15*(3), 32.

Schwinn, E. (2006a, September 28). IRS warns charities to avoid electioneering. *Chronicle of Philanthropy, 18*(24), 18. Retrieved July 2, 2007, from www.philanthropy.com

Schwinn, E. (2006b, October 30). Red Cross proposes sweeping governance changes. *Chronicle of Philanthropy.* Retrieved May 13, 2005, from http://philanthropy.com/free/update/2006/10/2006103001.htm

Schwinn, E. (2006c, November 9). Two Kansas churches accused of playing politics. *Chronicle of Philanthropy, 19*(3), 18. Retrieved July 2, 2007, from www.philanthropy.com

Schwinn, E. (2007, May 17). Seven American lung association affiliates sever ties with National charity. *Chronicle of Philanthropy.* Retrieved May 13, 2008, from http://philanthropy.com/free/update/2007/05/2007051001.htm

Sciolino, E. (2001a, May 30). Citing differences, director of a Smithsonian museum resigns. *New York Times,* Section A, p. 20.

Sciolino, E. (2001b, May 26). Smithsonian group criticizes official on donor contract. *New York Times,* Section A, p. 8.

Sciolino, E. (2001c, May 10). Smithsonian is promised $38 million, with strings. *New York Times,* Section A, p. 20.

Scott, W. R. (1995). *Institutions and organizations.* Thousand Oaks, CA: Sage.

Seiler, T. L. (2003). Plan to succeed. In H. A. Rosso & Associates, & E. T. Tempel (Eds.), *Achieving excellence in fund raising* (pp. 23–29). San Francisco: Jossey-Bass.

Selingo, J. (2003, February 28). The disappearing state in higher education. *Chronicle of Higher Education, 49*(23), A22.

Senge, P. M. (1990). *The fifth discipline: The art and practice of the learning organization.* New York: Doubleday.

Senge, P. M. (1994). *The fifth discipline fieldbook: Strategies and tools for building a learning organization.* New York: Currency.

Seymour, H. J. (1966). *Designs for fund-raising.* New York: McGraw-Hill.

Shin, S., & Kleiner, B. H. (2003). How to manage unpaid volunteers in organisations. *Management Research News, 25*(2/3/4), 63–71.

Shoham, A., Ruvio, A., Vigoda-Gadot, E., & Schwabsky, N. (2006, September). Market orientations in the nonprofit and voluntary sector: A meta-analysis of their relationships with organizational performance. *Nonprofit and Voluntary Sector Quarterly, 35*(3), 453–476.

Shore, B. (1999). *The cathedral within.* New York: Random House.

Silverman, L., & Taliento, L. (2006, Summer). What business execs don't know—but should—about nonprofits. *Stanford Social Innovation Review, 4*(2), 36–43.

Simon, J., Dale, H., & Chisolm, L. (2006). The federal tax treatment of charitable organizations. In W. W. Powell & R. Steinberg (Eds.), *The non-profit sector: A research handbook* (2nd ed., pp. 267–306). New Haven, CT/London: Yale University Press.

Simon, J. G. (1987). Research on philanthropy. In K. W. Thompson (Ed.), *Philanthropy, private means, public ends* (pp. 67–87). Lanham, MD: University Press of America.

Simon, J. S. (2001). *The 5 stages of nonprofit organizations.* St. Paul, MN: Amherst H. Wilder Foundation.

Skinner, B. F. (1953). *Science and human behavior.* New York: Free Press.

Small, L. M. (2001, May 31). Mr. Smithson's was the first. *The Washington Post,* p. A25.

Smith, D. H. (1991). Four sectors or five? Retaining the membership-benefit sector. *Nonprofit and Voluntary Sector Quarterly, 20*(2), 137–150.

Smucker, B. (1999). *The nonprofit lobbying guide* (2nd ed.). Washington, DC: Independent Sector. (Full text available at www.independentsector.org)

Smucker, B. (2005). Nonprofit lobbying. In R. D. Herman & Associates (Eds.), *The Jossey-Bass handbook of nonprofit leadership and management* (2nd ed., pp. 230–253). San Francisco: Jossey-Bass.

Steiss, A. W. (2003). *Strategic management for public and nonprofit organizations.* New York: Marcel Dekker.

Stem v. Lucy Webb Hayes National Training School for Deaconesses and Missionaries, 381 F. Supp. 1003 (D.D.C. 1974).

Stephens, J., & Ottaway, D. B. (2003a, June 14). Conservancy abandons disputed practices: Land deals, loans were questioned. *The Washington Post*, p. A01.

Stephens, J., & Ottaway, D. B. (2003b, May 5). How a bid to save a species came to grief. *The Washington Post*, p. A01.

Stephens, J., & Ottaway, D. B. (2003c, May 6). Nonprofit sells scenic acreage to allies at a loss. *The Washington Post*, p. A01.

Stephens, J., &. Ottaway, D. B. (2003d, May 5). The beef about the brand. *The Washington Post*, p. A10.

Stephenson, M., Jr., & Chaves, E. (2006, September). The Nature Conservancy, the press, and accountability. *Nonprofit and Voluntary Sector Quarterly, 35*(3), 345–366.

Stevens, S. K. (2001). *Nonprofit lifecycles: Stage-based wisdom for nonprofit capacity*. Long Lake, MN: Stagewise Enterprises.

Sumariwalla, R. (1983). Preliminary observations in scope, size, and classification of the sector. In V. Hodgkinson (Ed.), *Working papers for the spring research forum: Since the filer commission* (pp. 433–449). Washington, DC: Independent Sector.

Taylor, B. E., Chait, R. P., &. Holland, R. P. (1999). The new work of the nonprofit board. In *Harvard Business Review on Nonprofits* (pp. 53–76). Boston: Harvard Business School Press.

Thomas, D. C. (2002). *Essentials of international management*. Thousand Oaks, CA: Sage.

Thompson, B. (2002, January 20). History for sale. *The Washington Post*, pp. 14–22, 25–29.

Trescott, J. (2005, April 13). The Smithsonian's concession to the bottom line: Museums cash in with food, shops. *The Washington Post*, p. A01.

Trescott, J. (2006, December 16). Smithsonian deal with showtime passes muster. *The Washington Post*, p. C01.

Tuan, M. T. (2004). Cultivating a culture of measurement. In Grantmakers for Effective Organizations (Eds.), *Funding effectiveness: Lessons in building nonprofit capacity* (pp. 105–142). San Francisco: Jossey-Bass.

United Nations. (2008). *UN millennium development goals*. Retrieved July 16, 2007, from www.un.org/ millenniumgoals

United Way of America. (1996). *Measuring program outcomes: A practical approach*. Alexandria, VA: Author. Retrieved February 11, 2006, from www.national.unitedway.org/outcomes/resources/ mpo/model.cfm

United Way of Greater Milwaukee; Greater Milwaukee Foundation; University of Wisconsin at Milwaukee's Center for Urban Initiatives and Research and Helen Bader Institute for Nonprofit Management; & Nonprofit Management Fund. (2004). *Nonprofit collaboration and mergers: Finding the right fit* (Report on the United Way's Collaborative Learning Project). Retrieved June 19, 2007, from http://epic.cuir.uwm.edu/NONPROFIT/collaboration.pdf

Van Til, J. (1988). *Mapping the third sector: Voluntarism in a changing social economy*. New York: Foundation Center.

Van Til, J. (1992). Foreword. In R. A. Lohmann (Ed.), *The commons*. San Francisco: Jossey-Bass.

Van Til, J. (2000). *Growing civil society: From nonprofit sector to third space*. Bloomington/Indianapolis: Indiana University Press.

Viesca-Sada, A. (2004). The current state of philanthropy in Mexico and Central America. In *Global perspectives on fundraising* [Special issue] (New Directions for Philanthropic Fundraising, No. 46, pp. 13–25). San Francisco: Jossey-Bass.

Vroom, V. H. (1964). *Work and motivation*. New York: Wiley.

Wagner, L. (2003). Trends in major donor behavior and innovative approaches to philanthropy. In H. A. Rosso & Associates, & E. T. Tempel (Eds.), *Achieving excellence in fund raising* (pp. 215–225). San Francisco: Jossey-Bass.

Wagner, L. (2005). Fundraising, culture, and the U.S. perspective. In L. Wagner & J. A. Galindo (Eds.), *Global perspectives on fundraising* (pp. 5–12). (New Directions for Philanthropic Fundraising, No. 46, Winter 2004). Hoboken, NJ: Wiley.

Wagner, L., & Galindo, J. A. (2004, Winter). *Global perspectives on fundraising* [Special issue] (New Directions for Philanthropic Fundraising, No. 46, pp. 1–4). San Francisco: Jossey-Bass.

Wallace, N. (2005, May 12). Bridging old divides. *Chronicle of Philanthropy, 17*(15), 31–34. Retrieved June 26, 2007, from www.philanthropy.com

Weisbrod, B. A. (1975). Toward a theory of the voluntary non-profit sector in a three-sector economy. In E. S. Phelps (Ed.), *Altruism, morality, and economic theory* (pp. 171–195). New York: Russell Sage Foundation.

Weisbrod, B. A. (1988). *The nonprofit economy.* Cambridge, MA: Harvard University Press.

Weisbrod, B. A. (2004, Winter). The pitfalls of profits. *Stanford Social Innovation Review, 2*(3), 40–48.

Weisman, C., &. Goldbaum, R. I. (2004). *Losing your executive director without losing your way.* San Francisco: Jossey-Bass.

Weitzman, M. S., Jalandoni, N. T., Lampkin, L. M., &. Pollak, T. H. (2002). *The new nonprofit almanac and desk reference.* San Francisco: Jossey-Bass.

Wilhelm, I. (2005, April 28). Fired habitat founder establishes rival charity. *Chronicle of Philanthropy, 17*(4), 37.

Williams, G. (2006, September 28). A new report sheds light on nonprofit accountability practices. *Chronicle of Philanthropy, 18*(24), 59.

Williams, R. L. (2000, January). Closing remarks: Out with the old, in with the new. *Currents, XXVI*(1), 63–64. Retrieved May 16, 2007, from www.case.org/currents

Wolf, T. (1999). *Managing a nonprofit organization in the twenty-first century.* New York: Fireside.

Wolverton, B. (2003a, August 21). Key senator introduces foundation-payout proposal. *Chronicle of Philanthropy, 15*(21), 22. Retrieved December 15, 2006, from www.philanthropy.com/premium/articles/v15/i21/21002201.htm

Wolverton, B. (2003b, September 4). What went wrong? Board's actions at issue at troubled D.C. United Way. *Chronicle of Philanthropy, 15*(22), 27.

Worth, M. J. (1993). *Educational fund raising: Principles and practice.* Phoenix, AZ: Oryx Press and American Council on Education.

Worth, M. J. (2005). *Securing the future: A fund-raising guide for boards of independent colleges and universities.* Washington, DC: Association of Governing Boards of Universities and Colleges.

Yankey, J. A. (1996). Corporate support of nonprofit organizations. In D. F. Burlingame & D. R. Young (Eds.), *Corporate philanthropy at the crossroads* (pp. 7–22). Bloomington/Indianapolis: Indiana University Press.

Yankey, J. A., & Willen, C. K. (2005). Strategic alliances. In R. D. Herman & Associates (Eds.), *The Jossey-Bass handbook of nonprofit leadership and management* (pp. 254–274). San Francisco: Jossey-Bass.

Yoffe, D., & Brunetti, R. M. (2004, Winter). Fundraising in the Southern Cone. In *Global perspectives on fundraising* [Special issue] (New Directions for Philanthropic Fundraising, No. 46, pp. 27–36). San Francisco: Jossey-Bass.

Young, D. R. (1983). *If not for profit, for what? A behavioral theory of the nonprofit sector based on entrepreneurship.* Lanham, MD: Lexington Books.

Young, D. R. (2001a). Contract failure theory. In J. S. Ott (Ed.), *The nature of the nonprofit sector* (pp. 193–196). Boulder, CO: Westview Press.

Young, D. R. (2001b). Government failure theory. In J. S. Ott (Ed.), *The nature of the nonprofit sector* (pp. 190–192). Boulder, CO: Westview Press.

Young, D. R. (2006). *Corporate partnerships: A guide for the nonprofit manager.* Alexandria, VA: National Center on Nonprofit Enterprise. Retrieved February 9, 2006, from the National Center for Nonprofit Enterprise Web site: www.nationalcne.org/papers/corp_partner.htm

Zietlow, J., Hankin, J. A., & Seidner, A. (2007). *Financial management for nonprofit organizations.* Hoboken, NJ: Wiley.

Index

About the Author

Michael J. Worth is Professor of Nonprofit Management in the Trachtenberg School of Public Policy and Public Administration at The George Washington University in Washington, D.C. (GW). He joined the GW faculty in 2001. He teaches courses related to the governance and management of nonprofit organizations, fundraising and philanthropy, nonprofit governing boards, and nonprofit enterprise. He has more than 30 years of experience in philanthropic resource development. He served as Vice President for Development and Alumni Affairs at GW for 18 years and previously as Director of Development at the University of Maryland College Park. At GW, he planned and directed two major campaigns and held responsibility for trustee relations and board development. He has been a frequent speaker at conferences of the Council for Advancement and Support of Education (CASE), the Association of Fundraising Professionals (AFP), and the Association of Governing Boards of Universities and Colleges (AGB). He has served as a member of CASE's Commission on Philanthropy, as Editor of the *CASE International Journal of Educational Advancement*, and as a faculty member at the Harvard Institutes for Higher Education. He is active in the Washington, D.C., nonprofit community. He has served as a member of the Board of Directors of Miriam's Kitchen, a nonprofit organization providing services to the city's homeless, and as a member of the selection committee for the Washington Post Award for Excellence in Nonprofit Management. He consults with educational institutions and nonprofit organizations in the areas of fundraising, board development, and strategic planning. In addition to numerous papers, articles, and reviews, he has written or edited five books, including *Public College and University Development* (1985); *The Role of the Development Officer in Higher Education* (1994, 2000); *Educational Fund Raising: Principles and Practice* (1993); *New Strategies for Educational Fund Raising* (2002); and *Securing the Future: A Fund-Raising Guide for Boards of Independent Colleges and Universities*, published by the Association of Governing Boards in 2005. He holds a BA in economics from Wilkes College, an MA in economics from The American University, and a PhD in higher education from the University of Maryland.